Loss of Eden

ALSO BY JOYCE MILTON

The Yellow Kids:
Foreign Correspondents in the Heyday of Yellow Journalism

The Rosenberg File: A Search for the Truth (with Ronald Radosh)

Vicki (with Ann Bardach)

Loss of Eden

A BIOGRAPHY OF

CHARLES AND ANNE MORROW

LINDBERGH

JOYCE MILTON

HarperCollins*Publishers*

Quotations from the letters of Harold Nicolson and Vita Sackville-West are by permission of Nigel Nicolson and the Lilly Library, Bloomington, Indiana. Excerpts from the reminiscences of Marjorie Hope Nicolson, George Rublee, and Vice Admiral Emory Scott Land are by permission of the Office of Oral History Research, Columbia University, New York City. Quotations from the Dwight W. Morrow Papers are by permission of the Amherst College Archives, Amherst, Massachusetts.

HarperCollins books may be purchased for educational, business, or sales promotional use. For information, please write: Special Markets Department, Harper-Collins Publishers, Inc., 10 East 53rd Street, New York, NY 10022.

FIRST EDITION

Designed by Alma Hochhauser Orenstein

Library of Congress Cataloging-in-Publication Data
Milton, Joyce
    Loss of Eden: a biography of Charles and Anne Morrow Lindbergh/Joyce Milton—1st ed.
        p.   cm.
    Includes bibliographical references and index.
    ISBN 0-06-016503-0
    1. Lindbergh, Charles A. (Charles Augustus), 1902–1974. 2. Lindbergh, Anne Morrow, 1906– . 3. Air pilots—United States—Biography. 4. Authors, American—20th century—Biography.
    I. Title.
    TL540.L5M52   1993
    [B]629. 13'092—dc20   92-53319

93 94 95 96 97 ❖/RRD 10 9 8 7 6 5 4 3 2 1

CONTENTS

Illustrations follow page 216.

ACKNOWLEDGMENTS

I WOULD LIKE TO GIVE SPECIAL THANKS to my editor, Terry Karten, for her encouragement and guidance; to copy editor Sue Llewellyn, for her careful corrections and comments on the manuscript; and to my agent, Barbara Lowenstein.

This book would never have come about without the inspiration of my mother, who waved a flag to celebrate the triumph of a fellow Swedish American, and of my father, who never did get a glimpse of Lindy when he landed in Pittsburgh but returned to the airfield soon after for his first airplane ride.

ONE

Prophets

*O*N A LATE SUMMER DAY in the year 1900, Evangeline Land stepped off the train in Little Falls, Minnesota, and a hired a wagon to transport her trunk to the Antlers Hotel on Broadway. If any members of the school board were waiting on the platform to greet her, they must have been quite pleased with the new high school science teacher, whom they had hired sight unseen to teach five courses—chemistry, physics, biology, physical geography, and physiology—all for a starting salary of fifty-five dollars a month. Twenty-four years old, Miss Land was a slight, active woman with curly brown hair and large gray-blue eyes. She was pretty but not distractingly so, and unusually well educated for a small-town schoolteacher. A graduate of Miss Ligget's Academy in Detroit, she had earned a B.A. in chemistry from the University of Michigan.

There were few opportunities for women scientists at the turn of the century, and Evangeline had decided to use her bachelor's degree as a passport to see something of the world beyond her comfortable middle-class neighborhood in Detroit. After reading *Down the Great River,* Willard Glazier's 1881 account of his search for the true source of the Mississippi, she had set her sights on Little Falls. Glazier's popular and highly romanticized narrative told how he and his party had explored the headwaters of the river, canoeing across lakes with picturesque names like Winnibegoshish, where they encountered noble "copper-skinned" Chippewa as well as elk, bears, deer, and numberless flocks of migrating ducks, brants, cormorants, pelicans, and trumpeter swans.

Their journey of exploration completed, Glazier's party had continued downriver, stopping at a series of trading posts and rough lumbering camps before arriving at Little Falls, the first truly civilized town on the Upper Mississippi. There, wrote Glazier, "a brass band saluted us with a lively air while cheers and words of welcome met us on every side." The explorers were led off in triumph to a comfortable hotel, where a delegation of townspeople, led by Moses LaFond, said to be the town's first settler, questioned Glazier about the river's geological origins and brought, for his inspection, a collection of relics, evidence of some unknown race that had inhabited the northern forests long before the arrival of the Chippewa and the Sioux.[1]

When she accepted the school board's offer, Evangeline imagined herself teaching science to the children of humble lumberjacks and miners, perhaps with a faithful dog to carry her books to and from the one-room schoolhouse. But two decades had passed since Glazier's visit, and progress had come to Little Falls. The Pine Tree Lumber Company's state-of-the-art sawmill was busy round the clock, and local businessmen were buying up tracts of real estate on the west side of town and building worker's housing and blocks of stores on speculation. The windswept prairies to the west of town, where warriors of the Sioux nation had risen up against the whites as recently as 1861, were divided into prosperous farms. The primeval pine forests to the north and east were fast being clear-cut.

A county seat with a population of something over five thousand, Little Falls was far past the one-room schoolhouse stage, and the superintendent, probably reasoning that Miss Land was young and energetic enough to climb stairs without strain, promptly assigned her to a classroom on the top floor of the five-story high school building. The room was cramped and poorly equipped, and when winter came the winds blowing off the prairie penetrated the cracks around the windows. Evangeline's test tubes and beakers were icy, her fingers stiff and numb as she struggled to prepare her classroom demonstrations. She complained about the temperature in her classroom—"about 54 degrees"— only to be told that this was Minnesota and she would just have to get used to it.[2]

Back at the Antlers Hotel, Evangeline discussed her problems with a fellow boarder who also happened to be the town's most prominent attorney. Charles August Lindbergh, usually called C.A., was a remarkably handsome man, still lean and fit at forty-one, with startling blue eyes and a deep dimple in the center of his chin. Recently widowed, he had been married to Mary LaFond, a daughter of the same Moses LaFond who had welcomed Willard Glazier to Little Falls in 1881. Mary had died unexpectedly at thirty-one, of complications following minor surgery, and C.A.'s two little girls, Lillian and Eva, were living at his mother's house while he boarded at the Antlers. Lonely and bored, he was delighted to discover that the attractive new schoolteacher was, like himself, a graduate of the University of Michigan. In her letters home, Evangeline called C.A. "the widower" and teasingly described him as a rich old man, ugly and objectionably "Norwegian," with a name "suggestive of cheese." None of this was meant to be taken seriously—Evangeline was as giddy as a teenager over her success in capturing the heart of the town's most eligible man, winning out over several competitors, including a certain Miss Cooper. She and C.A. had rooms that faced each other across the hotel courtyard, and within a few weeks their romance had progressed to the point where they worked out a set of signals so that they could communicate with each other first thing in the morning and last thing at night.[3]

At the high school Evangeline had given up trying to reason with the administration. When her room was too cold, she took it upon herself to move her students to a vacant classroom on a lower floor. One day she was carrying a bulky piece of apparatus down the narrow staircase when she ran into the superintendent of schools. He ordered her to take the equipment back to the top floor. Evangeline, her "Irish temper" aroused, ignored him. The confrontation ended with her setting the apparatus down on the landing and walking out of the building, never to return.

Mailing in her resignation, Evangeline returned to Detroit. But C. A. Lindbergh continued his courtship by letter, and on March 21, 1901, the couple was married in the living room of her parents' home. After a honeymoon trip to California, where they visited Yosemite and the cattle ranch of C.A.'s older half-brother, Perry, the newlyweds returned to Little Falls.

Shortly before the death of his first wife, C.A. had purchased a 110-acre farm two miles south of town, with extensive frontage on the west bank of the Mississippi. The property included a fine home site on a twenty-foot bluff overlooking the river. In a burst of expansiveness, the normally thrifty C.A. approved plans for a three-story frame house complete with hardwood floors and red oak paneling downstairs, five bedrooms, and a third-floor billiards room. If not quite the equal of the Weyerhaeuser mansion, the home of the local branch of the St. Paul family that owned the Pine Tree Lumber Company, it would certainly be one of the finest homes in Morrison County.

While the house was going up, C.A. and Evangeline camped out near the riverbank, sleeping in a temporary two-room cabin. By the time the weather turned cold, the main house was nearly finished and the new mahogany furniture, ordered from Grand Rapids, had arrived. A year after she quit her teaching job, Evangeline had three full-time servants and her own carriage and was entertaining the Weyerhaeusers, the Mussers, and the other leading families of the county.

At the time of his marriage to Evangeline, C. A. Lindbergh had a typical country lawyer's practice. He took criminal cases, and during a stint as county attorney he had even prosecuted a few murderers, but most of his income came from handling the local business affairs of the Pine Tree Lumber Company and of national firms like the Singer Sewing Machine Company and McCormick Harvesters. He dabbled in real estate, both on his own behalf and as the local agent of a "New York millionaire" named Howard Bell, who speculated in rural land.

Even among his central Minnesota neighbors, a group not noted for their demonstrative ways, C.A. had a reputation for being unusually introspective, a deep thinker who revealed himself only in occasional flashes of sardonic humor. The town intellectual, he pored over volumes of Abraham Lincoln's speeches, Prescott's histories, and Populist tracts like *Coin's Financial School.* He had read and pondered the classics of philosophy and literature more deeply than many an eastern college professor, but like many self-educated men he expressed himself poorly and had a tendency to wrestle with the big questions in isolation, often reinventing solutions that were already intellectual clichés.

C.A.'s net worth was about two hundred thousand dollars, making him a rich man by Morrison County standards, but most of that was tied up in rural acreage and he had always lived simply. He wore the same suit day in and day out, used country expressions like "begorry," and before his remarriage his social life had consisted of attending country weddings and the "river pig" banquets and log-rolling exhibitions organized several times a summer by the big lumber companies. He had a reputation for never taking a case unless he believed his client was in the right, and on more than one occasion, he accepted a mortgage payment from a hard-pressed farmer only to turn around and hand the money back in the form of an unsecured loan.

Many of C.A.'s clients and tenants owed him money, and one suspects they were none too happy to see him marry a woman who was socially ambitious, with expensive tastes and no ties to the community. Evangeline had a penchant for wearing large, showy hats, and surviving examples of her wardrobe—a blue velvet traveling suit and a bead-trimmed gown that she wore to a reception at the White House during the Wilson administration—testify to her love of rich fabrics and stylishly cut clothes. She called the river house "Lindholm," an affectation that grated on the sensibilities of her unassuming Lindbergh in-laws, and she even persuaded C.A. to take up horseback riding.

There is a tradition in central Minnesota that another local boy, Sinclair Lewis of Sauk Centre, knew the story of C. A. Lindbergh's second marriage and used Evangeline as the inspiration for the character of Carol Kennicott in *Main Street*. The connection can't be proved, but C.A.'s parents had homesteaded in Melrose, near Sauk Centre, and there are other hints in Lewis's novel that he was at least aware of the Lindbergh family's colorful past.[4]

C.A.'s father, known in his youth as Ola Månsson, had been a famous man in the old country, a self-educated scholar and for eleven years a leading member of the Swedish Riksdag, where he almost single-handedly pushed through a program of liberal reforms. Månsson campaigned in favor of equal rights for Jews, other religious minorities, and women, and brought about the repeal of an old law that banned Bible reading and worship services in private homes. Another of his bills made it a crime for employers to beat their servants, and his longest and most controversial crusade resulted in the outlawing of the whipping post, the last vestige of corporal punishment in the Swedish legal system. Månsson's ultimate goal was the overthrow of the class system. In this he failed—"The Lords are ever Lords as they were before," he wrote sorrowfully some years after leaving office—but as the private secretary and close personal friend of the crown prince, later Charles XV, he was able to influence Sweden's development into a constitutional monarchy.

In 1859 a scandal brought Månsson's career to an abrupt end. He had used his position as a director of the Bank of Sweden to guarantee business loans for friends, and when the debts went unpaid he was charged with criminal embezzlement. According to the late Dr. Grace Nute, a Minnesota historian whose researches were partially sponsored by the Lindbergh family, Månsson was guilty at worst of a technical violation of the banking laws and was basically set up by his political enemies. A less charitable view might be that he had been careless and far too trusting of his wealthy friends.

Rather than fight the charges against him, a deeply embittered Månsson liquidated his property to cover the debts and announced his intention to turn his back on his ungrateful countrymen forever. In the summer of 1859, he sailed for America with his second wife, the former Louisa Carline, and his infant son, named Charles August in honor of the crown prince.

It happened that around the time of Månsson's emigration, the Swedish people were changing over from the old-fashioned system of patronymics—adding the suffix *son* or *dottir* to the father's first name— to standard surnames. Månsson's sons by his first marriage had already adopted the surname Lindberg, and he decided to do the same. In a more unusual move, he changed his first name as well, becoming August Lindberg. Soon after arriving in America, he anglicized his new last name by adding a final *h*. So determined was he to put the old country behind him that he put away his Swedish books, immersed himself in American literature, and was soon writing even his personal diary in English.

Louisa Carline Lindbergh was just twenty, thirty years younger than her husband and a member of one of the very aristocratic families whose power Ola Månsson had fought in the Riksdag. There is some question as to whether the couple was ever legally married, and C.A.'s birth on January 20, 1859, was registered from the home of the mid-wife who delivered him, a practice commonly resorted to when illegiti-mate children were born to upper-class families. All this suggests that the scandal that brought to an end Månsson's political career, and his and Louisa's subsequent decision to leave the country, may have been somewhat more complicated than surviving accounts indicate.

At any rate, the couple settled near Melrose, on the Sauk River in Stearns County, Minnesota, where August traded a gold medal awarded to him by the Riksdag for his first plow. Homesteading on the frontier was challenging enough for the able-bodied young. August Lindbergh, though he came from a peasant background, had done no farm work for thirty years, and the struggle to house and feed his family took a brutal toll.

In 1861 August Lindbergh was delivering a load of logs to a sawmill in Sauk Centre when he slipped and fell into the machinery. A rotating saw nearly severed his left arm and sliced through his rib cage— one witness said he could actually see Lindbergh's throbbing heart. The village's only doctor had gone to St. Cloud, and a local preacher, the Reverend Harrison, loaded the wounded man into the back of his wagon and took him back to Melrose so that he could die in his own bed. The next morning the doctor arrived and charged twenty dollars to amputate Lindbergh's arm without benefit of an anesthetic.

But August Lindbergh refused to die. By the end of the year he was chopping down trees again, using a specially weighted one-handed ax that he had designed himself. He lived to father six more children, three of whom died in infancy. He and Louisa helped establish the first public school in Melrose, and gave food and shelter to hundreds of Swedish immigrants who came through Melrose on their way to starting new lives in western Minnesota and the Dakotas. In later years August was frequently consulted by students aware of his historical role in bringing the values of the Enlightenment to Sweden.

As an adult C.A. would take tremendous pride in August's accomplishments. In his youth, however, he was terribly ashamed of his shabbily dressed, one-armed father. In addition, although the Lindberghs were literate in English, they all spoke with a strong accent, and C.A. recalled with shame the laughter that broke out when he was called upon to recite "The Charge of the Light Brigade" for a school program, enthusiastically declaiming: "Hof a lee-gyew, hof a lee-gyew, hof a lee-gyew onvart."

At the age of ten C.A. dropped out of school to help support the family. He ran trap lines, fished, and hunted deer for the table. He did not set foot in a classroom again until he was twenty years old, when he enrolled in a private academy that allowed young men like himself to make up for years of lost schooling by pursuing an intensive program of reading and independent study. Two terms spent studying law in Michigan completed his formal education.

C.A.'s limited higher education was typical for a professional in that rural part of the state, and it is not surprising that when Evangeline became pregnant she insisted on returning home to Detroit for the delivery. On February 4, 1902, her uncle Edwin Lodge, a well-known homeopathic physician, presided at the birth of Charles Augustus Lindbergh. (Technically, the child was not a "junior.") C.A. called his infant son "Charley." Evangeline occasionally fell into the habit as well, but on the whole she subscribed to the then fashionable notion that nicknames were demeaning. In her case this was a highly inconvenient principle—

her father, only brother, husband, and son were all named Charles; and her mother, another Evangeline, had long been called Eva, which also happened to be the name of one of her husband's daughters.

Charles's earliest memory was of sitting at the mahogany dining room table, which had been elaborately set with gleaming silver and stemware for one his mother's dinner parties, while his father fed him raw carrots. He also recalled being taken in a carriage to play with little Charles Weyerhaeuser, the lumber mill heir. His mother had planted irises, her favorite flower, around the front of the house, and played popular songs on the upright piano in the living room.

These very early memories, no doubt augmented by his mother's stories and his own imagination, were of a time when his parents were handsome, prosperous, and carefree. But the Lindbergh marriage had been troubled from the beginning. C.A.'s daughters, Lillian and Eva, fourteen and ten at the time of their father's remarriage, were not quick to accept the authority of a twenty-five-year-old stepmother who was living in a style their own mother had never enjoyed. The rest of the Lindbergh family in town, including C.A.'s widowed mother Louisa, his married sisters Juno and Linda, and his younger brother Frank, were no more accepting. The Lindberghs seldom criticized Evangeline outright, but their reminiscences about the late Mary LaFond—sweet-natured, unassuming, and a thrifty housekeeper—pointedly suggested the areas in which they found the second Mrs. Lindbergh lacking.

Evangeline was an emotional woman, impulsive and affectionate at times but also quick to sense rejection. Unfortunately, she was married to a man who loved her deeply but had few resources for expressing his feelings apart from teasing. Evangeline later recalled with indignation how, shortly after she and C.A. were married, while they were strolling along the riverbank, she lost her footing in the mud and slid into the chilly water up to her armpits. Instead of rushing to her rescue, C.A. doubled up laughing.

On another occasion C.A. told a nosy client who asked too many questions about the age difference in the marriage, "Oh, my wife is really much older than she looks. She is older than I am." The story got around town and Evangeline was not amused. The Lindbergh view of the situation was that Evangeline simply was not tough enough to adapt to Minnesota ways and lacked a sense of humor. But she was trying to cope with two unhappy stepdaughters and a hostile town, and C.A. often seemed oblivious to her problems. "I don't tell people when I am pleased," he wrote some years later, accusing himself of being "an old grouch."[5]

For his part C.A. was not entirely comfortable as a country gentleman playing cards and billiards with Weyerhaeusers and Mussers. Getting rich in farm real estate often meant profiting from the misfortunes of one's neighbors, a situation that troubled his conscience. Poring over his Populist tracts, he brooded about the powerlessness of the poor farmer, so often a hostage to the whims of eastern credit markets and the railroad magnates. Why, he wondered, should a downturn in commodity prices in New York and Chicago have the power to cause a good, hard-working farmer to lose his land? Why should the fate of an entire region be determined by the railroads, whose rate schedules made it more expensive to ship goods to Chicago from Minnesota than from New England?

In February 1905, in response to these problems, C.A. formed the Industrial Adjustment Company, whose initial investors included his younger brother Frank; his father-in-law, Dr. Charles Land; and his longtime friend, Little Falls contractor Carl Bolander. The company's assets included an empty warehouse near the railroad yards, which was to be turned into a cold-storage facility. The plan was to buy stock from local farmers, "finish" the animals on a tract of land just outside of town, and then butcher them right in Little Falls. In addition the company would serve as a sort of rural credit union, making loans on commodities and acting as an "adjustment agency between creditors and debtors."

While the other partners may have thought of the company as primarily a commercial venture, C.A. saw it as the beginning of a movement. He began publishing a quarterly bulletin, cumbersomely titled *The Law of Rights, Realized and Unrealized, Individual and Public,* preaching the need for rural self-help and the elimination of wasteful competition. The trouble with towns like Little Falls, C.A. argued, was that they had too many small merchants, each competing against the others. Instead of sixteen separate grocery stores, for example, Little Falls would be far better off with one or two retail cooperatives.

No doubt there was merit in this idea, but the town's competing small businessmen were not eager to put themselves out of business for the common good. Moreover, C.A. was better at envisioning sweeping solutions to social inequities than at following up on the day-to-day details of running a business. The Industrial Adjustment Company soon went broke, and C.A. eventually lost his entire investment—more than $20,000. But this business failure was to be the least of the Lindbergh family's problems that year.

One hot Sunday afternoon in August, three-year-old Charles was playing quietly on the first floor when he heard his mother and the servants rush through the house screaming. A nursemaid snatched him up in her arms and carried him across the road to the barn. "Don't look! You mustn't look!" she admonished. Charles managed to wriggle free and peer around the corner of the barn. He saw neighbors running out of his house carrying furniture, and black smoke pouring out of one of the third-floor windows.

The cause of the fire was never determined, although there would be speculation that a maid had carelessly left a hot curling iron in the linen closet. The Lindberghs' neighbors arrived in time to rescue most of the downstairs furnishings, including the piano and Evangeline's pride and joy, a set of imported blue willowware, purchased on her honeymoon trip to San Francisco. But it was too late to save the house. The next morning Charles stood hand in hand with his mother and looked down into the smoldering pit that had once been the basement. "Father will build us a new house," his mother promised him.

But the river house never was rebuilt. The following year, in the summer of 1906, it would be replaced by a much smaller structure, a typical summer cottage, with rooms clustered around a tiny central foyer, an unfinished attic, a pump in the kitchen, and no indoor plumbing or central heating system. Although C.A. had recently suffered financial reverses, lack of money was apparently not the main reason for this decision.

After the fire, the entire family—C.A., Evangeline, Lillian, Eva, Charles and his nursemaid, and for a time at least, the two dogs (one a Great Dane called Sweet Snider)—moved into a suite in the Buckman Hotel in town. If family relationships had been strained before, the cramped quarters made matters all the worse.

Despite pressing business and family problems, C.A.'s energies were now absorbed by his plan to challenge Representative Frank Buckman (owner of the Buckman Hotel) for the right to represent Minnesota's Sixth Congressional District. Theodore Roosevelt, the charismatic trust-buster, was in the White House, and the Progressive wing of Minnesota's majority Republican party was attracting new blood, mainly smart country lawyers like C.A., with creative ideas for attacking problems like discriminatory railroad freight schedules and unfair banking regulations. The Lindbergh name was still revered by the region's Scandinavian American voters, and sometime during the winter of 1905–6, C.A. had been approached by a group of Progressives who urged him to run in the Republican primary against the incumbent, Buckman.

Evangeline supported her husband's political ambitions. Although she had never attended church in Little Falls, she now dressed Charles up in an itchy flannel suit and long black stockings and brought him to services at the Lutheran church.

The Lindberghs were less enthusiastic. In addition to being his brother's law partner, Frank Lindbergh happened to be married to Buckman's daughter, and after C.A., in a moment of rhetorical excess, characterized his mission as a "battle against ignorance," the campaign took on overtones of a personal feud. Frank sided with his brother, but not happily.[6]

C.A. eked out a narrow victory over Buckman in the September primary and went on to win the general election, promising the Sixth District's voters that he was the candidate of "the masses against the classes" and in agreement with Theodore Roosevelt on "all the great issues that are before the American people today."[7]

Shortly after the election, the Lindberghs moved to an apartment in Minneapolis. According to the landlady, Charles, already scientifically curious at age five, dropped her cat out of a second-story window as an experiment to see if the animal would land on its feet. (It did.) Charles denied this story, remembering instead that a serious case of measles kept him indoors and inactive all winter long.

Congressional sessions were much shorter at the turn of the century than now, and the Sixtieth Congress would not officially open until December 1907. C.A., however, intended to be a full-time congressman, and months before the session began he moved his family to the capital, renting rooms in a modest apartment house on V Street. Immediately he began working twelve-hour days, sometimes sitting down at his desk as early as 5:00 A.M.

Among the other newcomers to Congress that term was Senator Robert ("Fighting Bob") La Follette, who soon became C.A.'s friend and political ally. La Follette was determined to organize midwestern Progressives into a powerful congressional voting bloc that would challenge the conservative wing of the party, led by Nelson Aldrich of Rhode Island. At first it was hard going. The Aldrichites treated the Progressives as pariahs, sometimes retiring to the cloakroom when one of them rose to speak. But for C.A. these battles were a bracing experience. After a lifetime of intellectual isolation, he suddenly found himself part of a vigorous insurgency, surrounded by first-class thinkers who shared his concern for the problems of rural America.

If there was a single event that symbolized for the Progressives all that was wrong with unfettered capitalism, it was a meeting held in the library of the Madison Avenue home of New York financier J. P. Morgan in December 1890. At that conference Morgan had convinced the presidents of seventeen major railroads to call a halt to their cutthroat competition and form a cartel. The meeting marked the beginning of the era of the trusts, and during the next fifteen years Morgan would personally preside over the organization of more than a half dozen megacorporations—among them United States Steel, the Guggenheim copper trust, and International Harvester, which controlled 85 percent of the farm machinery market.

The majority of the Progressives, even Fighting Bob La Follette, accepted that big business was here to stay. They looked to antitrust and consumer protection legislation to balance the overweening power of the giant corporations. At the beginning of his congressional career, C.A. shared these goals and, as he later told his journalist friend Lynn Haines, he "voted with the herd." But he was already developing a radical perspective that would win him a reputation as a "lone wolf" and the "most leftish" of the Progressive faction.[8]

C.A.'s special interest was reform of the banking industry and, looking for the power behind the railroad and tractor moguls, he focused on the one trust that controlled all the others, the Money Trust, dominated by the firm of J. P. Morgan. The influence of the Money Trust was everywhere—even Roosevelt, a hero to most Progressives, had a former J. P. Morgan partner, George W. Perkins, among his advisers. Lindbergh's theory that the Money Trust was the root of all evil would take several years to evolve, but its essentials were already apparent in his 1905 prospectus for the Industrial Adjustment Company. The concentration of financial power in the hands of a few men was poisoning the democratic process. For that matter, large cities were themselves unnatural and parasitic, the product of a distorted financial system that discriminated against the small towns and villages of the heartland.

Why is it, C.A. asked again and again, that bankers, "who are no smarter than the rest of us," continually get richer? Why do the most productive people in society, the farmers and laborers, bear the brunt of every economic downturn?[9]

At first C.A. believed that banking could be effectively regulated through the creation of a Federal Reserve system. But by 1913, when legislation to create the Federal Reserve banks was finally enacted, he had become cynical, convinced that the bill was so compromised that the system would be merely another tool of the Money Trust. In his frustration he eventually came to believe that inflation and panics were purposely created by bankers to rob the people, all as part of what he called their "selfish plan to rule the world by the manipulation of finances."[10]

While C.A. was engrossed in Progressive politics, his family life was disintegrating around him. Eva, a vigorous, intelligent girl who adored her father, went to live with relatives in Minneapolis. Her elder sister Lillian—who had inherited Mary LaFond's doe eyes, high cheekbones, and frail constitution—attended a private school in Detroit for a few months and studied briefly at the University of Michigan before returning to Little Falls to marry a young general practitioner, Dr. Loren Roberts.

Evangeline, meanwhile, had already begun writing letters to her mother in code. Whether this stratagem was intended to keep her thoughts from the prying eyes of her husband, stepdaughters, or servants is unclear, but it is evidence of her growing feelings of isolation. The move to Washington, at first welcomed as an escape from Little Falls, only made her more miserable. Scorned as a maverick by the leaders of his own party, C.A.—a teetotaler—had no interest whatsoever in the social life of the capital. He and Evangeline appeared at a few official functions together, and in the spring of 1907, she took Charles to the annual Easter Egg Hunt on the White House lawn; otherwise there were few opportunities to meet congressional wives or savor the rewards of her husband's position.

Stung by the Buckmanites' charges that he had profited from farm foreclosures, C.A. had begun to sell off his real estate holdings. In 1905 he estimated his net worth at about $165,000; three years later his holdings were reduced to about ten thousand acres, worth about $75,000. Increasingly critical of the trusts, which he saw as parasites feeding on the farmers' labor, he gave up his corporate clients. What legal business he retained was often neglected. He never again had a dependable cash income.

Evangeline sympathized with C.A.'s political goals, but she hadn't counted on marrying a prophet who was prepared to sacrifice his family's comfort for a hopeless cause. Her dim view of C.A.'s preoccupation with politics was communicated, passively or otherwise, to Charles, who stolidly resisted his father's attempts to get him interested in the affairs of Congress. C.A. proudly brought his son onto the floor of the House to witness important moments, including the passage of the act of Congress determining that the Panama Canal would be a high-level, lake-and-lock waterway, which he had enthusiastically supported. But the only aspect of congressional life that captured Charles's imagination was the tunnel that ran between the Congressional Office Building and the Capitol. The black-suited congressmen, he thought, were like ministers, except that they were even more red eyed and paunchy looking and they smoked large, smelly cigars. Instead of preaching about God, they went on about something called "Good Government." People who were in favor of it—the political equivalent of faithful Christians—were called Republicans. Those who weren't, were called Democrats. (The subtlety that only Progressive Republicans were like good Christians was lost on his six-year-old mind.)[11]

By 1907 it was apparent that the Lindberghs could no longer live under the same roof. That spring and again the following winter, Evangeline took Charles to Detroit for extended stays at her parents' home. Many years later, Charles told his father's biographer, Bruce L. Larson, that the failure of his parents' marriage was a "tragic" case of two people who were deeply in love but emotionally incompatible. As for the exact cause of the separation, he hadn't known at the time and still preferred not to speculate. This deliberate effort to close his mind to a subject he found painful would be characteristic of Charles throughout his life. His father was the same, which was no doubt a large part of the problem with his marriage. Evangeline was rather proud of her Irish temperament—though in fact she was three-quarters English and her "Irish" grandmother, Emma Kissane, apparently hailed from the Isle of Man. C.A. found emotional displays highly distasteful, and he considered many topics too private to talk about, even with his wife. As his friends Lynn and Dora Haines later wrote, "Backwards and forwards, all the Lindberghs have been like that. They do not discuss themselves even with each other."[12]

For Charles the separation was the end of what he would later call a "gray" period in his young life. In contrast to the stuffy apartments he had lived in in Minneapolis and Washington, his grandparents' house at 64 West Elizabeth Street in Detroit was a magical place, filled with fascinating objects—the stuffed head of a longhorn sheep, a human skull, trays of mounted and labeled butterflies, microscopes, lenses, an Edison phonograph, and more. His maternal grandfather, Dr. Charles H. Land, was not only a practicing dentist but an inventor, and nothing about his residence was quite like any other house in America. Dr. Land designed furniture, including a self-rocking cradle that Charles had used when he was younger, and he had wired his own home for electricity, using fixtures and hardware of his own creation. Even the flowers in the backyard garden were unique wildflower hybrids that the doctor and his wife cultivated from specimens he had collected while hiking in the woods.

The house was also the site of Dr. Land's dental surgery and inventor's laboratory. Land's waiting room was often filled with patients from all over the world, many of them wealthy and distinguished individuals who had been disfigured in accidents or by cancer. Land specialized in constructing prosthetic devices that would enable such patients to eat and speak normally and appear in public without embarrassment. For one man, who had lost all his lower teeth and part of his jaw to oral cancer, he fashioned a denture complete with pink-tinted porcelain gums and a realistically modeled lower lip. Hair from the man's own beard was fused to an "artificial skin" below the lip. Although Charles H. Land was a savior to such patients, he operated on the fringes of professional respectability, repeatedly denounced by the American Dental Association (ADA) and the dean of the University of Michigan School of Dentistry as a charlatan.

Land was an unusual sort of dentist—one who had never attended a single medical lecture, passed a qualifying examination, or even attended high school. He was descended from the first settler of Hamilton, Ontario, a Pennsylvania Tory who had fled north at the time of the Revolutionary War. By the time of Dr. Land's birth in 1847, the family fortunes were at a low ebb. His father, John Scott Land, was an unsuccessful wholesale grocer who moved his growing family to Keokuk, Iowa; Detroit; New Orleans; and finally New York, always just one step ahead of the debt collectors. In 1859, when gold was discovered in California, John Land went west to seek his fortune. The family never heard from him again, and Charles H. Land became the sole support of his family by the age of fourteen.

Land resettled his mother and siblings in Detroit, where he became a pharmacist's assistant. Drugstores of that era often repaired false teeth, and Land became so adept at this sideline that he was offered a job in Chicago, doing benchwork for Dr. Gordon Allport, an expert in gold-crown restoration. Although dental apprentices were already uncommon, Allport was so impressed by Land's skill that he trained him to do fillings and extractions. When Allport's practice was scattered by the Great Chicago Fire of 1871, Land moved to Detroit, where he married Evangeline (Eva) Lodge, whose father was both a pharmacist and the publisher of a magazine promoting what would nowadays be called holistic medicine.

Eva Lodge Land shared her husband's enthusiasm for laboratory work, and with her help he embarked on a series of ambitious projects. He experimented with nitrous oxide and other anesthetics, using himself as a guinea pig. He devised an improved formula for silver amalgam and invented a clean-burning furnace that fired porcelain inlays without discoloring them. But by far his most important invention was the full porcelain jacket crown. The gold and silver crowns used by Dr. Allport and his contemporaries were not airtight. It was actually considered desirable to leave the crown loose so that the pulp of the tooth could enjoy a healthful "bath in the sea of air that surrounds it." All too often the result was, in the words of one medical historian, "mausoleums of gold over a mass of sepsis." Land's peers greeted his airtight crown with a storm of outrage, and more than two decades passed before it won universal acceptance, but it then became the standard restoration method until the emergence of synthetics in the 1940s.

Land's lack of formal credentials accounted for much of the prejudice against him, but it was by no means the only cause. After an early run-in with another researcher who sued him for patent infringement, Land had begun to apply for patents on the procedures he developed, a practice many dentists considered unethical.[13]

Worse still, he advertised for patients in the newspapers. For this the American Dental Association refused to accept him as a member. In 1887 he was barred from attending the dentistry section of the International Medical Congress, and his chief critic, the dean of the University of Michigan School of Dentistry, denounced him as a "six dollar dentist." Land's reply was that a man with only six dollars in his pocket might not think this was such a bad thing. Striking back at the establishment in a pamphlet entitled *The Inconsistency of the Code of Dental Ethics,* he charged that "thousands of people are suffering from badly decayed teeth and resorting to barbaric methods of extraction simply because you have failed to provide a literature that the public might be made aware of the rapid progress made in the dental art."[14]

As a result of the slurs on Land's reputation, the company that manufactured his high-temperature furnace refused to produce an improved model. A libel suit against the University of Michigan dean consumed all Land's savings and ended in a hung jury. Another lawsuit against the furnace manufacturer drove him into bankruptcy. The final blow to his pride came when he decided to move his practice to Chicago: Although several dentists he had trained were using his methods very successfully there, the state of Illinois refused to grant him a license to practice.

Land seemed at times to glory in the role of the despised prophet. He wasted few opportunities to point out that many of his formally trained peers were ignorant of the basic principles of physics and mechanics, and he condemned his critics as not only "idiots" but crooks, out to discredit porcelain dentistry because, as he put it, they could make more money "plastering with silver." Land's colleagues at times suspected him of courting controversy because he knew that the more the ADA denounced him, the more the public regarded him as a miracle worker. He was certainly eccentric, however, and one former patient recalled that Land, irked by those who refused to accept the theory of evolution, hung a framed drawing of a prehistoric man on the wall of his surgery so that all who sat in his dentist's chair would be forced to contemplate humankind's descent from the apes.

Nevertheless, according to Dr. Laszlo Schwartz, a friend and close student of Land's life, the crotchety tone of Land's polemics did not reflect his personality. Schwartz describes Land as an essentially cheerful man whose myriad intellectual interests kept him young in spirit. He took his grandson for long walks in the woods, teaching him to recognize the various species of birds, flowers, and mushrooms. And though he despised the movies—which he regarded as a marvelous invention that had fallen into the hands of purveyors of mindless comedies and romantic mush—this did not stop him from giving the boy money so that he could attend the nickelodeon down the street.

Like Thomas Edison and Henry Ford, whom he greatly admired, Land had boundless faith in technology but no great confidence in the ability of human beings to use it wisely. He was fascinated by the automobile and looked forward to the day when it would drive horse-drawn carriages from the streets. But he predicted to Charles that the internal-combustion engine might lead to the human race becoming extinct like the dinosaurs, and by 1910 he was already so worried about the rising level of pollution in Detroit that he designed an air filtration system for his home.

Dinnertime conversations at the Land house ranged from heated arguments over a new design for a laboratory apparatus to philosophical speculation on evolution, religion, or the question "What is death?" Land's work with prostheses had led him to speculate that life might be essentially a mechanistic phenomenon. If it was possible to replace teeth, portions of jawbones, and even lips, then why not other organs as well? And if the body was just a collection of replaceable parts, then perhaps death could be postponed indefinitely.

Since his work, hobbies, and family were all consolidated under one roof, there was no need for Dr. Land to leave the premises, and except for his Sunday hikes, he rarely did. For that matter, none of the Lands ever seemed quite at ease away from the family circle. Like characters in an Anne Tyler novel, they basked in each other's eccentricities and found the rest of humanity disappointing by comparison.

Charles H. Land, Jr., Evangeline's only sibling, trained as a geologist and spent a few years prospecting in western Canada, then returned to his parents' home to live out his life as a bachelor. "Brother," as he was called, had built his own crystal set and spent hours tinkering in the lab, producing homemade fireworks, among other marvels.

Both Evangeline and her mother were artistic and used the laboratory to fire hand-painted porcelain plates. Evangeline's efforts in this medium were exquisite, decorated with delicate floral patterns in muted pastels, especially lavender, her favorite color. The plates were professional in quality, but there is no indication that either woman viewed them as anything more than just another hobby.

Young Charles seems to have regarded his Land relatives more as delightful playmates than adults to be reckoned with, and they, in turn, took little notice of his age. Early in 1908, soon after he turned six, his grandfather gave him his first gun, a .22 Stevens short rifle. Brother built a shooting gallery in the basement, where he and Charles took turns banging away at a target hung in front of a mattress-insulated partition. Brother had rigged the target so that when one of them scored a bull's-eye, a bell rang and a wrought iron figure of a man popped into view.

Charles also had the run of the surgery and the laboratory and was allowed to handle the most delicate equipment while his grandfather patiently answered his questions—"often while patients waited," says Schwartz. The boy was a little afraid of the dentist's chair, especially after he had a tooth filled and learned how painful it was to be under the drill. For some weeks after this experience, he avoided the surgery when there were patients around because he could not stand the thought of how miserable they must be. The dentist's chair and his grandfather's surgery, he recalled much later, became connected in his mind with the devil, just as the Capitol, where his father worked, was associated with God and religion. Yet it was the devil's workshop that he found the more fascinating.[15]

TWO

"I Worshipped Science"

ROM DETROIT, Evangeline and Charles returned to Little Falls, to spend the summer of 1908 at "the Camp," as the Lindberghs' rebuilt farmhouse was called. Seeing his son for the first time in some weeks, C.A. was taken aback to find him dragging around a rifle that was almost as long as he was tall. C.A. thought the six-year-old "a little young" to have his own gun, and he was skeptical of Brother as an instructor—for good reason, no doubt, since Charles would later remember having practiced his aim by training the .22 on the stuffed ram's head in his grandparents' living room. Since he couldn't control what happened at the Land house, C.A. decided that the time had come to teach his son to handle a gun safely. He had recently taken title to an abandoned farm within walking distance of the Camp, and that summer he and Charles began hunting there regularly.

The concept of sports clothes was unknown to C.A., who hunted in the same well-worn business suit that he wore to his office in town. He used a twelve-gauge shotgun and considered it highly unsporting to take aim at a stationary target. After Charles shot a sitting duck in the head at a distance of more than fifty yards, the rule against potshots applied to him as well. Although C.A. was a conservationist and an avid nature lover, he was also a product of the frontier, where it was taken for granted that boys and men spent a fair proportion of their leisure time shooting. Many years later Charles would provide a Minnesota historian with a list of things he and his father shot at, including pheasants, prairie chickens, hawks, rabbits, turtles, floating logs in the river, and rocks. C.A. talked often about going for "big game," meaning deer or moose, but nothing came of the plan, and one suspects that he looked forward to these hunting trips mainly as an excuse for spending time with his son. Long before the day was over Charles would be exhausted, and when C.A. saw that the boy was too tired to hold his rifle safely he would carry it for him.

Charles's parents, meanwhile, were at odds over the fututre of their marriage. Evangeline wanted a divorce or a legal separation, but in the absence of a claim of adultery or desertion she could get neither without C.A.'s cooperation, and he was resolutely opposed. The German and Swedish farm families of the Sixth District would have been scandalized by a divorced congressman, but C.A.'s main objection was that he did not want Evangeline to be free to take his only son back to Detroit. His argument that it would be unfair to deprive the boy of contact with his father made sense to Evangeline, who was unsure of herself and defensive about her refusal to live with a husband who was faithful, sober, and well-respected by his community.

Rather than take her chances with the courts, which might well have awarded custody of Charles to his father, Evangeline agreed that she and her son would spend winters in Washington, occupying separate quarters from C.A., who stayed in an inexpensive boardinghouse or, on occasion, slept on a couch in his office. In the summer they would have the use of the Camp while C.A. lived in a boardinghouse in Minneapolis or stayed with his family in Little Falls. C.A. still loved his wife and often sought her advice on political and business matters (though one suspects he seldom followed it). Despite tension over money, relations between the two of them settled into a reasonably amicable truce, and the arrangement appeared to guarantee a degree of stability for Charles. In the long run, however, it had the opposite effect.

As a grown man, Charles would remember the Washington, D.C., of his youth as "a prison."[1] He and his mother occupied a series of rented rooms—at the old Hotel Continental, in a slightly seedy apartment house on East Capitol and First streets across from the Library of Congress, and, for a somewhat longer time, at Houlton's boardinghouse on Massachusetts Avenue, within sight of the statue of Winfield Scott—who, Charles was told by his mother, was a relative of his great-grandfather John Scott Land. Evangeline had no productive work, no kitchen of her own to cook in, and, it seems, no friends—or certainly none who shared her intellectual interests.

At times she was a doting, even overprotective mother who organized educational visits to the Smithsonian and all-day excursions to Mount Vernon, Fort McHenry, and Arlington. On one memorable occasion the two of them attended an exhibition in Fort Myer where Charles, aged ten, saw his first airplane. The pilot demonstrated aerial bombardment by dropping oranges onto a chalk outline representing a battleship. At other times Evangeline was either distracted or depressed, and Charles was left to his own devices. He roller-skated on the Mall and the plazas of federal buildings, played in the self-service elevator at the Library of Congress, and hung around his father's office, where the staff found him none too easy to supervise. When C.A.'s secretary, Arthur Gorman, tried to show him the correct way to open packages, Charles snapped back, "You can't tell me what to do. You just work for my father." C.A. overheard and corrected him. "No one works for anyone else in this office. We all work together."[2]

When Charles learned in later years that Gorman had told this story to a reporter, he denied ever saying any such thing, but his own memoirs make it clear that he was a Capitol Hill brat who learned early on that the phrase "My father's a Congressman" had the power to intimidate security guards. Charles was twelve when C.A. was assigned a suite on the top floor of the new House office building, and he soon discovered that he could shinny through the crawl space in the ceiling and spy on neighboring offices. His favorite activity, however, was stealing the globular light bulbs from the lavatories and dropping them out the windows. Much to his amazement, the pedestrians on the sidewalk below were so absorbed in their own affairs that they paid scant attention to the glass bombs exploding around them. At least no one took the time to report the incidents, and he was never caught.

Frank Coxe, who was the maintenance superintendent at the time, later recalled that several congressmen's sons "ran wild" through the still-unfinished building. One day Coxe caught Charles teaching some of the younger boys how to slide down the package chute that connected the fourth floor to the basement mail room. "I grabbed him and shook him a little," Coxe said. Charles was made to promise that he would set an example and not let the boys use the chute again, and he kept his word.[3]

A few students of Charles Lindbergh's life have been almost obsessed by the notion that C.A. was a rigid disciplinarian who subjected his son to

Spartan ordeals in order to toughen him. It is true that C.A. lectured all three of his children about self-discipline and frugality and how much tougher he had had it when he was a child, but more often than not these sermons were a prelude to letting the youngsters have their own way. An associate of C.A.'s was shocked when Charles, about nine years old and tall for his age, interrupted a political discussion by leaping onto his father's back and hanging there, his arms clasped around his throat. C.A. never uttered a word of remonstrance but carried the boy around piggyback until he got bored and jumped down. When separated from his son, C.A. wrote him playful letters decorated with stick-figure drawings, and he delighted in sending "wonder packages" filled with small gifts.

It is doubtful that Charles ever lacked for anything he really needed, but C.A.'s perpetual cash crisis left little money for toys and other luxuries, and he felt deprived—as in comparison with some of his private-school classmates he no doubt was. It fell to Evangeline, trying to manage on the allowance she received from her husband, to explain that she could not afford to give him what the boys he went to school with had. Charles soon learned that if he appealed directly to C.A., his father would sometimes come up with the money, but playing off one parent against the other did not always work and for the most part he relied on his imagination and homemade toys for amusement.

There was a vacant lot near Houlton's boardinghouse where Charles, inspired by a visit to the Smithsonian, played at being a paleontologist digging for dinosaur bones. One day he arrived at his "dig" and found a pile of toys—a big, fluffy teddy bear, a bright red fire engine, and other dazzling treasures. Thrilled, he scooped them up in his arms and ran home. Evangeline took one look at his haul, dumped it into the trash, and marched him off to the tub, where she scrubbed him from head to foot with a stiff brush and laundry soap. Later Charles learned that a child in the neighborhood had died of scarlet fever and his mother was afraid the toys were contaminated. Looking back on the incident in middle age, he accepted this explanation but left no doubt that he considered it a paradigm of his relationship with his overcontrolling mother. "As a child, I discovered that most worthwhile things of life involved a struggle," he commented.[4]

In fact, Charles was deprived not so much of material things as of childhood itself. Looking back on this period of his life, Lindbergh once commented that he took it for granted that he had little in common with others his age, did not think to wonder why that was, but considered himself basically happy though aware of a certain isolation. Other evidence, including some of his own reminiscences, paints a darker picture. After his parents' separation he quickly became his mother's chief companion and protector. As sometimes happens in these situations, it was almost as if their roles were reversed: He had become the adult and, in effect, a substitute spouse. From an early age he handled travel arrangements and other errands, was no stranger to housework, and learned to read his mother's rapidly changing moods and cope accordingly. Evangeline, for example, was terrified of lightning, and at the first clap of thunder, he would rush to her bedside and hold her hand until the storm passed.

Eva Lindbergh, who otherwise had nothing positive to say about her stepmother, conceded on several occasions that Evangeline could be very good with young children. There can be no doubt that Mrs. Lindbergh's lively imagination and sense of fun made her a delightful companion and teacher—so much so that it is little wonder that Charles found school dull by comparison. But there was also a streak of controlled paranoia in Evangeline's personality. She was hurt when C.A. did not send news of Eva and Lillian, and vaguely suspicious and hostile when he did. No one, from tradesmen on up to her own husband, ever treated her in quite the way she felt she deserved to be treated. The only exceptions to this rule were members of her own family, especially Charles.

For a growing boy it must have been a struggle to avoid being smothered by the attentions of this volatile and at times unconsciously flirtatious mother. As an adult Charles Lindbergh would remain very protective of Evangeline, and he always declined to discuss his relationship with her in any detail. However, in an unpublished response to an early biography that portrayed his mother as cold and physically undemonstrative, he hinted that the problem was really quite the reverse.

Perhaps out of a need for security, Charles became a compulsive collector. He collected not only stamps, toy soldiers, and cigarette cards, but pebbles, sharks' teeth and, at one point, empty tin cans. Deciding that it would be fun to collect autographs as well, he screwed up his courage and approached the Speaker of the House, the famously irascible Joe Cannon. "Son, my signature isn't worth anything, even on a check," Cannon chortled.

Charles was so mortified by this response that he never requested an autograph from anyone again. One suspects that this extreme reaction was not so much a symptom of shyness as of his chronic uncertainty about how to present himself. He was, in a sense, an adult masquerading in a child's body and thus, in the eyes of the adult world, effectively invisible. Far from lacking self-confidence, he had a somewhat exaggerated estimate of his own capabilities, but figuring out how to get strangers to take him seriously was a problem. When grown-ups talked down to him he tried to accept it stoically, but it hurt his pride.

Relations with children his own age were even more difficult. Perhaps the most telling fact about Charles Lindbergh's childhood is that in 1927, when he had become the most famous man in the world, Washington reporters desperate for childhood anecdotes were unable to track down a single friend from his school days. By his own count Charles attended at least eleven different institutions, public and private, between the ages of eight and sixteen. Sidwell Friends, where he was enrolled two years in a row, in the seventh and eighth grades, was the institution where he stayed the longest. Even there he did not attend classes for the full academic year. Evangeline's habit of spending a few weeks in Detroit on her way to and from the summer house in Little Falls meant that Charles invariably started the school year late and was withdrawn before it ended. During the rest of the year he was often absent and almost always inattentive. His grades were poor, though he usually managed to do well enough on exams to avoid outright failure.

Neither of his parents found this situation worrisome. Evangeline disapproved of rote learning and believed she could do a better job teaching her son at home. When teachers complained that Charles was falling behind in his work, her solution was to pull him out of class and place him elsewhere. C.A. occasionally prodded his wife to find a permanent school for their son, but in general he had little respect for formal education and thought it unnatural to keep healthy youngsters cooped up in a classroom. In any event, he was suspicious of the American educational system, whose "censored textbooks" prevented teachers from telling the truth about the evils of capitalism.

C.A. was a restless man, constantly shuttling between Washington and Minneapolis with visits to Progressive colleagues in the Midwest sandwiched in between. For years he talked of taking eight or nine months off from politics to make a trip around the world; the journey was repeatedly postponed, but the itinerary—including an overland trek through China—had been worked out in his mind to the last detail.

Evangeline, too, adored travel, though she could never afford to do as much of it as she would have liked, and it is little wonder that Charles, from an early age, longed to see faraway places. In 1908 C.A. visited Panama as part of a congressional delegation investigating the Canal Zone Treaty, and from that time on, the desire to see Panama himself became almost an obsession with Charles. The journey was an expensive one, seven days each way by steamer, but when Charles wanted something nothing could distract him, and in 1913, after five years of listening to her son's pleading, Evangeline decided to grant him his wish. Fascinated by romantic tales of seafaring adventure and buccaneers, Evangeline and Charles toured the castle of the "pirate Morgan" and were thrilled to see one of the last of the square-rigged sailing ships plying its route between two Caribbean islands, but for Charles the highlight of the journey was watching giant earth-moving machines chew their way through the side of a mountain at the Culebra Cut (later renamed the Gaillard Cut for the army engineer in charge of its excavation). During the first decade of the twentieth century, engineering, previously associated with mechanics and artisans, had come to be considered a profession, and a rather glamorous one at that. Like both his father and his grandfather Land, Charles considered the canal the greatest triumph of American civilization.

Most years Charles lived for the moment when he and his mother returned to Little Falls. After spending the winter and spring with his mother, crowded into their cramped quarters at the boardinghouse, he was outdoors from dawn to dusk. He went wading in Pike's Creek, which joined the Mississippi just south of the house, played in the hayloft of the tenant farmer's barn, and built a playhouse out of odds and ends of lumber. (The design included a trapdoor at one end, so that his father could stretch his legs when he crawled inside for a visit.)

Although the farm was only two miles from Little Falls, Evangeline did not keep a horse and carriage, so mother and son were rather isolated. Ferguson's grocery wagon came around weekly to deliver Evangeline's standing order of groceries. If his mother needed other items or had letters to post, Charles would pedal into town on the folding bicycle that had been given to him by Grandfather Land. They never attended church or social events. It was common gossip that the congressman's son had never been seen in a white shirt, and C.A.'s family complained that Evangeline discouraged Charles from visiting them. His aunt, Juno Lindbergh Butler, described her nephew as "shy and a little odd."[5]

According to Lindbergh, his mother did encourage him to play with two boys who lived nearby, Alex Johnson and Bill Thompson. (In fact, he recalled that she paid them to play with him—supposedly because otherwise they would have been earning money doing chores!) Together the three youngsters visited the Pike's Creek swimming hole and fished for suckers in the river. Charles thought of Alex and Bill as his best friends. But Thompson, at least, saw it differently and when later asked about his impressions of the young Lindbergh, he commented laconically, "He was not what could be called a buddy."[6]

No doubt they had few interests in common. Used to entertaining himself, Charles had a long attention span and would become engrossed in his own projects for days at a time. Some of these could almost serve as textbook illustrations of the benefits of home schooling. At the age of seven, he designed a system for moving heavy blocks of ice from the ice-house to the kitchen, using pulleys, levers, inclined planes, and a toy wagon. In his mid-teens, when he decided to make a cement birdbath for the ducks, he began by reading everything he could on the theory of concrete construction, beginning with government pamphlets recommended by his father. He spent hours observing the ducks' behavior and calculated the optimum shape for the pond, so that its sides would retain water but still not be too steep for the ducks to negotiate. The result of these efforts, a small, basinlike pond—called *Moo Pond* because someone had told him that *moo* was the Chippewa word for dirty—is still in existence, undamaged by ice after more than eighty-five Minnesota winters.

Not all Charles's pastimes were so serious. He was fascinated by guns and spent many hours banging away at targets he set up along the riverbank. By the age of nine he had acquired a formidable arsenal. His father had passed on his old Savage .22-caliber repeating rifle, a Winchester twelve-gauge shotgun, and a .38 Smith & Wesson revolver. Grandfather Land had given him a pistol in addition to the Stevens .22, and his granduncle, Edwin Lodge, let him have an old ten-gauge saluting cannon, formerly used to signal the start of yacht races. Charles's fantasies of himself as a quick-draw artist survived into early adulthood, and at age nineteen, while staying alone at the Camp, he accidentally shot a hole in the living room door.

He was also extremely fond of dogs. Sweet Snider and the other pets of Charles's babyhood were followed by Todo, a dachshund cross; a hunting hound called Spot; and a spaniel named Hunter. Dingo, a lop-eared, nondescript mongrel, came into his life as an abandoned puppy who raided the garbage at night and snarled at anyone who came near. One morning Evangeline accidentally cornered the pup on the porch. The dog bared its teeth, and Evangeline reacted—"characteristically," Charles recalled—by scooping the pup up in her arms and hugging it close. Dingo became, quite literally, Charles's best friend. It was impossible to keep a dog in Washington, however, and the moment when Dingo was turned over to the farm family that cared for him over the winter was always emotionally wrenching.

But by far the greatest of the Camp's many attractions was that there—as seldom happened in Washington—Charles could enjoy his father's undivided attention. The timing of C.A.'s visits was always unpredictable; he dropped in when congressional business required his presence at his office in town. C.A. would leave his bicycle up the road and approach the house on foot, whistling *whip-poor-will, whip-poor-will.* Hearing this secret signal, Charles would drop whatever he was doing and come running.

Father and son swam naked in the river, and C.A. thought nothing of hoisting the boy onto his back and carrying him to the opposite shore, slicing through the swift current with his powerful breaststroke. On other visits he took his son fishing on Squaw Lake, where he made a game of sneaking up on mud turtles, scooping them into the boat with an oar. "How many do you want, Boss?" he called out as the bottom of the boat filled with turtles of all sizes and varieties. Later all were released except, on one trip, for a pair of babies that Charles kept as pets.

At five feet eleven inches and about 175 pounds, C.A. was not an especially imposing physical specimen, yet in the eyes of his contemporaries he loomed larger than life. Lynn Haines told of accompanying C.A. to the hospital for what he was told would be a minor procedure. When the doctor arrived it developed that C.A. was to have an operation for a ruptured hernia. Refusing an anesthetic or even a snort of whiskey, C.A. discoursed on the Federal Reserve system as the surgeon sliced through the wall of his abdomen. Later he apologized to Haines for subjecting him to an unpleasant experience.

Although he was often described as a dour, rigid man, C.A.'s letters reveal a spontaneous side to his personality and, on occasion, a sense of humor worthy of Wotan. Once, visiting a friend's hunting cabin, he decided to sleep fully dressed on a cot on the porch only to be awakened in the middle of the night by a sudden downpour that left him sopping wet. Describing the experience to Eva, he allowed that spending the remainder of the night and all the next day in his wet clothes had been rather inconvenient, but "it was fun, just the same."

Even God seemed small to C.A. Rejecting the vengeful God of traditional Protestantism as a "puny creature," he communed with nature and read Unitarian tracts and poetry, searching for a deity more worthy of his respect.[7]

To a young boy this dynamic man must have seemed a giant indeed. Charles longed for C.A.'s approval and was delighted in 1914 when C.A. informed him that he was thinking of touring the headwaters of the Mississippi in connection with pending flood control legislation and would like Charles to come along. Father and son navigated lakes and streams in a roughly built boat and camped out with a band of Chippewa. The following summer the journey was repeated, this time in a boat equipped with an outboard motor. Both expeditions were made at the height of blackfly season with a minimum of food and gear. Charles met every challenge and earned C.A.'s ultimate praise. "You and I can take hard knocks," he told the boy. "We'll get along no matter what happens."

But C.A. was gone more than he was around, and in his absence the Lindbergh farm became a favorite target of rowdies. Once a bullet whizzed by Evangeline's head as she was standing by the flower beds. On another occasion a man walking on the road just north of the Lindbergh property was hit in the leg.

Determined to defend his mother and the house, Charles dug a trench in a spot with a clear view of the meadow on the opposite bank of the river. A year went by without incident, and the trench became overgrown with grass and weeds. Then one day, as he was trying out a homemade raft he had built from leftover fence posts, the water around him was peppered with gunfire. Quickly he poled for shore and dashed into the house to retrieve his .22 rifle and the ten-gauge saluting cannon. Bill Thompson happened to be playing on the property, and the two boys sprinted for the trench.

Peering across the river, Charles saw a grown man with a rifle and four or five teenage boys singing, "shoot the old nigger up in the tree." He fired his .22, not aiming for a hit but coming close enough to leave some doubt as to his intentions. Simultaneously Bill shot off the cannon. Blank shell or not, its boom echoed across the valley, scaring the attackers out of their wits. "The group scattered into bushes and trees, and there was no more firing that year," Lindbergh recalled with no little pride.[8]

Charles and his mother were outsiders, an attractive woman and a child living alone, and as such they were easy prey for troublemakers. But there appears to have been more to these incidents than Lindbergh ever admitted. Perhaps the Camp was targeted because of C.A.'s politics, always controversial even in his hometown. Perhaps they were inspired by Evangeline's enemies. Mrs. Lindbergh was not a snob, as some in Little Falls thought, but she had a sharp tongue at times, and when she disliked someone, she made her feelings all too clear. It is not uncommon for farm dogs that wander to wind up shot, but the Lindberghs lost a suspicious number of pets over the years, including Dingo, whom Charles found lying dead on their own property during the summer of 1915.

By 1912 C.A. had become nervous about his family's isolation, and one day he appeared in a brand-new Model T Tourabout, driven by Clifton Roberts, the town's first automobile dealer and the brother of Lillian's husband, Dr. Loren Roberts. He announced that he had purchased the car for campaign trips but planned to leave it at the Camp the rest of the year.

In Evangeline's eyes the car was a mixed blessing. She named it *Maria* (pronounced with a long *i*) and suffered through a few driving lessons without overcoming her terror of shifting into second gear. The Ford had a crank starter with a recoil powerful enough to break a grown man's arm, and she and Charles often labored for more than half an hour to get the motor to turn over. Once behind the wheel, she drove the two miles into town with her foot clamped down hard on the gearshift pedal. These trips were so nerve wracking that Charles, then eleven, decided to take over the driving.

Charles gave Bill Thompson and Alex Johnson rides, and he boasted that the Model T was "his" car. This claim got back to Eva Lindbergh and caused some friction between C.A. and his daughters, but on the whole Charles's pride of possession was justified. Like all cars of its vintage, *Maria* required a good deal of maintenance. Even on short trips, the driver had to be prepared to tinker with the engine, change tires, and make adjustments to the gas headlamps (powered by a stream of water dripping onto lumps of calcium carbide). All these jobs were left to Charles, and by the summer of 1913 he was driving C.A. to speaking engagements around the state. Between campaign swings, he planned outings for himself and his mother. Equipped with a picnic lunch, they would set out for St. Cloud, Brainerd, or some scenic spot like Mille Lacs. "Maria gave us a freedom to travel that we had never dreamed of before," he would recall.

For an eleven-year-old it was a heady experience. The geographic horizons of both his parents had suddenly expanded, and it was his mastery of *Maria* that made it all possible. To his mind the mysteries of the internal-combustion engine were far more compelling than his father's speeches about the evils of the gold standard. At political rallies Charles distributed handbills and copies of his father's books, but when it was time for C.A. to take to the podium, delivering his indictment of "evil" New York bankers in piercing, high-pitched tones so unlike his normal speaking voice, Charles was usually found with his head buried under the hood or scribbling in the notebook in which he kept a log of the car's travel and maintenance history.

C.A.'s attacks on the Money Trust and its lackeys, including what he called the "subsidized press," had become more rabid over the years, and he found it increasingly difficult to imagine how the evils of capitalism could be curbed, short of social revolution.

In many respects C.A. was an enlightened man. He was an early champion of conservation laws and advocated the absolute protection of free speech and voting rights for women. He urged his daughter Eva to take up a career; thinking perhaps of Evangeline, he warned her that early marriage "is usually enough to squelch a woman for good."

However, some of C.A.'s other opinions would be an embarrassment to a later generation inclined to view him as a crusading socialist. Like many Progressives, he was deeply influenced by the theories of Social Darwinism. He believed that the genetic inferiority of blacks was a scientific fact; however, he also predicted that America's racial problems would be resolved in the long run by intermarriage, a position unlikely to endear him to the typical racist. In Minnesota politics, where the ethnic struggle that counted was between German Catholics on the one hand and German and Scandinavian Protestants on the other, he stirred controversy by making common cause with a fringe group called the Free Press League, which charged that parochial schools were part of the pope's master plan to subvert American values.

However, Lindbergh's opinions on race are known only from a single article written early in his career, and his flirtation with the Free Press League would prove fleeting. Similarly, though it has sometimes been said that he was a rabid anti-Semite, evidence for this is hard to find in his surviving writings. At the very least, in contrast to many agrarian radicals, C.A. understood that economic power in America was in the hands of wealthy Anglo-Saxons—and it was this group, the "anglophiles" as he called them, to whom he ascribed sinister influence.

His worst suspicions were proved to his satisfaction in 1914. After war broke out in Europe, C.A.'s bête noire, J. P. Morgan & Co., set out to finance the Allied cause by sponsoring the sale of five hundred million dollars in English and French war bonds. The Morgan bank then set up its own production division to help the Allied governments spend the proceeds from the bond issue. Shipments of American-made arms and supplies across the Atlantic inevitably became targets for German U-boat attacks. To C.A. it was self-evident that the United States was being pushed to the brink of war by a cabal of profiteers. In addition to Morgan & Co., the conspirators included the "Wall Street speculators" who had purchased the war bonds, the press, probusiness lobbies like the Chamber of Commerce and a few collateral institutions like the Carnegie Foundation, the Rockefeller Institute, and the American Red Cross, whose president was Henry P. Davison, Sr., a J. P. Morgan partner. "At no period in the world's history has deceit been so bold and aggressive as now in attempting to engulf all humanity in a maelstrom of hell," C.A. thundered.[9]

To critics who maintained that other issues were at stake—freedom of the seas, national honor, and the future of the Western democracies— C.A. proposed nationalization of the munitions industry—"thus removing any suspicion of conflict of interest." If America's security were indeed at stake, then the crisis was too important to be left in private hands: "Let there be no profit in any war enterprise."[10]

In 1916 C.A. abandoned his safe seat in the House and entered the Republican senatorial primary. His isolationist sentiments proved popular with the German and Scandinavian farmers of Minnesota. But the Progressive vote was split, and he lost to a moderate St. Paul attorney, Frank B. Kellogg.

Charles was his father's driver during this campaign and was deeply disappointed when "we" lost. Though he would insist in later life that he was scarcely aware of the issues, this recollection is not to be taken literally. C.A. talked to his son often about politics, and sent him autographed first copies of his books. Charles knew, moreover, that his Land and Lodge relatives in Detroit, many of whom were active in mainstream Republican politics, regarded C.A. as a fanatic.

C.A. himself was resigned to the fact that many of his goals would not be achieved or even understood in his own lifetime. "These things will come about after I'm gone," he would tell his son. Charles disliked this kind of talk because it reminded him that there would be a time when his father would no longer be with him.

Fortunately Charles had an excuse for not thinking too deeply about his father's beliefs. "Like most modern youth, I worshipped science," he would recall. "I was awed by its knowledge. Its advances had surpassed man's wildest dreams. Its benefits and powers appeared unlimited. In its learning seemed to lie the key to all the mysteries of life." Science had already made religion obsolete. It would soon do the same for politics. That being the case, he could support his father out of personal loyalty without bothering to decide whether he was right or wrong.[11]

The summer of 1916 was a bitter time for C.A. At fifty-seven his political future was in doubt. Eva, who had become her father's closest confidante as well as his research assistant, was engaged to a reporter, and the couple planned to purchase a small newspaper in the northern part of the state. Worse, the always-fragile Lillian, now a twenty-nine-year-old mother of two, had tuberculosis and was sinking fast. In a desperate effort to arrest the disease the family decided to take her to Santa Marguerita, California, where C.A.'s older half-brother, Peder, also called Perry, still ran a cattle ranch.

Evangeline was not on good terms with Lillian and her husband Loren Roberts, and she and Charles were not invited along. Charles was heartbroken—ostensibly because he was not going to see California but no doubt because the snub also made it all too clear that he would always be excluded from his father's other family. C.A. had recently replaced the Model T with a new Saxon Six sedan, and Charles begged to be allowed to drive the car to the West Coast. Amazingly, Evangeline agreed to let him. The two of them decided to take along Wahgoosh, a mixed-breed terrier Charles had recently purchased to replace the beloved Dingo. In addition Brother Land was talked into accompanying them for company and protection.

In 1916 there was nothing routine about a cross-country automobile trip. Rural roads were often treacherous, facilities few and far between, and the Saxon, while a more comfortable car than the Model T, was also a good deal less rugged. Like Evangeline, Brother did not drive. The planning as well as all the driving and car maintenance were left entirely up to fourteen-year-old Charles, who confidently predicted that the trip could be accomplished in ten days.

The Saxon broke down for the first time in Iowa, where it was necessary to wait for shipment of a replacement timer. In Kansas it threw a spring. What with one mishap and another, the journey took four times as long as expected. Charles described these problems in a letter to his father, so impersonal that it might as well have been the report of a hired chauffeur. Since C.A. was no doubt going to be unhappy about the damage to his car and the extra expenses, Charles may have been trying to make a businesslike impression. Nevertheless, the letter, bereft of any comments on the scenery, the company, or any extramechanical adventures en route, much less any expression of concern for Lillian, reeks of suppressed resentment.

Soon after they reached their destination, Brother Land returned to Detroit by train, and Evangeline, Charles, and Wahgoosh settled down in a small cottage in Redondo Beach. Charles enrolled in the public high school but rarely went, skipping classes to explore California's still-unspoiled beaches with his mother.

The Roberts-Lindbergh party, meanwhile, crossed the country by train, reaching Uncle Perry's ranch in mid-November. Two weeks later Lillian died, and her grieving family accompanied her coffin back to Little Falls. Evangeline remained in California with Charles until mid-April 1917, when Brother wrote saying that their mother had been diagnosed with cancer. She and Charles immediately packed up the Saxon and headed back east.

After Lillian's funeral, C.A. had returned to Washington, where he spent the final weeks of his lame-duck term trying to muster support for a bill that would have required a national referendum to ratify a declaration of war. The effort was futile. Shortly after Woodrow Wilson's second inauguration in March, the president sent his war message to Congress. C.A. immediately announced that he would cease his antiwar activism for patriotic reasons, but privately he was scornful: "There is no such thing as a war for democracy," he told Lynn Haines that spring.

In his gloomier moods he wondered if the war wasn't the beginning of the collapse of European civilization. On February 4, 1917, he wrote, "Charles is fifteen today.... The world has gone mad, and the white race stands in jeopardy from its own folly or craze."[12]

Despite his avowed intention to refrain from speaking against the war, C.A. decided to go ahead with the publication of an already completed book, which set forth his reasons for thinking that the Money Trust would use the conflict as an excuse to undermine civil liberties, overturn what few conservation laws were on the books, and turn working people into "industrial slaves." The book, cumbersomely titled, *Why Is Your Country at War and What Happens to You After the War and Related Subjects,* circulated mainly in the Prairie States, in areas with established agrarian-Progressive constituencies.

Although C.A. had talked for years about his longing to return to private life, he soon agreed to run in the Republican primary for governor on a slate sponsored by the Non-Partisan League, a group whose platform called for the nationalization of grain elevators and flour mills, government-sponsored crop insurance, and other federal programs that would guarantee farmers a stable income. By the time the campaign got under way, war hysteria had risen to a fever pitch. Beethoven was banned from concert halls. Butcher shops that continued to sell bratwurst, as opposed to "victory sausage," were picketed. After the Soviet Union made a separate peace with Germany, in March 1918, feeling against Bolsheviks—a term loosely interpreted to include anyone with socialistic inclinations—was if anything even more intense. The panic culminated with the notorious Palmer Raids of 1919–20, when agents of the Departments of Justice and labor rounded up thousands of radicals without benefit of warrants or formal charges.

According to an unconfirmed account by C.A.'s sometime law partner, Walter Eli Quigley, his publisher, the National Capital Press, was among the raids' targets, and federal agents used the occasion to smash the plates of *Why Is Your Country at War.* It is also said that a group of Little Falls residents, including some of the LaFonds, had put out a standing offer to buy up copies of the book in order to burn them. For whatever reasons, it soon came to pass that just about the only people who had access to the book were editorial writers at hostile papers who delighted in quoting C.A.'s attack on the Red Cross and other more extreme passages. The *New York Times* styled C.A. a "Gopher Bolshevik," but this was mild compared to some Minnesota papers, which urged that he be charged with sedition or worse.

At C.A.'s rallies, howling mobs tore up his campaign banners, threw rotten eggs, and shouted him down. In the town of Red Wing, he was hanged in effigy. In Martin County he was met by one hundred armed sheriff's deputies, who ran him out of town and arrested one of his campaign workers on a charge of "conspiracy." In Duluth, a center of the steel and armaments industries, no organization would rent him a hall. As he was leaving an outdoor rally in Rock County, a shotgun blast slammed into the side of his car. C.A. never so much as flinched. "Don't drive so fast, Gunny," he instructed his driver. "They will think we're scared."[13]

Despite this show of bravado, C.A. expected that he would be either dead or in jail by primary day, and he had instructed his family, including the loyal Eva, to stay out of the campaign. Amazingly, he not only survived but polled a respectable 150,626 votes to his opponent's 199,325. Although he did not run in the general election, he continued to stump the state, speaking on behalf of the newly formed Farmer-Labor party, a coalition formed by the Non-Partisan League and pro-labor interests.

For the first time in four years, Charles took no part in his father's political activities. He was too busy to do so, even if C.A. had not been determined to keep his family out of sight. Both of Charles's maternal grandparents were ill—his grandmother with cancer and Dr. Land with a shaking palsy that may have been Parkinson's disease. Brother Land and Evangeline decided they had no choice but to divide the burden, and so Evangeline brought her mother to Little Falls where she could nurse her full-time. The Camp still had no central heating, insulation, or proper indoor plumbing (just a pump in the kitchen), and though C.A. agreed to pay for a furnace, much of the work of getting the house ready for winter occupancy fell to Charles. Furthermore, the government had announced that it was the patriotic duty of all farmers to keep their land in production, and since—with so many able-bodied men off to the war—it was impossible to find a tenant, Charles persuaded his mother to let him try his hand at running the farm.

Eva Land was dying a slow, agonizing death, and when winter came, Charles, who was in the habit of sleeping on the porch, put off moving his camp bed indoors. In December the nighttime temperatures dipped to thirty below zero, unusually cold even for central Minnesota. Charles would wrap himself in an old raccoon coat of his father's, jump through the porch window directly onto the bed, and burrow under the quilts as quickly as possible to keep his face from freezing. He got up at dawn to stoke the furnace, chop wood, and feed the chickens and geese, then hiked two miles up the snow-covered road to Little Falls High School, where he was enrolled in the senior class.

Charles's preparation was spotty to begin with, and with no energy left for schoolwork he fell farther behind in his studies. Just when it seemed that his chances of graduating were nil, the principal called an assembly to announce that the high school was participating in the Food for Victory program. Because of the critical shortage of farmhands, senior boys who dropped out to work full-time on the land would be graduated automatically. Rescued by this miracle, he left school immediately and did not return until the diplomas were handed out in June.

Even after he was freed from the burden of attending school, Charles did not have much time for keeping up with the war news, but like many boys his age he did manage to follow the exploits of the great air aces—Americans Eddie Rickenbacker and Frank Luke, the Briton Edward ("Mick") Mannock, Frenchmen Charles Nungesser and René Fonck, and even the Germans Baron von Richthofen and Ernst Udet, as well as his favorite, the fictional "Tam o' the Scoots," hero of a magazine series. In the popular imagination if not in fact, aviators were knights of the air who met in single combat and fought according to gentlemen's rules. Aerial warfare had nothing to do with the grubby realities of trench warfare, much less the killing of civilians. In fact, no less a figure than Orville Wright had predicted that the growth of aviation would increase understanding among the peoples of the world and eventually lead to the elimination of war. People were beginning to talk about air-mindedness—a term that meant not just interest in airplanes but the belief that aviation would become the instrument of sweeping social change.

If the war lasted another year, Charles decided, he would try to enlist as army pilot. But one day in November 1918, while he was waiting at an auction for a chance to bid on some stock, a farmer came running up, shouting that an armistice had been signed. The army promptly canceled airplane contracts and began selling off existing planes as surplus, and hundreds of trained pilots, many of whom had never even made it overseas, found that their skills were redundant. Charles gave up all thought of learning to fly for the time being.

THREE

"This Strange Unmortal Space"

IN HIS EAGERNESS TO BE A SCIENTIFIC FARMER, Charles invested heavily in machinery and stock. He ordered a metal-wheeled LaCrosse tractor, one of the first in the area, and became the local sales representative for the Empire Milking Machine Company. His stock-breeding plans got under way with the purchase of a registered Guernsey bull, a full-blooded Guernsey cow, and a registered Shropshire ewe, and the dining room of the Camp was soon filled with incubators, including one he had designed and built himself. In a single season he hatched more than one thousand chickens. The only hired help was Daniel Thompson, a retired lumberjack in his seventies, whom C.A. had invited to live in the tenant's house. He and Charles set to work to repair the barn, refence several fields, and—using barbed wire and a few ash poles—construct a swinging bridge across Pike's Creek. In the future Charles hoped to raise Duroc-Jersey hogs and Toulouse geese. The only detail he hadn't worked out was how to make his capital investments pay off on a farm of only 110 acres, many of them untillable.

Charles's second shortcoming as a farmer was a tendency to make pets of the animals. When a herd of black-faced ewes C.A. had purchased out west began to drop their lambs during a late winter snowstorm and, for some reason, proved to be poor mothers, Charles hiked through the snowdrifts to rescue the lambs and carried them in his arms back to the garage, where Evangeline fed them by hand and gave them all names. A calf born under difficult circumstances was soon added to the growing brood. C.A. chided his son for running up a vet bill for a sick cow that was more than the cow was worth, and on one occasion he warned Charles to find new homes for his menagerie before he next returned to Little Falls, otherwise "they wouldn't be pets long."

However proud he was of Charles's enterprise, C.A. was also more than a little alarmed to think that he might have a vocation for farming. Although he had built his political philosophy on the premise that the farmer was the mainstay of the democratic system, he had no great desire to see his son become one. Under the current economic system, he warned Charles, the farmer existed only to be robbed blind by the capitalists. In any case the Little Falls property had been a drain on his income for twenty years, and C.A. hinted repeatedly in his letters that he would have sold the Camp long before, if only Charles and his mother hadn't been so attached to the place.

Evangeline, who had more influence over Charles than his father did at that point, got him to promise that he would try farming for only a year or so and then give it up to enter college. She had seen firsthand how the lack of academic credentials had blighted her father's career, and, of course, the passing years had made a degree not just desirable but essential.

Charles was probably as well prepared for college as the average high school graduate, especially in the sciences, but his dismal school experiences had left him without much confidence in his ability to master unfamiliar subjects. Inspired by his grandfather Land's example, he thought about becoming a doctor but became discouraged when he was told that Latin was a prerequisite for medical school. MIT, which had the only aeronautical engineering program in the country, was another intriguing possibility, but his high school record did not meet the school's standards. In the end he decided to enroll in the University of Wisconsin at Madison for no better reason than because it was situated on a large lake.

With nothing to keep her at the Camp, Evangeline applied for a job teaching junior high school science in Madison, and in the late summer of 1920 she went ahead to rent an apartment for both of them. A few weeks later Charles turned the farm over to a new tenant and rode his Excelsior motorcycle to Wisconsin.

Almost immediately he was roundly disillusioned with college life. The routine, he complained to classmates, was just a rehash of high school. "Presumably a man comes to college because he wants an edu-

cation," he groused. "Why, then, all this taking of rolls, daily assignments, checks on your personal life, and so on?" He resented being
treated like a child, but, as he himself later admitted, he did not have the
motivation to study on his own and did the required work grudgingly
when he did it at all. The only activity that commanded his full attention
was the ROTC rifle team. In several competitions he hit fifty bull's-eyes
in succession, and at the end of his freshman year he won a medal as the
team's best all-round shooter. His favorite trick was to get a friend to
hold a quarter between his index finger and thumb. Charles would then
plug the coin from a distance of fifty feet.[1]

When not target shooting, he spent a great deal of time tooling
around Madison on his Excelsior, often in the company of two other
avid cyclists, a country boy named Richard Plummer and Delos Dudley,
the son of a university librarian. The three friends also spent many
evenings building an iceboat in the Dudleys' basement, and when winter came Charles removed the motor from his Excelsior and mounted it
on the boat. On test runs the iceboat proved underpowered, and before
the joint owners could figure out a way to soup up the engine, it was
wrecked in a collision with another boat.

Lindbergh's grades in his mechanical engineering courses were
mediocre to begin with and sagged still lower as his level of boredom
rose. However, unusually for an engineering student, he showed a flair
for creative writing. One of his themes took the form of a dialogue
between a dating couple on their way to see a movie entitled "Sinful
Sin." The coed, Miss Justrite, is an expert on Theda Bara's films, but
when the subject of the Panama Canal comes up, she airily dismisses the
project as "a big graft." Miss Justrite and her smug, vacuous beau, Mr.
O'Kay, are compared unflatteringly to a pair of earnest sailors who lack
formal education but are smart enough to know that the canal is the
greatest engineering feat of the century.[2]

Miss Justrite was apparently a reflection of the college women
Lindbergh had met in Madison and whom he'd had no success dating.
Delos Dudley told him that his approach was too intellectual. "Just grab
a breast," he advised. Lindbergh was shocked. He couldn't imagine any
circumstance in which he would be desperate enough to resort to grab-
bing. If he were in love, he reasoned, it wouldn't be necessary. And if he
weren't, he wouldn't even want to.[3]

Charles's attitude toward women, formed largely in the abstract,
was at once highly idealized and slightly contemptuous. The reason he
didn't date in college, he later explained, was that getting to know girls

inevitably involved a lot of time-wasting activity—hours spent sitting stiffly in parlors dressed in uncomfortable clothes, making inane small talk, and playing silly parlor games. Lindbergh, it seems, was looking for someone like his mother, whose hobbies included studying organic chemistry and experimenting with colloids; even at the University of Wisconsin such women were rare and not easy to meet. Nor would they necessarily be interested in Charles Lindbergh. Richard Plummer's girl-friend Eunice, for one, considered Charles a grubby youth whose most noticeable characteristics were engine grease under his fingernails and a surly demeanor.

Charles's lack of commitment to the university was no doubt influenced by C.A.'s warnings that he would be unable to afford the next year's tuition. C.A. had said the same when Eva was a student Carleton College, yet somehow the money had been found. This time, however, he was talking about selling or mortgaging the farm, and Evangeline, who was already paying her and Charles's living expenses out of her teaching salary, was not sympathetic. Instead of devoting his time to the practice of law and thereby solving his cash-flow problems, C.A. was involved in launching yet another radical magazine, which promptly folded. As far as Evangeline was concerned, the Camp and the surrounding acreage were the only real home her son had ever known and his rightful inheritance, and she resented the suggestion that Charles might have to choose between the farm and a university education. That the Camp was destined for Charles was not necessarily the understanding of Eva Lindbergh Christie and Loren Roberts, however—after all, the property had been bought originally for Mary Lindbergh, C.A.'s first wife—and it may be that C.A. hoped to avoid future conflict by getting rid of it.

At any rate Charles, previously the link who held his parents together in a semblance of an amicable relationship, was now a source of contention. Midway through his freshman year, he was already talking about dropping out of college. He and Delos Dudley fantasized about finding jobs in Africa, though neither of them could imagine where to look for such jobs or why any company that needed a representative in Africa should be interested in hiring them. Dudley was also passionate about aviation and had amassed a stack of brochures from flying schools all over the country. Since he had no money of his own, Dudley's dream of becoming a pilot was unlikely to get beyond the talking stage. But Charles had a bank account, saved mainly from his part-time job selling and servicing milking machines, and what began as wild talk soon became a firm intention. When it became apparent that Charles was serious about leaving school, Dudley was guilt stricken. He saw the pained expression on Evangeline's face when the subject came up in her presence and felt sure that she blamed him for influencing her son to give up engineering.

No parent in 1921 could have been pleased to learn that a son (or daughter, for that matter) was thinking of going into aviation. Flying was considered so dangerous that even Charles's ROTC buddies tried to dissuade him. One showed him an article that claimed that, on average, a pilot could expect to fly only nine hundred hours before suffering a fatal accident. "Why do you want to throw your life away?" he asked. Charles interpreted this statistic to mean that a careful pilot could expect to last a good deal longer. He'd had several close calls on the farm—once he was digging a silo when the excavation caved in on him; another time he was driving a wagon next to the railroad tracks when lightning struck the rails, so close that his horse was knocked to its knees. Nine hundred hours' flying time sounded like quite a bit to him.

Aside from being risky, aviation was not so much a career as semidisreputable escapism, like running away to join the circus. In Europe airlines were already experimenting with scheduled commercial passenger service, but in the Wright brothers' homeland the skies still belonged to the gypsy fliers who crisscrossed the country in rickety war-surplus biplanes, putting on stunt-flying exhibitions and taking up passengers for five or ten dollars a ride. There was much talk that airplane racing would soon establish itself as a rich man's sport, like polo, but for the time being the glamour of aviation was for farm boys, not middle-class youths with other options.

Evangeline, who had spent much of her life longing for adventures she would never have the freedom to pursue, was more sympathetic than most mothers. Her chief fear was that once Charles left Wisconsin he would never return to finish his degree.

Convincing C.A. was more difficult.

Since 1918 C.A. had been spending a part of each winter in Florida, tending to what he grandly called his real estate interests. These consisted of a pair of residential lots on the outskirts of Miami. He camped out there in a tent and was putting up two small cottages made of stuccoed cement blocks, which he hoped to rent out eventually. C.A. had become an enthusiastic booster of Florida and, considering his life-long identification with Minnesota, he felt surprisingly little sentimental attachment to the North Country. Writing to a woman acquaintance who had expressed an interest in relocating to Miami, he assured her that she would not miss the prairie winters; without exception, the Minnesotans he knew in the South would not consider returning home "under any condition." Besides, he predicted, it would soon be possible to drive from Minneapolis to Miami in a mere twelve days.

When Charles began to hint that he wanted to leave Madison, C.A. urged him to come to Miami. True, he hadn't made much money so far, he wrote. At this stage of his life he was content to "go easy." But there were great opportunities in Florida for a young man. Working as partners, the two of them would be worth one hundred thousand dollars in no time at all.

Instead, when June came, Charles was off to Kentucky to attend ROTC training camp at Fort Knox. He rode his Excelsior down from Wisconsin and, when camp ended, spent some time exploring the countryside before returning north. The highlight of the trip was spelunking in the Mammoth Cave, where his guide was Homer Collins, brother of the Floyd Collins who later became the object of an intensive and highly publicized rescue effort when he got stuck in a narrow passageway inside the caverns. (Despite all attempts to save him, Collins died of exposure.)

Returning to Madison in the fall, Charles found it harder than ever to resign himself to the sedentary routine of lectures and study sessions. In February he received official notice that he was being dropped from the university's rolls on the grounds of failing grades and "immaturity." According to Charles, he had already decided to leave and had not bothered to take his finals or register for spring semester classes. As soon as the weather warmed up, he was planning to head for Ray Page's Flying School in Lincoln, Nebraska.

Charles's imminent departure forced Evangeline to think about her own future. She applied to teach high school science in Little Falls but was rejected, ostensibly because she lacked credits in education. She therefore made plans to return to Detroit, where she joined the faculty of the highly regarded Cass Technical High School. Her father passed away later that same year, and she and Brother Land eventually sold 64 West Elizabeth Street and purchased a smaller home together.

In his usual methodical way, Charles had studied promotional brochures from aviation schools all over the country before settling on Ray Page's operation in Lincoln, mainly because it was connected with a factory—the Nebraska Aircraft Corporation, which was in the business of refurbishing army-surplus Lincoln Standard biplanes. Page had informed Lindbergh by letter that a course of lessons would cost five hundred dollars. He neglected to mention that the "flying school" described in Nebraska Aircraft's brochure was nonexistent, a come-on to lure potential airplane purchasers.

Lindbergh reached Lincoln on April Fool's Day (appropriately enough) and paid his tuition in full. Page took one look at this tall, skinny, and very naive college boy and decided to call him Slim, a nickname that stuck. With that, Page's sense of responsibility was pretty much satisfied.

Slim spent the next week hanging around the factory, watching the mechanics work on the remarkably compact 150-horsepower Hispano-Suiza engine and helping to stitch fabric wing covers. A week later a biplane was ready for final assembly. The mechanics pushed the plane out of the hangar, its wings lashed to the fuselage. Slim stood by, fascinated, as they fastened the wing struts and hooked up the ailerons and rudder. The following morning, April 9, the plane was ready for a shakedown flight, and the factory supervisor, Otto Timm, offered to take Slim up for a ride. Timm flew the plane from the rear cockpit. Slim sat up front, sharing the passenger seat with the factory handyman, Bud Gurney. A stocky sixteen-year-old, Gurney had dropped out of school and left his parents' farm, determined to find some way to work around airplanes even if it meant sweeping the floor of the factory shed. With Slim's arrival his life had become infinitely more interesting, and he looked up to the twenty-year-old Lindbergh with something akin to hero worship.

A mechanic spun the propeller, the engine caught. Within seconds the Standard was airborne, rising harmlessly over a stand of tall trees that bordered the end of the field. Timm wrung the plane out pretty well, much to the delight of his passengers. For Slim it was the most thrilling moment of his life so far, one he would relive so many times in imagination that decades later he could still recall the cough of the engine, the clatter of the axle as the plane barreled across the bumpy field, and the sensation of watching one wing rise above the horizon when Timm banked into a turn. Within seconds the world had been reduced to a "topsy-turvy stage," the works of earthbound man to toys. Flying was the ultimate experience he had pursued but never attained on his motorcycle: "I live only in the moment in this strange unmortal space, crowded with beauty, pierced with danger."[4]

After this glimpse of heaven, Page's indifference to the progress of his school's only pupil became all the more frustrating. Slim had been assigned an instructor, a grizzled Signal Corps veteran named Ira ("Biff") Biffle. His face a network of scars and premature wrinkles, Biff looked the part of an ace flier, and he swore prolifically in a tinny voice, worn out from years of competing with roaring engines. Biff made many appointments for lessons but kept few of them. Early morning was a problem because he didn't roll out of bed much before eleven. At midday he judged the air too turbulent. At sunset, more often than not, the weather looked threatening. In two months Slim accumulated a mere eight hours of dual instruction. The mechanics advised Slim that Biff had watched his best friend spin out and crash, an experience that permanently soured him on aviation.

Slim had been cheated, but there is no evidence that he ever directly confronted Page. Apparently he reasoned that it was his own fault for being such a greenhorn. The economic realities of the airplane business made genuine flying schools quite uncommon. The engines of World War I–vintage planes were prone to conk out in midflight. When that happened the pilot had to learn to scan the ground for a likely landing spot in order execute a dead-stick landing. Forced landings were so much to be expected that Orville Wright had urged that "to make flying perfectly safe, good landing places must be provided every ten to twelve miles."[5] Minor accidents—always called crack-ups, never crashes—were inevitable. Insurance was nonexistent. As a result few owners would allow a novice to fly their planes under any circumstances. The way to learn to fly, assuming one had money, was to purchase a well-used plane and get the owner to throw in lessons as part of the bargain.

Still, five hundred dollars was a large sum in the world of gypsy fliers, and Page's behavior was unconscionable. He compounded his unfair treatment by telling Slim that if he wished to solo he would have to post a sizable bond in addition to what he had already paid. Even this condition became moot at the end of May, when the only Standard equipped with dual controls was sold a to pilot named Erold Bahl, who was planning to go barnstorming around Nebraska and Kansas. Slim had figured out by this time that his education at the Nebraska Aircraft Flying School was over, and he begged Bahl to take him along as an assistant. Besides paying a share of the expenses, he would look after the plane and work the crowds, lining up paying passengers. After a few days he suggested to Bahl that they would draw bigger crowds if he stood on the wing as they flew over the town. Bahl, who had a reputation for being overcautious, warned him, "Don't go farther than the inner bay strut the first time."

Erold Bahl was a serious young man. He did not touch alcohol and talked about remaining pure for his fiancée, whom he planned to marry as soon as he had earned a nest egg from barnstorming. He was also an unusually skillful pilot and saw himself as a sort of missionary for aviation. Slim undoubtedly saw him as a role model, and in that sense the tour was worthwhile. But Bahl, like Page, had no intention of risking his plane by allowing a tyro to take it up alone.

By the end of June Slim and Bahl were back in Lincoln. Low on funds, Slim moved to a cheaper roominghouse and joined Bud Gurney doing odd jobs around the factory. Unless he could find some place for himself in the barnstorming trade, he would soon have to return to Detroit with little to show for his abandoned college career and squandered savings. At this point Charley and Kathryn Hardin arrived in town for an exhibition sponsored by Nebraska Aircraft. The Hardins were parachute makers who promoted their products by demonstrating trick jumps.

Charley Hardin's specialty was "cutaway jumping." After his chute opened, he would use a hinged knife attached to a guy rope to cut the line that secured his body harness to the chute's shroud rings. A second chute was stuffed into a pack strapped to his back. The vent opening at the top of this chute was attached to the shroud ring of the first with a piece of twine. As Hardin fell away from the first chute, the second would be pulled from his backpack, ready to billow open as soon as the twine snapped. Hardin claimed to have performed up to ten cutaways in one jump, which—if true—would have been a record. On the day Slim Lindbergh saw him, he contented himself with a double jump.

The day after the exhibition, Slim strode into Page's office and announced that he wanted to try the same stunt. Page thought the kid was crazy. "He always had some wild idea," he later said. "About the only way to get him out of the office was to let him to do them."[6] Hardin was mildly shocked but changed his mind after Lindbergh hinted that he might be interested in spending one hundred dollars on a chute of his own.

Slim was invited to watch as the Hardins folded the home-sewn muslin parachute he would be using, placing sheets of paper between the shroud lines to prevent tangles. The parachute bag was lashed to a wing spar, and when it came time to jump, Slim eased himself out onto the wing of the plane, sat down, and attached the chute's lines to his body harness. He then lowered himself over the edge of the wing.

This was the moment of no return. With trembling hands, he

untied the bowknot that held the canvas parachute bag shut. The chute began to play out of the bag, and for a heart-stopping second, he was in free-fall. Then he felt a tug and saw the canopy blossom open. So far, so good.

Charley Hardin had warned him to leave plenty of altitude for the second stage of the jump, so as soon as he was dropping smoothly, he tugged on the knife-rope that would saw the first chute loose. Once again he was in free-fall, the ground rushing toward him. The second chute seemed to take much longer to open. He had just enough time to pull his camera from his pocket and snap a few pictures before he slammed into the sod of Lincoln's municipal golf course.

The landing was a bit rougher than he'd expected, but Slim had no idea how close he'd come to dying until he saw Charley Hardin running toward him, his face a mask of anxiety. The break cord between the two chutes had snapped too soon. The second chute, still wadded into a tight ball, had indeed taken a long time to open.

On the way back to the factory, Bud Gurney, who had been waiting with Charley Hardin on the golf course, confided to Slim that Hardin, having no cord on hand, had tied the two chutes together with a piece of rotting grocery string.

Only the brave or the foolhardy would consider making a parachute jump in 1922, for reasons that become obvious when one considers that the Hardins were reputedly expert parachute makers. No one could remember a novice who had made a cutaway jump his first time out. Slim wasn't sure of his own motives—though he suggested in his autobiography that he wanted to overcome a childhood fear of heights once and for all, elsewhere he downplayed this explanation. Perhaps he just wanted to be noticed. He had no doubts, however, about the rewards—not so much the excitement of speed or the gambler's high of cheating death but access to a state of "exhilarated calmness." Psychologists have since realized that this mental state, an exaggerated form of the "natural high" familiar to long-distance runners, can be almost addictive and is a motivating factor for many individuals drawn to high-risk endeavors. Lindbergh had already made this discovery on his own. Several decades later he recalled that while the jump itself lasted but a few moments—opening a window of danger "where existence [is] both supreme and valueless at the same instant"—before and for many hours after he operated on a heightened plane of awareness unlike anything he had experienced before.[7]

The double jump changed Slim's status at Municipal Field. Even Biff treated him with respect. A few weeks later Nebraska Aircraft sold a Standard biplane to Banty Rodgers, a well-to-do farmer from Bird City, Kansas, who had hired an experienced pilot named Harold J. ("Shorty") Lynch to take the plane on a barnstorming tour. Slim had talked Page into buying him a Hardin chute, in settlement for the flying lessons he never received, and Lynch invited him to come along as a combination mechanic, jumper, and wing walker.

Old-timers considered parachute jumping and wing walking about equally dangerous. This assessment was probably accurate as long as jumpers persisted in lashing their chute packs onto a wing. In addition to injuries caused by defective chutes, accidents occurred when the jumper lost his balance while lowering himself under the wing or the chute was snagged by contact with the plane. Ironically, however, the most-feared part of the jump was free-fall. Despite experience to the contrary, it was still widely believed that a jumper ran a high risk of losing consciousness or even suffering a heart attack. The prevalence of this notion explains why Slim's double jump was considered so courageous.

Wing walking, by contrast, was looked upon as a straightforward proposition, suitable for anyone with a good sense of balance, and many of the celebrated early wing walkers were women, like the great Gladys Ingle, who specialized in climbing from the top wing of one biplane to the lower wing of another. Stunts like this were not difficult, at least not until the wing walker made her first misstep or grabbed a loose strut. After his double jump Lindbergh had no trouble persuading some of the old-timers around the airfield to teach him a few wing-walking tricks. Like many of the younger flying-circus performers, he wore a steel safety cable attached to a harness under his jacket for all but the simplest maneuvers. Thus secured he could perform dramatic feats like "dangling by his teeth" from a leather strap. Another trick that was reasonably safe as long as one's safety gear was well designed involved balancing on the top wing while the pilot looped the loop. For this one, Slim wore four cables, and his feet were held fast by steel heel cups fitted with leather straps.

Safety cables were of no help, however, in the thrilling car-to-air change, popularized in an early Fox-Movietone newsreel, which involved leaping from a moving car onto a rope ladder dangling from the wing of a low-flying plane. This stunt became notorious in October 1921 when Madeline Davis, a partner of the celebrated aviatrix Ruth Law, lost her grip on the ladder and fell to her death during an exhibition at Long Branch, New Jersey. Before leaving for Wyoming with Shorty Lynch, Slim tried to persuade Ray Page to let him try an even trickier variation, a motorcycle-to-plane change, an idea Page nervously vetoed.

Shorty Lynch, however, printed up handbills touting the performance of DAREDEVIL LINDBERGH and sent out letters announcing the team's availability for the purposes of aerial advertising, county fairs, "stampedes and home comings," and "all special occasions." The response was good enough to keep him and Slim busy for four months, during which they performed in western Kansas, eastern Colorado, Wyoming, and Montana. They traveled with a mascot, Banty Rodgers's fox terrier, Booster, who for some reason went wild with excitement at his first sight of an airplane and begged to be taken along. Worried that Booster might fall out of the cockpit, Lindbergh rigged a harness to the fuselage, just behind the pilot's cockpit, where the dog rode contentedly, barking at cows hundreds of feet below.

The status of the gypsy flier in 1922 was somewhere between that of a sideshow freak and a living god. There were still many towns whose inhabitants had never seen an airplane, and a pilot, no matter how scruffy looking or inexperienced, was an impossibly glamorous figure— "the Superman of Now," as one Wright advertisement put it. The reality of flying might be grubby, but there was no end to the utopian claims made by air-power enthusiasts. The triumph of the airplane would render national boundaries obsolete and usher in an era of universal peace and prosperity. It would erase barriers of class, money, and geography. Flying, many Christian ministers seriously believed, would create a generation of spiritually attuned Americans. Feminists looked forward to the day when the average woman, like the average man, would have a pilot's license. In their zeal to make converts, barnstormers in the South even sold rides to black customers, making flying one of the few activities then not strictly segregated, and one optimistic black pilot predicted that his race would achieve economic prosperity by cornering the air-taxi market. The more mystical side of the aviation craze was represented by a lecturer named Alfred Lawson, who prophesied that in ten thousand years air-minded human beings would evolve into a distinct species he called "alti-man," destined to rule over their earthbound brethren.[8]

Although their immediate goal was to earn money, most young

pilots, and some like Slim Lindbergh, who weren't yet full fledged, felt themselves to be informal evangelists, initiating the public into the miracle of flight. Often, however, this mission required the showmanship of a carnival barker and the ethics of a patent-medicine salesman. Fliers earnestly preached the safety of aviation, turned their own close calls into funny stories, and shamed the reluctant with a line of patter, promising, "Your money back if we crash."

Slim's first partner, the clean-cut Erold Bahl, had taken himself seriously as a missionary of the airways, even wearing a business suit instead of flying gear because he believed that a well-dressed pilot inspired confidence in his passengers. Shorty Lynch was more flamboyant. On one tour he and Slim tossed a dummy over the side of the plane into the Yellowstone River to get the attention of the locals—a stunt that can hardly have promoted their faith in the safety of aviation.

Shorty, whose other nickname was Cupid, was given to socializing with rodeo riders, carny folk, and some of the less-reputable elements in the small towns they visited. He liked his "hooch," and there were persistent rumors that he made the occasional run north of the border to pick up a cargo of Canadian whiskey. Slim did not drink or use tobacco—his grandfather Land had told him that cigarettes contained poison, and his attitude toward liquor had been formed by his father, who never passed a saloon in Little Falls without commenting on the sickening smell of stale beer. He and Shorty got along well enough, but for the most part he kept to himself, occasionally pumping gas for a station in Billings when no money was coming from flying.

In October, when the barnstorming season was nearly over, Slim bought a used boat for two dollars and made plans to run the rapids of the Yellowstone River, then float down the Missouri as far as the Platte. Shorty pointed out a tent-show dancer who always made a fuss over the tall, skinny, wing walker. "She'd go if you invited her," he insisted.[9]

Slim shrugged off the suggestion. He couldn't imagine that being alone on the river with a complete stranger for two weeks would be an enjoyable experience for either of them. And as it turned out, he was probably right. The boat had been badly caulked, and by the time he had gone twenty miles he was doing more bailing than rowing. After two miserable days, he abandoned the craft on the riverbank and took a train back to Lincoln, where he had stored his motorcycle.

Slim spent most of that winter in Little Falls, trying to repair the Camp's balky plumbing system and searching once again for a tenant who might make a go of the farm. After six months as an aerial stunt man, his future in aviation was problematic unless he could come up with the cash to buy a plane of his own. Shorty Lynch had given him a few hours' instruction, but even he didn't trust his partner to solo in Banty Rodgers's Standard. Charles made frequent trips to Minneapolis, hoping to talk his father into cosigning a note for nine hundred dollars. As before, he insisted that his ultimate goal was to get into airplane design; he just needed a little flying time to establish his credentials.

C.A. had often enough told friends that a parent should allow his children to follow their natural inclinations, but now he was having trouble taking his own advice. When spring came he was still unconvinced, and Charles followed him to Miami on the understanding that he would look over the situation and at least consider going into the real estate business. He had a pleasant two weeks camping in the Everglades, but the idea of working with his father, whose business affairs lurched from one crisis to the next, could hardly have been very appealing even if his heart hadn't been set on flying.

The impasse was resolved in late April by the death of Minnesota senator Knute Nelson. A special election was scheduled to fill Nelson's unexpired term, and C.A. quickly made up his mind to file as a candidate in the Farmer-Labor primary. He had little hope of winning, but, he wrote Eva, he was pleased to think that his return to the Minnesota political scene would "scare" his old enemies.[10]

With the primary set for June 18, just seven weeks away, Charles suggested that the best way for his father to get his message before the voters would be to canvass the state by air. On that understanding, C.A. agreed to cosign for the bank loan, and Charles, who had only recently returned to Little Falls, headed south again, bound for Americus, Georgia, where the army had recently auctioned off a large number of World War I surplus planes. He was hoping to buy a Standard, but there were none for sale in Americus, so he settled for a Curtiss JN 4D with a brand new eight-cylinder OX-5 engine. The Jenny, as it was affectionately called, was a popular World War I–vintage training plane—light, very maneuverable, and cheap to operate since it could fly for an hour on ten gallons of gas. But the Jenny was also underpowered. Under favorable conditions it could do seventy miles per hour; if the wind was blowing the wrong way, it might not get off the ground at all. The plane Charles purchased happened to be equipped with an extra twenty gallon fuel tank that made it more unwieldy than most, but it was available for a mere five hundred dollars.

Slim had his own plane at last, but he faced the embarrassing problem of getting it off Souther Field in Americus. Abandoned by the army, the once-bustling airfield was all but deserted, and the speculator who was unloading army-surplus stock at bargain prices had given no thought to such amenities as flying lessons. Slim had never soloed, and those few hours of lackadaisical instruction from Biff were dim in his memory. As he taxied the little Jenny around the field, trying to get the feel of the controls, he accidentally went airborne. The plane skimmed over the field, then plonked down on one wheel and a wing strut. Luckily there was no damage.

A few pilots were lounging near the hangars, where they had a good view of this demonstration of ineptitude. One of them, a man named Henderson, approached the Jenny and tactfully observed that lots of pilots got "a little rusty" over the winter. The training controls were still hooked up, and Henderson volunteered to spend an hour or so helping Lindbergh practice takeoffs and landings. Slim returned to the field just before sunset to make his first solo.

He had promised his father that the trip north would take at most two weeks, allowing for a detour into Texas, a state he had heard described as the ultimate barnstorming territory. This prediction proved unrealistic. A week went by before Slim felt confident enough to leave Americus, by which time it was already mid-May. In one day of flying, he reached Meridian, Mississippi, where he took up his first paying passenger, a three-hundred-pound man who claimed to have flown with the Lafayette Escadrille during World War I. The overloaded Jenny barely cleared the barbed-wire fence at the end of the hayfield. On his second day out, Slim became disoriented during a rainstorm and flew north instead of west. Surveying the farmland below, he picked an inviting-looking greensward as a landing spot. It was a typical novice's mistake. The grass was so thick and tall that it completely hid a deep ditch running the length of the field. The Jenny's wheels sank into the trench with a thud, and the plane tipped forward, cracking the propeller.

Slim hiked to the nearest town, which happened to be Maben, Mississippi, and telegraphed Souther Field requesting one of the spare twenty-dollar propellers he had left in storage there. In the three days it took for the spare part to arrive, he lined up half a dozen requests for rides from local farmers who had helped him pull his plane out of the ditch.

Once the repair was complete, he would recall, his new friends lost their nerve. It required "psychology, diplomacy, and ridicule" to coax the first passenger into the front cockpit, but after this volunteer survived unscathed, business was brisk at five dollars a ride.[11]

One of his passengers that day was a black sharecropper. Some white farmers had anted up fifty cents apiece to pay the man's fare, giving Slim instructions to do a few "flip-flops" for their amusement. The intended victim of the joke was well aware of his so-called benefactors' motives but still eager to go up, and except for a tendency to clutch at the throttle of the dual controls, which were still operable, he conducted himself bravely. Slim, who had never stunted in any plane and had no idea how the Jenny would respond, was less confident. Cautiously he tried out a few spins and rolls. Next, he attempted to loop the loop. He pulled back on the throttle and the Jenny's nose tilted upward to a ninety-degree angle. Instead of going over, the underpowered plane lost airspeed and slid backward into a slip stall, then went tail-up, dropping like a stone for two hundred feet before he regained control.

The inexperience of the Jenny's pilot was matched only by the naïveté of the passenger, who was waving to some friends on the ground, quite unaware that this maneuver was unintentional. In fact, none of the spectators was any the wiser, and word of the visiting pilot's skill spread through the countryside. The weather had been so unpredictable that Slim was loath to try another cross-country hop anyway, and he stayed in Maben for a week, taking up about five dozen passengers.

Surviving assorted mishaps and heavy rains that had turned much of Arkansas into a floodplain, Slim eventually pushed on to Lincoln, Nebraska, where Bud Gurney, who had followed the Hardins into the parachute business, was looking for a pilot willing to take him up for his first jump. A test flight with a sandbag lashed to the wing nearly killed them both, but Gurney eventually made a successful jump from two thousand feet.

Although he still had a lot to learn about piloting, Slim had come to consider himself an expert on the subject of publicity. Writing to his father, who was awaiting his arrival in Shakopee, Minnesota, he advised that success in aviation was 90 percent advertising and gave explicit instructions on timing press releases to ensure maximum coverage of their forthcoming aerial campaign. However, press releases became unnecessary when, a few miles short of his destination, Slim ran into a thunderstorm and made a forced landing in a swamp. The Jenny did a ground loop, leaving its pilot hanging upside down, suspended by his jammed safety belt.

Twelve-year-old Roman Arnoldy was returning from a fishing trip with a friend. "We heard this plane just popping and spitting," Arnoldy would recall. "It was obvious that it was out of fuel or whatever." Running to the spot where the craft went down, they arrived in time to help Slim crawl out of his belt and right himself. For Arnoldy and the rest of the children in town, the crack-up was an exciting event. Slim had to wait for yet another propeller to be shipped from Georgia, and in the meantime he hung around the train station, surrounded by a crowd of admiring young people, telling stories about his experiences in aviation. "It was something really new to us," Arnoldy said. "It was new to everyone then."[12]

In this fashion even crack-ups became occasions for winning new converts to flying. Newspaper coverage, at least so many pilots believed, was calculated to have the opposite effect. AIRPLANE CRASHES NEAR SAVAGE, screamed the Minneapolis papers. The congressman's son's airplane "suddenly went into a nose dive and landed on its propeller," a typical story said. Scribes too ignorant to grasp the distinction between a crash and a routine crack-up were the despair of the enlightened disciples of air power. "After reading this and similar accounts of equally minor accidents of flight, it is little wonder that the average man would far rather watch someone else fly," wrote a peeved Lindbergh a few years later.[13]

C.A., in an admirable demonstration of paternal trust, was still willing to carry on with the plan for an aerial tour. As soon as the fresh propeller arrived, father and son took off from Marshall, Minnesota, intending to distribute campaign leaflets from the air. When Slim rocked the Jenny's wings, the agreed-upon signal to let fly, the nervous C.A. dumped the entire bundle of five hundred leaflets over the side of the plane at once, cracking a wing stabilizer.

On their next flight, several days later, there was a more serious accident. A few seconds after taking off from a farmer's field near Glencoe, Slim lost control of the Jenny and had to ditch it in a field. In a letter to Shorty Lynch, he indignantly reported that someone had sliced the rudder-control wires partway through, so that they snapped at the first hard turn.

But despite his fascination with global conspiracy theories, C.A. was always reluctant to attribute hostile intentions to his fellow Minnesotans. After the accident he reported to Eva that the control wires had been "munkied [sic] with ... [however] I figure it was not a plot, but just some boys."[14]

In any event, by the time the Jenny was repaired it was too late to resume the campaign by air and C.A. ran a dismal third in his party's primary. Although his 1918 campaign had helped to forge the Farmer-Labor coalition, he had become so controversial as to be unelectable. Some of his political heirs would remember him as an embarrassment; others would look up to him as a hero-martyr, in the words of one, "the untamed polar bear who fought for truth and justice."

Charles spent the rest of the season barnstorming in Minnesota, Iowa, and Wisconsin. As he learned the limits of his plane and became more experienced in judging field conditions and weather, there were many fewer mishaps, and by August he was confident enough to wire his mother, asking her to join him in Janesville, Minnesota. In the event, Evangeline was a bit nervous but game. ("I'd go with you no matter if my heart jumped out of my mouth," she replied when Slim first suggested the trip.) She took to flying instantly, tried her hand at the controls, and promptly joined her son on a ten-day tour around central Minnesota, making Slim Lindbergh probably the only Jenny pilot ever to go barnstorming with his mother.[15]

FOUR

Cadet and Airmail Pilot

*A*BARNSTORMER HAD TO TRAVEL LIGHT. The little Jenny had no room for a suitcase, and Slim carried only an extra shirt and pair of trousers, a toothbrush, and a few tools and spare spark plugs, wrapped in a blanket. Mail might take weeks to catch up with him. When it did there was a stack of letters from Evangeline, who worried that her son wasn't getting enough to eat and sent along boxes of homemade "glacés" to supplement his diet. Slim's flying buddies also kept in touch by letter, and he answered when he could, usually just with a few hasty lines scrawled on the back of a postcard with a dull pencil.

By September 1923 the news Slim received mainly concerned flying buddies who were dropping out of aviation. Death, injuries, and financial need all claimed casualties, but by far the major cause of attrition was marriage. Shorty Lynch was thinking of barnstorming his way through South America but probably wouldn't go because he now had a steady girlfriend in Billings. Erold Bahl had set a wedding date at last and was planning to take a nine-to-five job. Ray Page was engaged. A young man named Heston Benson who had flown with Slim in Glencoe reported that he was resisting the trend toward marriage though, he added: "I would like to try it for a few months. *Hot Dog.*" Even shy Bud Gurney acknowledged that he could no longer afford to tease Bahl because he was being pursued by no fewer than three women who were friends of Bahl's fiancée.

"Are you next?" Gurney wondered.[1]

The answer was no. Slim was interested in females in the abstract but avoided them in the flesh. As he later explained it, he had neither the patience nor—he added more insightfully—the "flexibility" to bother with the rituals of courtship.

Of course, there were alternatives to dating "nice girls," as they were called in those days, but Charles, as we have seen, found them unsavory in the extreme. There is no question that, as a farm boy, he was hardly naive. Moreover, by the standards of the day, both of his parents were unusually frank in their attitudes toward bodily functions and regarded sex as a normal part of life—though, significantly, it had not been a part of their lives for a very long time. It was not the physical aspect of sexuality but its emotional dimension that frightened the young Lindbergh. Emotions, whether love or animal lust, drove men and women to pair off with the wrong partners and ruined their lives forever. The lesson he had learned from his parents' experience was reinforced by the fate of his buddies: Love and aviation were incompatible.

Thus Slim's avoidance of romantic entanglements, as much as his luck and skill, would make it possible for him to keep flying a while longer. But the pressure to rethink his goals was growing. Even in the smallest villages of central Minnesota, the sight of an airplane was no longer a novelty. Competitors working the same territory were offering rides for a mere $2.50, and it was becoming impossible for a full-time barnstormer to compete with these weekend fliers, who were happy to make enough to pay for gasoline.

Still looking for a way to "get into design," Lindbergh sought out the advice of airplane manufacturer Marvin Northrop, at his factory in Robbinsville, Minnesota. Northrop sized up the lanky Jenny pilot as an unusually serious, intelligent young man who had been knocking about the countryside so long that he was beginning to get a little squirrelly. He advised that the future of commercial aviation in the United States was still a few years away. In the meantime he suggested that Lindbergh apply to the Army Air Service Cadet Program. C.A., despite his isolationist views, had no objection to military preparedness, and he wrote to several former congressional colleagues, asking them to recommend his son for the program.[2]

In October, while waiting for word from the army, Slim flew to St. Louis to attend the International Air Races, at which Bud Gurney would be showing off a new emergency chute that he hoped to sell for $150. Lambert Field was crowded with the planes of air-race celebrities, and the roominghouses near the airfield were full. Looking for a cheap hotel, Slim ventured into downtown St. Louis, where his shabby clothes and blanket roll filled with tools caught the eye of a policeman who mistook him for a burglar. Slim was carrying a Colt .45 as protection against airplane thieves and knew he might be in serious trouble if the policeman decided to search him. Luckily the officer accepted his explanation, and after a tension-filled dialogue he was allowed to go on his way.

This nasty scare made a deep impression. The fact was, he had been afraid, and it was difficult for Lindbergh to acknowledge that he was afraid of anything. The fear of physical phenomena could be overcome. In personal relationships this was not possible, so he resorted to rationalization. Thinking it over, he decided that the policeman's attitude had been an insult to aviation as well as evidence of the unnatural values of urban life. In the city appearances counted for more than substance, and the greasy clothes and dirty hands that were a working pilot's badges of honor put him on a par with the lowest sort of criminal.[3]

Slim's performance at the air show was almost as ill fated as his foray into downtown St. Louis. Demonstrating his new chute, with Lindbergh as pilot, Bud Gurney tried a double jump and landed in a ditch, cracking a shoulder blade. This inglorious performance was written up by the *St. Louis Post-Dispatch,* which quoted Gurney's explanation: "The air was too 'light' yesterday to hold me, and I came down awfully fast."[4]

In spite of these difficulties, Slim liked the personnel at Lambert Field and decided to make it his base of operations while waiting to hear from the army cadet program. However, he had outgrown the underpowered Jenny, even though he had yet to earn enough to pay off his bank loan. When a teenager offered him more than he had paid for the plane, Slim eagerly accepted a down payment and a note for the balance. He even threw in free delivery to the kid's hometown of Oelwein, Iowa. After just two flights, however, the teenage pilot lost interest and joined a traveling carnival as a violinist. Slim found himself engaged in a frustrating correspondence with the boy's mother, who explained that she had sold the Jenny for five dollars to a neighbor who promptly wrecked it. The lady professed to be mystified and then offended by Slim's polite insistence that she and her son still had an obligation to pay off the note.

Bud Gurney also owed Slim money—as, it seems, did half the pilots in Nebraska and Kansas. To shore up his bank balance, he gave flying lessons at Lambert Field and occasionally went barnstorming in a rented Lincoln Standard with a pilot and wing walker named Randy Enslow. Enslow recalled that he and Slim were willing to try anything that would "bring in dimes," but they got tired of answering the same questions day after day. After they had flown into one town with Slim balancing on the wing of the plane, a woman asked them, "Which one of you boys rode in on the fender?" Slim and Enslow decided that the time had come to print up some explanatory handbills:

COME AND GET ACQUAINTED
THE SHIP IS MADE OF WOOD
AND WIRED TOGETHER
THE WINGS ARE NOT COVERED WITH TIN
IT DON'T BACK UP

To save gas money, they always planned their route so they could fly with the wind. As Enslow put it, "Wherever we went, we always blew in." For a time they were so poor that they were reduced to sleeping in the hangars at Lambert Field. Once they left St. Louis with $.75 between them, then made $175.00 in a single day in Greenfield, Missouri, and felt so rich that they took a hotel room and dumped the money on the bed, marveling that it made a pile "as big as a strawstack."

Enslow's family lived nearby, and they became so fond of Slim that they invited his mother for a visit. "I suppose the boys might get hurt flying," Evangeline told Mrs. Enslow. "But they are careful and they want to do it, so we will have to let them." Overhearing this conversation, Enslow, like Delos Dudley before him, was overcome by guilt. In fact, he and Slim weren't the least bit careful. They made a game of buzzing Wabash-line freight trains, coming in so low that the brakemen had to duck for cover. Worse, they never bought gas until their tank was bone dry, and once made five dead-stick landings in one day. "It takes about 2,000 hours in the air to get over being foolish," explained an older and wiser Enslow some years later.[5]

Early in the new year, Slim joined forces with an automobile dealer named Leon Klink, who had just bought a Canuck, a Canadian version of the Jenny. Klink hadn't yet soloed, but he had the aviation bug and wanted to see something of the country. After a leisurely series of cross-country hops to Florida, he and Slim got it into their heads to try to fly across the continent from east to west. They got as far as the Pensacola

Naval Air Station in Florida before their first accident: On takeoff, the engine suddenly died and Lindbergh nosed the plane into a sand dune.

The Canuck had a smaller fuel capacity than Lindbergh's original Jenny, and after a scant hour of flying time, he and Klink had to start looking around for a place to get fuel. To increase the plane's range, they tied a five-gallon can of gas to each wing. Refueling during flight was the job of the copilot, who climbed out onto the wing, untied the can, and poured the contents into the Canuck's tank through a steam hose.

In Camp Wood, Texas, they landed the Canuck in a public square just on the edge of town, only to discover the next day that the wind had shifted and their only chance to get airborne was to taxi down Main Street. There was a pair of telegraph poles midway down the block, but Slim figured that he had a one-foot clearance on each side. Unfortunately he hit a bump at the crucial moment and the plane veered. One wing tip grazed a pole, and the Canuck spun around, crashing through the show window of a hardware store. No one was hurt, and the owner of the store good-naturedly refused compensation for his broken window. The pace of life was slow in Camp Wood, and he figured that customers would be coming from miles around to see the store that was hit by an airplane.

By now it was mid-March 1924, and Slim and Leon still hadn't made their way out of Texas. When Slim received his orders to report to Brooks Field, near San Antonio, on March 15, Klink decided to leave the battered Canuck with him and take a train to the West Coast. Slim had, at this point, 330 hours of flying time to his credit, including stunt work, and he was the only member of his class of 104 cadets to report to Brooks Field in his own plane.

It was a proud but fleeting moment. The sergeant on duty took one look at the battered Canuck with its torn wing covers and patched-together landing gear and bellowed, "Get that damn crate off the field!"

Slim found a civilian airfield willing to store the plane for him and hiked back to Brooks, where more shocking developments awaited him. In addition to flying instruction, he discovered, the curriculum encompassed twenty-five ground-school courses in such subjects as "Property Accounting" and "Army Paperwork." Written examinations up to eight hours long were administered at regular intervals.

Even for cadets who flew skillfully, excelled in class, and strictly obeyed regulations, including the 10:00 P.M. curfew, the odds of remaining in the program long enough to earn their wings were dismally small. The Army Air Service was shrinking every year, and instructors were under orders to wash out 75 to 80 percent of the class. If no other reasons could be found, violations of "cadet etiquette" would do.

After his first round of exams, Cadet Lindbergh found himself just one point above the cut for immediate termination. For the first time in his life he was motivated to study, and he worked so hard that he rose to become first in his class. Even so, he would recall, the atmosphere was one of "constant apprehension."

As if he weren't troubled enough, a letter from Evangeline arrived almost every day. Charles's barracks mates teased him about getting so many letters, and he could not bring himself to admit that they were from his mother. He begged Evangeline to desist. Instead she resorted to using pseudonyms and different return addresses and disguising her handwriting. This was Evangeline's idea of a private joke, and, she pointed out, Charles's buddies would now conclude that he had many girlfriends, not just one. Though he was not amused, he showed remarkable forbearance under the circumstances.

At this stage in his life, Charles was making a deliberate attempt to gradually loosen his ties to his mother while strengthening those to his father. A letter to C.A., mailed not long after his arrival at Brooks, is filled with the sort of detailed information C.A. loved and Charles himself normally cared little for. He began by observing that irrelevant course work and petty regulations would, in his opinion, deprive the army of the services of some of the best pilots in the class. Still, he wasn't surprised that the army considered these men expendable, since he had recently learned that it cost an outrageous fifty thousand dollars to train a single military pilot. He included two full pages of statistics on the costs of the cadet-training program, warning C.A. to let no one know the source of the information as he would be in serious trouble if anyone guessed that the figures came from him.

This was no understatement. The sad state of the army and navy flying services was a hot political issue in 1924. Just six months earlier, the controversial assistant chief of the Army Air Service, General Billy Mitchell, had gained national attention for his advocacy of an independent air corps by arranging a demonstration bombardment of two decommissioned battleships. Both ships were sunk—one, the *Virginia,* in just twenty-seven minutes—but the navy, which opposed Mitchell's ideas about long-range bombers and a separate air force, insisted the tests were inconclusive. The disgruntled Mitchell, officially a Democrat, was quietly supporting Progressive candidate Bob La Follette in his presidential campaign in the hope that La Follette would swing Republican votes in favor of higher appropriations for military aviation. Thus Slim's suggestion that the army wasn't making the best use of the money it had—made to his father, who was La Follette's friend and ally—was heresy indeed.

Perhaps because of the high washout rate and the supercompetitive atmosphere, barracks life at Brooks Field was even more boisterous than usual. Practical jokes, the cruder the better, were the favorite form of entertainment. At Lambert Field Slim had already been introduced to such standards of the genre as the snipe hunt (in which the victim spends the night in a swamp, making snipe noises and waiting for the prey to leap into an open burlap bag), and he quickly established himself as the leader by inventing a new version of the hot seat. Cutting a shotgun shell just below the wadding, he attached a fuse made of waxed grocery string. Army-issue shells at the time were still loaded with black powder, which, when it caught, produced a dramatic whooshing sound and a plume of evil-looking smoke guaranteed to evoke, in Lindbergh's own words, "a delightful reaction."

An Army Air Service colonel discovered that Lindbergh was the inventor of this device and was so impressed that he taught him his secret method for attaching explosive caps to the underside of toilet seats. Oil of valerian, dead skunks, and venomous snakes played key roles in other pranks that were considered highly amusing at the time.

The joke that Lindbergh recalled most proudly was played on a fellow cadet who frequented the brothels in the section of San Antonio known to the cadets as "spic town" and was given to regaling his less-experienced barracks mates with exaggerated accounts of his sexual prowess. This cadet, a large man in every respect, was a heavy sleeper, and one particular weekend afternoon, when everyone was lazing around trying to ignore the one-hundred-degree-plus heat, he was discovered sprawled on his cot, dead to the world except for a very prominent erection. Slim got the idea of painting the penis green, and when the victim still did not wake up, he and his buddies got tired of waiting around to see the reaction. One of them screwed a small hook into the ceiling over the sleeping cadet's cot, and another carefully tied one end of a string around the bobbing penis, passed the string through the hook and entrusted the business end to a cadet who was stationed just outside the barracks window. On cue, this accomplice jerked the string. When the victim opened his eyes and discovered that his private parts had turned green while he slept, he did not leap from his cot or even appear unduly alarmed, but remarked in his usual slow drawl, "Wulll ... Jeee ... zusss ... Keee ... rist," a reaction that brought down the house.[6]

Judging from a letter Slim subsequently received from another one of his chief victims, there were no hard feelings about these pranks. They were in tune with the mood of the camp, and he was admired for his ingenuity.

Lindbergh was still struggling to survive academically when, on April 24, he received a telegram calling him back to Minnesota. A few days earlier Walter Quigley had found C.A. wandering the streets of Minneapolis, only a few blocks from their law office but utterly lost. The elder Lindbergh was taken to the Mayo Clinic in Rochester, where exploratory surgery revealed a massive glioma, an inoperable tumor of the brain. By the time Charles arrived at his father's bedside, C.A., only sixty-five years old, was in a childlike state of befuddlement. Since no more could be done for her father at the clinic, Eva Lindbergh Christie was making arrangements to transfer him to a hospital nearer her home in Red Lake. Charles returned to San Antonio, where he received the news of his father's death a month later, on May 24.

In retrospect, both Slim and Eva remembered comments that led them to suspect their father had known he was dying months or even a year or more before the tumor was discovered. In a letter to Charles, for example, he had mentioned that when he died he wanted to be cremated and his remains "thrown to the wind." Certainly, his last book, *The Economic Pinch,* which appeared in 1923, reads as if he foresaw that it was destined to be his political testament. The book begins with the usual fulminations against the banks and big business but concludes with a stirring peroration calling for an end to racial prejudice and war. Like some other agrarian radicals of his generation, C.A. had been educated by World War I. He had seen where ethnic strife could lead, and he was appalled. "The national is not national for the purposes of death," he wrote, "but is national for the purposes of the life of the national human family—which ultimately will include the people of all the world."

These sentiments were followed by a warning against what C.A. saw as the dangerous modern tendency of the people to put their faith in "great men":

> Unless the hero of our mind happens to be really great and good
> enough to lead us to our own individuality and make us feel our own
> importance as thinking beings, thinking out all things for ourselves,
> our mind hero [*sic*] has served no good purpose…. The one great
> person must be the individual for himself—to make himself consistent
> with the rights of every other to be as high and as important as is he.

The "untamed polar bear" had ended his career on a high note. Unfortunately, his private affairs were not so well ordered. During the final year of his life, C.A. had explicitly promised Charles that he and his mother would inherit the Little Falls farm. But when Evangeline returned to Minnesota for the funeral, she learned that C.A. had never transferred the title—and, in fact, the property was mortgaged after all. Under Minnesota law Evangeline had the right to lifetime residence in the marital home, but legal ownership would then pass jointly to Charles, Eva Christie, and the children of Lillian Roberts.

Almost as dismaying, C.A.'s business and financial records were in utter disarray. A number of deeds, both to his own and clients' real estate, had never been registered, and many of C.A.'s properties were tied up in a partnership agreement, with rights to pass to the surviving partners. Charles and Eva suspected Walter Quigley of taking advantage of their father's periods of mental confusion to defraud him, but this was difficult to prove since C.A. was notoriously lax about paperwork. A lawsuit by the heirs against the partnership was complicated by squabbles between Evangeline on the one hand and her stepdaughter Eva and Dr. Roberts on the other. In the meantime the estate could not be probated, and the Little Falls property stood vacant. It was a measure of Charles's bitterness that ten years were to pass before he got around to honoring his father's last wish by distributing his ashes from the air over the old Melrose homestead.

Back in San Antonio, Slim applied himself to his studies with renewed determination. In September he was one of thirty-three survivors of the class to be promoted to flying De Havillands out of Kelly Field. Better known as the Flaming Coffin (because the location of the gas tank between the engine and the cockpit made it prone to explode during forced landings), the DH was a World War I–vintage plane and already technologically obsolete. In addition to weak landing gear, it had, one critic complained, "the gliding angle of a brick." Training consisted of flying figure eights over such landmarks as trees and haystacks. In view of the plane's unforgiving nature, departures from the programmed maneuvers were strictly forbidden.

This rule was occasionally difficult for the former Jenny pilot to keep in mind. One morning when the visibility was exceptionally poor, in Slim's estimation "an ideal day to do the things we were not supposed to do,"[7] he was hedgehopping along under a cloud bank when he noticed another DH nearby and challenged the pilot to a stunt duel— "chandelles, vertical banks, wingovers and every other thing we could think of," all at an altitude of something less than three hundred feet. Too late, he noticed that the plane he had challenged contained two men, one of them an instructor. The mandated punishment for his offense was ejection from the program. For a week after that, he waited for the dreaded order to pack his bags and leave the base. But the instructor had failed to report him.

One of the best pilots in his class, he had been chosen to specialize in pursuit, the elite assignment for a flying cadet. Pursuit training included practice with Browning machine guns, which in those days were mounted on the front of the plane and synchronized to fire between the blades of the whirling propeller. Another segment of the course involved practicing close-formation tactics such as Lufbery circles and crossover turns.

During the final weeks of the course, the class was checked out on other models, including the SE-5 scout plane. On March 9 Lindbergh was piloting one of nine SE-5s assigned to practice diving out of a formation in a coordinated attack. Group leader Phil Love, Lindbergh's closest buddy, dived at an "enemy" DH, and Lindbergh and a Lieutenant McAllister swooped down after him to confirm the "kill." Somehow their planes lost visual contact. The next thing Slim knew, he "felt a slight jolt followed by a crash." His official report tells what happened next:

> My head was thrown forward against the cowling and my plane seemed to turn around and hang motionless for an instant. I closed the throttle and saw an SE-5 with Lieutenant McAllister in the cockpit, a few feet on my left. He was apparently unhurt and getting ready to jump.
>
> Our ships were locked together with the fuselages approximately parallel. My right wing was damaged and had folded back slightly, covering the forward right hand corner of the cockpit. Then the ships started to mill around and the wires began whistling. The right wing

commenced vibrating and striking my head at the bottom of each oscillation. I removed the rubber band safetying the belt, unbuckled it, climbed out past the trailing edge of the damaged wing, and with my feet on the cowling on the right side of the cockpit, which was then in a nearly vertical position, I jumped backwards as far from the ship as possible.[8]

If the accident had occurred a year earlier, it would have surely been Charles Lindbergh's last. The Army Air Service flying school had first requested parachutes in 1918, but because of budget restrictions the 1924–25 cadet class was the first to be equipped with them. Cadets Lindbergh and McAllister became the twelfth and thirteenth members of the army's Caterpillar Club, the unofficial fraternity of flyers who had saved their lives by hitting the silk under emergency conditions.

There was another noteworthy aspect to the incident: Army regulations required a "full and accurate" report of every flying accident. But the average cadet was a stranger to the art of narrative writing, and a typical incident report was more likely to resemble Air Service pilot Jimmy Doolittle's summary of a similar mishap, which read: "Wings broke. Thrown out." Lindbergh's terse, suspenseful description of his brush with death was reprinted in an army newsletter and later by the *New York World,* a newspaper distinguished for its appreciation of lively prose.

Lindbergh never explained just how this came about, but judging by his scornful reaction to the comments of an early biographer, who suggested that Cadet Lindbergh did not realize that his report would be of interest to the general public, it was more than a lucky accident that brought the piece to the attention of the *World's* aviation correspondent. At any rate Lindbergh would soon be submitting other articles to aviation publications. The ultimate goal for an American pilot in 1925 was to become an air racer, and Slim had realized early on that getting his name in print would help him to attract sponsors.

Of the 104 cadets who had entered training a year earlier, only 18 graduated. Lindbergh was at the top of the class, with the best overall ratings in flying as well as classwork. He still had to face a board of examiners to get his regular army commission. The first question he was asked involved binomial equations. The second had to do with the names of the rivers of Texas. Although a sympathetic examiner hinted that wrong answers wouldn't count too heavily against him, Slim was panicked at the thought of having a failure on his army record and withdrew from the exam.

However, another event that year dramatically improved his

chances for full-time work in aviation. Congress had passed the Kelly Bill, authorizing the Post Office to lease airmail contracts to private companies. William and Frank Robertson, co-owners of the St. Louis–based Robertson Aircraft Company, were bidding on the Chicago–to–St. Louis route. Bill Robertson had been impressed with Lindbergh when he was barnstorming out of Lambert Field, and he offered him the position of chief pilot.

It would take nearly a year for the Robertsons to get their contract and set up operations, however. Lindbergh filled in the time giving flying lessons and serving as an instructor with the 110th Observation Squadron of the Missouri Air National Guard. Like other military flying units at the time, the 110th was so poorly equipped that the pilots often had to pay for gas and repairs out of their own pockets.

In May he survived another crash. He was test-flying a plane with a widened fuselage, designed to carry passengers, when the controls stuck while the plane was in a left spin. Lindbergh bailed out at 350 feet. By the time his chute opened, he had fallen beneath the twisting plane, which spun downward, missing him by a few feet. He escaped with a dislocated shoulder.

Soon he was back in the barnstorming game, and in June he was hired by Capt. Wray Vaughn to perform at country fairs in Colorado and Wyoming in an outfit called the Mil-Hi Circus. Besides the usual wing walking, stunting, and parachute jumps, the circus specialized in fireworks displays. Arriving in town earlier in the day, Lindbergh would purchase a selection of fireworks from a local store, build a frame out of scrap lumber, and attach it to the wing to support them. He began the show by lighting aerial bombs with a cigarette lighter. The trick was to toss the lit bombs over the side quickly enough to avoid getting burned but with enough control to keep them from grazing the struts. Next he set off the candles and flares attached to the frame, igniting them by means of a battery hookup in the cockpit. The Roman candles produced breathtaking trails of fire emanating from the wings, and the magnesium flares lit up the sky brilliantly.

Slim also took up passengers at ten dollars a ride. In Red Lodge, just north of Yellowstone, a passenger asked him to make a low pass over the town. As they buzzed Main Street, the man suddenly produced a brace of pistols and began firing wildly out over the wings. "I've shot up this town on foot, I've shot it up on horseback, and now I've shot it up from a plane," he told Slim proudly when the ride was over.

* * *

Barnstorming, however, was tame compared to flying the mail, statistically the most dangerous occupation in the country. Of the forty pilots hired by the Post Office during the period when pilots were government employees, thirty-one had been killed in crashes. Airmail pilots flew at night without navigation lights or beacons to guide them, landing in cow pastures and cornfields. In the event of a crack-up, the pilot was expected to hitch a ride to the nearest railroad station and see that the mailbags got aboard the next train.

Robertson Aircraft owned four De Havillands, open-cockpit observation planes that had been modified so that the pilot sat in the rear seat, formerly used by the military observer. The mail sacks were stowed in front. Lindbergh surveyed the 285-mile route between Chicago and St. Louis early in 1926, and flew the first official airmail flight between the two cities on April 26. For the next six months he and his fellow pilots, former army buddies Phil Love and Thomas Nelson, made a total of five round trips a week.

Slim and the carrot-haired Phil Love shared a two-room apartment on the second floor of a house in Bridgeton, not far from Lambert Field. An airplane mechanic named Clyde Brayton and his large family occupied the ground floor. Bud Gurney, still struggling along in the parachute business, had a room down the hall. Bud, Phil, and Slim ate many of their meals at a place called Louie's Shack, on the edge of the airfield, where Phil and Slim sometimes recruited air-minded patrons willing to come along as paying passengers on mail runs for the sheer thrill of the ride. Of the three friends, Slim was the one who showed signs of adapting permanently to the bachelor's life. He cooked hearty breakfasts, typically eggs with a steak or pork chop accompanied by home fries, toast, and sliced tomatoes. Still not dating, he teased his housemates mercilessly about their relations with women.

Bud Gurney was a notoriously poor housekeeper, and among his other derelictions, he neglected to refill the bucket of drinking water that the boarders obtained from a well in the backyard. One day Slim, still an inveterate practical joker, decided to teach Bud a lesson by filling the bucket with kerosene. Knowing that Norwegian farmers often took a snort of kerosene for its supposed medicinal value, he did not anticipate any serious consequences. Unfortunately Gurney happened to have a mouthful of chocolate-covered cherries when he ladled himself a cooling drink and swallowed two big gulps before he realized that anything was wrong. Gurney was wretchedly ill, but did not hold a grudge and came to see the incident as a good joke on himself. Slim, as usual when one of his pranks went awry, was outwardly composed but inwardly mortified. Recalling the episode in 1968, he commented that he still could not think of it without embarrassment.

Pilots in 1926 soared over a landscape innocent of suburban sprawl, interstates, and, everywhere but over the larger cities, the heavy palls of pollution that now blanket large areas of the country for days at a time. When night fell the stars sparkled overhead and the ground below was dark. There were few cars on the roads, few towns with street lights and even those farm families with electricity, still by no means universal, went to bed after sunset. One boy who had heard Lindbergh's DH flying overhead wrote Robertson Aircraft to say that he would keep a 100-watt light burning in his backyard every night. The light became a welcome landmark, and on his first overflight, Lindbergh circled over the house, tipping his wings in a gesture of thanks.

Fog was the mail pilot's worst enemy. If a Robertson pilot found himself in a fogbank and wished to land he was supposed to drop a parachute flare, which would give him a minute or so to survey the terrain and prepare for an emergency landing. The DH's were equipped with only one flare, and the first time Lindbergh tried to use his, it failed to ignite. He flew on to Chicago, which at least had landing lights, but even though the ground crew there heard his plane and lit gasoline torches to guide him in, he could not find the airport. Nor could he locate the Chicago beacon, one of the few navigational aids the federal government had provided to date.

Running out of fuel, Lindbergh discovered that his flare had failed to drop because of slack in the release cable. By tugging on the cable he was able to shake the flare loose, but it dropped uselessly through the fogbank like a candle sinking into the ocean.

When the engine died there was nothing to do but jump blind. Lindbergh bailed out, and the nose of the empty plane dropped. The sudden change in altitude caused the last ounces of fuel to run into the carburetor. The engine kicked on, and the plane began flying in descending circles about a mile in diameter. On its first pass the DH missed Lindbergh's chute by thirty yards. Lindbergh tried to guide himself away from the danger area, but he could only guess at the plane's path and rate of descent. Every few seconds the plane would reappear out of the mist like a ghost avenger.

After the plane completed five spirals and five near-misses, Lindbergh sank into the fogbank. For the last one thousand feet he drifted

blind—unable to see his still-circling plane, the ground, or, for that matter, his own chute. All he could do was brace himself for the impact.
Luckily, he landed safely in a field of tall corn.

Later Lindbergh learned that his plane's 110-gallon fuel tank had
been removed for repair and temporarily replaced by an 85-gallon one.
No one had thought to inform him of the change.

In November Slim again narrowly escaped death when a sudden
change of weather over Peoria trapped him above a heavy layer of fog at
fourteen thousand feet. He flew around looking for a break in the cloud
cover until he was almost out of gas, then had no choice but to bail out.
As he was hoisting himself over the side of the cockpit, ready to leap,
the right wing of the DH began to dip. Remembering the sickening
feeling of being pursued by his own machine, he climbed back into the
cockpit and stabilized the plane before making his jump. The fog was so
thick that he could not see the ground, and his rain-soaked chute
bobbed and weaved, threatening to collapse with each gust of wind.
Remembering the advice of his army instructors, he kept his legs
crossed. He landed smack on top of a barbed-wire fence, which, he
noted laconically, "helped break my fall."[9]

Ironically this crash made Slim Lindbergh something of a celebrity,
at least among those who followed aviation news. He was the only pilot
in the United States to have saved his own life four times by bailing out
of a doomed plane, and his first-person account of the crash was published in the November 1926 issue of the *National Aeronautic Association Review*. The article ended with a description of how he returned to
Chicago for a fresh plane and then rescued the oil-soaked but otherwise
undamaged mail from the twisted wreckage of the DH. The mail was
delivered just one day behind schedule.

Such dedication contributed to the civilian airmail service's 99 percent delivery record, truly amazing considering the conditions under
which the pilots operated. But the business community was not
impressed. Much to the dismay of Lindbergh and his fellow pilots, the
volume of mail they carried actually declined as the novelty of the service wore off. By the end of 1926, the canvas mail sacks often weighed
more than their contents, and the Robertsons, who were paid by the
pound, were on the brink of bankruptcy.

The company was now down to two planes, Lindbergh having
crashed the others. Moreover, he and Nelson were the only pilots left.
Phil Love, who had pulverized the bones of his face during the crash of
a crop-dusting plane a year earlier, had a silver plate in his jaw that kept

shifting. The pain was so intense that he had taken medical leave to have his jaw reconstructed a second time.

American mail pilots regarded with envy their peers in Europe, where scheduled passenger service was already a reality, linking not only London, Paris, Berlin, and Rome but Prague, Warsaw, and Budapest. In Germany alone Deutsche Luft Hansa, the government-sponsored holding company, operated twenty-six airlines. In the United States, by contrast, flying was still better established as a sport than as a business, and American pilots, largely for lack of other opportunities, held thirty-three out of forty established world speed and distance records. Slim had already had a taste of the journeyman air-derby circuit. At the end of his summer with the Mil-Hi circus, he and Wray Vaughn had joined a cross-country air race but were forced to drop out after repeated breakdowns, an experience that taught him that without luck as well as good financing, racing could too easily become just another dead end.

Piloting the night run, across the Mississippi and across Illinois, with the wind whipping in his face and the stars so bright overhead that he felt he could almost reach out and touch them, Slim allowed his imagination free rein. Just as he had begun his career as a parachutist by completing a double jump, he dreamed of starting at the top, with a plan so daring that it would capture the imagination of the aviation world.

FIVE

The "Walled Garden"

*I*N AUGUST 1926, while Charles Lindbergh was flying the mail between St. Louis and Chicago, two American girls touring Europe with their parents were looking forward to their first taste of Parisian nightlife. A bachelor friend of the family, the American architect Chester Aldrich, had offered to take the sisters out for an evening on the town, and the unexpected invitation set them rummaging through their steamer trunks, desperate to put together suitably sophisticated outfits. Elisabeth, the older sister, settled for a flowered chiffon frock of her mother's and a beige hat. The younger girl, Anne, wore a dress she called her "rose leaves and cream," topped off incongruously by a black velvet hat with a floppy brim.

The little group, rounded out to a foursome by the addition of a young musician from New Zealand who was a friend of Chester's, found their way to a *boîte* called La Maisonette Russe, where a White Russian orchestra and singers performed the "Song of the Volga Boatmen" and the popular tango "Florida." Anne, all but overcome by the glamour of it all, made a mental inventory of the surroundings so that she could record them in her diary—the orange lampshades decorated with little silhouettes in the shape of masks, the party of Russians at the next table who filled the air with incomprehensible murmurings and a haze of cigarette smoke, the gypsy accordion player who held his instrument high, as if physically reaching for the high notes, a woman dancer in leather boots and a red sash who made even the familiar moves of the Charleston look wild and exotic.

Anne had just turned twenty and was about to enter her junior year of college, but it scarcely occurred to her that she was old enough to be a part of the scene in her own right. She was all too aware of herself as a little person in an absurd hat, more child than woman, for whom the evening was a delicious if overrich treat.

The evening after the visit to La Maisonette Russe, Anne's family had General John ("Black Jack") Pershing to dinner at the Ritz Hotel. Then, after a quick trip to Grenoble to help Elisabeth settle in for a year of graduate studies, they moved on to Geneva, where Daddy conferred with statesmen like Edvard Beneš of Czechoslovakia and Jean Monnet of France, while Anne and her mother attended a luncheon for diplomats' families at the International Club and heard British Foreign Secretary Austen Chamberlain lecture on "the Spirit of Locarno." The final stop on the tour was Britain, where the family stayed at Wall Hall, the country house of J. P. Morgan, Jr. Jack, as he was called, had decorated the house himself with his immense collection of Bavarian beer steins and a profusion of fur pelts, which were scattered about on the floors, draped over the furniture, and even tacked to the backs of the doors. The proud host gave Anne a tour of his greenhouses, which was followed by a "very nice" dinner, at which Anne sat mute, unable to think of a thing to say.

When Anne had a spare moment she lost herself in reading *Tess of the D'Urbervilles*, a biography of Rupert Brooke, and *The Dance of Life* by Havelock Ellis, the last of which, she conceded, went completely over her head. She had been making these European tours with her family since she was a child, and this year she was bored and restless. Nevertheless, she could not suppress a shiver of excitement when she sat down to breakfast and saw the monogram JPM on the knife she was using to butter her toast.

The Morrows had come a long way from the modest brown-shingled house on Spring Lane in Englewood, New Jersey, where Anne Spencer Morrow was born on June 22, 1906. At the time Anne's father, Dwight Morrow, was a young associate in the Wall Street firm of Reed, Simpson, Thacher & Barnum. Her mother, Betty, a former Cleveland schoolteacher, had a cook and a part-time handyman who came around in the mornings to stoke the furnace, but otherwise she did her own housework, taking pride in her ability to stretch the budget by, for example, transforming an old packing case into a vanity table for the guest room by draping it with leftover fabric. The Morrows' social life revolved around the Englewood Presbyterian Church, where both Betty and Dwight taught Sunday school classes, and a bridge group known as the Simple Club. A bit later the couple joined the Shakespeare Club, whose members, all young marrieds, read a different play each month.

Even this modest suburban affluence seemed a dream come true for Dwight and Betty, who were the first members of their families to "come East." Both of them hailed from hardworking midwestern clans whose members had served with dedication as teachers, ministers, and soldiers, achieving local distinction yet never managing to accumulate a nest egg that would give the next generation a head start.

Dwight Whitney Morrow, the fifth child in a family of eight, was born in 1873 in Huntington, West Virginia, and grew up in Allegheny, Pennsylvania (later part of the city of Pittsburgh), where his father, James Elmore Morrow, was a mathematics teacher and, later, principal of the Fifth Ward elementary school. Strict Presbyterians, James and his wife Clara taught their brood that hard work and a sound education were the keys to success—a formula that admittedly hadn't worked very well for them. In a less optimistic moment, Clara Morrow once summed up the history of her marriage with the phrase, "too many books, too little money."

Jay, the eldest son, became a high school football player of some renown, placed first in his district on the competitive examination for West Point, and won a congressional appointment to the military academy in 1887. Dwight, three years younger, was not a promising candidate for the military life. An undersize youth with a head that seemed far too large for his body, he suffered from migraine headaches, bronchitis, and recurrent stomach pains. His left arm, badly set after a childhood accident, hung at an improbable angle, so that (as one friend observed) he always appeared to be walking sideways. But, like Jay before him, Dwight knew of no other way to get a free education, so after high school, he took a job as a board boy on the Pittsburgh stock exchange and spent every evening and weekend for a year cramming for the West Point exam. Like Jay, he received the top score, only to be passed over in favor of the son of one of his congressman's financial backers. When the congressman justified his decision on the grounds that it would be unfair to appoint two boys from the same family just three years apart, Dwight was prompted to write a letter of protest to President Benjamin Harrison: "I have always thought and had always been taught to think, that in America where everyone is supposed to fight for himself, no family ties can either aid or retard one."[1]

The president did not reply, and Morrow went to work as a stock-market clerk, remaining one until an old friend of his father's, a professor at Amherst, arranged a partial scholarship for him. Eking out the rest of his fees through tutoring jobs and small loans from relatives, Morrow lived off campus in a cheap boardinghouse favored by poor boys from his class, including a taciturn local kid named Calvin Coolidge. A brilliant student with top grades in math and English constitutional history, Morrow wrote essays in the *Amherst Literary Monthly* denouncing snobbery and special privilege. However, he learned early on to conceal his sense of the unfairness of life behind a facade of self-deprecating wit. In his sophomore year he was elected to the Beta Phi Pi fraternity, and one of his fellow Betas, upperclassman Mortimer L. Schiff, got into the habit of giving Dwight his cast-off clothes. Questioned about the significance of the monogram MLS on his shirt pockets, Dwight joked that the letters stood for "Morrow's Little Shirts." In his senior year he was elected "most popular" and edged out classmate Calvin Coolidge for the title of "most likely to succeed."

Still a junior when he first met Elizabeth Reeve Cutter, a Smith sophomore, at an off-campus dance, Dwight knew at once that this was the girl he was destined to marry. "She kind of reminds me of you sometimes," he wrote to his favorite sister, Agnes.[2]

Betty Cutter failed to share this sense of inevitability, however. Dwight Morrow was an odd-looking youth, a little shorter than she was, who tripped over his own feet on the dance floor and never stopped talking. They dated sporadically but, on Betty's part, there was not an iota of physical attraction. When Jay Morrow, tall and handsome in his first lieutenant's uniform, visited Amherst, Betty wrote in her diary, "Mr. M. brings his brother to see me. I like his brother more than I like Mr. M."

In the short run Betty appeared to be most attached to her college friend Amey Aldrich, to whom she dedicated amateurish undergraduate poetry. During Betty's senior year, the recently graduated Dwight Morrow returned to Amherst to attend his first reunion and made a detour to Northampton hoping to renew his courtship. According to a memoir written by one of her daughters, Betty "recoiled in indignation from the man's physical presence."[3]

Like the Morrows, the Cutters of Cleveland were hardworking

Presbyterians, who lived, as the same memoir puts it, in an atmosphere of "acute financial anxiety." Nevertheless Betty considered herself a notch above Dwight Morrow socially. The Cutters owned a modest amount of property and scrimped on necessities in order to provide themselves with "good" furniture. "New-law" Presbyterians, they approved of dancing and cardplaying; the more fundamentalist branch of the church, to which the Morrows belonged, was considered déclassé. Betty's family had sacrificed to send her to Smith, and she wasn't about to waste the opportunity by marrying a poor boy with no prospects.

Moreover, Betty had some justification for doubting that Dwight Morrow had a future. In his senior year, while he was busy campaigning for class honors, less distinguished but more savvy classmates were quietly lining up jobs, often through family connections. After graduation Dwight found himself back in Pittsburgh, working as an office boy for the law firm of his sister Agnes's husband, Richard Scandrett. Desperately "homesick" for Amherst, he wrote to a college friend, "Life does not have much knight errantry left in it now." He sank into a depression that lasted two years, until his family once again came to his rescue, pooling their funds to send him to Columbia University Law School.

Betty, meanwhile, finished Smith and taught at a private school in Cleveland until 1898, when her parents decided that she and her sister Anne ought to have the opportunity to pursue advanced studies in Europe. To make this possible, they rented out their house and decamped to England for a year, where they lived with relatives while Betty and Anne studied languages, literature, and fine art in Paris and Florence.

Five years had gone by, and Dwight Morrow continued to describe Betty Cutter to his friends as "the girl I'm going to marry." He wrote her weekly letters she seldom bothered to answer. And when she suggested that he confine himself to sending holiday greetings, he interpreted the word *holiday* so liberally that his letters were almost as frequent as before.

In the summer of 1901 Betty Cuttter returned from Europe, stopping in Northampton to visit friends on her way home to Cleveland. When she checked into her hotel, she found Dwight Morrow already in residence. He had learned of her visit through mutual acquaintances and arranged a "coincidental" meeting. Betty's friends expected her to be annoyed and were amazed when, at the end of the weekend, she told them that she and Dwight had become engaged. Two more years passed before the young couple felt they could afford to marry.

* * *

Nothing counts for less in New York society than a poor but modestly distinguished midwestern background. Not quite ready to expose themselves to the rigors of Manhattan social climbing, Betty and Dwight settled in Englewood, New Jersey. Although they had chosen Englewood partly out of economic necessity—they could not afford the rents being asked in good neighborhoods on Manhattan's East Side—the Morrows soon developed a sentimental attachment to the town that seems, in retrospect, a little excessive. (A section of Dwight Morrow's authorized biography is entitled "Love of Englewood.")

This is not to deny that Englewood was a fine place to live, and never more so than during the early decades of the century, when the town resembled a vision out of a Currier & Ives print. Manhattan was only twelve miles down the Hudson and an hour's commute away by train, but since there was no automobile bridge into the city many residents felt no need to own a car. Well into the 1920s, Englewood grocery stores continued to make deliveries by wagon, switching in the winter to horse-drawn sleighs invariably mobbed by boys who made a game of trying to hitch rides on the runners. Similarly, the "taxi" service consisted of a rickety horse-drawn carriage, fitted with musty green baize upholstery. Englewood's picturesque Victorian homes had been discovered by upwardly mobile New Yorkers like Steward Prosser, soon to be president of Banker's Trust, and Harry Davison, who became a partner in the firm of J. P. Morgan & Co. in 1908, and the Morrows' tireless efforts on behalf of Englewood charities and civic groups gave them an opportunity to mix with and be noticed by business and financial leaders they could scarcely have counted as friends in the city.

The Morrow family, meanwhile, was growing. Elisabeth Reeve and Anne Spencer, born in 1904 and 1906, were followed two years later by a son, Dwight Whitney Morrow, Jr., and in 1913 by a third daughter, Constance Cutter Morrow. By 1909, Dwight senior had become a full partner in his law firm, and he and Betty purchased a sprawling frame house on Palisade Avenue. "If we keep to our present resolutions, and ill fortune does not overtake us," Dwight wrote, "we will live here for the rest of our lives."[4]

Betty, no doubt, hoped this particular prophecy would not come true. Her tastes had been influenced by her friend Amey Aldrich and Amey's architect brother Chester, and she considered stained-glass windows, turrets, and interior woodwork gloomy. Since a modern house was beyond the family's means at the moment, she settled for hiring a contractor to rid this one of its gingerbread trim and dismantle the unfunctional tower that perched over the front porch.

The Palisade Avenue house was a paradise for children. Each of the younger Morrows progressed in turn from the backyard sandbox, to the homemade swing that hung from a limb of the nearby sweet gum tree, to exploring the perimeters of the one-acre garden. The nearest neighbor was an elderly German lady, who would summon the youngsters over to the fence and ceremoniously present them with gifts of home-baked strudel and pastries. Two blocks away lived the four Lamont children, who had a tennis court in their backyard. Elisabeth and Anne became especially fond of skinny, jug-eared Corliss ("Toughie") Lamont, who rode around the neighborhood on his white pony, Cream of Wheat.[5]

In the evenings the Morrows gathered in the den, where Betty read aloud to the children, working her way through Kipling, R. L. Stevenson, *Tom Sawyer*, and later, lengthy historical novels like Lew Wallace's *Ben Hur*, with its climactic Roman chariot race, spiritedly rendered by Betty down to the crowd noises and the whinnies of the horses. Elisabeth and Anne, however, were far more impressed by the theme of leprosy. The novel implied that this dread disease could be communicated instantly by a single touch of the hand, and for weeks the girls examined their fingers and toes at bedtime for signs that they were about to fall off. They also exchanged solemn vows that if one of them caught the disease, she would immediately touch her sister.

Dwight Morrow's place in the family circle was that of the brilliant but lovably absent-minded father. According to family legend, he was so unaware of his surroundings that he once got into the bathtub wearing his pajamas and couldn't figure out why the soap wouldn't work up a proper lather. Forbidden to smoke cigars at home, Morrow eased his nerves by tearing strips of paper and rolling them into matchstick-size cylinders. By the end of the evening, the floor around his chair would be littered with these sticks, many of which had been used in the interim to clean his fingernails or ream out his ears.

Business frequently kept Morrow in the city until long after the dinner hour, but he made a point of presiding at breakfast. He would come into the dining room whistling a jaunty off-key tune, and the children would line up for their morning hugs. "Where's my morning kiss?" he would demand of the girls. "No cheekies, now. No cheekies." And he would plant on each daughter's mouth a kiss that Anne would later describe as "the loud Morrow smack." While the children giggled

behind their hands at Daddy's terrible table manners, he would entertain them with funny monologues interspersed with pop quizzes in
mathematics and history. Anne later recalled that halfway through the
meal, his mind focused on other topics, he would say distractedly, "But
you haven't given your Dad a morning kiss!" And then the ritual of
morning hugs and wet kisses would begin all over again.[6]

Quoting a remark originally made about Alexander Hamilton,
Morrow's biographer said of him, "The power of his intellect was hardly
suspected under the ambush of his extraordinary charm." Morrow had a
facility for making his opponents in negotiations believe they were sacri-
ficing their petty demands for the sake of some higher principle; by the
time the deal was struck, he had exactly what he wanted and the other
side felt not like a flock of newly shorn sheep but somehow ennobled. It
helped that he often had a better grasp of the details of his clients' businesses than they did, and Daniel Guggenheim once said that Dwight
Morrow knew more about copper than he and his six brothers combined.

But Morrow was bored by corporate law. He hadn't struggled to
come east and get an education in order to spend his life poring over
utility company balance sheets. He often talked of chucking his career to
teach mathematics or constitutional law in a university as soon as he had
set aside a nest egg for his children's education. However, it wasn't easy
for a self-made man with a family to support to turn his back on prosperity. Betty Morrow told the story of how, early in his career, Dwight
awoke in the middle of the night in a cold sweat, complaining of a terrible nightmare. "It was all so vivid, so ghastly," he shuddered. "I dreamt,
Betsey, that we had become rich. But *enormously* rich."

In 1913 the nightmare came true. Florence Lamont, the mother of
Corliss, had been a Smith College classmate of Betty's, and now that
they were near neighbors in Englewood, the two women had become
close friends. In 1911 Florence's husband Thomas, a former newspaper
editor and chocolate importer, had been recruited by Harry Davison
into the firm of J. P. Morgan & Co. Two years later another partnership
slot fell empty, and Lamont lobbied on behalf of Dwight Morrow.

Morrow, now forty years old, was earning a very comfortable but
unspectacular income of about $38,000 a year. He had never owned an
automobile or a second home. A Morgan partnership would make him a
multimillionaire in short order and catapult him into the elite inner circle of international finance. Much to Tom Lamont's exasperation, however, Morrow asked for two weeks to think the offer over, agonized over

the decision night and day, and in the end came back to him with the obvious answer.

Even by the relatively sedate standards of pre–World War I Wall Street, J. P. Morgan & Co. was a kingdom unto itself. Inside the firm's walnut-paneled headquarters at 23 Wall Street, the partners set aside their business at four o'clock every afternoon so that liveried valets could serve an English-style tea. Seeing that the new partner often forgot to replace his suspenders after visiting the lavatory, the firm solved the problem by hiring an attendant whose sole job was to stand at the lavatory door and assist Mr. Morrow in arranging his attire. Tom Lamont, whose lifelong motto was Easy Does It, had made it a condition of his partnership that he be permitted to take at least two months of uninterrupted vacation every year, and he urged Morrow to do the same.

Dwight Morrow entered the House of Morgan at a time when the dowager banking institution of the Gilded Age was undergoing a subtle but profound change. John Pierpont Morgan, Sr., had died the year before—killed, some said, by the shock of being subpoenaed to testify before the Pujo Committee, the congressional investigation of the Money Trust inspired by C. A. Lindbergh. His son, JP junior, was a different breed, an easy-going family man who spent at least six months a year in Britain, much of them shooting game at his seventeen-thousand-acre hunting preserve in Scotland. The older partners were slow to take advantage of Jack's phlegmatic nature, and the ambitious Tom Lamont, his personality as smooth as his trademark pearl gray suits, was soon able to remake the firm in his own image.

Radicals like Congressman Lindbergh might charge the House of Morgan with being a trust of trusts, engaged in what he called "a selfish plan to rule the world by the manipulation of finances." Needless to say, the view from inside 23 Wall Street was quite different. JP senior had believed that he was saving the American economy from the ravages of unfettered competition. Tom Lamont, more manager than entrepreneur, carried this philosophy a step farther. In the 1930s, when the author Harold Nicolson innocently referred to the House of Morgan as a bank, Lamont was grievously insulted. "Banking!" he fumed. "Yes, of course, individuals and corporations, believing in the judgment of the house, made it their depository. So that, like any other bank, it had certain banking operations. But do you think that for a moment these were the chief operations of the firm members?" Lamont preferred to think of the House of Morgan as a sort of supragovernmental institution and, as he put it, "a glorious opportunity for public service, with enormous prestige and legitimate influence ready-made at hand."[7]

Soon after Dwight Morrow's partnership became official in 1914, war broke out in Europe, and Morrow was sent to London to organize shipping convoys for war matériel imported from America through the Morgan-sponsored purchasing agency. In 1918 he took a temporary leave to become a civilian adviser to General Pershing, handling the delicate problem of allocating ordnance shipments among the various Allied armies.

After the war Tom Lamont spent five months in Versailles, drawing up a schedule for Germany's payment of war reparations. Unless the Germans indemnified England and France, those nations would never be able to repay on their own the millions in bonds sold through Morgan & Co. syndicates. Needless to say, Lamont denied any mercenary motives, and in fact he spent much of his time trying to persuade French and British diplomats to moderate their demands. On returning home, he became a prominent advocate of the League of Nations, as was Dwight Morrow, who wrote a series of popular articles in defense of the League for the *New York Evening Post*.

While the other Morgan partners lived like uncrowned royalty behind the walls of their estates on the North Shore of Long Island, Lamont and Morrow cultivated a more modern, socially concerned image. They and their wives socialized with writers like Robert Frost, H. G. Wells, and Walter De la Mare; with political analyst Walter Lippmann and noted jurist Learned Hand; and with a circle of reform-minded college administrators and academics. Florence Lamont was a liberal who eventually channeled millions of dollars of J. P. Morgan profits to causes like the ACLU, the Women's Trade Union League, and Russian War Relief. Betty Morrow, only slightly more conservative, was a patron of Planned Parenthood, the YMCA, and the Union Theological Seminary.

Dwight Morrow somehow still found time to devote hours every week to Englewood civic affairs and committee work for his alma mater. He was a trustee of more than a dozen nonprofit organizations, including the Carnegie Endowment, and a member of the Board of Regents of the Smithsonian Institution. He wrote personal letters that ran to six or seven single-spaced typed pages and turned out dozens of articles, speeches, and book forewords without benefit of a ghostwriter. It is difficult to imagine this small, disheveled man with twinkly blue eyes and a perpetually misbuttoned vest as an international financier, and Morrow certainly didn't think of himself that way: "I never made Morgan & Co. any money," he once said of his years as a partner. Morrow's image as Morgan & Co.'s house intellectual, a man above mere pecuniary motives, was not always appreciated by his fellow partners, however. Jack Morgan privately considered him a publicity hound, and Tom Lamont, on reading the comment quoted above in Morrow's posthumous biography, sniffed, "He was the canniest there was."[8] Still, Morrow's growing reputation served the interests of the firm, and during the boom years after the war, differences among the partners were rarely more than a minor irritant.

Regardless of who was making it, the money kept rolling in. The partners' bonuses mushroomed with the bull market of the twenties, topping out in 1928 at 1 million preinflation dollars a year. In 1927, when the Morrows decided to reorganize their children's trust funds, they transferred excess securities so that each of the four would have an identical principal of $450,000. Dwight and Betty were also quietly subsidizing numerous poor relatives, including his sister Alice, a Pittsburgh schoolteacher, who kept a *pied-à-terre* on Riverside Drive in Manhattan, ran up department store and limousine bills to the tune of $20,000 a year, and wrote playful, self-mocking letters explaining that she had already cut her expenses to the bone and Dwight mustn't worry himself about budgets, just sign the checks.

The Lamonts soon purchased a Manhattan town house at 170 East Seventieth Street, returning to Englewood only on weekends, but Dwight and Betty Morrow still took pride in their loyalty to their hometown. Long after they had become multimillionaires, the Morrows continued to reside in the sprawling but unpretentious home on Palisade Avenue, and their children attended ballroom-dancing classes at a neighbor woman's home and Sunday school at the Englewood Presbyterian Church.

When Dwight Morrow went to Europe on business he took the entire family along. They traveled with more than three dozen pieces of luggage, including an entire trunk packed with books, and between appointments Morrow would take his brood sightseeing by chauffeured car. The itinerary was planned around visits to literary and historical "shrines" chosen by the children from their winter reading list. Daddy provided the historical commentary, reading aloud from a dog-eared copy of Henry Adams as the family hiked en masse around Mont-Saint-Michel, and from Washington Irving at the Alhambra.

These educational tours were in addition to summer vacations, when the Morrows and Lamonts decamped to the island of North Haven in Penobscot Bay, Maine, a retreat they had chosen precisely because the summer community was too small to support an organized social life. The summers were for children, and the four Morrow and four Lamont offspring whiled away the time swimming, sailing, beach-combing, and playing tennis and golf. (Finished in 1927, the Morrows' "cottage," known as Deacon's Point, had a private golf course.) Occasionally the young people borrowed the Lamont motor launch *North Star* for all-day outings to Isle au Haut, now part of Acadia National Park, or to Hurricane Island, where they would explore the "ghost village" formerly inhabited by the families of workers at the island's abandoned stone quarry.

But the highlight of the summer was the "Tildsey picnic," an event for all ages. Every year the Tildseys, whose summer cottage was some distance away on Little Deer Isle, would choose an uninhabited island in the bay as the site of their annual get-together. The Tildseys served their famous fish chowder, and the day would end with everyone gathered around the fire while the grown-ups declaimed poetry from memory—in Tom Lamont's case "You're a better man than I am, Gunga Din!" or "An' they're hangin' Danny Deever in the mornin'." [9]

SIX

"Don't Take Yourself Too Seriously"

*R*EMINISCENCES OF THE MORROW-LAMONT CIRCLE inevitably con-
jure up the image of a golden world in which great fortunes were
made in a single generation without the sacrifice of old-fashioned family
values, the adults used their power and influence to further humane
causes, and the children were ever dutiful and appreciative. "Much rub-
bish is written (and more talked) about the evils of great wealth.... Few
people in modern times, even among the generous Americans, can have
made more generous and enlightened use of their great wealth,"
enthused British poet laureate John Masefield in a posthumous tribute
to the Lamonts.[1]

Corliss Lamont, though he grew up to become an enthusiast (some
would say an apologist) for Stalinist Russia, staunchly insisted that he
never rebelled against his parents. Although his father was a sometime
admirer of Mussolini, supported Franco in the Spanish Civil War, and
was often called "the First Consul de facto of the invisible world of postwar high finance," Corliss described his own politics as a "natural continuation" of his parents' liberal views on international affairs and social
questions. Indeed, he remained a keen student of family history, attending meetings of Clan Lamont in Scotland and editing volumes of family
memoirs.[2]

Anne Morrow Lindbergh, with greater objectivity, would acknowledge that there was something limiting, even stifling, about the over-privileged environment of her youth, leaving her feeling at times as if she were secluded inside a "walled garden," like Sheltered Emily in Chaucer's "The Knight's Tale." Nevertheless, well into middle age she would continue to look back with longing to the "warm, safe," and "tolerant" world of her childhood. In her introduction to *Bring Me a Unicorn*, written when she was nearly seventy, Anne Lindbergh explains that she deliberately chose to publish her early diaries and letters, in preference to writing an autobiography, which would involve "sifting, picking and choosing" and a consequent temptation to "gloss over" the truth. Of course, many memoirs are written in the spirit of concealment, but most thoughtful people assume that the sifting process essential to writing a serious autobiography leads to greater self-knowledge, not as Anne would have it, a step backward in the "painful journey toward honesty."

One can only wonder, in retrospect, at the power of this artfully constructed myth of an idyllic family life, so compelling that even grown children, individuals of uncommon intelligence and international reputation, continued to be mesmerized by it. Certainly the Morrows were exceptional people, but like any other family, they had their problems. What made them different was not so much the problems per se as the enormous amount of energy that went into denying their existence.

To begin with Dwight Morrow had a lifelong drinking problem. The label *alcoholic* was seldom applied to successful men during the early decades of the twentieth century, and friends and family collaborated in transforming Dwight's more embarrassing lapses into anecdotes about his fabled "absent-mindedness." All those family stories about Morrow's mismatched socks and uncombed hair, the meals he forgot to eat, and the sloppy kisses he planted on his daughters' mouths at breakfast become less amusing when one realizes that he was frequently operating in a whiskey-induced fog.

Blond, pretty Elisabeth, known to the family as Ebba, was the eldest child and her father's "Number One." From an early age Elisabeth aspired to become a teacher, fulfilling Dwight Morrow's own frustrated ambitions in that direction. While still a student at Smith, she and her friend Constance Chilton were already planning to found their own nursery school, a dream that came to fruition in Englewood's Little School, financed in large part through a trust set up by her parents. Elisabeth's notions of the ideal educational environment seem, by today's standards better suited to a sanatorium. The children were to be shielded from loud noises, overstimulating games, and, of course, competition. Even the colors of the custom-designed furniture, toys, and the serving ware used at snack time were muted—limited to Elisabeth's favorite shades of taupe, rose, and dusky lilac.

A natural leader as well as a magna cum laude student, Elisabeth had inherited her father's poise and charm, the ability, as her younger sister Anne put it, "to make a party wherever she was." But in some ways she was also immature, her romantic life a series of crushes that came and went with devastating rapidity. Always frail, she had what in those days was called a "murmuring heart," which the family ascribed to a childhood bout of rheumatic fever. She seems also to have had a tendency to anorexia. Ebba never had to be encouraged to study, but getting her to eat was a concern.[3]

Anne, two years younger, was terribly shy, a serious disability in a family as ambitious and determinedly gregarious as the Morrows. A precocious and talented writer, Anne worked at her own deliberate pace and had a tendency to panic at exam time. Although (or, more likely, because) her father often conducted impromptu math drills over breakfast, she had a mental block against any subject that required doing calculations. "I never passed an arithmetic examination in my life," she later acknowledged.[4]

The only Morrow child who never went away to boarding school, Anne remained at Miss Chapin's—the New York private school whose founder, the eponymous Miss Chapin, was a close friend of the family. Surrounded by girls from similar backgrounds who in most cases had been her friends since first grade, Anne played basketball and was even elected class president, yet she lacked confidence and seemed much younger than her years. Filling out the traditional class questionnaire in her senior year, Anne responded a question about her ideal husband, "I want to marry a hero."[5]

For Dwight Whitney Morrow, Jr., the only son, nothing came easy. Dwight junior idolized his father and copied his every trait, even taking to wearing a pince-nez when he was still a teenager. Unfortunately, also like his father, he was physically uncoordinated and moody. Despite a pronounced stammer and a notable lack of athletic ability, young Dwight was packed off to Groton in 1924 at the age of fifteen.

Constance was the baby of the family, and like many a youngest child, she seemed to escape the pressures to excel that weighed so heavily on her older siblings. Con had her moments of what she called "weak-kneed" rebellion but usually found it easier to follow "meekly along in the path prescribed for me."[6]

Betty Morrow was in many ways the most complex and certainly the saddest member of the family. Once a promising writer, she attended Smith during an era when educators, defensive about "wasting" advanced learning on females, preached that a college woman could find no higher calling than creating a cultured home. Betty was an energetic woman whose sweet, slightly flustered manner disguised a will of iron. Her family was her masterpiece, and if her husband and children did not live up to expectations, they were not failing on their own account but hers as well. Betty would no doubt have been horrified at the suggestion that she imposed her will on her loved ones. Nevertheless, the rest of the family often appeared to be engaged in a conspiracy to avoid disappointing Mother. Dwight repeatedly assured his wife that he had given up smoking (a vow he had never had any intention of keeping), and Anne's letters to her mother from college are filled with false assurances that Dwight is getting along well at Groton, that Elisabeth is feeling fine, and that she herself is coping with the pressures of her demanding schedule.

Betty had submerged her own personality so completely that even her diary, kept faithfully throughout her married life, was not a record of her own emotional highs and lows, but of her husband's. Tom Lamont, who had occasion to read some excerpts, commented acerbically, "It isn't all of us that have a wife who takes the time to record our moods at the end of each day." Lamont hinted that the neurotic, intensely moody Dwight Morrow portrayed in the diaries was not the same man he had known as a friend and colleague but in large part a projection of Betty's own anxieties.[7]

Both Mrs. Morrow and her friend Florence Lamont were passionate about culture and dedicated to the cause of education for women, yet their intellectual horizons were limited. Betty wrote amateurish verse, which was occasionally published thanks to her friendships with literary editors like Ellery Sedgwick of the *Atlantic Monthly*. Florence Lamont had a master's degree in philosophy from Columbia, a rare accomplishment for a woman of her generation, and aspired to invent a new philosophical system that would reconcile science and religion, rescuing humanity from, as one friend put it, "the chaos into which life had fallen." Yet, as Anne Lindbergh later observed, modern intellectual movements like Freudianism had no place inside the "walled garden." There was even less room for literary modernism or for American writ-

ers of any school, with the exception of a few friends like the Amherst
poet Robert Frost.

In fact, the Englewood of the Lamonts and Morrows was like some
remote province of the British Empire where Kipling never went out of
fashion and second-rate English writers were extravagantly courted. Florence Lamont formed an intense friendship with John Masefield, writing him more than two thousand letters over the years. Masefield, in
turn, dedicated several of his lesser efforts to Florence and her husband,
among them a quite dreadful poem about the Palisades, perhaps the
only modern verse in English to employ the word *glid*, as in:

> Often I wondered what the rampart hid.
> What was it the cruising eagle saw
> Below the forest treetops as he glid
> Searching the rock for quarry for his claw?[8]

Needless to say, the existence of popular culture was never
acknowledged. Corliss's younger brother Austin, home on vacation
from Phillips Exeter, was astounded to learn that his mother had never
heard of Babe Ruth. The children still at home were unlikely to hear
about sports and popular music even from the servants, who were nearly
all imported from the British Isles or Scandinavia.

Strangely, considering Anne's memory of her girlhood as a time
when the world really was a "polite and gentle" place, untroubled by
the specters of concentration camps, the atom bomb, and street crime,
there was nothing peaceful or secure about the existence of a J. P. Morgan partner. The House of Morgan had become the favorite target of
lunatics and radicals of all persuasions, including anarchists, Communists, and German nationalists. As early as the beginning of the 1920s,
proto-Nazi clubs in Brooklyn and the Bronx were distributing copies of
a pamphlet, purportedly a reprint of a British secret service report of
1917, outlining a plot by the J. P. Morgan bank and the British government to subvert American democracy, nationalize the Red Cross, and
use the Boy Scouts and the YMCA "to make obedient little Britons out
of our native young."

Not all the enemies of the House of Morgan were content with circulating scurrilous pamphlets. In 1915 a German named Erich
Muenter, a self-described pacifist, broke into Jack Morgan's Long Island
home, took his children hostage, and wounded Morgan twice in the
groin. Muenter was eventually dispatched by the butler, who hit him

over the head with a lump of coal. (According to J. P. Morgan chroni-
cler Ron Chernow, the news that Jack Morgan had been wounded was
celebrated in Vienna with "fireworks, speeches and jubilant crowds.")[9]

Morgan recovered from this attack; then, in 1919, an anarchist
took a shot at him in church, killing his physician by mistake. And just
six months later, a bomb hidden in a wagon loaded with iron window-
sash weights went off in front of 23 Wall Street. Thirty-eight people
died, including two Morgan clerks, and the bank's main trading floor
was reduced to rubble. Dwight Morrow, who was in his office on the
partners' floor when the blast went off, strolled through the disaster
scene minutes later on his way to lunch, oblivious to the smoke, debris,
and agonized cries of the wounded—another example of his famous
"absent-mindedness."

Badly frightened, Jack Morgan hired the William J. Burns detective
agency to investigate crank letters, including kidnapping and extortion
threats against the partners and their families, and began to display signs
of paranoia about Bolsheviks, Germans, and Jews. (Jewish-American
bankers were suspected at this time of being German sympathizers.)
During the early 1920s, Tom Lamont and Dwight Morrow were not
well enough known to the public to be obvious targets, at least so it
seemed. And since both men came from modest backgrounds and took
a more liberal view of the world, they were almost more worried about
protecting their families from paranoia and social isolation than from
the actual threat of violence. Nevertheless, potential danger from fanatics undoubtedly accounted for some of Betty and Dwight Morrow's
tendency to overprotect their children. Anne and her siblings were not
taken out to restaurants or permitted to play with (or, as they grew
older, to date) strangers. Anne's likening of the world of her childhood
to a "walled garden" was not just a metaphor; invisible walls were deliberately erected by her parents in the hope of keeping their children
safe—and, as much as possible, innocent of the fact that there were people in the world who would hate them because of who their father was.

Perhaps the chief difference between the Lamont and Morrow families was that the Lamonts were not gifted with self-doubt, while the
Morrows were so introspective that their sudden rise to great wealth
instigated a prolonged identity crisis. After the Lamonts moved to New
York City, the Morrows made much of their decision to continue living
on Palisade Avenue in a house far beneath their means—a decision
treated at length in Morrow's authorized biography. In fact, however,
the Morrows' residence in Englewood during these years was a myth.

Commuting was a strain on Dwight and difficult for the children, who were attending private schools in the city, so from 1919 through 1928, their primary residence was New York City. The Palisade Avenue house was used mainly on weekends.

For most of this period, the Morrows lived in a rented apartment on East Sixty-sixth Street near Fifth Avenue. Later, in 1928, they purchased a co-op on East Seventieth Street. Both apartments were sumptuous and fully staffed. The Seventieth Street co-op occupied an entire floor and had a marble foyer, a ballroom, and more than a dozen bedrooms. Betty Morrow entertained vigorously, hosting formal dinner parties for thirty and receptions for three hundred. As early as the spring of 1920, Dwight wrote his daughter Elisabeth, then a student at Milton Academy, saying how much he missed the serenity of life on Palisade Avenue. In the city, he had so many social obligations that he scarcely had time to read or take walks.[10]

Morrow was active in New Jersey Republican politics, an obvious practical motive for maintaining the fiction that Englewood was his chief residence. However, even among themselves, the family tended to speak of the Manhattan apartments as mere *pieds-à-terre*, or, in Morrow's own words, "[places] to sleep in the city." Betty Morrow remembered the old days on Spring Lane as the happiest period of her life—"I was never alone for a minute!" she confided to one acquaintance, who thought this an odd definition of bliss. New York made both her and Dwight feel anonymous. Betty longed for a proper home in New Jersey, commensurate with the family's income and status. It was Dwight, it seems, who clung to the notion that he was a man of the people, different from the senior partners who were holed up with their families on their North Shore estates, protected by stone walls and hired security guards. In 1927, when the Palisade Avenue house was condemned in connection with a road-building project, Betty won out. The family purchased a tract of land not far from the center of Englewood and commissioned Chester Aldrich to design a stately home for the site. The Morrows hoped to move in shortly after Constance started boarding school.

Betty and Dwight's sentimental feelings about Englewood were exceeded only by their loyalty to Smith and Amherst—this was a couple who had planned their honeymoon around visits to their respective alma maters. Over the years their attachment grew even stronger, until they came to regard the college communities as surrogate families. Both institutions acquired Morrow dormitories, among other valuable gifts. Dwight became a life trustee of Amherst; Betty would cap a lifetime of service to Smith with an appointment as interim president of the college in 1940. As fortunate as this situation was for both institutions, which benefited not only from the money but from the Morrows' dedicated leadership, there was something overdone—or, to put it bluntly, phony—about this outpouring of devotion, as if Betty and Dwight were desperate to shed their nouveau-riche image by identifying themselves with the New England Brahmin tradition.

Worse, the children were expected to replicate their parents' undergraduate triumphs. The Morrows assuaged their Protestant consciences by reasoning that they had earned their great wealth by virtue of their hard work and superior intellectual attainments. Unfortunately, this reasoning demanded that the next generation also justify the privileges it enjoyed. But of course it wasn't the same—the younger Morrows were not ambitious scholarship students from the Midwest but overadvantaged scions of prominent alumni. They had neither their parents' raw drive nor any excuse for falling short of absolute perfection.

Even the dutiful, academically talented Elisabeth occasionally found the pressure to live up to her mother's stellar record too much to bear. Her father commiserated. Still, it never seemed to occur to either him or Betty that it might not be strictly necessary for all the children to attend their respective alma maters. From the day Dwight junior was born it was taken for granted that he would attend Groton and then Amherst. The girls, as Constance put it, were "just inundated with talk of Smith" from the time they were three years old. Constance would long to go to another college—even though it was "heresy" to entertain such ideas.[11]

In contrast to Elisabeth, who invariably managed to shrug off her bouts of insecurity in time to produce straight A's and win election to class office, Dwight junior had trouble just getting through prep school. Tormented by campus bullies, the myopic youth complained of hearing voices. He was admitted to the infirmary, and Groton headmaster Endicott Peabody relayed to Dwight senior the faculty consensus that Dwight was "socially immature" and ought to drop back a class. Repeating the previous year's work would give him a rest from academic pressure, and a chance to make friends with boys who were more compatible.

Morrow reluctantly agreed to follow Peabody's advice but could not reconcile himself to the prospect of sixteen-year-old Dwight junior taking it easy for an entire academic year. He wrote reminding Dwight that simply because he was repeating the same classes was no excuse for slacking off—such a course would be "fatal"—and he promised that he and Mother would send him history books to peruse in his free hours.[12]

Anne, meanwhile, was none too enthusiastic about entering Smith's class of 1928. Not only would she have her mother's record to emulate, but the popular Elisabeth would be a senior during her freshman year. A number of Anne's friends at Miss Chapin's were planning to go to Vassar, and in a moment of bravado Anne confided to her diary that she wanted to go to Vassar too. Even before she raised the issue with her mother she could anticipate the response—What about class reunions? What about Ivy Day? All the women of the family will be making the pilgrimage back to Northampton, and you will be the only one left out! In the end Anne rationalized that there was really no great difference between Smith and Vassar—except that by choosing Vassar she would break her mother's heart. So in the autumn of 1924, she went to Smith after all. Betty Morrow went along to unpack daughter's trunks for her; then mother and daughter dropped in on President Neilson and his wife for tea.

During her freshman year, Anne, though only five feet one, played varsity basketball and thrived on the approval of her English composition teacher Mina Curtiss, the sister of poet-balletomane Lincoln Kirstein and an accomplished author in her own right. Curtiss encouraged Anne to submit her work to the college literary magazine, which promptly accepted her first submission, an admiring review of A. A. Milne's *When We Were Very Young*. In the meantime she was fighting a losing battle with Greek and mathematics. At the end of the year the class dean called her in for a conference and suggested that perhaps next year she should include some less demanding courses in her schedule—perhaps "Home Gardening." Anne was insulted and horrified: "Who did she think I was? A fat old matron?" To prove the dean wrong, she signed up for an even more demanding schedule, including eighteenth-century literature and physics.[13]

But the dean was not wrong. Anne had a mental block against math and science, and even when it came to the humanities she was a slow, methodical worker. Although certainly intelligent and already an accomplished prose stylist, she was simply not up to the demands of a competitive academic environment. Her parents hired a tutor, who met with her in the basement of an off-campus church, trying his best to coax her through physics, one quiz at a time. The possibility that Anne and Smith were not really suited to each other was unthinkable, but in a letter to her father Anne wistfully remarked on how much she had enjoyed a biography of Erasmus borrowed from his library, adding that she would love to spend her time reading about Erasmus (or anything else) "in depth" rather than wrestling with courses like physics that held no interest for her.

Morrow replied to this plea with an extraordinary seven-page letter, a bizarre mixture of fatherly concern and displaced anxiety:

He began by reminding Anne of the advice of "an old Scotchman" of his acquaintance, Sir Joseph MacLay, the British minister of shipping during World War I, who had told him to always follow "rule six"— "Don't take yourself too seriously." The maxim sounds apt enough; but by way of illustrating how MacLay followed this rule in his own life, Morrow related that on the day MacLay's only son was killed in battle, the Scotsman attended a full schedule of cabinet meetings, never alluding to his personal tragedy for fear of making his colleagues uncomfortable!

Morrow also recalled how, as a first-year lawyer, he and his fellow associates at Reed, Simpson had stayed up into the small hours of the morning researching precedents until, at some point, one of the group threw down his pencil and announced, "What the hell, Bill"—a catchphrase that signaled it was time to call it a night. Perhaps, he advised, Anne and some of her friends could found a "What the Hell, Bill" club at Smith. Of course the name would have to be changed to avoid any suggestion of profanity. More important, the members must be carefully chosen. It wouldn't do to admit shirkers or those who might simply be tempted to close their books too soon.

Finally Morrow reminded his daughter of the example the old lama in Kipling's *Kim,* who wanders all over India trying to get off the Wheel of Things. The old man eventually succeeds in attaining enlightenment only to fall into the river in mid-trance and nearly drown.[14]

Bemused by his own meandering train of thought, Morrow admitted he wasn't quite sure exactly what lesson he expected his daughter to draw from the fate of this crazy old man, and Anne must surely have been even more confused. Her father was obviously very much attached to the Wheel of Things himself, and though he wanted to advise Anne not to worry so much about her grades, every anecdote that came to his mind conveyed the opposite message. Anne's reaction was to withdraw from activities like the drama club and field hockey. She spent her days holed up in the library and saw less of fun-loving friends like the none-too-studious Edie Sedgwick—a niece of Ellery Sedgwick, a distant cousin of the namesake Warhol superstar in the sixties, and definitely not a suitable candidate for a "What the Heck, Bill" society.

Anne eventually pulled up her grades and achieved distinction by publishing poems and stories in the *Smith College Monthly,* but unlike Constance, who would overcome her "prejudice" against her mother's alma mater to become a class officer and enthusiastic Smith booster, Anne never really adjusted. What Anne needed most was self-confidence— the one thing Smith could never teach her. While Anne struggled with her too-ambitious course load, everyone from President Neilson on down was solicitously looking out for her welfare.

During the years Anne spent at Smith, the social revolution of the Jazz Age had begun to have an impact on the social mores of the children of wealth and privilege. "Nice" girls—even Smith girls—bobbed their hair, wore makeup, and purchased off-the-rack clothes. In 1927, for the first time, Smith women were permitted to smoke in the public lounges after dinner—a change that prompted some students to wonder what they would do now for forbidden thrills. The more adventurous already had ideas on the subject and were dating young men who kept flasks of whiskey in the glove compartments of their roadsters. To the extent that Anne might have been tempted to experiment along these lines, she was inhibited by the knowledge that any rebellion, however timid, would be duly reported to her parents. Nor could she ever be quite sure that any attention she received from teachers was fairly earned—even Mrs. Curtiss, who had singled out her work for special praise, was a protégée of Betty Morrow's good friend *Atlantic Monthly* editor Ellery Sedgwick.

Marjorie Hope Nicolson, a distinguished member of the Smith faculty as well as dean of students—though apparently not the same "class dean" who advised Anne to switch to "Home Gardening"—knew the Morrow family well and was acquainted with Anne's academic struggles through her roommate, the novelist Mary Ellen Chase, who taught one of Anne's literature courses. Nicolson would recall that Anne's misery was well known to the faculty. Anne, she said, "hated Smith. She never really liked it.... She retired into herself." Always more comfortable with the older generation, Anne became the sort of girl who was the special pet of the housemothers, like the white-haired Mary Cooke of Emerson House, who would remember her as "the most exquisite girl I ever knew."[15]

Pretty and petite, Anne was attractive to boys but found dating an ordeal. A character in *Dearly Beloved,* a novel she published more than forty years later, would observe that all eligible men can be divided into four categories: Lumps, Worthies, Twinklers, and Sparklers. Lumps are the sort of boys who rely on female cousins to line up dates for them. Worthies are the presentable but harmless sons of your parents' friends. During her own college years Anne went out with her share of both, and, looking into the future, she assumed her destiny was to marry a Twinkler—perhaps an amusing conversationalist like Corliss Lamont, who had dated both her and Elisabeth. She even confessed to her diary that she wished she could dispense with the agonies of courtship altogether and move directly to the more secure status of the young matron.

There was a romantic, rebellious side to Anne's nature—one that dared to believe it would be her fate to fall in love with a Sparkler—but since arriving at Smith she had learned to keep that aspect of her personality under wraps. It found expression only in her writing. A typical poem, which Anne wrote after attending a performance by the Spanish dancer Raquel Meller, begins:

> I should like to be a dancer,
> A slim, persuasive Spanish dancer,
> A scarlet Spanish dancer....

The narrator of the poem presents herself to an impresario only to be told that "just now" there are no such parts available. However, there is a place for a Quaker maiden—"a blue-eyed Quaker maiden."

"So I play the role of Quaker and I do not blame my maker," the lyric concludes, on an unconvincing note of resignation.[16]

At the time this poem was written, the Morrow name was well known to those who followed business and financial news, but it could hardly be said that Dwight Morrow was a figure of national stature. However, the sudden death of President Warren G. Harding in August 1923 had set in motion a series of events that would earn Morrow his moment in history and bring even his shy, overprotected daughter a measure of celebrity.

In 1920 Morrow had formed a committee of Republican businessmen to promote the presidential candidacy of his former Amherst classmate Calvin Coolidge. Coolidge was the governor of Massachusetts at the time, and best known for putting down a strike by Boston policemen. Morrow, however, professed to see qualities in Silent Cal that had so far escaped the notice of the world at large, extolling him as "part practical politician and part transcendental philosopher." The intent of the Draft Coolidge campaign was to lay the groundwork for a presidential bid in 1924, but the nominating convention deadlocked, and after what Morrow called "a terrible jumble" of votes, Coolidge emerged as Warren Harding's running mate. "Coolidge did not want the Vice Presidency, and there was absolutely no plan on the part of anybody that he should have had it. But the convention just ran away with the idea," Morrow wrote Tom Lamont.[17]

When Harding died in office and Coolidge took over the White House, it was widely predicted that Dwight Morrow, his friend and adviser for nearly three decades, would be rewarded with a cabinet appointment, probably either secretary of state or secretary of the treasury. But as it turned out, Coolidge the "transcendental philosopher" really did march to the beat of a different drummer. Morrow not only failed to get a cabinet post, he was passed over for a number of lesser appointments he badly wanted, including an appointment as special European commissioner for the Dawes Plan (which dealt with German war reparations), a position he would have been eminently qualified to fill. Coolidge's motives for treating his chief booster so coldly are obscure. Perhaps he was afraid of appearing to be a tool of the Morgan bank, a definite liability even for a Republican. Or perhaps Coolidge did not really like Dwight Morrow very much and resented the assumption of pundits like Walter Lippmann that he could not run the country without taking cues from his worldly and brilliant adviser. As Tom Lamont waspishly observed, no president in his right mind wanted to elevate a man who would be sure to "talk rings around him."

Coolidge kept Dwight Morrow at arm's length until the summer of 1925, when the administration suddenly found itself under attack from the Army Air Service's General Billy Mitchell. Irate over his failure to convince senior military planners of the need for long-range bombers, Mitchell had taken his case to the people. In a series of articles featured in the *Saturday Evening Post,* he warned:

1. The modern battleship was vulnerable to attack from the air.
2. The next major war the United States fought would begin in the Pacific.
3. The war could be won only by adopting an island-hopping strategy, using land-based bombers as opposed to fighters launched from carriers.

To meet these challenges, Mitchell called for the creation of an independent air force. He also strongly criticized the government's failure to subsidize commercial aviation. The nation's lack of air transport capacity alone, he observed, would make it a second rate power in the event of a major war.

Although Mitchell had the president's permission to write the *Saturday Evening Post* series, he got carried away by his own rhetoric, at times forgetting that he and the navy's "fossilized admirals," as he called them, both reported to the same commander in chief. Mitchell's articles created a sensation. In Washington the controversy became so heated that navy officers would no longer speak to those in army uniform, cutting them dead at official receptions and on the streets. The secretary of the navy threatened to resign if Mitchell was not demoted, and Rep. Fiorello LaGuardia, a Mitchell supporter, introduced legislation that would have prevented the president from punishing a military officer for criticizing his policies in public. In the end Mitchell was knocked down to captain and exiled to Texas.

Just as the debate was beginning to cool down, on September 1, 1925, the navy's German-built dirigible *Shenandoah* was struck by lightning during a goodwill flight over the Ohio Valley, killing the ship's captain and fourteen crewmen. The crash was the most horrifying aviation disaster America had ever seen—sections of the burning airship drifted for miles, strewing a trail of charred debris and human remains. Mitchell promptly joined the captain's widow in charging that the *Shenandoah*'s crew had been ordered to make the flight despite unfavorable weather reports, all for a mission that had no purpose other than to sell the public on the navy's outmoded and pointless commitment to dirigibles.

Coolidge now had little choice but to order the secretary of war to court-martial Mitchell for insubordination. But public opinion was running high in favor of the maverick airman. Will Rogers promised his radio audience that "the Flying Napoleon" would soon return from his "Texas Elba" to conquer Washington, and when Mitchell did indeed show up in Washington, the American Legion staged a parade in his honor. At this juncture, with the military all but out of control and the whole brouhaha threatening to spark a rebellion in Congress, Coolidge at last found a high-profile job for his old college friend. Dwight Morrow was named to head a blue-ribbon panel that would evaluate the proper role of aircraft, if any, in the national defense. Morrow knew absolutely nothing about aviation, nor did he need to. The panel's true mission was to discredit Mitchell, and he proceeded to use his famous negotiating talents to steer the experts to the desired conclusion.

The President's Aircraft Board, better known as the Morrow Board, heard more than seventeen hundred hours of testimony and issued a report that remains one of the masterpieces of collective wisdom. Mitchell's warning of an air attack from across the Pacific was dismissed as a fantasy. Moreover, the panel concluded that air power would not play a significant role in warfare in the near future: "The next war may well start in the air, but in all probability it will wind up, as the last one did, in the mud."

Finally, the Morrow Board prophesied:

> Wars against high-spirited peoples will never be ended by attacks on important nerve centers such as manufacturing plants, depots, lighting and power plants and railway centers. The last war taught us that man cannot make a machine stronger than the human spirit.[18]

One could debate whether the atom bomb qualifies as a machine "stronger than the human spirit." In any event, the Aircraft Board had done its job of political damage control and, being a Dwight Morrow project, had actually managed to come up with some positive recommendations—a five-year program for the development of commercial aviation that would include the licensing of commercial pilots, a program to map the airways, twice-daily weather reports for aviators and the construction of beacons for night flying. These recommendations, promptly enacted into law as the Air Commerce Act of 1926, had an immediate impact on mail pilots like Charles Lindbergh, who took part in testing the Chicago beacon, one of the first night-flying aids erected under the new program. The U.S. government had at last committed itself to promoting "the business of the air."

Ironically Morrow, who basically supported the administration's policy of benign neglect, had emerged as the Republican party's chief aviation expert and something of a hero to commercial pilots and other air-minded Americans, a development that illustrates why he was both admired and despised by his contemporaries. The Mitchellites could hardly oppose the results but were privately furious that, in the process of discrediting their spokesman, the Aircraft Board had co-opted ideas they had been advocating for years. Meanwhile Coolidge, who rejected the very idea of government regulation of private industry—his motto, in governing as in life, was "Never do anything that someone else can do for you"—was stuck with a reasonably ambitious five-year plan for civil aeronautics for which Morrow, not he, got all the credit.

SEVEN

"Like Brave Lochinvar Out of the West"

*A*SIDE FROM THE PASSAGE OF THE AIR COMMERCE ACT, the big aviation news of 1926 was that Lt. Comdr. Richard Evelyn Byrd and his pilot Floyd Bennett had become the first human beings to fly over the North Pole. The heroes of the hour, Byrd and Bennett were honored with a ticker-tape parade in New York and a gala reception in Washington, at which President Coolidge awarded them the National Geographic Society's Hubbard Medal. Bennett then departed with the "Polar Plane" on a national tour sponsored by the Daniel Guggenheim Fund for the Promotion of Aeronautics—during which he confided to his copilot, Bernt Balchen, that he wasn't sure he and Byrd had reached the pole at all. Meanwhile, the well-connected Byrd, the "white-haired boy" of the admiralty, one naval officer called him, was already quietly planning his next triumph, a nonstop flight from New York to Paris.

The Atlantic had been flown before, notably by Britons John Alcock and Arthur Brown, who made the 1,890-mile hop from Newfoundland to Ireland in 1919. Two years after Alcock and Brown's success, Raymond Orteig, owner of the Brevoort Hotel in New York, promised to give $25,000 to the first pilot to fly direct from his adopted city to Paris. Orteig originally expected that his prize would be claimed within a few months, but the distance from New York to Paris was much greater than Alcock and Brown had covered, an additional 1,500 miles, and beyond the range of existing aircraft.

It wasn't until 1926 that the flight became technically feasible. The new generation of radial engines that came into use that year were not only more powerful but far more reliable, and aviation experts were predicting that the New York–to–Paris record would fall easily. In fact, Dick Byrd's chief worry in the fall of 1926 was that his rival, the French air ace René Fonck, would get to Paris before his own new Fokker trimotor was delivered.

Fonck and his crew were already at Roosevelt Field on Long Island, testing a Sikorsky biplane equipped with three 425-horsepower Gnome-Rhone-Jupiter radial engines. By the standards of 1926 the Sikorsky was a giant, an ocean liner of the air, equipped with seats upholstered in red leather, a convertible sofa bed, specially designed survival gear, and full-course meals of Long Island duckling and roast turkey, kept warm in insulated compartments. Fonck had even stocked champagne for the victory celebration in Paris—on the theory, one supposes, that the French might have none on hand.

On the morning of September 20, 1926, a crowd gathered at Roosevelt Field to cheer Fonck's departure. The Sikorsky lumbered across the unpaved field, shedding parts as it went. Never close to attaining airspeed, it reached the end of the takeoff strip, tumbled over a twenty-foot embankment, and burst into flames. Fonck and his navigator escaped alive. The radio operator and the mechanic were less fortunate.

Various ideas were advanced as to the cause of the tragedy. The coroner's inquest cited poor communication between the pilot and his flight engineer. The press assumed that the trimotor, weighing in at more than twenty-eight thousand pounds, was simply overloaded. Designer Igor Sikorsky blamed himself for giving in to pressure from commercial sponsors who were eager to see Fonck make the flight that autumn. For the rest of his life, Sikorsky would reproach himself for not insisting that Fonck wait until spring, allowing time for a full schedule of test flights. If he had, Sikorsky believed, his wonderful plane would have been first across the Atlantic.[1]

In St. Louis, mail pilot Slim Lindbergh read newspaper accounts of the Fonck disaster and drew his own conclusions. You certainly didn't need a convertible sofa bed to get to Paris. Or hot meals. For that matter, you didn't necessarily need three engines and a four-man crew. The idea that a big, multiengined plane was necessarily safer was based on the assumption that there was a substantial risk of any one engine going dead during a long flight. But the new radial engines were designed to perform eight thousand hours or more without failure, and in any case, neither the Sikorsky nor any other existing trimotor was designed to fly indefinitely on just two engines. With the new technology, the most dangerous part of the flight was the takeoff—and a heavily loaded trimotor required a longer takeoff strip than a single-engine plane. Such "huge" planes might be the coming thing, but American airfields at the moment were not designed to accommodate them, as the crash of Fonck's Sikorsky had demonstrated.[2]

Lindbergh saw the transatlantic flight as an engineering problem, and as he well knew, the simplest, most elegant solutions were usually the ones that worked. He was by no means the only pilot thinking along these lines, but he was unique in taking the reasoning to its logical conclusion: "It would be easier to do it alone."

Europe, was, after all, a big target. Finding France wasn't the same as finding, say, the Hawaiian islands. You could miss your landfall by hundreds of miles and still set your plane down safely, scoring an astounding aviation first. And with enough fuel it might even be possible to miss one's target by three hundred miles and still work one's way back along the coast toward Paris.

Dispensing with a navigator also meant there would be less pressure to take along parachutes, a radio, and other gear of doubtful utility. The available air-to-ground radio systems were highly unreliable in bad weather when they were most needed, and parachuting into the frigid waters of the North Atlantic was not likely to save any pilot's life. No, a solo flight would be cheaper and less complicated, and the pilot would be in total control of the plans, as he would not be if another man's life were at stake. Slim recalled an old saying of C.A.'s that pretty much summed up the Lindbergh attitude toward cooperative ventures: "One boy's a boy, two boys are half a boy, and three boys are no boy at all."[3]

The conventional wisdom was that setting out across the Atlantic without a navigator would be suicidal. (In Byrd's case it would have been impossible, since he was not primarily a pilot—he navigated while Bennett flew.) Not only would the flight be long and tiring, but few pilots had much experience flying at night or in bad weather, and fewer still were accustomed to flying by their instruments. In 1927 flying instructors still regularly told their students that "a good pilot looks at the ground, not at his instruments." But Lindbergh, partly out of boredom, often practiced finding his way at night or through fog by following a compass heading. Although an unknown, he was as well (or better) prepared to make such a flight as any of the celebrated aviators in the race. As for the danger, it was not that he set a low value on his life—on the contrary, the prospect of burning alive in a "flying coffin" for the sake of getting a few business letters from St. Louis to Chicago definitely did not appeal to him. If he were going to die, he might as well do it while pursuing some really audacious goal.

With excitement over the New York–to–Paris race building, finding financial backers was no longer an insurmountable problem. The Robertson brothers volunteered small contributions, as did Maj. Albert Bond Lambert, the former balloon pilot for whom Lambert Field was named. Harry Knight, a St. Louis businessman who had recently begun taking flying lessons from Lindbergh, was also enthusiastic about his idea, and he and Lambert arranged for Lindbergh to make a presentation to Harold Bixby, the head of the St. Louis Chamber of Commerce. Lindbergh assured Bixby that the publicity from the venture would be enormous, boosting St. Louis's chances of becoming the midwestern hub of the commercial aviation industry. He even suggested that the plane used in the Orteig race could later be modified to fly a direct mail route from St. Louis to New York. Bixby organized a group of civic leaders and quickly raised $8,500.

Convincing manufacturers to risk their reputations on an unknown pilot with a seemingly foolhardy plan was another matter. When a salesman for the Fokker manufacturing company showed up at Lambert Field, Lindbergh took the opportunity to sound him out. The bemused salesman told Lindbergh that he was out of his league. A properly designed trimotor would cost a minimum of $80,000, exclusive of the engines. In any event, under no circumstances would the Fokker company consider selling a single-engine plane for the Orteig Prize race.

Slim read all the aviation magazines he could get his hands on, and for a working airmail pilot he was very well informed about the latest developments in aeronautics. As he well knew, there was one plane already in existence that was uniquely suited to challenging the Atlantic. This was the aerodynamically advanced, single-winged Bellanca, built by an Italian immigrant named Giuseppe Bellanca, who worked out of his garage in Brooklyn. The Bellanca—only the prototype was actually in existence—was being used by the Wright Aeronautical Corporation to demonstrate its new nine-cylinder Whirlwind engine.

Hoping to convince the Wright company to make the plane available to him, Lindbergh introduced himself as the representative of a consortium of St. Louis businessmen via a long-distance phone call.

This was the 1927 equivalent of sending one's résumé by fax, and he was quite proud of himself for having the sophistication to know that it would make a good impression. He then invested in a one-hundred-dollar custom-made wardrobe for a trip to the Wright Corporation headquarters in Paterson, New Jersey. The hand-tailored suit, blue overcoat, gray felt hat, and silk scarf and tie failed to work their magic, however. Once the Wright executives heard his plan, they, like the Fokker company, wanted no part of it.

Dejected, Lindbergh returned to St. Louis, where he fired off telegrams to every manufacturer in the country, asking if they would consider building a plane to his specifications. He received only one positive response, from the Ryan Aircraft Corporation in San Diego. Ryan was a small company without much of a track record, and its bid of six thousand dollars was so low that even the thrifty Lindbergh was suspicious. On February 6, meanwhile, he received a wire from Giuseppe Bellanca urging him to return to New York "in quickest manner." Bellanca and a businessman named Charles Levine had repurchased the rights to the Wright-Bellanca design. Levine and Bellanca had set up a manufacturing company called Columbia Aircraft, and in the meantime, they were willing to sell the prototype to Lindbergh for fifteen thousand dollars. Lindbergh took the next train back to St. Louis, where Knight and Bixby hurriedly obtained a bank loan to cover the additional cost. By February 12 Lindbergh was in New York again with a cashier's check for the full amount of the purchase.

The check was already on Charles Levine's desk when Levine mentioned, as if an afterthought, that Columbia Aircraft, "of course," would retain the right to select the crew that flew the plane across the Atlantic.

Levine's demand was outrageous, but many a more experienced negotiator would have been tempted to agree, in the hope that he could be induced to select Lindbergh, who was, after all, the choice of the financial sponsors. Other competitors for the Orteig Prize were poised to take off as soon as weather conditions over the North Atlantic permitted, and Levine controlled the only suitable plane not already spoken for. Lindbergh, indignant, pocketed his check and went home to St. Louis.

It was now mid-February, and the newspapers were predicting that the Orteig Prize might be claimed as early as the middle of April. Assuming it was already too late to get into the race, Lindbergh was prepared to scuttle his plans. Perhaps he should shoot for Australia via the Hawaiian islands instead—a longer and, for various reasons, much riskier flight. Knight and Bixby advised him not to give up. He could at least go out to San Diego and see what Ryan had to offer.

Lindbergh didn't know it, but Ryan Aircraft was on the verge of declaring bankruptcy. Franklin Mahoney had recently bought out his partner Claude Ryan, and without a single order on hand he had no idea how he would make his March payroll. The Ryan factory—Mahoney hadn't gotten around to changing the name—was located in an old cannery building on the waterfront, permeated by the smell of dead fish and equipped with a secondhand lathe, a drill press, and a few other miscellaneous pieces of machinery. The fabric covers for wings and fuselages were assembled by a woman named Mrs. Bray, working on a home sewing machine. Aeronautical engineering as practiced at Ryan was definitely a low-tech science. Factory manager Hawley Bowlus boasted that he had developed a system he called "fingertip aerodynamics"—on test flights he and the pilot would lean out the windows and wave their arms to determine the width of the slipstream. Mahoney could not afford to be choosy, but his first impression of the young pilot who had been writing to him on Robertson Aircraft stationery was not reassuring. Slim was twenty-five, but at six feet two and a half and about 128 pounds, with an adolescent slouch and a slow, midwestern drawl, he seemed more like eighteen. Like the Fokker and Wright people, he would gladly have passed on the project, but he could not afford to say no to a cash customer.

On February 28, the morning after Lindbergh's arrival, he and Mahoney went out to the Ryan hangar at the Dutch Flats proving grounds for a test flight, where the company's Danish-born chief mechanic, Harm Jon van der Linde, took one look at Slim and assumed that the boss was giving someone's teenage son a tour of the facilities. Van der Linde had been told to get the company's demonstration plane ready for a test flight, and when Slim climbed into the cockpit he became alarmed. "Instead of one of our pilots getting in, this young boy got aboard and I wondered if it was all right for him to fly the plane," he recalled. "So I walked over to Red Harrigan, who was chief pilot at the time, and asked if 'the kid' was supposed to fly it. He said 'yeah' and told me who he was. He flew that ship for about an hour, wrung it out like nothing I'd ever seen."[4]

Lindbergh had no time for another false start, and he told chief engineer Don Hall that he would give him twenty-four hours to come up with preliminary specs for a plane capable of getting to Paris. The plane was to be called the *Spirit of St. Louis*, a name suggested by Harold Bixby. It was to be equipped with an earth-inductor compass—a new and highly accurate instrument—and a Wright J5C engine, the latest version of the Whirlwind. Otherwise the craft would be little more than a flying gas tank, with no room for a parachute, radio, or even a copilot: "If we're going to break the world's record, we've got to put range above everything else," Lindbergh stressed.

Hall hadn't known that Lindbergh was planning a solo flight. "Are you sure you can stay awake?" he wondered. "How many hours will you be up?"

Lindbergh didn't know. He had been promoting the flight for five months, but he had never actually sat down and figured out the mileage. He and Hall drove to the nearest public library, where they used a pencil and piece of string to measure the distance on a globe.

Hall worked overnight to come up with a rough design. There was no time to develop a completely new concept, so he adapted two existing Ryan models, the M-2 and the Brougham. The wingspan would be increased to forty-six feet, the fuselage lengthened, and the tail skids moved back. The main design problem was the positioning of the gas tank. Lindbergh wanted it moved forward—like so many DH pilots he had developed a dread of being crushed between the gas tank and the engine in the event of a crash. However, since the tank would have to be very large, there would be no room for a windshield. Used to flying from the rear cockpit of a modified DH, Lindbergh was not especially concerned about the lack of forward visibility. "I don't expect I'll run into much traffic where I'm going anyway," he told Hall.

To avoid premature publicity, Mahoney at first didn't let his mechanics know what they were working on. The team of welders who worked at Dutch Flats was completely befuddled when they received an order to assemble an enormous tank, cleanly welded and "without a scratch" on it. "I assumed it was a gas tank for a doggone fishing boat," one of them later told Ryan company historian Ev Cassagneres. "It was a *mammoth* thing."[5]

Lindbergh wired Harry Knight that what impressed him most about Ryan was "the character of the people." When the factory hands learned that they were building an entry for the Orteig Prize race they became almost as excited as Lindbergh, volunteering to work extra shifts without pay. Among the most enthusiastic was a young Ryan test pilot named Douglas Corrigan, who temporarily reassigned himself to the metal shop where he put in four-hour shifts hand finishing metal fittings. Some years later, after filing a flight plan for California, Corrigan himself would set out across the Atlantic, earning himself a brief moment of fame as "Wrong Way" Corrigan.

Don Hall had moved into his office, where he worked round the clock, stopping only for brief naps. Lindbergh spent much of his time at a desk in the corner, charting a great circle route to France via Newfoundland and the Irish coast. With no navigational equipment on board to confirm his position, a small error early on could throw him many miles off course, so he checked and rechecked his calculations. He had also purchased charts of the Pacific and spent his spare moments plotting a course for Hawaii. If the competition beat him to France, he was quite prepared to strike out in a westerly direction.

Mid-April arrived, but the weather refused to cooperate. Aviation writers on the East Coast agreed that four candidates stood an excellent chance of capturing the prize, depending on who took off first. The front runners were Richard Byrd, whose Fokker trimotor would have a crew of four, and Charles Levine's Bellanca, now scheduled to be flown by Wright test pilot Clarence Chamberlin and celebrated stunt flyer Bert Acosta. Another promising entrant was Lt. Comdr. Noel Davis. Although Davis held a commission in the naval reserves, he was a protégé of the Army Air Service's commander General Mason Patrick, who had helped him obtain his Keystone biplane. Davis was getting financial assistance from the American Legion and was considered the army's unofficial candidate in the race. In France, meanwhile, World War I ace Charles Nungesser had announced that he would attempt to fly from Paris to New York in a single-engine biplane he called *L'Oiseau Blanc (White Bird)*. And the Sikorsky factory in Connecticut was working day and night on a new plane for René Fonck, who might yet surprise everyone and be ready to take off by the first of June. Lindbergh was counted as a dark horse, along with several other American and French pilots who were said to be preparing for the race in secret.

Dashing Dick Byrd, a boy's magazine hero come to life, was the Establishment candidate, and from the moment he declared his intentions, he received the lion's share of the publicity. The last of the gentleman explorers, Byrd enjoyed the sponsorship of the National Geographic Society and the financial support of such wealthy patrons as John D. Rockefeller, department store magnate Rodman Wanamaker, and Dwight Morrow. His trimotor plane, naturally called the *America*, was, like Fonck's Sikorsky, hailed as the avatar of the transoceanic liners of the future. It had a seventy-one-foot wingspan and was loaded from stem to stern with custom-designed (and therefore largely untested) equipment.

All that spring Byrd, who communicated with the public exclusively through the *New York Times,* issued statements disclaiming any "commercial" motive and insisting that he was flying to Paris purely in order to advance the cause of aviation science. So eager was he to separate himself from mere airplane jockeys like Clarence Chamberlin that he had elected not to file as an official entrant for the Orteig Prize. Cynical aviation correspondents groused that if Byrd made it to Paris he would get the twenty-five thousand dollars anyway and be none too proud to take it, but such quibbles never found their way into print.

On April 16 the *America* was scheduled for a test run out of Teterboro Airport in New Jersey. The plane's Dutch designer Anthony Fokker was at the controls, and Byrd, Floyd Bennett, and radio operator Lt. George Noville were riding with him in the cockpit. The trimotor's huge auxiliary gas tank was empty, as was the rear crew compartment, and when Fokker attempted to land, the nose-heavy plane flipped over on its back. Fokker was unhurt. Byrd escaped with a cracked bone in his wrist. Floyd Bennett, the most seriously injured of the passengers, was trapped inside the cockpit for almost an hour, his right thigh crushed, a shard from the propeller piercing his lung. The plane itself was not badly damaged, but the injury to Bennett—a Congressional Medal of Honor winner and one of the best-liked men in aviation—put an end to the mood of premature celebration.

Two days later Comdr. Noel Davis and his navigator Lt. Stanton Wooster took off from Langley Field in Virginia in their Keystone biplane. Perhaps mindful of Fokker's error, Davis insisted that the gas tanks be fully loaded so that he could get the "feel" of his plane. The feel was not good, however, and minutes after takeoff the *American Legion* sank into a swamp. Trapped inside the cabin, Davis and Wooster suffocated.

The Bellanca plane *Columbia,* meanwhile, was beset by a different order of problems. Although those in the know considered it the best ship in the race and rated Clarence Chamberlin the best pilot, Charles Levine seemed driven to manufacture obstacles where none existed. Levine now announced that he had hired navigator Lloyd Bertaud to fly to Paris, leaving room for only one of his two pilots. "On the day of the flight," he said at a press conference, "Chamberlin and Acosta will appear on the field in flying togs. Their names will be written separately on slips of paper. One slip will be drawn." Hearing this, Acosta promptly defected to the Byrd camp, replacing the injured Floyd Bennett.

Levine then reneged on a promise to provide both Chamberlin and Bertaud with $50,000 life insurance policies, and he pressured both of them into signing management contracts giving him half of all prize money and endorsement contracts they would earn if successful, in exchange for a salary of $150 a week. Levine's associates were beginning to suspect he was not the multimillionaire he claimed to be, and Giuseppe Bellanca hired a lawyer in an attempt to regain majority control of Columbia Aircraft. Bertaud was seeking an injunction on the insurance issue, and Chamberlin's lawyer filed suit to break his management contract. While the lawyers haggled, the wonderful Bellanca sat at Curtiss Field on Long Island, the hangar doors padlocked under court order.

In San Diego the *Spirit of St. Louis* was scheduled to make its maiden flight on April 28, exactly sixty days after Lindbergh placed his order with Ryan. On the night before the test, as the ground crew was fueling up the plane for the first time, a mechanic dropped a piece of rubber hose into the main tank. Since the hose could potentially clog the fuel lines, it was necessary to cut a six-inch hole in the bottom of the tank and remove it. There was no time to wait for gas fumes from the drained tank to evaporate, and rather than risk an explosion by welding a patch over the hole, the mechanics repaired it with solder and hoped for the best. Neither Lindbergh nor Franklin Mahoney was told about the accident.

The troubles of the American entrants in the transatlantic race had created an opportunity for Charles Nungesser and his copilot François Coli. One could tell a lot about the personalities of the competitors by the food they chose to take on board—Byrd had his pemmican and Fonck his *canard à l'orange*, but Nungesser had outclassed everyone by announcing that he and his copilot would be snacking on bananas and Caspian caviar. Practical like Lindbergh, the veteran pilot had stripped the *White Bird* of all but the bare essentials. The plane's fuselage was designed to float, and minutes after takeoff he planned to jettison the landing gear—a weight-saving tactic that Lindbergh had seriously considered but rejected as too dangerous.

Nungesser and Coli took off from Paris during the early morning hours of May 8. They planned to set the *White Bird* down in New York

Harbor just off the Bowery, where a launch and tugboat would be standing by to pluck the plane and its crew out of the water. Hundreds of New Yorkers had chartered boats in order to ensure themselves of a good view of the historic moment, and there and in Paris crowds gathered outside newspaper offices for the latest bulletins on the *White Bird*'s progress. The plane had been sighted over Newfoundland, then off the coast of Nova Scotia, and again near Portland, Maine.

But the *White Bird* never appeared over the skies of New York, and escort planes sent out to greet the triumphant fliers returned alone. The numerous eyewitness sightings were either honest errors or hoaxes, and the fate of Nungesser and Coli remains a mystery to this day.

The great Atlantic air race had now claimed the lives of six celebrated aviators, and Floyd Bennett, believed by many to be the true hero of Byrd's polar expeditions, would never fully recover from his injuries. The competition, which had been expected to usher in a new era of international aviation, had turned into a nightmare.

Rescue planes were still searching the waters off Newfoundland for signs of the *White Bird* when Charles Lindbergh took off from San Diego at 3:55 on the afternoon of May 10. The cross-country flight was intended partly as routine shakedown cruise, and involved no unusual feats of navigation. Lindbergh had purchased a set of Rand McNally road maps at a San Diego bookstore and planned to find his way by following railroad lines and natural landmarks. But five hours later, over the southern tip of the Rockies, the *Spirit*'s supposedly foolproof engine began to cough and sputter. It was the worst possible moment for a forced landing—nothing but boulder-strewn mountain slopes below, and nearly two thousand gallons of fuel left in the *Spirit*'s tanks. While circling in search of an emergency landing site, Slim discovered that he could keep the plane in the air by tinkering with the throttle and fuel mixture. This was good news, since it meant that the engine problem could be easily corrected by installing a carburetor heater in New York. But Lindbergh soon realized that while he was preoccupied with the engine problem, he had drifted more than fifty miles off course, a sobering precedent for one about to strike out across the North Atlantic.

Despite his troubles over the Rockies, favorable tail winds enabled Lindbergh to make good time. When he landed in St. Louis for refueling, he realized he was in a good position to set a new cross-country record. After a ham-and-eggs dinner at Louie's Shack and a good night's sleep, he took off again at 8:30 the next morning, and by 3:15 in the afternoon, St. Louis time, he was over Manhattan.

Sixteen minutes later the *Spirit of St. Louis* touched down at Curtiss Field on Long Island. Its total elapsed flying time from San Diego was a mere twenty-one hours and forty-five minutes, an impressive new record. Slim Lindbergh had arrived "like brave Lochinvar out of the west," one pundit said—a lanky, impossibly youthful-looking man with a dazzling smile, flying a blind silver bird. Suddenly, it seemed that the race might not be jinxed after all.

It would be easy to dismiss the reaction to Lindbergh's arrival as media hype, but this was not the case. The newspapers had already assigned their senior reporters to other teams, and while the mob of reporters and photographers that greeted Slim on his arrival was unlike anything he had ever experienced in St. Louis or San Diego, the press still considered him a dark horse. It was the public that went wild for "Lindy," almost before the first newspaper stories about him hit the streets. Since the beginning of May, aviation buffs had been showing up by the hundreds at the adjacent Curtiss and Roosevelt fields, hoping to see Byrd, Clarence Chamberlin, and Bert Acosta. On the first Sunday after Lindbergh's arrival, thirty thousand fans made the trip. Astonished reporters saw one middle-aged woman break through the security barrier, briefly grasp Lindbergh's leather flying jacket, and rush off screaming, "I touched him! I touched him!" Another matron of apparently modest means was overheard betting a stranger a thousand dollars to his one hundred that Lindbergh would succeed.[6]

Undoubtedly it was Lindbergh's plan to challenge the Atlantic alone that captured the imagination of the public, but his photogenic looks went far to sustain their enthusiasm. Press photographers swarmed around the St. Louis mail pilot and his Rube Goldberg–ish plane. Amateur shutterbugs, not far behind, would soon be trading tips on stalking Lindbergh in popular photography magazines. Showgirls and starlets schemed to get their pictures taken with the boyishly handsome pilot—one promoter wanted to pose a model doing a split on the blades of the *Spirit of St. Louis*'s propeller and was quite put out when he was told this would not be possible. Reporters interviewed Lindbergh as if he were a Hollywood star, plying him with questions like "Do you prefer blondes or brunettes?" and "What's your favorite kind of pie?"

No one would have dared ask Commander Byrd such questions. And as for Clarence Chamberlin, no one much cared what his favorite pie was. Charles Levine saw a phenomenon in the making and immediately announced that he was thinking of replacing Chamberlin, who was "not a movie type."

Slim himself was far from publicity shy. Indeed, up to this point he had considered himself very modern in his appreciation of the importance of public relations. But he was doggedly serious about aviation and disconcerted to find himself being treated as a pop hero. Busy with preparations for the flight, he assumed that if he just refused to answer silly questions or pose with actresses, this unwanted attention from the tabloids would cease. On the contrary, his aloofness made him all the more intriguing.

With his arrival in New York, Lindbergh had acquired an instant entourage, another development he had not counted on. The Wright Corporation, which had so recently turned down his request to fly in the Bellanca, had assigned a team to assist him, including mechanics Eddie Mulligan and Ken Boedecker and freelance PR man Dick Blythe of the Bruno and Blythe Agency. The Pioneer Instrument Company, manufacturers of the earth-inductor compass, also had a representative on hand, as did the Vacuum Oil Company, whose products Lindbergh had agreed to endorse. Franklin Mahoney had flown out from San Diego, and the St. Louis backers had sent a Lt. George Stumpf, a Missouri National Guard pilot, to serve as Lindbergh's aide-de-camp. Stumpf was a nice enough man, Lindbergh would recall, but completely out of his element in New York, and Lindbergh spent more of his time taking care of him than the other way around.

Despite all the attention, Lindbergh was still working on a tight budget, and a spirit of improvisation prevailed. When he decided that a mirror on the dashboard would make it easier to check on the earth-inductor compass, which was mounted on the ceiling of his plane's cockpit, he borrowed one from the compact of a young woman in the crowd and used a piece of chewing gum to fasten it in place.

To save money he also agreed to share a room at the nearby Garden City Hotel with Dick Blythe. For three days, Blythe recalled, Slim scarcely spoke a word and the two of them "bedded down like two wildcats, each in his own hole." On the third morning, Blythe was awakened by a shower of ice water and opened his eyes to find Slim standing over him with a pitcher, joking, "That'll teach you to wear pajamas."[7]

A pilot and war veteran himself, Blythe was no stranger to barracks humor, and he and Slim were soon getting along famously. Blythe took Slim to Coney Island—they fled when Lindbergh was recognized and mobbed by a screaming crowd—and out to lunch with a showgirl from *Earl Carroll's Vanities,* who was forced to swear on her word of honor that she would never talk to the newspapers about her meeting with Lindy. (Amazingly, she kept her promise.) On May 16, after a Department of Commerce representative decided that Lindbergh would need a passport when he arrived in France, the two of them hopped into Blythe's yellow roadster, and Blythe treated Slim to a demonstration of city driving skills, running red lights all the way down Fifth Avenue to the passport office, successfully evading a pursuing police car.

Even with Blythe running interference, Slim continued to have run-ins with the press, however. The late twenties were the age of jazz journalism, and newspaper photographers were even more numerous than today. Miniature cameras, hidden in the heels of shoes or in fake cigarette packs, were common. The rules of the photojournalism game were not clear, and if the papers could not get the shots they wanted, they routinely printed composites. The content of both photos and stories was usually, though not always, tamer than today, but the tactics for gathering them were often outrageously aggressive.

One evening, two photographers burst into Lindbergh's room at the Garden City Hotel, demanding that the flyer pose in his pajamas, and Blythe had to do some fast talking to convince Slim that it would not be a good idea to punch them in the nose. Meanwhile, reporters in Detroit were camping out on Evangeline Lindbergh's front porch, asking her how she felt about the fact that she might never see her son alive again. Mrs. Lindbergh became so alarmed that she took the next train to New York. A *New York Times* reporter named John Frogge, who happened to be in the hangar when Evangeline arrived, observed that Slim barely acknowledged his mother's presence and did not interrupt his work. Thus began the rumor that there was something almost unnaturally cold about Lindbergh's relationship with his mother. More likely Slim was afraid that if he appeared happy to see her, Evangeline would never leave. Over lunch at the Garden City Hotel, he managed to talk her into returning home by the next train.[8]

In a passage that he later excised from an early draft of his autobiography, Lindbergh commented that the real reason for his growing antipathy to the press was that newspapermen had become linked in his mind with failure. He had seen the photographers positioned at the end of the runway watching him take off on test runs and could not erase from his mind the impression that they were rooting for him to crash. This feeling was by no means uncommon. A few years later the great Jimmy Doolittle would retire from air racing after he learned that photographers had gathered around his wife, waiting to catch the expression on her face if his plane went down.) Lindbergh was far more sensitive to any hint of failure than most, yet the newspapers harped on the theme that he was a reckless gypsy flier. His decision to fly without a parachute was considered almost suicidal. (Though he had little faith that he would last long enough in the event of a crash to get it launched, he did have a rubber raft.) Worst of all, some enterprising reporter had resurrected the nickname Flyin' Fool from his days with the Mil-Hi Circus. Lindbergh, who thought he had put those days behind him, was not amused.

Lindbergh always insisted that his motivation for entering the Orteig race was the sheer love of adventure. No one could reasonably take issue with this, but those who met him in New York had already concluded that he was a complex and inscrutable young man. Dick Blythe's partner, Harry Bruno, believed Lindbergh had been ragged mercilessly by the other pilots at Lambert Field for losing three planes in little more than a year and had set out to prove himself. Lindbergh denied this, and his friends in St. Louis certainly never had any serious doubts about Slim's skills as a pilot. Still, Bruno was on the mark in observing that Lindbergh was driven by insecurity and the need to win the acceptance of the aviation establishment: "He was not particularly interested in what the public thought about him and his flight. But from the little things he said to Dick and me, I knew he was getting a tremendous kick out of the fact that at last rival flyers had to take him seriously."

And despite the newspapers' insistence on portraying him as the Flyin' Fool, he was being taken seriously at last. At the Garden City Hotel, where members of the Byrd and Bellanca teams were also staying, an atmosphere of friendly competition prevailed. Several of the Wright Aeronautics mechanics were working simultaneously on all three planes, and a group of dinner guests unrelated to the competition was surprised to overhear Lindbergh, Clarence Chamberlin, and Lloyd Bertaud deep in conversation on the balcony, speculating in matter-of-fact tones on the fate of Nungesser and Coli and their own chances of making it. Dick Byrd was not personally present at the hotel, but he had sent word to his rivals that they were welcome to move their takeoffs from Curtiss Field to Roosevelt, which he had paid to have lengthened to accommodate his big trimotor.

Hedging its bet on Dick Byrd, the *New York Times* had purchased exclusive rights to Lindbergh's story for five thousand dollars and was predicting "the most spectacular air race ever." Nevertheless, insiders tended to agree with the tabloids that called the *Spirit of St. Louis* "a fly-ing coffin." Harry F. Guggenheim, president of the Guggenheim Fund for the Promotion of Aeronautics, visited Curtiss Field, sat in the *Spirit*'s cramped cockpit, and wished Lindbergh luck, but he was think-ing all the while, "He'll never make it." And though few would admit it later, there was some feeling in the business that a Lindbergh victory would be bad for aviation; his plane was useless as a commercial vehicle, and the public might come to see his solo flight as just another stunt.

The storm system over the North Atlantic that had no doubt been the undoing of Nungesser and Coli persisted into the third week of May, and weather forecasters were calling for continued rain squalls and heavy fog. The *America* had been repaired, but Dick Byrd, unnerved by Floyd Bennett's serious injuries, was insisting on further test flights. Byrd, moreover, had learned that Bert Acosta had no experience flying at night and wanted to sign on Bernt Balchen, but having promised his chief sponsor, Rodman Wanamaker, that he would use an all-American crew, he couldn't take off until Balchen, a Norwegian, was able to take out his first citizenship papers. Charles Levine, meanwhile, had been heard to say that he would give Lindbergh twenty-five thousand dollars to take him along as a passenger. Clarence Chamberlin wryly passed the message along to Slim, who replied, "I will try to think of a place to put Mr. Levine." Everyone laughed, but Levine was quite serious about making the crossing himself, and on May 19 he fired Lloyd Bertaud.

That same morning, Dick Blythe drove Lindbergh, Lieutenant Stumpf, and Franklin Mahoney to New Jersey where they were to tour the Wright factory. It was pouring rain, and after the tour Blythe offered to drive Wright executive Kenneth Lane home. "I'll drop you at your front door," Blythe promised, and when the front door turned out to be set well back from the road, Blythe, egged on by Slim, jumped the curb and drove across the lawn. Lane was none too pleased, but his wife later decided not to have the scarred lawn reseeded—the ruts would remain for years, proudly pointed out to visitors as a souvenir of Lindy's visit.

That evening Blythe and Harry Bruno had arranged for Lindbergh to attend the Broadway hit *Rio Rita,* watching the show from back-stage. On the way to the theater, they stopped off at Blythe and Bruno's midtown office, where Blythe called Dr. James H. Kimball of the U.S. Weather Service, who told him that the latest forecasts showed the storm system breaking up.

"Bad news for the show, Slim," he reported after hanging up the phone. "You'll hop off in the morning."[9]

Blythe immediately drove Lindbergh and Stumpf back to Long Island. On the way they stopped for dinner at a diner in Queensboro Plaza, and Blythe ran around the corner to a soda fountain where he ordered five sandwiches to go. Arriving at Curtiss Field, they found the hangars all but deserted. Dick Byrd was planning an elaborate christening ceremony for the *America* the following afternoon, and knowing that Lindbergh was supposed to be at the theater, the aviation correspondents who had been camping out at the airfield had taken the night off. Wright engineer Ken Boedecker later told an interviewer that Clarence Chamberlin had also been shooting for an early-morning takeoff, but around midnight "some complications" developed, apparently legal rather than mechanical in nature.

Frank Tichenor of *Aero Digest,* who had spent the day in New Jersey with Lindbergh's party, was one of the few members of the press on the scene. Tichenor took one look at Lindbergh's brown-bag lunch and burst out laughing. Byrd's elaborate provisions for his crew, including a three-week supply of survival rations and distilled water, had been the subject of numerous newspaper stories.

"Is that all you're taking?" Tichenor asked.

"Wu-ll, if I get to Paris I won't need any more food, and if I don't, I won't need any either," Lindbergh replied.

Lindbergh supervised the installation of a barograph, as required by the Orteig Committee, to provide an official record of the flight. The Wright engineers then took charge of moving the plane to the adjacent Roosevelt Field. It was midnight by the time Lindbergh got back to his hotel, and he locked himself in his room alone, hoping to get a few hours' sleep before his 2:30 A.M. wake-up call. George Stumpf sat outside in the hall, delegated to chase away reporters and others who might disturb Slim's rest. But no sooner had Lindbergh closed his eyes than he was awakened by a knocking on his door. It was Stumpf, teary eyed and overwrought. "Slim, what'll I do when you're gone?" he wailed.

Stumpf's "fool question," as Lindbergh called it, destroyed his last chance for a nap. By takeoff time, 7:52 on the morning of May 20, he had already been awake for almost twenty-four hours straight.

Word of Lindbergh's plans had spread during the night, and about five hundred people were gathered at Roosevelt Field in the drizzly gray dawn. Among those present were Dick Byrd, Clarence Chamberlin, and a young aviation promoter named Juan Terry Trippe. The unpaved takeoff strip was soggy from a week of intermittent rain, and because of the high humidity, the *Spirit*'s Whirlwind engine was turning at less than maximum capacity. The Ryan monoplane weighed 2,150 pounds and was carrying 2,750 pounds of fuel, and the mechanics had tried every trick they could think of to make sure it got off the ground, including draining the grease from the wheels and replacing it with lightweight lubricating oil.

Frogge of the *Times* counted three heart-jolting bumps as the plane lumbered down the field. Another witness said that the *Spirit* reminded him of a kangaroo as it bounced along on the spongy turf. Somehow Lindbergh managed to hold the plane steady and get airborne, clearing the telephone wires at the end of the field by twenty feet.

In retrospect the most startling statistics in the *Spirit of St. Louis*'s log are the altitude figures—200 feet over Long Island and a mere fifty feet above sea level during the crossing between New England and Nova Scotia. Over Newfoundland, Lindbergh impulsively altered his carefully planned course, veering off ninety miles to the south to buzz the city of St. John's. Suddenly it seemed vital to him that someone should spot his plane and know he had made it this far.

He did not begin to feel nervous until the thirteenth hour of the flight. The gray ocean was dotted with icebergs, and an enveloping fog forced him into a steep climb. At ten thousand feet ice began to form on the *Spirit*'s wings, and Lindbergh wondered how cold it would have to get before the carburetor heater installed at Curtiss Field was no longer effective. There was nothing an airmail pilot dreaded so much as getting caught above a closed carpet of clouds. Descending through a mantle of gray mist could be instantly and fatally disorienting, even in daytime. At night it was suicidal. The *Spirit* at least had an altimeter, but it was a relatively primitive model that needed to be recalibrated often, and Slim had no great confidence in its accuracy.

Describing this critical moment of the flight more than two decades later, Lindbergh wrote: "A victory given stands pale beside a victory won. Every pilot has a right to choose his battlefield—that is the strategy of flight. But once that battlefield is attained, conflict should be welcomed, not avoided. If a pilot fears to test his skill with the elements, he has chosen the wrong profession."[10]

During the fifteenth hour the sky began to clear. The ice on his plane's wings was melting, and Lindbergh was able to pick his way between cumulus clouds that towered over him like mountains. The moon was rising in the north, not at all where he would have expected it to be. Both the earth-inductor and liquid compasses were oscillating. He could see the North Star high in the sky to his left and decided to trust that he was still more or less on course.

For the next ten hours, his chief adversary was sleep. A doctor had given him a few ammonia capsules. He broke one under his nose, but his senses were so deadened that he could smell nothing. Shivering with cold, he resisted the temptation to pop the plastic side windows into place. Too tired even to record instrument readings in his log, he nosed the *Spirit* up and down through the patchy fog. At times he was skimming along just five feet above the waves, the salt spray hitting his face through the open windows.

Now he began to see what he later called "fog islands" and "phantoms," ghostly hallucinations from his past that crowded into the tiny cabin. He had been awake more than forty-eight hours straight and was operating in a half-world, somewhere between consciousness and blind instinct. Passing into the twenty-seventh hour of flying time, he spotted a flotilla of fishing boats. No one was on deck, but leaning out of the porthole of one boat, he saw a man, mouth agape, staring up at him. He throttled down and skimmed within fifty feet of the porthole, leaning out the window, shouting, "Which way is Ireland?" The man stared, his face a mask. Lindbergh knew the fisherman probably couldn't hear him, yet it was strange that the sight of an airplane dropping out of the sky, perhaps the first the man had ever seen, provoked no reaction whatsoever. He began to feel as if he had entered a different plane of reality, and perhaps the man really had not seen him.

An hour later he spotted land. Amazingly the indentations of the coastline exactly matched the outlines on his charts for Dingle Bay, on the southwestern coast of Ireland. He was almost exactly on course!

Six hours later, at 10:22 local time, the *Spirit of St. Louis* was over Le Bourget airport. Although the floodlights had been turned on at 9:00 P.M. in anticipation of his arrival, the entire field was not illuminated and Lindbergh was disoriented after nearly thirty-four hours in the air and uncertain of the boundaries of the landing strip. Nor did he realize, as he set his plane down in the darkness, that an immense crowd, estimated at one hundred thousand, had broken through the barriers and was rushing toward him. As he prepared to taxi back toward the hangars he saw a wall of people running in his direction, arms waving, clutching at the fuselage of his plane and climbing up onto the wings.

The newspapers would later circulate several apocryphal versions of

Lindbergh's first words, including the equally unnecessary "Is this Paris?" and "I'm Charles Lindbergh." According to Lindbergh himself, his first words were, "Are there any mechanics here?" followed by the usual query of the American tourist, "Does anybody here speak English?"

It didn't matter what he said. The pandemonium was so great no one heard him. Two *New York Times* reporters, under orders to interview Lindbergh immediately after he landed, crawled under his plane and cowered there in fear of their lives. When Lindbergh tried to climb out of the cockpit he was lifted into the air, and for nearly thirty minutes he was passed around over the heads of the crowd, a living trophy. At last two French pilots, a civilian stunt flier named Michel Detroyat and an army pilot, Charles Delage, fought their way through the mob. One of them grabbed Lindbergh's helmet and clapped it on the bare head of a tall American reporter. Pointing in the reporter's direction they yelled, "Zaire he eeesss.... C'est Leenbairg!"

The vainly protesting reporter was hustled into the terminal, where American ambassador Myron T. Herrick was waiting. "But I'm not Lindbergh," the involuntary impostor kept saying. Herrick assumed the strain of the flight had caused the pilot to become disoriented. "Of course you are," he said soothingly.[11]

The real Lindbergh saw to it that his plane was safely tucked away in a hangar; then Detroyat, Delage, and another French flier, Maj. Paul Weiss, hustled him into a car and drove him to the center of the city, avoiding the main arteries, which were still jammed with cars trying to get to the airfield. While half of Paris, including the press and two companies of the French army, was searching the aerodrome for the missing pilot, the trio of aviators drove Slim to the Arc de Triomphe and led him to the Eternal Flame that marked the tomb of the French Unknown Soldier. Lindbergh spoke no French, his hosts little English, and it is not clear whether he understood why the pilots had thought it appropriate to show him this place, which for them epitomized the special relationship between France and the United States: It was here on Bastille Day 1919 that General Pershing and his doughboys had been cheered by two million Parisians, grateful for America's role in the liberation of their country.

EIGHT

"The Glory"

*C*ETTE FOIS, ÇA VA!*" Parisians cheered on the night the *Spirit of St. Louis* landed: "This time, it's done!"

The next morning Paris awoke with a hangover. Out at Le Bourget ground crews cleaning up the debris from the previous night's mob scene would collect more than a ton of personal belongings abandoned during the melee, including a woman's sable coat and half a dozen sets of false teeth. The press, in its eagerness to rush the story of Lindbergh's arrival into print, had dispensed with the niceties of copy editing. Correspondent Janet Flanner was especially taken with the Paris *Herald*'s instant biography of the hero, which reported a garbled version of the story about Lindbergh, aged five, and his Minneapolis landlady's pet: "Downstairs a family had a larger self than most boys. He was never an angora cat." In a less surrealistic vein, the Comtesse de Noailles wrote: "More generous than Columbus, he has given us the continent of the sky."[1]

Telegrams were pouring into the American Embassy by the bushel-basketful. Adolph Zukor wanted to sign Lindbergh to a $350,000 film contract. One of the Gimbel brothers wanted to subsidize his salary as an executive of "any airline company" to the tune of $100,000. A British promoter, undoubtedly a charlatan, clamored to sign the aviator to a five-million-dollar contract for a world tour. Parmely Herrick, son of Ambassador Myron Herrick, took it upon himself to sift through the mountains of mail. Anticipating that Lindbergh would be unprepared to deal with the onslaught of contract offers, Ambassador Herrick was already suggesting that a committee of three distinguished businessmen be appointed to act as his financial advisers.

The hero himself slept until early afternoon. The first thing he saw when he opened his eyes was the ambassador's valet standing next to his bed, holding a bathrobe. He had never owned a bathrobe, much less had a valet to help him dress. It occurred to him that his life was going to be very different from now on.

Over a ham-and-eggs breakfast, Lindbergh sat down for his first interview, with Carlisle MacDonald, the *New York Times* reporter assigned to ghostwrite his first-person account of the flight. "They call me Lucky Lindy, but luck had nothing to with it," MacDonald's story would begin. Many years later Lindbergh would acknowledge that he did, indeed, believe he was extremely fortunate to have held his course while fogbound over the Atlantic. At the moment, however, he was eager to emphasize a different message: The flight was not a stunt but a triumph for American engineering. He wanted to talk about the remarkable performance of the American-engineered earth-inductor compass and Charles Lawrance's air-cooled Whirlwind engine.

MacDonald, who had a more realistic notion of what even the *Times*'s readers wanted to know, politely ignored these protests and turned out a young-man-against-nature narrative. In any event, American investors had already gotten the message. With the announcement of Lindbergh's landing in Paris, Wright Aeronautical had shot up five and three-quarter points on the New York Stock Exchange. Other publicly traded aviation stocks were up by comparable amounts. Wall Street analysts, who had recently been warning of an overheated market, with too much money chasing too few overvalued stocks, were euphoric.

In a sidebar article, MacDonald quoted Lindbergh as saying that his own plans for the future were vague though "I hope to do a little flying here in Europe." In fact Lindbergh, who was nothing if not methodical, knew exactly what he wanted to do next. In his pocket he had a draft on a Parisian bank for fifteen hundred dollars and a tentative itinerary for a European tour. Funds and flying luck permitting, he hoped to continue across Asia, returning to North America via the Bering Straits, thus becoming the first human being to fly solo around the world.

Aware that there was already talk in Washington of an official welcome-home ceremony, Lindbergh gave few details of his own plans except to say that he did not expect to return to the United States immediately. On May 25, however, the chairman of the Italian Olympic Committee announced in the Chamber of Deputies that he had received, in reply to his congratulatory wire, a telegram from Captain Lindbergh: "Thanks for your message. Long Live Mussolini and the Youth of Italy." In an interview with MacDonald that same day, Lindbergh did not deny sending the telegram, and he disclosed that his plans for a European tour were shaping up: "The Swedish government is very anxious I go to Sweden. So is the German government and Premier Mussolini of Italy."[2]

Lindbergh's desire to meet Mussolini could hardly have come as a surprise to those who shared his passion for aviation. *Il Duce* was still receiving relatively favorable coverage in the American press, in which he was typically portrayed as a benevolent technocrat. More importantly, he was the most air-minded head of state in the world, well known for his patronage of Roald Amundsen and his American partner, Lincoln Ellsworth, who had used a 348-foot Italian navy dirigible in their 1926 aerial assault on the North Pole. When Amundsen objected to flying under the fascist flag, Mussolini had obligingly allowed him to lease the dirigible so that it could fly under Norwegian auspices.

Lindbergh's desire to go "barnstorming around Europe," as contemporary newspaper accounts put it, has usually been dismissed as an example of the delightful naïveté of the hero whom the French were already calling "*le boy*." Not only was it by no means unrealistic, but other American entrants in the Orteig Prize race had been thinking along exactly the same lines. Just two weeks later, on June 4, the Bellanca plane *Columbia* would follow the *Spirit of St. Louis* to Europe, with Clarence Chamberlin as pilot and Charles Levine riding in the copilot's seat as a passenger. Levine then proceeded to take the *Columbia* on a European victory tour, beginning with a tumultuous welcome at Berlin's Templehof Airport. Again like Lindbergh, Levine planned to continue the flight across Asia. He departed on what was to be a nonstop flight to New Delhi, but got no farther than Vienna, where the Bellanca was grounded by engine failure.

Levine being who he was, his victory tour degenerated into an orgy of bad publicity. There were more arbitrary personnel changes and a near calamity at London's Croydon Aerodrome, where Levine, a novice pilot, insisted on making his first solo landing. In Rome he embarrassed the American Embassy by hailing Mussolini as the "world's greatest statesman."

No doubt Lindbergh would have handled himself with more dignity, but the Coolidge administration—including Secretary of State Frank Kellogg, the same St. Paul attorney who defeated C. A. Lindbergh in 1916—was not about to take that chance. Apparently it was Kellogg who first suggested to the president that he honor America's new hero by sending a U.S. navy vessel to escort him and his plane home from Europe.

Britain's King George V had expressed a desire to meet Lindy, and, partly as a consolation prize, Lindbergh was asked to make goodwill visits to Belgium and England. In Brussels security was tight, and the crowds large but restrained. At the Croydon Aerodrome, the scene was a replay of the hysterical welcome at Le Bourget. The official ceremony canceled because of the uncontrollable crowds, Lindbergh was driven to Buckingham Palace, where he was told that His Majesty had something to ask him that could only be discussed in private. Wondering what the ruler of the British Empire could possibly want to know from him, a nervous Lindbergh was shown into the king's study, where George V wasted no time getting to the point. "Tell me," he asked in confidential tones, "How do you pee?"[3]

Back at the American Embassy, where Lindbergh was staying during his London visit, Ambassador Alanson B. Houghton had been assigned the task of breaking the news that visits to additional European capitals would be out of the question. Lindbergh heatedly objected that the plan to ship the *Spirit of St. Louis* home on a navy vessel—and not even a destroyer but a slow cruiser—was an insult to himself and to his plane. Houghton, who was just delivering the message from the State Department, persisted. President Coolidge had already ordered the cruiser and postponed his summer vacation expressly in order to be in Washington to greet him and it would not do to disappoint his commander in chief.

"Is that an order?" asked Lindbergh, thinking of his commission as a captain in the army reserves.

"Almost," said Houghton. "It is not an order. But it *is* advice."[4]

Lindbergh wasn't even allowed to fly the *Spirit* back to France. It would be more convenient, he was told, for the plane to be left at the British army facility at Gosport, where mechanics would remove the wings in preparation for shipping. Disgruntled, he returned to Paris in a borrowed plane, where he attended worship services at a Swedish church in lieu of his intended visit to Stockholm. On June 4 he boarded the *Memphis* at Cherbourg, accompanied by Carlisle MacDonald. The

Spirit was already on the ship, packed inside a wooden crate lashed to the deck. Having just demonstrated the power of the airplane to free humankind from the constraints of distance and time, Slim Lindbergh had never felt less free.

The *Memphis* was scheduled to take seven days to cross the Atlantic. To Lindbergh it must have seemed a lifetime. On June 5, his first full day at sea, Clarence Chamberlin and Charles Levine set the Bellanca plane *Columbia* down in a German cow pasture, exceeding his New York–to–Paris distance record by 295 miles. Two days later the Bellanca team was honored by Germany's leading airplane manufacturers and a delegation of World War I aces at a luncheon originally planned for Lindbergh. With Byrd's *America* poised to take off any day, and several teams of French aviators preparing to cross the Atlantic from east to west, Slim had good reason to fear that his moment of glory would be fleeting indeed.

Several days off the coast of North America, the *Memphis* rendezvoused with the destroyer *Goff.* Dick Blythe, who had used his navy connections to hitch a ride, was on board, and he gave Lindbergh a firsthand report of the incredible situation developing in the States. Lindy-mania was mounting almost by the hour, and the air waves were already jammed with musical tributes, including marches, ballads, and several competing tunes entitled the "Lindy Hop." The *Times* had devoted sixteen pages to his landing in Paris, and newspapers across the country were filled with poetic tributes and editorial cartoons proclaiming the clean-cut Lindbergh as a rebuke to the frivolity of the generation of Flaming Youth. Congress had voted into existence the Distinguished Flying Cross, of which Lindbergh would be the first recipient. The Post Office was about to issue an air mail stamp. Washington, New York, St. Louis, and Detroit were all planning receptions in his honor.

"You are in for it now," Blythe commiserated. "You're the great American idol. Your time is no longer your own."

"I don't know about the idol part," replied Lindbergh. "But I do know I'm in a terrible mess."

There were, however, compensations. An admirer had sent Evangeline Lindbergh a pound of chocolates packaged in an antique Robertson silver box, and other valuable gifts were piling up in Detroit, St. Louis, and at the office of the Bruno and Blythe Agency. Moreover, the commercial offers that Lindbergh had received in Paris were just a fraction of the overtures that would come his way. Blythe estimated that Lindbergh could turn down any proposals he considered undignified and still amass a fortune of between two and five million dollars from endorsements and personal appearances.

All this sounded wonderful to Slim. A fervent believer in the utopian future of air power, he was genuinely interested in promoting the cause of aviation. But he had never said that he didn't want to make money doing it. Before leaving the States, Lindbergh had already agreed to endorse such products as AC spark plugs and Vacuum motor oil. Nor did he see anything undignified or inappropriate in this. Even Dick Byrd had done commercial endorsements from time to time.

One of the minor mysteries of the Lindbergh phenomenon is that the legions of reporters—who were busily interviewing Slim Lindbergh's old flying buddies, distant family connections, and even a few people named Lindbergh who later turned out to be no relation to the pilot at all—somehow overlooked Lindy's connection to Captain Emory S. Land, a figure of some importance in the field of military aviation. It wasn't every obscure mail pilot who had a cousin who was the assistant chief of the United States Navy's Bureau of Aeronautics.

Captain Land's father, a younger brother of Dr. Charles H. Land, had gone to Colorado in 1876, lured by rumors that the missing family patriarch, John Scott Land, was prospecting for gold in the vicinity of Pike's Peak. No trace of John Land was ever found, but his son remained in Colorado and established a successful chain of fish hatcheries. Emory Land, usually known as Jerry, was born in 1879. He attended the U.S. Naval Academy, where he became a star halfback, and in 1910 he was assigned to the Department of the Navy in Washington, where he and his wife had renewed their acquaintance with his favorite cousin, Evangeline, and her young son, Charles.

In 1915, at the Pensacola Naval Air Station, Land became the first member of the family to take an airplane ride. The pilot was Lt. Earl Spencer, whose wife Wallis would one day become the Duchess of Windsor. On initial exposure Land proved immune to the lure of aviation. The flight "damn near killed me," he later recalled. "At any rate, it made me sick." Land opted to join the submarine service, but in 1921, much against his will, he was reassigned to the Bureau of Aeronautics, known in navy parlance as the Bu-Aer.[5]

It was not easy duty. Land's boss, Rear Adm. William Moffat, believed that the future of military aviation lay with lighter-than-air ships, and it became Land's unhappy task to defend the navy's dirigible program to Congress and the press. Otherwise Land divided his time between fighting the "Big Gun Navy" for appropriations and sparring with Gen. Mason Patrick of the Army Air Service and his assistant Gen. Billy Mitchell, a relentless critic of the Bu-Aer and all its works. In an oral history interview given in 1960, a quarter of a century after Billy Mitchell's death, Land would reluctantly concede that Mitchell was not the devil incarnate. "I'm his enemy while I'm talking to you," he told interviewer David Shaughnessy, "but ... he had more vision than the rest of us." In 1927, fresh from having to rebut Mitchell's charges about the *Shenandoah* crash before a navy court of inquiry, Land's views were a good deal less temperate.

There was also a personal aspect to this feud. Mitchell had divorced his first wife to marry the daughter of the mayor of Detroit, a longtime political associate of Evangeline Lindbergh's uncle John C. Lodge. Through this connection Land was privy to the latest gossip about Mitchell's private life which was, in his words, "pretty rough." Land considered Mitchell unfit to wear an American uniform and was suspected of passing on gossip that played a role in Coolidge's decision to court-martial him.

Land's relationship with Dick Byrd was more ambivalent. He had worked closely with Byrd over the years and admired him, but was irked by Byrd's demands for free equipment and technical support for his civilian ventures. Byrd, he complained, had come down with a bad case of "Potomac fever" and was becoming insufferable.

Strangely, although the Bu-Aer was a major customer of Wright Aeronautics, Charles had not approached his cousin for help when he was trying to convince the company to let him fly the Bellanca. This seems almost unbelievable, but Lindbergh was shy and proud and thought that asking favors of relatives was not quite moral. No doubt he also believed that Land was committed to aiding Byrd, which was more or less the case. After Lindbergh landed in Paris, neither Land nor Lindbergh's partners had any such scruples. A letter in Land's files, written to Lindbergh shortly after the flight, was never sent. His Detroit relatives had already sought him out, asking his help. Both they and the St. Louis sponsors were powerfully annoyed with Dick Blythe and Harry Bruno, who were issuing press releases describing themselves as Slim's agents and "close friends of the Lindbergh family." When they learned that Blythe was already on board the *Memphis,* they were beside themselves.

It was Land's idea to collaborate with the sponsors on what he called a "butter and eggs letter." Radioed to the ship through confidential navy channels, the message warned Lindbergh in the strongest terms to sign nothing until he had conferred with them. It was too late to prevent him from agreeing to a fifty-thousand-dollar contract with George Palmer Putnam for a quickie book to be ghostwritten by Carlisle Mac-Donald, but otherwise Lindbergh bowed to the sponsors' wishes. In the meantime Evangeline Lindbergh began telling reporters in Detroit that she was sure her son would do nothing to "commercialize" his fame, a choice of words that recalls Dick Byrd's preflight press releases.

The Army Air Corps (as the Army Air Service was now called) had its own plans for Lindbergh, and when the *Memphis* dropped anchor off Norfolk on June 10, a launch came alongside bringing a message from General Patrick informing him that he had been promoted to the rank of colonel in the army reserves. Also delivered was a package containing a brand-new dress uniform, hand tailored to his measurements. Byrd, though he flew as a civilian, had worn a navy uniform at his victory parade, and army aviation, it seemed, was looking forward to having a hero of its own.

Harry Bruno later reported his partner's version of what happened next:

> Lindbergh tried on the uniform in his stateroom and admired himself in the mirror. "Pretty good for an air mail pilot," he observed.
>
> "But you can't wear it," Blythe shot back. "You came into the limelight with no avowed religion.... You had no avowed politics.... And you were neither an Army man nor a Navy man.... Nobody would claim you, and nobody could be against you. This Army uniform would spoil the perfect picture."
>
> "I was a captain in the Air Corps Reserve and everybody knew it," Lindbergh protested.
>
> "Yes, but you went to Paris as a civilian."

A close reading of Bruno's account suggests that what bothered Lindbergh most was Blythe's suggestion that he would be seen to be siding with the army against the navy. He was an army man, but his mother's family, the Lodges and Lands, were navy all the way. A little worried that he might be accused of insubordination for refusing to wear the uniform, he suggested, "Why couldn't I wear a Navy overcoat over this?"

"It's June, Slim," said Blythe.[6]

Laughing, Lindbergh changed back into the blue suit that had been run up for him by a Paris tailor.

*　*　*

That same morning, at 15 Dupont Circle, where President and Mrs. Coolidge were living while the White House was undergoing renovations, there was a minor crisis. Evangeline Lindbergh, due in on the 9:00 A.M. train from Detroit, was missing. While having breakfast in the dining car, Mrs. Lindbergh had heard over the radio that several hundred admirers, including a delegation from Little Falls, were waiting at the station to greet her. Panicked, she got off the train in suburban Baltimore and accepted a ride from a stranger to the Belvedere Hotel downtown, where she spent the morning shopping for hats, then made an appointment under her own name at the hotel beauty parlor. Word that Lindy's mother was having her hair done in the salon sparked a near riot, and the Baltimore police had to dispatch twenty-five officers to restore order. The president's staff, who had been frantically trying to figure out how they would explain misplacing the hero's mother, sent Coolidge's personal car to pick her up.

Despite her detour Mrs. Lindbergh was in high spirits. A youthful looking fifty-one, she arrived at the temporary White House wearing an ermine-trimmed black silk coat over a green crepe dress, with gray kid pumps, gray doeskin gloves, and—waiting reporters noted approvingly—"a milan straw hat trimmed with gardenias." Coolidge, who had a cabinet meeting scheduled that evening, had asked Dwight Morrow in his capacity as the Republican party's chief aviation expert, to entertain Mrs. Lindbergh at dinner. A demanding conversationalist and by no means easy to impress, Morrow was utterly charmed. The pilot's mother was a delightful woman, he reported to his wife.

To others who met her during the next several weeks, Evangeline would remain an enigma. Extremely camera shy, she usually managed to thwart photographers by wearing floppy-brimmed hats. Nevertheless, she remained glued to her son's side from the moment he disembarked from the *Memphis* and was soon almost as much of a celebrity as he. The Lindbergh side of the family, by contrast, was officially invisible. At least one of Charles's first cousins had joined the convoy of supporters that drove from Little Falls for the occasion. Present as Lindbergh disembarked from the *Memphis,* he managed to get close enough to shout "Hey, Charley," before being swept away in the crush.

For the ceremony at the foot of the Washington Monument, the Mall was jammed with spectators from the Capitol to the Lincoln Memorial, the largest crowd Washington old-timers could recall. An estimated thirty million were listening on a nationwide network of fifty radio stations—another first, and such a novelty that the *New York Times* published the complete transcript of the announcer's commentary so that readers without radio sets could form some impression of how it was possible to broadcast a parade.

"I wonder if I deserve all this," was Lindbergh's reaction when he caught sight of the crowd. And many veteran aviation writers were asking themselves the same question—after all, Lindbergh's record had already been broken by Clarence Chamberlin.

It was already apparent that Lindy-mania was only partly about aviation. It was also the culmination of a craze for heroes that had been building for several years. The twenties were a prosperous, optimistic decade, and new developments in the mass media—movie newsreels, photo-journalism, and radio—had created an appetite for instant celebrities. Movie stars, baseball players, Channel swimmers, flagpole sitters, gangsters, and even some individuals whose names had cropped up in the news more or less by chance—all had their day. Too often, however, fame proved to be fleeting, and yesterday's heroes found themselves touring the vaudeville circuits, telling their stories from the stage to paying crowds—this form of entertainment, the 1920s equivalent of today's TV talk show, was known to vaudevillians as a freak act.

To the skeptically inclined, there was not a great deal of difference between an aviator and a Channel swimmer, and the hoopla over Lindy had already prompted sour speculation about his future. The most commonly voiced prediction was that he would feel compelled to top his Paris flight and kill himself trying. Another guess was that he would end up like Gerturde Ederle, who was already penniless and embittered a year after her conquest of the English Channel.

Of course, to some, aviators really were different. The newspapers loved them because their feats combined a ripping good story with genuine commercial, patriotic, and scientific interest. The air-minded were a ready-made, awestruck constituency. Even at this late date, however, aviation insiders were feeling a bit shell-shocked by the intensity of the response to Lindbergh.

Covering the parade for the *Times,* military correspondent Fitzhugh Green struggled to explain why the excitement was so much greater than at similar receptions for Dewey, Peary, and Byrd: "The stiff military bearing of the others, that touch of dramatic superiority which can suggest so much in the air of a military victor, was totally lacking in Lindbergh. His hair was mussed; his stance awkward. But it was a mussiness and an awkwardness that made men cheer and women weep to see.... It detracts in no way from Lindbergh's glory and success to say he bears no trace of suffering."

New York World correspondent Damon Runyon put it more concisely: "My, how young he is!" he sighed.

The ceremony at the Washington Monument ended with Coolidge pinning the Distinguished Flying Cross on the lapel of Lindbergh's suit—in his speech the president called Slim "this boy." The Army Air Corps was nowhere represented, and afterward an ebullient Jerry Land, in dress whites, joined Charles and his mother in their open car, and the three of them were whisked off to 15 Dupont Circle. When they arrived the president and the first lady were already home and waiting at the front door to greet them. At their side was the diminutive figure of Dwight Morrow.

Morrow pumped the hero's hand vigorously. His first words were, "Young man, I like your relatives!"[7]

Over lunch Morrow explained to Slim why government subsidies for airlines, as favored by Billy Mitchell and the Democrats, were a bad thing: Laissez-faire capitalism would, in the long run, produce a stronger network of passenger lines. Morrow also suggested that Lindbergh use his influence to promote the construction of airports by local governments and private investors.

Lindbergh's opinions on federal subsidies up to this point are unknown, but certainly the great majority of pilots favored them, if only because they would create jobs. Even Jerry Land, good Republican that he was, privately considered subsidies necessary and was only against them because Mitchell was for them. But Morrow, who had talked circles around some of the shrewdest politicians in the world, was persuasive, and Lindbergh dutifully incorporated his suggestions in the formal remarks he made that weekend. At times, reading over the texts of these speeches, one can almost hear him mentally backpedaling:

> All Europe is covered with a network of lines carrying passengers between all the big cities. Now it is up to us to create and develop passenger lines that compare with our mail routes.... The question comes up, "Why has Europe got ahead of us in commercial air lines?" The reason is, of course, is that the governments over there give subsidies. Now I don't think we want any subsidies over here. Of course, if we had them, they would create passenger lines overnight, so to speak, but in the long run the air lines, the distance they covered and the routes would be entirely controlled by the subsidies.[8]

The hero's schedule that weekend included another public rally, on the steps of the Capitol, where he was presented with the Cross of

Honor of the American Flag Association, and a state dinner so exclusive that even Comdr. Byrd was unable to wangle an invitation. On Monday morning, after a breakfast at the National Press Club, Lindbergh was hustled off to Bolling Field, from where he was to fly the *Spirit of St. Louis* to New York, arriving just in time for his ticker-tape parade.

Here, however, there was a glitch. The *Spirit*'s engine would not turn over. An army Curtiss P-1 biplane was hastily wheeled from its hangar, and Lindbergh, already more than an hour behind schedule, took off without a proper briefing. After takeoff, unfamiliar with the P-1's gas feed system, he flipped the wrong switch and fuel immediately began draining out of the main tank into an auxiliary tank. The gauge for the main gas tank was soon on empty, and Lindbergh assumed that he had a problem with his fuel line. Since he was being accompanied by a twenty-three-plane honor squadron, an emergency landing would have been somewhat embarrassing, so he flew on. He landed—safe but a little edgy—at Long Island's Mitchel Field, where he was whisked off to the waiting amphibious plane piloted by the celebrated Capt. Ira Eaker, who had recently flown the same aircraft on a demonstration tour of South America. The amphibian swooped low over the Narrows, setting down in New York Harbor. Rushing out to greet it, said the *Times,* were "four hundred ships which had run wild and 10,000 persons aboard them who had become frantic with excitement."

The ticker-tape parade honoring Lindy was the biggest New York had ever seen, and in some respects it has never been equaled. Hotels were filled four days before the event. The Stock Exchange had closed for the entire day in Lindbergh's honor—as well it might have, considering the impact of Lindbergh's accomplishment on aviation stocks—and brokers were auctioning off window seats in their offices to the highest bidders. Along the parade route ten thousand schoolchildren serenaded Lindy with a chorus of "Hail, the Conquering Hero Comes!" And this was just the beginning of four days of festivities, including a second parade in Brooklyn and a banquet for three thousand guests hosted by Mayor Jimmy Walker.

The New York welcoming committee, like scores of other civic groups that would entertain Lindbergh during the year to come, seemed incapable of saying no to anyone, and Lindy was trotted off to add luster to such forgettable events as a boxing match sponsored by the Catholic Boys' Clubs of New York, on the excuse that one of the fighters, Ace Hudkins, was a former barnstormer from Lincoln, Nebraska. Lindbergh, who did not seem to recall Ace, looked bewildered when the mayor pulled him into the ring between rounds to present him with a pair of "golden boxing gloves" inscribed "from the Ace of the ring to the ace of the air." The following day, in the ultimate dropout's fantasy, he was welcomed at a luncheon meeting of the University of Wisconsin Alumni Association by a cheer of "SIS BOOM, SIS BOOM, AHHHH—LINDY!" He told the group that when all the fuss died down he hoped to return to Madison and finish his engineering degree. The remark got a huge laugh.

In one week Lindbergh was awarded eighteen medals. Offers from lecture bureaus, promoters, and businessmen were piling up at Blythe and Bruno's Forty-second Street office. And of course, gifts continued to pour in. Some of these presents were valuable—a touring car with an air-cooled engine from the Franklin Motor Company and a set of hand-blown crystal presented by the government of Sweden. More typical were models of the *Spirit of St. Louis* in everything from gold to soap, portrait busts, crewelwork pillows and tea cozies, a set of Mexican ser-apes, autographed books, original poems, rosaries, gold watches, and lifetime memberships in organizations that ran the gamut from the Chauffeurs Association of Bogotá, Colombia, and the Society of Rus-sian Refugees in Wolomin, Poland, to something called the Walkers League of the World.[9]

Author Hendrik van Loon, who met Lindbergh at Mayor Walker's banquet, observed that the young colonel was looking haggard. "Another three days of this and the reflected glory hounds will chase him to his death," van Loon predicted.

Lindbergh himself would have been the first to say that such well-intentioned expressions of sympathy were a little misplaced. In an unpublished 1968 memorandum he recalled that the "fantastic" response of the public to his flight was by no means unenjoyable. On the contrary, he regarded it at the time as a "highly interesting" phe-nomenon, one he fully expected to exploit for his personal benefit as well as for the good of aviation. "I decided to let it develop, and to chart my course as time and circumstances changed."[10]

NINE

"Save Him from the Wolves"

$\mathcal{T}$O BE FAMOUS FOR BEING "INIMITABLY NAIVE," as Fitzhugh Green put it, was a dubious honor. Ambassador Herrick's suggestion that a committee be appointed (presumably not by Lindbergh himself) to handle his financial affairs was typical of the less than flattering ideas being put forth by well-meaning individuals who saw Slim Lindbergh as an unsophisticated country lad, ripe for exploitation. Lindbergh at times rebelled against such presumptions, especially when strangers tried to tell him when and where he could fly an airplane, but the situation also had its welcome aspects. After spending the first twenty-two years of his life yearning for his father's attention and only intermittently getting it, Slim was now surrounded by successful, accomplished men, eager to give him fatherly advice.

And he needed it. In some respects Lindbergh was indeed an exceptionally immature and impressionable twenty-five-year-old. His ideas about politics and business were amorphous, his social skills few. The Lindy dance craze was sweeping the country, but the man for whom it was named had never danced with a woman. Before arriving in Paris, he had never attended a dinner party either. "I was just a kid at the time," he would remark to a friend some years later.

Among the first to take an interest in Slim's future was Dwight Morrow. Shortly after meeting Lindbergh in Washington, he phoned his friend Harry Guggenheim with an urgent request: "Harry, almost everyone in the country is after this young man, trying to exploit him. Isn't there something you and the Fund can do to save him from the wolves?"[1]

Guggenheim duly arranged with the committee planning Lindbergh's New York ticker-tape parade and reception that the pilot and his mother would stay at the Long Island estate of F. Trubee Davison, a former assistant secretary of war—and, as it happened, the son of the late Harry Davison, Sr., the Morgan partner C.A. once accused of turning the American Red Cross into a front for the Money Trust. At the Davison estate, Lindbergh was introduced to a group of businessmen who would soon become his personal advisers, including Harry Davison, Jr., and Henry Breckinridge, another former assistant secretary of war and a prominent Wall Street attorney.

Far from sharing his father's views on the evils of the Money Trust, Lindbergh admired men of wealth and power and was interested in becoming one of them. He was especially impressed by Harry Guggenheim. Just twelve years older than Lindbergh, Guggenheim had served as a navy pilot during World War I and studied economics and philosophy at Oxford. Highly air-minded, he believed that aviation would break down the barriers between peoples and bring prosperity to the undeveloped nations of the world. "The sky is the universal highway," he liked to say.

After the official New York reception ended, Guggenheim invited Lindbergh to stay at La Falaise, his eighty-eight-acre estate near Port Washington, on Long Island's North Shore. Peacocks disported themselves on the lawn, and the Guggenheim living room was a vast gallery of Renaissance sculpture. But despite their surroundings, Harry and his wife Carol were unpretentious people. A fan of pilots the way some are fans of sports stars, Harry took Slim's rough edges and fondness for practical jokes in stride. In short order Lindbergh was accepted as a virtual member of the family.

The Daniel Guggenheim Fund for the Promotion of Civil Aeronautics had been founded at the height of the Billy Mitchell controversy with the specific approval of President Coolidge in order to demonstrate that private philanthropy could accomplish many of the functions the Mitchellites believed were the government's responsibility. Among other activities, the fund encouraged local governments to paint town names on the roofs of buildings as a navigation aid to pilots. It had also sponsored the Byrd Polar Plane tour of 1926 in order to encourage the development of airports. But none of its projects so far had had anything like the impact of Lindbergh's flight.

Before Lindy landed in Paris, few banks had been willing to lend money for any purpose connected with flying, and the typical aviation business was a small, privately held company with little or no outside debt. Now investors and venture capitalists were rushing to pour money into civil aviation. The Guggenheim group, as financiers are wont to do, was already looking at the downside of this phenomenon. The boom was based entirely on investor psychology. If anything happened to destroy the luster of Lindbergh's reputation—a plane crash, a scandal, or simply the devaluation of his name through overexposure—the bubble could burst and it would take the industry years, perhaps a full decade, to recover. Already, in Ohio, a promoter selling shares in something called the Lindberg [sic] Aviation Company had bilked unwary investors out of several million dollars. State agencies were swamped with requests from businesses seeking to register under variations of the names *Lindbergh, Slim, Lindy,* and *Lone Eagle*—this last, the nickname that was fast replacing Flyin' Fool. Within two days of the New York ticker-tape parade the Guggenheim Fund, with Lindbergh's approval, had engaged the William J. Burns detective agency to investigate and warn off persons seeking to exploit the Lindbergh name. Unfortunately, many of those threatened with legal action were small businesspeople who merely wanted to honor the aviator by opening their town's first "Lindy Laundry" or "Lone Eagle Luncheonette."

But the Guggenheim group's main task was to convince Lindbergh to pass up all those lucrative offers he was receiving. Henry Breckinridge, who had become Lindbergh's personal legal adviser, assured him that restraint now would pay off in the long run. His future was unlimited; if he handled himself well, he could even run for president in a few years. Moreover, Breckinridge warned, those who were urging him to commercialize his fame did not have the best interests of aviation at heart. In the short run, Harry Guggenheim suggested that Slim make a tour of the United States under the auspices of the fund, for the purpose of promoting airport construction. He would be paid fifty thousand dollars, plus an additional payment as a consultant the following year. This idea appealed to Lindbergh, in part because it involved flying and additional opportunities to demonstrate the reliability of the *Spirit of St. Louis.*

Without question, Breckinridge and Guggenheim believed they were advising Lindbergh in his own best interests. They really did mean to "save" him. What they were saving him from was the fate of becoming rich through personal appearances, movie deals, and endorsements.

Of course, as multimillionaires they could afford to look down on such activities as demeaning. And, inevitably, there were conflicts of interest. Juan Trippe, who was in the process of organizing what would become Pan-American Airways, was desperately eager to sign Lindbergh to a contract. Worried that he might be accused of taking advantage of the young airmail pilot, Trippe insisted on dealing with Lindbergh only in the presence of his attorney. But Breckinridge was also interested in getting into the airline business, and, not surprisingly, the contract with Trippe went unsigned.[2]

Eager to do the right thing for aviation and his own reputation, Slim came to trust Breckinridge and Guggenheim implicitly. Still, he was more than a little skeptical of the proposition that the entire future of American aviation rested on his shoulders. Airplanes were here to stay, he reasoned, even if he crashed tomorrow. Furthermore, ready as he was to take the long view, he felt a little nervous about passing up the chance to make himself independently wealthy.[3]

In late June, Guggenheim sent Slim to see Dwight Morrow at his New York apartment. Morrow promised to act as Lindbergh's personal financial adviser, opening an account for him at the Morgan bank, where the pilot's name was duly added to the firm's secret list of "preferred clients" who were given opportunities to buy stocks below market prices and to take advantage of other deals based on insider information. All this was technically legal at the time, and in any event Lindbergh had no idea how Morgan's favored clients became rich; he only knew that they did.[4]

In the course of this visit, Dwight Morrow mentioned that while he was in Washington, Coolidge had raised the idea of appointing him ambassador to Mexico. If he decided to take the job, he mused, perhaps Lindbergh would be interested in making a goodwill flight to Mexico City.

Morrow also took care of another of Lindbergh's concerns. Slim was still technically under contract to the Robertsons and felt a moral obligation to all the St. Louians who had contributed to the cost of his flight and were still trying to raise additional subscriptions to cover the bills. Morrow promptly got in touch with Harry Knight, inquiring about the budget for the flight and expressing a desire to make a contribution. Knight replied that the sponsors had raised $8,500 as collateral against a bank loan (actually a line of credit), of which the largest single contribution, $2,000, had been made by Lindbergh himself. By the time all the bills were in, he estimated, the flight would have cost between $16,000 and $17,000. Knight emphasized that he and Harold

Bixby had agreed between them that Lindbergh should get his $2,000 back. "We have, however, not yet told Lindbergh of this plan. He, as a matter of fact, is not only willing, but eager, to bear his full share of the expense."[5]

All this was a polite way of saying that a $2,000 contribution would be appreciated. But Morrow had not waited for Knight's reply. On the same day Knight wrote to him, he dispatched a check for $10,500, an amount just $80 short of the total cost of the *Spirit of St. Louis*. A day later, June 30, Morrow sent along a list of twenty-two individuals responsible for the donation, all J. P. Morgan partners and executives, including Jack and Junius Morgan.[6]

Knight, who was justifiably proud of his role in supporting Lindbergh without expectation of recompense, must have been a little put out that his generosity had now become superfluous. On the whole, however, the St. Louians had no complaints. Knight and Bixby soon became involved with Henry Breckinridge in trying to organize a New York–to–St. Louis airline, to be funded by a consortium of New York banks led by J. P. Morgan. The Robertson brothers, meanwhile, sold out their airmail route at a profit and went into the manufacturing side of the industry, becoming the builders of the popular Curtiss Robin monoplane.

Certainly there was one subject on which the St. Louis and New York groups were in total agreement: Dick Blythe had to go. Blythe talked to Slim like a big brother, affectionately calling him "dumbbell" and "you dirty bum," and encouraged his penchant for practical jokes, horseplay, and fast driving. More to the point, perhaps, Blythe and Bruno had hooked up with Franklin Mahoney of Ryan Aircraft, who was also interested in starting an airline with Lindbergh's participation. Blythe, moreover, made no secret of his opinion that Slim would be a chump to pass up a chance to become a millionaire in his own right from lectures and endorsements.

Immediately following the victory celebration in New York, Lindbergh was scheduled to fly to St. Louis for another round of parades and banquets. Harry Knight wrote Dwight Morrow making it clear that Blythe was not welcome. Several individuals, including Wright Aeronautics executive Guy Vaughan, were deputized by Guggenheim and Breckinridge to warn Lindbergh against Blythe. He ignored them, and Blythe showed up in St. Louis, where the guests at Harry Knight's estate were horrified to see Blythe and America's hero roughhousing on the lawn. At one point, Blythe rubbed Slim's face in the dirt, and

Slim stalked off in mock indignation. Later they had a good laugh over the pretentiousness of people who were taking "this hero guff" so seriously.[7]

Although he had accepted the Guggenheim group's argument that it would be bad for him and for aviation to cheapen his accomplishment by commercializing the flight, some of the offers coming Slim's way were difficult to turn down. William Randolph Hearst and the MGM studios had offered him five hundred thousand dollars plus 10 percent of the gross to appear in a documentary about the transatlantic race. On Hearst's assurance that he would tear up the contract if Lindbergh changed his mind, he signed it on the spot. That evening, at La Falaise, he broke the news to Guggenheim and Breckinridge, who were appalled. Breckinridge warned that Hearst would no doubt want to cast his mistress in the film. "Don't you know that Hearst's interest in movies begins and ends with Marion Davies?" he argued. Guggenheim agreed that the film would make Lindbergh into a laughingstock. The argument lasted half the night. The next day a sheepish Lindbergh showed up at Hearst's East Side town house, explaining that he had changed his mind.

Hearst insisted that the movie would be a documentary, as specified in the contract. "This is not a moving picture in the ordinary sense of the word. It is not a fiction story. It is the real story of your life—a thing the President of the United States ought to be glad to have done for him."

Lindbergh stared at his feet. "I said I would not go into moving pictures."

With a shrug Hearst handed over the papers. "All right. But you tear up the contract. I haven't the heart to do it."[8]

Around this time Lindbergh was invited to Blythe and Bruno's bachelor apartment for dinner. When he arrived, he discovered that the only other guest was a heavily made up blond. After some moments of awkward conversation, it dawned on him that the woman was, as he put it, "a professional prostitute." Concerned that Slim would never manage to relieve himself of his virginity, the partners had hired her as his date for the evening. Deeply embarrassed, Lindbergh made his excuses and fled. The next day he sent Harry Bruno a letter thanking him for his help in the past, and enclosing a check to cover any incidental expenses the firm might have incurred on his behalf. Later he was infuriated to learn that Bruno had framed the letter and hung it behind his desk. Slim chose to believe that Dick Blythe, whom he genuinely liked, was not to blame, but the incident left him with a lifelong distaste for the public relations field, and he never again used a personal agent or publicity representative.[9]

Adding to the pressure of these eventful weeks, a controversy was raging in the press over the armed services' handling of Lindbergh's flight from Washington to New York on the day of the ticker-tape parade. The misunderstanding over the Curtiss biplane's fuel system had caused Lindbergh some tense moments, but he refused to blame the army; it was a pilot's responsibility to know his plane, no matter what the extenuating circumstances. However, one of the ghostwritten stories appearing under his byline in the *Times* had Lindbergh saying that the *Spirit*'s engine failure was caused by its exposure to "salt moisture" during the trip across the Atlantic. Whether or not Lindbergh actually said this, it turned out on further inspection that the problem was a broken cam follower, the same engineering flaw responsible for aborting the Bellanca's flight to New Delhi.

The question remained, Why had navy engineers at Bolling Field not discovered the problem and repaired it? Assistant Secretary of the Navy, Adm. Edward Warner lamely explained that the Wright engine was not yet due for a routine overhaul (this after an unprecedented thirty-three-and-a-half-hour flight and the plane's partial disassembly for transport across the Atlantic) and in a statement that can hardly have been reassuring to navy pilots, he dismissed the engine problem as "one of the things which happen one time in a thousand against which it is impossible to guard."

At this point Billy Mitchell gleefully entered the fray. "It is the saying now, 'Join the navy and see the world, but join naval aviation and see the next world,'" he wrote in a letter to the *Washington Post*. "Today, the navy lives principally on hot air, spread by their Washington lobby." The Coolidge administration, he went on, had staged Lindbergh's return home on the *Memphis* to grab the glory for his accomplishment, only to make a hash of its own propaganda exercise. "How must Lindbergh feel now...?"[10]

In fact, Lindbergh was still seething over his forced homecoming and none too happy about the navy's treatment of his plane. But as Mitchell was about to learn, bullying Charles Lindbergh in public was a sure way to drive him into the opposite camp. He promptly issued a statement to the press absolving the navy of all responsibility. Naively enough, since Mitchell never needed an excuse to stir up trouble, Lindbergh seemed to feel that if Carlisle MacDonald had not written such an indiscreet story, he wouldn't have been put on the spot.

Just as the Mitchell-Warner flap reached its peak, the hapless Mac-Donald delivered the manuscript of his quickie book. It was already in galleys when it was sent to Lindbergh, and much to George Putnam's distress, he refused to approve it. Lindbergh later insisted that he had not known the book would be written in the first person, though since it was based on "Lindbergh's Own Story" as it appeared in the *Times* it is difficult to imagine how he could have failed to realize this. However, he was quite right in thinking that MacDonald's effort did not serve him well. Lindbergh's flat midwestern drawl and old-fashioned locutions—like many barnstorming-era pilots he pronounced "aviator" with a short *a*—would soon be imitated by pilots across the country, including his fervent admirer, the Pennsylvania-born actor and flier Jimmy Stewart. But MacDonald's effort to render Lindbergh's speech in print made Slim sound like a dumb hayseed.

Putnam was still owed a book, however, and now Guggenheim encouraged Lindbergh to write the thing himself. For three weeks Lindbergh shut himself up in his bedroom at La Falaise, working fourteen hours a day to fill ruled yellow pads with 30,000 words. His spelling and punctuation were as atrocious as ever, but he produced an informative, tersely written account of his early experiences in aviation. The book was in the stores by July 27 and was an immediate commercial success, selling 190,000 copies in two months.

But the publication of *We* was not a happy experience. It had been too late to change the title, which was based on MacDonald's observation that Lindbergh was given to speaking of himself and his plane in the first person plural. Reviewers waxed sentimental on this theme, comparing Lindy and the *Spirit* to Alexander the Great and Bucephalus and other such heroic duos. Lindbergh called a press conference and lectured reporters on their failure to grasp that the "we" of the title referred to himself and his St. Louis partners. Since there was absolutely nothing in the book to support this interpretation, the journalists felt abused. Lindbergh would continue to insist to the end of his life that the title of *We* had been misunderstood, yet his own description of the plane in his 1953 autobiography, *The Spirit of St. Louis*, suggests MacDonald was not wrong at all. "It's like a living creature, gliding along smoothly, happily," Lindbergh himself wrote. "We have made this flight across the ocean, not I or it."[11]

One suspects that the real reason for Lindbergh's disgruntlement was that the Guggenheim Fund directors had serious reservations about the book's contents. Barnstorming pilots loved to tell stories about their close calls, a practice known as "ground flying," and Lindbergh had served up some of his best anecdotes in *We*. But tales of daredevil antics and multiple crack-ups—not to mention Lindbergh's frank admission that he taught himself stunt flying while carrying paying passengers—were hardly calculated to reassure a nervous public that flying was safe. Apparently at the insistence of the fund's publicity director Ivy lee, Putnam's prefaced Lindbergh's account of his barnstorming career with a lengthy disclaimer: "It should be borne in mind by the reader that the experiences and incidents related in this book in no way describe modern commercial flying conditions ... etc."

Even as the public was thrilling to the story of his great adventure, it had dawned on Lindbergh that aviation was now a business whose success would depend on making the pilot's job routine. Although he understood that the change was inevitable, he had mixed feelings about his role in bringing it about.

With his book about to reach the stores, Lindbergh turned with some relief to planning the final details of his forty-eight-state tour. The response to the initial announcement had been overwhelming, and he and the Guggenheim Fund staff decided on an itinerary that would include sixty-nine overnight stops as well as numerous "touch-downs" and "fly-overs." Lindbergh would fly the *Spirit of St. Louis* alone, accompanied by a Department of Commerce plane containing a pilot, a mechanic, and Commerce spokesman Donald Keyhoe, a congenial ex-Marine pilot who had escorted Bennett and Balchen on the Polar Plane tour of 1926. Local arrangements were to be left in the hands of civic organizations in the respective cities, though an advance man, Milburn Kusterer, would visit each stop before Lindbergh's arrival. The fund sent letters to the mayors of every city on the itinerary, warning of the need for crowd control and exhorting them not to overload Lindbergh's schedule. Otherwise the arrangements were similar to those for the 1926 tour.

Eager to be flying again, Lindbergh expected the tour to be fun. He had arranged for the escort plane to be piloted by Phil Love, now a Commerce Department inspector, and he wrote Shorty Lynch and a number of other old flying buddies arranging for them to meet him en route. He planned to demonstrate the reliability of the modern airplane by scheduling his arrival at each of the sixty-nine overnight stops at precisely two o'clock in the afternoon—a goal he would fail to meet only once, when a summer storm prevented his landing at Portland, Maine. Still, he was able to lay out a route that would take him over some natural wonder or other point of interest every day: the Green Mountains of Vermont, Churchill Downs in Kentucky, Niagara Falls, the Indianapolis Speedway, the Dakota Badlands, Yellowstone National Park, Lake Tahoe, the Golden Gate Bridge, and Death Valley. Lindbergh and Keyhoe believed, no doubt correctly, that no pilots before them had ever made such a comprehensive aerial survey. They would be seeing America as it had never been seen before.

The airborne part of the tour more than lived up to expectations. The *Spirit* and its escort flew over cities and prosperous farms, Indian reservations and forests. In the Dakota Badlands, Lindbergh and his companions spotted a herd of wild mustangs. In Montana they departed from their planned route to soar and dart among the snowcapped peaks of Glacier National Park. Over Sacramento they joined a large flock of pelicans and were astonished by the birds' unlikely grace and precision maneuvers.

When there was nothing special to see, Lindbergh and Love would amuse themselves by doing a little stunt flying. Love had discovered that by suddenly dropping the nose of his plane he could cause all the loose objects in the cabin, and sometimes the passengers as well, to hang suspended in midair. He applied himself to perfecting this levitation trick, inevitably choosing the moment when Keyhoe and the mechanic were dozing off for a brief nap. Lindbergh's favorite stunt was to dive sharply and skim along, thirty or forty feet above ground level, savoring the sensation of exaggerated speed as the ground flashed beneath him.[12]

When 2:00 P.M. on the day of a major stop approached, the fun abruptly came to an end. The enormous crowds that turned out everywhere defeated the best efforts of local law enforcement. At Wold-Chamberlain Field in Minneapolis twenty thousand spectators broke through police barriers and surged toward the *Spirit of St. Louis* as it approached the terminal; Lindbergh managed to avoid the onrushing masses by turning abruptly and taxiing away at top speed. In Kansas City and Portland, Oregon, he had to abort his landings and set the plane down in nearby fields. Even where security forces managed to contain the crowds, news photographers routinely leapt the barriers and positioned themselves on the runway.

Except for a makeshift periscope, which had too narrow a range of vision to be useful on takeoffs or landings, the *Spirit* had essentially zero forward visibility. Used to flying from the rear cockpit of the Robertson DH's, Lindbergh had no trouble sideslipping in for a landing, but there came a moment, after his wheels touched the landing strip, when he had no way of knowing who or what was directly in front of his moving plane. Whirling propellers were dangerous. Even experienced pilots and mechanics occasionally grew careless around the rotating blades, which spun so fast that they were invisible to the naked eye. Lindbergh had once seen a man sliced in half, and fear of a fatal accident began to take a toll on his nerves.

Of course, the way to avoid such close calls was to erect fences around landing strips, as was already routinely done in Europe. Ironically, this solution was considered undemocratic by many air-minded Americans. How could the sky be a universal highway if access to airfields was restricted? Morris Markey, advocating the construction of fences in a *New Yorker* profile of Lindbergh, felt it necessary to point out that "Lindbergh himself does not suggest such a thing."[13]

Immediately after landing, a rattled Lindbergh would be turned over to a waiting crowd of photographers and reporters shouting the usual questions: "How's the weather up there? " "Have ya got a girl-friend yet, Lindy?" "Say, which do you prefer, blondes or brunettes?" Lindbergh, whose talent for small talk was nil at the best of times, responded to such efforts to draw him into banter with a standard reply: "If you can tell me what that has to do with aviation, I'll be glad to answer."

The fund, in its wisdom, had planned exactly the same program at each of the sixty-nine stops on the *Spirit*'s itinerary. But an arrangement that had been quite adequate for the Bennett-Balchen tour failed to take into account the intensity of the public's response to Lindbergh. As historian Joseph J. Corn has noted, air-mindedness was a sort of secular religion: "Aviation enthusiasts," Corn writes, "tended to view flight as a 'holy cause.'... Over the years, the collecting of aviation relics became common, a form of airplane worship analogous to the reverence for relics shown by traditional religions." The Lindbergh flight happened to coincide with the peak of this phenomenon, and in the eyes of many of the fans who were flocking to airfields along the tour route, he was more than just a celebrity; he was almost literally godlike. To cite just one dimension of the scope of this hero worship, a 1980 study by Lawrence Goldstein concluded that Lindbergh's flight inspired more works of poetry than any other person or event in history. This outpouring included verse by such established poets as Babette Deutsch and

William Rose Benét as well as thousands of amateur efforts with titles like "Lord of the Air," "A Chantey for Celestial Vikings," and "Master of the Empyrean." A couplet from a fairly typical effort enthused:

> Our gaze drew upward—from the skies you taught,
> "Man is divine, and meant by God to soar!"[14]

Donald Keyhoe noted with amazement that far from getting a swelled head, Lindbergh seemed completely unaffected by all the adulation. On the contrary, at several stops on the tour he disappointed promoters by refusing to ride on the perches mounted on the backseats of flower-bedecked convertibles. "I hate to cause any trouble but I'd rather not sit up there," he said, excusing himself. To Keyhoe he confided that the elevated seats reminded him of thrones.

During the Minneapolis–St. Paul victory parade, Eva Lindbergh Christie saw a person in the crowd fling a bouquet of roses into the car Charles was riding in. Unfortunately the awestruck fan had neglected to remove the roses' thorns, and the bouquet struck Charles in the face, drawing blood. She could tell Charles was annoyed, but he quickly composed himself and pretended to be oblivious of the scratches on his cheek and forehead. For Eva the incident summed up her half-brother's situation.

But despite his discomfort at finding himself the object of hero worship, Lindbergh, too, believed that aviation was almost a sacred cause. He was shocked to discover that many reporters—especially those who thought the federal government, not private investors, should be building airports—saw him as a shill for big business, while local politicians and businesspeople used his appearances as opportunities for self-promotion.

The pretour package sent out by the fund had emphasized that Lindbergh was especially interested in speaking to children and wished that a certain number of seats be set aside for young people at all official tour events, including banquets. In Detroit, where his granduncle John C. Lodge had recently become acting mayor, he got his wish and made a highly successful talk to twenty thousand schoolchildren, telling them that they would be the true "flying generation." Elsewhere, almost inevitably, his time was monopolized by people who were less interested in spreading the gospel of aviation than in personal profit and publicity. When he complained to his advance man, he was told to grin and bear it. "Slim, these are powerful people and they are used to getting what they want," Kusterer warned.[15]

There was scarcely a charity or pressure group in the country that did not hope, in some way, to capitalize on the Lindy craze. Left-wing groups, perhaps hoping that C.A.'s son was a secret sympathizer, were especially insistent. In Chicago, for example, the International Labor Defense League announced that its members intended to corner Lindbergh during his visit and force him to reveal his "sentiments" about the impending execution of the anarchists Sacco and Vanzetti. When the police assigned Lindbergh round-the-clock bodyguards, the league accused them of plotting to separate Lindbergh from "the people."

Surprisingly enough, it was the antitobacco lobby that managed to provoke Lindbergh's first public display of pique. A national women's temperance organization had begun circulating a pamphlet urging young men "to follow Lindy's example and abstain from smoking cigarettes." Lindbergh indeed did not smoke or drink, but he was hardly the mama's boy the women's groups made him out to be.

"I won't be played for a tin saint," he told Phil Love. "I never said I would not smoke."

At a banquet in Cincinnati that evening, he accepted an after-dinner cigarette. Strangely, no one noticed except one sharp-eyed AP reporter, who got the rest of the story from Phil Love.

The next day at his press conference, Lindbergh denied telling Love, as quoted by the AP, "If these women don't leave me alone, I'm going to take a drink next." This was not enough to satisfy the fund or the temperance ladies, however, and additional clarifications and partial retractions followed, until eventually Lindbergh insisted that he had never smoked at all.

Lindbergh's defensiveness, combined with his total inability to banter with reporters, who after all only wanted a quip to liven up their stories, led some of them to take cheap shots. Many had noticed that Lindbergh, like his mother, felt an extreme distaste for public displays of affection. In Wisconsin, for example, a demonstrative teenager assigned to present Lindbergh with a bouquet attempted to kiss him, and he instinctively took a step backward, holding the flowers in front his face to ward her off. It was said that the girl ran offstage and burst into tears. From then on, at every press conference someone was sure to ask, "Lindy, is it true that you don't like girls?"

Such speculation to the contrary, Lindbergh *was* interested in girls, which no doubt accounted for his increasingly sour mood. It is perhaps necessary to state that in 1927 a twenty-five-year-old male virgin was not necessarily considered abnormal. Nevertheless, a young man who found himself in this situation could hardly welcome the knowledge that the entire civilized world was taking a lively interest in his sex life—or rather the lack of it.

Women threw themselves at Slim, and at times he enjoyed it. Arriving at a function held in the dining hall of a South Carolina women's college, he was informed that the coeds had formed a double line and were insisting that Lindy "walk the gauntlet." Far from objecting, as Keyhoe expected, Lindbergh thought this an excellent idea. On the other hand, he had narrowly escaped several attempts by the newspapers to lure him into compromising situations, experiences that left him wary and resentful. "If I talked to a girl for five minutes," Lindbergh later wrote, "gossip started as though we were beginning a courtship on stage."[16]

Donald Keyhoe considered Slim a "super-pilot" and a "good scout" who was bearing up under pressures that would have destroyed a lesser man. Unfortunately, added Keyhoe, Lindbergh's habitual "lack of effusiveness" was often mistaken for glumness. "It was as impossible for him to break into superlatives in thought or speech as it would have been for him to hurt anyone deliberately." Keyhoe found the private Lindbergh extraordinarily considerate, an observation that would be echoed by many who knew him over the years. It was Lindbergh who kept up the morale of his escorts, was careful to thank the local police who provided security, and invariably remembered to see that the gifts of flowers, candy, and food sent to his hotel suite were distributed among hotel employees or sent to children's hospitals.

Eager to expose this side of the hero to the press, Milburn Kusterer began to set up photo opportunities. In Pittsburgh, for example, the tour motorcade stopped, apparently spontaneously, so that Lindbergh could greet a little boy in a wheelchair; later, reporters discovered that the child was the son of an Alleghany Airlines executive, whose presence at that particular spot had been arranged in advance. When Slim caught on, he objected vehemently to these "staged good deeds" and did his best to frustrate Kusterer's efforts. In Omaha, confronted by an elderly stranger who was supposedly a distant relative, he announced that he was so deeply touched that he could only express his feelings in private, and before the assembled photographers could snap their pictures he hustled the old man off to a private room.

By mid-August, with slightly less than a third of the tour completed, relations between Lindbergh and the press had deteriorated into an undeclared war. While the newspaper people were not exactly blameless, Lindbergh acknowledged in later years that he did his share to stoke the fires. Concluding that the entire celebrity phenomenon was bogus, he had vowed he would absolutely refuse to do or say anything simply in order to placate the press, a totally unrealistic premise considering that he was getting paid fifty thousand dollars to serve as a spokesman for aviation.[17]

After a spate of newspaper reports that Lindbergh was looking haggard and might be headed for a nervous breakdown, Harry Guggenheim dispatched a physician to give the flier a complete checkup. The doctor's report was released along with a statement from Lindbergh's mother (!) attesting to her son's good health. Apparently the Guggenheim group was not convinced by its own public relations ploy, and Dwight Morrow wrote a fellow fund trustee suggesting that the remainder of the tour be canceled. Instead Jerry Land was persuaded to take time off from his duties at the Bu-Aer so that he and his wife could join Lindbergh in Montana, where he was vacationing for a few days at the Elbow Lake lodge, owned by John D. Ryan. Under the Lands' steadying influence, Lindbergh settled down, and the western half of the tour, while hardly placid, proceeded more smoothly.

Although the forty-eight-state tour generated almost as much bad publicity as good, with hindsight it was an overwhelming success. For thousands of young people, the pilgrimage to catch a glimpse of Lindy and his plane would be the beginning of a lifelong fascination with aviation. Moreover, as Jerry Land later reported, "From a dollars and cents point of view, the Lindbergh Tour was the most outstanding accomplishment of the Fund. Conservative estimates indicated that the tour was responsible for the expenditure of well over one hundred million dollars in airports alone."[18]

The tour also worked out well for Land personally. In August 1928, he temporarily resigned from the navy to become the fund's vice president. One of his first decisions was the selection of another of his protégés, Lt. Jimmy Doolittle, as the fund's chief test pilot.

Lindbergh himself, however, faced an uncertain future. Early in the tour, Donald Keyhoe had been startled to hear a gushing matron tell Slim that he owed it to the world to give up flying. "You're too valuable to lose! You belong to the world now!" she cooed. Keyhoe thought the woman quite mad, but six months after Lindbergh's triumph the sentiment that he ought to give up all "dangerous" flights (whatever those were) had become commonplace. A total of twenty-three men and two women had lost their lives attempting to fly either the Atlantic or the Pacific, and Secretary of Commerce Dwight Davis was pressuring famous aviators to call for a halt to further transoceanic air races. Dick Byrd, whose own attempt to fly to Paris had ended in a forced landing on a Normandy beach, complied, saying: "We've got to prevent those attempts that leave no margin for error, no leeway for accident. Dicing with danger has no place in aviation. Blind luck is a blind pilot. Adventure? Adventure is a plan gone wrong." In fact, Byrd's attempt to leave no margin for error had made his own assault on the Atlantic overcomplicated and doomed it to failure. But Byrd was still considered careful and responsible while Lindy was the reckless youth who gambled with fate and won.

Thus it came about that after performing the most celebrated aviation feat since the invention of the airplane, Lindbergh had no offers of commercial sponsorship for future flights. Nor had Dwight Morrow, concerned about reports that Lindbergh was burned out, renewed his suggestion that Lindbergh make a goodwill flight to Mexico. Shortly before the Guggenheim tour ended, Lindbergh wrote to Harry Davison, Jr., who had taken over the job of handling his account at the Morgan bank, asking him to find out whether Morrow would still be willing to arrange an invitation from the president of Mexico. The *Spirit* still had a few more good records in her, including, he thought, the first nonstop flight from Washington, D.C., to Mexico City.

Morrow was now on the spot. A visit from Lindbergh would delight the Mexican people and increase his own political visibility. On the other hand, he risked being remembered forever as the man who lured the Lone Eagle to his death. The ambassador decided to take a chance, but he was not reassured when Lindbergh wrote saying how pleased he was that the invitation was for the second half of December: He had recently installed a new and highly accurate altimeter and was looking forward to testing its performance under extreme weather conditions.

Though he had failed to sign a contract with Juan Trippe, Slim had been impressed by Trippe's plans to develop the first major American overseas airline, competing with the Germans for routes in Latin America. After receiving his invitation from Morrow, he decided to make Mexico City the jumping-off place for a tour of the Caribbean, with stops in Nicaragua, Panama, Venezuela, and Cuba. Sentiment in favor of grounding Lindy had by now grown so strong that even Adolph Ochs of the highly air-minded *New York Times* cabled Ambassador Morrow begging him to persuade Lindbergh to end his trip in Mexico. Ochs raised the point that the visit to Venezuela might offend other South American nations not similarly honored, reducing the chances of a major goodwill tour later on.

In fact, as Ochs well knew, the chances that the administration would officially sponsor Lindbergh on a South American tour in the foreseeable future were small indeed. In early July, before the Guggenheim tour began, the State Department had asked Lindbergh, who was then in Detroit visiting his mother, to fly to Ottawa in honor of Canada's Diamond Jubilee. What should have been a routine landing ended in tragedy when two Canadian army planes flying as the *Spirit*'s escort collided in midair, killing one of the pilots. Although Lindbergh personally was never in danger, the incident made government officials wary of initiating further visits, especially to South America, where airfield conditions and crowd control were likely to be unpredictable at best.

It seems likely that Ochs, too, was mainly worried about what he called the "incidental risk and peril" of the Venezuela flight. Lindbergh "must not overlook [the] bad effect of any mishap upon aviation to which he has contributed so much in creating [a] feeling of confidence and security on [the] part of [the] world at large." Ochs added, "Everyone on Times staff approves this telegram."[19]

Lindbergh ignored this plea, as he had all the others. Though no one could stop him from flying where and when he chose, his situation was nevertheless extremely frustrating. His transatlantic flight had earned him an estimated $500,000 from various sources, including prizes, the Guggenheim Fund honorarium, book sales, and $125,000 in syndication fees, which the *Times* voluntarily turned over to him. However, any illusions he might have had that the Orteig Prize would guarantee him a blank check for future flights of exploration had been rudely dispelled. The consensus that Lindbergh was a national treasure, too valuable to risk, discouraged patrons from coming forward. The price of being Lord of the Air was that he found himself paying for the Caribbean trip out of his own pocket.

CHAPTER 10

"The Last of the Gods"

DWIGHT MORROW had accepted the appointment as U.S. ambassador to Mexico over the strong protests of his wife, who indignantly compared Calvin Coolidge to a father who distributes his wealth among his ungrateful children, reserving for his one loyal son "this little tin whistle." The Mexican government had extensive dealings with the House of Morgan, and to avoid conflict-of-interest charges, Morrow was forced to resign his partnership and place his investments in government bonds in order to accept the post. With stocks riding high and Morgan partnership bonuses nearing a million dollars a year, Morrow's family and friends could be forgiven for suspecting that Coolidge was taking sadistic advantage of his eagerness to enter the public sector.

Mexican American relations were at an all-time low. The revolutionary movement was firmly in power and President Plutarco Elías Calles had closed the churches, canceled American oil leases, and was threatening to repudiate foreign debts. "Some hotheads here, who wanted to annex Mexico, thought we should just go in and take it," Morrow's good friend George Rublee would recall. "The Mexicans were excited and disturbed and hostile." A perplexed Rublee asked Morrow what he could possibly hope to accomplish by going to Mexico. "Well, at least I can like them," replied Morrow, who had faith that there were few problems that could not be solved through a combination of his keen intelligence and abundant goodwill.[1]

Morrow had little use for foreign-service professionals—"cookie pushers with the milk of Groton still on their lips," he once called them—and he quickly established a flair for personal diplomacy. He and his wife socialized with leaders of the revolutionary party, hitherto viewed by the embassy with suspicion and scorn. Betty learned Spanish and visited dozens of villages to promote the handicrafts industry. Constance was enrolled in a Mexican school, and Elisabeth took a leave of absence from her teaching duties in Englewood to give English lessons in a Mexican primary school. Some of these efforts seem condescending by today's standards—Elisabeth's lesson plans consisted of having the children write essays based on advertising photos she clipped from *Town and Country* and *Vanity Fair*—but they made a favorable impression on President Calles, who soon invited Morrow to a private breakfast at which they hammered out a compromise on the oil-lease question.

The pundits observed that Dwight Morrow had replaced "gunboat diplomacy" with "ham and eggs diplomacy." Morrow noted quizzically that Calles had actually served him popcorn sprinkled with chocolate, but he was delighted to find himself mentioned as a possible presidential candidate.

Charles Lindbergh, meanwhile, was in Washington, D.C., where on December 8, he received the Smithsonian Institution's Langley Medal. He was staying at the home of Jerry and Betty Land, and on December 10, Land invited him to attend a meeting of the House Appropriations Committee. Speaker Nicholas Longworth promptly invited Lindbergh onto the floor of the House, where the representatives gave him a standing ovation and passed a special resolution in favor of awarding him a Congressional Medal of Honor.

Early on the afternoon of the thirteenth, Lindbergh took off for Mexico. Washington's Bolling Field still did not have a paved runway, and one reporter described the airfield that rainy December day as "a hammocky, soggy, puddle-bespattered morass." Loaded with 375 gallons of fuel, the *Spirit of St. Louis* barreled along through the muck for three thousand feet before becoming airborne. During the twenty-two-hour flight, Lindbergh's hope that he would have a chance to duel with the weather was fulfilled. Dogged by heavy clouds, rain, and intermittent fog he crossed the Smoky Mountains, passed over Houston, and continued south, hugging the coastline. At Tampico he turned right. Crossing into the Valley of Mexico, he encountered the worst fog yet. His new altimeter enabled him to thread his way among the mountain peaks, but he had wandered off course. Spotting railroad tracks winding through the desert, he followed them to the nearest station, swooping low to read the sign posted on the adobe wall. CABALLEROS, it said.

Much to his annoyance, there was no Caballeros on his map. He flew on to the next station, but there too the sign said CABALLEROS. Eventually he realized that the signs marked the locations of the men's rooms.[2]

In Mexico City an enormous crowd had gathered at the airport. Lindbergh was two hours behind schedule and Dwight Morrow, George Rublee observed, was a nervous wreck. At last, after many false reports, the *Spirit* appeared in the sky.

Lindbergh's reception in Mexico City was at least the equal of any-thing he had experienced in the States. "The throng on the field shout-ing and screaming with joy was indescribable," Betty Morrow wrote in her diary. "As we went to the car our clothes were almost torn off." Fourteen-year-old Constance, seated at Lindbergh's feet in the open touring car that carried him and her parents through the jam-packed streets, was almost buried under the bouquets of flowers tossed by Lindy's adoring fans.

At the official embassy reception, Constance wrote her sister Anne, a thousand guests ignored the punch bowl and the buffet in order to stand around gaping at the hero. Her schoolmates had talked her into taking their autograph books home for Lindy to sign, and he obligingly inscribed a "cartload" of them before her parents found out and put a stop to it. When one of the signed books was stolen, the victim's parents showed up at school in tears, begging Con to have Lindbergh auto-graph its replacement. (He did.)[3]

In the grip of a teenage crush, Con baked fudge as a present for her idol and sent Anne a portrait she had drawn to prove her contention that the flier's looks were more "refined" than they appeared in news photos. The other guests and the embassy staff, however, noticed that while Lindbergh was polite to everyone, his attentions were focused on the brilliant and ever-poised Elisabeth, who had a way of getting even this most reserved of young men to talk about himself. Rumors of a romance soon filtered out to the Mexican press.

And Lindbergh was indeed looking for a wife. The problem with being the world's most eligible bachelor, he later wrote, was that "girls were everywhere, but ... the mixture of awe, respect and curiosity with which I was treated rose like a haze around me." He had already con-cluded that he would find his future bride among the daughters of his wealthy advisers, the only young women he had a chance to meet under reasonably normal circumstances. For the moment, however, he had other things on his mind.

Two days after he reached Mexico, there was another tumultuous reception at the airport to welcome Evangeline Lindbergh, who arrived in a Ford Tri-motor lent for the occasion by Henry Ford. Mrs. Lindbergh had already turned down an invitation from the Morrows to join Anne and Dwight junior, who were traveling to Mexico in the family's private railroad car, the *Henry Stanley*. Charles, however, was eager to impress Dwight Morrow with the merits of Ford's new twelve-passenger airplane, and one suspects that he had urged his mother to make the flight.

Evangeline, who had so charmed Dwight Morrow when they met in Washington, did not repeat her success on this occasion. More than a little skeptical of the ambassador's motives for inviting her, she had little to say except for occasional barbed comments about the media hullabaloo over her son.

No such reservations troubled Jerry Land, who wrote Ambassador Morrow expressing his delight over Evangeline's presence in Mexico City. There was already talk in Washington of a Morrow-Lindbergh ticket in the 1932 presidential campaign. "The whole nation is not only proud of the combination of Morrow and Lindbergh, but is exceedingly proud of the marvelous way you are handling all matters in Mexico," Land wrote, sounding suspiciously like a political matchmaker.[4]

Any worries the ambassador might have had that Lindbergh would be hard to manage proved unfounded. He was on his best behavior, and the Morrows had far more headaches over their other holiday guest, Will Rogers, whose dinner-table jokes about military coups and political corruption did not go over well with President Calles and his aides. Rogers, however, was a starry-eyed Lindy fan and so grateful to the ambassador for bringing him together with his idol that he forgot his previous criticisms of Coolidge's aviation policies.

On December 20 Anne and Dwight junior joined the family. With them aboard the *Henry Stanley* was a party that included Dwight's Groton classmate Richard ("Dicky") Bissell and the ambassador's sister Alice Morrow. The intellectual, adventure-loving Alice developed an instant rapport with Evangeline. About to depart for Turkey, where she was to spend a year teaching English at a girls' high school, she offered to arrange a similar appointment for Mrs. Lindbergh, who readily accepted.

Forewarned by Constance's letter, Anne was irritated that her holiday with her parents was to be spoiled by all the fuss over Lindbergh, whom she had written off in advance as a sort of "baseball player"—a type of which she had absolutely no experience but was sure she could not possibly find interesting. Unlike Con, who was thrilled by all the tumult and cheering, Anne was unsettled and a little frightened by the hysterical crowds that gathered outside the embassy each evening, refusing to disperse until Lindbergh appeared on the balcony. Under the circumstances she was all the more impressed by Colonel Lindbergh's poise. Notoriously ill at ease with the press, Lindbergh was at his best meeting dignitaries and delegations of Mexican students. In such situations his low-key manner served him well, and he had the knack of communicating interest and friendliness without seeming to pander.

Like others meeting Charles Lindbergh for the first time, Anne discovered that his most surprising physical characteristic was his hands. Lindbergh had long, elegant fingers (an artist's hands, one acquaintance would remark), and his precise gestures and deft touch with everything from silverware at a formal dinner to the controls of an airplane were unexpected in a man of action. When Lindbergh offered to take Betty Morrow and a party of her guests for a ride in the Ford Tri-motor, Anne and her sisters were invited to ride in the cockpit. Entranced, she described the flight in her diary in terms no doubt unconsciously sexual. Colonel Lindbergh, she wrote, was perfectly, wonderfully in control— "he moved so *very* little, yet you felt the harmony of it.... It was a complete and intense experience."

Anne was now as infatuated as Constance. The "arty" intellectual college boys of her acquaintance were revealed to be hopelessly shallow and ordinary. But the colonel seemed scarcely to notice her existence. In fact, he had seen Anne briefly some months earlier at the Morrow apartment in New York and assumed she was still in high school. Nothing happened in Mexico to alter that first impression, and it was Elisabeth who boldly hinted that she and her sisters would love to take flying lessons from him. Anne was in despair, since Colonel Lindbergh, like every other young man she had ever been attracted to, obviously preferred her sister.

On Friday, January 13, just one week after Anne's return to Smith College, a windstorm whipped through the campus, rattling dormitory windows and ripping branches off trees. The next morning the sky was leaden, an omen of the first major snowstorm of 1928. In the dining hall freshman Joy Kimball tarried over her breakfast, waiting for her friend Frances St. John Smith. Concerned because Frances had skipped her Friday classes even though she was on academic probation, Joy had left a note in her friend's room suggesting they have breakfast together.

When Frances failed to appear, Joy climbed the stairs to her friend's single on the third floor of Dewey House. There she discovered the window wide open, as it had been on the previous afternoon, and her note lying on the bed untouched. None of the girls in the dormitory could recall with any degree of certainty when they had last seen Frances.

Within forty-eight hours Frances had become the object of an international search. Boy Scout troops drawn from all over western Massachusetts were combing the woods around Northampton, and reporters from Boston and New York descended on the college town, drawn by reports that the eighteen-year-old heiress was worth two million dollars in her own right. Young women answering Frances's general description—five feet six inches tall, average weight, brown hair, and believed to be wearing a brown coat—were detained by the authorities in Troy, New York; San Antonio, Texas; Coatesville, Pennsylvania; and Olive Hill, Kentucky. In Paris an American student who registered at the Ritz under the name of Frances Smith was held in custody for three days until the embassy was satisfied that she was not the same girl who had gone missing in Massachusetts.

On Sunday morning the St. John Smiths arrived from New York and moved into a suite in the Northampton Hotel, where they began supplying police investigators with the names of their daughter's acquaintances. Summoned to a meeting with the police, Anne Morrow was disconcerted to learn that her name was near the top of the short list. Frances, whose mother had served with Betty Morrow on numerous committees, was one of those alumnae children whom Anne was expected to befriend. Shortly before the holidays she had sought Anne out, confiding that she was desperately lonely, jealous of Joy Kimball, who was making new friends while she was not, and despondent over her first-semester grades, which would surely be a bitter disappointment to her father. Anne had listened sympathetically to this litany, not so different from her own freshman year complaints, but in the excitement of getting ready for her extended Christmas vacation in Mexico, Frances and her problems had slipped to the back of her mind. Since her return she had spoken to Frances only once, briefly and in passing; preoccupied with her new classes and thoughts of Colonel Lindbergh, she had taken Frances's assurance that she was feeling much better at face value.

Now Anne was in the awkward position of having to defend her behavior to teams of local and state police detectives, as well as to the St. John Smiths, who were under the impression that Anne was one of only three girls on campus Frances had considered a true friend. Grieving not just for Frances but for her own lost sense of invulnerability, Anne turned to President Neilson and his wife for comfort. "If life is really this sad, I don't think I can find the strength to bear it," she exclaimed.

Mrs. Neilson, who had recently lost a son, wisely assured her that she could. "In some ways, it's easier when the sorrow is your own."[5]

Like the police, Anne suspected suicide, but there was to be no quick solution to the St. John Smith mystery. Frances's parents, convinced that their daughter was over her case of freshman blues, believed that she had suffered an accident while hiking in the woods or perhaps had been abducted while trying to hitchhike to the family's summer house in nearby Amherst.

When Frances failed to turn up after a week, the governor of Massachusetts assigned the case to State Police Detective Joseph Daly, a former chief of security for Calvin Coolidge and himself the father of a Smith student. Daly ordered the dragging of the Connecticut River and brought in a special "submarine spotlight" to search the depths of the partially frozen Paradise Pond on campus. The *Northampton Gazette*, meanwhile, published a letter from the father of Alice Corbett of Syracuse, New York, reminding the Smith community that Alice, a member of the class of 1928, had also disappeared from the campus on a Friday the thirteenth, in 1925, never to be seen or heard from again.[6]

The state police questioned scores of local men, including a former Cornell basketball star with a history of mental illness who managed a teahouse frequented by Smith women, and wild rumors circulated on campus about a certain faculty member who happened to have taught both Smith and Corbett. Moreover, five students swore affidavits describing their encounters with a suspicious-looking male who had been seen wandering through one of the dormitories a few days before the disappearance. The college warden dismissed these reports as "fantastic" and "absolutely impossible."

Family and college officials who visited Frances's room after her disappearance had noticed a sharp, chemical odor, an observation that led, for a time, to speculation about chloroform and poisons. But when the room was thoroughly searched, the detectives discovered that the smell came from a collection of rotting oranges stashed in a bureau drawer. Other girls in the dormitory recalled that Frances had been obsessed with her weight, going on crash diets while hoarding food in her room. Parents, already up in arms over lax campus security, began complaining that the college was in the grip of an epidemic of self-starvation. President and Mrs. Neilson invited Anne to tea and interrogated her about her eating habits. Anne, who was as obsessed with dieting as any of her friends but hardly anorexic, complained that she was growing weary of being used as a conduit to student opinion.

The Boston and New York tabloids were playing the Smith case as front-page news, and the girl's parents had begun receiving crank letters. After they had paid at least one ransom without results, Daly proposed setting a trap for the next person who demanded money, and a family representative left a suitcase, filled with shredded newspaper in lieu of the twelve-thousand-dollar ransom, on a stairwell in a Springfield, Massachusetts, department store. The more-than-two-dozen undercover detectives stationed on the sales floor were so easy to spot, one Boston paper complained, that it was hardly any wonder that the extortionist made no effort to collect the money. Lieutenant Daley countercharged that the ransom demand was "so well written" that it could well have been a newspaper hoax.

One day, while Anne was shopping in town, a boy jumped out of the shadows at her and shouted gleefully, "Frances Smith, I have you now!" This sort of thing was happening to other Smith students, but Anne wondered self-consciously if there was something about her face or her manner that telegraphed her connection to the case. Pursued everywhere by reporters frantic for an interview with the girl to whom Frances had confided her innermost thoughts, Anne became protective of her privacy almost to the point of paranoia.

Three months after Frances Smith's disappearance, in April 1928, Lieutenant Daly died after a brief illness. The official cause of death was complications resulting from an acute gall bladder attack, but his widow and daughters publicly blamed the stress of the investigation. In June a boater on the Connecticut River discovered a badly decomposed corpse, later determined from dental records to be that of Frances St. John Smith. It was too late to establish the cause of death. The tabloids, refusing to accept even the identification, continued to speculate that the heiress was still alive and suffering from amnesia. The Smith case became a staple of tabloid gossip, periodically revived over the years as women purporting to be the real Frances came forward to claim her fortune.

In the meantime Smith College followed the time-honored policy of drawing a veil of silence around a possible student suicide. Frances St. John Smith would be nowhere mentioned in the school yearbook or official publications at the end of the 1928 school year or at the time of her class's graduation. For that matter, the index to the *Northampton Gazette,* which ran front-page stories about the case on an almost daily basis, does not even list Smith's name.

While the search for Frances dragged on, Anne had more disturbing news from Groton. Dwight junior was having what was described in those days as a "nervous breakdown" but would today be called a manic episode. With the ambassador and Mrs. Morrow on a state visit to Havana, it fell to Elisabeth to rush to Dwight's school and persuade him to put himself under a physician's care.

Dwight's problems had actually begun a year earlier, in spring 1927, when he was elected to the editorial board of the *Grotonian.* Dwight had been able to attract a number of distinguished speakers to the school, including the poet Robert Frost, and supporters of his opponent charged that he would never have won a spot on the board if it weren't for his ability to trade on his parents' connections. Brooding over these allegations, the distraught boy had shown up at the office of Headmaster Endicott Peabody early one morning, demanding that the election results be reversed. Dwight was sent to the infirmary, and Peabody reported laconically in a letter to Betty his diagnosis that the boy was "a bit over-trained."[7]

Dwight recovered after a few days, but during the fall semester his symptoms returned. Ironically, as sometimes happens, the onset of a manic phase transformed him overnight from a lumpish, pedantic boy into a dazzling personality. He became a debating-team star—inundating his father with requests for research materials—challenged his teachers in class, fearlessly broke all the rules, and, on several occasions, led his classmates on unsanctioned expeditions into Northampton. Dwight even bragged that he had spent the night in a Smith dormitory; apparently this occurred during a Thanksgiving weekend visit with Anne and was entirely innocent, but in the 1920s such escapades were the stuff that prep school legends were made of.

At the beginning of February, Dwight had crashed. He was delirious, tormented by inner voices that he believed belonged to a clique of classmates who were persecuting him. Betty Morrow rushed home from Havana, and she and Elisabeth spent the next month nursing Dwight at home in Englewood.

Few outside the immediate family knew of Dwight's illness, but one who did was Charles Lindbergh, who visited the sick youth shortly after returning from his Caribbean tour. This kind gesture was much appreciated by the Morrows, though they all assumed that Lindbergh's chief interest was in renewing his acquaintance with the eldest Miss Morrow. Elisabeth, who certainly thought so, invited Lindbergh to come to North Haven that summer, and Anne and Constance began to indulge in giddy, envious fantasies about their sister's forthcoming marriage to the most famous man in the world.

By mid-March, Dwight was much calmer, and Mrs. Morrow returned to Mexico with Anne, who had added a few days to her Easter vacation in order to see her parents' new weekend house in Cuernavaca. Elisabeth was supposed to go to Mexico as well but canceled her plans when Dwight begged her to accompany him on the train trip to the Southern Pines resort, where he was to recuperate under the supervision of his grandmother Cutter, a Swedish nurse, and a young Yale graduate who had been recruited to serve as his paid companion and golf tutor. Dwight had made up his mind to devote this recovery period to learning golf, the only sporting activity his father enjoyed. Astoundingly, after just a few rounds with his tutor, he managed a feat that eludes many dedicated players all their lives. In a telegram to his father, he gloated over scoring a hole in one and pronounced himself cured.[8]

The burdens of being a child of Dwight and Betty Morrow are nowhere more evident than in the family's reaction to Dwight's illness. Ambassador Morrow obviously loved his son dearly and protested against the doctors' advice that the young man would be better off at Southern Pines than with his parents in Mexico. But at the same time he dwelt obsessively on his fear that Dwight would lose a year of school and thus be unable to enter Amherst with the class of 1932. This dread consequence was averted when Morrow persuaded Endicott Peabody to grant Dwight his diploma in June, even though he had done no work all semester. Even mental illness was not to be permitted to interfere with Dwight's progress toward the academic goals his parents had set for him.

Anne, meanwhile, was in the final semester of her senior year, a time when her classmates were planning careers and announcing wedding plans. A former beau had recently announced his engagement, and another young man whom she had been seeing casually, so she thought, raised the subject of marriage in more or less hypothetical terms. Unprepared to make the commitments that seemed to come so naturally to her peers, Anne began to fret that the safe, all-enveloping world of her childhood was disintegrating and there was nothing to take its place. Spending the weekend in Englewood in early March, she had a sudden premonition that "one of us [the children] is going to die. It won't be me."

With her mother preoccupied with Dwight's problems, Anne's icon of strength was Colonel Lindbergh—"the last of the gods," she called him. In her diary she made a list of Lindbergh's best qualities, citing, tellingly enough, "impersonality" (meaning aloofness) as well as "courage" and "clean cutness." Having a tooth filled, Anne found that the whirring of the drill reminded her of an airplane motor and thus, by association, with "HIM"—a word she surrounded with little hand-drawn suns. The news that Lindbergh had flown over Northampton on his way to deliver serum to Floyd Bennett, who was fatally ill with pneumonia in a Quebec hospital, left her positively giddy with excitement. So did the experience of watching a newsreel, "40,000 Miles with Lindbergh."[9]

One day in mid-April, a barnstormer showed up in Northampton, and Anne convinced a college friend to go halves on the cost of an airplane ride. The plane was a wreck, held together with spit and twine, but Anne was so enthralled that she went up twice more, paying ten dollars for fifteen minutes in the air. On one of these flights her companion was Elisabeth, who happened to be visiting Northampton. Anne was careful not to tell her parents about these excursions. Ambassador Morrow, the aviation expert, had been horrified by Elisabeth's talk of learning to fly.

There are few hints in Anne's diaries that she even considered the possibility of competing with Elisabeth for the colonel's attentions. Elisabeth's place as the "number one" sister was unchallenged within the family. By common consent she was not only the brilliant sister but also the beautiful one. Family photographs reveal that Elisabeth had indeed been a lovely child, a blue-eyed blond with a perfect oval face and angelic features. But at twenty-five Elisabeth was too thin, her smile slightly off kilter, and her taste in clothes prematurely spinsterish. If anything, she was the plain sister. Moon-faced, button-nosed Constance was developing the "cute kid" looks still very much in fashion in the late twenties, while Anne, with her high forehead and thick, straight eyebrows, was more the classic beauty.

A short story of Anne's that appeared in the June 1928 issue of the *Smith College Monthly* reveals that in her heart of hearts she knew the score. The story's heroine, a girl named Jane, has listened all her life to adults singing the praises of her older cousin 'Lida, now a "young married" of twenty-nine: "Always, as far back as she could remember, she had the incomparable 'Lida held up to her as a model of goodness and beauty. And she wondered wearily, *was* 'Lida so beautiful? It did seem to her sometimes that 'Lida was just a little—well—*dowdy*." Even Jane's current beau, Tom, a decidedly ordinary young lawyer, is another of 'Lida's pass-alongs. But one day, as Jane scans one of Tom's chatty, absent-minded letters, her eyes fall on a few disconnected references to a recent encounter with her cousin: "saw 'Lida—become disgustingly fat." The offhanded comment fills Jane's heart with malicious joy. But the process of repression is immediate. That evening, smiling to herself at the dinner table, Jane can no longer recall just what the "lovely thing" was in Tom's letter that has made her so very, very happy.[10]

Despite passages of overwrought prose, this story reveals a maturity lacking in Anne Morrow's other college writing. No longer content merely to appreciate the glistening surfaces of life, she was beginning to grapple with unpleasant realities, including the possibility that emotions like jealousy and the humiliation of a rival might be among life's sweeter pleasures.

But it was a work in a very different vein that won Anne her first major writing award, the Elizabeth Montagu Prize for the best undergraduate essay on the topic "Women in Dr. Johnson's Time." Anne chose to write about Sophie, comtesse d'Houdetot, whose contribution to the canon of French literature consists of a single eight-line lyric on "Amour," but who is perhaps best remembered as the lover of Jean-Jacques Rousseau. Anne saw her subject as a model of detached aestheticism: "Madame d'Houdetot had no consciousness of evil. She saw only the good.... Even during the horrors of the Revolution, a friend described her as being able to forget for a moment all her painful memories in the contemplation of a flower, a butterfly, a passing fragrance or a patch of brilliant color."[11]

The essay was a bravura performance, revealing an impressive grasp of French literature and history, but the choice of subject was as unsettling to some readers then as it is today. Certainly, from the feminist point of view Madame d'Houdetot can only be seen as a stunted personality who sacrificed her own talent in order to become the mistress of a salon and muse of a genius. Moreover, can one truly admire a woman who was an ornament of the court of Louis XVI and a survivor of the Terror yet never developed a "consciousness of evil"? A woman reporter for the *New York Telegram* who encountered this essay while preparing a biographical portrait of Anne tactfully called it "a very young girl's idea of the perfect woman."

Anne had vague ideas of joining her parents in Mexico after graduation, where she would "try to write," and her accomplishments so far suggested that she indeed had a future as a poet and novelist. In addition to the Montagu Prize for her essay on d'Houdetot, she received the college's Augusta Baker Jordan Prize for literature for a selection of poetry. Moreover, Betty Morrow, unknown to Anne, had submitted one of her poems to *Scribner's Magazine,* which published it in its April 1928 issue. Informed that her verse was about to appear in a major national publication, Anne felt mixed emotions. "Height" was a childish poem about growing up and had been written long before Lindbergh's transatlantic flight, yet now, in spring 1928, its lines about reaching for the sky ("... fixing on a star I grew./I pushed my head against the blue!/... And sometimes standing in a crowd/My lips are cool against a cloud.") seemed to be proclaiming Anne's infatuation with flying, and by extension with Colonel Lindbergh, to all the world. Indeed, one suspects that the editors of *Scribner's* had made this very connection and would not have been interested in publishing such doggerel if its author were not Ambassador Morrow's daughter.

Given this slightly embarrassing debut in print and the experience of being pursued by reporters interested in the Smith case, Anne had become extremely protective of her own privacy. A few weeks later, when the college press office distributed questionnaires to all seniors, the memory of her innocent answers to a similar form handed out at Miss Chapin's four years earlier must have come back to haunt her. Anne was the only member of her class, and indeed the only senior in memory, who refused to give the press office any information whatsoever about her future plans.

ELEVEN

"Anne and Lindy Wed"

*W*HILE ANNE WAS FINISHING HER SENIOR YEAR AT SMITH, Charles Lindbergh was busy "getting out of the hero business," as he put it. He still had a number of commitments, including a March visit to Washington, where President Coolidge presented him with the Medal of Honor, voted by Congress the previous December.

In appreciation Lindbergh offered to give free airplane rides, in navy planes, to members of Congress. Going up in an airplane was still considered an act of daring, and Lindbergh and the Bu-Aer expected that only a few dozen senators and congressmen would have the courage to accept. Much to the amazement of everyone—including the Army Air Corps, which belatedly insisted that Lindbergh use its planes for half the rides—the congressmen turned out in droves, bringing with them their wives, their daughters, and, in a few cases, their mistresses. In one week Lindbergh gave rides to an astonishing 835 people, a statistic bound to impress any investors who still doubted that the American public was ready for commercial air travel.

The *Spirit of St. Louis* was on exhibit at the Missouri Historical Society in St. Louis, where it was expected to remain until April, when Lindbergh planned to donate it to the Smithsonian. In February, however, Dwight Morrow wired Lindbergh on behalf of a committee that included Harry Davison, Harry Guggenheim, and Morgan partner Tom Cochrane, asking permission to bring the *Spirit* to New York, where it would be shown for ten days at a charity benefit.[1] The St. Louis sponsors, already disappointed that the plane would not be remaining in their city permanently, were utterly opposed to losing any more exhibition time, and Lindbergh turned down Morrow's request with the excuse that he had already said no to hundreds of organizations that would feel slighted if he said yes to one group now. Morrow was too tactful to remind Lindbergh that he and his partners were not just another importunate charity committee. They had paid for the plane—an arrangement that had, of course, never been made public.

That same month Lindbergh joined Harold Bixby, Maj. William Robertson, Harry Knight, and Henry Breckinridge in Detroit, where they hoped to persuade Henry Ford to back their idea for a New York–to–St. Louis passenger airline. Ford told the group that he knew nothing about the service side of transportation and never invested in businesses he didn't understand. Furthermore, he had no plans to expand his airplane manufacturing operation. The death of Ford's friend Harry Brooks in the crash of a single-seat Ford Flivver had left him with little enthusiasm for building planes.

"The meeting with Ford was one of the great disappointments of my life," Lindbergh told an acquaintance many years later. "I was expecting Henry Ford to manufacture a Model T of the air. But he wasn't interested."[2]

This vision of a "Model T of the air" or, as Dick Blythe once put it, "an airplane in every garage," was a dream shared by many air-minded Americans of Lindbergh's generation. Just as the automobile had created the suburbs, the family airplane would revitalize rural areas, making it possible for people to live on farms while commuting to factory jobs many miles away. Dirty, unhealthful cities would become obsolete. In fact, the private plane would accomplish what fifty years of Populist and Progressive agitation had failed to do—reverse the drain of population and political power to urban areas.[3]

A true believer in this utopian fantasy if there ever was one, Lindbergh was fast coming to realize that the business community had another vision entirely. The Bixby group soon found its angel in the person of Clement Keys, a former *Wall Street Journal* reporter turned entrepreneur who had recently acquired a controlling interest in the Curtiss Aeroplane Company. "Why stop at St. Louis?" Keys wondered aloud. "Why not organize a truly national airline, linking America from coast to coast?" Keys estimated that start-up costs would be about ten million dollars, a sum so fantastic that Bixby, Lindbergh, and the others thought he was joking. Within a few weeks, however, Keys and Breckinridge had raised the money through a consortium of investors including Curtiss, the Wright Aeronautical Corporation, J. P. Morgan & Co., and four other New York banks. The new airline would be called Transcontinental Air Transport, or TAT.

Despite its name TAT did not propose to fly passengers directly across North America. Night flying was still not practical, especially over the so-called "hell stretch" between Philadelphia and Pittsburgh and the even-more-treacherous Rockies. TAT passengers would depart from New York on a Pennsylvania Railroad Pullman train and transfer to a plane the next morning in Columbus, Ohio, stopping in Indianapolis, St. Louis, Kansas City, and Wichita. A second train would carry them across the southern Rockies to Clovis, New Mexico, where they would again transfer to a plane for the flight to Los Angeles, via Albuquerque, New Mexico, and Winslow and Kingman, Arizona. If all went according to schedule—a big if—the trip would take forty-eight hours.

Keys had stressed Lindbergh's participation in his presentations to investors, and as soon as the financial package was complete, he called Slim to discuss exactly what title he would have in the new corporation. Much to his shock, Lindbergh said he didn't want any title at all. The prospect of a full-time desk job did not much appeal to him.

Keys felt ill used. Whether his reaction was justified is a matter of opinion. Even before his transatlantic flight, Lindbergh had discussed organizing a New York–to–St. Louis airline with Bixby and the other St. Louis backers. By taking part in the formation of TAT he was fulfilling a moral obligation to his partners, but the airline that emerged from the negotiations was certainly far different from the one they had originally envisioned. In the meantime Lindbergh was once again talking with Keys's rival Juan Trippe, whose dream of pioneering international air routes and forging links among nations had a visionary scope the TAT concept lacked. Lindbergh, who always hated to disappoint people he considered his friends, often found it easier just to go along against his better judgment. Unfortunately, sooner or later there usually came a time where he began to feel that he was being pushed around and dug in his heels. These unpredictable changes of heart left associates feeling betrayed and caused more hard feelings than if he had made his wishes clear at the outset.

Although at this point he was far from sure what he wanted to do with the rest of his life, Lindbergh did not find the idea of working for a corporation appealing, and it was beginning to dawn on him that one of the rewards of being Lindy was that he didn't have to. Rather than be so closely identified with a "commercial undertaking," he told Keys, he felt he could do more for aviation by remaining independent. The rhetoric of Henry Breckinridge and the Guggenheim group was now coming back to haunt them. We can be sure that when these men urged Lindbergh to avoid commercializing his fame, they had never meant that he should not take a job with a commercial airline, especially this one. As Breckinridge was beginning to discover, Slim could be astonishingly literal-minded at times, especially when it came to carrying the advice of his mentors to extremes they themselves had never intended. In this case, as usual, it was difficult to tell whether Slim was as obtuse as he seemed or actually rather canny in using the advice of others to justify doing what he wanted to do in the first place.

After several weeks of frantic negotiations, Lindbergh agreed to join TAT as an independent consultant with the title Chairman of the Technical Committee. He would receive a relatively modest salary of ten thousand dollars a year plus an additional consultant's fee from the Pennsylvania Railroad, as well as a one-time bonus of twenty-five thousand shares of TAT stock, valued at ten dollars a share. The appointment was announced on May 22, 1928, and met with a mixed response. As *New York Times* aviation correspondent Lauren D. Lyman observed, "aero stocks rocketed" at the mere mention of Lindy's name. On the other hand, "some cynical observers" assumed that Lindbergh had been given a no-show job as a public relations gimmick.[4]

Despite this perception Lindbergh's title was not an honorary one. Besides personally surveying TAT's routes, he had the ultimate responsibility for hiring and training pilots, recommending which planes the airline should purchase, setting safety standards, and developing airport facilities. In the western states, TAT had to build its own hangars and terminals and bring in engineers to upgrade landing strips that had never before been used for multiengined planes. The technical committee also had to work out the logistics of transporting passengers and their luggage to and from connecting trains and organize its own network of seventy-nine weather stations to supplement the government's inadequate system.

Lindbergh obviously did not do all these things himself. Recruiting, for example, was handled mainly by his assistants, Maj. Thomas Lanphier and veteran pilot Casey Jones. However, Lindbergh did not hesitate to make tough decisions, sometimes to the dismay of TAT's executives. Regretfully he chose Kansas City over St. Louis as the site of the airline's midwestern headquarters, and picked tiny Waynoka, Oklahoma, over Wichita as the spot where passengers would disembark for the train trip to Clovis, New Mexico.

One of the most difficult decisions the committee had to make was whether TAT planes should carry parachutes for its passengers. Once viewed as an exhibitionistic means of committing suicide, the parachute was now, Lindbergh thought, almost an obsession with the public. Realistically, most accidents occurred on takeoff or landing, and a if trimotor crew had time to evacuate a planeful of passengers, all novice jumpers, there would probably also be time for the pilot to make an emergency landing. However logical, the committee's decision that parachutes were unnecessary dismayed TAT's marketing staff, which felt that asking passengers to fly without parachutes was like asking them to board an ocean liner that was not equipped with lifeboats.

Within the company Lindbergh's most controversial action was in steering the technical committee to recommend purchase of Ford Tri-motors over a half dozen other models, including the wooden-winged Curtiss Condor, manufactured by Keys's own company. The Tri-motor, soon to be nicknamed the Tin Goose, had a squared-off bottom and a corrugated skin that made it look like a flying Quonset hut. In the Ford engineering tradition, the steering was balky. The landing-gear lever required superhuman strength to operate, and the trim lever was mounted on the ceiling of the cabin so that all but the tallest pilots had to strain to reach it. As an added challenge, the instruments were attached to a strut *outside* the cockpit, where they quickly became frosted over in bad weather.

Engineers and pilots who preferred the elegant Condor grumbled that Lindbergh was blinded by his hero worship of Henry Ford, but in the long run, his decision proved justified. The Tri-motor had power to spare and required relatively little maintenance. After a Condor belonging to a rival airline shook off a wing in midflight, Lindbergh's preference for the Tin Goose came to seem all the more prescient.

Lindbergh's fame made it possible for TAT to attract some of the most skilled pilots in the country, many of whom remained with TAT and its successor, TWA, throughout their careers. And finally, despite his reputation for shunning publicity, he did his share of promotional work, giving interviews, making speeches, and greeting the Hollywood stars and executives who were soon to become the airline's most loyal customers.

All in all TAT got more than its money's worth out of Lindbergh, but just as the "cynics" suspected, what Keys and the major investors really wanted was the publicity value of his name. Harry Bruno had been hired to do public relations for the new airline and, as he later told the story, he was editing a routine press release when he was inspired to pencil in the phrase *The Lindbergh Line,* in brackets after the letters *TAT.*

Bruno continued:

> The moment Keys saw it his face lit up. "Great!" he said. "We're not using Lindbergh's name in advertising, but we can through constant repetition of the slogan, 'The Lindbergh Line,' in news stories get the public to realize what Lindbergh has done for air transportation."[5]

Bruno was being disingenuous. Lindbergh's name was not being used in TAT advertising because his contract didn't permit it. Nevertheless, the Lindbergh Line motto was eventually printed on tickets and luggage stickers and even painted on the sides of TAT planes and Pennsy railroad cars. No fan of Bruno's to begin with, Lindbergh was irate and considering suing TAT but was advised against it by Henry Breckinridge, who was a director of the corporation as well as Lindbergh's personal attorney. As a practical matter Breckinridge may have been right. The removal of Lindbergh's name from TAT's planes, much less a lawsuit, could well have destroyed the fledgling airline and the value of Lindbergh's stock with it. Still, his advice was somewhat ironic coming from one who had urged Lindbergh so strenuously to resist any "exploitation" of his name.

Traveling around the country on TAT business, Lindbergh continued to have his problems with the press. If he announced his flight plans in advance, he was met at his destination by unmanageable crowds. If he didn't, the newspapermen guessed and then reported him missing and presumed dead when he failed to show up. Kent Cooper of AP and UP's Karl Bickle told Slim that he could make life a lot easier for all concerned if he issued an occasional press bulletin, posed for pictures, and stopped limiting interviews to a favored few like Lauren Lyman of the *Times* and C. B. Allen of the *World.* Lindbergh tried to follow this advice, but his efforts were inconsistent and he was too easily discouraged when they failed to bring immediate results. During a visit to Cleveland, for example, he called a paper that had printed some critical remarks about him and volunteered to answer questions, only to be rewarded by a mocking headline: NOW LINDBERGH

ASKS TO BE INTERVIEWED. The humor of this completely escaped him.

In the end his effort to make peace with the press was a failure, and Lindbergh became more secretive, using false names, disguises, and other ruses to avoid reporters. At Roosevelt Field a Minnesota-born teenager named George Dade was delegated to act as a decoy, delivering Lindbergh's Franklin touring car to a distant part of the field that he used for takeoffs and landings. "You have to understand," Dade says, "Lindbergh was two different people. If it was anything to do with newspapers, he was one way. If the newspapers weren't involved he was fine."[6]

Survey flights and other TAT business kept Lindbergh busy through the summer of 1928. Unable to get up to North Haven, he sent word to Elisabeth that he would try to see her in Englewood before she left for France, where she was planning to continue her graduate studies. But Elisabeth's sailing date came and went. Dwight junior started at Amherst, Constance left for Milton Academy, and Ambassador and Mrs. Morrow returned to Mexico. Only Anne, who was scheduled to have minor surgery in early October, remained in Englewood.

Two days before Anne went into the hospital, Lindbergh called the house, asking for the ambassador, Mrs. Morrow, or Miss Morrow. He seemed surprised to learn that Elisabeth was gone, but since Anne, too, had expressed an interest in learning to fly, he offered to take her up for a lesson. Anne assumed that she was being asked out by default. In fact the timing of the call had been carefully planned. Although the "sparkling vivacity" of the eldest Miss Morrow made a deep impression on Charles in Mexico, it was Anne's face that had remained alive in his memory.[7]

Anne Morrow was like Evangeline Lindbergh in so many ways— petite, shy, intellectual, warm hearted, moody—that one cannot doubt Charles's word that he had fallen in love with her even before their first date. However, there was another reason for him to focus on the younger sister: He had a dream that he and his mate would become fly-ing partners. In a ponderous and rather embarrassing passage in his posthumously published *Autobiography of Values,* Lindbergh lists the abstract qualities he required in a wife—including a good figure and good health—suggesting that he had learned, probably during his visit to Englewood earlier in the year, about Elisabeth's "murmuring heart."

Charles planned that first date (the first of his life, he later said) with the same methodical single-mindedness he brought to the preparations for his assault on the Atlantic. It began with lunch at La Falaise, where Anne, who still thought of him as a trifle uncouth, had a chance to see him *en famille* with the Guggenheims. Next came a flying lesson in a borrowed open-cockpit Moth biplane. Unable to bear the thought of being seen by her idol in boots, Anne dressed for the occasion in gray golf socks and high heels. Anne had only recently learned to drive a car—a few months earlier she had been brimming with pride over her success in taking the station wagon across the ferry from North Haven to Rockland—and she considered herself the least mechanical person in the world. But she was a good sailor and a far better athlete than she gave herself credit for, and in time she would become a more-than-competent pilot.

Their second outing consisted of a leisurely drive in the Franklin over backcountry New Jersey roads. A novel Anne published many years later, in 1960, describes just such a date, which begins with the young man delivering a mystifying discourse on the dangers of carbon monoxide emissions. While his companion is still trying to puzzle out the point of this lecture, he suddenly makes an awkward lunge across the front seat and blurts out a proposal of marriage. Dazzled by her vision of the amazement of her friends, who consider this fellow a great catch, the young lady says yes.

At any rate Charles and Anne were now engaged—but secretly. Worried about her parents' reaction, they hoped to keep their romance out of the newspapers until they had a chance to break the news to them face to face. This, of course, proved impossible. Ryan Aircraft had given Charles a five-seater Brougham to replace the *Spirit of St. Louis*—a "dolled-up" plane that was pretty but unstable, Lindbergh would recall—and he soon invited Anne and the Morrows' housekeeper, Jo Graeme, for an excursion to Lakehurst, New Jersey. Reporters saw the trio at Teterboro airport, and guessed that the women were two of the Morrow girls. Anne returned home to find reporters camped on the porch and phone messages from all the New York papers, including the *Times*. She instructed the servants to tell all callers, "Miss Morrow is in Europe." (Only Elisabeth, the eldest sister, was properly known as Miss Morrow; Anne was Miss Anne Morrow.) The effect of this statement was to encourage the press to think that there was a romance between Charles and Elisabeth, a misconception reinforced when Elisabeth paid a visit to her Aunt Alice in Turkey and was seen in public with Evangeline Lindbergh.

Anne joined her mother and father in Mexico in November but did not feel up to breaking the news alone. Few parents in 1928 could have been enthusiastic about a daughter's decision to marry an aviator, much less become one. Certainly it was assumed that Charles Lindbergh's life expectancy was short. The ambassador's sister-in-law, Mrs. Jay Morrow, relayed what she understood to be the family's position to reporters: "If Lindbergh wants to marry a Morrow he'll have to give up flying."[8]

Fortunately, Col. Alexander McNab, the American military attaché in Mexico, had invited Charles to join a group of Mexican officers at a hunting party on a ranch in Coahuila owned by American businessman Hal Mangum. After a few days, McNab was called back to Mexico City on business, and Colonel Lindbergh was invited to the Morrows' week-end house in Cuernavaca. Casa Mañana, as the family called it, was a series of detached bungalows, picturesquely arranged on a steep hillside and connected by red-tiled walkways planted with bougainvillaea, aza-leas, and sweet jasmine. There was a swimming pool and a patio where Charles and Anne could sit at breakfast sipping fresh-squeezed orange juice while enjoying a splendid view of the twin volcanos, "Popo" and Ixtacihuatl. For a couple newly in love it was an idyllic setting, and the depth of their commitment was soon obvious to everyone except Sandy McNab, who kept apologizing to Lindbergh for having abandoned him to the company of the ladies.

Many years later Anne would vividly recall her father's reaction to the stunning news. "He's going to marry Anne! What do we know about this young man?"[9] Dwight Morrow had never met a man he con-sidered good enough for any of his daughters, but he was tickled by the prospect of having a national icon as a son-in-law and rather proud of his timid, bookish daughter's unexpected show of enterprise. "At least he's a nice clean boy," he told one amused friend.

Betty Morrow was not so easily reconciled. Anne, after all, was the child who seemed destined to fulfill her own thwarted dream of becom-ing a writer. And now she planned to attach herself to a man who in Betty's eyes was little more than a glorified mechanic. Not necessarily social snobs, the Morrows were intellectual snobs. Brains—defined as verbal agility, wit, attendance at the right schools, and familiarity with the right books, music, and paintings—meant everything to them. Meanwhile, Anne herself was having second thoughts about marrying a man who proudly told her that he knew a little about poetry himself. He was a great admirer of the works of Robert Service, and had memo-rized his ballad "The Cremation of Sam McGee" in its entirety. ("That just hurt terribly," she wrote.) Charles, moreover, did not get the point of *New Yorker* cartoons and his familiarity with the modern novel began and ended with Helen Hunt Jackson's bestseller *Ramona*. There were so many things she cared passionately about that were meaningless to him. How would they communicate? This was a valid question, but when her mother and even Constance expressed similar reservations Anne became all the more determined to go ahead with the marriage.

A professor of Anne's at Smith had often told her students, "Never marry a man to reform him." Anne was incapable of making such a banal mistake. On the contrary, she was marrying to reform herself. On one of their early dates, when Anne confessed that her ambition was to become a writer, Charles had exclaimed in amazement, "You want to *write!* I want to do the things other people write about!" No response could have impressed Anne more. Disturbed by her own passivity and tendency to depression, which she would later characterize as a sense of being "separated from life," she had decided that the antidote was marriage to a citizen of what she called "that world of action and non-introspection—that superb, objective, vigorous world of his and Elisabeth's."[10]

At the same time Anne could not detach herself from her parents' values. She did her best to draw Charles into the family's intellectual conversations and word games and was almost pathetically proud when he measured up. In the course of one game that consisted of matching famous people with foods, someone called out "Calvin Coolidge" and Charles instantly shot back "Grape Nuts!"—a riposte that Anne thought worthy of recording in a letter to Elisabeth. She laced her letters to Charles with quotations in French and classical Greek, which she then warned him not to ask anyone to translate.

Charles can hardly have failed to be aware of the family's thinly disguised condescension, and he responded by roistering around the embassy with a group of Mexican officers and playing inane practical jokes on Sandy McNab. At the dinner table he amused himself by tossing nuts into the air and catching them in his mouth. Meanwhile Frederick Hibbard and Alan Dawson, the embassy's second and third secretaries, gleefully mocked Lindbergh's attempts to contribute to conversations that were over his head and joked about his "one-track mind."

At times, however, Charles could be impressive. He took his prospective mother-in-law for a scenic flight over the twin volcanoes and earnestly assured her that aviation was not really so dangerous, especially when the pilot was as safety conscious as he was. Betty, resigned to the inevitable, told her daughter, "Well, at least you'll have the sky."[11]

Realizing that word of Lindy's romantic involvement would set off a media feeding frenzy, Charles and Anne wanted to be married as soon as possible. Betty and Dwight, perhaps hoping that Anne would change her mind, insisted on a waiting period. In the meantime the engagement would remain secret.

A few months later, Anne Morrow confided to her diary that Charles Lindbergh had dropped a "bomb" that exploded in the midst of her "college-bred, forever book-reading, introspective family."[12] In the context of Anne's published letters and diaries, this seems melodramatic to say the least. But if one considers certain events Anne chose to exclude from her account, the metaphor is more justifiable.

In mid-October, almost simultaneously with Anne's decision to marry Charles, Elisabeth fell ill with bronchial pneumonia. After a brief stay in a London nursing home, she boarded a ship for America, where a protective Jack Morgan shielded her from reporters who guessed she was returning home to marry Lindy. Elisabeth was hardly the jilted sweetheart some would later imagine her to be, but it was not easy to fend off questions about a nonexistent engagement at the very moment when her doctors were warning that her activities in the future might have to be sharply curtailed.

That same autumn Dwight junior was cutting a wide swath through Amherst where, early in the first semester of his freshman year, he distinguished himself by founding an Al Smith for President club. Learning of this development from an article in the newspapers, the ambassador, who happened to be one of the architects of Herbert Hoover's candidacy, was more bemused than angry. But though he managed to joke about the press coverage of the club's activities in his next letter to Dwight, Morrow was clearly alarmed.[13]

Fearful that he would never be able to equal his father's accomplishments, Dwight junior had often worried that he was destined to become the "forgotten Morrow." Anne's engagement to Charles Lindbergh was his worst nightmare come true, and he reacted by trying to attract as much attention to himself as possible. "Dwight Morrow was probably the brashest freshman in the history of Amherst," college chaplain Arthur Lee Kinsolving recalled many years later.[14]

Lindbergh exacerbated the competition, no doubt unwittingly, when he interrupted his Mexican sojourn to fly to St. Louis, where he cast his ballot in the presidential election, later informing the press that he had voted for Hoover. Apparently the endorsement of Hoover was Jerry Land's idea. Whoever thought of it, it was not a good one.

Though privately skeptical, to say the least, journalists had joined in the glorification of Lindy, portraying him as the universal American hero. Now it developed that this paragon was a Republican, and the working press, largely Democratic, felt that Lindbergh had violated his promise to refrain from exploiting his fame. Up to this point, few overtly hostile stories about Lindbergh had appeared in the press. That was soon to change.

In December Anne and her parents returned to Englewood for the holidays. After Anne's departure a month earlier, the last of the family's belongings had been removed from the Palisade Avenue house and transferred to the new Chester Aldrich mansion, which Betty Morrow had decided to call Next Day Hill. Mrs. Morrow had been looking forward to celebrating the move for months, and neither Elisabeth's illness nor Anne and Charles's desire to keep a low press profile could deter her from throwing herself a gala housewarming party. Invitations went out to 960 guests for New Year's Eve, inevitably reactivating rumors that Ambassador and Mrs. Morrow were about to announce their daughter's engagement to Colonel Lindbergh. There was still a good deal of confusion as to exactly which daughter was Lindbergh's sweetheart. The Associated Press correctly guessed Anne, but the photo it sent out over the wires was of Constance, leaving many readers with the impression that the Lone Eagle was dating a fifteen-year-old.

On the night of the party, several dozen photographers took up positions on the street leading to the house and the ambassador's private secretary Arthur Springer was forced to eject several reporters who had managed to cadge invitations from invited guests. The press stakeout of Next Day Hill became a permanent fixture, at least when the Morrows were in residence. The family eventually got the town of Englewood to pass an ordinance restricting photographers from approaching within eight hundred feet of their property; however, the Morrows' baronial life-style, far more conspicuous in Englewood than it had ever been in Manhattan, proved an irresistible magnet for the tabloids. One loyal servant, offered five thousand dollars to steal Anne's love letters, turned it down. Even so the newspapers appeared to be extremely well informed about the family's comings and goings. Unable to imagine that their trusted servants were selling tips to the press, the family suspected that their phone was tapped.

Less than one month into the new year, on January 28, 1929, Ambassador Morrow received an urgent summons from Amherst:

Dwight junior had suffered another breakdown. The details of this episode remain obscure, and Dwight's problems may or may not have been related to a mysterious fire that had broken out in the college's Morrow dormitory a few days earlier. At any rate Morrow took his son out of school and drove him by chauffeured limousine to a private hospital in Stockbridge. The sanatorium, known at the time as the Riggs Foundation for Psychopathic Diseases, catered to wealthy patients. Even so, Dwight junior did not live on the grounds. He stayed in an apartment in town, watched round the clock by private-duty nurses. Three weeks later another mysterious fire did twelve thousand dollars' worth of damage to the hospital's occupational therapy room, and Dwight was moved to a more secure facility, New York Hospital's Bloomingdale Center in Beacon, New York, where he remained for the better part of a year.

The Morrows worried that Dwight's illness would become public knowledge, destroying his chances for a successful career. In fact the press paid no attention, but this was a situation that seemed unlikely to last long. Frustrated over being denied photos of the world's most famous lovers, the newspapers were getting desperate. On February 12 the wire services picked up an item reporting that Evangeline Lindbergh, returning from Turkey on a Dollar Lines cruise ship, had become engaged to the captain. Mrs. Lindbergh had made friends on board with a lively young Southern belle named Jean Faircloth, later Mrs. Douglas MacArthur, and was having a fine time. She found the rumor about her engagement to the captain (who happened to be a married man) rather amusing. The Morrows, however, decided that enough was enough. That same afternoon, the ambassador summoned the press corps to his office in the Mexico City embassy and distributed copies of a press release announcing his daughter's engagement to Col. Charles A. Lindbergh.

Even as Morrow was enjoying being the one to tell the correspondents the news they had been waiting to hear for so long, Charles Lindbergh was flying from Belize, British Honduras, to Havana on the last leg of a highly publicized inauguration of Pan-American's new Caribbean airmail route. The tour, which had begun in Miami, where five thousand people showed up to cheer his takeoff in a Sikorsky S-36 amphibian, with former air-race celebrity Basil Rowe as copilot, took nine days to complete, including a detour to survey possible landing sites in British Honduras.[15]

Lindbergh's financial arrangement with Pan-Am was comparable to his TAT contract. He received ten thousand dollars a year (or, if Lindbergh's own memory on the subject was correct, twenty thousand) plus options on thirty thousand shares of stock—but he displayed an enthusiasm for his work for Pan-Am that was never quite evident in his dealings with the domestic airline. The charismatic and canny Juan Trippe was proving remarkably successful in winning government contracts for foreign airmail routes and in lobbying Congress (with Lindbergh's assistance) for favorable rates. For Lindbergh Pan-Am was less a moneymaking proposition than a tool for pursuing the cause to which he was devoted with an almost missionary zeal. "The thing that interests me now," he would tell Anne later that year, "is breaking up the prejudices between nations, linking them up through aviation."[16]

Anne was skeptical, and more than a little surprised to hear such an idea coming from the fiancé she still thought of as an unreflective man of action. She was even more taken aback when he confessed that he envied her talent for writing. If he were not a pilot, he would have liked to be an author, he said.

By the end of February Charles had joined Anne in Mexico, where the two of them avoided public appearances and photographers as if their life depended on it. Occasionally they escaped from the embassy and flew off in a borrowed Travel Air cabin plane to isolated mountain meadows for romantic picnics. One morning a mechanic at Valbuena Field who was asked to grease the Travel Air's axles neglected to tighten the bolts when he replaced the wheels. As Charles and Anne were taking off from their picnic spot in the hills, one of the loose wheels fell off. Charles circled Valbuena until the gas tanks were empty and showed Anne how to pack herself in seat cushions.

Below them on the airfield there was pandemonium. The ground personnel were afraid that Lindbergh did not realize he had dropped a wheel—an occurrence difficult to ignore in a plane as small as the Travel Air—and as he passed low over the hangars, he could see a man running around on the field holding a tire over his head. He brought the plane in for a two-point landing, on the left wheel and tail skid, but at the last minute the landing gear grazed the ground, causing the light craft to flip over. Anne was unhurt. Charles's right shoulder—which he had dislocated when bailing out over Lambert Field—had popped out of its socket. News photographers on the scene complained bitterly that Mexican soldiers, on Lindbergh's orders, confiscated cameras and destroyed their exposed film. Years later Lindbergh said he couldn't remember whether he had told the soldiers to do this or not. He was powerfully annoyed, however, when the newspapers described the mishap as a "crash"—a dreaded word that all air-minded people agreed was bad for aviation.

Constance, now an honors student at Milton Academy, was so far the only member of the family apparently unaffected by the glare of publicity. That changed dramatically on April 24, when she picked up her mail at her dormitory and found herself reading an anonymous letter, written with a pencil in crude block letters:

> You read this and keep your mouth closed.... Don't open your trap to a living soul.... The smith girl received a letter just the same as this she told her friends at school. And her Father had her under guard But you see how she Dropped out of the Picture. just so will you if you talk to anyone about this note.

The letter, which also mentioned Alice Corbett, ordered Constance to ask her father for a fifty-thousand-dollar extortion payment: "Tell him to have Morgan Co. send you the cash in $5–10–20–50 100 500–1000 Bills," it specified.[17]

Headmaster W. L. Field brought in Burns Agency security guards just to be on the safe side, but neither he nor Ambassador Morrow took the threat seriously. On May 13, however, a second letter arrived giving detailed instructions for delivery of the money. Constance was to travel by bus to Westwood, Massachusetts, and throw a suitcase containing the fifty thousand dollars over the wall of a Catholic cemetery adjacent to the estate of Gen. Clarence Edwards. Burns detectives rented an apartment across from the drop location, and on the appointed day a policewoman who bore a remarkable resemblance to Constance Morrow delivered a suitcase stuffed with dummy bills.

For forty-eight hours the suitcase lay untouched, and the police concluded that the extortionist had been stalking Constance and was not fooled by the decoy. Seriously concerned now, the Burns Agency recommended to Gen. Jay Morrow, who was handling the situation in his brother's absence, that Constance be packed off to the family's summer home on North Haven. The island estate was reachable only by car ferry, and the agency could provide absolute security there. General

Morrow, recently retired from his duties as commander of U.S. army forces in the Panama Canal Zone, was not in the best of health and highly excitable. Somewhat carried away by the responsibility of protecting his niece, he gave his assent to an elaborate security operation. The following morning all three Morrow sisters were driven to a small Connecticut airfield, where Colonel Lindbergh was waiting in a borrowed Sikorsky amphibian to fly them to North Haven.

Unfortunately it happened that aviation correspondents from all over the country were gathered that day at Old Orchard Beach, Maine, to cover the possible arrival of a transatlantic flight. Tipped off by an airport employee that Lindbergh and his fiancée's family were due in Portland for refueling, the correspondents leapt to the conclusion that the party was on its way to North Haven for a secret wedding. Hopping into their cars, they sped to the Portland airfield, where a volunteer approached the plane to ask Lindbergh if he and his passengers would come out to pose for a few pictures. Lindbergh's language in rejecting the request would later be described by one member of the group as "blunt."

Having no idea that they had just spoiled an elaborately planned clandestine operation, the reporters were irate. Minutes later the Sikorsky, now heavily loaded with fuel, taxied across the wet field and promptly got bogged down in the mud. Morris Markey recounted what happened next in his New Yorker profile of Lindbergh:

> There were no attendants on the field, and the twenty newspapermen stood close by and jeered while Lindbergh struggled with the mess alone. They refused, by unanimous accord, to give him the moment's help, the shove out of the mud and the turn of the engine crank, that would have solved his difficulties. It was an hour before he could get away.[18]

Even if the Sikorsky had not been spotted, the descent of several dozen Burns security guards could hardly go unnoticed in peaceful Rockland, Maine. Like the reporters in Portland, the town interpreted the guards' arrival as evidence that Lindy and Anne were about to be married at the Morrow summer house. The press and curiosity seekers converged on the village, but instead of a wedding they witnessed a two-day manhunt for a suspicious stranger who had been spotted on the island. When finally captured in the woods near the Morrow cottage, the interloper proved to be a Mexican citizen named Robert Tondero, who told police that he had only wanted to show Lindbergh the plans for an invention that would prevent airplane crashes. The sheriff of Knox County, irate over Burns operatives who were interrogating locals and issuing orders to his deputies, complained that this apparently harmless eccentric was the first person arrested on North Haven in two hundred years.

The following day, May 22, the *Boston Post* broke the story of the threats on Constance Morrow's life. The *Post* quoted Chief Driscoll of the Westwood police as saying that the notes were similar to a score of others received by well-to-do Bostonians and a few nationally prominent individuals, including Mrs. Douglas Walsh, the mother of millionaire socialite Evalyn Walsh McLean. Driscoll also said the police had identified the writer of the notes and would be making an arrest any day. The suspect Driscoll had in mind was George Long, a former army codes specialist who worked as a private secretary to Gen. Clarence Edwards. Long, who came under suspicion because he had a previous conviction for mail fraud, was brought in for questioning, but according to Edward Dean Sullivan, who reported on the case in his book, *The Snatch Racket,* he was able to offer conclusive evidence that he had nothing to do with the letters. Neither Long nor anyone else was ever formally charged.[19]

Charles and Anne had indeed hoped to be married quietly at Deacon Brown's Point in June. Charles had purchased a thirty-eight-foot Elko motorboat, the *Mouette,* and after the ceremony he and Anne were looking forward to spending a quiet honeymoon cruising the Maine coast. Since the flap over Tondero's arrest had spoiled their plans, they decided to move the wedding date forward. On Sunday May 26 Betty Morrow, who never allowed family crises to interfere with her social calendar, held an afternoon reception for 260 guests at Next Day Hill to celebrate Alice Morrow's recent return from Turkey. Among those present was Evangeline Lindbergh. The following morning Betty called two dozen old friends of the family and suggested that they come over for a few hands of bridge. When the guests arrived they noticed that Dr. William A. Brown of the Union Theological Seminary, whose recently deceased daughter had been a classmate of Anne's at Miss Chapin's, was stationed in the living room. Betty Morrow circulated among the tables, whispering, "When Dr. Brown stands up, please draw close." Dr. Brown stood and the dining room doors were flung open, revealing Anne in a traditional white chiffon wedding gown, her proud father at her side.

Anne's dress had been run up by a family seamstress. Her bouquet consisted of flowers picked by Elisabeth on the grounds of the estate. There was no best man, and except for Evangeline, none of the groom's family or friends were present. Minutes after cutting the wedding cake, Anne and Charles escaped from the house, hunkered down in the back-seat of a guest's car. Henry Breckinridge was waiting with Charles's Franklin on a side street, and the newlyweds drove immediately to his yachting club on Long Island where the *Mouette,* which neither Charles nor Anne had yet seen, was waiting, lights ablaze. Meanwhile, tall, skinny Randy Enslow, Lindbergh's old barnstorming buddy from St. Louis, had agreed to act as a decoy. Dressed to enhance his resemblance to Slim, Enslow took off from Teterboro Airport in Lindbergh's Curtiss Falcon sport plane, with a planeload of newspaper reporters in hot pursuit.

These honeymoon-getaway plans—romantic, complicated, and, of course, doomed to failure—would unfortunately become the paradigm for Charles and Anne's efforts to avoid publicity. If the couple really wanted a few days of privacy, important people all over the world would have been happy to put their estates at their disposal. Moreover ,it seemed not to have occurred to Charles and Anne that a brand new thirty-eight-foot motor launch is not exactly inconspicuous. When the *Mouette* docked at a marina for supplies and fuel, Anne hid in the cabin while Charles, who had given up shaving to make himself less recognizable, handled the errands. His stubbly beard can hardly have fooled anyone—one old salt even joked with a friend in his presence, "Hey, this guy told me that he's Lindbergh!"—but for nearly a week, the *Mouette* did manage to stay one jump ahead of the newspaper search parties.

This was long enough for Anne to discover that her new husband was a quite competent cook, capable of whipping up three-course meals in the tiny galley, as well as meticulously neat. After Anne, whose concept of domesticity consisted of giving orders to the executive housekeeper, spent the better part of a day helping him swab the decks and reorganize the galley, she tried to convince herself that it had all been an interesting experience.

On June 6, as the *Mouette* cruised into York Harbor, Maine, it was buzzed by a press plane with a photographer hanging out the window. Minutes after Charles dropped anchor, a boat approached, and a second photographer using a bullhorn called out a request for the newlyweds to come on deck and pose. Charles, who was "pretty annoyed," made up his mind that he wasn't going to give the man the satisfaction of a picture. For eight hours he and Anne hid out belowdecks while the press boat circled. When it became clear that the photographer intended to wait them out, Charles gunned the engine and the *Mouette* lurched by fits and starts toward the mouth of the harbor, dragging its anchor behind it.

TWELVE

"Our First Romancers of the Air"

*I*N JULY 1929 MEMBERS OF A CARNEGIE INSTITUTION archaeological dig, marooned in Arizona's Canyon del Muerto by a flash flood, were surprised to see a small airplane circling their camp. The plane disappeared from view and minutes later two figures, a tall, skinny man and a small woman wearing knee-high boots, came clambering down the steep trail from the canyon rim to the campsite.

"How are you fixed for grub?" the tall man asked as he approached the bivouac. "Er ... excuse me. This is Mrs. Lindbergh. It's for her."

The Lindberghs explained that they had spotted an abandoned cliff dwelling in an adjacent canyon and decided to drop in on the camp, hoping to organize an impromptu expedition. The next day, accompanied by the archaeologists and several Navaho guides they hiked to the Canyon de Chelly and located the site, whose lower rooms contained shards of prehistoric pottery. Anne decided to explore one of the upper chambers. Shinnying through a narrow opening, she landed on her knees and found herself nose to nose with a skeleton. The guides assured her that there was nothing to be alarmed about; the bones were not genuine Anasazi remains but "quite recent," so no harm had been done.[1]

The Lindberghs' pioneering ventures in aerial archaeology were just one example of the adventures that were quickly establishing them as America's premier flying couple—"our first romancers of the air" as one *Vanity Fair* profile put it. Under her husband's rigorous tutelage, Anne had become a very competent pilot. She, in turn, had brought to the marriage a lively interest in geology, archaeology, and primitive cultures. The Morrows were active patrons of New York City's Museum of Natural History and of the Carnegie Institution, and during the summer of 1929, Charles and Anne took time off from their survey work for TAT to visit the digs of Dr. and Mrs. Earl Morris, Dr. Alfred E. Kidder, and other Carnegie scientists who were working in the Southwest. Charles, an enthusiastic amateur photographer, was fascinated by the possibility that it might be possible to map archaeological sites from the air. While Anne flew in circles over the digs, he would lean out the window snapping pictures.

In September the Lindberghs were in the Caribbean, touring Pan-Am's mail routes with Juan Trippe and his wife, the former Betty Stettinius, who was, like Anne, the daughter of a onetime Morgan banker. After the tour they joined Carnegie staffers Dr. Oliver Ricketson and Dr. Kidder in making an aerial survey of Mayan sites in Guatemala, Campeche, and Quintana Roo. Flying a Pan-American S-38 twin-engine amphibian out of Belize City, the expedition flew over Tikal, Uaxactún, Rio Bec, Chichén Itzá, and Tulum, searching for unexcavated temples and ceremonial sites. Many such sites were known to exist, but since they were covered with heavy jungle vegetation, finding and evaluating them could be a major undertaking. By airplane Kidder and Ricketson could accomplish within a few hours what would have taken weeks, even months, of slashing their way through the jungle. Not only were vine-shrouded pyramids visible as bumps on the horizon, but, Kidder and Ricketson noted, changes in the character of the vegetation clearly marked the locations of the natural limestone reservoirs known as cenotes, abandoned maize fields, overgrown stelae, and stone walls.

Camping on the beach near Tulum on the coast of Quintana Roo, Lindbergh found that his fame had penetrated even this remote part of the hemisphere. The locals were mainly *chicleros,* who made their living by gathering sap from the *zapote* tree, which is used in the manufacture of chewing gum. Two of them were working in the area and came down to the beach to introduce themselves, and one was soon overheard reproaching his companion for not knowing who "el Coronel Lindbergh" was—"He is the man who flew around the world in a single day!"

The Carnegie scientists saw aerial archaeology as an interesting possibility for the future, but it did not seem to occur to them that this might be anything but a diversion for the Lindberghs. Much to Anne's dismay, one of them naively enthused that the main value of the Belize expedition lay in "having the name Lindbergh associated with archaeology."[2]

Even this advantage became problematic after magazine writer William Van Dusen published a colorful but highly inaccurate two-part article in the *Saturday Evening Post* about the Lindberghs' Central American expedition. Van Dusen misplaced Tulum, describing it as being on the shore of large lake, and erroneously credited the Lindberghs with discovering a Mayan city. (Lindbergh speculated that Van Dusen had misunderstood a conversation between him and Dr. Ricketson about Tikal, a site that had been discovered and partially excavated long before the Lindberghs set eyes on it.) The *Saturday Evening Post* articles were a lighted match dropped into the tinderbox of academic rivalries. Several experts in Mayan studies wrote to the *New York Times* in protest, and one published a journal article exposing what he interpreted as scientific fraud, an attempt by the Lindberghs and Ricketson to claim credit for the work of others. Charles had not approved the contents of the Van Dusen article and was quite stung to discover that he had become persona non grata in the field of archaeology.

So much was happening in the Lindberghs' lives in the year and a half following the wedding, however, that there was little time to brood over this disappointing turn of events. During this period Charles and Anne made eight transcontinental survey flights for TAT (in addition to flights Charles made on his own), inspecting the airline's new facilities in places like Waynoka, Oklahoma, a sleepy western town that, to Anne, seemed as exotic as any Mayan ruin. Between trips to L.A. in the summer of 1929, they managed to find time to spend a week at the National Air Races in Cleveland, where Charles stunted with the navy's High Hat squadron; the better part of a week with President and Mrs. Hoover at their summer retreat (later Camp David) in Rapidan, Maryland; and a few days as guests of Charles Edison, son of the inventor, who had invited Lindbergh to be a judge of a high school essay contest.[3]

Anne, who had been reclusive even in college, was totally unprepared for the pressures of her new role. She had little experience of—and frankly not much interest in—people who were not physically attractive, well educated, and articulate, and now she was meeting the hoi polloi under circumstances that would have tried anyone's patience. Few individuals are at their best when meeting the very famous: Bores become positively boorish; the shy babble inanities. Like many celebrities, Charles had developed the ability to let importunate fans talk at him, and if matters got out of control he felt no compunctions about being rude. Anne, on the other hand, focused her full attention on everyone, was unfailingly charming, and finished each day exhausted and out of patience. Warned by her husband that even private conversations might be overheard and letters stolen, she practiced constant self-censorship. She gave up keeping her diary out of fear that it might fall into the hands of reporters. "I have to keep so reserved and taut and on edge for pitfalls," she wrote her sister Constance less than two months after the wedding.[4]

Charles, still attempting to gain a foothold in the world of science, somehow found time in his crowded schedule to promote a plan for a research program in rocketry. In 1929 designers like Igor Sikorsky still faced resistance from physicists who claimed that heavier-than-air craft had already reached their theoretical size limitations. Having disposed of this argument in his own mind, Lindbergh was already looking ahead, his imagination captivated by the possibility of building a rocket that could reach the moon. In the fall of 1929 he made a presentation on the subject to a group of engineers and executives at the Delaware headquarters of the DuPont corporation. Realizing that DuPont was unlikely to invest in his vision of exploring outer space, he tried to persuade the engineers that the principles of rocketry might have nearer-term applications. Perhaps, he suggested, a rocket might be attached to a plane "for the purpose of giving it one minute of thrust in case of engine failure on take-off."[5]

The engineers turned down the proposal with a curt letter, informing him that using rockets in connection with airplanes was a technological impossibility.

Not three weeks later, Carol Guggenheim showed her husband and Lindbergh a newspaper item about a man named Robert Goddard in Massachusetts who had tested a liquid-propelled "moon rocket." (Although neither Lindbergh nor Harry Guggenheim knew it at the time, Goddard had applied for a Guggenheim Fund grant, only to be turned down by Jerry Land, who wrote the rocket enthusiast off as just another nut.) In November Lindbergh visited Goddard at his farm near Clark University. Mrs. Goddard would later recall that he arrived with his arm in a sling, and when she wondered if he had been injured in an airplane crash, he told her rather sheepishly that he had dislocated his trick shoulder while trying to retrieve a puppy that was hiding under his bed. That evening Lindbergh and Goddard sat on the porch, facing the cow pasture where Goddard tested his rockets, and discussed the possibility of reaching the moon. "It might cost a million dollars," Goddard said. This was so outrageous that they both had a good laugh.

Lindbergh arranged for Goddard to meet with the DuPont engineers, who remained unimpressed by the potential of jet propulsion. He had more success in persuading the Carnegie Institution to give Goddard a five-thousand-dollar grant, and in early 1930, he approached Daniel Guggenheim, Harry's father, who agreed to underwrite Goddard's research for four years at twenty-five thousand dollars a year. This money enabled Goddard to move to Roswell, New Mexico, where he eventually succeeded in launching a rocket nine thousand miles into space. Lindbergh was still lobbying the *National Geographic* and the navy on Goddard's behalf as late as 1939. His own proposal, however, was quickly forgotten.

The people the Lindberghs were meeting in connection with their public relations work for TAT belonged to a different universe from scientists like Goddard, Ricketson, and Kidder. Movie stars were among the obvious potential customers for TAT's coast-to-coast service, and Charles and Anne did their part to drum up enthusiasm by visiting Hollywood as the guests of Douglas Fairbanks and Mary Pickford. Hollywood's favorite couple called their mansion in the hills Pickfair, prompting Charles and Anne to giddy speculation that when they had a home of their own they might name it Lindmor, Charlanne, or, perhaps—Charles's suggestion—Spengustus.

After numerous delays TAT carried its first paying passengers on July 7, 1929. Mary Pickford christened the Ford Tri-motor *City of Columbus* before its departure on the airline's maiden west-to-east flight by breaking a bottle of ginger ale over the metal hull—champagne was forbidden because of Prohibition. Charles then took the controls to fly the ship as far as Winslow, Arizona. Anne was riding in the passenger section along with Will Rogers and a number of aviation correspondents. In Arizona the Lindberghs left the plane to await the arrival of the first east–west flight, which Charles then flew back to Los Angeles. On this leg of the journey, Anne met Amelia Earhart, also a TAT consultant, with the title of "Assistant Traffic Manager."

TAT's publicity releases promised "an indescribable experience, complete, luxurious relaxation." In a letter to Constance, Anne loyally sang the praises of the plane's amenities, including seat cushions upholstered in green leather, curtains over the windows, and little aluminum tables the uniformed attendant handed out to passengers who wished to pass the time writing letters. At mealtime the same tables were covered with lavender linen tablecloths, and the attendant served tongue sandwiches and pineapple salad. Tactfully—or rather, on guard against the possibility that her comments might fall into the wrong hands—Anne omitted mention of the drawbacks of flying in a Tin Goose: In the unventilated, unpressurized cabin, passengers sweltered on the ground, then gasped for air when the ship climbed above ten thousand feet to cross the mountains. The ride was so rough that according to TAT's own statistics, 75 percent of all its passengers became airsick. Among the casualties on the east–west inaugural flight was Amelia Earhart, who hid behind a curtain to avoid being seen in the throes of uncontrollable nausea.

Earhart was in the habit of staying with Jack and Helen Maddux when TAT business brought her to the West Coast, and on several occasions the Lindberghs were her fellow houseguests. By no means the most accomplished female pilot of her day, Earhart had been plucked from obscurity by George Palmer Putnam, who was impressed by her striking resemblance to the hero of 1927 and promoted her as "Lady Lindy." Knowing how strongly Lindbergh felt about the exploitation of his name, Earhart was a little nervous about meeting him. But when the Madduxes organized an outing to a nearby Chinese restaurant, Earhart confided to Anne and Charles that she had just overheard two middle-aged ladies discussing her appearance in unflattering terms. One of the women, Earhart reported, closed the conversation by observing, "And she does look like Lindbergh, poor thing." Charles roared with laughter and later pronounced Earhart "a grand girl." Anne thought her "just as tremendous" as her own husband, and very much like him in many ways.

Earhart's feelings about the Lindberghs were mixed. A devoted feminist, Earhart saw her career as blazing a path for other women to follow. Much to her disappointment, Anne disclaimed any interest in serving as a role model, insisting that she was not a "modern career woman," just the "wife of a modern man."[6]

Anne, Earhart noted, was interested in feminist ideas. At a later meeting they shared their enthusiasm for Virginia Woolf's *A Room of One's Own,* which Betty Morrow tellingly called "the most important book published in America since *Uncle Tom's Cabin.*" But in Earhart's opinion Anne had far to go when it came to putting feminism into practice. Charles, she observed, made all the decisions for both of them, including telling his wife how to pack their suitcases.

Moreover, he expected to monopolize Anne's attention. One evening, when she and Earhart were having a discussion at the Madduxes' kitchen table, Charles stood behind his wife, attempting to distract her by dribbling water from his glass onto her silk dress. Earhart was delighted when Anne suddenly turned around and flung the contents of her glass of buttermilk in his face. But Colonel Lindbergh, she noted somewhat grudgingly, was a good sport and seemed rather proud of Anne's spunk.[7]

One evening during the same visit, when nine-year-old Jack Maddux, Jr., came downstairs in his pajamas to say good-night to the houseguests, Charles asked the boy if he would like to win a quarter. Jack junior said he sure would. Folding a piece of paper into a cone, Charles fastened it inside the elastic at the front of the boy's pajama bottoms, gave him the quarter, and challenged him to close his eyes, throw the quarter into the air, and catch it in the cone. Jack shut his eyes tight, but before he could toss the coin, Charles grabbed a glass of ice water and poured it into the cone. The child shrieked in surprise and mortification. Lindbergh appeared completely bewildered by this reaction. Earhart was appalled.

Needless to say, Charles's memory of this visit was somewhat different. According to him, Earhart was quite a prankster herself. She carried a small container filled with dried beetles and would challenge new acquaintances to taste them, claiming they were the secret ingredient in soy sauce. Amelia could be very persuasive, he recalled.

Earhart's impressions of the Lindberghs' marriage, echoed by many others who knew the couple over the years, require some qualification. The son of a mother who was not only a well-trained scientist but a fearless flyer, the young Charles Lindbergh had advanced ideas about women's place in society. Early in the marriage he persuaded Anne to bob her hair, shorten her skirts, and wear less matronly clothes. More important, he was enormously proud of her writing talent and would have been quite happy to support her in a solo flying career. Unfortunately Charles was also used to having his own way in everything. Happy to have a wife who was also his sidekick and flying partner, he rarely seemed to consider that Anne might have wishes and goals of her own that would require some compromises on his part.

It must also be said that Anne herself did not seem to consider her own needs.

After their first, romantic flying dates, Anne had discovered that learning to fly with the great Lindbergh as an instructor was more of an ordeal than she had anticipated. Charles was so worried about Anne's safety that he had purchased a special Bird training plane, said to be so safe it could land in a tree. But he was also a demanding teacher. During their lessons at the Long Island Aviation Club, he urged her on to practice landings and takeoffs for hours at a stretch. Tougher psychologically than she looked, Anne was also too proud and self-controlled to quit or to respond to her husband's sometimes withering criticisms in kind.

And this was just the beginning. Anne had set herself the goal of sharing her husband's activities, but she was far from a born adventurer and had married a man who was constantly seeking the extra element of physical risk. Deeply in love and enthralled with the novelty of her new life despite the annoyances of the press and a too-heavy schedule, at times even she couldn't be sure whether she was having fun or not.

On a visit to San Diego in January 1930, Charles tried out a glider designed by Hawley Bowlus, who had been the factory manager at Ryan during the construction of the *Spirit of St. Louis*. Charles was so enthusiastic that in March he and Anne joined Bowlus for a week of gliding off the Monterey cliffs. Anne's first effort at flying the glider was not very successful, however, so Lindbergh and Bowlus hatched a plan. Instead of pulling the sailplane behind a truck until it attained airspeed—the usual method for training novices—they decided to launch it off the summit of Mount Soledad, where ascending air currents would make for a more exciting ride. Strapped into the sailplane as six helpers tugging on ropes prepared to propel her over the side of the mountain, it occurred to Anne that she felt very much like the victim in some primitive sacrificial rite. Once launched, the flight was wonderful, but Anne was content just to get safely back to earth and made no attempt to ride the currents. Although she became the first woman in the United States to earn a glider pilot's license, sailplaning was a thrill she was pleased to have safely behind her.

After TAT's passenger operations got under way in July 1929, the Lindberghs expected to spend somewhat less of their time on airline business. Unfortunately it did not work out that way. Despite all the reassuring publicity, flying over the mountains at low altitudes was still a hazardous operation. So many flights were canceled due to bad weather that pilots joked that the airline's initials stood for "Take a Train." Even so TAT lost its first plane on September 4, after less than three full months in business. Charles and Anne, who were planning to leave for the

Caribbean in two weeks, flew out to New Mexico to take part in the search. After five days the wreckage of the Tri-motor was discovered on a mountainside in the Sierras. All aboard had perished. TAT tried to compensate for the bad publicity by offering hot meals and Fox-Movietone newsreels in flight, but to little effect. A second TAT Tri-motor went down over Pleasanton, California, in January 1930, killing sixteen. These two accidents, combined with another crash—the one on Wall Street in October 1929—left the company on the brink of bankruptcy.

In a letter to her mother, Anne acknowledged that the search for the missing TAT plane brought back horrible memories of the Frances Smith affair. Flying in bad weather set her nerves on edge; nevertheless she and Charles were looking forward to surveying a Great Circle route across Alaska and the Bering Strait to Tokyo as the first leg of an ambitious round-the-world flight.

On the day of her wedding, Anne wrote that she pictured herself striding forward into the future between Charles and her mother, holding hands with both of them. Anyone with more experience of marriage than she had at that moment would have recognized that this was unlikely to be a very comfortable position.

From the beginning there were in-law troubles.

For the ambitious, work-ethic-oriented Morrows, perhaps the greatest shock was the realization that Lindbergh, with his choice of attractive career options, had no intention of taking a full-time job. Moreover, while far from a spendthrift in most areas, Charles had celebrated his engagement by ordering the *Mouette*. Next he purchased the little Bird biplane to give Anne flying lessons. Still another plane, more advanced and also more expensive, would be necessary for his and Anne's planned survey of the Great Circle route to Asia. After meeting Lockheed engineer Jerry Vultee at the Cleveland Air Races, Charles ordered a custom-designed, low-wing monoplane that was to cost him $17,825 on delivery. And this was just the beginning of the expenses the Arctic venture would entail.

As the result of her marriage, Anne had come into control of her trust fund, and in mid-September, three and a half months after the wedding, Ambassador Morrow instructed his personal attorney Charles Fay to draw up a new will for his daughter to sign. Fay's draft is not among Morrow's papers, but it apparently stipulated that if Anne died childless, her fortune would be equally divided among her widower and her three siblings. If she left surviving offspring, the money would go into a professionally administered trust for their benefit. The Morrows had set up their children's trusts partly for tax reasons, and their assumption that the money should remain in the family in the event of Anne's premature death was not unusual. Nevertheless the implication was there to be drawn that Charles might get his wife killed in a flying accident while he survived to live off her fortune. Worse, in the event that children were involved, the Morrows, through their trustees, would control the inheritance and thus, for all practical purposes, the children's education and upbringing.

The details of the will were already worked out by the time the ambassador raised the subject with his daughter and son-in-law. To his surprise, Colonel Lindbergh objected.

Charles's reaction can be better understood if one recalls that the ambassador was not only his father-in-law but the generous and much-admired mentor who had only recently urged him to pass up the chance to become wealthy in his own right through endorsements and personal appearances. Morrow and his friends had assured Lindbergh at the time that if he did what was right for aviation his future would be taken care of. Characteristically, Charles took these promises at face value. Now the cold print of the draft will made it all too clear that he was something less than a surrogate son. Lindbergh brought the conference to an abrupt end by announcing that rather than have his wife sign such a document he would just as soon she gave the money back.[8]

To keep the peace, this is exactly what Anne did.

Needless to say, renouncing her fortune did not make Anne more independent of her parents. Dwight and Betty promptly established a new trust in her name with the survivorship provisions they had wanted all along. The chief difference was that Anne no longer controlled the principal of her own money.

This incident notwithstanding, Charles thought Dwight Morrow a great man and spent far more time playing the role of the agreeable son-in-law than most men in his situation would have found bearable. Although the Lindberghs kept a suite at the Berkshire Hotel in Manhattan, Anne was still very much attached to her family, and the couple were often in Englewood, where Charles did his best to adapt to what the family insisted on calling "the Morrow way."

For people who talked often about their preference for the simple life and reminisced nostalgically about the good old days before they became rich, Dwight and Betty Morrow had managed to surround themselves with the best of everything. They now had four homes—Next Day

Hill, the Seventieth Street co-op in Manhattan, their architect-designed cottage at Deacon Brown's Point in Maine, and Casa Mañana in Cuernavaca. Meals at Next Day Hill, heavy on lobster, avocados, and richly sauced dishes, were served by uniformed waitresses; Charles preferred simple food and liked to smother his scrambled eggs in ketchup. The Morrow way of traveling, even on relatively brief trips, invariably involved mountains of luggage, as well as golf clubs and trunks full of books and papers, and, on occasion, one or more servants and their luggage. Anne, headed to Mexico for a brief stay with her parents before her marriage, had taken with her, among other items, her phonograph and a collection of records. Indeed, considering the amount of gear the family hauled around as a matter of course, Amelia Earhart was perhaps too hasty in condemning Charles for trying to limit his wife's luggage.

While the Morrows were avid accumulators, Charles, who had lived most of his life in boardinghouses and toured the country with nothing but a blanket roll, felt in danger of being engulfed by a rising tide of unwanted possessions. He was happy to be able to sign over the huge accumulation of gifts he received after the transatlantic flight to the Missouri Historical Society, keeping only the few items he really wanted, including the Franklin touring car and the Ryan Brougham. In St. Louis the Lindbergh collection was placed under the guardianship of a curator named Miss Beauregard, who was given to announcing to visitors, her eyes fixed heavenward, "I have fuh-*lown* with Col. Lindbergh." Miss Beauregard did an admirable job of maintaining the collection, but her hero worship was so embarrassing to Charles that he avoided visiting the society's headquarters.

No such relief was at hand from the hundreds upon hundreds of wedding presents he and Anne received—many from total strangers, but quite a few from Morrow connections whose feelings had to be considered. Orderly almost to the point of compulsion, Charles evolved what he called his "brown paper system." Purchasing an enormous roll of wrapping paper, he energetically packed up articles unlikely to be used in the immediate future into neatly labeled parcels. This activity was a little disconcerting to the Morrow servants, who earned their wages taking care of the family's superfluous things.

Even more eccentric from the Morrow point of view was Lindbergh's cavalier handling of his mail, which ran to almost a million letters a year. Much of the mail was junk—after the Caribbean tour, Western Union had offered customers a choice of eight standard congratulatory messages—and rather than pay secretaries to open sacks of form telegrams, Charles simply had them burned. The probability that there might be personal messages from important people mixed in with the others did not bother him in the slightest, though it certainly did his in-laws.

While Charles was often easygoing and eager to please, he had inherited his mother's moodiness. Highly punctual and well organized, he was none too patient with those who were not, and punctuality and efficiency were unfortunately not among the Morrow virtues. Moreover, he had a temper. Although there is no evidence that he was ever violent, to be in the presence of an angry Charles Lindbergh could be a memorable experience. (An acquaintance of later years, asked to describe how Lindbergh behaved when upset, was momentarily at a loss for words. "Well," he said at last, "he suddenly became *very large*.")

When the moment passed, these outbursts were forgotten, at least by Lindbergh. But among the Morrow family unpleasant emotions were scarcely acknowledged, much less openly displayed. The only one of the in-laws who was completely unintimidated was Constance, who teased Charles by calling him Lindy (a nickname he despised) and laughed at the disguises he and Anne had taken to wearing to avoid being recognized.

Eluding the press was a private game that the Lindberghs played in deadly earnest. As much as he craved anonymity for himself, Charles was far more upset when the press harassed his wife. Anne was having a tough time adjusting and complained that she often felt like an escaped criminal, but the knowledge that her husband viewed every item in the press or candid photo as a personal defeat can hardly have helped her to relax.

This attractive young couple, who could easily have been the toast of New York, lived as virtual hermits. Shortly after the flight, Charles had attended a performance of Will Rogers's one-man show, and when he was spotted in the audience there was so much commotion that Rogers had to interrupt his act and could not resume until Charles left the theater. After one or two more such experiences, Charles gave up going to shows altogether. Restaurants were equally out of the question. Before the meal was over, he and Anne were sure to be spotted by a fellow diner who would lurch toward the table with the inevitable opener: "Colonel, I just want to shake your hand." This apparently innocuous remark opened the floodgates. Soon other diners would be standing in line for chitchat and autographs. On more than one occasion, the line stretched out the restaurant door and a crowd gathered in the street. A dinner party at the home of George Palmer Putnam and Amelia Earhart, attended by big-game hunter Roy Chapman Andrews and balloonist Auguste Piccard, was amusing, but the next day Charles and Anne felt betrayed to see an account of their dinner-table conversation in the newspaper, sold to the press by one of their fellow guests.

When they were in residence at the Berkshire, Charles and Anne would don disguises—often a cap and eyeglass frames with no lenses for him, a scarf and heavy makeup for her—and sneak out to a movie or for a stroll in Central Park. Even if they were not approached, they had come to dread the flash of recognition that would occasionally light up the eyes of a passing stranger. The problem with being so famous, Anne observed years later, is that life loses all its spontaneity. Like Medusa, one has the unwanted power to turn other human beings to stone.

Although it is easy to dismiss this reaction as oversensitive and even hysterical, acquaintances who spent time with the Lindberghs discovered that they, too, became sensitized to that look of recognition, which could so easily set in motion a chain reaction of events that were inconvenient, annoying, and occasionally frightening in their unpredictability. Donald Keyhoe was driving with Charles in Lower Manhattan near the entrance to the Holland Tunnel one day in 1931 when the motorist in the next car glanced their way and recognized Colonel Lindbergh. At the next red light, the man abandoned his car to ask for an autograph. This drew the attention of other drivers and brought traffic to a halt. Two policemen promptly arrived on the scene but showed no interest in unsnarling the traffic. What they wanted was a ride uptown so they could tell their buddies at the precinct house that they had hitched a ride with Lindy. Charles happened to be headed in the opposite direction and had a full day's work waiting at his office, but since the New York police had always been helpful to him, he did not feel able to refuse. The officers climbed into the car, and the four men drove off, leaving a morass of traffic, and no doubt some powerfully irate drivers, behind them.

Friends, family, and sympathetic newspapermen repeatedly warned Charles and Anne that if they would just give in, grant a reasonable number of interviews, and get used to being fussed over, they would have fewer problems in the long run. By cloaking activities in an aura of mystery they only made themselves more tempting targets. Charles didn't agree. He and Anne had noticed there was a direct correlation between the appearance of a photo of themselves in the newspapers and the reactions of strangers on the street. In fact, they were much more likely to be recognized if they were wearing the same clothes they had been photographed in, and it irked Anne to have to give up wearing some of her favorite dresses because they had been pictured in the papers. Charles was convinced that if they refused to give in to the demand that they make their lives public property, the press and the merely curious would eventually lose interest. At times, however, it was hard to imagine that that day would ever come. On a TAT cross-country tour, the commotion at their hotels was so great that Charles sarcastically suggested to Anne that they ought to walk through the lobby naked: No one could possibly stare any more, and some people might even be embarrassed into letting them alone.

The Morrows, too, had become quarry. Tabloids like the *Daily News* and the *Post* still assigned photographers to stake out the estate and snap pictures of arriving guests. Hosting a party for Republican party workers, the Morrows were forced to give out the name of the ambassador's nephew and political manager as a password; only guests who used the phrase "Dick Scandrett sent me," were admitted. On another occasion a car full of joyriders drove past the watchman at the gate and sped around the oval driveway, striking and killing Daffin, the white terrier who had been Anne and Con's favorite pet. Charles must have felt responsible for causing all this trouble—it certainly seems that the Morrows thought he was. On the other hand it was obvious that the press would long ago have lost interest in Lindy if he had married a doctor's daughter from St. Louis or Detroit. The quickest way to obtain peace for all concerned, it seemed, was for him and Anne to establish a home of their own, away from Englewood.

Anne wanted a home as much as Charles did, but the thought of breaking her ties to her family was wrenching. She had turned her whole life upside down to marry Lindbergh—learned to fly, let herself be propelled off mountaintops, and steeled herself to the exposure of making small talk with thousands of strangers. Now Charles was talking about finding a dairy farm that he could run as a hobby, and Anne worried that she would have to learn how to keep "cow accounts." She was sentimentally attached not just to her immediate family but to the entire circle of her parents' friends. It was difficult to imagine, for example, that there were doctors elsewhere as competent and trustworthy as Dr. Foster, who had been her family physician since childhood. "My homesickness for my family seems incredibly naive for a young wife, and rather hard on a young husband," Anne wrote many years later.[9]

Charles's attempts to guard his and Anne's privacy soon became a staple of newspaper and magazine commentary. The flood of articles, with titles like "The High Cost of Fame" and "Feet of Clay— Or Eyes of Envy," were largely sympathetic, and a man in California had even announced the formation of a "Let Lindy Alone Club," though it wasn't clear what the activities of this organization would consist of. Few would deny that the Lindberghs had a right to enjoy their honeymoon undisturbed or to be outraged when a tabloid reporter offered a servant a large bribe to steal Anne's letters. On the other hand, their definition of what constituted an intrusion into their private lives was so totally unrealistic—as evidenced by their refusal to pose together after announcing their engagement—that there was a growing feeling among the press that they were becoming unwilling participants in a psychological contest whose rules they did not fully understand.[10]

The struggle escalated in the spring of 1930, when five New York papers carried items confirming long-standing rumors that Mrs. Lindbergh was pregnant. Since Anne Lindbergh was a public figure in her own right, this was arguably legitimate news. Charles and Anne didn't see it that way, and he, in particular, was furious. As was often the case when Charles's reaction seemed disproportionate to the offense, the newspapers had unwittingly touched on a sore subject. Anne was not only a pregnant wife, she was a pregnant copilot. In 1930 it was generally accepted that physical activity was bad for expectant mothers, and many upper-class women still avoided being seen in public in the later stages of their pregnancies. Anne's determination to keep on flying was definitely controversial within the aviation community. The airlines were struggling. Every crash of a commercial plane had a bad effect on business, and some people seriously suggested that it was socially irresponsible for the newspapers to report them. If anything untoward happened to Anne or her baby, it would be "bad for aviation"—a phrase Charles must have been thoroughly sick of hearing.

With the confidence in her own invulnerability that comes from youth and excellent health, Anne was quite unfazed by the risks to herself and the baby—which were probably a great deal less than everyone supposed. Although the decision was hers to make, her parents knew that she invariably deferred to Charles's judgment, and felt he was pushing Anne too far.

Anne was already six months pregnant when she earned her glider pilot's license in March 1930. In April, after numerous delays, she and Charles expected to take delivery of the new Lockheed Sirius monoplane, and Charles was looking forward to setting a transcontinental speed record on the flight back east. More important than the record itself, the trip was to be a demonstration of the superiority of high-altitude flying. The public, and for that matter even some pilots, still held to the irrational belief that the key to aviation safety was flying "low and slow." Lindbergh intended to smash this myth once and for all by proving that flying above the weather was not only faster but safer and more comfortable.

In November, beset by morning sickness, Anne had looked forward to the long flight with dread. As the day of the flight drew near, however, she had worked up some enthusiasm, though she confided to her family that climbing in and out of the Sirius was a little difficult. Ironically, what worried her most of all was not the flight itself but having to walk through the terminal before and after, her ungainly form swathed in an unflattering electrically heated flying suit. Among the most-admired women in the world and still petite even in an advanced state of pregnancy, Anne truly believed that the reporters and fans would be laughing at her behind her back.

The Sirius's maiden voyage took place on Easter Sunday. Cruising at fifteen thousand feet, the powerful Lockheed with its 450-horsepower Pratt & Whitney engine flew from Los Angeles to New York in a mere fourteen hours and forty minutes, slicing four hours off the old record. But the journey was far from comfortable for Anne. The altitude, combined with engine fumes leaking into her cockpit, left her dreadfully nauseated for most of the flight. The Sirius had a single isinglass hood which enclosed both cockpits, but Anne could communicate with her husband, who sat in the front, only by signaling or passing notes. Not wanting to spoil the record, she suffered in silence.[11]

By the time they landed at Roosevelt Field, Anne was too ill to leave the plane and Charles, obviously rattled, met the large contingent of aviation reporters alone, angrily denying their suggestions that there was anything wrong with his wife. Thirty minutes later, however, Anne was spotted, ashen-faced and teary-eyed, being hustled into a black limousine. Tabloid headlines proclaimed that Anne had suffered a nervous breakdown. At the other extreme the "responsible" papers made no mention of the incident whatsoever.

Anne was by now so nervous about photographers and aggressive fans that she did not trust any New York hospital to guarantee her security. As her delivery date approached, the Morrows had portable hospital equipment installed in a room of their New York apartment, and it was there, on her twenty-fourth birthday, June 22, that Anne gave birth to a son.

Seventeen days passed. The birth was acknowledged by the *New York Times,* but the parents issued no announcement and refused to respond to phone inquiries. Inevitably, perhaps, the family's silence gave rise to rumors that something was dreadfully wrong. One rumor had it that the child was deformed. Others whispered that the baby had been stillborn, and the parents planned to obtain another infant to pass off as their own. Even the most sensational of the American papers limited themselves to veiled allusions to the gossip, but the foreign press were not so circumspect, and Lindbergh's office in New York received requests for comment on the stories appearing abroad.[12]

Finally, on July 9, Colonel Lindbergh summoned the press to his office on lower Broadway in Manhattan to announce that he and Anne had a son, Charles Augustus Lindbergh, Jr. He then distributed copies of a baby picture that he had taken and developed himself. All present were asked to promise that the picture would be printed with a copyright notice crediting Lindbergh. Reporters from the five New York papers that had disclosed Anne's pregnancy and reported her alleged "nervous breakdown" were excluded from the press conference, and Charles hinted that if they published the photo of his child they would be courting a lawsuit. "My wife and I are through trying to deal with them," he said.[13]

A few days later, in an extraordinary two-hour interview with Marlen Pew of *Editor and Publisher* magazine, Lindbergh explained that his decision to punish the five "irresponsible" papers was a protest against American journalism's preoccupation with personalities to the exclusion of "things, ideas and ideals," which he called "non-constructive," "a social drag," and a "waste of time." Pew timidly suggested that perhaps this was taking too lofty a view. The popular press provided a degree of "vicarious satisfaction and uplift." Was this really so wrong? And surely, it was inspiring to know that "an expectant mother in this day of emancipated womanhood may tour the heavens with her husband." Lindbergh, Pew noted, considered these arguments as if hearing them for the first time, but he remained unconvinced.

As the interview progressed, Lindbergh spoke earnestly about the need to get on with his "work" of promoting the development of aviation. Aggrieved as he was, however, he had difficulty deciding who was to blame for his troubles. Although he wished that the journalists who badgered him would get into "some more decent business," he understood that publishers and editors "force reporters to do these unjust and intolerable things." On the other hand, he conceded, his feelings toward those publishers he had actually met were cordial.

Pew, obviously trying to puzzle his way through this conundrum, pointed out that Lindbergh had the option of complaining directly to the publishers about those reporters whose conduct exceeded the bounds of propriety. But Lindbergh demurred. He could never do this, he explained, because the reporters might lose their jobs, and his personal code of ethics prevented him from doing harm to any individual.[14]

Charles's attempt to teach the offending newspapers a lesson came at an awkward time for his father-in-law, who happened to be running in a special election for the United States Senate seat vacated by the appointment of Walter Edge as ambassador to France. Morrow had agreed to enter the race in the fall of 1929 when his reputation was at its peak. By June 1930, however, the ambassador's efforts to negotiate a restructuring of Mexico's foreign debt had used up his goodwill with that country's government and involved him in a feud with his old friend Tom Lamont, who was pushing a rival plan that would give preference to holders of Morgan-sponsored bonds. His reputation as a foreign-affairs genius unraveling, Morrow was even less prepared to deal with the pressing domestic issues of the day—the plunging stock market and the depressed economy. In his campaign speeches the ambassador lamely suggested that the current economic downturn might provide a useful lesson in "self discipline"—superfluous advice from one who had been fully invested in government bonds at the time of the crash and who still employed more than three dozen servants, mainly British subjects.

Obviously in need of a campaign issue, Morrow had decided to come out for repeal of Prohibition, a decision that was perhaps less courageous than it seemed at the time. With the onset of the Great Depression, the public was rapidly becoming disenchanted with this idealistic but also expensive and patently unsuccessful experiment in regulating private morality. Significantly William Randolph Hearst had also had his fill of the Eighteenth Amendment, denouncing it in a signed editorial on January 6, 1930, which charged that Prohibition had "increased crime enormously" and made "every man and every man's house subject to a system of espionage that is only equalled by that of Soviet Russia." Both the *New York Times* and the *World-Telegram*, where the Morrows' friend Walter Lippmann held sway over the editorial page, endorsed the ambassador's candidacy, but it was the enthusiastic support of the normally Democratic Hearst press, read by millions of

New Jerseyans, that enabled Morrow to eke out a victory in the June 7 Republican primary.

Hearst executives were stunned when Lindbergh announced less than a month later that he intended to prevent them from publishing a photograph of the ambassador's first grandchild. "We beg you to interpose with the Colonel," the editor of Hearst's INS news service pleaded in a telegram to Morrow.[15]

The telegram must have prompted Morrow to reason with his son-in-law, because just two days later the Hearst-owned *Daily Mirror* printed the Lindbergh baby picture on its front page. There was no lawsuit, and the other tabloids promptly used the picture as well. Morrow's honeymoon with the press was over, and a flurry of hostile stories appeared portraying him as a front for big business. (Even so, the press ignored the fact that the ambassador was a heavy drinker who served liquor in his home during Prohibition.) In any event the negative stories were too late to reverse Morrow's commanding lead over his Democratic opponent.

For Charles the hours he spent in the air had become a rare respite from his overbusy schedule and a chance to assess the direction his life had taken. Flying over the southwest on TAT business some months earlier, he had landed his plane in the desert and camped out under the stars, lying awake late into the night trying to chart a course for the future. Despite all his resolutions to the contrary, his life had become impossibly complicated. Although there were still things he hoped to accomplish in aviation, what he really wanted was to become a scientist like his grandfather Land. To his way of thinking, at least, science was a means of confronting the big questions: What is the relationship between mind and body? Is death necessary?

Lindbergh was still in this twenties, not too late, at least by today's standards, to start a new career. He hadn't been joking when he told the Wisconsin alumni association in 1927 that he hoped to return to college and finish his degree, but their reaction showed just how impractical a goal this was—the thought of Col. Charles Lindbergh as an undergraduate was ludicrous. Henry Breckinridge, a Princeton alumnus, came up with a possible solution. He introduced Charles to his alma mater's president, the noted liberal educator Dr. John Hibben, who promised to put Princeton's resources at his disposal. Charles could use Princeton's laboratories and libraries to pursue a course of independent studies, and the college would endeavor to keep publicity to a minimum.

The university was also close to the Lakehurst Aerodrome, a major aviation facility suitable as a home base for the Sirius.

When Charles junior was a few months old, the Lindberghs renewed their search for a country home, this time concentrating their efforts around Princeton. Exploring the area by plane, they were drawn to the Sourland Mountain region near Hopewell, about twenty miles northwest of the university. Except for a few illegal stills tucked away in the woods, the postwar boom had left the Sourlands virtually untouched, and the locals, said to be descended from Hessian mercenaries who deserted the British army during the Revolutionary War, were still commonly referred to as "mountain folk." It seemed a lucky omen that the owner of the first piece of property they picked out from the air happened to be a man named Land, a direct descendant of Charles's great-great-grandfather.

By October an agent acting on the Lindberghs' behalf had put together a parcel of five hundred wooded acres, and the firm of Aldrich & Delano was drawing up plans for a house. In the meantime, the Lindberghs settled into a rented house in Mount Rose, about four and a half miles away on the Princeton-Hopewell Road. The white-frame farmhouse had a picket fence and a barn, but it was also sparsely furnished and hard to heat. Anne's idea of the country was North Haven, with its private golf course, sailboats, and congenial neighbors. In Mount Rose she had nothing much to do and missed her family all the more. Keeping house for the first time, she was amazed that Charles wanted his food set on the table all at once, "farm style," even though they had a perfectly nice live-in couple to serve their meals.[16]

Charles, meanwhile, attended a few demonstrations at Princeton but was soon deflected from his study plan. As the result of a conversation with Dr. Paluel Flagg, the anesthesiologist who had presided at the delivery of Charles junior, another, more tempting opportunity had come his way. While Anne was in labor, Charles had begun to tell Flagg about the tragic situation of his sister-in-law Elisabeth, who had recently suffered a mild heart attack. Elisabeth's doctors warned her that one of her heart valves was permanently damaged; she would have to restrict her activities severely, and she might never be able to have children. Charles refused to accept that the life of his vital, intelligent sister-in-law might be cut short because of a heart valve, a mere scrap of tissue. Why, he asked Flagg, couldn't the doctors simply replace or repair the valve?

Other doctors to whom Lindbergh posed this question had told him that heart surgery was impossible because there was no way to maintain the patient's circulation while repairing the damaged organ. Flagg, however, happened to know the head of Rockefeller University's experimental surgery laboratory, who was working on just this problem. The winner of a Nobel Prize in medicine for developing a method of suturing blood vessels, Dr. Alexis Carrel had begun experimenting with kidney transplants in dogs as early as 1905. He had also attempted to develop a technique for restoring amputated legs, sometimes attempting two-way transplants, exchanging legs from a pair of dogs. Carrel's prediction that not only open-heart surgery but organ transplants and even the restoration of severed limbs would one day be routine sounded like science fiction in 1930, and he himself was a controversial personality. Attacked on the one side by the antivivisectionists, he was also a devout Catholic who had written a book on the miracles at Lourdes and drawn fire from the scientific community for his interest in extrasensory perception and telepathy.

Carrel enjoyed being provocative, and even his admirers at the Century Club in New York City, where he often held forth, sometimes found it difficult to decide whether he really believed the things he was saying. Worried about the dehumanizing nature of factory work, he corresponded with Henry Ford about a plan to create model "organic villages," in which each worker would spend part of the day on the assembly line and the rest tilling his own plot of land. He fretted that educated women who chose careers over the rearing of large families were contributing to the "decline of the white race," and believed that "unassuaged" sexual energy was the source of all creativity in the arts and sciences: "A workman's wife can request the services of her husband every day. But the wife of an artist or of a philosopher has not the right to do so as often," he once wrote. This, however, may have been wishful thinking. The imperious Madame Carrel, who had a son by a previous marriage and no desire to bear any more children, refused to make her home in America, and for many years Dr. Carrel saw her only during his summer vacations.[17]

Happy to serve as "Col. Lindbergh's Tiresias," as he put it in a letter to Carrel, Flagg arranged a meeting. For Lindbergh, his first visit to Carrel's laboratory was a revelation. It could hardly fail to be memorable since Carrel wore a black gown and hood in the operating theater and insisted that his assistants and observers do likewise—to cut down on glare, he said, but from sheer love of self-dramatization, according to his detractors.

"When I donned my gown and hood of black outside the operating room," Lindbergh later recalled, "I prepared for a supernatural experience.... In that room mortality was being analyzed in its ultimate physical form. Life sometimes merged with death so closely I could not tell them apart."[18]

Carrel showed Lindbergh a culture of cells from a chicken's heart that had been kept alive in solution for more than two decades. He then explained that his latest project was to develop a chamber that would keep whole organs alive and functioning. Aside from its value as a tool for basic research, a functioning perfusion pump, as Carrel called the apparatus, might someday be used to produce human insulin and other hormones *in vitro*. Carrel even envisioned the possibility of removing diseased organs and tissue (such as kidneys and arterial sections) from humans, repairing them while they were maintained in suspension, and then restoring them to the patient. A German engineer named Heinz Rosenberger had made a preliminary design for a glass pump, but had been unable to solve a number of basic problems, including figuring out a way to enable scientists to introduce nutrients and manipulate the organ without causing bacterial contamination. Back home in Princeton, Lindbergh sat up until late at night sketching his ideas for improving the pump. Although he did not immediately solve the problems that had defeated Rosenberger, his design was so promising that Carrel offered him a place in his laboratory and the services of a master glassblower, Otto Hopf.

That a college dropout with no formal training in biology could join Carrel's group at Rockefeller University and immediately begin producing world-class work is less astounding than it sounds. Medical research had been slow to take advantage of the revolution in applied science and technology that had occurred in the late nineteenth and early twentieth centuries. Bio-engineering was in its infancy. Lindbergh's childhood puttering in his grandfather Land's laboratory, as well as the knowledge he had gained from his mother's continuing interest in improving her laboratory equipment, gave him a grasp of the basic problems and techniques that many university-trained engineers lacked. The single-track mind that often proved a liability in daily life was an asset in research, and without question he possessed a genius for the work. By 1935 he had developed an improved pump based on a three-chambered Pyrex vessel; compressed gas was used to maintain a continuous circulation of fluids through the pressurized container. In the meantime he had also designed a flask that could be used for cultivating large numbers of cells and developed an improved method of separating red cells from blood plasma.[19]

Following his 1930 interview with Lindbergh, Marlen Pew had made the perceptive comment that Lindbergh's problem with the popular press was that he loathed the image of himself he saw reflected there; he wanted to be accepted as a scientist, but reporters insisted on seeing him as a mere "showman." Lindbergh's affiliation with the Rockefeller University made the public's misperception easier to bear. Carrel rarely interfered with his associates, and Lindbergh had great freedom to manage his own research goals. At the same time, Carrel's worldwide reputation inspired his associates with the excitement of being on the cutting edge of science. "I once looked up from my work to see him step into the room with Albert Einstein discussing extrasensory perception," Lindbergh recalled.[20] Eager to avoid the sort of premature publicity that had spoiled his relationship with the Carnegie Institution, Lindbergh seldom discussed his work outside the lab. The Morrows, more than a little skeptical of their son-in-law's decision to start a career in science at the age of twenty-eight, would be taken by surprise when one of his papers was accepted for publication in the prestigious journal *Science* in 1932. Even Anne knew little about her husband's work; talk of decerebrate cats and immortal chicken-heart tissue did not appeal to her fastidious nature, and she was reassured and a little relieved when she overheard a conversation between her husband and his mother and realized that Evangeline understood the work and accepted its importance.

The Lindberghs' quiet existence in Mount Rose was too uneventful to attract the attention of the press, and even though the house was almost a two-hour commute from New York by car, country living agreed with Charles. It was now four years since the flight. Even in the city, incidents like the traffic jam that he got into with Donald Keyhoe in Lower Manhattan were becoming less common, and when they did occur Lindbergh took them philosophically. "I'm all right as long as I keep moving," he assured Keyhoe.

One sign of Charles's more relaxed attitude was his decision to cooperate when Keyhoe was asked to write an article on Lindbergh for the *Saturday Evening Post*. He even allowed Keyhoe to spend time at the farmhouse and describe the visit in print. Keyhoe found Charles Lindbergh at home a completely different person from the brooding, overburdened youth he had known in 1927. Over dinner Charles and Anne chatted animatedly about everything from the baby's progress to the latest developments in aviation policy. Knowing his remarks would be published, Charles praised his wife's skills as a pilot and emphasized that she was fully qualified to become the first woman to fly the Atlantic alone, a prospect that obviously appealed to him much more than it did to Anne herself.

After dinner, Keyhoe's report went on, Charles retired to the den to study his biochemistry textbooks. The only sign of his old restlessness was that he immediately flicked on the radio, turning up the volume full blast until the strains of a symphony orchestra flooded the house. Keyhoe was amazed that Lindbergh could concentrate, and still more amazed that the baby, who had just been put to bed upstairs, managed to sleep through it all.

One rather disturbing incident that occurred during Keyhoe's visit did not find its way into his *Saturday Evening Post* article. Earlier in the evening, while Charles was busy elsewhere, Keyhoe sat in the living room watching Anne as she entertained little Charley. As Anne was playfully singing the popular song "You Must Have Been a Beautiful Baby," Keyhoe looked up and saw a disheveled, wild-eyed man peering in at them through the living room window. As soon as the Peeping Tom realized he had been seen, he turned and fled into the night.[21]

Shaken, Keyhoe suggested to Anne and Charles that they ought to think about hiring a watchman, but they protested that they moved to the country precisely to get away from the need for watchmen and security guards. The man was a little feeble-minded perhaps, but surely nothing to worry about. In fact, the Mount Rose farmhouse was not far from a state home for "epileptics"—in most cases, the inmates were mildly retarded adults—and the Lindberghs were probably quite right in dismissing the prowler as harmless. On several occasions, however, strangers who were not so obviously innocuous had found their way to the house. One woman had knocked on the front door loudly demanding to be allowed to inspect the baby and was angry and indignant when Anne refused to let her come in. The housekeepers, Ollie and Elsie Whateley, were recently arrived from Scotland and Anne was a little anxious about leaving Charley at home with them for any length of time. With the long-deferred Arctic flight scheduled for the summer of 1931, Anne decided to send the baby to North Haven, in the care of her mother and the newly hired nursemaid Betty Gow.

As was usually the case with a Lindbergh project, the main purpose of the Arctic flight was adventure. Foreseeing that the Great Circle route to Asia would one day be of commercial importance, Charles wanted to be the one to blaze the trail. Many of the tundra lakes and remote islands the Lindberghs would be exploring had never before been visited by an airplane. The Lockheed Sirius had been refitted with pontoons and a more powerful engine, and caches of fuel had been sent ahead by ship. Anne had qualified as a radio operator in preparation for the flight, taking lessons from the renowned navigator Harold Gatty, but in case of trouble, help would be many hours, perhaps days, away. Prepared for everything from engine trouble to a forced landing in the Bering Sea, the Lindberghs would be carrying extensive survival gear, including spare parts, their electrically heated flying suits, a rubber life raft, parachutes, two pistols with ammunition, and forty-five pounds of food, selected by Anne with the help of a manual on nutrition.

Pan-Am would be providing technical support for the journey, and there was much talk that the Lindberghs' planned visit to Shanghai would promote Juan Trippe's ambition to expand his operations in China, where Harold Bixby already had his hands full trying to keep alive a Pan-Am subsidiary known as China Airways. But the Lindberghs were paying for the expedition themselves, and the preparations went forward in an atmosphere of dedicated but economical amateurism. The rented house became a temporary supply depot, and Anne purchased her clothes for the journey in the "Growing Girls" section of a New York department store. Departing from New York on July 27, the Lindberghs made the Morrow house in Maine their first stop so that they could say good-bye to their son, and when they took off the next morning from Penobscot Bay, Anne was bemused to see that the neighbors who turned out to wish her luck were the same people who, two years earlier, had watched her back the family Buick into a fence.

That evening they landed in Ottawa, where a committee of experts tried to persuade Charles to switch to an established airway over the Mackenzie River. His northerly route was over desolate territory, and they warned of high tides on Hudson Bay, dangerous fog conditions, and other hazards.

"I wouldn't take *my* wife into that territory," one of the experts said, shaking his head.

"You forget, she's crew," replied Lindbergh. Anne, overhearing the remark, called it the proudest moment of her life.[22]

Although Anne would confess to feeling "slightly insulted" when reporters pressed her for the feminine angle, asking questions like, "What do you serve for lunch?" this was exactly the tone she would take in her own account of the journey, published as *North to the Orient*. Her sense of herself as something of an impostor, journeying under false pretenses into the rough-and-ready world of outdoor adventure, may not have been much fun in real life, but it made her book agreeable reading for the armchair adventurer: Landing at a fur-trading post near Baker Lake, grimy and disheveled after a long flight through an arctic white night, Anne discovered that the local Eskimo population had turned out to inspect the first white woman ever to visit the area, and reflected that she was no doubt a great disappointment. At a Soviet village on Kamchatka, she heard the grizzled cannery workers who turned out to cheer Colonel Lindbergh muttering a phrase in Russian as she passed by. Pressed for a translation, her interpreter apologetically explained that the men were saying, "But who is *she?*"

In fact the experts' warnings had not been exaggerated, and the journey had its share of life-threatening moments. The Sirius was forced down three times, once damaging its propeller during a hard landing. Over Japan's Chishima Islands, marked on the Lindberghs' navigation chart as a Japanese "fortified area," the ceiling was zero. Charles opened the cockpit cover and peered out through mist until he located the peak of a volcano, then dived, following the dim outline of the mountainside while Anne furiously worked the radio. The transmitter worked off an antenna that trailed below the plane, and every time they neared ground level, she had to reel it in, forty-eight turns of a stiff hand crank. When they were unable to locate open water Charles climbed again and Anne reeled out the antenna. They continued "tobogganing down volcanos" in this fashion until they finally found the roiling waters of Buroton Bay.[23]

The following morning the Sirius's anchor line was accidentally severed and they were rescued by a Japanese ship, the *Shinshiru Maru,* as they were about to smash against the rocky coastline. That night, sleeping in the cargo compartment of the seaplane, atop a mound of gear as usual, they were buffeted by gale-force winds.

Anne met every test, displaying remarkable courage and stamina, but took little credit for her success. In her mind it was her husband, "Charles the Invincible" she called him, who had brought them through.

Arriving in China, the Lindberghs found the Yangtze Valley in full flood. Villages were inundated up to the rooftops, and thousands of homeless peasants were living on sampans, crowded together with their pitiful belongings, trying to survive by trolling muddy waters for fish. Meeting up with a famine relief team from Rockefeller University in

Nanking, the Lindberghs interrupted their journey to assist in making an aerial survey of the flood plain. Charles and a Chinese doctor then flew the Sirius to Hinghwha for a load of medical supplies. On their return they were mistaken for a relief plane bringing food, and hundreds of sampans converged on the plane. Some of the boatmen made begging gestures, cupping their hands in a mute request for rice. Others shouted curses at the foreigners. One sampan had a small cooking fire burning on deck. The flames flickered within inches of the Sirius's wood-and-canvas wing.

"Have you a gun?" shouted an American relief worker who had poled his boat up to the plane to help unload the medicines.

Lindbergh did, a .38 Winchester. At the last moment, as half a dozen desperate men were attempting to clamber up onto the Sirius's fragile pontoons, he fired into the air and the sampans began to back off. A large parcel of desperately needed vaccines was torn apart in the melee. One Chinese relief worker's boat was swamped, and he narrowly escaped being drowned in his struggle to regain the Sirius.[24]

From Nanking the Lindberghs moved on to Hangkow, where the swollen waters of the river were so dangerous that they accepted an invitation to store their plane on the deck of the British aircraft carrier *Hermes*. Three days later, ready to depart for Shanghai, they boarded the Sirius and sat ready, engine idling, as a steel cable lowered the plane to the river's surface. When the pontoons touched the water, the sailors tried to release the cable, but it jammed and the plane swung sideways to the current, one wing dipping below water level. Charles screamed, "Jump!" and he and Anne plunged into the roiling Yangtze.

They came up swimming. Anne surfaced in time to see a heavily loaded sampan pass safely under the overstressed cable just seconds before it snapped. A friend consoled her by telling her of the Chinese superstition that each of us has three devils who follow us throughout life. A brush with death can separate us from one or more of those devils. The passengers on the sampan had been freed from all three of their evil spirits, and surely she and Charles had also shed their bad luck.

The badly battered Sirius would have to shipped home by way of Shanghai. Charles and Anne still hoped to visit Peking, but before they could depart, they received a cable from Mrs. Morrow. Anne's father had suffered a stroke and died hours later without regaining consciousness. Although Mrs. Morrow stoically volunteered that there was no reason for Anne to cut short her trip, she and Charles made immediate plans to return home.[25]

Morrow, not yet sixty, had served just one year in the Senate, and his death came three weeks after Constance, his youngest child, started college. Despite his differences with his father-in-law, Charles had considered the senator a great man. He had never developed a rapport with Betty Morrow, however, and now, somewhat uneasily, he was thrust into the role of the man of the family.

Later that winter Charles visited Constance at Smith College and sat in on her freshman English class, which was taught by Dean Marjorie Nicolson. "Miss Nickie," as she was known to generations of devoted students, was as starry-eyed over Lindy as any teenager, but she was also not a woman to be intimidated by anyone. On an earlier visit to North Haven, Nicolson had found herself part of a group Colonel Lindbergh was ferrying somewhere on the *Mouette*. Lindbergh was not familiar with the local waters, and when he took a little too long getting under way to suit her, Nicolson impatiently shunted him aside and commandeered the wheel, telling him, "If you let *me* manage this I'm sure we'll get where we're going."

"I did, and I made a sensation," she later recalled with great satisfaction.

Charles, used to being treated with bone-chilling deference even by his in-laws' friends, was delighted, and one suspects that he had planned a little surprise for Nicolson in return. When he showed up in the classroom, he was wearing his favorite disguise of tinted wire-rimmed eyeglasses, and Con had warned Nicolson in advance, "Don't tell the girls until after who he is, because he's tired of being 'Oh, Wonderful!'" The day's lecture happened to be on book 2 of *Paradise Lost*, and when the question period began, the mystery auditor in the back of the classroom raised his hand and, to Nicolson's utter astonishment, began to quote from memory the lines describing the descent of Satan.

"When I have picked up my wife's *Paradise Lost*, and you know she's read it a great deal," he added, "we have said that this second book is very interesting. The descent is what we call a parachute, and someday we might have to descend ourselves. Not to Hell, I would hope."[26]

THIRTEEN

"The Eaglet Is Taken"

DURING THE WINTER OF 1931–32, all New York was mesmerized by the career moves of one Vincent Coll, an ambitious hood who was challenging Dutch Schultz and Owney Madden for control of organized crime on the island of Manhattan. Hoping to pressure the established bosses into offering them a territory of their own, Coll's gang kidnapped a Madden henchman named Frenchy McFadden and collected a thirty-five-thousand-dollar ransom. Coll's next victim was Sherman Billingsley, the owner-manager of the posh Stork Club, who was held prisoner in a basement and beaten daily until his friends anted up twenty-five thousand dollars. A few weeks later, a bungled attempt to kidnap Dutch Schultz himself led to a shoot-out on a midtown street corner that killed a four-year-old girl.

On February 7, 1932, *New York Mirror* columnist Walter Winchell received a tip from speakeasy hostess Texas Guinan that the Vincent Coll menace was about to be eliminated. An unnamed gangland boss had summoned a posse of hit men from Detroit's notorious Purple Gang, also known as the Jewish Navy because its leaders were Jewish and its activities consisted mainly of ferrying Canadian whiskey around the Great Lakes. In his column the next morning, Winchell reported: "Five planes brought dozens of machine guns from Chicago Friday to combat the town's Capone.... Local banditti have made one hotel a virtual arsenal and several hot spots are ditto."[1]

Coll was gunned down hours after the column hit the newsstands, and the Purple Gang, annoyed by the accuracy of Winchell's prediction, put out a contract on his life. For several weeks he showed up at work in the company of an armed bodyguard provided by Owney Madden, who happened to be a fan.

Coll's brief reign of terror sowed panic out of proportion to the casualties. With the end of Prohibition in sight, the mob had been moving in on legitimate businesses, extorting protection money from contractors, truckers, storekeepers, and labor organizers. Now the super-rich, already fearful that their prosperity in the midst of the depression would make them targets of crime, wondered if the Coll experiment was just the beginning of a wave of kidnappings for ransom, otherwise known as "the snatch racket."

Highfields, the Sourland Mountain estate of Charles and Anne Lindbergh, seemed remote from the hysteria that gripped New York that dreary depression February. Far from the haunts of the rich and fashionable, the stone house was located off a narrow, unpaved country lane, at the end of a gravel driveway nine-tenths of a mile long. The house boasted many features that reflected Charles Lindbergh's interest in engineering and design, including a seven-zone heating system and heavy-duty wiring to accommodate the biological laboratory he planned to install in the basement. Most ingeniously, three skylights made of smoked-glass bricks were set into the slate roof; all but undetectable from the exterior of the house, they flooded the attic with natural light.

Although Charles and Anne had purchased the acreage through a nominee, the press had quickly discovered the location, and an aerial photo of the house, then still under construction, was featured on the front page of the *Sunday Mirror*, headlined THE LONE EAGLE BUILDS A NEST. After the story appeared, sightseers beat a path to the estate, often departing with "souvenirs" in the form of carloads of lumber, plumbing supplies, and tools, and the contractor hired a local man to guard the site at night and on weekends. When the construction crews departed, however, the Lindberghs dismissed the night watchman, much to his disappointment. Eager to be on good terms with their neighbors, they also let it be known that the locals were welcome to continue using Featherbed Lane, an abandoned right-of-way that ran through their property roughly parallel to their new cinder driveway.

Charles loved the woodland hideaway, but the two-hour drive to New York made it somewhat impractical for everyday living. Eventually he planned to add an airstrip, so that he could commute by plane. No doubt he and Anne would also have done some landscaping. For the moment, however, the Normanesque country farmhouse deep in the woods resembled a vision out of a fairy tale, and not one of the sunnier fairy tales either.

Anne, though she claimed to be as enchanted by the house as her husband, had not yet really warmed up to the place. After three years of marriage, her family was still the emotional center of her life. Since the completion of Highfields the previous October, she and Charles had spent only fourteen weekends there, usually not arriving until late Saturday afternoon. Early on Monday morning Charles drove directly into Manhattan, and Anne returned with the baby to Next Day Hill. Ollie and Elsie Whateley, who had their own apartment in the west wing of the house, remained behind to keep an eye on the property.

On Leap Year Day, Monday, February 29, Anne departed from her usual routine. The baby, now twenty months old, had a bad chest cold, and Anne was reluctant to take him outside. She spent a quiet day in the house and slept over Monday night with only the Whateleys for company. Charles, who had a very full schedule of appointments the next day, stayed in Englewood.[2]

On Tuesday morning Anne awoke to the sound of a late-winter rainstorm pounding on the slate roof. Charley was much better, but she felt achy and feverish. Three months pregnant and bothered by morning sickness, she had also caught the baby's cold. At ten-thirty, she called Next Day Hill and told Charley's nurse Betty Gow that she was planning to stay at Highfields another night. During the two-and-a-half-month-long Arctic flight the baby had become very attached to Gow—he learned the word "Betty" before he could say "Mummy"—and Anne had decided that she would use her visits to Hopewell to get reacquainted with her son, caring for him herself with a little help from Elsie Whateley. Gow, therefore, had been to Highfields only once, and she was none too happy when Anne asked her to take the train down to Princeton. The nursemaid had an important date that night with her boyfriend, a Norwegian sailor named Finn Henrik ("Red") Johnson, whom she had met in North Haven, where he crewed on Tom Lamont's yacht, the *Reynard*. Johnson had been living in an Englewood boardinghouse, supporting himself over the winter by doing odd jobs, but he was about to move to Connecticut to stay with his brother's family, and Betty wasn't sure when she would see him again.

At least Betty didn't have to wait at the train station in the driving rain. Violet Sharpe, the downstairs maid who answered Anne's call, had mentioned it to the Morrows' assistant chauffeur, Charles Ellerson, who volunteered to drive Betty to Hopewell in one of the family's Cadillacs. They arrived a little after one o'clock. Ellerson came inside for a quick cup of tea and then drove back to Englewood alone.

In the middle of the afternoon, there was a brief lull in the rainstorm, and Anne decided to go out for a walk. Returning at about a quarter to five, she stopped under the southeast corner window of the nursery and tossed pebbles at the windowpane until Betty heard the noise and brought the baby to the window to wave to his mother.

After giving Charley an early dinner, Anne and Betty spent more than an hour in the nursery getting him ready for bed. Anne rubbed the toddler's chest with Vicks VapoRub, and gave him his nose drops and then his medicine, which he promptly spit up all over his clothes. Betty fetched another Dr. Denton's sleeping suit from the dresser. This one had never been worn, and it seemed a shame to have the brand-new outfit get all gooey with VapoRub.

"Why don't I run up a little flannel shirt to put next to the baby's skin?" she suggested.

An experienced seamstress and a thrifty one, Betty cut two pieces from an old petticoat and basted them together with some blue silk thread saved from an expensive French negligee. When the baby was dressed again, she tied on the plastic thumb guards that had been recommended by the pediatrician to discourage thumb-sucking. Tucking the baby in, she pinned the top edge of the crib covers to the bottom sheet with two large safety pins so that he couldn't push them off in his sleep.

Charley fell asleep almost immediately. Anne went downstairs, but Betty sat quietly in the nursery until she was sure that the baby was settled. Before she left the room, she latched the shutters of the French windows on the south side of the house and one of the two windows that faced east. The shutters on the corner window were warped—the contractor and the carpenters were still arguing about who was responsible—so she left those unfastened but closed the window.

It was now about eight o'clock, and at the Waldorf-Astoria in New York, the alumni of New York University were eagerly awaiting Colonel Lindbergh, who was to be the featured speaker at their annual fund-raising banquet. Lindbergh, who had attended a lifetime's worth of formal dinners in the year after his transatlantic flight, would resort to almost any excuse to avoid getting into a dinner jacket, but he had found it impossible to refuse an invitation from Frank Bartow, who was a Morgan partner as well as a member of the NYU Board of Regents. Lindbergh's appearance had been announced in the morning newspapers, and a small crowd had gathered in the rain outside the hotel, hoping to catch a glimpse of the elusive hero. As it happened, however, they were to be disappointed. The date of the banquet had been changed twice, and in the confusion Lindbergh's personal secretary, Elizabeth Sheetz, somehow neglected to mark the correct date in his appointment book. Lindbergh himself had forgotten the date, or perhaps saw his secretary's oversight as a perfect opportunity to duck an unwelcome obligation. Shortly after six he started for Hopewell, calling en route to let Anne and the Whateleys know he would be there for dinner.

By 8:00 P.M., when Henry Breckinridge phoned from the Waldorf wondering what had become of Charles, the weather had turned nasty again. Gusts of wind whipped through the trees and rattled the French doors that opened off the living room onto a flagstone veranda. Anne sat down at her desk in the living room to write some letters and finish her day's entry in her diary. "I stayed at my desk, listening for Colonel Lindbergh from about 7:30 until about 8:25, looking at my watch all the time, waiting for him," she later told the police. "I once thought I heard the sound of a car on gravel, but it was a very windy night. I didn't get up to see what it was.... About 8:25 I heard Colonel Lindbergh's car and his horn."[3]

The horn was the usual signal for Ollie Whateley to open the garage doors. Whateley had taken the message from Breckinridge, and Charles immediately called the attorney back, asking him to pass his apologies to the NYU alums. Charles and Anne ate a light supper in the small dining room on the west side of the house, then went into the living room to sit in front of the fire. Almost as soon as they sat down they heard a crash, which Charles later described as "the sound of slats from an orange crate falling off a chair." At the time he and Anne assumed that the noise came from the pantry, where Whateley was putting away the dinner dishes.

A minute or two later Charles decided that he wanted to take a quick bath, then work for the rest of the evening in his study. He and Anne went upstairs together and spent ten or fifteen minutes talking in the master bedroom. While Charles then took his bath in the large bathroom down the hall, Anne collected her toiletries. She had left her tooth powder in the smaller connecting bath between the master bedroom and the nursery. The nursery door was ajar, and rather than turn on the light and disturb the baby, she fumbled around in the semidarkness, guided by the dim orange glow of the space heater that Betty Gow had left on in the nursery.

Downstairs Whateley had finished straightening up the kitchen and was reading a magazine in the tiny servants' sitting room, just off the pantry. Elsie had asked Betty Gow to come up to the Whateleys' apartment over the garage to help her pin up the hem of a new dress. The women worked on the dress for about twenty minutes, until about nine-thirty, when Anne, who had finished her bath and was reading in bed, rang the servants' bell to ask Elsie for a glass of hot lemonade. Betty decided to pop into the nursery to check on the baby.

The electric heater was still burning, but Gow noticed immediately that the room was surprisingly cold. Without turning on the light, she bent over to the four-poster maple crib and reached in to check the baby's covers. Charley was not in the crib. But, strangely, the blankets were still neatly pinned to the bottom sheet, as if someone had pulled the baby feetfirst out from under the covers.

Several times in the past Colonel Lindbergh had played practical jokes on the serious-minded nursemaid, stealing the baby away when her attention was momentarily distracted and hiding with it. These pranks had been frightening enough, but they always occurred during playtime. Tonight the child needed his sleep. Swallowing her annoyance, Betty went to the door of the master bedroom, where Anne was still reading in bed, "Mrs. Lindbergh, does the Colonel have the baby?" she asked.

"Why, I don't know," said Anne. "He must have."

Betty went downstairs to the study. "Colonel, have you got the baby? Please don't fool me."

He shook his head.

The nursemaid persisted. "You must have the baby. He is gone."[4]

Charles dropped his pen and bounded up the stairs, three at a time. Anne was already in the nursery, rummaging through the closet and peering under the bed in the desperate hope that this was another of her husband's jokes. One look at his face told her it wasn't. At that moment they both noticed that the southeast corner window was wide open.

Shouting to Whateley to call the police, Charles grabbed a rifle and ran outside. Anne went into her bedroom, threw open the window, and leaned out. Over to her right, in the general direction of the woodpile, she heard what sounded like a baby's cry. Elsie had come up behind her. "That was a cat, Mrs. Lindbergh," she said quickly.[5]

Charles ran down the driveway but saw no sign of an intruder. The bare trees were creaking and moaning in the wind, making it difficult to hear any unusual sounds. After a few minutes, he decided to go back inside to fetch a flashlight. He was surprised to learn from Whateley that the phone lines had not been cut.

He and Whateley found the women gathered in the nursery. The room had scarcely been disturbed, but there were traces of mud on a leather suitcase that lay just under the corner window. Lying atop the built-in radiator was a white envelope. Realizing that the police might be able to lift fingerprints, Charles resisted the impulse to tear it open.

There were no flashlights in the house, so Ollie Whateley took the car and went out to find some. However, soon after he turned into the one-lane dirt road known locally as Lindbergh Lane, he met up with Hopewell chief of police Harry Wolfe and Constable Williamson. They had extra flashlights in the car, and Whateley followed them back to the house. Charles, meanwhile, had phoned Henry Breckinridge, who advised him to call the state police. By 10:50 P.M., an all-points alert for the missing baby had been issued, and state troopers were setting up roadblocks on major arteries into New York City, Newark, and Trenton.

The first state policeman to reach the house was Cpl. Joseph Wolf (no relation to Hopewell police chief Harry Wolfe). A second-year trooper, Wolf rose to the occasion, making detailed notes on the layout of the nursery and taking preliminary statements. That done, he went outside, where Constable Williamson showed him a three-quarter-inch Bucks Brothers chisel lying under the southeast corner window of the nursery. He also pointed out what appeared to be at least two sets of muddy footprints under the nursery window, a man's and a woman's. The man's footprints led them about seventy-five feet from the house, where they found a folding ladder lying in mud near the edge of the forest. The ladder was constructed so that its three sections telescoped together for easy carrying, but whoever built it had done a hasty job, using odds and ends of several kinds of lumber. Williamson pointed out that one of the rungs, on what would have been the ladder's bottom section, was broken.

Corporal Wolf went back inside and asked the women if any of them had left the house after the crime was discovered. None of them had. "The kidnappers apparently consisted of a party of at least two or more persons," Wolf wrote in his report. Based on his information that a woman's footprints had been discovered under the window, troopers manning roadblocks around the state began paying special attention to cars carrying couples or perhaps several men traveling with a woman.[6]

Two more troopers, Cain and Sullivan, showed up at the house a few minutes later. Wolf sent Cain back down the driveway, with orders to have all new arrivals park their cars on the public road in order to avoid destroying tire-track evidence. Sullivan was assigned to keep newcomers from trampling ground in the immediate vicinity of the house. By 11:15, at least thirteen state police officials were on the scene. Among them were detectives Nuncio de Gaetano and Lewis Bornmann, investigators assigned to the state police headquarters in Trenton; head of detectives Capt. John J. Lamb and his deputy, Lt. Arthur ("Buster") Keaten, who had played a central role in the notorious Hall-Mills murder case, uncovering evidence that convicted a New Jersey minister of slaying a member of his church choir; and three more detectives, Zapolsky, Leon, and Haussling. Among the last to arrive was Col. H. Norman Schwarzkopf, founding director of the New Jersey State Police, and his aide, Maj. Charles Schoeffel.

Schwarzkopf asked Colonel Lindbergh who he thought might have done it. Did he have any enemies?

"I have no idea," Lindbergh said.

Everyone stood around waiting for the crime scene investigator, Cpl. Frank Kelly, who showed up a few minutes after midnight. Schwarzkopf, realizing that it was crucial to keep the contents of the envelope confidential, dismissed all but a few senior aides and Colonel Lindbergh from the room before Kelly started work. Unfortunately, except for a useless smudge, the envelope and letter were clean, and the note itself was barely legible:

> Dear Sir!
>   Have 50,000 $ redy 25000 $ in 20 $ bills 15000$ in 10 $ bills and 10000 $ in 5 $ bills. After 2–4 days we will inform you were to deliver the Mony.
>   We warn you for making anyding public or for the Polise
> the child is in gut care.
>   Indication for all letters are singnature and 3 holds.[7]

This "singnature," as the note's author called it, consisted of two interlocking blue circles, shaded red where they overlapped. The design was perforated by three square holes apparently made with a hand punch.

While the senior state police officials were gathered in the nursery,

A proud Evangeline Lindbergh holds up Charles, age five months, for his first encounter with the camera. *(Minnesota Historical Society)*

C. A. Lindbergh in 1901, the year of his marriage to Evangeline. An artist's rendering of this portrait of the handsome forty-two-year-old attorney was used on his campaign posters when he ran for Congress in 1906. *(Minnesota Historical Society)*

Charles and his beloved Dingo, his favorite among the many dogs he owned as a child. Dingo was shot by persons unknown in 1915. *(Minnesota Historical Society)*

The Lindberghs and their friends on an expedition to Lake Emily, near Brainerd, Minnesota, in 1907. Seated in the front row *(left to right)* are Lillian, Evangeline, Charles (holding his rifle), and Eva. C.A. is standing, *third from right. (Minnesota Historical Society)*

Charles, age nineteen, on his twin-cylinder Excelsior motorcycle. He used the motorcycle in his part-time job selling and servicing milking machines. Later he rode it to Madison, Wisconsin, where he started college in the fall of 1921; on a tour of the South the summer after his freshman year; and eventually to Lincoln, Nebraska, where he began his career in aviation. *(Minnesota Historical Society)*

The Morrows in their backyard on Palisade Avenue in Englewood, New Jersey, about 1917. *Left to right*: Dwight Morrow and his wife Betty, Elisabeth, Anne, Dwight, Jr., and Constance. *(Amherst College Archives)*

Evangeline Lindbergh, wearing one of her many stylish hats, showed up unexpectedly at Curtiss Field as her son was preparing for the long flight. Although her refusal to pose kissing her son good-bye led some to characterize Mrs. Lindbergh as cold, she was in good spirits and told reporters, "If it weren't for the fact that I would be excess baggage, I would gladly go with him."

(AP/Wide World Photos)

Christened by the press the "Flyin' Fool,"
the young airmail pilot from St. Louis was
the dark-horse candidate in the great
transatlantic air race of 1927. The
Guggenheim Fund later used this photo
in its publicity for Lindbergh's
forty-eight-state goodwill tour, making
it perhaps the best-known image of
"Lucky Lindy." *(AP/Wide World Photos)*

Fueling up the *Spirit of St. Louis* in the early morning hours of May 20, 1927.
(AP/Wide World Photos)

Wearing a borrowed suit, Captain Lindbergh appears with Ambassador Myron T. Herrick *(right)* and his jubilant staff on the steps of the American Embassy. *(AP/Wide World Photos)*

Actress Mary Pickford with the Lindberghs and two unidentified TAT executives at the christening of the TAT Tri-motor *City of Los Angeles.* Hollywood stars were among the most loyal customers of TAT, which promised to speed passengers "Coast to Coast by Train and Plane" in a mere forty-eight hours. *(AP/Wide World Photos)*

The Lindberghs at Grand Central Airport in Los Angeles on Easter Sunday 1930, about to depart on their record-setting, one-stop transcontinental flight. Anne was pregnant and self-conscious about her appearance in her bulky, electrically heated flying suit. *(AP/Wide World Photos)*

After a twelve-hour flight from Baker Lake, the Lindberghs landed at Aklavik, Alaska, where parka-clad Eskimos invited Anne to pose seated on a traditional sledge. The Lindberghs' arrival on August 9, 1931, opened a new era for the village, previously served only by a supply boat that made one visit a year. *(AP/Wide World Photos)*

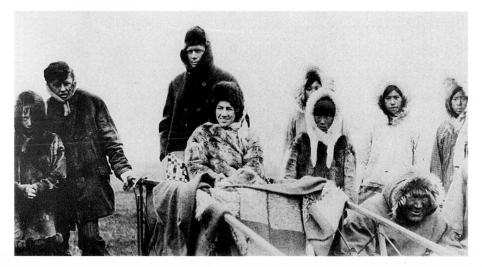

Anne and Charles junior, about three weeks old, in a quiet moment on the terrace of Next Day Hill. *(AP/Wide World Photos)*

Charles Lindbergh took this snapshot of his son in February 1932. Two weeks later the boy was kidnapped. *(AP/Wide World Photos)*

Highfields, the Lindberghs' home near Hopewell, New Jersey, as it appeared in 1936. The three French doors in the center open into the living room; the nursery was at the far right of the second floor, under the gabled roof. The driveway *(top, right)* runs for nine-tenths of a mile to an unpaved country lane. *(AP/Wide World Photos)*

Designed by architect Chester Aldrich, with suggestions from Colonel Lindbergh, Highfields is somewhat less grand than it appears in aerial photographs. The rooms are modestly proportioned, as one can see by comparing them with the three-car garage. *(Courtesy Highfields)*

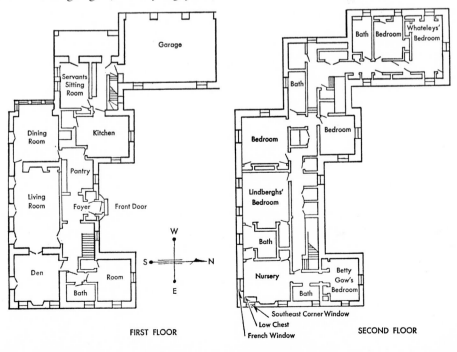

FIRST FLOOR

SECOND FLOOR

Crowds kept vigil in the streets outside Walter Swayze's funeral parlor in Trenton, where the Lindbergh baby's body had been brought for autopsy. Here they make way for the hearse carrying the child's white-satin-lined casket to the crematorium. *(AP/Wide World Photos)*

Right: The Lindberghs wave good-bye to a crowd of well-wishers at Lerwick in the Shetland Islands. Their reception in the Shetlands, which Anne called "*really* informal," made for one of the more relaxed stops on the tour. *(AP/Wide World Photos)*

Just two months after her marriage to Aubrey Morgan, Elisabeth Morrow Morgan, twenty-eight, was spotted by press photographers with an unidentified escort at the Nice railroad station. Elisabeth's doctors, fearing she could not survive the damp climate of her new home in Wales, had suggested an extended stay on the French Riviera. *(AP/Wide World Photos)*

In the summer of 1933, the Lockheed Sirius was refitted with pontoons and a powerful Wright Cyclone F engine in preparation for the Lindberghs' survey of North and South Atlantic air routes. Here Charles makes a solo test flight over Long Island Sound. *(AP/Wide World Photos)*

After living out of their airplane for five and a half months, Anne and Charles look relieved to be back in the States. Arriving at the Pan-Am seaplane base in Miami, Florida, they carried only twelve ounces apiece of personal luggage; the rest had been jettisoned in Gambia twelve days earlier to save fuel. *(AP/Wide World Photos)*

Arrested near his home in the Bronx, Bruno Richard Hauptmann was first taken to NYPD headquarters in Greenwich Village, where this mug shot was made. *(AP/Wide World Photos)*

Accompanied by Col. H. Norman Schwarzkopf, Charles Lindbergh leaves the Hunterdon County Courthouse in Flemington, New Jersey, after testifying before the grand jury that was about to indict Hauptmann for murder. Excluded from family councils in the aftermath of the kidnapping, Schwarzkopf had become Lindbergh's trusted adviser. *(AP/Wide World Photos)*

Anne Lindbergh appeared at the trial only twice, once on the day of her own testimony and again to offer moral support to her mother, who was called as a character witness for her late housemaid Violet Sharpe. Colonel Schwarzkopf (sporting a mustache grown after the grand-jury deliberations) escorts the two women the day Mrs. Morrow testified. *(AP/Wide World Photos)*

Minutes after identifying Hauptmann as "Graveyard John," Dr. John F. Condon talks to reporters in the hallway outside the courtroom. Condon's attempt to play Good Samaritan had made him the target for death threats and cost him his part-time job. Later, when he went on the lecture circuit to explain his role in the case, he was vilified as a publicity seeker. *(AP/Wide World Photos)*

Colonel Lindbergh talks with Göring's second in command, Gen. Erhardt Milch, at a banquet given by the Lilienthal Aviation Society in Munich in October 1937. "In those days, a kind of international brotherhood of airmen existed," Anne later commented, recalling that Charles had heard rumors that Göring and Milch were protecting non-Aryan officers within the Luftwaffe. *(AP/Wide World Photos)*

The Lindberghs' retreat from the world culminated in their secret purchase of a tiny islet off the coast of Brittany. Illiec consisted of a run-down house and pocket-size garden, surrounded by rocky outcroppings. *(AP/Wide World Photos)*

Unable to convince either his wife or the Lindberghs to leave Europe, Alexis Carrel returned by ship to New York in October 1938. Enjoying the celebrity gained through his partnership with Lindbergh, Carrel had signed a contract to write for *Reader's Digest*. A month later, he was frantic when *The New Yorker* associated his "artificial heart" with Nazism. *(AP/Wide World Photos)*

Charles Lindbergh's long self-imposed silence—he never issued a single public comment on the arrest and trial of Hauptmann—had enveloped him in an aura of mystery. His first radio speech, broadcast from the studios of WOL in Washington, D.C., on September 15, 1939, was covered by all three major networks. *(AP/Wide World Photos)*

On Christmas Eve 1940, Anne went on the air to urge support for the Quakers' plan to distribute food aid in occupied Europe. The distribution was opposed by Britain, and the newsreels headlined the story, "Anne Lindbergh Wants to Feed Hitler's Europe." *(AP/Wide World Photos)*

In 1953 Jon Lindbergh, twenty, donned a diving suit and Aqua-Lung to explore Bower Cave in Mariposa County, California. Jon became a record-setting deep-sea diver and inventor, active in underwater exploration and fish farming, but, like his younger brothers and sisters, he has avoided personal publicity. *(AP/Wide World Photos)*

The Lindberghs' youngest son Scott, and his wife Alika, outside their chateau in St. Chamassy, France, which they had converted into a primate rehabilitation center. Scott, who had shunned publicity since his student days, had just announced his intention of representing the family in Paris at the fiftieth anniversary celebration of his father's transatlantic flight. *(AP/Wide World Photos)*

By 1970 Charles Lindbergh's conservation activities had focused on the Philippines. Here he converses with members of the Ubu tribe in their settlement of Datal Tabayong ("Home of the Clouds"), in South Cotabato on the island of Mindanao. The settlement had been attacked repeatedly by gunmen, and Lindbergh met with the mayor and police officials of the nearby lowland town to encourage tolerance. (*John Nance*)

Returning from the meeting, Lindbergh greets Datu Ma Falen, an Ubu leader. Lindbergh carries an automatic rifle, which was not unusual on the Mindanao frontier. He wears the traditional "mountain-shaped" hat of the Tboli tribe, a gift from Tboli leaders. (*John Nance*)

Overcome by emotion, Anne Lindbergh grasps the hand of a statue depicting her husband as a young aviator about to challenge the Atlantic. The dedication ceremony, held in St. Paul, Minnesota, in May 1985, was one of Mrs. Lindbergh's rare public appearances in recent years. The Paul Granlund sculpture also includes a representation, *at right*, of Charles Lindbergh as a boy. (*AP/Wide World Photos*)

Corporal Kelly had gone downstairs with Lieutenant Bornmann to examine the ladder. Rough surfaces do not take fingerprints well, and Kelly was not surprised that he was unable to raise any useful prints. Equally unsuccessful with the three-quarter-inch chisel, he set aside his fingerprinting kit and began taking photographs of the crime scene. He got a shot of the muddy footprints under the southeast corner window but did not attempt to take plaster casts, perhaps because the ground was too wet.

Realizing that bulletins about the crime were already on the radio, Anne rushed to phone her mother and mother-in-law. Charles decided to go with detectives Keaten, Haussling, and Horn to question the neighbors. When the group stepped outside, they found two ambulances parked in the car turnaround at the front of the house; both carried teams of INS photographers who kept the leased vehicles equipped with complete portable darkrooms, knowing that flashing lights and sirens guaranteed them access to crime scenes. The INS "ambulances" were just the beginning of an invasion of reporters. The *Times* sent half a dozen, the *Daily News* nine, and the *American* and *Evening Journal* a total of twelve, led by their publisher's son, William Randolph Hearst, Jr.

Solving mysteries is a small part of the work of any state police force, and Schwarzkopf's organization was less prepared than most to deal with what was soon to become the most notorious crime in America's—and perhaps the world's—history. Founded shortly after World War I, the Jersey state police had been preoccupied, not to say overwhelmed, for most of its brief existence by trying to stanch the flow of contraband liquor through what was, by common consent, the wettest state in the nation. Its detectives lacked up-to-date forensics equipment and had little experience in dealing with a class of suspects who could not be tricked or bullied into disgorging information. The Hall-Mills murder investigation, though it ended in a conviction, had been a mess, and the Lindbergh case was about to prove that Keaten and his associates had learned little from their mistakes.

Nevertheless, much subsequent criticism of Schwarzkopf and his organization would be unjustified and unfair. In kidnapping cases it is customary to allow the victim's family to negotiate and pay the ransom. And the Lindberghs were by no means ordinary victims. Charles Lindbergh assumed control of the investigation from the outset and was responsible for many of the decisions for which Norman Schwarzkopf and the state police would later be blamed.

Surprisingly, considering his notorious dislike of the press, Lind-

bergh refused to allow the state police to bar reporters from his property. Publicity, he believed, would be useful in mobilizing the public to
join in the hunt for his child. As representatives of the press arrived, they
were invited inside the large three-car garage in the west wing of the
house, where Ollie Whateley served coffee. The Lindberghs appeared
briefly and spoke to the reporters; then Henry Breckinridge, who had
driven down from New York soon after Charles called him with the
news, gave a briefing on the facts.

Contrary to most published accounts—"the press, with the collab-
oration of the bungling police, had unwittingly destroyed real clues,"
wrote Daniel J. Boorstin in his book *Hidden History*—the situation was
under control at this point.[8] Since the newspapers had early deadlines
and local phone lines were jammed, nearly all the reporters departed
promptly for Princeton to file their stories. Chaos did not descend until
shortly after daybreak, when the general public began pouring into the
area, bringing traffic on the narrow country roads to a standstill. Hundreds of would-be helpful or simply curious individuals hiked across
adjoining farms and onto the Lindbergh estate, trampling the under-
brush and leaving behind them trails of muddy footprints, cigarette
butts, and trash. Scores of visitors also began turning up at the house to
offer condolences and help—ministers, local politicians, and, notably,
"famous detectives," a breed as common in the 1930s as famous lawyers
are today. No doubt many of these visitors were sincere; others seemed
quite content to have their presence on the scene recorded for posterity,
and Anne Lindbergh watched from an upstairs window as a parade of
strangers took turns having their pictures taken leaning against the running board of the Franklin touring car.

At least one visitor had a practical suggestion: Dr. John Hibben
arrived at midmorning, prepared to organize the Princeton student
body into a human chain to search the countryside. But an intensive
search would be useful only if the baby were dead, and on the off
chance that the kidnappers were hiding somewhere in the woods, it
might even cause them to panic and kill the child. In any event, Colonel
Schwarzkopf's first priority was to restore order. The last thing he
needed was several hundred more strangers tramping around the area.
Securing five hundred acres of unfenced land would have required an
army, but in fact by midafternoon the state police did have the situation
more or less under control once again.

Schwarzkopf moved quickly to turn the three-car garage into a
communications center. As early as 9:00 A.M., the phone company was

at work, laying an auxiliary cable along the Hopewell–Princeton road and installing twenty additional phone lines in the house. Colonel Lindbergh, meanwhile, had called on Oscar Bush, a local man with a reputation as an expert hunter and tracker. Bush quickly realized that the woman's footprints under the nursery window had been made by Mrs. Lindbergh during her midafternoon walk. But he also concluded that the larger "nubby" footprints had been left by two different individuals, both wearing burlap bags tied around their shoes. Bush followed the double trail to Featherbed Lane, where he found tire tracks indicating that two vehicles had been parked on the muddy verge of the road.[9]

State police detectives, still busy interviewing the neighbors, were hearing vivid but often confusing and contradictory accounts of strange vehicles that had been seen around Highfields over the past several days:

Ben Lupica, a student at the Princeton Preparatory School, whose family lived half a mile from Highfields, reported that at 5:00 P.M. the previous afternoon he had been driving along Lindbergh Lane when he passed a 1929 green Dodge sedan with nickel bumpers and what he believed was a Mercer County, New Jersey, license plate, driven by a clean-shaven man dressed in "city" clothes. Lupica said he had noticed what appeared to be several ladders in the backseat of the car.

The Harry Conover family, who lived near the spot where Featherbed Lane joined the public road, also had a story to tell. At about 6:45 they were returning home from an outing when they noticed the headlights of a car moving toward them along the lane. The Conovers were surprised. Although locals occasionally disregarded the ROAD IMPASSABLE sign posted at the entrance, Featherbed Lane was mainly used as a footpath. Conover stood on the porch watching the car as his wife let herself into the house. When Mrs. Conover turned on the lamp in the living room, the driver of the car in the lane flicked off his headlights.

Archie Adam, manager of the state village for epileptics in nearby Skillman, told troopers that he was driving toward Hopewell on the Hopewell–Wertsville road at about 7:40 P.M. when two cars traveling together passed him going quite fast, nearly forcing him off the road.

John Donnelson Guinness, operator of a gas station in Hopewell, had noticed another strange car, possibly a Willys-Knight, Buick, or Packard, in the vicinity of the Lindbergh estate on February 28, the Sunday before the kidnapping. Guinness became suspicious when the car turned off into another country lane that he knew to be a dead end. The car proceeded for a few hundred yards and then turned around and

passed him again on the main road. There was a woman in the passenger seat and the driver, Guinness recalled, was a rather peculiar-looking
man, blond and light complexioned with "jowly" face and "pop eyes."

Teresa Dersi, a nineteen-year-old music student whose family also
lived near Featherbed Lane, told police that on February 22, eight days
before the kidnapping, she was stopped by three men riding in a blue-
green sedan with New York license plates. The men asked her for directions to the Lindbergh house. At least four other Hopewell residents
reported seeing a similar car on that day.[10]

Lt. Arthur Keaten considered the Lupica and Conover stories solid.
As for the other witnesses, it was anyone's guess whether the strangers
they had seen had any connection with the crime. For the time being,
however, the police were operating on the assumption that the crime
was the work of at least two men, possibly with a female accomplice.

Fresh from covering the Vincent Coll killing, many of the reporters
who gathered in the Lindberghs' garage during the early hours of
Wednesday morning speculated openly that the kidnapping was the
work of the Purple Gang. A number of highly imaginative theories were
hatched as to the motive. One often-mentioned possibility was that Al
Capone, recently convicted of income tax evasion, had arranged the
snatch and was planning to barter the child's freedom for his own.

Schwarzkopf and his detectives never believed this for a second.
The crime had all the earmarks of amateurism—the failure to cut the
phone lines, the crude note, the absence of any plan for a quick payoff.
To the detectives' way of thinking the key piece of information so far
was that the child had never before spent a weekday night at Highfields.
Furthermore, Anne and the baby had never stayed there without
Colonel Lindbergh. It seemed obvious that the kidnappers, knowing
they could never penetrate the security of Next Day Hill, had been waiting for just such an opportunity. And on Tuesday evening, even his family had believed that Colonel Lindbergh would be at the Waldorf.

Any victimized family would have been horrified by the suggestion that
one or more of their own servants had betrayed them. Charles Lindbergh found this possibility more difficult to accept than most. The
complexities of human emotions were a closed book to him. He truly
believed that people he knew and liked must be good and decent.
(When he concluded otherwise, as in the case of Harry Bruno, his contempt was total and unforgiving.) This attitude was partly based on idealism but partly on an almost childlike egocentricity. It was always diffi-

cult for him to imagine that people who were opposed to him had redeeming qualities, and it would prove even harder to convince him that otherwise efficient employees might be subject to temptations, weaknesses, and desires compelling enough to override their loyalty to him.

And there were certainly compelling reasons for wanting to believe that Charles Lindbergh, Jr., had been taken by gangsters. Professional criminals would be more likely to keep the child alive and return it unharmed. It wasn't just the press who were in a panic over the gang theory; many of the people the Lindberghs most trusted, including Henry Breckinridge and the Morgan partners, were completely taken in by it.[11]

FOURTEEN

The "Inner Circle"

ARLY ON MARCH 2, the morning after the kidnapping, Congress-woman Ruth Pratt was on the phone to Col. William ("Wild Bill") Donovan. "You've got to bring Mickey Rosner in on this Lindbergh thing," she urged him. "He's done great work for the government. I have two Senators who'll vouch for his absolute honesty."

Donovan, now best remembered as the director of the OSS during World War II, was an attorney in private practice and had no official connection with the Lindbergh case, but he had often undertaken confidential missions on behalf of the Morgan bank, and Congresswoman Pratt was just one of a half dozen callers that morning who assumed the family would call him in. Moreover, as a former U.S. attorney in Buffalo and acting attorney general in the Coolidge administration, Donovan was considered an expert on organized crime. Minutes after speaking with Pratt, Donovan learned that Rosner had already called his some-time law associate, Robert Thayer, touting his credentials as an intermediary. Rosner said that he had spent the early hours of the morning with Owney Madden, who had told him "something dramatic"—a well-known gangster who "had recently dropped out of sight" was behind the Lindbergh snatch. Rosner further hinted that he was in contact with "the chief of the Unione Sicilione," who had offered to mobilize the underworld to ensure the child's safe return.

Donovan was skeptical. A career con artist facing a long sentence in connection with a two-million-dollar stock fraud, Rosner had been ped-dling his services around Washington as a potential government informant. Donovan passed the messages on to Henry Breckinridge but warned that Rosner was probably lying. "I can't vouch for this man," he emphasized.

"At this point we're accepting offers of help from any and all sources," Breckinridge said. "We're completely in the dark on this thing."[1]

Breckinridge and a friend, Washington attorney Bill Galvin, arranged a meeting with Rosner that same evening in Thayer's apartment. A short, dapper man with a rat-a-tat verbal delivery, Rosner showed up in a pin-stripe suit with a white silk handkerchief in his lapel pocket and a pearl gray fedora. "I'm not coming into the case for the money," he assured Breckinridge. Nevertheless, he added, he would need an advance of $2,500 to buy the cooperation of various gangland informants.

Breckinridge nodded his assent, and Thayer went upstairs to retrieve the cash from his bedroom safe. Rosner then got on the tele-phone and summoned two individuals who, he implied, were messenger boys for Owney Madden. When the men arrived, Rosner ceremoniously removed $1,000 from the envelope Thayer had just given him and made a show of giving each messenger $500, personally stuffing the bills into the men's trouser pockets. One of the "messengers" later admitted to the FBI that he and his confederate had received only $20; Rosner had palmed the larger bills. They were so elated over their suc-cess in pulling the oldest con game in the world on three silk-stocking lawyers, he added, that it was all they could do to keep from confessing then and there just for the pleasure of seeing the expressions on their marks' faces.

After Breckinridge and Galvin left the apartment, Rosner asked Thayer to drive him to the corner of Forty-seventh and Broadway. While Thayer waited in the car, Rosner went into a known speakeasy, emerging an hour later to announce that he had received a personal message from the kidnappers. Thayer and Rosner drove hell-bent for Princeton, where at 3:00 A.M. they met Breckinridge in an all-night diner and relayed the alleged kidnappers' demands:

1. The Lindberghs must pledge that the kidnappers would not be prosecuted, pending the safe return of the child.
2. Rosner was to have a clear, untapped phone line from the Hopewell house, which he would use to conduct further nego-tiations.

Breckinridge agreed to these terms, and he, Thayer, and Rosner drove immediately to Hopewell, arriving shortly after dawn. There was a long conference with Colonel Lindbergh, and a few hours later Breckinridge issued a statement to reporters who were keeping a watch at the gatehouse near the entrance to the Lindbergh property. The statement, actually drafted by Bill Galvin, said in part, "Mrs. Lindbergh and I desire to make personal contact with the kidnappers of our child.... We promise that we will keep whatever arrangements that may be made by their representative and ours strictly confidential and we further pledge ourselves that we will not try to injure in any way those connected with the return of our child."

"Col. Lindbergh is not afraid," Breckinridge elaborated. "Certainly the kidnappers cannot believe he would trifle with them in a matter of extreme importance to him. He will meet with them anywhere, under any conditions they may wish to lay down, even going into the underworld itself, to meet with the men who have his baby and arrange its safe return."

But the underworld, in the person of Mickey Rosner, had already occupied Highfields. Rosner moved into the den, sleeping on the couch at night and monopolizing the phone lines by day, screening incoming calls, and using his private line for conferences with his supposed intermediaries.

"This is X," Rosner would demand. "Do you have any news for me?"

These calls invariably ended with Rosner shaking his head in dismay and passing the word to Thayer and Breckinridge that the arrangements would take "just a little more time."

Colonel Schwarzkopf, who was putting in eighteen-hour days supervising the state police command post in the Lindbergh garage, was furious but helpless to do anything about it. As he told a conference of federal agents some weeks later, "He [Rosner] was to be the contact man ... it was decided in private conference by the family in which the police was [sic] not included. We did not know him except that Colonel Lindbergh told us Rosner was all right. We looked at him and thought maybe he was a gangster. We were told no, that he was vouched for. He was always in the inner circle of the family."

Charles Lindbergh appeared downstairs every morning dressed in a clean white shirt and his leather flying jacket. Lieutenants Bornmann and Keaten marveled that he appeared well rested and never lost his hearty appetite. Anne, herself remarkably composed under the circumstances, proudly compared him to a general marshaling his forces. If so, he was a general operating in alien territory without a strategy. He loathed Mickey Rosner but seemed mesmerized by his claim to have ties to powerful gangsters. It seems churlish even now to criticize a desperate father for doing whatever he thought necessary to get his child back. Nevertheless the endorsement of Rosner was a disaster. The last person any kidnapper would wish to deal with was a notorious con man, rumored on the street to be interested in turning federal informant. At the same time the family's credulity made them open season for other scam artists. While few had the heart to question the bizarre decision publicly, reporters and law-enforcement personnel were so astonished by it that some began wondering if all was as it seemed. A *Boston Herald* reporter named Laura Vitray came up with the theory that the crime was a hoax, perpetrated by the Morgan bank and the mob to "distract" the public from the depression. Fired by her paper, she churned out a quickie book claiming that the Lindbergh baby had not been kidnapped at all: The child had been stashed somewhere for safekeeping and would reappear in due time.[2]

In the meantime, partly—though by no means wholly—as a result of the Lindberghs' express call for maximum publicity, the entire country had literally been mobilized to hunt for the missing child. Many radio stations had canceled all programming and were broadcasting bulletins day and night. Evangeline Booth called out the Salvation Army, and the head of the A.F. of L. challenged each and every union member to dedicate himself to the search. Over a thirty-five-day period, the Lindberghs received more than twenty-eight thousand pieces of mail, including eight thousand tips and twelve thousand letters from people who believed that their dreams held the key to solving the mystery. The mayor of Englewood, previously named a spokesperson by the Lindberghs, received additional thousands of letters, as did the FBI, which was not yet even officially involved in the hunt. Still more tips poured into the office of the prominent New York attorney Dudley Field Malone, whom the Hearst press named as *its* intermediary. (Malone, who had not been consulted in advance, was irate.)

At Highfields all was chaos. Breckinridge, Galvin, Thayer, and several other family advisers, in addition to about a dozen state policemen, were camping out at the house, sleeping on mattresses on the floor. Twenty-one phones rang off their hooks day and night. A dozen troopers were kept busy patrolling the estate. On clear days the house was buzzed by a sightseeing plane, operated by a private pilot who was charging the curious $2.50 each for an aerial tour of the estate.

On Wednesday afternoon, the day after the crime, Betty and Elisabeth Morrow arrived in a chauffeured car, prepared to take Anne back with them to the seclusion of Next Day Hill. When Anne insisted her place was with her husband, Mrs. Morrow moved into one of the guest bedrooms to look after her. Betty Gow wrote to relatives in Scotland that Mrs. Lindbergh was holding up well, but Anne still had a bad cold, and Mrs. Morrow and Anne's obstetrician were worried that the shock might bring on a miscarriage. There was no privacy to be had in the house—on more than one occasion Anne was rousted out of bed in the middle of the night so that her husband and his advisers could confer out of earshot of the police and Rosner. More amazingly, perhaps, there is no indication in police or FBI papers that the child's mother took any active part in strategy meetings.

Three state troopers had been assigned full-time to read and sort the mail coming into Highfields, but since the troopers were not aware of the kidnappers' secret signal, Colonel Lindbergh, Breckinridge, and Thayer spent a part of every morning in the garage opening each and every letter that arrived. On Friday Lindbergh found himself reading a hand-printed, cryptically worded postcard that brought back eerie memories of the threats against his sister-in-law three years earlier. The state police concluded that the postcard had indeed been written by the same individual who attempted to extort money from Constance, but they dismissed the note as unconnected with the kidnapping.

Frustrated by the family's refusal to allow his men to interrogate the Lindbergh and Morrow servants, Lieutenant Keaten had made it his mission to win the confidence of Betty Gow. That same day, Friday, Gow happened to mention over tea that her Norwegian boyfriend Red Johnson had called the house at about eight-thirty on the evening of the kidnapping to acknowledge her message about their canceled date. Hearing this, Keaten felt sure that the pieces of the puzzle were beginning to fall into place. Johnson's nationality, he thought, would explain the Germanic-sounding spelling errors in the ransom note. Keaten leapt to the conclusion that the phone call had been made from the Hopewell area to confirm that the child was asleep in the nursery, and that Gow herself was probably in on the conspiracy.

In a strangely precipitous move, Keaten asked the Hartford police to pick up Red Johnson. The arresting officers found an empty milk bottle in the back seat of the sailor's green sedan and were not impressed by his explanation that he was in the habit of swigging milk while driving. Johnson was quickly extradited to New Jersey, where he was turned over to a portly, florid-faced Jersey City police detective named Harry Walsh, who had a reputation for extracting confessions by fair means or foul.

Johnson, the ideal suspect, was innocent. Telephone company records showed that he placed the 8:30 P.M. call from Englewood. Moreover, he spent the rest of the evening in the company of Margaret Junge, a seamstress at Next Day Hill, and her disabled husband. Johnson knew nothing, but since he was in the United States illegally, the authorities were able to hold him without charges until April 11, when he was deported to Norway. By then he and Gow had been all but convicted by the *Daily Mirror*, which ran a series of articles stating that the nursemaid was a sister of Scotty Gow, a member of Detroit's Purple Gang (she wasn't) and had a criminal past in Canada and Seattle (in neither of which she had ever set foot). In subsequent issues the *Mirror* reported that Gow had committed suicide—another fantasy—and after Colonel Lindbergh was seen walking in the woods with a rifle (he was taking target practice with the state police), it announced that the distraught father had also attempted to take his own life.

Unfortunately Lieutenant Keaten's impulsiveness had given the Lindberghs good reason to mistrust the police. Gow was no stranger to the family—her cousin Mary Beattie had been been Elisabeth's maid for many years—and a less likely conspirator than this slender, no-nonsense Scotswoman could hardly be imagined. Moreover, stories depicting Gow as a gun moll for the Detroit mob had upset Beattie and thus Elisabeth, whose poor appetite and insomnia were already worrisome enough. The police's blunder worked to the advantage of Rosner, who did a masterful job of playing on the Lindberghs' credulity. Anne Lindbergh wrote her mother-in-law that she and Charles had reached an arrangement with "two of the biggest men in the underworld—men who have tremendous power over the gangs even though they are not in touch with them."[3] Norman Schwarzkopf, hoping to discredit Rosner, had arranged for a state trooper at the Hopewell telephone exchange to tap his private line. When Colonel Lindbergh accidentally learned of the phone monitoring, he threatened to eject the state police from his property. Schwarzkopf was now completely excluded from the strategy sessions of what he disparagingly called the "inner circle."

* * *

On Saturday, March 5, Charles Lindbergh and Robert Thayer were sorting through the morning mail when they found a letter bearing the kidnappers' symbol. Mailed from downtown Brooklyn the previous afternoon, the letter said:

> Dear Sir. We have warned you note to make anyding Public also notify police now you have to take consequences. Ths means we will holt the baby untill everyding is quiet.... It is rely necessary to make a world affair out off this, or to get yours baby back as sun as possible ... now we have to take another person to it and probable have to keep the baby for a longer time as we expected.[4]

In view of these complications, the letter went on, the ransom demand was being raised to seventy thousand dollars. (A psychologist consulted by the police later observed that the letter contained a classic example of a Freudian slip. Presumably the author had meant to write: "Is it really necessary to make a world affair out of this?" By reversing the word order, the kidnapper betrayed his satisfaction at being the object of worldwide attention.)

Although Lindbergh had previously agreed that only a few trusted associates would see communications from the kidnappers, he was so disturbed by the note that he carried it into the living room to show it to Bill Galvin. While Galvin was reading, Mickey Rosner wandered in from the den. As Robert Thayer later described the scene, when Rosner saw the letter in Galvin's hands he "turned very white and was trembling all over." "This is the break we've all been waiting for!" he announced, and he persuaded Lindbergh to let him deliver the note to Henry Breckinridge, who was in New York conferring with Morgan partner Frank Bartow, who was in charge of raising the ransom payment. Furious at this breach of security, Schwarzkopf assigned two troopers to follow Rosner to New York.

Bartow had already virtually liquidated Colonel Lindbergh's portfolio. Although press accounts regularly estimated the Lindberghs' net worth at between two and three million dollars, in reality they had far less. Anne received only the income from her trust fund, which by 1932 had dwindled alarmingly. Charles had spent heavily on various aviation projects, and in any case, much of his money was in aviation stocks, now selling at rock-bottom prices when one could find a buyer at all. Bartow had sold off securities worth about $350,000 in predepression days to raise the first $50,000 demanded by the kidnappers. Now, the kidnappers were demanding an additional $20,000, and the Lindberghs only had $5,000 left in their account. Of course, Betty Morrow would have been more than willing to advance the additional cash, but money was still such a sore subject between Charles and his mother-in-law that even now he refused to ask for her help. Instead Bartow arranged for J. P. Morgan & Co. to advance the additional sum—an arrangement that gave the bank a certain standing in deciding how the negotiations should be handled.

By the time Rosner arrived at Breckinridge's office he had acquired two companions, Salvatore ("Sonny") Spitale and Irving Bitz. Rosner introduced Spitale to Breckinridge and Bartow as "a former associate of Legs Diamond." (Indeed, the FBI suspected Spitale of arranging Diamond's assassination.) Bitz, a hulking speakeasy bouncer, was described as "an associate" of Spitale's. Bitz and Spitale lacked even Rosner's patina of respectability. However, Rosner's name-dropping worked its magic on Frank Bartow, who apparently believed that the criminal world was organized like a Wall Street firm—anything could be accomplished if only one had access to the top man. Bartow and Breckinridge shuttled back to Hopewell, where they talked the increasingly skeptical Charles Lindbergh into issuing a press release adding Spitale and Bitz to the list of authorized intermediaries.

Spitale and Bitz moved into the house that evening. The two of them promptly took over the living room, where they sprawled on the couch, shoes up on the coffee table, smoking smelly cigars and reading newspapers while issuing peremptory orders to Anne, who scuttled in and out of the room serving them sandwiches and coffee and emptying their ashtrays. Incensed over this treatment of Mrs. Lindbergh, Bill Galvin and John Fogarty, a private investigator employed by Breckinridge's law firm, decided to make it their business to get Rosner and his pals out of the house. Galvin and Fogarty happened to be sharing the downstairs guest bedroom opposite the den, and they began eavesdropping on the gangsters' conversations.

On Sunday morning, March 6, a telegram arrived from the Rev. Peter Berritella, the minister of a storefront church at 164 West 127th Street in Harlem, claiming that he had important information on the baby's whereabouts. Rosner, for some reason, insisted that Berritella was an important contact, so Henry Breckinridge set up a meeting in a rented room at the Princeton Inn. Berritella showed up accompanied by Mary Cirrito, a spiritualist medium who gave seances in New York under the pseudonym Mary Magdalene. Cirrito said that she had an important message for the Lindberghs "from the spirit world," which could be delivered only at a seance in the missing baby's nursery.

"That's impossible," Breckinridge snapped. "The condition of the mother won't permit it."

At this, Cirrito's eyes rolled back in her head. In a quavery voice she proclaimed that the baby boy was at that moment four and a half miles northwest of Highfields. (It would later be discovered that he was four and a half miles to the southwest.) Cirrito then described, quite accurately, a lightning-struck tree that stood behind the Lindbergh house.

"Spiritualist nonsense," harrumphed Breckinridge.

At this Cirrito snapped out of her "trance." Suddenly all business, she warned that nothing could be resolved until the police were called off. "Have you received any letters from the kidnappers?" she demanded. There had been a letter, but Breckinridge denied it. Cirrito muttered that Breckinridge was spending too much time away from New York. From now on, she said, he must make it a point to be in his office at 9:00 A.M. every morning.

Irritated at this waste of his time, Breckinridge declared the meeting over, but he offered to drive the pair to the Princeton train station. "No, no," said Berritella. "They bought us round trip tickets to Princeton *Junction* [a few miles away from Princeton proper]." It occurred to Breckinridge that spirits do not purchase railroad tickets, and he began to wonder whether Rosner had arranged the meeting to get him out of the house.

While Breckinridge was in Princeton, Galvin and Fogarty decided to seize their opportunity to talk some sense into Colonel Lindbergh. Rosner, however, got wind of the plan and got to Lindbergh first. Summoning the colonel and Bob Thayer to "his" office, he announced that his gangland sources had just relayed a warning that the kidnappers had two confederates *who were actually living inside the house*. The accomplices were none other than Bill Galvin and John Fogarty! Even Thayer, so far Rosner's chief supporter, found this too much to believe. But Lindbergh eyed Galvin and Fogarty warily and seemed half convinced of their guilt. Disgusted, the two men packed their belongings and left the house.

No sooner had Galvin and Fogarty departed than Owney Madden showed up in Hopewell, demanding to see Colonel Lindbergh. The speakeasy czar had figured out that Rosner was trying to pin the crime on him and was determined not to let that happen. Madden called the house repeatedly after that, and a few days later he spent two hours clos-eted with Lindbergh and Breckinridge giving them his views on the case. Madden's speech was such an impenetrable mélange of under-world argot, locutions borrowed from his favorite columnist, Walter Winchell, and sheer double-talk that Lindbergh and his attorney were unable to figure out if he was denouncing Rosner or offering to help him. Nevertheless they invited Madden to attend future meetings of the "inner circle," much to Schwarzkopf's disgust.

Strangely, on the Tuesday morning following his meeting with Berritella and Cirrito, Breckinridge received an excited call from his sec-retary, who described a letter that had come with the morning mail. Bearing the kidnappers' symbol, the letter was in the same handwriting and on identical paper as the first two notes:

> Dear Sir. Dit you reccive ouer letter from March 4. we sent the mail in one off the letter post near Burror Hall—Brooklyn. We know Police intefere with your privatmail; how can we come to any arrangements this way. In the future we will send our letters to Mr. Breckenbridge at 25 Broadway. We belive Polise capturet two letter and let not forwarded to you. We will not accept any go between from your sent. We will arrangh theas latter. There is no worry about the Boy....
>
> Is it nessisery to make a world-affair out of it, or to get your boy back as soon as possible. WHy did you ignore ouer letter which we left in the room the baby would be back long ago. You would not get any result from Polise becauce this kidnnaping was pland for a year allredy. Byt we were afraid the boy would be strong enough.[5]

Again, the letter ended with a demand for seventy thousand dollars to be paid once "the polise is out of this cace and the pappers are quite." Colonel Lindbergh was to place an ad in the personals column of the New York *American* acknowledging his receipt of the message. The warning—"We know Police intefere with your privatmail"—was so similar to what Mary Cirrito had told Breckinridge that he and the state police now suspected that she and Berritella had been sent by the kid-nappers after all. How else could she have known that the kidnappers intended to forward their next letter through Breckinridge's office? Another disturbing feature of the message was the complaint that the police had captured two previous letters. Unless this referred to the note

left in the nursery, which for various reasons seemed unlikely, a communication from the kidnappers must have gone astray in the mails or else
simply had not been recognized as genuine.

While Mickey Rosner held the Lindberghs in thrall, Charles's cousin
Capt. Emory Land had joined forces with the Washington socialite Evalyn Walsh McLean in an independent attempt to locate the missing
baby. An heiress with a fabulous wardrobe and a voice like a rusty hinge,
Evalyn McLean was best known to the public as the owner of the Hope
diamond, which allegedly brought its owners a lifetime of bad luck.
McLean herself scoffed at the legend, saying that her troubles—and she
had plenty of them—were merely "the natural consequences of
unearned wealth in undisciplined hands." The daughter of a Colorado
prospector who struck it rich late in life, McLean was the estranged wife
of the owner of the *Washington Post* and the capital's most eccentric
hostess. At her Virginia estate, Fair Haven, she kept a pet llama, which
her daughter rode bareback through the upstairs bedrooms, and a long-
tailed monkey named Babe, famous for pouring a glass of lemonade
over the head of President Warren G. Harding.[6]

After the birth of their son, Vinson, nicknamed by the press the
"million-dollar baby," the McLeans had received a series of letters
threatening the boy's life. Vinson grew up surrounded by bodyguards,
sluggish and depressed despite fifteen-thousand-dollar birthday parties
and the twenty-four-hour-a-day companionship of a black child named
Julian Winship, whom the McLeans had purchased from his parents.
(Mrs. McLean rationalized that Winship was not a slave since the agreement only gave her "legal custody for ten years.") The unfortunate Vinson died in a freak accident when he was nine years old. Fourteen years
later, still racked by guilt, McLean hoped to compensate for her mistakes by saving the Lindbergh baby.

Three days after the kidnapping, McLean sought out Gaston Means,
one of the more unsavory "great detectives" of the era. Once a key operative of the William J. Burns Agency, Means joined the Bureau of Investigation (precursor of the FBI) only to be fired by J. Edgar Hoover for taking bribes. He became a bootlegger, served time in the federal penitentiary in Atlanta, and was tried and acquitted for the murder of a rich
widow in North Carolina. His reputation in Washington rested on his
coauthorship of a bestseller, *The Strange Death of Warren G. Harding,*
which alleged that the president had been poisoned by the first lady.

McLean had been a close friend of Mrs. Harding and knew

Means's salacious charges weren't true, but, she later said, "I wanted Means for precisely what he was—for the lack of straightness in his smartness." A day after he was hired, Means reported that he had spoken with the leader of the Lindbergh kidnapping gang, a man known as "the Fox," and struck a deal to purchase the baby's freedom for one hundred thousand dollars. (One hundred thousand dollars, or for that matter the mere seventy thousand dollars demanded in the ransom notes, was a lot of money in 1932. The average per capita income was still under fifteen hundred dollars, and many were trying to support a family on less.) Mrs. McLean, however, was ready to put up the cash, but she wanted a partner who was close enough to the Lindbergh family to identify the baby. Her first recruit was Robert Guggenheim, who hastily withdrew after meeting Gaston Means.

McLean next turned to Jerry Land, whose parents had known her father in Colorado. Even by the standards of the inner circle, Land was extraordinarily trusting. Without setting eyes on Gaston Means, he agreed to join McLean in what he would later call "the most miserable experience of my lifetime."[7]

On March 6 Land drove through a late-winter blizzard to Hopewell, where he found Anne and Mrs. Morrow in the kitchen, assembling a mountain of sandwiches for their "sundry assistants," as he put it. Charles, who had probably heard something of Evalyn McLean's plans from Robert Guggenheim, was not enthusiastic about dealing with Gaston Means, but he told his cousin that he was accepting any and all offers of help. Naturally, he added, if the ransom were eventually paid, he would insist on reimbursing Mrs. McLean.

Land carried this message back to Washington, where he was astounded to learn that McLean had already given Means the full hundred thousand without asking to see any evidence that his contacts actually had the baby. Means sent word that Mrs. McLean and Captain Land, together with a Catholic priest invited along "for the sake of propriety," were to go to Fairview, a summer home in Maryland owned by Mrs. McLean's mother, and wait there for the child to be delivered into their custody. Fairview had been boarded up for the winter; the heat was turned off, the furniture shrouded under tarps. Land, McLean, and the priest camped out in the living room, consuming gallons of coffee and (in Mrs. McLean's case, at least) equal quantities of spirits. They never saw any sign of a baby, but Means showed up on several occasions and managed to talk Mrs. McLean into handing over an additional three thousand dollars.

After two weeks Land and the priest gave up. McLean, however, was persuaded by Means that the baby had been moved south and would be turned over to her at her winter home in Aiken, South Carolina. Traveling under the alias "Mrs. Land," McLean went down to Aiken, where she was introduced to "the Fox," who was actually Means's accomplice Norman Whitaker. The Fox sorrowfully reported that the rest of the kidnapping gang, fearing a trap, had fled to El Paso, Texas, with the child. McLean then followed Whitaker and Means to El Paso, where she was told that the gang was now in Juarez, Mexico, and would give up the child for an additional thirty-five thousand dollars.

Her judgment somewhat clouded by a three-week-long drinking binge, McLean was quite ready to go on to Juarez, but first she had to return to Washington, where she attempted to raise the thirty-five thousand by selling some of her jewelry to wealthy friends. One of these women, realizing that Evalyn's chances of returning from Mexico alive were not good, managed to persuade her friend to turn the whole matter over to her attorneys.

The attorneys arranged for McLean to send Gaston Means a message, luring him back to Washington, where he was arrested and eventually pleaded guilty to larceny and embezzlement. Means's active role in the Lindbergh kidnapping mystery was finished, but Jerry Land's problems had just begun. Although Evalyn McLean was reputedly one of the richest women in America, the combined ravages of the stock market crash, ruinous legal battles with her ex-husband, and decades of extravagance had left her deeply in debt. She had mortgaged her Washington town house to raise the hundred thousand dollars she gave to Gaston Means, and her attorneys, who knew that she was an alcoholic and often irrational, held Captain Land responsible. When they learned of Colonel Lindbergh's promise to reimburse McLean if the ransom was paid, they concluded that Mrs. McLean had been acting as an agent of the Lindbergh family and was legally entitled to the money. Land was caught in the middle of this dispute, which would drag on for several years. Although he eventually arranged a meeting between McLean and Charles Lindbergh, the money never changed hands.

Once the kidnappers had begun communicating with the family via Henry Breckinridge's office, there appeared to be no further reason for the Lindberghs to place any faith in Mickey Rosner. Nevertheless, events contrived to keep Rosner's scam alive a few days longer. On March 5 Gov. A. Harry Moore of New Jersey met with a delegation of

Chicago police officials to ask about rumors that Al Capone had something to do with the Lindbergh case, and a few days later, Capone himself summoned Hearst executive Arthur Brisbane to his jail cell in Chicago for an exclusive interview. Capone told Brisbane that the crime was obviously gang related since "nobody else could get away with that job at a spot surrounded by bridges." (Brisbane did not ask what bridges Capone had in mind.) Although he emphasized that he had no idea who had done it, Capone boasted that he could solve the case in forty-eight hours if a federal judge would agree to release him on $250,000 bond.

After March 6, when the first hints of Capone's involvement surfaced in the newspapers, the whole country began debating the morality of exchanging Capone's freedom for the Lindbergh baby. Rosner, needless to say, claimed to be in touch with various Capone associates. "Capone is so feared," he told Lindbergh, "if he were free he could find the baby in a matter of hours." Simultaneously, at least six other individuals representing themselves as Capone's agents were negotiating with Breckinridge's law firm. One Washington, D.C., attorney asked that Lindbergh's TAT colleague Maj. Robert Lanphier stand ready to drop a ransom payment of $200,000 from the air at a prearranged spot in rural Illinois. In a phone call to Secretary of the Treasury Ogden Mills, Colonel Lindbergh emphasized that he would never ask the government to release Capone. But Lindbergh sounded far from convinced that Capone was bluffing, so Mills asked Elmer Irey, the head of the IRS Enforcement Division and the man primarily responsible for Capone's conviction, to go up to Hopewell to offer moral support.[8]

Accompanied by Arthur Nichols of the IRS's Philadelphia office, Irey dropped in at the house on Tuesday, March 8. Like Jerry Land, Irey was taken aback to find Mrs. Lindbergh, ashen faced but outwardly calm, running errands for Spitale and Bitz. "To meet Lindbergh is to know that he has no time or desire for polite talk," Irey later wrote, "so I told him very bluntly, 'Capone doesn't know who has the child, Colonel Lindbergh. He is simply trying to get out of jail.'"

Lindbergh produced the three ransom notes for Irey's inspection. He now felt there was a good chance of getting his child back, he said, and he was "desperately anxious that no police or civilian interference bungle things." As an example of the kind of meddling that was going on, Lindbergh showed Irey a copy of the *Bronx Home News*, a neighborhood newspaper with a circulation of about one hundred thousand. DR. JOHN F. CONDON OFFERS TO ADD ONE THOUSAND DOLLARS OF HIS

OWN SAVINGS TO RANSOM LINDBERGH CHILD, proclaimed a page-one headline.

"I'm at a complete loss, Mr. Irey," Lindbergh said, adding, "I have only policemen to turn to for help. I would like it very much if you folks could stay."[9]

Irey replied that there were already too many outsiders camping out at the house, but he offered to place an undercover agent in Peter Berritella's storefront congregation and to work with Frank Bartow in assembling the ransom payment.

FIFTEEN

"Jafsie"

*A*NATION ALREADY ANXIOUS over the depression, crime, and the rise of totalitarian regimes abroad found it all too easy to believe that the kidnapping of their hero's first-born son reflected some deeper flaw in society. To a degree, all Americans were responsible. A popular ditty of the period asked:

> Who stole the Lindbergh baby?
> Was it you? Was it you?
> After he crossed the ocean wide,
> Was that the way to show our pride?
> Was it you? Was it you? Was it you?[1]

The same idea was expressed less flippantly in an Associated Press cartoon that appeared in newspapers across the country a few days after the crime. It showed a grief-stricken Lindbergh with the caption: LINDY WE HAVE FAILED YOU IN YOUR HOUR OF NEED.

Among the millions who saw this drawing and were touched by its message was a seventy-two-year-old retired Bronx school principal named John F. Condon. Sentimental and garrulous but also deeply idealistic, Condon was committed to the very core of his being to the ideal of melting-pot America. He had served forty-six years in the public school system, organized Little League teams, coached generations of

Golden Gloves boxers, and occasionally contributed articles to the *Bronx Home News* under pseudonyms like "L. O. Nestar" and "P. A. Triot." A few days after the AP cartoon appeared, Condon overheard a stranger in a Fordham Road restaurant tell his companions, "Your Department of Justice, your Secret Service ... what can they do? In my country, such a crime would never have happened!" This remark so aroused his "American spirit" that he gave an interview to the *Home News*, offering to act as an intermediary.

By the time the interview appeared, Condon was feeling a bit sheepish. So many high-level people were already on the case—why would the kidnappers be interested in dealing with him? In any event, the one reply he received, a note to him that arrived along with a sealed enclosure addressed to Colonel Lindbergh, was so crudely spelled and worded that Condon put it in his pocket and forgot all about it until that evening, when he mentioned it to his two best friends, Maxie Rosenhain and Milton Gaglio. Rosenhain insisted that Condon call the Lindbergh house right away.

Robert Thayer answered the phone and was about dismiss Condon as just another nut when Condon mentioned that the note contained a "trigamba."

"A what?" asked Thayer.

Condon described the peculiar design of interlocking circles. Gaglio had told him it was a Sicilian symbol whose name meant "three legs."[2]

Hearing this, Thayer became very excited and urged Condon to come down to New Jersey that very night.

Since Condon did not own a car, Rosenhain and Gaglio volunteered to drive him. At 2:00 A.M., they finally located the all-night diner near Princeton where Henry Breckinridge was waiting to meet them. Condon, a man of many words, had prepared a little speech introducing himself and his friends as Good Samaritans from the Bronx, "the most beautiful borough in the world."

"A Wop, an Israelite and a Harp," Rosenhain added helpfully.[3]

Following his conversation with Elmer Irey, Charles Lindbergh had somewhat belatedly decided that Mickey Rosner must not be allowed to see any further ransom notes, so Breckinridge hustled Condon, Rosenhain, and Gaglio up the back staircase of Highfields to a second-floor bedroom. Before producing the kidnapper's letter, Condon asked to be allowed some time in the nursery to pray beside the baby's crib. Next he insisted on being introduced to Mrs. Lindbergh, who was awakened from a sound sleep for a brief meeting. All in all Condon was even less confidence-inspiring than Mickey Rosner or Mary Magdalene Cirrito. But he did have a letter in the kidnapper's handwriting.

It said:

> Affter you gett the Mony from Mr. Lindbergh put them 3 word's in the *New York American*
> money is redy
> .... Don't be affrait we are not out fore your 1000 $ keep it. Only act stricly. Be at home every night between 6–12 by this time you will hear from us.

The enclosure addressed to Lindbergh merely reiterated the demand for seventy thousand dollars.

Condon spent the night at the house, and the following afternoon Breckinridge and Lindbergh drove him back to his home on Decatur Avenue in the Bronx. Lindbergh, wearing one of his many disguises, was carrying a suitcase containing seventy thousand in cash. The suitcase sat in the kitchen for several days until Condon's wife, Myra, insisted that Breckinridge deposit the money in a vault at the Corn Exchange Bank.

Condon's message to the kidnappers appeared in the personals column of the New York *American* on March 11. In order to keep the press from discovering his identity, he had signed the ad "Jafsie"—a play on his initials, J. F. C. At seven o'clock that evening, his home phone rang. "I saw your ad in the *American*," a male voice said. Condon chatted with the man for a few minutes and got the impression that the caller was relaying his comments to a third party.

"Where are you calling from?" Condon asked.

"Westchester."

In the background Condon heard a voice say, "*Statti citto* [*sic*]"— Italian for "shut up." The man hung up.

The following Saturday Bronx cabbie Joseph Perrone was driving past the intersection of Gun Hill Road and Knox Place when he was flagged down by a man who offered him fifty cents to deliver a note to Condon's house. The note directed Condon to an abandoned frankfurter stand on Jerome Avenue. There a second note ordered him to a rendezvous in Woodlawn Cemetery. Condon's friend Al Reich (pronounced *Reech*), a retired heavyweight boxer, drove him to the cemetery and sat waiting in the car, suspiciously eyeing a man in a brown fedora who appeared to be acting as a lookout. Reich later described the lookout as "a medium-sized Italian."

Seconds after Condon entered the cemetery, he saw a man waving a white handkerchief. He approached and found himself sharing a stone bench with a muscular, clean-shaven man who held up his coat collar to shield his face. Condon had not spent three decades as a high school principal for nothing. "Take that collar down and be a man," he scolded.

The stranger complied.

There followed a fifteen-minute conversation between Condon and the man he decided—for reasons never made clear—to call "John." John said he came from Boston, had been a sailor, and represented a gang of three men and two women.

"Are you German?" Condon guessed.

"Scandinavian."

"Well, Colonel Lindbergh is Scandinavian too, so you should have nothing against him," Condon observed.

John replied that he had nothing against Lindbergh, but, "*they* have something against me." The baby, he added, was being held on a boat, where he could signal to it from shore. In the next breath, however, he said the boat was five or six hours away. It was obvious to Condon that many of John's answers were drawn from newspaper stories about Red Johnson and other suspects, no doubt in a deliberate attempt to mislead him. But one remark John made chilled Condon to his very bones. Interrupting his own rambling description of the gang, John blurted out, "Vat if the baby iss dead? Vould I burn if the baby iss dead?"[4]

Suddenly cautious, Condon told John that the family wanted to see proof that he actually had the child. Condon had been instructed to ask for the baby's Dr. Denton's sleeping suit since the police had purposely released an incorrect description of the garment to the newspapers in order to foil extortionists. On Monday John called to say that producing the clothing would take a little time. Finally, on Wednesday afternoon, a package arrived in the mail containing a freshly laundered Dr. Denton's. Charles Lindbergh, disguised in oversize amber glasses and a workman's cap, drove in from Hopewell to inspect the garment. "That appears to be my son's," he told Condon.

Judging by the postmark on the package, the sleeping suit had not been mailed until sixty-five hours after the meeting in Woodlawn Cemetery. Condon believed there could be only one reason for the delay. The child was dead, and the kidnappers had returned to the grave to retrieve it. Far from saving the Lindbergh baby, he would merely be helping the criminals bilk the parents out of a small fortune in ransom. Although Condon didn't have the heart to tell Colonel Lindbergh what he suspected, he began to insist on what he called a "C.O.D. delivery." He wanted to see the baby with his own eyes before handing over any money, even if he had to offer himself as a hostage in exchange for the child. Lindbergh, who had been advised by the Treasury agents to pay the money quickly without setting conditions, delegated the job of managing Condon to Henry Breckinridge.[5]

Condon's ad—"I accept. Money is ready. The package is delivered and is okay"—ran in the *American* for a week. Every evening at six o'clock Henry Breckinridge showed up at Decatur Avenue and sat in the kitchen until midnight, chain smoking and drinking black coffee, prepared to arrange a payoff on an hour's notice.

Still, there was no word from Graveyard John, who had apparently been scared off by continuing developments in the saga of Mickey Rosner. On March 11 Lindbergh had finally told Rosner that his services were no longer needed, and the gangster and his associates were ejected from the house by a half dozen burly state troopers. Rosner, however, was far from ready to bow out of the case. After a trip to the Midwest, supposedly to confer with Davey Fleisher of the Purple Gang, Rosner gave a press conference at a mid-Manhattan speakeasy, announcing that he had "proof positive" that the baby was alive and being held in Detroit. In fact, he said, *he had seen the baby with his own eyes.*

Condon, meanwhile, had become convinced that he was being watched. At a charity rummage sale, where he was attempting to sell several old violins, a young woman approached him and whispered, "Nothing can be done until the excitement dies down." The woman then asked him to meet her at the Tuckahoe, New York, station of the New York Central Railroad in four days. Condon showed up at the appointed time, and the woman—"the violin prospect," Condon called her—appeared out of the crowd. "You will get a message later," she whispered hoarsely. "Keep advertising until you hear more."

On another occasion a "swarthy" man who appeared to be a peddler came striding down Decatur Avenue, bypassing neighboring houses, and knocked on Condon's door. The man left hastily after catching a glimpse of Colonel Breckinridge in the living room.

The police, meanwhile, were worried about Condon's penchant for talking about himself. He had already discussed his role in the case with

Reich, Rosenhain, and Gaglio, as well as his son-in-law, Ralph Hacker. Moreover, scores of people, including the city editors of the major metropolitan newspapers, had no doubt made the connection between the "Jafsie" ads appearing in the *American* and Condon's public offer to act as intermediary. Amazingly, however, everyone was sitting on the story. But on March 17 a Decatur Avenue neighbor of the Condons', while interviewing for a job at the *Daily News,* "accidentally" mentioned that he knew Jafsie well. The next morning the sidewalk in front of the Condon house was six deep in reporters. Condon escaped from the house by dressing up in his wife's clothes. Pulling a scarf over his face to hide his walrus mustache, he fled on the arm of Al Reich.

That evening the "inner circle" held a strategy session at Frank Bartow's Manhattan apartment. Among those present, besides Colonel Lindbergh, Henry Breckinridge, and Bill Galvin, were J. P. Morgan partner Harry Davison and three Treasury agents—Elmer Irey, Arthur Nichols, and Frank Wilson. Far from being grateful for Dr. Condon's efforts on the family's behalf, the advisers dismissed him as a publicity-seeking eccentric who had pushed his way into the case, destroying their chances of setting up a channel of negotiations through Henry Breckinridge. Ironically, Breckinridge himself had become Condon's lonely defender. Although Condon's endless monologues often tried his patience, Breckinridge pointed out to the group that this seventy-two-year-old man had shown considerable courage in meeting a desperate criminal in a deserted cemetery after dark.

Now that the newspapers had learned Condon's identity and were planning to spread it all over the front pages of the morning editions, the group was all but resigned to the fact that Condon's usefulness was ended.

"Why don't you just ask them to hold off on this?" Irey suggested.

No one had considered this possibility. Bill Galvin now began calling editors and discovered that every paper except the *Daily News* was willing to kill the story. The *News,* too, fell into line after Frank Bartow relayed an appeal to the paper's owners through a mutual friend.

Next, much to dismay of the Treasury agents, the group decided to accept Owney Madden's offer to investigate Peter Berritella and Mary Cirrito. Some days later Madden sent two henchmen to bring Berritella and Cirrito to his office for a little talk, an experience which left them so terrified that they would scarcely leave their apartments for the next six months. Berritella's storefront church was closed, rendering Wilson's undercover agent useless. Wilson had no doubt that Berritella and Cirrito were acting as messengers for the kidnappers, probably as accessories after the fact, but since both of them were more frightened of Owney Madden than of jail, there was not much chance of getting them to tell what they knew. (In July 1932 Berritella and Cirrito would get married—a move that Wilson interpreted as a ploy to protect themselves from having to testify against each other before a grand jury. Although both the Treasury agents and the FBI continued to regard the two of them as suspects, inexplicably the New Jersey and New York police lost interest in them—perhaps because Keaten and Walsh had already made up their minds that the pair worked for Rosner.)[6]

Elmer Irey then took over the meeting and explained that Treasury agents working with tellers at the Morgan bank were preparing a second package of ransom money. This time the serial number of every bill would be recorded. The package would also include a number of gold certificates. Gold notes were about to be withdrawn from circulation and would therefore be easier to trace. Lindbergh objected strongly. He and Anne had promised in their appeal to the kidnappers that they were not interested in prosecution, only in getting their child back alive. A promise was a promise, he argued, even if made to a criminal.

Flabbergasted, Irey protested what he called Lindbergh's "extraordinary ethics," insisting, "We cannot compound a felony." Unless the ransom was paid with marked money, the federal agents would withdraw from the case. Lindbergh, Irey would recall, "pursed his lips and said nothing." At this point, the Treasury agents walked out of the meeting.[7]

Although Condon was still in the picture, Breckinridge's arguments on his behalf had made little impression. Bartow and Davison, especially, simply could not bring themselves to believe that this "interloper" who claimed no high-level connections, legitimate or otherwise, might yet prove useful. On the other hand, even at this sensitive stage of the negotiations, almost anyone who could drop the right names was being given a chance. Shortly after Elmer Irey walked out of the meeting, Frank Bartow told Lindbergh that he had been approached by Murray Garsson, a special assistant secretary of labor, who claimed that he could solve the case within forty-eight hours if he were allowed to visit the scene of the crime. Bartow had no notion of how Garsson planned to pull off this miracle, but he recommended that Lindbergh arrange for Garsson to visit Highfields that very night. At 1:00 A.M., Lindbergh, who planned to be in conference with Breckinridge and Galvin until dawn, called home and asked his wife to be prepared for Garsson's arrival.

Bartow drove Garsson to Highfields, where Mrs. Lindbergh, her mother, and Aida Breckinridge, Henry's wife, had roused themselves from bed and dressed hastily, not quite knowing what to expect. Garsson entered the house carrying a bulky duffel bag, and when Anne saw it she nearly fainted, imagining for a second that it contained the body of her child. Garsson began his presentation by ordering Anne to run upstairs and walk around in the nursery, to prove his contention that it was impossible for a kidnapper to have entered the room without being heard downstairs. He ended some four hours later by leading the women down to the basement, where he pantomimed the act of throwing a dead baby into the furnace and then picked up a poker and began sifting through the ashpan in search of bone fragments.

At long last it had become clear what Garsson's theory was: He believed that Charles Lindbergh had killed his son in a fit of temper and that Anne and the servants were lying to protect him. Astonishingly Bartow made no attempt to interfere—he later explained that Colonel Lindbergh had instructed him to assist the visitor in any way possible!

The next day Bill Galvin called Irey and told him that Colonel Lindbergh had been persuaded to use the marked bills after all. Lindbergh later apologized to Irey for his behavior at the meeting, saying, "The kidnappers have me over a barrel." Although he knew that Irey's demand was reasonable, he still worried that the kidnappers would find out the serial numbers were on record and retaliate by killing his son.

As for Murray Garsson, he showed up at Highfields at least twice more, demanding to be allowed to search the basement. His visits finally ceased after Elmer Irey complained directly to the White House.[8]

Frantic over Graveyard John's continuing silence, Lindbergh was now willing to deal with almost anyone, however implausible their story might be. Shortly after the kidnapping, the family had begun to receive phone calls from two prominent citizens of Norfolk, Virginia, Adm. Guy Burrage and the Rev. Harold Dobson-Peacock, formerly the pastor of the Episcopal cathedral where the Morrows had worshipped in Mexico. Burrage and Dobson-Peacock urged Charles to speak with a Norfolk boatbuilder named John Hughes Curtis, who claimed to be in touch with one "Sam," the leader of a gang that was holding the baby on a boat somewhere off the Atlantic coast of the United States. A flashy dresser who lived in an ostentatious beachfront home, Curtis sold speedboats to rum runners and was associated with the Philadelphia gangster Sam ("the Gas Man") Goldberg, a circumstance that lent his story an aura of plausibility.[9]

The problem with Curtis's account was that he had absolutely no knowledge of the ransom notes; nor could he supply any proof that Sam had the baby. Nevertheless, on March 22, Curtis, Burrage, and Dobson-Peacock were invited to Highfields. Lindbergh listened intently to what Curtis had to say and then told the three men that in his opinion Sam was a phony. Although all three visitors promised not to discuss the meeting, Dobson-Peacock, apparently befuddled by his moment in the spotlight, soon told a reporter that John Curtis had Colonel Lindbergh's "complete confidence." A few days later the clergyman also announced that he had met Sam at a Manhattan hotel. Partly on the basis of this confirmation from a respected clergyman, Curtis negotiated a contract to sell his exclusive story to the *Daily News* for twenty-five thousand dollars. At the last minute, however, the *News* insisted on a clause stipulating that Curtis would not be paid a cent until and unless the child was returned to his parents alive.

Four days later Dr. Condon received a testy note from Graveyard John, who complained: "How can Mr. Lindbergh follow so many false clues he knows we are the right party ouer singature is still the same as in the ransom note."

Another letter, received on March 31, gave final instructions for the delivery of the seventy thousand dollars.

On the appointed night, Saturday, April 2, representatives of the police, the three Treasury agents, and the rest of the "inner circle" gathered at the Morrow apartment on East Seventy-second Street. Norman Schwarzkopf and the NYPD urged that Graveyard John be followed after he left the cemetery, but Lindbergh decided to rely on the advice of the T-men, who warned that an effort to trap the kidnappers might endanger the baby's life. Patrolmen walking beats in the Bronx and Manhattan were actually notified that the Lindbergh ransom payment would be made that night and they were not to interfere in any suspicious situations.

Shortly before eight o'clock, a cab driver arrived at Dr. Condon's front door with a note containing last-minute directions. Lindbergh, wearing a .38 pistol strapped under his coat jacket, personally drove Condon to the rendezvous in Al Reich's car. Condon was carrying the money in a wooden box, constructed by his son-in-law, Ralph Hacker, according to Graveyard John's specifications. Still quite upset at being ordered to turn over so much money with no guarantee that the child was alive, Condon told Lindbergh that in his opinion "John" was desperate and would settle for a good deal less than seventy thousand dollars. Lindbergh replied that the family wanted no further delays: "The ladies are impatient."

As before, a series of notes, secreted in out-of-the-way spots, directed Condon to the final meeting place, this time St. Raymond's Cemetery in the East Bronx. While Lindbergh waited in the car, Condon paced up and down by the cemetery gate until he was hailed by a figure hiding behind a mausoleum, who called out, "Hey, Dok*tor!*" It was the man Condon knew as Graveyard John. Condon impulsively told "John" that he was only getting fifty thousand dollars, and he agreed without much argument.

Condon then returned to the car to fetch the money. "Colonel, I tried to do you a little favor," he explained. Lindbergh nodded his agreement and removed a packet containing twenty thousand dollars from the box. Condon carried the box back into the cemetery and handed it over in exchange for a note, which, he was told, contained instructions for finding the child. John warned that the note was not to be opened for six hours.

Much to Condon's frustration, Lindbergh was prepared to obey. The two men drove to a Westchester playground called Kiddy Corners, where Condon badgered Lindbergh until he finally agreed to open the letter. Inside the sealed envelope they found a few scrawled lines:

> the boy is on the Boad Nelly. it is a small Boad 28 feet long.
> two person are on the Boad. the are innosent. you will find the
> Boad between Horseneck Beach and Gay Head on Elizabeth
> Island.

Lindbergh knew the waters around the Elizabeth Islands well. He and Anne had sailed there on their honeymoon, and Arthur Springer still owned a summer cabin near Gay Head. Energized, he drove Condon to East Seventy-second Street. While Henry Breckinridge arranged to borrow a Sikorsky amphibious plane from a banker friend, Lindbergh raced around the apartment collecting Charles junior's favorite blanket and diapers and a baby bottle. Irey, meanwhile, berated the hapless Condon for his efforts to save Lindbergh twenty thousand dollars; the packet that was held back had contained fifty-dollar gold certificates, the easiest of all bills to trace.

Several hours later, the four men, giddy with anticipation and dread, boarded the Sikorsky at an airfield near Bridgeport, Connecticut. Breckinridge took the controls and flew like a madman; every time he saw a likely looking boat, he dived so precipitously that all hands on board hit the deck in panic. Lindbergh, apparently in an attempt to distract himself, began fiddling with the control wires so that the plane would turn right when Breckinridge wanted to go left or lose altitude when he wanted to climb. Breckinridge took these antics in stride, but the passengers were prepared to die. Dr. Condon, seated next to Irey in the rear of the plane, was reciting passages from the Song of Solomon at the top of his lungs.

Coast guard and navy vessels had sealed off Long Island Sound and were scouring every inch of coastline. Five boats named "Nelly," or something remotely similar, were boarded and searched without result.

As the hours passed it became obvious that John's directions were a hoax, and the passengers of the amphibian lapsed into a grim silence. When darkness fell Breckinridge headed for his flying club in Hicksville, Long Island. Lindbergh, in his frustration, turned on Condon. "When can I expect the bill for your services?" he demanded.

Mortally offended, Condon snapped, "I never take money from a man poorer than myself."[10]

Condon, however, could not remain angry for long. He later wrote that he had assumed that everyone involved knew the odds of getting the baby back alive after so many days were vanishingly small. Not until he saw Lindbergh rushing around his mother-in-law's apartment clutching the baby's blanket had he realized how totally unprepared he was to face the truth.

Understandably, if unrealistically, the Lindberghs refused to give up hope. Anne even found comfort in the comment of a no-doubt well-meaning friend, who told her, "A dead baby is a lot harder to hide than a live one."

For the next four days, fifteen thousand circulars listing the serial numbers of the ransom bills sat in Elmer Irey's office in Washington, withheld from circulation at the family's request. However, when a twenty-dollar ransom bill promptly turned up in a shipment to the Federal Reserve from the East River Savings Bank in Manhattan, Irey decided to act. On April 6 circulars were distributed to banks in all forty-eight states. Although tellers were not told why the Treasury was interested in the bills, the reason was not difficult to guess.

Since beat patrolmen in the New York area had been informed of the ransom payment in advance, the newspapers already knew as well. Once again they had agreed to suppress the story at the request of the family's advisers, but when the *Newark News* carried a description of the Treasury Department circular on April 8, the papers felt they could hold back no longer.

Suddenly Dr. John Condon became everyone's favorite scapegoat. The kinder newspaper accounts described Condon as the man who had been "duped" into giving the Lindberghs' money to the kidnappers; others hinted that he was a coconspirator. Condon was deluged with hate mail, and a Bronx grand jury was convened to consider whether he had broken any laws by conducting private negotiations with a felon. Fordham University, where Condon had lectured on education three times a week since his retirement, informed him that his contract was being terminated. Federal officials began monitoring his mail and tapping his phone. Police in New York City and New Jersey interrogated his friends and family.

Disheartened by the failure of the negotiations, the "inner circle" was breaking up, and the Lindberghs found themselves with no one to turn to. The state police detectives noticed that even Henry Breckinridge was seldom at the house. Supposedly Breckinridge was in New York, working on a lead—"another butterfly," the troopers called it— but it was also true that a certain coolness had set in between the attorney and Charles Lindbergh. Breckinridge was the one who had talked Condon into handing over the money without seeing the baby first. Now Condon had been thrown to the wolves, and he felt responsible.

The Lindberghs themselves were inclined to blame the press. "The tabloids I believe have cost us this terrible delay and waiting and we don't know what in the future," Anne Lindbergh wrote her mother-in-law. "I think such papers are really criminal outside of their inaccuracies." Certainly it was true that the newspapers had much to answer for. On the other hand, they had made efforts to cooperate when asked and had received nothing in return—not a promise of a future interview or even a call of thanks from the family. The editors of the *Daily News,* the first to confirm Condon's identity, felt especially aggrieved, and soon after the ransom payment they began headlining the story of John Curtis's ongoing negotiations with the mysterious Sam, running front-page stories like BABY'S CLOTHES SIGHTED ON RUM SHIP, LINDY TOLD.[11]

Ironically, after this story was published, Lindbergh did reopen discussions with Curtis, who now said that Graveyard John was a member of Sam's gang. According to Curtis, Sam had received the fifty-thousand-dollar ransom but was holding out for an additional twenty-five thousand. Curtis's descriptions of the gang, including the well-built

Scandinavian sailor named John, another sailor called Dynamite Larsen, and a registered nurse named Inez, became more vivid by the day.

Curtis was still unable to produce a scrap of evidence, but the idea that the kidnappers were holding out for a second ransom had become the parents' final hope. In any case it must have been all but impossible to sit at home doing nothing while the *News* issued ever-more-detailed bulletins about Sam and his gang. Once again Lindbergh ordered the state police and the federal authorities not to interfere, and he and Curtis began setting out to sea in search of the gang. Sam failed to keep a rendezvous off Block Island, and another near Norfolk. Sailing in the *Cachelot,* a yacht loaned by a sympathetic Brooklyn businessman who had been following Curtis's story in the *News,* Lindbergh continued his search. Eventually he made his way down the coast to Cape May, where he checked in to a hotel near the courthouse under the alias Alex Swanson and spent his days at sea, searching for a Gloucester fishing vessel named the *Mary B. Moss,* on which the gang was supposedly holding the missing child.

Colonel Lindbergh was still in Cape May on May 12, when a truck driver who had parked near the summit of the Hopewell–Princeton road walked into the woods to relieve himself and discovered the body of a young child lying facedown in the mud. The remains were in an advanced state of decomposition; both hands as well as the right leg and arm were gone, and the vital organs had been eaten by scavengers. A burlap bag lying nearby was later found to contain strands of the baby's hair.

Insp. Harry Walsh was among the first on the scene. Walsh—who needless to say was not trained in forensics—picked up a stick and used it to support the corpse's head as he turned it over. What he saw made him suck in his breath. The face, which had pressed into a mulch of leaves and damp earth, was an ashy white color, the features clearly recognizable as those of the child whose picture had stared out from the front pages of the papers for the past ten weeks. Even as Walsh watched, the skin began to turn brown from exposure to the air.

The corpse had been found not far from the farmhouse the Lindberghs had rented in 1931. For that matter, it was also near the place where telephone workers had laid an auxiliary cable on the morning after the kidnapping, suggesting that John Condon may have been right in thinking that the body had been buried shortly after the crime and then dug up by the kidnappers to retrieve the sleeping suit. Local newspapers noted that the seemingly peaceful country road was used regularly by bootleggers ferrying Sourland moonshine to the speakeasies and illegal casinos in the resort community of Lakewood. Moreover, Highfields—about four and a half miles by road but less than two miles in a straight-line distance across the valley—was clearly visible from several vantage points nearby.

The "Eaglet," as the press called him, was still clad in the little undershirt Betty Gow had made up on the night of the kidnapping. Hopewell police chief Harry Wolfe went to the house to retrieve the remains of Gow's flannel petticoat as well as a sample of the blue silk thread she had used. It then fell to Norman Schwarzkopf to inform the child's mother. Mrs. Lindbergh was waiting in her bedroom with Betty Morrow. Schwarzkopf was struck by how young and fragile she looked. To his relief she accepted the news calmly.

The child's body had been taken to Walter Swayze's funeral home in Trenton, and early that evening Betty Gow and the family's pediatrician, Dr. Philip Van Ingen, were brought in to confirm the identification. After Van Ingen left, the Mercer County medical examiner, Dr. Charles H. Mitchell, prepared for the autopsy. Mitchell was not a trained pathologist, and, for that matter, his hands weren't as steady as they had once been. Some years earlier he and Walter Swayze, who was both a mortician and county coroner, had made a confidential arrangement: Swayze would do the actual autopsies while Mitchell observed and signed the final report.

Swayze quickly located a massive fracture on the left side of the child's head. His report, which would later be presented in court as if it were Mitchell's, noted that directly opposite this large wound "there was also a suspicious opening at a point about one inch posterior to the right ear, the opening was about one-half inch in diameter, somewhat rounded, and resembled a bullet wound but, on examination of the cranial vault I could not locate a bullet." The report went on to speculate that the bullet might have fallen out when the body was moved. The official cause of death was listed inconclusively as "fractured skull due to external violence."[12]

It was not an easy autopsy, even for Mitchell and Swayze, who had performed hundreds over the years, and by the time they left the funeral home they had put back a few drinks. On the sidewalk they ran into two news photographers, Pat Candido of the *Mirror* and Frank Merts of the Acme News Picture Service. Mitchell, Candido later recalled, "was in an advanced state of intoxication." By some never-disclosed means, the two photographers persuaded Mitchell to let them take a look at the baby's body, which had already been placed in an infant-size casket lined with white taffeta.

Mitchell threw open the lid. Candido nearly gagged on the "terrific odor," but he snapped away. In the fiercely competitive world of the press photographer there was a ghoulish joke that the "coffin shot" was the ultimate prize. Now Candido had captured the ultimate coffin shot, but one so horrible that he knew no newspaper would be willing to publish it.[13]

Notified of the discovery when the *Cachelot* put ashore for the evening, Charles Lindbergh had rushed back from Cape May. By this time the Hopewell–Princeton road was one long traffic jam, and vendors had materialized, seemingly out of nowhere, selling hot dogs, pretzels, and even souvenir postcards featuring aerial views of the Lindbergh house. Hundreds more were gathering in Trenton outside Swayze's funeral parlor. Colonel Schwarzkopf was concerned about security, and he warned the Lindberghs that they should think very carefully about the funeral plans. The baby's grave would be sure to become a tourist attraction and possibly even a target for grave robbers. Horrified, they decided on immediate cremation.

Although Schwarzkopf had hoped to spare both parents the ordeal of seeing the remains, Charles insisted on making a personal identification. He had to be sure. The following day, Friday, Henry Breckinridge drove him to the mortuary. Once again the coffin was opened, and Lindbergh confirmed, "That is my son." He and Breckinridge then followed the hearse to the crematorium. While they waited in an adjoining room, Norman Schwarzkopf witnessed the disposal of the remains.

By the end of the weekend, prints of Pat Candido's "coffin shot" began turning up in Trenton speakeasies, for sale at five dollars apiece. Not only was the truth about how the pictures came to be taken embarrassing to state and local authorities—already under fire for their failure to make a thorough search of the woods around Hopewell—but it could create serious problems for the prosecution if the killer were ever apprehended. Rather than acknowledge publicly that the autopsy on the Lindbergh baby had been performed by a drunk, the police opted for a cover-up. Even the child's father was not told the truth. When he learned about the pictures, he was told that the two photographers had gained entrance to the mortuary during the middle of the night by throwing a rock through the window.

For Charles Lindbergh, the discovery that photos of his dead child were being bought and sold on the streets was in some ways more devastating than the kidnapping itself. All his efforts of the past two and a half months had turned out to be a charade. Graveyard John, Rosner, and Curtis had manipulated him like a puppet, and now he proved incapable of protecting his son even in death. Under the circumstances it is curious that Lindbergh did not question the police's explanation. (Since the mortuary was under guard, it is difficult to imagine how anyone could have gained entrance through a broken window without being caught.) But, somewhat disillusioned with his influential friends, he had belatedly come to appreciate the hard work and discretion of Norman Schwarzkopf, and when Lindbergh trusted people, he needed to trust them completely.[14]

Few events are so destructive to a marriage as the death of a young child, especially when that child is a murder victim. Anne, now six months pregnant, needed to work through her grief and prepare for the birth of her second baby. For ten weeks her husband had been so preoccupied with chasing down leads and holding strategy conferences that the two of them had spent hardly any time together. Now, much to her dismay, she discovered that nothing was about to change. Charles was totally consumed by the hunt for his son's murderer. What made the Lindberghs' situation unusual was that their home continued to function as an unofficial police station.

Keaten and Walsh, still not sure whether John Curtis was a hoaxer or the innocent dupe of the man who called himself Sam, had managed to lure him to Highfields for debriefing. Curtis was detained for the better part of four days, for much of that time closeted in the den with Harry Walsh, who played checkers with him, cried with him, and cajoled him with false promises of immunity.

When he was not actually being questioned, Curtis sat outside in the driveway, unkempt and haggard looking. Charles, who had come to accept that Curtis shared his belief in Sam's existence, now refused even to acknowledge him, passing by without making eye contact. Anne and her mother, unable to effect the same show of indifference, did their best to stay out of his way.

While Curtis was being interrogated in the den, Dr. Condon and Rosner were also summoned to the house for further questioning. The state police made it all too clear that they regarded Condon as a suspect, a development so upsetting to Henry Breckinridge that he prevailed upon Charles to write an open letter to Condon expressing his appreciation "for the great assistance you have been to us."

At last, during the early morning hours of Tuesday, May 17, John Curtis broke down and confessed to Inspector Walsh that he had invented the story of Sam and his gang, hoping to sell it to the newspapers in order to raise money to pay his gambling debts. It had soon become apparent that he would not succeed—he had yet to receive a penny from the *Daily News*—but at some point, "a kind of sickness took over." Dobson-Peacock, the newspapers, and then Colonel Lindbergh were all pressuring him for information, and it had simply become too painful and embarrassing to admit that the entire story was a fantasy. "I became insane on the subject for the time being."[15]

Even after he signed a statement admitting everything, Curtis was kept at the house, locked in the basement overnight until a judge could be brought in to arraign him on the spot. And on Thursday, after Curtis was finally removed from the premises, Colonel Lindbergh called a conference of all the investigators who had worked on the case to review all the evidence. The meeting ended with the group going outside to test one detective's theory that the kidnapper had accidentally dropped the child when the rung of his homemade ladder snapped as he was descending from the nursery window. Using a burlap bag filled with sand to simulate the weight of a twenty-month-old, the troopers practiced backing down the ladder, allowing the weighted sack to splatter onto the flagstone border of the flower bed below. Anne huddled indoors, doing her best to ignore the demonstration.

Although it would be impossible to erase such scenes from her memory, Anne had developed an attachment to Highfields, perhaps because the house was a link to her dead child and a happier, more hopeful past. Strangely, it was Charles, who hated living in his mother-in-law's house, who insisted on moving back to Englewood. Preparing to return to work at his New York office and the lab at Rockefeller University, he was understandably nervous about leaving his wife in Hopewell with only the servants for company. But there was also another reason, as Anne first learned through a chance conversation with Norman Schwarzkopf. The state police were planning to concentrate their investigation on the servants at Next Day Hill, and Charles planned to be very much involved.

SIXTEEN

"Life Is Getting So Sad"

$\mathcal{S}$ ET ON FIFTY-TWO ACRES OF PRIME REAL ESTATE within walking distance of downtown Englewood, Next Day Hill was the sort of establishment the average American was likely to encounter only between the covers of an Agatha Christie novel. In May 1932, the presence of Colonel Schwarzkopf and Inspector Walsh interviewing servants in the library made the resemblance complete.

The handsome white house with its manicured gardens and commanding oval driveway was intended to make a statement about the family's dramatic ascent from obscurity. When Senator Dwight W. Morrow died at the age of fifty-eight, less than two years after the house was completed, his widow had made up her mind to continue showing the flag. Although the big house had only two permanent residents, Betty and her semi-invalid daughter Elisabeth, the late Senator Morrow was still very much present in spirit. Mrs. Morrow's stationery was imprinted not with her own name or the name of the house but with the legend "The Estate of Dwight W. Morrow." Writing to a friend who was interested in spiritualism, she confided that she still felt Dwight's "presence" in the house.[1]

To care for her and her daughter's needs, Mrs. Morrow employed a staff of thirty-two servants, not counting security guards and other contract workers. Establishments of this size were rare at the height of the depression, when many of the nation's richest families had closed off all but a few rooms of their ostentatious residences and were making a show of living simply. Mrs. Morrow, however, subscribed to the philosophy of Harry Guggenheim, who often told friends: "Firing my chauffeur isn't going to solve the unemployment problem." Some of her servants, like the butler Septimus Banks, had been with the family for many years, formerly staffing their palatial Manhattan apartment. Quite a few were foreign nationals, who could be deported if they lost their jobs.

Although the Morrow servants were well paid and hardly overworked, they were also far from being a happy family. A vast social distance separated estate manager Arthur Springer from the two black laundresses and the part-time yardmen. Between those two extremes were the downstairs maids like Bessie Binn, who had been with the family almost twenty years; Ida the cook; Mary Beattie and Isabelle MacDonald, who were the personal maids of Elisabeth and Betty Morrow; two female secretaries; and Banks the butler. Mary Smith, the dressmaker who had made Anne's wedding gown, lived in town and sometimes served as Mrs. Morrow's traveling companion. Margaret Junge, also a seamstress, had formerly been one of the most prosperous citizens of Hamburg, Germany; after she and her husband lost their fortune in 1929, Mrs. Morrow had taken her on as a favor to mutual friends.

Near the apex of the pyramid, a notch below Arthur Springer, stood the executive housekeeper, Mrs. Rhoderick Cecil Grimes-Graeme. The widow of a British army officer long stationed in South Africa, Jo Graeme kept her own apartment in Manhattan. Just as she had been Anne's confidante at the time of her engagement to Charles Lindbergh, Graeme was now close to Constance Morrow, who occasionally spent the night at her place in the city, but she was by no means popular with the other servants. After the FBI entered the Lindbergh kidnapping case in mid-May on the orders of President Hoover, several members of the staff eagerly pointed out to agents of the bureau that Graeme received "commissions" from merchants on everything she ordered for the estate, a practice that had enabled her to accumulate a tidy fortune.

The FBI, however, was far more interested in Mrs. Graeme's grown sons. The Graeme family had long summered at Oak Bluffs on Martha's Vineyard, not far from the spot where Graveyard John's note had directed Colonel Lindbergh to search for the "boad Nelly." Moreover, the Graeme boys, as South Africans, presumably would have been capable of faking the Germanic-sounding diction of the ransom letters. But when the FBI and New Jersey State Police asked the young men for samples of their handwriting, Mrs. Graeme had indignantly protested to the British consul in New York, who warned both agencies that British subjects could not be questioned without a specific agreement between their embassy and the State Department.

Following a short stay with the Guggenheims at La Falaise, Charles and Anne Lindbergh moved back to Next Day Hill on May 23, just in time to bear the brunt of Mrs. Graeme's indignation. Colonel Lindbergh had been kind to Jo Graeme in the past—he had even invited her along on one or two flying dates with Anne—but his obliviousness to the subtleties of social interaction with the servants had earned her contempt. At any rate she certainly blamed him for persuading Mrs. Morrow to allow the authorities to question the servants at Next Day Hill. When Anne asked Mrs. Junge to do some sewing for her new baby's layette, Graeme huffily countermanded the order, reminding Anne that all requests for assistance from the servants must be channeled through her office. Anne meekly complied, only to be told that Mrs. Junge was too busy to help just now. The seamstress, along with some of the other servants, was soon reduced to sneaking behind the housekeeper's back to do chores for the Lindberghs. Meanwhile, Graeme dropped snide hints that Anne and Charles were freeloading off Mrs. Morrow and ought to be grateful for what they had. Anne was indignant, but since she was reluctant to upset her mother, who depended on Graeme to keep the house running smoothly, there was little she could do.

In the three years since her marriage, Anne had continued to think of her mother as her best friend and Next Day Hill as her true home. Now she found herself making lists of the reasons why the house made her nervous, from the sound of strange feet clattering down the uncarpeted hallways to Betty Morrow's constant, frenetic activity.

On returning from her stay at Hopewell, Mrs. Morrow had resumed her usual social schedule. Almost every day there were guests, sometimes in three shifts for lunch, afternoon tea, and dinner. If anything, the family was busier than usual. Elisabeth, Betty, and Dwight junior were about to leave for Europe and were shuttling off to doctor's appointments, farewell visits, and shopping expeditions, all immensely complicated by the Burns Agency's advice that the family make all their arrangements under assumed names in order to keep their travel plans a secret from the press.

Mrs. Morrow believed that unhappiness, like physical illness, was best dealt with by keeping busy and refusing to dwell on one's problems. Unfortunately, this prescription proved inadequate for her children, three of whom suffered from psychological troubles that could not simply be willed away. Anne's extreme shyness and her sense of being on the fringes of life, an onlooker rather than a full participant, probably indicated a low-grade depression present since childhood. In any event, while the early months of her marriage had been stressful but also exhilarating, the word *weariness* now began to appear often in her diary and letters. Coping with the meaningless routines of everyday living exhausted her energies. Since Anne was not a complainer—the unhappiness so evident in her diary was seldom overtly expressed to those close to her—neither her mother nor her husband realized just how deeply troubled she was, and no doubt they wouldn't have known how to deal with it if they had.[2]

Mrs. Morrow, after spending the better part of two months at Highfields, was already preoccupied with the problems of her eldest daughter. Ever since Elisabeth's damaged heart valve had been diagnosed, her periodic romantic crushes had become a matter of deep concern to Betty Morrow, who feared that Elisabeth might rush into an unsuitable match. One such relationship, with Rev. Clyde Roddy, had been broken off after his family had already released an engagement announcement to the press; Roddy, it developed, had been married before and had obtained an annulment under somewhat questionable circumstances. Now Elisabeth had made up her mind to marry Aubrey Neil Morgan, the heir to a Welsh department store fortune (and no relation to the J. P. Morgans), whom she had met in January 1930 when she accompanied her father to England for the deliberations of the London Naval Conference. Mrs. Morrow, understandably distressed over the prospect of her daughter settling permanently in Britain, was looking forward with some trepidation to meeting the prospective groom's family. Elisabeth herself was so exhausted by the flurry of last-minute preparations for the trip that she checked into the hospital for a few days' rest. While she was a patient, a team of physicians from the Rockefeller Institute performed a series of tests and warned that the damage to her heart had worsened in the past year.

Neither Anne nor her mother had the slightest interest in the hunt for the kidnappers (it was assumed by all concerned that there was more than one), and they were not terribly sympathetic to Charles's preoccupation with the subject. Catching those responsible would not bring little Charley back to life. Moreover, the insistence of the police that the kidnappers must have had an informant among the staff of Next Day Hill had thrown the household into turmoil. Mrs. Morrow found it impossible to imagine that the theory might be correct. For that matter

Charles was almost equally resistant to the idea, but he had made up his mind to cooperate with Colonel Schwarzkopf's investigation. He was torn between his desire to get at the truth and his responsibility for seeing that none of the household employees were as unfairly treated as Betty Gow and Red Johnson had been.

As it turned out, Detectives Keaten and Lamb's interest in the Graeme brothers was something of a passing fancy. Several other employees were more obvious suspects, especially Charles Henry Ellerson, the assistant chauffeur who had volunteered to drive Betty Gow to Hopewell on March 1. Before he was hired by the Morrows in the summer of 1931, the twenty-nine-year-old, Danish-born Ellerson had a checkered employment history. For some unknown reason, however, he had quickly found favor with Arthur Springer, who later described him to the FBI as "a little wild, but harmless." Springer promoted Ellerson from gardener to assistant chauffeur, and during the months just prior to the kidnapping one of Ellerson's chief duties had been driving Charles Lindbergh, Jr., across town to the Little School, where Elisabeth Morrow had arranged for her nephew to attend an infant play school class.[3]

Ellerson was known to frequent a Fort Lee, New Jersey, speakeasy called the Sha-Toe, a hangout for horseplayers, and was rumored to have been seen there often during March and April, flashing a sizable bank roll he claimed to have acquired as the result of a streak of "hot tips." The Morrow butler, Septimus Banks, told the state police that he was at the Sha-Toe himself on the evening of March 1, and had seen Ellerson pull a stack of bills from his pocket and peel off twenty dollars to lend to an acquaintance who complained of being short of cash. Banks was suspicious but admitted he had no specific reason for believing that Ellerson would be a party to a serious crime. However, according to FBI records, "one of the most trusted Morrow servants, a woman who has been with the family twenty-five years" told bureau agents that she knew Ellerson was somehow involved even though she had no evidence to back up her conviction.

Around the time the baby's body was discovered, Ellerson came to the attention of the police in nearby Fort Lee when he reported that his personal automobile had spun out of control on a hill. Alone in the vehicle, he had opened the door and jumped to safety, but the car slid over an embankment, where it caught fire and burned. The police were unconvinced by this account, and it occurred to them that the accident might have been staged to destroy evidence.[4]

However questionable his character, Ellerson had been conspicuously present at the Sha-Toe on the evening of the kidnapping, and the police were unable to prod him into making any damaging admissions. This was not the case with their other prime suspect, the downstairs maid and waitress Violet Sharpe. When first questioned Sharpe claimed to have been at the movies on the night of March 1. Later she said she had been at a roadhouse called the Peanut Grille on a double date with a man named Ernie and another couple. Sharpe said that she had met Ernie a few days earlier when he struck up a conversation with her and her sister Edna as they were strolling along Palisade Avenue. A pretty brunette with a slight overbite and a flirtatious manner, Sharpe was informally engaged to Septimus Banks, which could well have accounted for her reluctance to admit that she was out with another man. But Sharpe's account of her evening routine changed every time she told it, and her insistence that she had no idea of Ernie's last name or how to reach him seemed suspicious. Furthermore, her sister Edna, who had been on extended visit to the States, had changed her steamship tickets and returned to England on April 6, four days after the Lindbergh ransom was paid.

In early May Sharpe was admitted to Englewood Hospital for a tonsillectomy, and the Morrow family physician, probably acting on Mrs. Morrow's orders, had told police the maid was too ill to answer any more questions. One reason for Charles Lindbergh's decision to move back to Englewood was his determination to break this standoff. On May 23, the first day he and Anne took up residence, he arranged for Sharpe to be interviewed in the library after dinner by Lt. Arthur Keaten and Insp. Harry Walsh. Also present was Norman Schwarzkopf and Harold Nation, an assistant director of the FBI (technically still known at this time as the BI, or Bureau of Investigation). Lindbergh also sat in on the session, having promised his mother-in-law that he would not allow Sharpe to be badgered.

When Sharpe entered the library, Keaten and Walsh were shocked by her appearance. Once plump and unabashedly cheeky, Sharpe had lost more than forty pounds in two months and appeared subdued, even frightened. Walsh began with a few questions about the Peanut Grille, then abruptly changed the subject. "Do you have any boyfriends besides Banks and this Ernie?" he demanded.

Violet insisted she didn't.

"What about a man named McKelvie who works for the *Daily News?*"[5]

Sharpe warily admitted that she had met McKelvie when he was staking out the house for the *News*. She dated him a few times but insisted she hadn't seen him since February. McKelvie, however, had already told a different story to the New York police. Shortly before midnight on March 1, he said, Sharpe had called him at home to tell him about the kidnapping and the family's reaction. Much to McKelvie's disappointment, the *News* had not given him a byline for this scoop, but having a source inside the Morrow household, he frankly admitted, had certainly raised his stock at the paper.

Next Walsh began asking Sharpe about the substantial balance in her savings account. Where had all that money come from? Had she been selling tips to the *News* all along?

Sharpe said the money was saved bonuses and Christmas gifts. Mrs. Morrow was very generous.

Before she could finish her explanation, Sharpe began to tremble violently and the color drained from her face. As she slumped down in her chair, apparently unconscious, Colonel Lindbergh summoned the family doctor, who was waiting outside in the hall. The physician helped Sharpe to her room and returned to tell the detectives that the maid was running a fever and there would be no more interrogations until further notice.

Two weeks later Violet Sharpe wrote to her sister in England, reporting she had been hospitalized with a "poisoned throat" and now weighed only seven stone (ninety-eight pounds). "You have no idea what we have been through when the Police had me for questioning," she went on. "I fainted 2 [times] in 2 hours so you can guess how weak I was.... Gee, life is getting so sad I really don't think there is much to live for any more."

But the interrupted interrogation had not been unfruitful. While Sharpe was being questioned, two state troopers and an FBI agent had conducted a search of her room and found a business card belonging to one Ernie Brinkert, a driver for a White Plains, New York, car service. Just before lunch on June 9, Walsh returned to Next Day Hill alone and confronted Sharpe in Arthur Springer's office. Waving a copy of Brinkert's cab driver's license he demanded, "This is the man you were with, isn't it?"

Sharpe studied the photo and shook her head. She had never seen this man before in her life.

Walsh cut her off. "Don't give me that. We know he's the one."

"Yes, yes. All right. Since you say so. He's the one then."

Although Sharpe had sounded quite convincing, as she left the room she favored Arthur Springer with a conspiratorial wink. Springer tried to explain to Walsh that Violet was simply telling him what she thought he wanted to hear, but Walsh believed he was on the point of cracking the case and was so pleased with himself that Springer's warning made no impression.

The following morning Charles Lindbergh left the house early carrying the urn that contained the pitiful remains of his infant son. He and Anne had decided that the ashes should be scattered from an airplane over the Atlantic, quietly and without informing anyone else in advance in order to avoid attracting the notice of the newspapers.

Not long after Charles departed, Harry Walsh called to say that the state police wanted Miss Sharpe to come to their headquarters in Alpine for questioning. When Banks relayed the message to Violet, she burst into tears and ran up to her room. Hidden in the corner of her closet shelf she had a can of cyanide of potassium, a highly poisonous crystalline substance sometimes used for polishing silver. Pouring a handful of crystals into a glass of water, she gulped the mixture down and staggered back downstairs, where she collapsed on the pantry floor.

Banks at first thought Violet was having another of her fainting spells and he and Dwight junior, who had recently arrived home from Amherst, labored in vain to revive her. When it became obvious that Violet was dead, Dwight, acting on some naive notion of propriety, carried Sharpe's body upstairs to her bed.

Lindbergh returned from his gloomy errand to find the house in an uproar. Banks, an alcoholic who had recently given up drinking in his attempt to win Violet's affections, had sought solace in whiskey and was incoherent. (He would be committed to a sanatorium within the year.) The police, meanwhile, were questioning Dwight junior, whose impulsive decision to move the body struck them as mildly suspicious.

At first it was thought that Sharpe's suicide was an admission of guilt, but this assumption quickly began to unravel. The following morning, after reading of Sharpe's death in the newspaper, a twenty-three-year-old bus driver from Closter, New York, named Ernest Miller stopped by the state police barracks at Alpine and identified himself as the man who had taken Sharpe to the Peanut Grille. As Miller's friends and other witnesses soon confirmed, the outing had been quite innocent. Worried about returning home with liquor on her breath, Sharpe had drunk only coffee.

Sharpe's suicide became a scandal of international proportions. The *Daily Mirror*, expressing the prevailing view that the New Jersey authorities had browbeaten and perhaps even physically abused the helpless maid, pronounced her death MURDER BY THIRD DEGREE. The British press agreed, and a Labour MP promised to investigate the conduct of the British consul in New York, who had shielded the middle-class Graeme brothers while failing to advise the other British subjects among the servants of their rights. In the shabby North of England village of Tult's Clump, Edna Sharpe called a press conference and read Violet's last letter as evidence that her sister had been a victim of police brutality. Edna also announced that Violet could not possibly have been engaged to Septimus Banks, as the American press suggested, because she was already secretly married to an Englishman named George Price.

Harry Walsh was quite capable of roughing up suspects on occasion, but Violet Sharpe had been questioned only very briefly and then always in the presence of at least two witnesses. However, this was small comfort to the rest of the staff. Betty Morrow took the unusual step of issuing a statement to the press declaring her complete faith in Sharpe's innocence, but Colonel Lindbergh, whether or not he was totally convinced, maintained his usual sphinxlike silence.

Sharpe was buried in Englewood on June 14. That same afternoon, Mrs. Morrow, Dwight junior, and Constance sailed for England (Elisabeth had departed on an earlier ship). Although the voyage had been planned for some time, it now appeared that young Dwight was being hustled out of the country, and a few of the tabloid papers, which so far had ignored Dwight's existence, indulged in some pointed speculations about the relationship between the downstairs maid and the senator's "lunatic son."

In the weeks to come the lion's share of the criticism was borne by Norman Schwarzkopf and his staff. Nevertheless press stories about the suicide managed to imply that the Morrows had something to hide, or at the very least that Colonel Lindbergh, in his haste to find a scapegoat, was subjecting his mother-in-law's servants to an inquisition. (Hypocritically enough, the papers that professed to be most outraged by the harassment of Miss Sharpe were the very ones that had all but convicted Betty Gow without a trial.)

In fact both the FBI and state police were mystified by the suicide. The bureau's files state as fact that Sharpe had an illegal abortion early in 1932, and while Banks and Arthur Springer both denied this, the fear that an autopsy might reveal evidence of an abortion would explain Edna Sharpe's strange insistence that her sister was secretly married. (George Price, the putative husband, admitted knowing Violet, but he had been married to another woman for more than thirty years, and Scotland Yard could find no evidence that Sharpe ever considered herself Price's wife.) The night before Sharpe killed herself, FBI records go on to say, another servant (apparently Betty Gow) visited her room in an attempt to cheer her up, but their talk ended with Violet sobbing inconsolably and saying that she had killed her own child and now the police were trying to blame her for murdering Colonel Lindbergh's baby too.

Obviously Sharpe had also been distraught over being exposed as a spy for the *Daily News*. The police and federal agents tended to dismiss Sharpe's call to McKelvie as a minor embarrassment, but in the Morrow household selling secrets to the press was just about the worst crime it was possible to commit. Even if Sharpe were not dismissed—as she surely would have been—she would have had to face the scorn of the other servants, some of whom had turned down substantial bribes out of loyalty to the family.

Of course there remained the possibility that Sharpe really had known something about the kidnapping. If what she knew implicated another of the servants, the chances of identifying that individual were now greatly reduced. Mrs. Morrow, whose friendships with important Republicans and pundits like Walter Lippmann made her a formidable woman to oppose, wanted no further investigations of her employees. The police were stymied.

Over the weekend between Violet Sharpe's death and her funeral, the Lindberghs escaped to the serenity of La Falaise, where, as Anne recorded in her diary, Charles and Harry Guggenheim got into "a terrible argument over ... [Charles's approach to] handling publicity."

Guggenheim made the mistake of trying to tell Charles that he would simply have to get used to the fact that he was a public figure. "The only thing to do is to change your whole attitude," he urged. "Conquer it inside of you. Get so you don't mind."[6]

This prescription outraged and bewildered Charles and Anne, who insisted all they wanted was to be left alone.

Reluctant to remain at Next Day Hill while Mrs. Morrow and the rest of the family were in Europe, the Lindberghs soon moved back to Highfields. Since their pet fox terrier, a gift from Evangeline, had failed to raise an alarm on the night of the kidnapping, Charles purchased a German shepherd guard dog from a trainer in Princeton. The trainer locked the snarling animal in the garage, with the warning that it would take two weeks for Pal, as he was called, to transfer his loyalty to his new owners. The following day, Charles entered the garage—armed with a baseball bat just in case—and succeeded in making friends with the dog.

Charles's ability to communicate with the shepherd, soon renamed Thor, struck some who saw them together as almost uncanny. Anne was a little nervous about trying to manage the fierce-looking animal along with the two smaller dogs she and Charles now had with them at Highfields, but Thor, who was not only well trained but much gentler than he appeared, soon became her devoted companion.

But no guard dog could exorcise the spirits that haunted Highfields. Charles was spending his days at the trial of John Curtis, who was eventually sentenced to one year in jail for obstruction of justice. Shortly after the proceedings ended, the Lindberghs packed their things and moved back to Englewood.[7] Reluctant to sell the house, which one promoter hoped to open for public tours, they asked Morrow family attorneys to draw up papers deeding the Hopewell property to the state of New Jersey, "to provide for the welfare of children, including their education, training, hospitalization and other purposes without regard to race or creed."

Although Thor frightened some of Mrs. Morrow's visitors, the guard dog was actually a moderate security measure, and in the months immediately following the kidnapping the Lindberghs demonstrated a courageous resolve to continue living as normally as possible. At times, it seemed that they were less frightened than many of their acquaintances. Oddly enough, considering the millions of words that had been published about the crime, few journalists connected the crime with the long history of attacks on the Morgan bank and its partners. This was not, however, the perception of the partners and others of their class. Smith dean Marjorie Nicolson recalled that for a time the alumni seemed incapable of discussing anything else. "The question was," she recalled, "Was it a Morrow child? Was it a Lindbergh child? Why had it been done?"[8] When Constance Morrow returned to Smith in the fall she was accompanied by a private security guard—"one of the silent police," Nicolson called him—who escorted her around the campus, even sitting through her classes. Other Morgan partners, including Russell Leffingwell and Tom Lamont, hired bodyguards for their children. In some instances these precautions were maintained for more than a decade. Margot Lamont Heap, the eldest daughter of Corliss Lamont, would recall that her otherwise happy visits to her grandparents' Torrey Canyon estate on the Hudson during the late 1940s were overshadowed by what she called "a slight menacing atmosphere." When the grandchildren slept over, an armed guard supervised their outdoor play and another sat up all night in the hallway outside their bedrooms.[9]

Others who knew the family were attempting to draw some larger moral:

Harry Guggenheim, an activist by inclination, became an organizer of the Citizens Committee for the Control of Crime, a civilian watchdog organization that monitored the prosecution of racketeers. Until 1940, the campaign for reform of law enforcement and the court system occupied much of his time.

Alexis Carrel's reactions were incorporated into the manuscript of a book he had begun to write at the urging of his friends at the Century Club, his home away from home in Manhattan. Modern democracies, especially the United States, Carrel often told his friends, made a fetish of individual liberties to the detriment of the common good. Mass culture, progressive education, and sexual license—not to mention flabby, underexercised children and women who drank cocktails—were all symptoms of the dislocations caused by the Industrial Revolution. But no effect was more alarming than the tendency to elevate the welfare of criminals above the interests of normal, law-abiding people.

During the years after World War I, it was taken for granted that science could solve humanity's problems. People who considered themselves modern in outlook believed in eugenics almost as surely as a later generation would imbibe the doctrines of Freud. Charles Lindbergh had certainly been brought up in this tradition, which was identified not only with scientists like the Lands but with Progressive politics. The goal of improving the human race through genetics may not have been unworthy in itself, but the primitive state of scientific knowledge at the time offered few clues as to how this might be accomplished. Prejudice and crackpot social theories rushed in to fill the gap. By the mid-thirties the intellectual shortcomings of eugenics were being all too vividly dramatized in the actions of totalitarian fanatics. Carrel's book, a sort of last stand of the old guard, mixed a naive confidence in socially responsible science with sweeping social prescription. Government policy, Carrel wrote, should be devoted not to making the weak more numerous but to "mak[ing] the strong still stronger." Carrel also advocated euthanasia for kidnappers and other violent criminals as well as those who "misled the public on important matters."

Editors who saw early drafts of Carrel's manuscript told him it was unpublishable. In early 1935, however, it was released by Harper &

Brothers under the title *Man, the Unknown* and became one of the
most-talked-about books of the year. A few reviewers accused Carrel of
offering a blueprint for a watered-down version of fascism, but most
were favorable, and the book evoked admiring responses from, among
many others, Upton Sinclair, Henry Wallace, and Rabbi Stephen Wise.
The last called it "an epochal book … an oasis of beauty in a wilderness
of things that are just muck and ruck and truck."[10] Such readers found it
possible to overlook Carrel's outdated ideas about race and Social Darwinism, blinded by his promise that pure science could clean up the
mess the politicians had made of the world.

Carrel was perhaps the ultimate ivory-tower scientist. His fame as
the man who brought the first Nobel Prize in medicine to United States
was so great that he was insulated even from pressure to publish. Rockefeller University unquestioningly supported the projects of his laboratory, including a vague nutritional study involving twelve thousand mice
who were housed in a special annex to the lab called the "Mousery."
His circle of admirers at the Century Club, which included the international attorney Frederick Coudert and Frederick Woodbridge, the dean
of Columbia University, rarely challenged his pronouncements. Carrel
had been deeply troubled by the kidnapping, and as a Frenchman,
frightened by the ominous developments on the European scene. His
private papers make it clear that the more hysterical passages of *Man, the
Unknown* accurately reflected his everyday state of mind. Carrel was
convinced that America was on the brink of anarchy—its young people
suffering from endemic "nervous debility." Morover, the "white race"
(because it was the most thoroughly corrupted by the Industrial Revolution) was well along on the path to genetic suicide. By 1938 he would
write: "Humanity is in the process of rapid deterioration and the very
future of civilization is in grave and mortal danger."

Carrel truly believed all this, along with some other things directly
contradictory. He was an intellectual. He liked to talk. Everyone who
knew him understood this, including Lindbergh who liked to quote the
remark of Boris Bakhmeteff, the former Russian ambassador to the
United States who had emigrated after the fall of Kerensky and begun a
second career in New York as a civil engineer: "If Carrel is right 20% of
the time it is enough."

In retrospect, it is unfortunate that the Lindberghs were unable to
assuage their grief by making some positive social contribution. In contrast to Harry Guggenheim, who had his crime-fighting committee, and

Betty Morrow, who continued to work for the expansion of higher education and for soical welfare agencies like the YMCA, they were not
drawn to activism.

Influenced by Charles Morgan's *The Fountain,* a novel about a
young woman whose husband is horribly disfigured during World War
I, Anne had retreated into a study of the literature of mysticism and
contemplation. Try as she might, she could not bring herself to embrace
the doctrines of any established religion. Rather like her childhood
friend Corliss Lamont—who resolved his mother's philosophical conundrum by eliminating the religious component and developing the theory of secular humanism—Anne was trying to find a way to be a mystic
without God. It is difficult to imagine a lonelier undertaking.

Charles, meanwhile, had his scientific work at Rockefeller. There
was a walk-in incubator at the institute where he spent long hours, often
sitting until after midnight observing the function of cells through a
microscope. He soon succeeded in maintaining a cell culture for 105
days in a circulating flask of his own design, and his next goal was to
design an improved model of the perfusion pump, capable of preserving
whole organs, beginning with the thyroid gland of a cat. Charles's scientific labors had great potential, not only for his personal satisfaction but
in the long run for the conquest of cancer and heart and kidney disease.
However, lacking formal education and credentials, he was wholly
dependent on his mentor. And although he remained skeptical, to say
the least, of some of Carrel's more bizarre pronouncements, he could
hardly help but be influenced by his conviction that the rapid pace of
technological change had thrown Western civilization into a crisis that
threatened its very survival.[11]

SEVENTEEN

"Around the North Atlantic"

O N AUGUST 16 ANNE LINDBERGH gave birth to a son. She and Charles had been expecting a girl, and the one boy's name they had considered earlier in her pregnancy was John, which they now hesitated to use for fear that the press would draw unwarranted conclusions that the child was named after Dr. Condon or, worse, Graveyard John himself. After debating for two months and rejecting any number of alternatives, they settled on the Scandinavian variant Jon, which Anne had discovered in a book of fairy tales.

Outwardly it was a hopeful time. Dwight junior had recovered from the trauma of Violet Sharpe's suicide and returned to Amherst. Elisabeth and her sweetheart Aubrey Morgan had made up their minds to defy the doctors' dire predictions, and they were married at Next Day Hill on December 28, in a ceremony attended by an array of old family friends including Jack Morgan, Jean Monnet, and the Lamonts. And though Anne still felt that the glare of celebrity made it difficult to contemplate writing anything too revealing of her inner self, she had begun to turn her notes on the Great Circle flight of 1931 into a nonfiction book, a project Charles strongly encouraged.

She and Charles were even beginning to go out socially. Heavily disguised, they managed to attend a Broadway show without being recognized. They also appeared at a private banquet at the Waldorf-Astoria, where the guests included the Kermit Roosevelts, Henry James (nephew of the author), and Vita Sackville-West and her husband Harold Nicolson. Anne was fascinated by Nicolson's conversation, though he took little notice of her except to observe that she had an aura of tragedy about her and was "rather interested in books." Charles, however, struck Nicolson as "a surprise.... He has a fine, intellectual forehead, a shy, engaging smile, windblown hair, a way of tossing his head unhappily, a transparent complexion.... He looks young with a touch of arrested development."[1]

Evangeline Lindbergh had turned down several invitations to come east to see the baby—probably because she feared that a visit would generate unwanted publicity at a time when the family was doing its best to keep Jon's name out of the papers. So in March 1933 Charles and Anne decided to drive to Detroit to see her, stopping along the way to call on Anne's grandmother Cutter in Cleveland. Anxious about leaving Jon behind at Next Day Hill despite the presence of a state police guard, they made their plans at the last minute and told no one of the trip until an hour before they left, including Betty Gow and members of their own family. While they were gone, Jon was moved from his nursery to another part of the house, where the trusty Septimus Banks (now recovered from his stay in the sanatorium) would sleep every night in an adjoining room. With the baby's security provided for, Charles and Anne turned the trip into an adventure. Anne wore a curly wig and bright red lipstick. Charles had tinted his eyebrows and hair black. Staying at modest hotels and roominghouses, where their claim to be young marrieds from Hackensack went unchallenged, they managed to make the ten-day journey to Detroit and back without being recognized and had a grand time.

Privately, however, Anne was still reeling from the shock of her son's murder. As she noted in her diary, this was not the kind of "normal" grief such as she had felt at her father's passing, which could be expected to heal with time. Charles junior's death was something that never should have happened. Pain, bewilderment, and the unanswered—perhaps ultimately unanswerable—question, Why? were her constant companions. She was not sleeping well and felt perpetually tired. During a rare foray into the New York subways, she found herself staring nervously at her seatmates, wondering if one of them was her child's killer.

Anne's published diaries from this period—entry after entry consisting of little more than cries of naked anguish—give a misleading impression. Although it was apparent to a stranger like Harold Nicolson that Anne Lindbergh was an unhappy woman, with family and friends she hid her feelings behind a facade of stoicism. The atmosphere at Next Day Hill was not conducive to the free expression of emotion. There were always servants hovering in the background who might overhear a too-personal conversation. In any case there was no one for Anne to discuss the subject with. During a trip to Hopewell to retrieve a few personal possessions, Anne attempted to talk about her feelings with Charles and he cut her off, saying, "I went through it last spring—I can't go through it again."[2]

Unfortunately it wasn't that simple. The investigation into the kidnapping, which Charles had originally expected would be concluded within a matter of days or weeks at the most, continued to plod along, and in his capacity as the unofficial administrator of the inquiry he was faced with the problem of getting the various state and federal agencies involved in the case to work together. While the New Jersey State Police and federal agents were wearing themselves out pursuing tips from the public, which invariably led nowhere, the focus of the inquiry had shifted to New York City and neighboring Westchester County, where ransom bills were trickling into the banks at a dishearteningly slow rate—three in August 1932, only one in September, and then a flurry of nine in October.

The job of tracing the ransom bills had been assigned to Lt. James Finn of the NYPD. Just five years earlier, Finn had been a member of the honor guard chosen to escort Lindy during his ticker-tape parade up Broadway. The wiry, cerebral New York cop had made an impression on Harry Bruno, and after the kidnapping Bruno had asked New York's police commissioner to make sure that Finn was assigned to the crime. Much decorated and nearly as often demoted, Finn was a maverick. He was thoroughly versed in modern police methods and the first truly intuitive detective to have a crack at solving the case, but he made no secret of his contempt for the blundering efforts of Arthur Keaten and Harry Walsh, and his relations with the New Jersey State Police had gotten off to a disastrous start. The Jersey detectives, suspecting the NYPD of wanting to take over their investigation, gave Finn and his team the cold shoulder, and as late as the fall of 1932 they were still refusing to provide him with copies of the ransom notes.

In spite of the lack of cooperation from the Jersey police, Finn hoped to use the ransom bills to build a profile of Graveyard John. Most of the bills had passed through a number of hands by the time they came to the attention of bank tellers, and except for the fact that two of them had shown up in the cash receipts of Childs restaurants, there was no apparent pattern in how they were being spent. But there were intriguing physical similarities. Most of the money had been folded in a characteristic manner—eight times over. Lab tests detected the presence of emery and glycerin on the bills, suggesting that they had been handled by an individual who had occasion to sharpen tools. Some bills also showed traces of lipstick, and some had a musty odor, as if they had been buried or stored in a dank place.

At the suggestion of Hearst reporter Leigh Matteson, Finn asked a clinical psychologist, Dr. Dudley Shoenfeld, to study the bills and other evidence in order to produce a profile of Graveyard John. Shoenfeld concluded that the suspect was a German-speaking ex-convict, about forty years old, probably a schizophrenic with homosexual tendencies. Such a man might develop an obsession with Charles Lindbergh, Shoenfeld suggested, because Lindbergh "lived in the world ... yet was alien to all that was going on around him," causing the public to endow him with "the characteristics of one omnipotent." To a deranged mind the kidnapping of the Lone Eagle's firstborn would be the equivalent of appropriating the hero's virility. Shoenfeld also speculated that Graveyard John carried a single bill folded eight times over hidden on his person as a talisman against his feelings of sexual inadequacy.[3]

Finn's reliance on advice from a psychologist was ridiculed by the New Jersey State Police, who found it especially hilarious that Shoenfeld had deduced homosexual tendencies from the way the suspect folded the ransom bills. Lieutenant Keaten complained to federal agents that the NYPD detective was a "nitwit" who was complicating an already difficult situation with his "fruitcake" speculations. But Charles Lindbergh had faith in the scientific approach, and on November 5—alerted to the existence of the profile by Henry Breckinridge—he invited Dr. Shoenfeld to present his theories to New Jersey and federal agents at a conference held in the library at Next Day Hill. At this meeting it developed that the lawmen's chief objection to Shoenfeld's theories was his insistence that Graveyard John, being insane, had of necessity to be a lone wolf, who had planned and executed the kidnapping without benefit of accomplices. (In retrospect the assumption that the mentally deranged are incapable of enlisting accomplices in the pursuit of their obsessions seems more than a little simplistic, and even Lieutenant Finn, who was not present at the conference, did not accept this aspect of the profile.)

Although Lindbergh thought Shoenfeld's idea of Graveyard John as a homosexual loner a bit far fetched, he was intrigued by the specificity of the psychologist's predictions. While Schwarzkopf and the federal agents listened in skeptical silence, he played devil's advocate, listing one by one the reasons why the police believed there had to be more than one person involved. But for all his objections, Lindbergh wanted to be convinced. The notion of a single, deranged kidnapper was certainly easier to live with than the state police's conviction that Graveyard John had been tipped off by someone in the family's employ. By the end of the evening, Lindbergh had come around to the lone wolf theory. He managed to persuade Colonel Schwarzkopf to release photostats of the complete ransom notes to Lieutenant Finn, and they were delivered to NYPD headquarters the following morning.[4]

Shoenfeld's associate Leigh Matteson was of the opinion that Norman Schwarzkopf wanted to cooperate more fully with the NYPD but was unable to do so because he was under heavy pressure from Governor Moore, who had made it all too clear that Schwarzkopf's job, and perhaps the very survival of the state police, depended on their getting credit for cracking the case. (The blundering Harry Walsh, Matteson noted, had close connections with the Democratic boss of Jersey City, but for which he would have been removed from the investigation long ago.) With no promising leads, Schwarzkopf and his staff found themselves retracing the same ground for the third and fourth times. They were as convinced as ever that there had been an informant among the Next Day Hill servants and none too sure of the innocence of Dr. Condon, who had recently exhibited himself in a department store window, posing beside a replica of the kidnap ladder, and was now talking about undertaking a nationwide lecture tour. Considering that Condon had lost his part-time employment at Fordham University and been branded as either a dupe or a conspirator, his decision to take his case to the public and earn a few dollars by doing so seems hardly surprising, but the authorities saw it as evidence of mercenary intent.

In March 1933, shortly before the Lindberghs' secret automobile trip to Detroit, Charles and Colonel Schwarzkopf cooked up a plan to lure Condon into incriminating himself. The two of them reasoned that if Condon was in league with Graveyard John, he would also jump at the chance to get an additional payoff from the Lindberghs. While Betty Morrow was abroad visiting with Elisabeth and Aubrey in Wales, Charles talked Anne into inviting Condon and his daughter, Myra Hacker, to dinner at Next Day Hill. Myra was a high school English teacher, and after the meal Anne offered to show her the manuscript of her book. Left alone with Dr. Condon, Lindbergh told him that the family would like to compensate him for his efforts on their behalf.

Condon thought the offer over. When he first came into the case, he had been given three toys from Charles junior's nursery to keep in case the child was turned over to him. "I don't want your money, Colonel Lindbergh. But if you would, let me keep the wooden animals."

Abashed, Lindbergh shook the doctor's hand and told him to consider the toys his. A few days later, he reported to a conference of state and federal agents that he was satisfied that Condon, however eccentric, was a fundamentally decent man.

In New York, meanwhile, Lieutenant Finn was looking forward to his first big break. On May 2, 1933, a presidential order against gold hoarding was scheduled to go into effect. After that date gold notes would still be legal tender, but since it would be theoretically illegal for a private citizen to hold more than one hundred dollars' worth of them, they would no longer be widely circulated. Finn and Treasury agent Frank Wilson were betting that the kidnapper would try to get rid of as many notes as possible before the deadline, and the Treasury Department distributed thirty thousand circulars asking bank tellers to exercise special vigilance.

On May 1 there were long lines at banks across the country. At the Federal Reserve Bank in New York City, teller James Estey was so busy that he didn't finish tallying the money in his cash drawer until after midnight. Checking his receipts against the Treasury's printed notice, Estey discovered that he had taken in $2,980 worth of Lindbergh ransom money in ten- and twenty-dollar gold certificates. He had handled so many large transactions that he had no memory of the individual who had presented the notes, but he did have a deposit slip signed by one J. J. Faulkner, who gave his (or possibly her) address as 537 West 149th Street. The search for Faulkner, identified in the FBI's CALNAP files as "unknown subject #5," immediately became Lieutenant Finn's top priority.[5]

The following day teams of investigators from the NYPD, the FBI, and the Treasury Department all beat a path to 537 West 149th Street, better known as the Plymouth Apartments. As they soon learned, the property was owned by Payne Louis Kretzmer, a sixty-three-year-old German immigrant who had suffered a mental breakdown after the 1929 crash. By a strange coincidence, Payne Kretzmer, now in an advanced state of dementia, was a resident of a private sanatorium located less than a mile from Next Day Hill.[6]

The 149th Street neighborhood was already familiar to the NYPD's Lindbergh-case squad. On March 2, 1932, the day after the kidnapping, an abandoned 1930 Buick Brougham had been recovered on the street, a few blocks east of the Plymouth Apartments. A woman living nearby told Det. John Genet of the NYPD's Auto Theft Squad that she had seen a blond, pop-eyed man park the Buick beside a fire hydrant in the predawn hours, leaving the windows open and the key in the ignition. Although under normal circumstances the car might have been a tempting target for thieves, neighborhood residents excited by the news of the Lindbergh kidnapping had promptly reported it to the police.

Detective Genet had immediately notified New Jersey state police headquarters that the vehicle was possibly connected with the kidnapping. The Buick and its contents—including two dirty bathrobes, a grapefruit knife, and a milk bottle with a section of rubber tubing attached—were turned over to investigators from Trenton, who determined that the car had been taken from the parking lot of the Pines Hotel in Lakewood, New Jersey, on January 28, 1932. Sometime between that date and the day it was recovered, the car's original Jersey plates had been exchanged for New York license plates stolen in Yonkers on January 2. That someone had gone to the trouble of exchanging one set of stolen plates for another strongly suggested that the Buick had been used in the commission of a crime. Nevertheless, in the confusion of those harrowing days, some overworked state police clerk had overlooked the significance of the information. The Buick was returned to its owner and Genet's report, including the eyewitness's description of the blond, pop-eyed man, was filed among the exhausted leads.

Although the Jersey authorities were originally interested in the information that Payne Kretzmer was a resident of Englewood, their enthusiasm cooled after they were reminded by the NYPD that they had lost track of a vehicle that might possibly have been used in the kidnapping. The error was arguably excusable—real-life police, unlike their fictional counterparts, do get bogged down in paperwork and make dumb mistakes—but following the Red Johnson fiasco and the Sharpe suicide, the story of the misfiled report would have been disastrous for the troop's image. Tempers were running so high that Schwarzkopf's staff almost felt that Lieutenant Finn was pursuing this angle of the case just to embarrass them.

Charles Lindbergh's conduct in the weeks immediately following the kidnapping had demonstrated that he was far too credulous to make a good detective and certainly too close to the case emotionally to make objective strategy decisions. Nevertheless the investigation had reached a point at which he now could have played a useful role in getting the various agencies involved to set aside their differences and work together. Instead, at the very moment when there was new hope of a solution, Lindbergh began to withdraw from his self-appointed role as coordinator of the investigation.

Anne Lindbergh made no secret of the fact that she was not looking forward to the day the case was solved. Simply knowing the name and seeing the face of her baby's killer would not answer the question of why this horrible tragedy had happened. An arrest would only mean more ugly newspaper publicity, another wave of threatening letters, and the necessity of publicly reliving events that already haunted her troubled sleep. Betty Morrow, on her part, saw her son-in-law's absorption in the details of police work as slightly *déclassé*, as well as hard on Anne's peace of mind and disruptive for the household. No doubt she was none too pleased on returning from Europe to discover that he had convinced Anne to entertain Dr. Condon at Next Day Hill. Charles was thus caught between his need to know the facts and his family's feeling that his selfish absorption in the case was contrary to his wife and child's best interests. He reacted by distracting himself with the prospect of new ventures in the field where he felt most at home—aviation.

Charles and Anne resumed flying together in April, making a trip to the West Coast on business for TAT (recently reorganized under the name TWA). Soon after, he began drawing up plans for a more ambitious trip surveying transatlantic routes for Pan-American Airways. Anne, though she looked forward to the long flight as a distraction, had decidedly mixed feelings about being separated from Jon on his first birthday, but she took comfort in the fact that Evangeline had agreed to look after the baby at the Morrow "cottage" on North Haven, where she would be assisted by Betty Gow, Elsie Whateley, and a contingent of armed guards provided by the Burns agency.

Six years after Charles's hop to Paris, crossing the Atlantic by air was still a risky business even though transoceanic flights were becoming ever more common. In July 1933, the same month the Lindberghs began their journey, General Italo Balbo of Italy led an unprecedented fleet of twenty-five planes across the Atlantic and back again—only two aircraft from Balbo's group were lost en route, a success rate considered highly impressive. As for commercial passenger service, technology had yet to catch up with the optimistic predictions made by Fonck and Byrd in 1927. Large aircraft with a full complement of paying passengers could not carry enough fuel to negotiate the Great Circle route pioneered by Charles Lindbergh, and some experts predicted that before air service from the United States to Europe became a reality, it would be necessary to build a network of refueling stations on artificial islands in the middle of the ocean.

The Lindberghs' mission in July 1933 was to investigate more realistic alternatives, surveying both a northern route—via Labrador, Greenland, Iceland, and the Faeroe and Shetland Islands to Denmark—and a southern route, westward from Lisbon via the Azores. The obvious danger of the northern route was that the weather could be unpredictable, even in midsummer. The southern route was not anticipated to be as risky; however, it involved a long hop over open water with nowhere to land in the event of an emergency.

Flying once again in their Lockheed Sirius, repainted red and black for the journey and equipped with a 710-horsepower Wright Cyclone engine that used a variable-pitch propeller, the Lindberghs hoped to test some newly developed equipment, including a powerful air-to-ground radio set and an improved navigation aid for measuring ground speed. They would also make use of an instrument of Charles's own invention called a "sky hook"—actually a simple device for exposing petroleum-jelly-covered slides in order to take samples of airborne microbes at high altitudes. (As later reported in a *Scientific Monthly* article coauthored by Lindbergh and a Department of Agriculture scientist, slides collected with the sky hook revealed that a surprising variety of microbes were present in the atmosphere at ten thousand feet and above.) Since weather conditions were expected to be treacherous on the northern crossing, the Sirius was also fitted out with extensive survival gear, including a rubber boat, a sledge, snowshoes, and a ground-to-ground radio for use in case of an emergency landing. Since the trip would be mostly over open water, the Lindberghs did not take parachutes—an omission some interpreted as reckless.

Pan-American Airways would be supplying technical support for the survey, including an escort ship, the *Jelling*, which would track the Lindberghs at sea. As with the 1931 Orient flight, however, the Lindberghs were paying most of the expenses, and the trip was a combination of business and pleasure, allowing plenty of time for adventurous flying and the exploration of their exotic destinations. In Greenland Charles and Anne tarried three weeks, tracking polar bears and muskoxen from the air and attending a dance at which Eskimo couples in native dress performed Scottish flings and Virginia reels taught to them by missionaries. In Godthaab Charles purchased a sealskin kayak and challenged the entire crew of the *Jelling* to try their hands at paddling the tricky craft in the freezing waters of the harbor.

Here Charles also threw a scare into the *Jelling*'s captain and the Danish bureaucrat assigned to act as his liaison by announcing that he and Anne planned to cross the Greenland ice cap by air, a feat that had been successfully accomplished only twice before. Like most nonaviators, the support staff assumed that on any flight in a region where the weather was unpredictable, the chances of a forced landing were reasonably high. They looked at the petite, deceptively frail-appearing Mrs. Lindbergh, tried to imagine her crossing the ice sheet on snowshoes, and concluded that Colonel Lindbergh had taken leave of his senses. Lindbergh, however, had faith in the Sirius's advanced engine.

According to British pilot John Grierson, one of the two aviators to have successfully flown across the ice sheet before the Lindberghs, the actual risks lay somewhere between these estimates. The Sirius had power to spare, but Charles, with his usual supreme confidence in his abilities as a pilot, somewhat underestimated the challenge posed by arctic conditions. Flying over the ice sheet, as Grierson described it, was like being "lowered into a bowl." The vast expanse of sparkling snow created an optical illusion, making it seem that the earth below was concave rather than convex, confounding the pilot's sense of altitude. Snow blindness as well as disorientation could strike without warning.

Despite an unseasonable August 1 snowstorm and unusual fog conditions near the coast, the Lindberghs made their traverse five days later. Charles located a chain of mountains not marked on the charts, and though they flew through a storm before touching down at Angmagssalik on the eastern coast, Anne had time to wonder at the scenery—fewer mountains than she had expected but a vast sweep of icy wasteland, a glittering desert of snow. In the week that followed, the Lindberghs flew across the cap twice more, once taking a longer route via Julianehaab on the southernmost tip of the island, before continuing their survey flight with a hop to Vidhey, Iceland. "As usual," Charles wrote in his official report to Juan Trippe, "in a country where little flying has been done, the difficulties have been greatly exaggerated."[7]

What the officers of the *Jelling* and the local officials had seen—as Charles seemingly had not—was just how frightened Anne was of the flight. His apparent disregard of her feelings struck them as so unchivalrous that after the third dash across the ice, the Danish liaison told Mrs. Lindbergh, "I think I'll just take that sledge out of that compartment so you can't go over the cap again."[8]

In fact Charles was not as oblivious as he seemed. Flying had always taken a toll on Anne's nerves, but in the long run there were also rewards—excitement, the satisfaction of sharing a great adventure with her husband, and perhaps most important, the knowledge that she had overcome her tendency to passivity. Anne herself saw flying as therapy, and Charles, for once in total agreement with his mother-in-law, believed that the best cure for grief was keeping too busy to have time to brood.

Certainly for Charles himself—and he was by no means as unaffected by the emotional strain of the past year as he liked to pretend—the cure seemed to work. Though he had doubts about the future of "flying boats" for commercial air travel, Lindbergh was never so happy as when flying a seaplane. In the Sirius he and Anne were freed from the need to rely on ground facilities, and landing on an unexplored cove or lake was always an adventure. If there happened to be a settlement nearby, the locals paddled out to the plane, offering their unexpected visitors a warm bed for the night and a supper of raw fish or, as on one occasion, pony meatballs. If the area proved to be uninhabited, he and Anne could dine on canned baked beans and bed down in the rear luggage compartment, their sleeping bags stretched over a mound of survival gear. Charles was in high spirits, and when a teenage boy in Iceland asked him if the Eskimo girls of Greenland were beautiful, he replied, "I'll tell you something you can take as a fundamental. There are beautiful girls in every country you go to!"[9]

But Anne, despite her efforts to get into the spirit of the trip, was growing more fearful with every leg of the journey. As Charles often reminded her, sitting in the rear cockpit of the Sirius working the radio was much like being a backseat driver in an automobile. If only she would take over the piloting occasionally in tight situations, she would realize that it is far easier on the nerves to be the one in control. Anne accepted this reasoning, but when the fog actually closed in around the Sirius it always seemed far more sensible to place her faith in the husband she still thought of as "Charles the Invincible."

John Grierson, who ran into the Lindberghs in Iceland, found them to be a likable but puzzling couple. Anne, though an expert radio operator and soon to capture the world's record for air-to-ground transmission, turned aside his requests for advice on equipment with a flustered wave of the hands. "She passed the question over to Charles and pretended she did not really understand such technical matters herself," wrote Grierson with a mixture of annoyance and frustration.[10] (Anne later explained away her transmitting record, noting that using the signal "Lindbergh Plane," instead of her call letters, as she did on occasion, was "a little like using live bait on your fishing rod instead of regulation fly.")[11] Grierson also thought Charles's approach to navigation a little lackadaisical, and a few years later, after reading Anne's account of the 1931 Great Circle flight, he would write Colonel Lindbergh a letter, chastising him for flying south across the Kurile Islands without realizing that in the Arctic a small difference in latitude could make for a critical variation in number of daylight hours suitable for flying. "A less skillful pilot would very likely have come to grief," Grierson commented in his book on arctic aviation.

From Iceland the Lindberghs flew to the Faeroes, where the miserable weather conditions were enough to convince Charles the islands did not have a future as a major stop on the North Atlantic route. They then proceeded to make a leisurely tour of Europe, beginning with the Scandinavian capitals, which they adored, and Leningrad and Moscow, where the lavish welcome they received from the Soviet aviation establishment could not compensate for their shock at the shabby clothes of their hosts, the underfed horses pulling wagons on the streets, and the general seediness of the cities.

In London Anne arranged to have dinner at a restaurant with the newlyweds, Elisabeth and Aubrey. On the excuse that his presence might attract unwanted attention, Charles stayed behind at the hotel, where he was descended upon by Florence Grenfell, the much-younger wife of the senior partner of the firm of Morgan Grenfell and a famous society beauty known for her tall, slender figure and vivacious personality. Charles, it seems, was not averse to going out in public with the right kind of encouragement, and Florrie, who had a Bohemian streak, swept him off to a nightclub to see Josephine Baker, who had brought her act to London and was the talk of the town.

Sadly for Charles, the low point of the tour was Paris, where ecstatic crowds cheered the return of *"le boy."* As much as he liked France and the French people, their tributes only served to remind him how different he was from the confident, carefree youth who had landed at Le Bourget.

By contrast, for Anne, the stays in London and Paris were a brief respite from the long hours in the Sirius, which had come to seem less a home away from home than a prison. She missed Jon and was becoming more nervous about flying by the day. More than once she seriously considered withdrawing from the flight and taking the next ship home, leaving Charles to find another copilot. The only thing that held her back was the knowledge that she would have to face scores, perhaps hundreds, of reporters demanding to know if her return meant that she and Charles were separating. (And the answer to this question was far from clear. Charles, so sensitive to any hint of criticism, would have found it difficult to forgive the humiliation of being deserted by his wife with the tour half completed.)

One day, heading out of Amsterdam for Geneva, the Sirius was trapped above a fogbank and Charles flew all the way to Spain and back in a vain search for a break in the clouds. Anne was so shaken that she decided if she lived to touch solid ground again not even the fear of publicity could keep her from taking the next train to Paris, where the French branch of the Morgan bank could wire New York for steamship fare. Just before nightfall the weather broke, and they were finally able to land in Rotterdam. There a friendly Dutch pilot, also marooned by fog, took them out to supper. "My wife and I always fly together and we think those are the happiest moments of our lives," the pilot remarked innocently. And it occurred to Anne that perhaps, in spite of everything, this was true for her and Charles as well. Someday, when the terrors of the moment had receded into memory, she might look back on these hours in the air as precious. Her resolution forgotten, she decided to stick with the itinerary.[12]

In theory the return flight across the southern route was to be the easiest part of the journey. But the Lindberghs' survey of the Azores failed to locate a harbor suitable for Pan-Am's big flying boats, and Charles decided to deviate from the original plan of hopping directly to Newfoundland and returning home via the Cape Verde islands and Brazil. But as it turned out, the harbors in the Canaries were also inhospitable. At Porto Praia, the prevailing winds blew landward, churning up powerful, rolling breakers that made it impossible for the Sirius to take off with a full load of fuel. The Lindberghs' host had a tubercular cough, the bed they were offered was infested with what the maid apologetically called "*des bêtes qui piquent*," and after a week they returned to Bathurst in Gambia. Here, too, the wind conditions were wrong—they needed a tail wind to take off, but for a week there was no breeze at all. Charles finally managed to get the Sirius airborne by jettisoning more than two hundred pounds of supplies, including tools and sleeping bags.

After a flight of more than sixteen hundred miles across the South Atlantic, the Lindberghs reached Natal, Brazil, on December 6. Even now Charles was in no rush to return home. He and Anne made a side trip up the Amazon to Manaus, followed by stops in Port-of-Spain, Trinidad, and San Juan, Puerto Rico, reaching New York thirteen days later, in time to spend Christmas week with Jon.

Charles Lindbergh would look back on the five-and-a-half-month, thirty-thousand-mile Atlantic survey flight as the high point of his career in aviation. In many respects it had been more dangerous and more physically demanding than his 1927 flight to Paris, and commercially and scientifically it was more productive. Not only did the tour lay the groundwork for Pan-Am's expansion into transatlantic passenger service, but the Lindberghs had shown the flag for American commercial aviation at a time when the industry was suffering through a crisis of confidence, plagued by the depressed economy and government indifference.

Following the flight, the Lindberghs decided to retire the Sirius— which during the course of the journey had acquired the nickname *Tingmissartoq,* an Eskimo word meaning "flies like a big bird." The plane became a popular exhibit at the Museum of Natural History in New York, where it remained until Charles and Anne decided to donate it to the Smithsonian. Aviation buffs and young people were excited, but on the whole reaction to the trip was strangely grudging. Unlike Wiley Post or Earhart, Charles Lindbergh was viewed as a sort of national treasure, and the feeling persisted that he was doing the country a disservice by continuing to fly. *Time* magazine editorialized that if Lindbergh refused to ground himself for the good of aviation someone else ought to: "He is worth keeping. And one way to keep him is on the ground."

Backhanded compliments like this must have been all the more frustrating to Lindbergh, given the Roosevelt administration's policies with regard to commercial aviation. While both Coolidge and Hoover had refused to endorse direct subsidies for the industry, as was the rule in Europe, the Republicans had evolved a system of de facto regulation, administered through the post office, whose payments to airmail contractors gave the airlines a guaranteed income, enabling them to expand into passenger operations. After the stock market crash, however, Post-

master General Walter Brown had concluded that the airmail subsidy
was not sufficient. More often than not, the winning bidders for airmail
contracts were small companies that owned only one or two light
planes, flew only the most profitable routes, and had no interest in serving passengers. When it became clear that even the larger airlines would
have difficulty surviving the depression, Brown summoned industry
leaders to Washington for a meeting soon to become known as the
Spoils Conference. Taking advantage of a regulation that permitted him
to bypass low bidders in the interests of safety, Brown doled out contracts to those airlines that seemed most capable of offering comprehensive regional service.

Brown's action created a nationwide system of trunk airlines
overnight and was arguably good for the consumer. However, the new
regulations strongly favored the big, well-capitalized airlines like TAT,
which gobbled up Western Air to become Transcontinental and Western
Airlines (TWA). Smaller entrepreneurs—who, coincidentally or not,
happened to be Democrats—were left with no choice but to merge their
operations with larger competitors or get out of the industry entirely.
Among the casualties were the Robertson brothers, who had returned
to the airline business only to lose their company in a forced sale to the
future American Airlines. The outrage of the losers was well expressed
by Gene Vidal, founder of the now-extinct Luddington Line, who railed
bitterly against this exercise in "Hoover socialism." And when the
Republicans were voted out of office, it was inevitable that there would
be a backlash.

The stage for the reaction was set, appropriately enough, by the
Senate Banking Committee inquiry known as the Pecora Hearings.
During the course of this investigation, the J. P. Morgan Bank was compelled to open its books to Senate investigators who discovered that
clients on the firm's "preferred list"—including prominent politicians
(among them Calvin Coolidge himself), leaders of industry and, of
course, Lindy—had been offered opportunities to buy stocks at bargain
prices. Moreover, when stock prices fell, many of these well-fixed clients
had been able to lower their income tax burden by claiming paper losses
on the sale of depressed securities. In fact, J. P. Morgan and nineteen of
his partners had paid no income tax at all in 1931 or 1932.

Hard on the heels of the Pecora hearings came a series of muckrak-
ing articles by Hearst columnist Fulton Lewis, Jr., charging that the
Spoils Conference was a classic exercise in restraint of trade, possibly

also involving influence peddling and outright bribery. This led to an investigation of Postmaster Brown's actions by the Senate Subcommittee on Postal Operations, chaired by Senator Hugo Black of Alabama, the future Supreme Court justice. In the manner of C. A. Lindbergh a generation earlier, Black was somewhat carried away by the theory that the airline reorganization was a J. P. Morgan plot. Ironically this made the younger Lindbergh an inviting target. Colonel Lindbergh had not attended the Spoils Conference, but he was an obvious link between the Morgan interests and TAT as well as one of the bank's private clients. The Black subcommittee requested Lindbergh's financial records, which he provided voluntarily. The figures were then promptly introduced into the public record through staff testimony which described Lindbergh's $250,000 signing bonus from TAT as a "gift," a word widely construed as a euphemism for bribe.

On February 9, 1934, without waiting for Black's subcommittee to finish its investigation, President Franklin Delano Roosevelt issued an executive order suspending all airmail contracts. Until new contracts were awarded, the U.S. Army would fly the mail. The president's action left the Army Air Corps brass in an embarrassing position. Long starved for appropriations, the corps had neither the equipment nor enough pilots experienced with night flying to take over mail deliveries at a moment's notice. By the same token the Air Corps had finally been offered a chance to prove itself by performing a highly visible public service, and it could hardly afford to plead that army pilots weren't up to the task of delivering a few sacks of mail.

Lindbergh had no such compunctions. With the encouragement of Henry Breckinridge, he fired off an open telegram to Roosevelt. Suspending the airmail contracts, he protested, CONDEMNS THE LARGEST PORTION OF OUR COMMERCIAL AVIATION WITHOUT TRIAL. A follow-up story in the *New York Times* pointed out that Colonel Lindbergh was deeply concerned for the safety of army pilots.[13]

And, indeed, in the first week after the army took over the mail routes, five pilots died in crashes and six more were critically injured. By the end of March 1934, the death toll had risen to twelve. Billy Mitchell, who believed the government should have simply nationalized TWA's fleet for the duration of the crisis, took out his frustration on Lindbergh in a speech before the Foreign Policy Association's convention in New York, calling him a "front of the Air Trust," a spokesman for "profit" (a dirty word in 1934) and "that son-in-law of Dwight

Morrow" (about the worst insult he could think of). But public opinion sided with Lindbergh, and a chastened Roosevelt was forced to rescind his order and return the airmail to private operators.[14]

In hindsight Lindbergh's role in the airmail controversy revealed a stunning lack of political savvy. In subsequent testimony before the Senate Subcommittee on Postal Operations, he admitted that he had no idea what went on at the Spoils Conference but indignantly defended the integrity of the men he called "my friends"—a group of sophisticated businessmen who may indeed have acted within the letter of the law but who were hardly innocents when it came to influence peddling. The art of behind-the-scenes negotiation was unknown to Lindbergh, and instead of making his stand solely on the safety issue, where his judgment proved all too correct, he had put his reputation on the line and made a personal enemy of the president in the name of a cause whose complexities he seemed not to grasp.

This was not, however, how it appeared at the time. After eleven months during which FDR had been able to impose his programs on Congress and the country virtually without opposition, he had been forced to retreat—a setback that "dented the myth of Roosevelt's invulnerability," as Arthur Schlesinger, Jr., put it in *The Coming of the New Deal*. Overnight Republican power brokers began to look at Charles Lindbergh as their man on a white horse, the hero who could slay the dragon of Rooseveltism, if only he could be induced to take up the crusade.[15]

EIGHTEEN

"Unknown Subject #5"

*I*MPORTANT AS IT WAS FOR AVIATION, the 1933 survey flight was also an exercise in escapism. The transatlantic routes the Lindberghs surveyed could have been covered in two months, and their visits to European capitals, while wonderful publicity for Pan-Am and American aviation in general, could easily have been shortened or put off to another year. Anne certainly had never anticipated that she would be separated from Jon for five and a half months, and the cool response to the trip in the United States no doubt reflected a certain unease over the way the Lindberghs, having just lost one son, had blithely (or so it seemed) flown off to Europe, leaving their second to celebrate his first birthday without them.

The dilemmas the Lindberghs faced on their return go far to explain why Charles had made the trip last as long as possible. First and foremost there was the perpetually troublesome question of where to live. Charles's dream, as always, was to make his home in the West or Midwest, on a ranch in Montana or Colorado or even a farm in Minnesota, at any rate somewhere far from the constant scrutiny of the eastern press. Anne was more dismayed than ever by the prospect of living out "in the sticks," as she put it, away from her mother and civilization as she knew it, and no doubt it is quite true that she would often have been left at home, with no friends nearby to rely on, while Charles flew off to interesting places on airline and scientific business. This unresolved debate was now immensely complicated by the problem of security. On their own the Lindberghs could not possibly afford the night watchmen and uniformed security guards that were ever present at Next Day Hill, and it was difficult to imagine how an ordinary country home could be made safe from intruders.

Before leaving for Europe Charles and Anne had agreed that the logical solution to their problem was a high-rise apartment in the city, where the building's doormen would screen all callers and they could live without the fear of some stranger creeping in through an open window. Thus, in the spring of 1934, they sublet a furnished penthouse in mid-Manhattan, an experiment that quickly proved disastrous. The kidnapping had injected an element of morbid curiosity into the public's reaction to Lindy, and Charles, who disliked the noise and crowds of the city streets to begin with, returned home every evening irate over some real or imagined indignity. Anne was trying to work simultaneously on her book, eventually published as *North to the Orient,* and on a long article for the *National Geographic* about the Atlantic survey flight, but she was depressed and lethargic. Just caring for Jon on the maid's day off was an overwhelming challenge. The dogs, unused to being cooped up all day, did their business on the penthouse balcony and urinated against the legs of the grand piano. The landlord soon asked for a substantial increase in the rent—a demand possibly related to the dogs' behavior—but the Lindberghs suspected that they were being overcharged because of *who they were,* and the demand became an excuse for retreating back to the security of Englewood.

At Next Day Hill Charles was rather like a houseguest who had overstayed his welcome, still idolized by some of the staff but resented by others, including Jo Graeme. Visitors to the house during this period often found him with a camera in his hand, snapping endless photographs as if to emphasize that he was more an observer of the scene than an actual participant. To be incapable of providing a safe home for his family would have been hard on the pride of any man, but the situation must have been especially difficult for Lindbergh, whose self-image had been formed by his role as his mother's companion and protector. Adding to the tension, Anne wanted another child and was disturbed by her inability to conceive when she had gotten pregnant so easily in the past.

In the wake of the airmail controversy, a number of Colonel Lindbergh's acquaintances were urging him to enter politics, assuring him that the presidential nomination could be his for the asking. Even Alexis

Carrel confided to one reporter that he thought Lindbergh would make an excellent candidate. But Lindbergh, as uninterested as ever in what he once called "the fluff of party politics," preferred to devote himself to the final stages of the development of Igor Sikorsky's latest high-wing flying boat, the S-42. Lindbergh had helped Sikorsky draw up the original plans for the S-42 back in 1931, during a Pan-Am flight from Miami to the Canal Zone, sketching the rough design on the back of a Pan-Am in-flight menu. Always an advocate of advanced engineering, Lindbergh had urged Sikorsky to incorporate such novel features as the variable-pitch propeller and a more streamlined silhouette, featuring flush riveting and engines mounted in cowls directly on the wing. On August 1, 1934, Lindbergh and Pan-Am test pilots Ed Musick and Boris Sergievsky took the S-42 up for its maiden flight, setting a phenomenal eight world records during the course of the eight-hour, twelve-hundred-mile shakedown cruise.

But even in his work for Pan-Am, politics intruded. Juan Trippe's efforts to open up airmail service to Europe, one of the goals of the Lindberghs' survey work, were frustrated by disputes with foreign airlines, including Britain's Imperial Airways, which was reluctant to grant reciprocal landing rights as long as it had no aircraft to compete with the S-42. Pan-Am and Sikorsky were also suffering from the fallout from the airmail controversy. Although Trippe had taken no part in the Spoils Conference, Pan-Am was perceived as another beneficiary of government favoritism, and the scandal complicated his efforts to obtain seaplane landing rights on Guam and Wake Island for his proposed trans-Pacific airmail route. Sikorsky's holding company, meanwhile, was being forced by the Black Committee to break up into three corporations (Boeing, United Aircraft, and United Airlines). The political climate being what it was, neither Trippe nor Sikorsky had anything to gain from being too closely associated in the public eye with Lindbergh. Trippe valued their personal association but made it a rule to avoid the kind of open confrontation Charles had generated by publicly attacking the president. Further S-42 test flights as well as Pan-Am survey work in the Pacific were assigned to Musick and others.

While the Lindberghs were in Europe, the NYPD's Lieutenant Finn had continued his dogged investigation into the identity of his unknown subject #5. There was no J. J. Faulkner living at the Plymouth Apartments on West 149th Street but a check of building and city records for the past twenty years revealed that until 1920 apartment number 64 had been occupied by a mother and daughter, Jane and Jane Emily Faulkner. Jane Faulkner had died in 1923. Her daughter then married Carl Oswin Giessler, an older widower who owned a nursery and wholesale seed business. In 1925 the Giesslers moved to Larchmont, subletting their apartment to Jane's uncle, an elderly musician who played in the Metropolitan Opera orchestra. What intrigued the investigating team, however, was the discovery that Giessler's son by his first marriage, Carl Donald Giessler, had gone to high school with Dr. Condon's son-in-law, Ralph Hacker. Suddenly Condon was an active suspect once again. The FBI also began monitoring the Giessler family's mail and bank records, and when Carl senior's married daughter Phyllis Leipold made a brief visit to Canada, her luggage was surreptitiously searched before she crossed the border. When the Giesslers learned they were under suspicion they cooperated fully, submitting to repeated interrogations. After months of scrutiny it became obvious that the family was thoroughly respectable and was as bewildered as the police by the J. J. Faulkner deposit slip.

In August 1933, shortly after the NYPD and the FBI agreed to close their files on the family, Phyllis's husband Henry Leipold placed the barrel of a .22 rifle in his mouth and blew his head off. Mrs. Leipold told Insp. John J. Lyons, Lieutenant Finn's superior, that her husband had a history of emotional illness and had become convinced that the FBI was persecuting him because of an adulterous affair he had been involved in years earlier. Terrified of being publicly identified as Lindbergh kidnapping suspects, the Leipolds and Giesslers cooperated with Lyons and the FBI in making sure that the press never found out that the CALNAP investigation had claimed its second suicide victim.[1]

While the Giesslers were still under suspicion, a member of Lieutenant Finn's team happened to return to the Plymouth Apartments to interview the building employees. As he waited in the basement for the super, the detective found himself idly staring at a row of boarded-up dumbwaiters located across from the door of the super's office. Taped above the shafts was a row of yellowing labels. The shaft directly opposite the office door was that of apartment number 64. Its label, still legible through the coating of soot and grime, read: "J & J Faulkner."

To Lieutenant Finn, who prided himself on his ability to think like a criminal, it seemed logical that whoever exchanged the gold certificates would not have risked using his own name. Unexpectedly confronted with a request for a signature, he might well have remembered a name that had been directly in his line of sight as he sat at his desk in the basement office.

At the time of the kidnapping, the NYPD soon learned, the super of the Plymouth Apartments had been one Duane William Baker. Prior to the spring of 1931, when he was hired by Richard Kretzmer, the deaf-mute brother of the Plymouth's legal owner, Baker had resided in a boardinghouse in Englewood, New Jersey. The Plymouth's tenants remembered Baker as an incompetent super who ran a gambling game in the basement, entertained women in his office at night, and stole "whatever was not nailed down." Richard Kretzmer, however, was a trusting soul and had ignored the tenants' complaints until the spring of 1932, when he learned that the super was often absent from the building and had been paying the elevator operators to cover for him. On April 15, 1932, just as Kretzmer was considering firing him, Baker came to Kretzmer with the story that his wife was desperately ill and needed an operation. The soft-hearted Kretzmer gave him twenty-five dollars. The next morning Baker did not show up for work, and Kretzmer discovered that he had absconded with the midmonth rent receipts.

Between April 15 and the end of May 1932, Baker moved at least four times, on one occasion paying a month's rent in advance only to bolt after four days without leaving a forwarding address. His common-law wife, described by the Plymouth's tenants as a brunette with a heavy foreign accent who kept very much to herself, dropped out of sight. Baker also stopped making payments on two small life insurance policies, and a girlfriend he had been seeing regularly lost track of him. When the NYPD finally caught up with him in November 1933, Baker was working as a super in a building on Knox Place in the Bronx, just one block from the spot where the cab driver Joseph Perrone had been flagged down by a man who gave him a note addressed to Dr. John Condon.

The moment he saw Duane Baker being escorted into the Bronx precinct house for questioning, Lieutenant Finn knew he was not looking at Graveyard John. Dr. Condon's description had been explicit—John was a "middleweight" with brown hair, high cheekbones, and almond-shaped eyes. Baker was blond and blue eyed, wore horn-rimmed glasses, and had a very distinctive face—long and thin with thick eyebrows, slightly protuberant eyes, suggestive of a thyroid condition, and "sunken jowls." Though of German extraction, he had been born in New York and spoke English without an accent. His handwriting was utterly unlike that of the ransom notes. Much to Finn's frustration, handwriting experts retained by the NYPD pointed out that his handwriting was also different from the J. J. Faulkner signature—

Charles, by contrast, was energized. Although it wasn't strictly necessary, he and Anne flew back east so that he could testify before a Bronx grand jury that was preparing to indict Hauptmann on a charge of extortion. (The decision of Bronx DA Samuel Foley to press for an indictment before extraditing Hauptmann to New Jersey amounted to a vote of no confidence in the Jersey attorney general; if a New Jersey jury failed to convict Hauptmann of kidnapping or murder, he could always be tried in New York.) After Lindbergh described to the grand jury how he sat in Al Reich's car outside St. Raymond's Cemetery and heard Graveyard John call out to Condon, "Hey Dok*tor!* Over here!" District Attorney Foley asked if he would be able to identify that voice if he heard it again. "It would be difficult," Lindbergh answered.

Meanwhile Dr. Condon, after picking Hauptmann out of a lineup, had become strangely evasive, insisting that he would not "declare his identification" of the suspect until he was actually sworn in as a witness at Hauptmann's trial. Condon said later that he was afraid Hauptmann would be lynched once it was known that he had been positively identified. The police suspected that the elderly educator was simply enjoying his moment in the spotlight and paying them back for all the grief they had caused him over the past two years. The possibility that Condon just wasn't sure Hauptmann was the right man cannot be dismissed either, but more likely he saw withholding his identification as a sort of insurance policy. The police had made numerous attempts to implicate him, and there was no guarantee that Hauptmann, under pressure, would not confess and attempt to strike a deal by naming Condon as his accomplice.

At any rate Condon's unpredictability made Charles Lindbergh's testimony potentially important. Norman Schwarzkopf and Inspector Lyons of the NYPD decided to set up a test. The day after Lindbergh's grand jury testimony, Hauptmann was brought before a group of federal and state agents who had gathered in Foley's office and asked to shout the words Graveyard John had used on the night of the ransom payment. Lindbergh, "disguised" by means of a pair of sunglasses, was seated among the detectives. After this demonstration Lindbergh told Schwarzkopf that he would be willing to swear that this was the same man he had heard outside St. Raymond's Cemetery. Charles Lindbergh was honest to a fault, and it is difficult to believe he would deliberately set out to commit perjury on such an important matter. Nevertheless some of the agents present wondered whether Lindbergh, in his eagerness to be of use to the prosecution, was not deceiving himself.[4]

As far as Lieutenant Finn was concerned, the investigation was far from over. Anna Hauptmann, when questioned at the police station after her husband's arrest, said that she could not specifically recall what she and her husband were doing on the night of March 1, 1932 ("Who can remember so long ago?"), but she insisted that Richard, as she called him, was a decent man and a good husband. Finn suspected that Mrs. Hauptmann, even if not involved in the crime, had reason to know that Richard was not quite the paragon she claimed. However, he soon discovered that Schwarzkopf and the New Jersey prosecutors wanted as little to do with Anna Hauptmann as possible. Mrs. Hauptmann had no police record, attended church regularly, and was the mother of an eleven-month-old son as well as a highly volatile personality. Still reeling from the Violet Sharpe scandal, they did not wish to give the press any excuse for portraying her as a victim of police brutality.

Like Finn, the FBI assumed that the next step in the investigation was to pursue Hauptmann's coconspirators. Four days after the arrest, the Associated Press quoted unnamed "high officials" in the Justice Department as saying that the bureau was still seeking an accomplice, "another man, whose connection with the case remained shrouded in mystery."[5] FBI agents who had actually worked on the case told reporters off the record that there were actually two other men involved.

A few days later, Arthur Keaten explained to a federal agent that the New York office of the FBI and Lieutenant Finn were simply not being realistic. The public was clamoring for a speedy conviction, and there was no doubt in any of the investigators' minds that Hauptmann was the main culprit. He was the man who had received the ransom money from Condon, and independent handwriting experts confirmed that he had also written every one of the ransom notes.

Ironically enough, rounding up Hauptmann's accomplices might actually make it more difficult to send him to the electric chair. Kidnapping had not been a capital crime in New Jersey in March 1932. Therefore the goal was to convict Hauptmann of murder. In theory, when a killing occurred during the commission of a felony, all involved were equally guilty and subject to the death penalty. But New Jersey law also permitted juries to recommend mercy, and faced with multiple defendants, each pointing the finger of blame at the others, jurors could be unpredictable.

New Jersey attorney general David Wilentz faced another problem that complicated his strategy. The border between Hunterdon and Mercer counties zigzagged across the Lindberghs' Hopewell estate. The house was in Hunterdon County, but most of Featherbed Lane (as well as the place where the body was eventually found) was located in Mercer County. Wilentz considered rural Hunterdon County to be the better venue for the trial. Therefore it suited his purposes to maintain that Charles Lindbergh, Jr., died within a few feet of the house. Since no one had heard a gunshot and no bullet was ever found, Wilentz decided to base his case on the theory that the Lindbergh baby died accidentally. On October 8 Wilentz told a Hunterdon County grand jury that Hauptmann had placed the sleeping twenty-month-old infant in a burlap sack and backed down the ladder from the nursery window, holding the sack under one arm. When a rung of the jerry-built ladder cracked under the added weight of the child, Hauptmann dropped the sack and the baby fell headfirst onto the paving stones below, dying instantaneously from a fractured skull. Presumably while carrying the dead child, Hauptmann then dragged the ladder seventy-five feet to the verge of the forest and made his escape via Featherbed Lane. Further, according to Wilentz, the small round hole in the baby's skull was not caused by a bullet, as Dr. Mitchell had thought at the time of the autopsy—it was made on the day the corpse was discovered, when Insp. Harry Walsh accidentally poked a stick through the skull as he was trying to remove the child's undershirt.

Wilentz's theory did not impress the experts at the time, nor has it since. Reviewing the autopsy evidence in an October 1983 article in the *Journal of Forensic Science,* Dr. Michael M. Baden concluded that Dr. Mitchell's report was so vague that there is simply no way to determine exactly how the Lindbergh baby died. Dr. Baden suggested several possibilities, including suffocation, a massive blow to the head, and a small-caliber gunshot wound; he did not think that the small hole in the cranium had been caused by Inspector Walsh's stick. (More likely Walsh had accidentally pushed the stick into an existing hole in the baby's skull.)

After being released by the police on the evening of Bruno's arrest, Anna Hauptmann immediately sought the advice of her cousin's ex-husband, Harry Whitney, an art supply salesman from Queens. Whitney, who was thrice married and, it seems, never legally divorced, had contacts in the Brooklyn court system and arranged for Bruno Hauptmann to be represented by James Fawcett, a defense attorney best known on Court Street for his wardrobe of purple velvet suits. Fawcett and Whitney, whose legal name was Harold Weisensee, set up an office in room 1101 of the Pennsylvania Hotel in Manhattan and began entertaining commercial offers. At one point Whitney even tried to sell a startling "new lead" in the case to the *Herald Tribune* for $450,000. The kidnapping, he claimed, had been committed by a certain "fairy dress designer" who later disappeared from a boardinghouse in Chelsea after sending a friend a note in which he said, "Dr. Condon is looking for me." Tracked down by a New Jersey detective, the woman who received the note said it was written as a joke. The dress designer wasn't missing either; he had simply skipped out on his last month's rent.[6]

On October 31 Anna Hauptmann and James Fawcett visited her husband in the lockup of the Hunterdon County Courthouse. Afterward she and the attorney got into a furious argument on the courthouse steps. In a 1935 deposition, Mrs. Hauptmann said Fawcett was pressuring her to sign a management contract giving him 25 percent of her earnings for twenty-five years. According to Fawcett the trouble started because he had just advised his client to plead insanity. The following day, as Anna was boarding the train back to New York, she was approached by a reporter from Hearst's New York *American*. "For God's sake, Mrs. Hauptmann, if you want to save Richard, get rid of Fawcett," he urged. She was all too happy to agree and soon signed a contract granting exclusive interview rights to the *American;* in return, the newspaper would pay a twenty-five-thousand-dollar retainer toward the fee of the celebrated defense attorney Edward J. ("Big Ed") Reilly.[7]

On January 6, 1935, on the eve of the trial, the New York *Daily Mirror,* also owned by the Hearst corporation, published an item saying that Reilly originally intended to base his defense on Hauptmann's testimony that another individual, so far not publicly named, killed the Lindbergh baby. On hearing this Judge Thomas Trenchard had called Reilly into his chambers and warned that if Hauptmann named an accomplice, he would adjourn the proceedings immediately. "Then, not until that person is in court can the trial be resumed." It was one thing for Hauptmann to push the blame onto an absent accomplice, but if that individual were actually in custody he would have every incentive to make a deal with the state and testify against Hauptmann. Reilly apparently decided the risk was not worth taking.

One would think that Charles Lindbergh, of all people, had a compelling interest in seeing that all involved in the kidnapping were identified and prosecuted. But Colonel Lindbergh had been ready to accept Dr. Shoenfeld's lone wolf theory as early as November 1932. Now many of Shoenfeld's predictions had proved uncannily accurate, and the prosecutor, albeit for reasons of his own, was relying on aspects of the psychologist's work. Not only was Shoenfeld's analysis based on a bio-logical view of human nature, an approach in which Lindbergh had inordinate faith, but the premise that the kidnapper was a victim of mental illness who had committed a solitary and impulsive act was in some ways attractive to the victim's family. Certainly it was less trou-bling than the possibility that Hauptmann had been in league with the very man the family had trusted to drive Charles junior to nursery school. Moreover, Wilentz's explanation of how the child died was based on the theory developed by Norman Schwarzkopf shortly after the body was discovered. Schwarzkopf's idea was known to Anne Lind-bergh, who took comfort in his assurance that her baby had died instan-taneously.

As acceptable as the lone-kidnapper hypothesis might be to the family, it was widely scorned by lawmen and journalists who had closely followed the development of the case, and rumors circulated in Trenton that Schwarzkopf himself was far from convinced and hoped to proceed against Hauptmann's accomplices later.

Lindbergh had come to rely heavily on the judgment of the gruff, plainspoken West Pointer, and as the trial got under way, the two men were inseparable, driving down to Hunterdon County together every morning—and stopping on one occasion to help one of the defense attorneys, whose car had skidded off an icy road into a ditch. It would be interesting to know whether Schwarzkopf suggested to Lindbergh that the trial might not close the books on the state's interest in the case, but it may be that the evidence against Hauptmann was at this point not even their major concern. Despite the courthouse's location in a rural county seat, huge crowds were predicted, and there had been threats against both the accused and his accusers, creating the very real possibility that justice would not be allowed to take its course.

NINETEEN

"It Was Enough to Make Me Want to Cable Hitler"

*I*N THE 1920S THE AMERICAN PUBLIC had an insatiable appetite for heroes. A decade later, heroes were passé, and the country was mad for children. A six-year-old tap dancer named Shirley Temple had become a major movie star. Little Orphan Annie was the queen of the funny papers. The custody battle over Gloria Vanderbilt, the ultimate "poor little rich girl," would be the scandal of the decade, and the Dionne quintuplets, born in May 1934, were treated by the Canadian government as a national treasure, removed from their parents' custody to a specially built compound where tourists observed them at play. The reasons for this epidemic of kindermania are not difficult to fathom. Millions of unemployed workers were struggling to hold their families together, and a generation of young adults had postponed marriage, often in order to help support their financially strapped parents.

More than any other child-centered story of those troubled times, the Lindbergh kidnapping tapped into the deepest insecurities of the depression generation. If the Lindberghs—courageous, handsome, wealthy, and popular—could not prevent their firstborn child from being snatched from his crib, then what family, anywhere, was safe? Though undoubtedly much of the fascination with the details of the crime was (and is) sheer voyeurism, the kidnapping set its mark on the psyche of the nation. A boy born in the late twenties and early thirties might not simply fantasize that he was adopted; he was likely to nurse the secret suspicion that he might be the "real" Lindbergh baby. For others the bogeyman would always wear the face of the Lindbergh kidnapper. Among the latter is author Maurice Sendak, who confesses to a lifelong obsession with the case. "All my books are really about the Lindbergh kidnapping."[1]

John Schenk, the young first-term mayor of Flemington, New Jersey, had lobbied vigorously to convince State Attorney General Wilentz that Bruno Richard Hauptmann should be tried in Hunterdon County, in the belief that the trial would help local businesses and bring publicity to the picturesque county seat. He was all too right on both counts. On opening day an estimated seventy to one hundred thousand people descended on the formerly peaceful village. The Union Hotel, across the street from the century-old courthouse, had been booked solid for months, and rooms in private homes were renting for fantastic sums. Soda fountains and luncheonettes in town were featuring such items as "Lindbergh sundaes" and the tastefully named "Hauptmann pudding." The spirit of commercialism had even infected Flemington's children; one grade school boy was doing a brisk business selling miniature kidnap ladders for a quarter, and at least two others were hawking "genuine" locks of the Lindbergh baby's hair.

Photographers were theoretically banned from the courtroom, but Sheriff John Curtiss had made a gentleman's agreement with five newsreel companies, including Fox Movietone News and Pathé, to allow them to film the trial provided no footage was shown until after the verdict came in. One camera was discreetly located inside a wall clock, but a second, "hidden" under a large wooden box mounted on the balcony railing, was impossible to overlook, and high-intensity bulbs installed in the lighting fixtures made the packed courtroom stifling despite the frigid January temperatures outside. Nevertheless, when newsreel film of the testimony began showing up in movie houses before the end of the trial, Judge Trenchard and the attorneys for both sides would indignantly protest that they never suspected the cameras were present.

Overwhelmed by more than fifty thousand ticket requests from as far away as Germany, the Philippines, and China, Sheriff Curtiss had decided to issue passes only to the press and members of the bar, seating other spectators on a first-come first-seated basis. On January 5, 1935, the day the first witnesses were scheduled to be heard, the line began forming before dawn, but when the courtroom doors were thrown open the pushing and shoving in the narrow hallways was so chaotic that brawny court officers simply plucked individuals out of the crowd at random. One bailiff's call for "skinny gents and slender ladies" to fill the few remaining spots on the benches nearly caused a riot when those who did not qualify heatedly protested being passed over.

Inside the courtroom Grace Noble of the London Newspaper Services was dumbfounded by the grandstanding of the attorneys and the bad manners of the spectators, who munched picnic lunches, laughed, and even broke into applause when Colonel Lindbergh and Norman Schwarzkopf took their seats just behind the prosecutor's table. "Oh dear, it is more like a cricket match than a trial," Noble protested to her American colleagues.

A strikingly large percentage of those fighting for seats were well-to-do. One Tuxedo Park socialite arrived before daybreak every morning in a chauffeured Rolls-Royce to stake out her place at the head of the line. Actress Lynn Fontanne showed up in a leopardskin coat. Comedian Jack Benny, actor Clifton Webb, and torch singer Helen Morgan were among the faithful standees, along with Mafia kingpins from New York and New Jersey.[2]

"It is considered chic to go to the Hauptmann trial," observed novelist Edna Ferber. "A mink coat, one of those Cossack hats, the word 'divine' in your vocabulary, and there you are, if a woman, complete for a day at Flemington.... All the mink coats were saying to all the Saville [sic] Row topcoats and burgundy mufflers, 'Hel-lo, dar-ling. How are you? Isn't this divine? Isn't it wonderful?'"[3]

There was an element of hypocrisy in such protests. Many of the same people who condemned the crowd's unseemly fascination with another family's tragedy were themselves mesmerized. The *New York Times,* which printed Ferber's scathing vignettes, was devoting more words to the trial than any tabloid. The *Herald Tribune,* a close second in terms of coverage, expected its chief correspondent Joe Alsop to file ten thousand words of copy a day. H. L. Mencken sarcastically called the trial "the most important event since the Resurrection" but later wrote to a pamphleteer who questioned the outcome, making a suggestion about tactics and expressing his opinion that Hauptmann had not acted alone.

Many of the nearly two hundred journalists covering the trial were celebrities in their own right. America's premier sob sister Adela Rogers St. Johns appeared each morning in a new ensemble created for her by

the Hollywood costume designer Edith Head. Hearst executive Arthur
Brisbane sat through the jury selection process, as intent as any cub
reporter. Damon Runyon and Alexander Woollcott rubbed shoulders in
the press box. The *Daily News,* in its wisdom, had assigned its top sports
commentators. Literary lion Ford Madox Ford, writing for the Associated Press, appeared to be attending another event entirely and compared the ambience of the courtroom to that of Westminster Abbey on
the day of George V's coronation.

In the beginning the press called it the "Lindbergh kidnapping trial"
and all eyes were on the victim's grieving parents. Spectators wept
openly as Anne Lindbergh, looking pale and nervous but unusually chic
in a jacquard silk suit with blue fox trim and a black pancake beret,
briefly described the moment when Betty Gow told her the baby was
not in his crib.

Charles Lindbergh's lengthier testimony was riveting for a different
reason—a number of spectators had noticed that he was wearing a .38
revolver in a shoulder holster under his suit jacket. The gossip in the
corridors was that Lindy was planning to take justice into his own
hands, though—as the New York *American*'s Jimmy Cannon noted—
Lindbergh looked a lot more likely to turn his gun on the ill-mannered
spectators. In fact Lindbergh was armed at the suggestion of Norman
Schwarzkopf, who feared an assassination attempt.

Yet, by the end of the first week of the trial, Colonel Lindbergh's
daily arrival in the courtroom caused little stir. "Strangely—unexpectedly," one AP reporter observed, "Lindbergh has found complete
obscurity.... Few ever see him, much less turn to stare." Indeed, by the
final day of the proceedings, when Anne Lindbergh returned to Flemington to lend moral support to her mother, who had been called as
character witness on behalf of the late Violet Sharpe, the two women
slipped into the courtroom through a side door and were in their seats
for more than an hour before their presence was noticed. The Lindberghs had become supporting players in the drama; what the crowd
wanted to know was, Who was Bruno Richard Hauptmann? And why
had he done it?

A young Hearst reporter named Dorothy Kilgallen was the first to
notice that the attention focused on Hauptmann was by no means all
hostile. "Hauptmann is definitely a hit," wrote an outraged Kilgallen.
"On paper this is hard to believe [but it] is as incredible as it is true." It
was not simply that Hauptmann was a muscular, good-looking man; he

appeared to practice "a kind of mesmerism," deliberately making eye contact with female witnesses, spectators, and jurors. According to Kilgallen, at least one of the female jurors was visibly smitten.[4]

Adela Rogers St. Johns, Kilgallen's older rival, agreed, but only up to a point. In a story headlined HAUPTMANN HAS SEX APPEAL, she suggested that the defendant was not a dominant personality but "a weak, handsome man who stirs either some sympathy of sex or of motherhood. The weakling—who must be protected."[5]

The first chance to unravel the enigma of Hauptmann's motives fell to New Jersey attorney general David Wilentz, a rail-thin thirty-eight-year-old whose impeccably tailored wardrobe was the outward badge of a scholarly, precise legal mind. Wilentz had never before tried a criminal case, but he was a rising star in state politics and securing the conviction of the Lindbergh kidnapper would make him a figure of national stature.

Aside from the notoriety of the crime, the killing of Charles A. Lindbergh, Jr., was the sort of murder case common in fiction but rare in real life—a genuine mystery that had been solved by brilliant police work and state-of-the-art forensics. The New Jersey State Police, making up for their initial shortcomings in the forensics area, had assembled a dazzling array of evidence from outside consultants.

Perhaps the most impressive expert witness was Arthur Koehler, the director of the U.S. Forest Service's Products Laboratory, often known as the "Sherlock Holmes of wood." Studying the collapsible ladder left at the scene of the crime, Koehler had concluded that while the design required a considerable knowledge of basic carpentry techniques, the execution was slapdash. The ladder had been pieced together from odds and ends of wood, some new and some previously used. Several of the rails were white pine and displayed microscopic irregularities caused when they were passed through a planing machine with a defective blade. Koehler had traced the blade to the M.G. and J.J. Dorn sawmill in McCormack, South Carolina, which had shipped some of the boards to the National Lumber Company in the Bronx. And National Lumber's books showed that one Bruno Richard Hauptmann had made a purchase of lumber on December 31, 1931.

Another component of the ladder, identified by Koehler as Rail #16, bore a characteristic pattern made by four old-fashioned, square-headed nails. After Hauptmann's arrest Koehler had matched this rung with floorboards in the unfinished attic of his apartment. Koehler offered no opinion as to why Hauptmann had torn up a floorboard to finish the job, but the inference was plain: He was in a big hurry.

But by far the most compelling evidence was the ransom notes. All eighteen notes bearing the kidnapper's symbol, including the one left on the nursery windowsill, matched samples of Hauptmann's handwriting, including his automobile registration applications and six notebooks seized from his apartment at the time of his arrest. Walter Winchell, who as usual had excellent contacts with both the prosecution and the defense, had obtained photos of the handwriting material even before the trial opened and conducted his own impromptu survey in the bar of the Union Hotel. "When this reporter reveals samples of the suspect's handwriting to the most skeptical," Winchell announced in his column, "they are immediately converted to Bruno's guilt."[6]

Handwriting evidence is notoriously subjective, more an art than a science. Attorneys for both sides can typically line up reputable authorities willing to testify to their liking, but in this case, the evidence was so striking that the defense had difficulty finding experts willing to risk the ridicule of their peers. J. Vreeland Haring, a noted authority originally consulted by Hauptmann's first attorney, James Fawcett, eventually wrote a book explaining why, in his opinion, the notes proved Hauptmann had been in the Lindbergh nursery on March 1, 1932. An impressive panel of prosecution experts concurred, producing an array of annotated charts and hundreds of pages of analysis to substantiate what was already clear to any unprejudiced observer.[7]

In addition to this damning circumstantial evidence, an array of eyewitnesses identified Hauptmann as Graveyard John.

Dr. Condon, after nearly giving the prosecutors ulcers by refusing to disclose what he planned to say on the stand, proved an impressive witness, more than up to the challenge of matching wits with defense attorney Big Ed Reilly. Commenting on Condon's description of Graveyard John as a "middleweight," Reilly observed, "And you and I are both heavyweights, so we start even."

"Right," replied Condon without missing a beat. "That is, physically."

Condon's identification was backed up by the cab driver Joseph Perrone; by Cecile Barr, the movie clerk who received a ransom bill at the Sheridan Square theater on November 26, 1933; and by Colonel Lindbergh himself, who said of the shout of "Hey Dok*tor!*" he heard at St. Raymond's Cemetery on the night the ransom was paid: "That was Hauptmann's voice!"

The prosecution also produced a surprise witness, a lanky blond fashion model, Hildegarde Olga Alexander, who said she had been in the Fordham Road station of the New York Central Railroad one evening in the spring of 1932, when she saw Dr. Condon, whom she had known since she was a high school student, standing in line at the telegraph window. She then became aware that someone else was standing back from the window watching Condon intently, a man she later recognized from newspaper photos as Bruno Richard Hauptmann.

Between these witnesses and the forensic evidence, Wilentz had an airtight case. Why, then, have doubts about Hauptmann's guilt persisted for sixty years? Why, for example, did a 1987 article in the *Stanford Law Review* cite the Lindbergh kidnapping trial as one of the most famous miscarriages of justice in the history of American criminal law?[8] In later years it has often been charged that the prosecution was guilty of cooking the evidence. Most of these claims simply do not hold up under close examination, and those that cannot be disproved fall into the category of prosecutorial overzealousness rather than an outright frame-up. Wilentz's problem was not the evidence, but his inability to present a convincing scenario of how the crime was conceived, motivated, and executed.

In his opening statement, Wilentz asserted that Charles Lindbergh, Jr., had died by accident when Hauptmann dropped him as he was climbing down the ladder from the nursery window. But there was an obvious problem with this theory. If the baby had lived, what did Hauptmann plan to do with it? Normally it takes at least two people to pull off a kidnapping—one to guard the hostage and another to negotiate and collect the ransom. Wilentz himself appeared to see the flaw in his scenario, and in his closing remarks he shifted ground, suggesting that Hauptmann deliberately bashed in the child's head.

Similarly, Wilentz had no clear explanation as to Hauptmann's motive. In his opening statement Wilentz said that Hauptmann "had nothing against Colonel Lindbergh"—his motive was "money, money, money"; in summation, he described the defendant as a man with "a peculiar mental makeup who thought he was bigger than Lindy ... an egomaniac ... a secretive fellow ... who wouldn't tell anybody anything." To suggest that Hauptmann was a gangster, Wilentz asserted, was an insult to our homegrown hoods: "No American gangster and no American racketeer ever sank to the level of killing babies!"

Finally the single-kidnapper theory made it more difficult to place Hauptmann in the vicinity of the Lindberghs' house. Most of the witnesses interviewed in Hopewell immediately after the kidnapping believed there were two men, and possibly a second car, variously described as a dark blue or black Buick or Willys-Knight sedan. Even Ben Lupica, the prep school student who had seen a man resembling Hauptmann driving a green Dodge, insisted that the car was equipped with a New Jersey license plate. Although the prosecutors had reason to believe that Hauptmann had switched plates—a ruse often used by professional criminals—this was a complication they were not prepared to introduce.[9]

Ben Lupica was ultimately called by the defense, and Wilentz was left with an unimpressive trio of eyewitnesses: Millard Whited, an illiterate Sourlands "mountaineer," was easily rattled under cross-examination, and eighty-seven-year-old Amandus Hochmuth, who had seen a man resembling Hauptmann driving a green Dodge past his house at the junction of the Princeton–Amwell Road and Lindbergh Lane, was the proverbial blind witness—legally blind, although he had not yet been so certified in March 1932. The third witness, Charles Rossiter, believed that he had encountered Hauptmann at the Princeton airport on the Saturday before the kidnapping, but since there had been nothing suspicious about their brief exchange at the time, he had not come forward until he saw the defendant's picture in the papers in the fall of 1934. All three witnesses may well have been sincere, but their credibility was an easy mark for an enterprising *Daily News* reporter who succeeded in getting a number of Hopewell residents, including Ben Lupica's father, to identify photos of Fiorello LaGuardia and Judge Crater as individuals they had seen lurking around Hopewell in March 1932.

Still other complications arose from the prosecution's attempt to prove that Hauptmann had not shared the fifty-thousand-dollar ransom with any accomplices. William E. Frank of the United States Treasury Department's Intelligence Division presented the jury with an intricate financial accounting that demonstrated that the Hauptmanns' known expenses between April 2, 1932, and September 1934, along with Anna Hauptmann's earnings during that period and the $14,590.00 found in his garage, all added together and subtracted from their net worth at the time of the kidnapping, came to exactly $49,950.44. Aside from its other questionable premises, this neat exercise in bookkeeping failed to take into account the possibility that Bruno Hauptmann had income from illegal sources either before and/or after the kidnapping. The prosecution thus appeared to be saying that Bruno Hauptmann was a law-abiding immigrant carpenter who suddenly, and for no reason the state was prepared to explain, took into his head to leave his apartment in the Bronx and drive down to Hopewell in order to murder Charles and Anne Lindbergh's twenty-month-old son.

In fact the prosecution had a great deal of information about Bruno Richard Hauptmann's background that was never presented in court— information suggesting that the dichotomy between the psychotic and the gangster had been too sharply drawn. Hauptmann was, perhaps, a little of each, secretive and even at times delusional, but not necessarily a loner.[10]

Bruno Hauptmann first set foot on American soil on his twenty-fourth birthday—November 26, 1923. A stowaway on the SS *George Washington,* he spent the ocean crossing hiding in a coal bunker, emerging every night to scavenge from the garbage pails that were brought up on deck for disposal by the morning watch.

It was his third attempt in five months to enter the United States. On his first try, in July, Hauptmann had stowed away in a bilge compartment of the German liner *Hannover,* only to be seized by customs officials when he tried to sneak off the ship. He gave the alias Karl Pellmeir and was deported to Germany after a brief hearing. On his second stowaway attempt, he was caught during a general search and locked in a bathroom for the return voyage. He escaped from the locked cubicle twice and eventually managed to leap overboard and swim to shore just before the ship docked in Bremerhaven.

The next time around Hauptmann got lucky. An engine stoker who stumbled on his hiding place in the coal bunker was planning to jump ship in New York and offered to help Hauptmann sneak ashore. The stoker had the address of a German family named Uhland on West Eighty-second Street, and he and Hauptmann walked there from the waterfront. Jacob Uhland was willing to put the merchant seaman up for a few days but wanted nothing to do with the disheveled, tough-looking stowaway. Hauptmann was sitting in the Uhlands' living room, wondering where to go next, when eighteen-year-old Fred Aldinger showed up, hoping to trade some stamps with Uhland, a fellow collector. Aldinger's father, a war veteran with a wooden leg and a heavy drinking habit, had recently lost his job, and his mother, Lena, was looking for a boarder to supplement her earnings as a laundress. Aldinger told Hauptmann that he could stay with his family for free until he earned his first paycheck.

At first Hauptmann was the ideal boarder. He landed a job washing dishes at a restaurant near South Ferry just two days after he moved in, and he spent his evenings studying an English grammar book. Although he never would learn to speak or write English fluently, Hauptmann was an intelligent man who prided himself on reading the *New York Times* every day, unlike so many other immigrants who relied on the German-language press or the tabloids for their news. He also played the mandolin and displayed impeccable manners, never failing to help Lena Aldinger with the heavy baskets of laundry she collected from her customers on Riverside Drive.

Lena was just forty, a decade younger than her alcoholic husband, and she was soon enamored of this athletic, well-spoken roomer with, as she put it, "such happy go lucky ways." She began calling him Richard or Rick, names he came to prefer to Bruno because they sounded more American. Before three weeks had passed it occurred to Rudolph Aldinger that his wife and the new boarder were getting along a bit too well. One night in mid-December, Aldinger came home blind drunk and accused the two of them of sleeping together. When Richard seemed reluctant to defend himself with his fists, Lena resolved the dispute by breaking a chair over her husband's head. Hauptmann departed to a nearby roominghouse, and two days later, while Rudolph was at work, Lena and her teenage sons moved to a new apartment on 117th Street. As soon as they were settled, Lena sent word to Richard inviting him for Christmas dinner. He showed up carrying his meager belongings and moved in.

By now Fred Aldinger rued the day that he had invited Hauptmann into his home. Richard had made contact with Albert Deibisch, a fellow German whom he had met on the docks in Bremerhaven before his second stowaway attempt. Deibisch, who came from a middle-class background and had brought some savings with him to the States, was now running a hole-in-the-wall coffee shop on Lexington Avenue known as the A.D. Coffee Pot. Almost every evening Deibisch and Hauptmann lounged around the kitchen table in the Aldinger apartment hatching get-rich-quick schemes. One that Fred Aldinger particularly remembered involved a formula for laundry soap, apparently obtained from an old-country acquaintance of Hauptmann's who worked for Procter & Gamble. Hauptmann and Deibisch were convinced that they could make a fortune by manufacturing soap from the stolen formula and selling it themselves, door to door. Like most of their ideas, this one never got beyond the talking stage.[11]

Lena, meanwhile, had begun playing mother hen to another greenhorn who worked as a maid for one of her laundry customers on River-side Drive. Anna Schoeffler was new in New York and didn't yet know her way around, so Lena invited her out one evening for a movie, then brought her back to 117th Street for coffee. By the time Anna left that evening, Hauptmann had asked her out on a date, and they were soon meeting secretly almost every weekend.

With her strong jaw, slightly protuberant eyes, and unruly straw-berry blond hair, Anna Schoeffler was not a pretty woman, but she had vitality. She also had more than a thousand dollars in the bank, and after a trip through the Tunnel of Love at Coney Island, Richard proposed marriage. Hauptmann had an older sister living in West Hollywood, California, and he promised Anna a honeymoon trip to the movie capi-tal. To save money for the journey, they would pool their savings in a joint account. A good manager, Anna lived frugally and deposited a substantial portion of her paychecks. Richard contributed to the account as well, but as he later admitted, he was also giving money to Lena and had a second bank account on the side with a balance of at least a thousand dollars—a substantial sum in 1924.

During their Sunday strolls in Riverside Park, Richard confessed to Anna that he had been in a little trouble with the law back in Germany. This, she would later discover, was an understatement.

Born in Kamenz, Saxony, in 1899, Hauptmann won a number of footraces as a teenager and enjoyed local celebrity as a promising ath-lete. After leaving school he was apprenticed to a carpenter until 1917, when he was drafted into the German army. He served as a machine gunner with the 177th Regiment near Verdun, where he was wounded in the head by a piece of flying shrapnel. After the war Hauptmann returned to Kamenz, where his boyhood friends found him a changed man. He talked constantly about money—a not-uncommon obsession, given the state of Germany's monetary system—yet seemed to identify with the Spartacists, an extreme left-wing splinter group.

Hauptmann and an army buddy named Hans Petzold soon went on a crime spree, committing a dozen robberies and burglaries within a two-week period. Among other crimes, they burglarized the home of the mayor, using a ladder to enter a second-floor bedroom window. A few days later, Petzold and Hauptmann robbed two women who were pushing baby carriages down the street. Hauptmann was sentenced to five and a half years for these crimes but was paroled after three. Sixteen days after his release, he was in jail again, this time for possession of stolen machine-shop tools. Before he could be tried, he brazenly walked out of the lockup while his guards were busy elsewhere.

In his eagerness to woo the freckle-faced housemaid, Richard skipped lightly over the details of his record. Anna knew that Richard was still wanted in Germany, but, understandably, she took the view that what had happened in the Old Country was history. The immediate obstacle to the marriage was Lena Aldinger. For some reason Richard could not bring himself to tell Lena that their affair was over. Instead he wrote Rudolph Aldinger a letter, giving him his wife's new address and urging him to press for a reconciliation.

When Lena finally realized what was going on, she was furious with Anna and accused her of using her bank account to steal Richard away. She did not blame Richard at all. In fact, when New Jersey State Police investigators interviewed Mrs. Aldinger after Hauptmann's arrest, she told them that she didn't care whether he was guilty or not. Rick, she said, had made "lots of money" almost from the first day he arrived in America, had given her a Victrola and other presents, and had treated her better than her husband ever had. She would be happy to take him back any time.

Anna and Richard were married on November 11, 1925. Immediately after the wedding they packed his car and headed for California. With them was Albert Deibisch. Richard told Anna that Deibisch owned a half share in his automobile and would help pay for the gas. Anna accepted this explanation, but when the car broke down before they got out of the Bronx, that was the end of the honeymoon. Instead the newlyweds moved into a thirty-three-dollar-a-month, five-room apartment in a well-kept building on Park Avenue and 118th Street.

All went well for a few months. Then the Hauptmanns abruptly stopped paying rent. The landlord, Nathan Drucker, later told investigators that when he threatened Mrs. Hauptmann with a dispossess notice she "cried with tears rolling down her cheeks" and told him that she didn't dare ask her husband for the money. Drucker concluded that Mrs. Hauptmann was an abused wife and was reluctant to force the issue until the janitress told him that Richard Hauptmann easily earned thirty-three dollars in three days and was just taking advantage of his leniency. An hour after the city marshal and his crew began moving the Hauptmanns' furniture onto the sidewalk, Richard showed up at Drucker's office with a check for the back rent. The Hauptmanns moved back into the apartment, and two days later they filed a police report charging that the marshal and his agents had rifled their bureau drawers, stealing a diamond ring and other items of value. Drucker doubted that the ring ever existed.

Despite recurring problems with their landlords, the Hauptmanns were prospering. They invested $800 in a new coffee shop to be managed by Deibisch, who eventually paid them $1,200 in small installments, and they took over the mortgage on a friend's house, on which they received $224 a year in interest. Various small investments, along with a savings account, put their net worth at more than $10,000, and in 1928 Anna was able to afford a trip to Germany to visit her mother. In Dresden Anna bought her husband a rather expensive present, a pair of Zeiss field glasses of a type that was being heavily promoted in the United States as ideal for aviation buffs who wanted to get a closer look at their heroes during parades and airport receptions.

A typical Zeiss ad, which ran in the *Times* on the day the German plane *Bremen* landed in New York after making an east-to-west flight across the Atlantic, urged, MEET THE FLYERS FACE TO FACE WITH A ZEISS BINOCULAR. Coincidentally, perhaps, this ad was positioned directly under an article about the "lost Smith girls," Alice Corbett and Frances St. John Smith. The *Times* reported that despite "hundreds of clues" and the best efforts of Joseph Daly, President Coolidge's former security chief, the fate of both girls remained "an impenetrable mystery."

The source of the Hauptmanns' income during this period is another mystery. Although Anna continued to work after her marriage, her earnings as a counter girl and waitress were modest. Richard, after his arrest, gave police an extensive work history, listing a number of high-paying jobs in machine shops and with construction projects. However, investigators learned that Hauptmann had stayed with these jobs for much less time than he claimed, often quitting after a few weeks or even a few days. Former neighbors reported that Richard was often away from home for long stretches of time.

Some months after the crash of October 1929, Richard began to play the stock market. Although his timing may seem odd in retrospect, depressed stock prices had become attractive to bottom fishers, including some amateur speculators who considered themselves too smart to have become caught up in the frenzy of the great bull market. No less an authority than Tom Lamont, the guru of Wall Street, had been widely quoted as calling the 1929 crash a technical correction, and John D. Rockefeller announced that he now considered common stocks a sound investment. Hauptmann bought and sold on margin, specializing in the same few companies. One of his favorites was Curtiss-Wright, long the glamour stock of the truly "air minded." (Another was Warner Brothers.) By early 1931 his highly leveraged brokerage account showed a balance of more than $25,000.

To celebrate their prosperity, Richard and Anna set out on their long-deferred trip to California. Once again, they were not to be traveling alone. Richard's friendship with Deibisch had cooled, but he had invited along his new sidekick, Hans Kloeppenburg, a tall, quiet bachelor whom the Hauptmanns called "long Hans." Driving a newly purchased 1930 Dodge sedan—of an indeterminate color that some people call blue, others green—the three of them drove cross-country to Yellowstone National Park, where they joined Richard's sister Emma Gloeckner and her family on a camping tour that took in Yosemite and Death Valley. In Los Angeles they attended a barnstorming exhibition at which Hauptmann paid three dollars for the first and only airplane ride of his life. After separating from the Gloeckners, the Hauptmanns and Kloeppenburg returned home via the Grand Canyon, the Gulf Coast, and Tybee Island, South Carolina.

While the Hauptmanns were enjoying their extended vacation, a chain reaction of international events plunged the financial markets into chaos: Unable to meet the burdens imposed by the Treaty of Versailles, the German government defaulted on reparation payments; the banking system of Central Europe collapsed, and Great Britain was forced off the gold standard. The New York stock market, which earlier in the year had seemed poised for recovery, plummeted to new lows. Hauptmann's account was wiped out, a minor casualty of the deteriorating European situation.

Many small investors in Hauptmann's situation blamed Lamont and Rockefeller for suckering them back into the market. The left-wing press in Britain asserted that the collapse of the gold standard and the subsequent fall of Ramsay MacDonald's Labour government were part of a rightist conspiracy engineered by Lamont. Pro-Nazi groups in the United States, meanwhile, churned out propaganda charging that Lamont and the House of Morgan were leaders of an anglophile plot to devastate the German economy.

Hauptmann, who checked in at his broker's office almost every day, spending hours in the waiting room watching the ticker tape, could hardly fail to be aware of such talk. He himself had a history of flirting with radical ideas without being overly fussy about ideological consistency. When he began playing the market in 1930, one of the stocks he traded most actively was Amtorg, the Soviet-American trading corporation. By 1933, however, a number of the Hauptmanns' friends, including some distant connections of Anna's in Philadelphia, were active in the proto-Nazi Friends of New Germany, and Hauptmann himself was briefly a member of this "lodge," as he called it.

The winter of 1931–32 is a blank period in Richard Hauptmann's history. He later claimed that he worked sporadically, taking free-lance jobs that were put up for bid at the National Lumber Company's yard in the Bronx. However, the foreman of the yard told investigators he had no memory of Hauptmann and was unable to recognize his photograph. After more than six months without steady work, Hauptmann finally visited an employment agency on February 27, the Saturday before the Lindbergh kidnapping. He was immediately offered a job on the construction site of the Majestic Apartments on West Seventy-second Street in Manhattan. The site was unionized, and the project promised to be the best-paying employment he had had in some time. But Hauptmann wasn't actually called to the site until March 21. He worked from then until April 1, missed the next two days, showed up on the fourth, then disappeared without giving notice. He never held a job again.

Nevertheless, in early April, Richard began making regular deposits of silver dollars and small coins in his account at the Central Savings Bank in Manhattan. Treasury agents later speculated that he was using ransom bills for small purchases and banking the change. On June 1 he opened a second account at the Mount Vernon Trust Company in Mount Vernon, New York, an area in which a number of ransom bills subsequently turned up.

Hauptmann was also spending freely. He purchased a new maple bedroom set, a fifty-six-dollar rifle, and a second pair of Zeiss field glasses to replace the originals, which were stolen from his car on the night of the Max Schmeling–Gene Sharkey heavyweight title fight. He also bought a floor-model radio that retailed for $669—an amount that would have paid the rents of many a family for an entire year. To friends who wondered at this display of prosperity, Richard boasted that he had, at long last, figured out a way to make big money out of the stock market.

As he had in the summer of 1928, another period of unexplained prosperity in his life, Hauptmann celebrated by sending Anna back to Germany. Mrs. Hauptmann sailed on July 3 and spent the summer visiting her family. By September she was in Kamenz, where she gave Pauline Hauptmann money to consult an attorney about her son's legal problems. The attorney advised that the statute of limitations had two more years to run. Richard Hauptmann could not return to Germany until October 1934, when he would be a free man as far as the German legal system was concerned.

A few weeks after Anna left New York, Clayton Moul, a salesman for the Strout Realty Agency in Spring Grove, Pennsylvania, received a letter in a language he recognized as *Hochdeutsch,* as opposed to the "low German" of the Pennsylvania Dutch, with which he was familiar. Moul took the letter to Pastor George Welsh of the Mount Zion Reformed Church, who explained that the writer, one Richard Hauptmann of the Bronx, was interested in purchasing a farm in the area. Hauptmann later visited Spring Grove twice to inspect likely properties. Relaxed and talkative, he told Moul that he had come from Germany "in steerage" and been lucky enough to find a wife fluent in English and German.

After reading of Hauptmann's arrest in the newspapers, Clayton Moul contacted the Philadelphia office of the FBI. He didn't get many customers from as far away as the Bronx, so he remembered a good deal of his conversation with Hauptmann, especially the latter's fond description of his blond, curly-haired infant son. Moul was incredulous when FBI agent John Sears told him that during the summer of 1932 the Hauptmanns had been childless.[12]

With Anna away, Richard spent most of his time that summer at Hunter's Island, a section of Pelham Bay Park frequented by working-class residents of the Bronx. He had purchased a new canoe, and in the evenings he played his mandolin at campfire sing-alongs. He had given up the idea of buying a farm in Pennsylvania, and he hinted broadly to some of the Hunter's Island crowd that he was losing interest in Anna as well. His new best friends were the Henkels, who lived in the same boardinghouse as Hans Kloeppenburg—located at 145 West 127th Street (just a few blocks across town from Peter Berritella's storefront church).

Karl Henkel was from Kamenz and was delighted to make the acquaintance of a countryman. Richard, however, showed more interest in Gerta, a pert blond with pencil-thin eyebrows. He soon fell into the routine of stopping at Gerta's every morning for coffee, on his way to the Yorkville brokerage office of Steiner & Rouse. Hunter's Island was abuzz with gossip that Richard and Gerta were having an affair and, strangely, Karl seemed not to mind.

But Karl Henkel could afford to be complacent. Hauptmann enjoyed flaunting his reputation as a ladies' man but showed no interest in pursuing a sexual relationship. Gerta, somewhat miffed by this, later told police that Hauptmann had "used" her, in order to have an excuse to meet with another resident of the boardinghouse, a frail, jug-eared man in his twenties named Isidore Fisch. A Polish Jew born in Leipzig, Fisch was a skilled fur cutter, but he had been forced to give up his trade when he contracted tuberculosis soon after his arrival in America. Fisch occasionally worked as a gofer for Gerta's father, a small-time bootlegger, but Fisch had a gambling habit, and debts combined with high medical bills kept him chronically broke.

Hauptmann and the Henkels gave differing versions of how he and Fisch first met, but the consensus was that the two men did not become acquainted until some weeks after the Lindbergh kidnapping. According to Hauptmann, he and Fisch entered into an informal business partnership in late June or early July 1932. Fisch gave him money to invest in the stock market, and he in turn invested in fur pelts that Fisch was importing from Europe. Curiously Hauptmann, who kept meticulous financial records even of small loans to friends, did not commit the details of these transactions to paper; the only evidence of the supposed arrangement found during the search of his apartment were a few cryptic notes indicating that he and Fisch had entered into some sort of deal "on a 20 percent basis."

Most likely the partnership had less to do with investing in furs than with money laundering. In 1936 sources told the *New York Times* that several months after the Lindbergh kidnapping, Izzy Fisch had been hanging around a pool hall on Eighty-sixth Street and Third Avenue in Manhattan, trying to shop "hot money" at forty cents on the dollar.[13]

With word out on the street that Owney Madden was assisting in the hunt for the Lindbergh kidnappers this offering of "hot money" cannot have found many takers, and by midsummer, Isidore Fisch was a scared and frustrated man. "Isidore got on my nerves," Gerta Henkel later complained to police. "He always got me nervous, pacing up and down and looking out the window to see if Hauptmann would come or not.... He would go away with Hauptmann, but sometimes Hauptmann didn't come and he would go away alone."

Richard Hauptmann actually admitted to police interrogators that around this time Isidore Fisch began trying to blackmail him. According to Hauptmann, Fisch had learned that he was in America illegally, a secret he had shared with no one but Anna and Albert Deibisch. At any rate, Fisch's initial demands were almost laughably modest. He told Hauptmann that two or three hundred dollars would "straighten out" the problem.

After Bruno Richard Hauptmann was arrested in September 1934, the FBI heard from a number of prisoners who claimed to have had previous dealings with him. Most of these would-be informants were obviously lying in the hope of winning a reduced sentence or other favors. However, one exception to the rule was a Massachusetts convict named J. R. Russell. Unlike the other tipsters Russell did not come forward voluntarily. He was being detained in the county lockup in Middlesex, Massachusetts, in connection with a minor parole violation, when his cellmate sent a message to the warden, saying that Russell had information about Hauptmann's past. Somewhat reluctant to get involved at first, since he expected to be released soon, Russell eventually gave the FBI an extraordinarily detailed twelve-page statement, explaining how Hauptmann had tried to recruit him to shoot Isidore Fisch.

According to Russell, he first met Hauptmann in a Childs Restaurant in Buffalo, New York, in June or July 1926. Hauptmann was in town working on a construction job, but as their friendship warmed he tried to convince Russell to become his partner in crime. First he proposed robbing a bank in Batavia, New York. Later he laid out a plan for kidnapping a wealthy Buffalo jeweler. Russell dismissed both schemes as too dangerous to consider.

Russell ran into Hauptmann again on a construction site in Vermont in 1929. Before they parted Hauptmann borrowed ten dollars, leaving him a nickel-plated revolver as security. He also gave Russell an address on Palisades Avenue in Yonkers, New York (across the Hudson from the Palisade Avenue where the Morrows owned a home). Russell wrote several letters and finally received a reply from Hauptmann, who hinted that he had a job for him.

Hopping a freight train to New York, Russell was stopped and searched by a railroad detective who found his gun. He was arrested and sentenced to a year in jail. Russell was assigned to a work detail near the Rockefeller estate in Pawling, New York. One day Hauptmann showed up with a carton of cigarettes and promised to help him find work as soon as he got out of jail. Russell, who was under the impression that Hauptmann was involved in smuggling whiskey from Canada, figured that Hauptmann owed him as much since it was his gun that had gotten him into trouble with the railroad police.

When Russell got out of jail in the summer of 1932, Hauptmann showed up again driving a car Russell remembered as either a blue Nash or a blue Buick, and told him he knew of a way for Russell to earn a quick five hundred dollars, but the job involved an automobile trip to Maine. A few days later the two men headed north on Route 1. Somewhere in Connecticut they stopped to pick up a man who was introduced to Russell as Isidore Fisch. Later, during a stop for gas, Hauptmann took Russell aside and explained that the "job" was actually a contract killing. Pointing to Fisch, he added, "This is the man I want you or somebody to bump off. He knows too much about me."

"Well, I don't think it is a very nice thing to do," said Russell, who had never been convicted of anything more serious than check kiting and auto theft. "In spite of it all, I am not a killer."

Russell wanted no part of murder, but he was penniless and figured that Hauptmann owed him fifty dollars for his time and trouble. The argument continued during a stop in South Boston, where Hauptmann and the unsuspecting Izzy Fisch had business with a man who appeared to Russell to be a gangster. Two days later, they drove on to Bangor, Maine. Hauptmann registered the three of them at an inn, then took Russell out to the parking lot for a conference. Reaching under the front seat of the car, he produced a snub-barreled single shot .22—a "regular starter's pistol," Russell called it—which he had brought along to do the job on Izzy.

Russell took one look at the doll-size gun and burst out laughing. "I explained to him and tried to show him that a .22 shell would not kill a man."

The next day, Fisch was ill and remained at the hotel while Russell and Hauptmann drove to Houlton, Maine, an area Hauptmann claimed to know well. Russell by now had no hope of getting fifty dollars, but he still wanted the price of some new clothes and bus fare. He continued to disparage the .22, saying "What's the use, the single shells won't kill a man."

"Yes it will," said Hauptmann. "I know it will. I killed a child with it."

Russell's statement continues:

So I looked at him and thought he must be crazy. I told him, "That gun will be no good [because it had been used in a homicide and might be traceable]," ... and he asked what will he do with the gun and I said to throw it away and he threw it in a clump of bushes alongside the country road.

Back in Bangor, while Fisch was at the movies, Hauptmann went into a pawnshop and came out with another gun not much bigger than the last, which Russell described as either a .25- or a .22-caliber automatic. The next day the three men drove on to Nashua, New Hampshire, where Fisch, who had run out of medicine, went off to look for a drugstore.

Said Russell:

> Bruno took me to the outskirts of Nashua past the railroad station, following the river. There we came to a little bridge alongside a railroad track. There were some boys fishing in there and Bruno said, "This is a nice place for a fellow to commit suicide." I said, "What do you mean?" He says, "Well, you know, you see this automatic? Well, Isidore can shoot himself and fall in the water and get drowned." He said, "or we can use some stones or something to weigh him down." I looked at him and thought, "The man was insane," but I didn't say nothing.

The two of them then drove back to town. There, Russell goes on:

> Bruno asked me point blank whether I was going to do it or not. I told him, "Gee, I will not. It is not my line." He said, "If you do it now I will give you one thousand dollars."
>
> I laughed at him and said, "You haven't got a thousand," and he pulled out a roll of bills which I could see was over a thousand. He said, "Come on, we've got fishing rods in the car. We can all go and pretend to fish and I will watch and see if there is anybody around ... you can do the work and I will help you dispose of the body."

When Russell continued to insist that he wanted no part of a killing, Hauptmann drove off and left him. Penniless, Russell hopped a freight to Concord, New Hampshire, where he and a hobo named Morgan were arrested for stealing from a Salvation Army poor box and sentenced to one to two years in jail.[14]

The FBI took Russell's statement seriously. Many details checked out—from Hauptmann's apparent preference for Childs restaurants to the fact that Isidore Fisch had a brother living in Stonington, Connecticut, on the coast road to Boston, something even the Bureau did not know until after Russell was interviewed. Of course, Hauptmann had never lived in Yonkers, much less on Palisades Avenue, but so many ransom notes had turned up either in Yonkers or in neighboring Mount

Vernon that it was not far fetched to assume that Hauptmann had some long-standing connections there. However, before Russell's story could be checked further, the FBI terminated the CALNAP investigation in deference to the New Jersey prosecutor who was determined to try Hauptmann alone. Even if admissible, Russell's statement was useless to the prosecutors since it implied that the Lindbergh baby had been shot, not bludgeoned to death. More important, perhaps, Russell had sized up Hauptmann as a man who had big ideas but lacked the nerve to carry them out alone.

Although the Maine trip described by Russell was never confirmed, Hauptmann and Karl Henkel did go hunting in Maine in November 1932. At the lodge where the two men stayed, the guests somehow got into a conversation one evening about the Lindbergh case. Hauptmann listened noncommitally for a while, then snapped, "They wouldn't make such a big fuss if it weren't a rich man's child."

Hauptmann and Henkel also did some hunting that fall in New Jersey, on land belonging to a friend, Henry Lempke, who had recently started a chicken farm about eight miles from Lakewood. Apart from being the site of several notorious illegal casinos, the Lakewood area was home to a substantial German community, dating back to shortly after World War I, when several hundred technicians emigrated from Germany to work on the zeppelins that were hangared at the nearby Lakehurst Aerodrome. Richard Hauptmann acknowledged that he had spent time in Lakewood as early as 1924, when he helped a friend who was building a summer cabin on the main road just outside town. By 1933 he and Anna were visiting the area once a month or so—ironically, they even stopped in the village of Flemington to purchase farm-fresh eggs.

Much to the frustration of the state police, they were unable to find a single member of the German community who would admit to seeing Hauptmann in the Lakewood area in the first half of 1932. The Lempkes insisted that they scarcely knew Hauptmann, and the entire community was terrified that the kidnapping would inspire a replay of the anti-German hysteria of 1918.

By the end of 1932, Izzy Fisch's health was failing fast, and Hauptmann apparently decided that killing him was not worth the risk. Nor did he follow through on his hints about leaving Anna, who returned to the United States in October. The following February, after seven years of longing for a child, Anna finally became pregnant, and on November 4, 1933, she gave birth to a son, whom she and Richard planned to name Mannfried after the great German air ace, Baron von Richthofen.

Soon after Anna returned home from the hospital, the postman delivered a letter addressed to Mannfried Richard von Hauptmann. "I read it and I was very upset," Mrs. Hauptmann told author Anthony Scaduto forty years later. "It said terrible things, 'I hope you live an awful life and die young,' things like that." Anna had always liked the gentle, well-spoken Izzy Fisch. She considered him a "real gentleman." But apart from the Henkels and her niece Maria Mueller, only Fisch had been told of the decision to call the baby Mannfried.

Accusing Izzy to his face of writing the poison-pen letter, Anna became hysterical. Fisch took the letter away, and when he returned it, he pointed to a date written in pencil near the upper-right-hand margin that Anna hadn't noticed before. "Look, it says here November 26," he told her soothingly. "This is for Richard, not the baby." Fisch then suggested that the letter had been written by Gerta Henkel and her sister Erika. Anna didn't believe this, and Gerta pointed the finger back at Fisch. The letter, she said later, was just another of Izzy's efforts to "stir up trouble" for Richard."[15]

Apparently it was a successful effort. According to Hauptmann's statements after his arrest, Fisch already owed him $5,000, supposedly losses from their fur-trading deals. He now agreed to loan him another $2,500, provided he would return home to Leipzig. Early in December, the Hauptmanns threw Fisch a going-away party. Fisch, said Hauptmann later, arrived with a shoebox, which he asked his friend to hold for safekeeping. Hauptmann placed the box on the top shelf of the kitchen broom closet, where it remained until September 1934, when he notiiced that the box had become soggy from contact with a leaky pipe. Only then did he open the box and discover that it contained more than $14,000.

By that time Fisch was dead, having expired in a Leipzig charity ward four months after he returned to Germany. Hauptmann dried out the money and buried the bulk of it under the floor of his garage. Since he figured Fisch owed him thousands, he had no compunction about spending some of the bills.

Although David Wilentz would heap scorn on Hauptmann's "Fisch story," it may well be that Izzy Fisch did show up at the Hauptmanns' apartment on the night of his going-away party carrying a shoebox, as several of the couple's friends confirmed. It may also be that the shoebox contained a substantial sum of Lindbergh ransom money, which Fisch had been unsuccessful in laundering. The problem, from the point of view of the defense, was that the Fisch story hardly proved Richard Hauptmann's innocence. For example, it did not explain how Cecile Barr could have received a ransom bill from Hauptmann a month *before* the going-away party. Nor did it account for the ransom notes, the evidence of the ladder, the .25 German automatic found buried in the Hauptmann garage, or the presence of Dr. John Condon's phone number scrawled on the door trim inside a closet in the apartment. (Richard told the Bronx grand jury that he was in the habit of jotting down interesting facts; later, he would deny any knowledge of how the phone number came to be there.)

Overall the investigators' files on Hauptmann show that while he may have been secretive and even a psychotic with an obsession with aviators—a possible motive never brought out in court—he was hardly a loner. While he enjoyed being thought of as a ladies' man, Hauptmann seldom went anywhere without a male buddy for company. Whether these friendships were actively homosexual, as many detectives involved in the case had come to assume, could be debated. Still it is difficult to imagine that Hauptmann, who even had Albert Deibisch along on his honeymoon, undertook to kidnap the Lindbergh baby alone.

The task of defending this enigmatic and thoroughly unsavory defendant fell to the celebrated Edward J. Reilly, a ruddy-faced, foghorn of a man who invariably appeared in court in striped pants, morning coat, and spats. Like many highly successful defense attorneys, Big Ed, as he was called, was primarily a showman. He had made his reputation in Brooklyn Supreme Court defending bootleggers, who were often neighborhood heroes, and women who had struck back against abusive husbands. "Over a period of 25 years," noted the *Times* on the occasion of his death, "Reilly had defended all but three of Brooklyn's female killers."[16]

Courthouse old-timers never tired of recalling Reilly's tactics during the trial of Annie Lonergan, the mother of Brooklyn waterfront boss Peg Leg Lonergan, who was accused of shooting her husband:

"The jury will never convict when they see how your husband knocked out your front teeth," Reilly told his client on the eve of the trial.

"But I have my front teeth!" the defendant protested.

"Tomorrow, you won't," Reilly assured her.

Mrs. Lonergan appeared in court minus her incisors and was duly acquitted.[17]

The Hearst corporation, which was paying Reilly's $25,000 retainer, certainly didn't expect him to get Hauptmann acquitted, but it did expect Big Ed to inject an element of drama into what otherwise promised to be entirely the prosecution's show. Anna Hauptmann, in turn, had signed a contract promising to speak only to the *Evening Journal,* the perennial loss leader of Hearst's New York newspaper empire. To make sure that Anna kept her word, she had been assigned three female reporters who kept her company day and night, even sitting outside her rented room as she slept.

Since the signing of the contract in October, the leader of this team had been Jeannette Smits, who produced the requisite three-handker-chief interviews detailing Mrs. Hauptmann's anguish when she brought her infant son "Bubi" to visit her husband in jail. When the trial began, however, a newcomer was assigned to the team. Dorothy Kilgallen was just twenty-one, and with her big brown eyes, chipmunk cheeks, and frilly shirtwaist dresses she looked more like thirteen. A devout Catholic, she seemed the perfect candidate to win the confidence of Mrs. Hauptmann, who rarely went anywhere without her minister-adviser, Pastor D. G. Werner.

Even in his prime, Ed Reilly would have been hard put to make Richard Hauptmann sympathetic. And by 1932 Reilly's best years were definitely over. An advanced alcoholic, he spent his nights "giving dictation" to a series of flashily dressed secretaries. The stationery he had made up especially for the trial misspelled the name "Linburg," not a good omen.

As the pressures of the trial began to mount, moreover, the defendant's demeanor soon shattered any romantic illusions the female spectators may have been entertaining. Hauptmann interrupted the testimony of FBI agent Thomas Sisk, shouting "Mister, mister you are lying!" hurled insults at other witnesses (*"Der Alte ist verrückt"*—the old man is crazy—he said of eighty-seven-year-old Amandus Hochmuth), and generally conducted himself like a man who was not used to controlling his temper. "Hauptmann was the most graceless prisoner I have ever seen in the role of a defendant in any sort of trial," wrote INS reporter Leigh Matteson. "His borderline incivility, with his life at stake, exceeded that of any surly hangover victim arraigned merely for drunk driving." On the stand in his own defense, Hauptmann appeared to relish the chance to match wits with David Wilentz but could not suppress an occasional smirk. His guards reported that he spent his evenings reading biographies of heroes, including Floyd Gibbons's life of Baron von Richthofen and Lowell Thomas's *Lauterbach of the China Seas.*

Courtroom regular Jack Benny observed laconically, "What Bruno needs is a second act."[18]

Reilly had better raw material in Anna Hauptmann. Thrifty, industrious, and pious, Mrs. Hauptmann had worked steadily as a bakery clerk and waitress up to the time of Mannfried's birth, often putting in six-day weeks while Richard was off on hunting trips or cavorting with the Henkels on Hunter's Island. Novelist Kathleen Norris, who was covering the trial for the *New York Times,* expressed the general opinion that Mrs. Hauptmann was a naive and probably much-neglected spouse. "How long should a woman stick by a man anyway?" Norris asked. "Does anything like love still linger for him, or is it only pity?"

But if Norris believed that Anna's loyalty was wavering she was wrong. On the contrary, Mrs. Hauptmann grew more convinced of her husband's innocence by the day. When interviewed by the police shortly after her husband's arrest, Anna had no specific memory of what her husband had been doing on the night of March 1, 1932. "If only I could remember three years ago everything would be all right," she had told reporters outside the courthouse.[19]

Four months later Anna's memory had improved dramatically. She was sure that Richard had dropped in at Fredericksen's bakery about seven o'clock and hung around there until she got off work at nine. Moreover, Richard had been home all evening April 2, the night the ransom was paid, playing mandolin-and-guitar duets with Hans Kloeppenburg. And on November 26, 1933, when Graveyard John handed a ransom bill to movie clerk Cecile Barr, Richard had been celebrating his birthday at home with friends.

A visibly nervous Hans Kloeppenburg backed up the story of the April 2 "musical evening," but admitted on cross-examination that he had told Detective Wallace of the NYPD that he couldn't recall being with Richard on any specific dates in March or April 1932. Anna's niece Maria Mueller and two friends, Otto and Louis Wollenburg, testified to being at the Hauptmanns' on the night of the birthday; asked why she had earlier told Detective Breslin and Captain Apple of the NYPD that there was no birthday party, Mrs. Mueller said that at the time she hadn't thought of the gathering as a party. Christian Fredericksen, owner of the bakery where Anna worked, said that since it was a Tuesday night, Hauptmann had probably picked his wife up at work, but "I couldn't swear to it."

Although the Lindbergh jury was sequestered, they were hardly unaware of press coverage. The jurors ate in the main dining room of the Union Hotel, their table separated from those of the journalists who also dined there by a flimsy curtain. Their rooms were located directly above the temporary press headquarters, and one juror later complained that the penetrating voice of radio commentator Gabriel Heatter doing his late night-trial roundups had kept her awake.

But if Reilly hoped that the Hearst newspapers would help win the jurors' sympathy, he was mistaken. Dorothy Kilgallen, despite her youth, had a high opinion of her own worth. She loathed Mrs. Hauptmann and refused to compromise her credibility by doing the kind of interviews her editors wanted, and as the trial went on, even Jeannette Smits's stories became fewer and more skeptical. The frustrated Mrs. Hauptmann was reduced to passing notes to other reporters, urging them to outwit her chaperones and come talk to her. A woman reporter from a Boston paper managed to catch the New York *American* contingent off guard and slipped into Anna's rented room one evening for an interview. Anna proudly showed off the picture of Christ praying in the Garden of Gethsemane that sat atop her bureau. From the top drawer of the same bureau she produced a thick stack of letters from supporters, many of them women who professed a romantic interest in her husband. The reporter came away with the impression that Anna's feelings for Richard were more maternal than wifely.

David Wilentz's official position was that Anna Hauptmann was just another of her husband's victims. In court, however, he took a more aggressive line, suggesting repeatedly that Anna could hardly have been unaware of her husband's activities. For example, he called as a witness Mrs. Ella Achenbach, a neighbor of the Hauptmanns on 222nd Street and once Anna's good friend. Achenbach said she was sitting on her porch one day in March 1932 when Anna and Richard drove up. "Anna came to my front porch and told me they just came home from a trip."

"Mrs. Achenbach, you are lying!" Anna shrieked.

Anna was ordered by the judge to keep quiet, and Achenbach continued her story, recalling that she had noticed that Richard was limping, and Anna had told her, "Oh, another thing, Richard hurt his leg."

Anna later testified that the trip Achenbach was referring to must have been in 1931, not 1932. As it happened, the prosecution had a file of evidence to back up its contention that it was in 1932 that Hauptmann had hurt his leg, a condition that later resulted in his being treated for phlebitis, but Wilentz never bothered to pursue the matter. As for the alleged "trip," the only journey anyone suggested Hauptmann had taken in March or April 1932 was to Hopewell to retrieve the Dr. Denton sleeping suit. Wilentz had no proof that such a trip ever took place and no evidence whatsoever connecting Anna in any way with the kidnapping. Still, the jury was left to ponder why Achenbach's mere mention of the subject had provoked such a strong response.[20]

With his clients out of control and his case disintegrating around him, Ed Reilly filmed a newsreel segment appealing for new witnesses to come forward. Few who responded were turned away.

Louis Kiss had earned his living in 1932 by manufacturing "rum" in his kitchen, a process that he estimated took "about ten minutes." Kiss testified that he had seen Hauptmann (whom he did not know) in Fredericksen's bakery on the evening of March 1. He was certain of the date because it was "exactly one week" after Washington's Birthday (until 1972 celebrated *on* February 22), when his infant son was admitted to the hospital with a serious kidney condition. A check of the calendar showed that 1932 was a leap year; one week after February 22 would have been February 29, not March 1.

A construction worker named Elvert Carlstrom also claimed to have seen Richard Hauptmann in the bakery; a rebuttal witness placed him in Dunellen, New Jersey, all evening.

August Van Henke recalled seeing Hauptmann walking the Fredericksens' dog that evening. Under cross-examination Van Henke admitted that he used two aliases and was the manager of a restaurant that was a front for a notorious betting parlor.

Peter Sommer claimed to have seen a man resembling Isidore Fisch and a woman who looked like Violet Sharpe carrying an infant on the mid-Hudson ferry some hours after the kidnapping. Sommer was duly exposed as a professional witness who had perjured himself for money in a dozen proceedings, including the Hall-Mills murder trial.

Anna Bonesteel owned a coffee shop in Yonkers, New York, near the terminus of the Alpine ferry (a different Hudson River crossing from the one described by Sommer). Bonesteel said that she knew Violet Sharpe by sight and saw her in her coffee shop on the night of March 1, 1932, carrying a baby wrapped in a gray blanket. Shown a photograph of Sharpe by Wilentz, she failed to identify it.

And so on.

Surprisingly, after this embarrassing defense, Reilly almost redeemed himself in his closing remarks. No sensible person could take seriously

Reilly's hypothesis of a grand conspiracy, involving Betty Gow and John Condon as well as the late Violet Sharpe and Isidore Fisch. But he was more persuasive in laying out the reasons why Wilentz's theory of a lone kidnapper was almost equally unlikely. Reilly never quite said that Hauptmann was not involved—leaving open the possibility that his client might indeed have been the man who collected the ransom. But, he declared passionately, "I believe this man is absolutely innocent of murder." It was the sort of last-ditch appeal that occasionally works if the jury happens to include one or more individuals of the sort who are suspicious of public officials on principle and take umbrage at being told half-truths.

Prosecutor Wilentz's summation should have been the final act of the drama, but there was one more bizarre twist to come. As Wilentz was concluding his remarks, a spectator in the rear of the courtroom interrupted, shouting, "Your honor! Please! A man has confessed—" The rest of the statement was muffled when a bailiff clapped his hand over the spectator's mouth and dragged him bodily from the room. After some debate Judge Trenchard decided against declaring a mistrial.

Outside the courtroom the spectator told reporters that he was Rev. Vincent Burns, pastor of a small congregation in Palisades, New Jersey, not far from Englewood. On Palm Sunday, 1932, Burns said, a man had come into his office after services and confessed to the Lindbergh kidnapping. Although he believed that it was his sacred duty never to reveal the man's name, he had been trying for weeks to tell his story to the state police, to Wilentz, and then to the defense. Strangely, Reilly, who had no compunction about putting Peter Sommer on the stand, also dismissed Burns's story. Later that afternoon the judge told Burns that if he continued to talk about the phantom confession he would be jailed for contempt of court.

The following morning, at 11:23, the case went to the jury. The first ballot was seven to five—seven in favor of the death penalty and five for life in prison.

By midafternoon a crowd estimated at ten thousand had gathered on Main Street. At first the scene resembled a street fair. Souvenir vendors were doing a brisk business, and spectators in a party mood mugged for the newsreel cameras. But dinnertime came and went with no word from the courthouse, and the mood began to turn ugly. Someone started a chant—"Kill Hauptmann! Kill Hauptmann!" A group of boys lobbed rocks at the courthouse, shattering a window. At last, at 10:45, the jury signaled that it had reached a decision: guilty, with no recommendation for leniency.

*   *   *

The conclusion of the Lindbergh kidnapping trial brought not catharsis but an outpouring of shame and soul-searching. The disorderly, emotionally charged courtroom scenes captured by the newsreel cameras made Hauptmann look like a wounded animal at bay. Whether or not the trial was actually unfair, the spectacle was so embarrassing that cameras would be banned from American courtrooms for years to come. The conservative *American Mercury* branded the proceedings "tabloid justice," and an article in *Scribner's Magazine* advocated restrictions on newspaper coverage of criminal proceedings similar to those in force, then as now, in Great Britain: "An English editor can be sent to jail for doing almost anything that an American editor would do as a matter of course," the author of the article noted with satisfaction.[21]

More surprisingly, a number of commentators drew the conclusion that the fundamental cause of the crime was the devastation of German society by World War I and the Treaty of Versailles. Ford Madox Ford, who had distinguished himself throughout the trial by his insistence on interpreting the proceedings as a paradigm of the class struggle, wrote that as a combat veteran of the Great War he could not bring himself to condemn a fellow survivor of the trenches: "There is too much class hatred in the world already, and the passion for bloodshed is too keen."

Edna Ferber, while not quite ready to give war veterans a license to murder, agreed that "guilty or innocent, this man, when he was not yet 17, his bones not yet a man's bones, his mind not yet a man's mind, saw and knew fear, agony, ruthlessness, murder, hunger, cold. He was a German soldier in the war and a product of the war." It was fashionable in 1935 to proclaim the decline of the West, and Ferber found in the undignified goings-on in Flemington sufficient reason to despair of the future of democracy. "It was enough," she concluded, "to make me want to cable Hitler saying, 'Well, Butch, you win.'"

TWENTY

"House of Atreus"

*H*AROLD NICOLSON—distinguished author, diplomat, younger son of an earl, and husband of novelist Vita Sackville-West—handled most social situations with aplomb. During the autumn of 1934, however, Nicolson found himself in a rather awkward position vis-à-vis the family of Dwight Morrow.

Searching for the ideal biographer for her late husband, Betty Morrow had been turned down by Walter Lippmann and several other American authors of note. At the suggestion of Anne and Elisabeth, who had read Harold Nicolson's life of his own father, Mrs. Morrow approached Nicolson through her agents with a handsome offer: if he were interested in writing Morrow's authorized biography, the family would pay his expenses, including the cost of travel to and from the United States. Nicolson did not normally write sponsored books, but Mrs. Morrow was quite winning in her insistence that he would have an entirely free hand, with no interference from the family. The first hint that all might not go as planned came while Nicolson was still on board the liner *Berengaria* on his way to meet his new patroness, and he found himself sharing a table with Jack Morgan's daughter, who warned that Dwight Morrow had been a shameless publicity seeker.

When the *Berengaria* docked in New York on September 24, the first sight that greeted Nicolson's eyes as he came down the gangplank was a mob of newsboys hawking papers filled with news of Bruno

Richard Hauptmann's arrest. The second was the Morrow welcoming party, a delegation of black-suited retainers who included Arthur Springer, Tom Lamont's private secretary, and a "dumpy little youth" in a pince-nez who identified himself as Dwight Morrow, Jr.

Nicolson, who resided at Sissinghurst Castle in Kent, was no stranger to luxury. Nevertheless he was somewhat taken aback to find that not one but two chauffeured Cadillacs had been placed at his disposal—the first to carry his luggage to Next Day Hill and the other to drive him to the appointments in the city that he had scheduled for the day of his arrival. The Morrow house itself continued Nicolson's education in the tastes of superrich Americans—acres of deep pile carpeting, wood paneling, and Chinese paintings on glass. In the absence of Mrs. Morrow, who was closing up North Haven for the winter, Jo Graeme was ready to turn the house upside down to make Nicolson's suite of rooms comfortable. Among other amenities, he was provided with a private phone system of bewildering complexity ("I press buttons which connect me with all the world") as well as an overstuffed chair in his private bathroom. Betty Morrow, for unknown reasons, was under the impression that Englishmen of a certain class were in the habit of lounging around their rooms wrapped in a bath towel and wanted to make sure her guest felt right at home.

Nicolson soon learned that while Mrs. Morrow was undoubtedly sincere in promising him autonomy, she also took it for granted that the biography would secure Dwight's place in history and would be broken-hearted if it were anything short of adulatory. And there were other complications as well. A retired army colonel named Lowrie, hired to do interviews and organize Morrow's papers, had been under the impression that he might eventually be chosen to write the book. Lowrie was not aware that the family had made other arrangements until he found himself shaking hands with Nicolson, the man to whom he was to turn over all his research. Devastated, he resigned on the spot, threatening to write his own biography to compete with Nicolson's. Tom Lamont, meanwhile, was nervous about the book's treatment of the House of Morgan; when Nicolson eventually sent him his first draft to read, Lamont responded with a one-hundred-page memo listing his objections.

The Lindberghs were still at Will Rogers's ranch in Santa Monica when Nicolson arrived in the United States, and before their return east he made a brief research trip to the Amherst area, where he had lunch with Mina Curtiss, who had acted as his intermediary with Mrs. Morrow. Curtiss, who was now a "great friend" of Constance Morrow, according to Nicolson, took the occasion to fill Nicolson in on family gossip. Dwight junior, she reported, was "the family tragedy": Unfortunately Betty Morrow could not hide her disappointment and was "not really kind" to her only son. Second on the list of family problems was Anne's husband, whom Curtiss described as none too bright and "not easy" to get along with. Anne had her hands full dealing with Charles, and the whole family sympathized.

Summing up the Morrows' view of their famous in-law, Curtiss explained that "he is really no more than a mechanic," and if it hadn't been for his flight across the Atlantic he would be running a gas station on the outskirts of St. Louis. "Although the Morrows were themselves of humble origin, yet they were always cultured people and distinguished," Nicolson wrote, summarizing what Curtiss told him: "Thus, Lindberg [sic] is really of a lower social stratum and they treat him with aloof politeness as one treats a tenant's niece."[1]

Thus forewarned, Nicolson returned to Englewood, where Banks the butler informed him that the Lindberghs were now in residence and waiting to meet him in the wing of the house that housed their private suite. As Nicolson entered the sitting room he found Colonel Lindbergh, with his hand resting on the head of an enormous police dog.

Nicolson described the ensuing conversation in a letter to his wife:

> "You will have to be a little careful at first, Mr. Nicolson," Lindbergh warned.
>
> "Is he very fierce?"
>
> "He is all that. But he will get used to you in time...."
>
> "Thor is his name, is it not? I read about him in the papers."
>
> I stretched a hand towards him. "Thor!" I said, throwing into the word an appeal for friendship which was profoundly sincere. He then made a noise in his throat such as only tigers make while waiting for their food. It was not a growl, not a bark. It was a deep pectoral regurgitation—predatory, savage, hungry. Lindbergh smiled a little uneasily. "It will take him a week or so," he said, "to become accustomed to you." He then released his hold upon the collar. I retreated rapidly to the fireplace, as if to flick my ash away from my cigarette. Thor stalked towards me. I thought of you and my two sons and Gwen and Rebecq and my past life and England's honour. "Thor! I exclaimed, "Good old man." The tremour in my voiiiice was verrrrry trrrremmmmmmulous."[2]

This was the sort of anecdote that a skillful raconteur like Nicolson could dine out on, and it is hardly surprising that a slightly edited version of the story was later included in the first volume of Nicolson's papers, published as *Diaries and Letters: 1930–1939*. But this daunting first impression did not last. "It is all nonsense people saying that Lindbergh is disagreeable," Nicolson was soon writing his wife. "He is as nice as nice can be, and runs everywhere for me to get me things."

The class differences that loomed so large in the estimation of Mina Curtiss were invisible to Nicolson. A self-confessed snob, he guiltily but gleefully noted that Lindbergh was the sort of good-looking but deferential chap an upper-class English family would be pleased to have as a chauffeur. But Mrs. Morrow, for that matter, reminded him of a very superior sort of upper house servant, while Elisabeth and Anne were rather like the postmistresses in their Kentish village.

On second thought, if anything, it was Colonel Lindbergh who was the natural aristocrat. When Mrs. Morrow hired a Mexican marimba band to play for a party, it was Lindbergh, Nicolson noted, who thought to send the musicians a bottle of champagne after their performance and then made a point of speaking with each member of the band, demonstrating his mastery of the sort of gracious but totally impersonal small talk practiced by the royal family. "He really is a true hero in this country and he never cheapens himself," Nicolson enthused. In another letter Nicolson added that Charles's "delicate prehensile hands ... disconcert one's view of him as an inspired mechanic." And again, "I may be under the glamour of the mouselike modesty of Anne and that staglike modesty of Charles, but oh my God, what charming people!"[3]

Charles had sized Nicolson up as a kindred spirit and all but talked his ears off, leaving Nicolson to wonder how this unassuming, garrulous man had ever acquired a reputation for reserve.

Lindbergh described his work on the perfusion pump, which had reached the point where he was able to keep a rabbit's kidney functioning for six weeks. He hoped that his research would lead to new treatments for cancer but added, shaking his head, "We have had such luck over that darned pump for the last two years that our luck is bound turn. Something is sure to go wrong."[4]

The Lindberghs had recently visited the Chicago World's Fair, separately and in disguise to avoid attracting the attention of photographers. Charles gave a hilarious description of the British pavilion, where a sideshow barker promised passers-by a glimpse of "the original Globe thee-ater," and of the French and Belgian pavilions, where the featured attractions were nude dancing girls. Although he condemned the latter as little more than brothels, Charles did not mind describing the performances in lurid and hilarious detail.

Lindbergh also argued with Nicolson about the British class system, which he found repellent, and recalled his outrage over FDR's high-handed canceling of the airmail contracts. He found fault with some aspects of the New Deal, arguing that the welfare state could only triumph at the expense of individual liberty, but he was less opposed to Roosevelt's policies than many of the Morrows' friends and described himself as "a Democrat by instinct and a Republican in practice."

"He is not a stupid man in the least," Nicolson wrote his wife, "though I doubt he knows who Goethe is." And further, "He is a sensible man without unthoughtful prejudices and with a direct approach to things."[5]

Nicolson's descriptions of the social round at Next Day Hill go far to explain Charles's notorious aversion to receptions and dinner parties: Mrs. Morrow's annual lawn party for eighty or so old friends—the people she and Dwight had known before they became millionaires—was excruciatingly boring and infused with a spirit of *noblesse oblige* that reminded him of the affairs held at British embassies in the more remote colonies on the king's birthday. At a dreadful dinner party hosted by the Cornelius Blisses in Manhattan, a male guest pontificated about "my aunt George Eliot," and one of the ladies went on about "my grandfather Matthew Arnold." Charles, noted Nicolson, "mooned about wretchedly," and all present gave him a wide berth, as if they were afraid of him.

A visit to the Lamonts' prompted Nicolson to remind Vita that "Mrs. Lamont is an ass, as you know." Florence and her "Communist son" (Corliss) bickered constantly, he complained. Worse, she and Betty Morrow sidetracked every worthwhile conversation, apparently on principle, since they held that it was not appropriate to discuss politics in mixed company. Colonel Lindbergh, Nicolson noted with amusement, managed to tactfully deflect Betty Morrow's hints that Florence, "who is not air-minded," would overcome her fear of flying if he invited her up for a ride. "Now that is just like these old dames," Charles said later, "just because I flew alone to Purris they think I am a safe pilot."[6]

Lindbergh's obvious boredom at the Blisses' dinner party was the exception. On the whole he was amazingly patient in situations that would have tried the good nature of any son-in-law. Charles Fay, Morrow's former attorney, invited to reminisce about the late senator over dinner, droned on interminably, lecturing on American history in terms that would have insulted the intelligence of a five-year-old. Mrs. Morrow and Anne excused themselves and went to bed, and Nicolson and Colonel Lindbergh were left awash in the verbal flood. Lindbergh, Nicolson noted with admiration, sat patiently, his features frozen in an expression at once benign and noncommittal, his fingers twiddling almost imperceptibly with a piece of string. At long last, the talkative old man departed, and Lindbergh turned to Nicolson and grinned. "Well," he said, "I have taught myself three new kinds of knots this evening."[7]

These jaundiced impressions of the Morrows' social circle were perhaps not as private as Nicolson thought. Miss Shiff, the secretary assigned to help him go through Morrow's files, warned him that his letters could be read through their envelopes, and Anne Lindbergh hinted in her diary that she suspected him of secretly condescending to all of them. Her reservations were hardly suspected by Nicolson, who thought Anne lovely, shy, and quite charming. He read the article Anne was writing about the North Atlantic tour for the *National Geographic* and admired it so much that he asked Anne's permission to send a copy to his wife. Vita, however, was not impressed. Realizing that Anne was timid about publishing and far from confident about the merits of her own work, Nicolson could not bring himself to tell Anne the truth. He led her to believe that Vita had praised the manuscript, a polite and apparently harmless equivocation.

On a stormy night in late November, Aubrey Morgan called from Pasadena with bad news. Elisabeth, who had recently undergone an emergency appendectomy, had developed pneumonia and was in critical condition. Despite the treacherous weather and her own fear of air travel, Betty Morrow was determined to fly to her daughter's bedside immediately. TWA officials decided that the storm made a night flight too dangerous, and Charles reluctantly agreed to arrange a charter.

Watching Mrs. Morrow as she stood in the entrance hall, waiting for Charles and Anne to drive her to the airport, Nicolson reconsidered his judgment of his patron. "She is an ugly little woman of 65 or so with a disagreeable mouth. And yet there is something about her which is inspiring," he wrote his wife. "She is not brilliant, she is not amusing and her poetry is very poor, but there is something about her which is so important and perplexing that I long for you to be with me so that we could discuss it together."[8]

Mrs. Morrow's night flight arrived safely in Pasadena, and for a time, Elisabeth appeared to be recovering nicely from her operation. During the early morning hours of December 3, Anne woke up shivering with cold and a strange foreboding of disaster. Minutes later the phone rang. It was her mother calling from Pasadena. Elisabeth was dead.

Although long predicted by her doctors, Elisabeth's death at the age of thirty was a devastating blow to the family. Elisabeth had been so much like her father that Betty Morrow felt she had lost the last link with her husband's memory, and Anne was once again plunged into a deep depression. It fell to Charles to make the arrangements for the funeral which was held in the library at Next Day Hill, the same room where Elisabeth and Aubrey Morgan had been married just two years earlier.

Harold Nicolson compared the Morrows to the House of Atreus, and it did seem as if the fates were extracting a grim revenge for the family's earlier run of luck. In addition to the deaths of Dwight Morrow, Charles Lindbergh, Jr., and now Elisabeth, so many others connected to the family had died suddenly that several popular magazines ran articles speculating on the existence of a "Lindbergh curse." Dr. John Hibben, who had comforted the Lindberghs in the immediate aftermath of the kidnapping, had been killed by a drunk driver. Hibben's wife was crippled in the same accident, and the couple's son had been stricken with a fatal brain tumor. Helen Maddux, barely in her forties, had died suddenly. Ollie Whateley, only a few years older, developed stomach cancer some months after the kidnapping and succumbed after a long and agonizing illness. Violet Sharpe, of course, had committed suicide, and several detectives connected with the kidnapping investigation had died prematurely.

And of course, the Lindberghs, like all those connected with the early history of aviation, lost friends and colleagues in plane crashes. Floyd Bennett had succumbed to pneumonia despite Charles's flight to Quebec with experimental drugs from Rockefeller University. The year 1935 would bring the deaths of Will Rogers and Wiley Post in Alaska. Charles and Anne themselves survived a number of close calls, more as the result of good airplanes, safety consciousness, and piloting skill than sheer luck. But no one who flew as often as the Lindberghs could ignore the very real possibility of a fatal crash. In September 1934, their brand-new single-engine Lambert monocoupe did a ground loop as they were attempting to take off from Wichita airport, and mechanics discovered that the brakes on one wheel had been installed backwards.

Continuing their flight in a substitute plane, they experienced engine failure over Oklahoma and made a forced landing in a farmer's field. Anne was increasingly terrified of flying in "experimental" airplanes, a fear that can hardly be dismissed as irrational.

Nicolson, living under the same roof as this tragedy-plagued family, was astonished by their stoicism. When the kidnapping trial got under way in January 1935, he came down to breakfast every day to find that morning's *Times* neatly folded on the breakfast table, its front page invariably dominated by news from Flemington. Even so, the kidnapping—or as the family preferred to call it, "the case"—was the one subject Charles Lindbergh never alluded to during their daily chats. "It *must* mean something to him," Nicolson wrote, amazed, yet he concluded that Lindbergh's refusal to allude to the headlines was "not a pose. It is merely a determined habit of ignoring the press." Whether Charles Lindbergh actually ignored the press or just pretended to could be debated; certainly he often enough seemed to be reacting to it, one way or another.

On February 13, the evening after the case went to the jury, the family broke with habit and left the radio on after dinner. At 10:45 the announcer broke into a program of swing tunes with a news flash: "Bruno Richard Hauptmann has been condemned to death without mercy. You have now heard the verdict in the most famous trial in history." The correspondent's microphone was picking up the screams of the mob in the street outside the courthouse, exulting over the prospect of Hauptmann's death by electrocution. Charles suddenly turned off the radio. "That," he said, "was a lynching crowd."

Everyone went to the kitchen for ginger ale, and Charles quietly began to review the evidence presented at the trial. "He pretended to address his remarks to me," Nicolson wrote. "But I could see he was trying to ease the agonised tension through which Betty and Anne had passed.... Never has circumstantial evidence been so convincing."[9]

Nicolson's summary of this monologue—more detailed in the original correspondence than in the published entry in his *Diaries and Letters*, has prompted several authors interested in the kidnapping to observe that Lindbergh appeared to be trying to convince himself as well as his family. Yet, they note, it wasn't circumstantial evidence alone that convicted Hauptmann; Lindbergh himself had positively identified the defendant as the man who collected the ransom money in St. Raymond's Cemetery. Ludovic Kennedy concludes, for example, in *The Airman and the Carpenter* that Lindbergh had not really recognized

Hauptmann's voice at all but had allowed himself to be talked into belief in Hauptmann's guilt by New York and New Jersey police.

But the issue left unsettled by the trial was not Hauptmann's guilt so much as the possible existence of accomplices. Ed Reilly, prevented by Judge Trenchard's threat from pointing the finger of guilt at individuals he was not prepared to call as witnesses, had nevertheless made a point of asking Lindbergh about the assistant chauffeur he called "Ellison." Lindbergh acknowledged that Ellerson had driven family members to Hopewell on a number of occasions, though he didn't know how often.

"Ellison [*sic*] is no longer a chauffeur on the estate, is he?" Reilly had then asked. "He is a watchman at the gate, isn't he?"

And it was true. Charles Ellerson had returned to Englewood, been rehired by Arthur Springer, and was working part-time as a night watchman at Next Day Hill. Reilly's knowledge of this, considering that he was otherwise so ill prepared and ignorant of many basic elements of the evidence, must have been disconcerting.

On February 16, the Saturday after the verdict was delivered, a passenger on an American Airlines flight from Boston to New York paid for his ticket with two ten-dollar Lindbergh ransom bills. The FBI collected the flight manifests and began interviewing passengers, only to abandon the investigation at the request of Norman Schwarzkopf, who insisted that the bills must have been in circulation for some time; their turning up in this fashion so soon after the trial was a mere coincidence. Schwarzkopf still hoped that Hauptmann would confess, but at least until the appeals process was completed, the last thing he wanted was for the FBI to suggest it did not accept the theory of the case presented in Flemington. J. Edgar Hoover and the chief of the NYPD agreed with Schwarzkopf that it was time to close the books on an investigation that had eaten up countless man-hours and a good percentage of their budgets for the past three years. Over the protests of some of the agents and detectives involved, the CALNAP investigation was abandoned.

The following week Anna Hauptmann introduced reporters to her new "personal manager," one David Webber, who was working with a group called the Bruno Hauptmann Defense Fund, whose headquarters were located at 226 East Eighty-sixth Street in the Yorkville section of Manhattan. Both the fund's chairman, Johannes Weiss, and its attorney, Alphonse Koelble, were associated with the pro-Nazi sect called the Friends of New Germany. At a Defense Fund rally, held in the Bronx on March 5, 1935, a crowd of fifteen hundred jeered every time Colonel

Lindbergh's name was mentioned and applauded loudly when Koelble referred to prosecutor David Wilentz as "Wilensky." Hawkers outside the hall were doing a brisk business in pro-Nazi pamphlets, including one entitled "The Gentile Front." At the end of the speeches, Weiss called on "our O.D. men," burly ushers wearing green armbands, to circulate through the crowd collecting donations. ("O.D." stood for *Ordnungsdienst,* a paramilitary group modeled on Hitler's storm troopers.) The duties of the O.D. men also included breaking the cameras of news photographers who attempted to photograph the rallies. After New York City authorities refused to grant permits for further meetings, the Defense Fund sent Anna Hauptmann on a fund-raising tour of the Midwest. Mrs. Hauptmann said later that she had no idea at the time that the organizers were using her to promote their own political agenda.[10]

But the Hauptmann Defense Fund had at least the tacit encouragement of the leadership of the National Socialist party in Germany. Throughout the trial the pro-Nazi press had portrayed Hauptmann as a scapegoat, and Julius Streicher's notorious *Der Stürmer (The Storm Trooper)* actually charged that the Lindbergh baby had been stolen by the Jews and used in a ritual of blood sacrifice. More typically, the *West Deutsche Beobachter,* an organ of the National Socialist party in Cologne, commented: "This case is for us principally an example of the lack of discipline that has spread throughout the United States." When it became obvious that their rallies were alienating more German Americans than they attracted, the American-based Defense Fund quickly folded, and pro-Nazi organs in Germany all but ceased commenting on the case. American correspondents were severely discouraged from attempting to contact Hauptmann's family and childhood friends.

Mrs. Hauptmann's appearances in Chicago, Milwaukee, and other Midwest cities netted less than fifteen thousand dollars, and when Ed Reilly claimed the money should be used to cover the unpaid portion of his bill, the Hauptmanns fired him, retaining Lloyd Fisher, the Flemington attorney who had served as Reilly's cocounsel, to handle the appeal of the death sentence. Fisher knew that the medical examiner, Dr. Mitchell, and the coroner, Swayze, were vulnerable witnesses, and he was convinced that Reilly should have built his defense on the contention that the corpse in the woods was not that of Charles Lindbergh, Jr. In fact there was no doubt that the identification was correct—even officers on the scene agreed that the child's facial features were recognizable, and the body had still been dressed in the homemade undershirt sewn by Betty Gow, but Fisher's claim that the Lindbergh baby was still alive made good copy. In August, six months after the trial ended, he announced that he had located the real Charles Lindbergh, Jr. on Long Island. Rejecting Norman Schwarzkopf's offer to settle the matter once and for all by comparing the baby's fingerprints with latent prints collected from the Hopewell house, Fisher publicly begged Colonel Lindbergh to come out to Long Island and meet his son face to face. When Lindbergh ignored this plea, Fisher implied that the family had something to hide.

Every time the press reported on the activities of Fisher and Mrs. Hauptmann, the Lindberghs received another spate of threatening letters. Betty Morrow, too, had become a target and was so nervous that she no longer opened her own mail or answered the phone. By the end of 1935, police in New York and New Jersey had tracked down thirteen mentally deranged men and women who were writing threatening letters to the family; in order to avoid inspiring still more threats, these cases were disposed of quietly, the individuals involved committed to mental institutions.

Suggesting that he still had some doubts about the resolution of the case, Colonel Lindbergh no longer relied on Mrs. Morrow's servants to insure the security of his second son. Jon spent most of the summer in North Haven, and when he was in Englewood, he was guarded round the clock by a retired detective. No longer permitted to roam the grounds with his nursemaid, he played in a wire-mesh enclosure, watched over by Thor and his private bodyguard, who was usually armed with a sawed-off shotgun.

But unresolved questions about the case inevitably took second place to the need to resume a normal family life. Anne and her mother had not actively followed the investigation since the summer of 1932, and Charles now began a determined campaign to "erase" his own memories of the crime.[11]

Somewhat unexpectedly, one aspect of this effort involved making his peace with the memory of his father. Although he had had little contact with his Lindbergh relatives since 1927, he and Anne now flew to Minnesota, where they visited Eva Lindbergh Christie and her family in Red Lake and C.A.'s sister, Mrs. Linda Seal, in Melrose, where Charles distributed his father's ashes over the site of the August Lindbergh homestead. The Lindberghs also stopped in Little Falls, staying at the home of the local hardware-store owner, Martin Engstrom. A lifelong friend of C.A.'s, Engstrom had made a valiant if largely unsuccessful effort to protect the Camp from the depredations of vandals and souvenir hunters. Now the dispute over C.A.'s will had finally been resolved, and the heirs had agreed to donate the property to the state as a memorial to the congressman.

During this visit or shortly afterward, Charles made contact with Dr. Grace Nute, a Minnesota historian who hoped to write a biography of C.A. He underwrote some of her research into the background of the Lindbergh family and began corresponding with her about his memories of his father.

Anne, meanwhile, had been awarded an honorary degree of Master of Arts and Letters by the trustees of Smith College. As the college's most celebrated living graduate, she certainly merited the honor, but Anne believed that such degrees should be reserved for women who succeeded on their own, not as the wives of famous men, and Charles and her mother had to talk her into accepting. In the event, Anne's appearance at Smith's commencement ceremony was not an unalloyed success. She and Charles spent their visit to Northampton in seclusion at the home of an old friend, refusing all requests for photographs and interviews, and many townies as well as some students felt snubbed.

Despite her fear that her efforts would be seen as just another Lindbergh publicity stunt, Anne seemed well on her way to a successful writing career. On Harold Nicolson's recommendation, she had submitted the manuscript of her book on the 1931 polar flight to Harcourt, Brace, the same company that was about to publish his life of Dwight Morrow. The book, entitled *North to the Orient,* appeared in the stores at the end of the summer, and none of the glowing reviews pleased her as much as the comment of her editor, who assured her: "I would have accepted the manuscript if it had been written by Jane Smith."

Charles and Dr. Carrel were also on the brink of a major breakthrough. In the spring of 1935 they had begun perfusing organs with oxygen during experimental surgery on animals, and that June, *Science* published their coauthored article reporting the successful perfusion of a cat's thyroid gland for 120 days. Promising as this development was, it hardly lived up to its ecstatic billing in the media. The perfusion pump was hailed by the popular press as an "artificial heart," and the *New York Times* called Carrel and Lindbergh's accomplishment "one of the most sensational in the annals of medicine."

Carrel's connection with Lindbergh had undoubtedly helped make his book *Man the Unknown* a best seller and him a celebrity in his own right, deluged with speaking invitations and interview requests. Carrel had always enjoyed being provocative, and the presence of journalists did not stop him from allowing his mind (and tongue) to wander unchecked. He told Anne New of *Cosmopolitan* magazine, for instance, that "we can produce telepathy at will in the laboratory." In the same interview he attempted to explain that he did not wish to use eugenics to "make supermen of a few persons" but to benefit all humanity. At other times, this distinction was by no means clear. Challenged by a *New York Times* reporter to explain the difference between his views and Hitler's, Carrel pointed out that the notion of a "pure" master race was a scientific absurdity; on the contrary, "crossing civilizations as we do in America" was the way to produce superior human beings. Then, unwilling to leave well enough alone, Carrel mused out loud, "Perhaps it would be effective if we could kill off the worst of these pure races and keep the best, as we do in the breeding of dogs."[12]

Such comments were an embarrassment to Rockefeller University, and Dr. Herbert Spencer Gasser, who replaced Carrel's mentor Simon Flexner as director in 1935, was determined to force Carrel into retirement. Although Carrel's controversial public statements were undoubtedly Gasser's chief complaint, the struggle between the two men was played out over internal policy disputes. Gasser wanted to introduce a system of project accountability, while Carrel believed that truly important discoveries came about when scientists were given the freedom to putter in their laboratories at will, free from pressure to publish papers every few months. The project system, he complained, created a situation in which scientists' careers depended on their ability to predict the results of their experiments in advance, a system that invited fraud and stifled creativity. Carrel had a point, though it was also true that his open-ended "Mousery" studies had cost the university a great deal of money without producing tangible results. Within a matter of months, relations between Gasser and Carrel had degenerated into bureaucratic sniping. Gasser refused to approve even routine expense vouchers and deluged Carrel with petty requests to rewrite reports and reorganize his bibliographies.

After returning from Minnesota, Anne had joined Jon at North Haven, and Charles flew up from New York whenever his airline work and research duties permitted. At times during these visits it seemed to Anne that she and Charles were the same people they had been in 1931, a young couple with more advantages than burdens and the best of life still ahead of them.

But the old problems had not been resolved and a few new ones added. On a sparkling September afternoon, Charles decided that the time had come to take Jon up for his first airplane ride. Jon, now three years old and already looking forward to the day when he would be big enough to "make everything go myself," was entranced. But Anne, who had pioneered the Great Circle route to Asia, confided to her diary that she was petrified, her knuckles white with tension as she held the excited child in her lap.

In October, when Anne and Jon returned to Englewood, what peace of mind she had achieved soon began to erode. The big house was filled with ghosts—Dwight senior, Elisabeth, little Charley—not to mention suspect servants and Mrs. Morrow's endless guests. Charles would return from a busy day in Manhattan to find several dozen Smith alumnae waiting in the foyer for their cars to be brought around, while, in the library, the servants were already setting out chairs in preparation for a charity bridge party. Anne decided to rent a studio apartment nearby, where she could escape for a few hours a day to write in peace. "It is a physical relief to get away," she wrote. "I try to remember: This is how Charles feels *all* the time here."[13]

On October 9 the New Jersey Court of Appeals voted to uphold the conviction of Bruno Richard Hauptmann, and several of the tabloids decided to take note of this development by assigning photographers to get a picture of Jon. A van leased by the *Daily Mirror* staked out the Little School, where Jon was attending nursery school classes. A few weeks later the Morrow's chauffeured Cadillac was forced off the road by another press van; photographers leaped onto the running boards and snapped away while the boy's nursemaid screeched in terror. The Lindberghs decided to keep Jon at home, but even there they could not feel entirely sure of his safety. One evening Charles was sitting in his bedroom when he heard a voice calling to him from outside. Captured, the man proved to be what Lindbergh later described as "off-and-on mental-institution case" and apparently harmless, but it was disturbing that all the family's precautions had failed to prevent him from wandering onto the grounds and zeroing in on the window of the Lindberghs' bedroom.

On December 3 the *Mirror* published the first installment of Bruno Hauptmann's ghostwritten autobiography—purchased for a small fraction of the one hundred thousand dollars originally demanded. Two days later the *News* reported that New Jersey governor Harold Hoffman was about to launch an independent investigation of the case. Hoffman and prosecutor David Wilentz had been rivals since they were children together in Perth Amboy, and the governor now hoped to discover evidence of malfeasance that would destroy Wilentz's career.

The same day the *News* broke the story of Hoffman's plans, Charles told Anne that he was thinking of taking her and Jon to live in England. (Like most family decisions, this one was unilateral.) Although the move meant that she would never have a chance to use the small apartment she had spent the last two months decorating, Anne confessed in her diary that she was secretly relieved to be getting away. Moreover, the business of packing, traveling, and then settling into a new home provided an excellent excuse to put off grappling with her next book. No doubt Charles's desire to protect Jon and Anne was similarly reinforced by his unhappiness with Englewood and the tense situation at the laboratory. Still relatively composed and even cheerful when Harold Nicolson last saw him in the spring, he was now irritable and angry much of the time.

Shortly before the family left for England, slipping away under assumed names on the freighter *American Importer* with diplomatic passports issued through the intervention of Treasury Secretary Ogden Mills, Charles told a friend, "We Americans are a primitive people. Our moral standards are low. We do not have discipline." No doubt it was a coincidence that this was precisely the conclusion of the Nazi press. Similar sentiments were being expressed by leading American papers. The *New York Herald Tribune,* for example, editorialized that the kidnapping had "laid bare the excesses of American habit and temperament." On the other hand, the *Daily News,* unrepentant, sarcastically compared Lindbergh to Greta Garbo, observing: "He would have been pestered less if he had acted more as a popular hero is supposed to act."[14]

With Harold Hoffman's advent on the scene, the Lindbergh kidnapping investigation made its final descent into surrealism and utter madness. Norman Schwarzkopf, foreseeing that Hoffman was planning to use the alleged misdeeds of the state police and Wilentz as an election issue, conducted a masterful holding operation. Schwarzkopf sent Hoffman lengthy memoranda reporting that there was nothing new to report and that, in Hoffman's words, "the usual conferences are being held."[15]

Frustrated, Hoffman began to rely increasingly on free-lance investigators and "famous detectives" who were happy to share their fantasies with him. One of Hoffman's informants was a Boston writer and radio commentator named Zoe Patricia Hobbs, who had noticed, correctly, that there were certain parallels between the kidnapper's notes and the extortion letters received by Constance Morrow in 1929. (Conceivably there was a direct connection; or possibly Hauptmann, or an accomplice such as the Boston-bred Duane Baker, knew about the extortion case from accounts that had appeared in the *Boston Post* and *Herald*.)

With the gusto of a true conspiracy theorist, Hobbs leaped to the conclusion that the mastermind behind both crimes was a member of the Morrow family. Her favorite candidate was Dwight Morrow, Jr., whom she suspected at one point of murdering Frances Smith, Violet Sharpe, and his own father, in addition to the Lindbergh baby. Hobbs began nosing around Amherst and the Riggs Institute in Stockbridge asking pointed questions about Dwight junior's mental illness. She soon became convinced, probably correctly, that she was being followed by private detectives hired by either the Morrows or the Morgan bank. This only made her more certain that she was on the right track.

An alternate scenario was provided by Gaston Means, who now "confessed" that he and Norman Whitaker had been hired to kidnap the Lindbergh baby by a certain "female member of the Morrow family." Means never publicly named names, but it was understood that he was accusing Elisabeth Morrow, who supposedly had been in love with Charles and insanely jealous of her sister for having a baby when her own ill health prevented her from bearing children.

Almost unbelievably this story found a supporter in Evalyn McLean, whose capacity for being fooled by Gaston Means apparently knew no limits. Still angry with the Lindberghs for their failure to reimburse her for the one hundred thousand dollars she had squandered, McLean decided that Charles and Anne had fled the country because they were afraid the governor's investigators would subpoena them to give depositions about Elisabeth's role in the crime.

McLean hired a criminalist named Robert Hicks who had earlier come to the conclusion that the Lindbergh child died of a gunshot wound. Hicks moved into the Hauptmanns' former apartment on 222nd Street in the Bronx to search for "new evidence." Some weeks later a Hoffman investigator announced with great fanfare that he had discovered proof that rail number 16 of the kidnap ladder had not come from the attic flooring after all—the nail holes did not match! Independent investigators from Columbia University eventually determined that the reason the holes no longer matched was because they had been partially filled with sawdust by a person or persons unknown. Hicks, meanwhile, had resigned from the case for reasons he refused to explain.

McLean's second brainstorm was somewhat more productive. She offered a prominent New York defense attorney named Sam Liebowitz, who had covered the trial for WHN radio, fifteen thousand dollars if he could get Hauptmann to confess and name his accomplices. Liebowitz believed that psychological pressure from his wife and his attorneys, combined with the belief that he would be executed anyway, had so far prevented Hauptmann from telling the truth. Calling on Mrs. Hauptmann, he persuaded her that only he could save Richard's life. (The idea that Hauptmann could avoid execution by telling the whole story was frequently expressed by Liebowitz and others; practially speaking, it would have been necessary to delay the execution for Hauptmann to testify against his accomplices. That his death sentence would actually be commuted was far from obvious, as Hauptmann himself must have known.) At any rate Mrs. Hauptmann immediately fired Fisher and talked her husband into granting Liebowitz an interview.

Liebowitz showed up in Hauptmann's cell carrying a cardboard model of the Hopewell house. Appealing to Hauptmann's ego, he coaxed him into discussing, hypothetically, how the crime might have been pulled off. Hauptmann ridiculed Wilentz's theory that the kidnapper had placed the sleeping infant in a burlap bag and carried it down the ladder, only to drop the bag when one of the ladder's rungs cracked under his weight. That wasn't how it would have happened at all, he told Liebowitz. The ladder would have broken on the way up. The kidnapper then left the house by the main stairway, carrying the baby in his arms.

Liebowitz was incredulous. "But Col. Lindbergh was in his study! He would have heard!"

Hauptmann shrugged. "I tell only the truth."[16]

In fact Liebowitz was mistaken. If the sound the Lindberghs heard in living room was made by Hauptmann on his way up the ladder, then he would have still been in the darkened nursery when they came upstairs to the master bedroom a minute or so later. The doors to the small connecting bathroom between the nursery and the master bedroom had been left ajar so that Anne could hear the baby if it cried, and the window through which Hauptmann had entered was directly opposite these doors. It would have been virtually impossible for him to leave the way he had come in without attracting attention.

After a few minutes, Charles Lindbergh had gone into the large bathroom at the far end of the hall and shut the door behind him so he could take his bath. Anne had been moving around in the master bedroom, hunting for her tooth powder. At that moment, Hauptmann may well have calculated that his best chance of getting away was to grab the baby and sprint down the front stairs.

By this time Ollie Whateley would have been reading his magazine in the servants' sitting room on the other side of the kitchen; his wife and Betty Gow were upstairs in the servants' wing. It was a windy night. No one would have heard Hauptmann shut the front door behind him.

If Hauptmann indeed left the house in this fashion, it is most unlikely that he would have risked going back around to the nursery to retrieve the ladder. An accomplice must have grabbed the ladder and scurried with it toward Featherbed Lane. Moreover, since the kidnappers did not make their getaway until twenty or more minutes later than the police estimate, the chances are good that they realized the crime had been discovered. Even if they were not still on the property when Colonel Lindbergh came running out of the house with his rifle, from the summit of the Princeton-Hopewell Road the Lindbergh house, ablaze with lights, could be clearly seen. Panicked, they killed the child and hastily buried the body.

After his extraordinary jailhouse conversation with Hauptmann, Sam Liebowitz made the mistake of telling several reporters he knew that he expected the condemned man to make a full confession soon. When Anna read in the papers that her new attorney wanted Richard to admit to murder, she fired him and quickly made her peace with Lloyd Fisher. Liebowitz never again had an opportunity to talk with Hauptmann.

Harold Hoffman's investigation, meanwhile, was foundering. Neither the FBI nor the NYPD would cooperate, and far from hailing the governor as a truth seeker, columnists like Walter Winchell assailed him for pandering to Nazi sympathizers. Desperate to come up with dramatic new evidence, Hoffman entered into a conspiracy with Ellis Parker, a Burlington County detective who was bitter against Schwarzkopf and Lieutenant Keaten for excluding him from the kidnapping investigation. Parker's son hired four men to kidnap a disbarred attorney named Paul Wendel and hold him prisoner in a Brooklyn basement until he signed a confession dictated by them. Wendel was then stashed in a New Jersey mental institution until the eve of the Board of Pardons hearing, at which Hoffman was to present the results of his inquiry. Parker told Wendel that if he stood by his confession, Hoffman would see that he was ruled incompetent to stand trial and released from the sanatorium in a few years. He could then live in luxury for the rest of his days off the fortune he would make from selling his story to the movies.[17]

Paul Wendel was a pathetic individual at the best of times. He had been beaten and probably drugged. However, he was smart enough to realize that Parker and the governor would have everything to gain by seeing that he did not leave the sanatorium alive. He knew the address of the Brooklyn house where he had been held, and he had managed to scratch his initials on the basement floor. At the first opportunity he repudiated his confession, charging the Parkers with kidnapping.

Wendel's accusations left the Hoffman investigation totally discredited, and Bruno Richard Hauptmann died in the electric chair in the state penitentiary at Trenton on April 3, 1936. Ironically, Ellis Parker senior and junior were eventually convicted under the federal kidnapping statute known as the Lindbergh Law. Gov. Harold Hoffman escaped indictment and survived in office long enough to punish Norman Schwarzkopf for refusing to cooperate in the political demolition of Wilentz. Schwarzkopf became, for a time, the moderator of the popular radio show "Gangbusters." He eventually rejoined the army, served as head of the U.S. Military Mission to Iran during World War II, and rose to the rank of major general. His son, H. Norman Schwarzkopf, Jr., born after the Hauptmann trial, continued the family tradition of military service.

The Lindberghs, in seclusion at Aubrey Morgan's family home in Llandaff, Wales, learned of many of these developments through letters from relatives and friends, and from the somewhat garbled accounts in the British press, which was inclined to view the Wendel kidnapping and assorted other follies of the Hoffman administration as one more proof that the United States was the land of cowboys, gangsterism, and charlatans.

Certainly for Alexis Carrel they demonstrated that America had succumbed to what he called ochlocracy—the rule of the worst. Just as he had become embittered against the French nation when his colleagues there failed to accept his revolutionary methods for treating battlefield wounds, Carrel—professionally embattled and distressed by his separation from Lindbergh—was rapidly souring on America. Although he had long avoided any comment on politics, "the isms" as he called them, Carrel began to tell his friends at the Century Club that the only way to curb the "reign of lawlessness" was for Lindbergh to return to the United States and run for president in 1940. "He will surely be elected."[18]

TWENTY-ONE

Exile

AFTER HAUPTMANN'S EXECUTION the Lindberghs did not return to the United States. They had recently taken a lease on Long Barn, Harold and Vita Nicolson's picturesque country place in the Kentish village of Weald, and were settled in for the indefinite future. Long Barn was an old house—sections of it dated back to the fourteenth century—but it had been enlarged by the Nicolsons some years earlier and had a fifty-foot living room, seven bedrooms, and four reasonably modern baths. Much lived in, it was stuffed from kitchen to attic with moth-eaten tapestries, books, family photos, and trunks of old clothing. There were even graffiti on the walls of some of the upstairs rooms, not only the scrawls of the Nicolsons' two sons but also marks indicating the heights of various friends—"Stephen Spender in bare feet," and so on.

A few days after Anne and Charles moved in, Vita Sackville-West came over from Sissinghurst Castle to help the new tenants get established. She reported to her husband, now living mainly in London, where he was serving as a Liberal MP, that the Lindberghs were "charming, but more muddle-headed than I could have believed possible. I arranged everything for them, even to ordering their coal!"

Except for their stint in the New York apartment they both hated, it was the first time Anne and Charles had lived on their own since 1931, and they did feel, Anne noted, a bit like "young marrieds" playing house. Anne had fallen in love with Long Barn at first sight, especially the lovely garden bursting with primroses and bluebells. She sent for her trunks and settled in happily to work on her second book, an account of the 1933 North Atlantic survey flight. For several years she had been worrying over her inability to conceive another child, but by the autumn of 1936, she was pregnant again. Her third son, named Land, was born in London in May 1937. During the early stages of her labor, Anne took her mind off the pain by reading Virginia Woolf's *The Years.*

Anne had decided that her book would cover only the last leg of the survey flight, when the Sirius was stranded in the Canary Islands and she and Charles were united in their goal of returning home. Even so, the work went slowly. "Isn't it possible for a woman to be a woman and yet produce something tangible besides children, something that stands up in a man's world?" Anne asked in a letter to her cousin Mary Scandrett. "In other words is it possible to live up to women's standards and men's standards at the same time?" She had decided that for herself, at least, the answer was a qualified no. She had resolved to stop trying to be the perpetual A student, and stop making herself unhappy because she hadn't become a successful "woman writer" according to the feminist standards that her mother held up to her. She would continue to write and hope something good came out of it, but she was quite content to think of herself as an amateur.

This all sounds realistic enough, but there is a plaintive undertone to this letter, as if Anne was not quite convinced by her own reasoning. She cites an aphorism from an anthology compiled by the British belletrist Maurice Baring—"God is an amateur"—but mentions Woolf's *To the Lighthouse,* Vita Sackville-West's *All Passion Spent,* and Rebecca West's *Thinking Reed* as examples of books that came out of a "truly feminine" sensibility as opposed to the "straight line" mentality of masculine-dominated society. But these authors were not amateurs; nor is amateurism necessarily a matter of not having enough time.[1]

The pressure to be a perpetual A student was no longer coming only from her mother. Charles felt sure that his wife had the talent to write a great novel and was disappointed with her for setting her sights so low. In his opinion, too, Anne had plenty of time—after all, there was a nurse, a cook, and a secretary to handle the business of the house. He chided Anne for devoting hours to her diary and the writing of beautifully crafted personal letters while refusing to bring the same degree of commitment to any work destined for publication. In an effort to spur her to finish the travel manuscript, later published as *Listen! The Wind,*

Charles wrote the foreword and the appendix, drew the maps, and spent hours on the manuscript itself, mainly critiquing the descriptions of flying from a technical standpoint.

Unlike his wife, Charles had time to burn. He had left behind his airline consulting work, and his research on the perfusion pump had been interrupted at the very moment when the device was on the brink of becoming a useful experimental tool. Many of Carrel's perfusion experiments had been performed at very low temperatures, and to keep himself busy, Charles decided to study the phenomena of hypothermia and suspended animation. He purchased a hyperbaric chamber, which finally arrived after many disputes with the British manufacturer, and he also began doing experiments with rats in a shed on the grounds of Long Barn. In order to avoid upsetting Jon, he tried to purchase enough animals so that the boy would not notice when some of them disappeared.

Charles and Dr. Carrel were still collaborating long-distance on a book about their research, *The Culture of Organs,* and Carrel was anxiously wondering when Lindbergh planned to return to the United States. Carrel's feud with Dr. Gasser had divided the Rockefeller Institute along generational lines, and Gasser had finally decided to rid himself of the opposition in one fell swoop by getting the trustees to establish a mandatory retirement age of sixty-five. His future uncertain, Carrel was circulating a proposal for what he called the Institute of Man, originally envisioned as a sort of think tank, where an elite group of scientists would attend three-day conferences "under conditions resembling life in a monastery" to discuss the "development of techniques for the production of a superior type of men and women." Later, when it became clear that Gasser planned to shut down the entire laboratory of experimental surgery, throwing his younger associates out of work, Carrel began to think of his institute as a traditional laboratory facility, where his protégés and others could continue their research into the causes of cancer and the techniques of organ transplants as well as such subjects as telepathy and extrasensory perception. Carrel's controversial statements about eugenics and social engineering scared off potential sponsors, however. He needed the backing of his celebrated associate to attract funding.

Lindbergh resisted Carrel's pleas to come home, insisting that one thing and one thing only stood in the way of his return: "The Press is really our greatest problem, for we could protect ourselves against the fanatic and criminal; we could maintain a home suitable for our children and lead a reasonably normal and happy life in our own country were it not for the attention which the newspapers concentrate on our movements and the interference in our affairs."[2]

Ironically Charles's expectations that the British press adhered to a more gentlemanly standard had proved to be somewhat naive. The *Times* of London, no less, published a photo of Jon on its front page, and there was an unpleasant incident when some British reporters threw rocks at Thor. After the Hauptmann execution, however, the London papers' interest in the Lindberghs had all but evaporated. The possibility that the American tabloids might eventually grow bored with the subject did not seem to occur to Charles. He was already fretting about how he and Carrel would deal with reporters at the institute, the least of their problems at the moment.

In May 1936, Charles showed up at Harold Nicolson's London office in need of advice. He and Anne had been invited by the military attaché at the American Embassy to come to tea and meet the new monarch, Edward VIII. Lindbergh, Nicolson reported to his wife, was in "a dreadful state" over the invitation: "Was he being used as bait to get the King to tea?" Was the embassy trying to manipulate him for "social profit"? "Evidently the thing had been going around in their poor minds." Nicolson thought this fear of exploitation exaggerated. Amused, he advised that there could be no harm in the Lindberghs going to tea at their own embassy.[3]

Nicolson soon had cause to regret his advice. Three weeks after meeting the king at the embassy, the Lindberghs were invited to an intimate dinner party at York House, Edward's residence. The only other guests were Prime Minister and Mrs. Stanley Baldwin and Mr. and Mrs. Ernest Simpson. The party marked the first time Wallis Simpson had been entertained by the king, at least officially, and the Lindberghs had indeed been used as bait to lure the prime minister into a social meeting with the king's mistress. Anne, apparently oblivious to this aspect of the occasion, thought Edward immature and rather sad but still the most "sensitive" Englishman she had met.

Back at Next Day Hill, in the days when Edward was still Prince of Wales, Charles had remarked to Harold Nicolson that the prince was the only man in the world who could truly understand his situation. The difference was that Edward at least had an entourage to protect him. On the other hand, "He has to care what they [the newspapers] say, and I don't," Charles added. Anne now discovered that the king also seemed to feel a certain kinship with her husband. An aviation buff, Edward had been inspired by Lindbergh's 1927 flight. Other similarities between the two men would shortly become apparent.

Despite being invited to dine with the king, the Lindberghs were feeling abandoned. At Next Day Hill, Harold Nicolson had been treated as a member of the family, and Charles, who did not warm up to people easily, liked Nicolson very much. Undoubtedly, he had expected that Nicolson and his wife would take him and Anne up socially and introduce them to their literary friends. For a variety of reasons, this never happened. As an MP, Nicolson was preoccupied with various political crises, including Edward VIII's stubborn refusal to give up Mrs. Simpson. Sackville-West had her hands full juggling her writing and the management of Sissinghurst Castle, and in her own understated way she was even more protective of her privacy than were the Lindberghs.

Even so, Vita did make an effort. On several occasions she invited her tenants to Sissinghurst, only to find that it was next to impossible to settle on a mutually agreeable date. The Lindberghs' reply to every suggestion, she complained, was, "Our plans are so indefinite." Stopping by Long Barn one day, Vita found that Charles and Anne had flown off to the Continent, leaving Jon in the care of the servants. The little boy was in bed with a stomachache, and when Vita asked him what the matter was, he replied, "Well, it might be apples, or it might be nuts." Vita found the answer charming but could not say as much for the household. The cook had just broken her ankle, and the secretary and the nursemaid were frantic. Betty Morrow and Constance, who had recently announced her plans to marry Aubrey Morgan, Elisabeth's widower, were expected for a visit any day. The servants weren't sure exactly where Charles and Anne were or when they would be returning, and they couldn't make up their minds what to tell Mrs. Morrow or how they should entertain her and Constance if they showed up before the Lindberghs got back. "Evidently they preserve their policy of secrecy even towards their own household!" Vita exclaimed.

Assuming that Charles and Anne wanted to be left alone, Sackville-West began confining her visits to those required by her duties as a landlady. And unfortunately, in her estimation, the Lindberghs left much to be desired as tenants. In December 1937, she had a call from the servants informing her that all the pipes had burst and the roof was leaking. "The Lindberghs, of course, were not there," she wrote Harold in exasperation. Furthermore, the house was "dreadfully ill-kept" and overrun with mice. This time not only Jon but the new baby, now seven months old, had been left in the care of the staff. Vita was shocked.

Six months later she dropped in again and found the situation even more chaotic. There were "dust and cobwebs everywhere." The garden, Vita's pride and joy, had been allowed to go to weeds, and all the furniture, including a pair of heavy antique Dutch cupboards, had been shifted to other rooms.[4]

The Lindberghs' frequent flights to Europe, so puzzling to their landlady, involved a variety of errands. Charles had taken up the study of primates with the idea that monkeys would eventually be used as experimental subjects in Carrel's new institute. He was visiting primatology centers on the Continent, including the Château de Claires, near Rouen, where a colony of gibbons lived on an artificial island ringed by a moat.

In the spring of 1937, when Sackville-West found the servants so frantic about the impending arrival of Mrs. Morrow and Constance, Charles and Anne had been in Calcutta, attending the Religious Conference of All Faiths. Several noted yogis were speaking there, and Dr. Carrel had suggested that Charles might learn something of interest about hypnosis and the psychomystical aspects of suspended animation. Charles was intrigued by the yogis and quickly mastered the trick of stopping his pulse, which he accomplished by pressing a wadded-up handkerchief under his armpit, but he thought the conference a waste of time from the scientific point of view.

The Lindberghs flew to India in their new English-built plane, a Miles Mohawk, stopping along the way for sightseeing in Italy, Egypt, and Palestine, as well as in Tunis, where they met the Italian air marshal Balbo. Charles later described the airborne portion of the trip as so routine it was almost boring. Anne, six and a half months pregnant and increasingly anxious about flying and the lengthy separations from Jon, did not agree. Over the Alps the Mohawk was trapped above a fogbank, and Charles had to make a blind descent through the mist without the help of his autogyro, which conked out in the middle of the maneuver.

This frightening experience became the basis for Anne's novella, *The Steep Ascent*, published in 1943 but written mainly in 1938 and 1939. Eve, an American married to a British stunt pilot nicknamed "the Flying Fool," is (like Anne) pregnant and anguished over leaving her young son alone in England in order to join her husband in a danger-fraught flight across the Alps. "Why was she going on this trip?" Eve asks herself. "She certainly wasn't doing it out of wifely devotion. She wasn't that unselfish. No, she was doing it for herself, she had to admit, because of something very strong in herself. A feeling for life, she guessed it was."[5]

For Eve life is a precious "jewel" that can be obtained only if she pays the price of exposing herself to danger. One may wonder if this was not a rationalization.

Anne was certainly not unaware of the symbolism of her heroine's name: While they are lost in the fog, Eve points out a mountain that Gerald recognizes as a mirage, and she reflects, "She had handed him a poisoned apple. But he had not taken it." But Charles had indeed bitten into the poisoned apple of domesticity. Doing what he considered necessary to protect his family, he had given up his work and was growing more restless and disgruntled by the day. These long flights were his only escape, and Anne, who had been withdrawn and preoccupied for so long, was determined to accompany him. It was a completely unsatisfactory situation, but neither of them could think of a solution.

Until the summer of 1936, Germany, once the aviation capital of Europe, had been conspicuously absent from the Lindberghs' extensive travel itineraries. That May, however, a letter arrived from Maj. Truman Smith, the American military attaché in Berlin, asking Colonel Lindbergh whether he would accept an invitation from General Göring to inspect German civil and military air installations. "From a purely American point of view," Smith urged, "I consider that your visit here would be of high patriotic benefit."[6]

The Treaty of Versailles had dismantled the Kaiser's air corps, leaving the Weimar regime with an air force consisting of seventy-two officers but not a single plane of any description. For some years it had been an open secret that the German government was using the subsidized national airline, Luft Hansa, as a front for a military buildup, and by 1936, even this pretense had been dropped. Officers in Luftwaffe uniforms were much in evidence on the streets and at train stations, and new fields and airplane factories were being constructed across Germany. At the same time, Smith noted, Göring had recently shown signs of wanting to establish friendlier relations with the United States. The Luftwaffe was being rebuilt with American-made parts, including Pratt & Whitney engines, and the Germans wanted to reassure the American government that these purchases were not being used to construct long-range bombers capable of crossing the Atlantic.

Inspired by his wife, Kay, who had read an item in the Paris *Herald* about Lindbergh's tour of a French airplane factory, Major Smith decided that a visit by Lindbergh to Germany could tempt Göring into allowing Americans to see the Luftwaffe's most advanced aircraft. Smith had no expectations that Lindbergh would take an active role in spying on the Germans; he was to be escorted at all times by the American air attaché, Capt. Theodore Koenig, who would use this entrée to produce more reliable estimates of the Luftwaffe's strength.

In his letter to Colonel Lindbergh, Smith promised disingenuously that his visit would be carried out under conditions of "strictest censorship." Not a word of his presence in Berlin would appear in the world press. Lindbergh knew better. "I do not think it will be possible for me to come to Germany and go to various German air establishments without the fact being known," he replied. "However, I see no objection to that. What I am most anxious to avoid is the sensational and stupid publicity which we have so frequently encountered in the past." Charles added that Anne was also eager to visit Germany and would be coming along with him.[7]

As Lindbergh anticipated, by the time the visit was arranged, the German Air Ministry had negotiated a schedule of official functions, including an appearance by the Lindberghs in General Göring's box at the opening-day ceremonies of the summer Olympics in Berlin.

The Lindberghs' presence on this occasion, as guests of Göring, was met with dismay in the United States. Yet, surprising as it may seem in retrospect, the reaction to the Lindberghs' visit to Germany was by no means all negative, largely because of a widely reported speech he made to an audience of German officers at a luncheon at the Berlin Aero Club:

> We, who are in aviation, carry a heavy burden on our shoulders, for while we have been drawing the world closer in peace, we have stripped the armor from every nation in war.... Aviation has, I believe, created the most fundamental change ever made in war. It has turned defense into attack. We can no longer protect our families with an army. Our libraries, our museums, every institution we value most, are laid bare to bombardment. Aviation has brought a revolutionary change to a world already staggering from changes. It is our responsibility to make sure that in doing so, we do not destroy the very things we wish to protect.

These words were widely interpreted as a stern rebuke to the Germans. They were that and far more. Göring, eager to impress the American flyer, had arranged for Colonel Lindbergh to see the aeronautical

research institute at Adlershof, and the Heinkel and Junkers airplane factories, where Lindbergh examined the Germans' new design for a liquid-
cooled engine. He also became the first American to examine the JU 87
Stuka dive-bomber, which, Truman Smith now discovered, was already
in mass production. Although hardly uninformed about developments
in military aviation, Lindbergh had somehow continued to have faith in
the airplane as an instrument of peace. It may be that the undermining
of this faith had been a long, slow process, but it was the sight of Stuka
dive-bombers and his conversations with German aeronautical engineers
that brought his illusions crashing down around him. The airplane, the
machine to which he had devoted his adult life, was actually a weapon,
capable of raining down unprecedented destruction on civilian popula-
tions and the very centers of a nation's cultural life. Worse, the peace-
loving nations of Europe could not protect themselves by building traditional defenses. The ultimate defense against aerial bombardment was
retaliation. A horrible war was inevitable, and once European civilization had been reduced to rubble, Communism would sweep across the
Continent.

The depth of Lindbergh's disillusionment cannot be overstated.
The utopian dream had been replaced by a nightmare of the apocalypse.

Much to his confusion, however, Charles was not unimpressed by
the authors of this nightmare. He had loathed the Soviet Union during
his stop there on the North Atlantic tour, and, primed by staunchly
antifascist friends like Harold Nicolson and Aubrey Morgan, he arrived
in Berlin expecting to be equally repulsed. On the contrary, he found
much to admire in the industrious, efficient, and above all science-
minded Germans. Here were people who were lovers of nature, good
music, and hearty food, not unlike the German American farmers he
remembered from his Minnesota summers. This reaction was not at all
unusual. William Shirer, who was representing the Universal Press association in Berlin at the time, was close to despair over his discovery that
many, if not the majority, of American tourists he talked to were favor-
ably impressed by what they saw of the Third Reich. "The Nazis have
won the propaganda war," he wrote.[8]

Lindbergh, however, had another reason for liking Germany. In a
letter to Harry Davison, he described what a relief it was to visit a country where he was not hounded by reporters and photographers, and
how depressed he felt on returning to London where he was forced to
walk among "headlines of murder, rape and divorce on the billboards."[9]
This was the paradox: The Third Reich, a regime that was really about

death, seemed to Lindbergh a haven from the specters that haunted him.

The 1930s were a decade when many thinking people found refuge in such delusions. The United States was filled with intellectuals who persisted in believing that the Soviet Union was an egalitarian paradise, despite abundant evidence to the contrary. The opposite casuistry, while not unknown in the States, was far more popular in Europe: Hitler was the only strong leader on the European scene, and if a devil, at least he was our devil, dedicated to holding the line against the advance of Soviet Communism.

In his posthumously published *Autobiography of Values*, Lindbergh alludes to another rationalization that seemed attractive at the time: Stalin had slain his millions and his tens of millions. The crimes of the Nazis, up to that point, paled in comparison. Moreover, "Hitler would not live forever." During his German visit Lindbergh had little or no contact with politicians. He saw Göring but apparently did not converse with him at any length. He associated almost exclusively with scientists and Luftwaffe officers, many of whom viewed Hitler as a necessary evil at best. There were constant rumors, certainly known to Truman Smith, that when and if *Der Führer* went too far, he would be removed in a military coup, perhaps led by anti-Nazi officers, perhaps by Göring himself.

Lindbergh accepted these arguments so completely that in September 1936 he wrote Henry Breckinridge that he found the situation in Germany "encouraging ... rather than depressing." He actually called the German nation "a stabilizing factor" in the European situation.

Further, in a January 1937 letter to Harry Davison, he observed that Germany and Italy were "the two most virile nations in Europe," and while he disliked the Nazis' fanaticism, he also found in Germany "a sense of decency and values which is way ahead of our own."[10]

Nevertheless, Lindbergh returned to England after this visit convinced that Britain must commit itself to a crash program to build up its air force, the only defense should Germany turn its sights westward. In December 1936 Harold Nicolson arranged for Lindbergh to have lunch with Labour party leader Ramsay MacDonald and Sir Thomas Inskip, the minister of defence. Lindbergh, wrote Nicolson, was "charming and shy and full of information." Unfortunately, at least according to Nicolson, MacDonald's mind appeared to have taken a leave of absence, and he was apparently under the impression that he was talking to Winston Churchill's scientific adviser F. A. Lindemann.[11]

Nicolson believed that Inskip, at least, had listened to Lindbergh's message and been impressed. "Some good will come of it," he concluded. None did. Much to Lindbergh's disappointment, the only follow-up was a half-hearted invitation for him to lecture on navigation to a class of cadets.

It was not really true, as Lindbergh concluded, that the British were oblivious to the threat posed by German air power. In the latter part of 1936 and early 1937, the intelligence division of the British Air Ministry was developing its own sources of information about the Luftwaffe and was in the process of revising its estimates of Germany's air strength. Far from being complacent, the air intelligence analysts agreed with Lindbergh's somewhat inflated impression of the Luftwaffe's strength. The danger, in the minds of some policymakers, was that after underestimating German rearmament for too long, Britain would now panic and conclude that it was too late to oppose Hitler's escalating demands.

This was precisely what was happening to Lindbergh. At a banquet meeting of the "Ends of the Earth Club," he seethed with frustration as a former Air Ministry official lectured him, "Of course they [bombardiers] can't hit anything, you know. Nothing is ever hit with bombs. Why, look at the last war; they never hit what they were aiming at! Have you ever seen anyone come down in a parachute? They never land where they want to, you know. Too many cross currents in the air. It's the same way with a bomb." Another sentiment Lindbergh heard often, and which never failed to incense him, was "Our American cousins will always be behind us."[12]

TWENTY-TWO

Mission to Berlin

*F*ROM TRUMAN SMITH'S POINT OF VIEW, at least, the Lindberghs' German visit had been an outstanding success, so productive that he arranged similar tours for other American aviation experts, including Dr. Jerome Hunsaker of MIT, Igor Sikorsky, and Glenn Martin. However, these visitors could not match Lindbergh's celebrity status (or, to put it another way, his potential propaganda value for the Nazis) and none were given the same degree of access. In the fall of 1937, therefore, Smith asked the Lindberghs to return to Germany. The pretext for the visit was an invitation to attend the congress of the Lilienthal Aviation Society, held in Munich from October 12 through 16. Smith arranged for Charles and Anne to stay at Hohenschau Castle, a thirteenth-century fortress high in the Bavarian Alps, where their hosts were the Baron and Baroness Kramer-Klett, well known for their anti-Nazi views.

Lindbergh's second tour was even more productive than the first. As in 1936, he normally traveled with the American air attaché, and it was the attaché, not Lindbergh, who actually wrote up the reports that were forwarded to army intelligence. However, Lindbergh hit it off with Gen. Ernst Udet, the World War I ace, who was now a high official in the Air Ministry. Udet was an inept administrator and, by some accounts, a rather foolish man, addicted to mistresses and dinner parties. He was also one of the world's greatest pilots, famous for being able to pick a handkerchief off the ground with the tip of an airplane wing.

Moreover, like the Lindberghs, he had explored Greenland by air. Jimmy Doolittle, who also encountered Udet during a Truman Smith–sponsored tour of Luftwaffe facilities describes him as being utterly charming—fluent in English and a skilled caricaturist who amused his guests by drawing funny cartoons. According to Doolittle, Udet hated Göring and did a mean imitation of Hitler, ranting in a high-pitched voice while holding a pocket comb under his nose.[1]

At any rate, Udet invited Lindbergh to tour the top-secret Rechlin airfield in Pomerania. Lindbergh was told that he would not be permitted to bring his escort since he was going to be shown some planes that even the Italian air attaché had not yet seen. When he and Udet arrived, seven aircraft were lined up for inspection, including the Messerschmitt 109 fighter, the Heinkel 111 medium bomber, and the Dornier 17 bomber/reconnaissance plane. Lindbergh was allowed to sit in the cockpits of these planes, and to test-fly another new model, the Storch infantry-artillery liaison plane.

Major Smith guessed that Udet expected Lindbergh to be suitably impressed without picking up a significant amount of technical information. But Lindbergh made careful notes of his observations and later collaborated with the air attaché, Maj. Albert Vanaman, on a memorandum which began with what was, for the time, a startling pronouncement: "Germany is once again a power in the air." The Luftwaffe, the report estimated, had "*at least* 174 nine plane squadrons, each with three additional planes in reserve." German engineering was developing so rapidly that the two-year-old JU 86 bomber was already considered obsolete, and the new German factories—at least forty-six of them—had been designed to withstand air attacks.

As Smith later conceded, this memorandum stressed the strengths of the Luftwaffe and made no mention of its weaknesses, including the lack of long-range bombers and the inexperience and ineptitude of many German officers. It was frankly designed to shake up military intelligence experts in Washington, and apparently it did. In December 1937 the Lindberghs made a short, unpublicized visit to America, so that Charles could brief the National Committee for Aeronautics (NACA) on the status of European aviation.

His second stay in Germany strengthened Charles Lindbergh's "fascination" (his word) with Nazi Germany, which grew in inverse proportion to his unhappiness with Britain. "It is impossible for me to describe the frustration I felt in England," he later told an American friend. The British military establishment (unlike the Germans) ignored him. The culture, with its myriad class distinctions and worship of past grandeur, was depressing.

Anne, meanwhile, complained bitterly that she had not made a single friend since moving to Long Barn. In fact, she and Charles had been invited to embassy functions and private dinners, but she found that the people who were so cordial on these occasions looked right past her the next time their paths crossed. Considering that the Lindberghs' desire to be left alone had been front-page news in all the London papers, this was not surprising. Anne, like many shy people, found it difficult to imagine that others might find her aloof and intimidating. The Lindberghs did no entertaining of their own—Anne wrote some years later that she had never given a dinner party in her life; nor, it seems, did she make any effort to cultivate the friendship of the literary figures she admired from a distance. She waited for the people she wanted to know to seek her out, and when they did not, she felt snubbed.

Of course, Charles's views on the European situation were unlikely to endear him and Anne to the intellectual circles whose acceptance they longed for. In May 1938 the Lindberghs, along with Mrs. Morrow, who was visiting from New York, were invited to tea at Sissinghurst Castle, where Charles did his best to convince Harold Nicolson of the necessity of an alliance between Britain and Germany. Nicolson, dismayed, observed that Charles had bought the Nazi "theology" and been blinded by his hatred of "degeneracy," American democracy, and the press. Although Nicolson was given to hyperbole, the world *theology* was apt. It was the revolutionary ardor of the Third Reich, as opposed to the specifics of the Nazis' program, that appealed to Charles. As for the preoccupation with decadence that Nicolson and other British acquaintances found more and more dominant in Lindbergh's conversation, this was more Carrelist than Nazi, though the two schools of thought were so similar that Lindbergh himself was having difficulty sorting them out.

During the spring of 1938, the Lindberghs were somewhat belatedly taken up by Nancy Astor, an old friend of Anne's parents. A redoubtable hostess and wit, Lady Astor was in the habit of popping her false teeth out in midsentence. She launched the conversation at one luncheon attended by the Lindberghs and George Bernard Shaw by commanding her guests: "Now be quiet. I want to know why G.B.S. has turned into a fascist." Lady Astor took Anne shopping for clothes—not an easy errand, since for some reason Anne always felt guilty about spending on her wardrobe—and saw to it that the Lindberghs were invited out more often. The Astors' circle—older and ultraconservative—consisted mainly of those who believed that a negotiated peace with Germany was not only inevitable but perhaps actually desirable. Charles was influenced by this reasoning even as he grew more contemptuous of the attitude behind it.

Edward VIII had abdicated, and, through the Astors, the Lindberghs were invited to a ball at Buckingham Palace, where they met George VI. Anne wore a lavender taffeta gown and a paste necklace that had belonged to Elisabeth. Charles was coaxed into knee britches for the first and only time in his life, but when the queen asked him to waltz with her he demurred, saying, "Madame, I have never danced a step in my life." Her majesty graciously suggested that they sit out the dance together. With no cameras present, Anne, who normally stayed off the dance floor for fear of being photographed, had a grand time.

But the Lindberghs had already decided to abandon England. After visiting Dr. and Mrs. Carrel at their home on St. Gildas, a small island off the Côte du Nord, they had fallen in love with Brittany. The Carrels owned St. Gildas as well as a number of smaller islands, and the Lindberghs arranged to purchase one of them secretly. Tiny Illiec was a rocky tor almost entirely occupied by a three-story stone house built in the late nineteenth century by the composer Ambroise Thomas. At low tide it was possible to drive or hike across the causeway to the mainland; when the tide came in, forty feet high, one reached Illiec by boat. The island's only well produced brackish water, and the long-neglected house had no plumbing. Stained-glass windows kept the downstairs rooms gloomy even on the brightest days, and the furnishings consisted of a miscellaneous collection of oversize mahogany pieces and horsehair settees, imbued with the dust of decades.

"I think poor Anne dreads the idea of this desolate and rocky island," Sackville-West told her husband after bidding good-bye to the Lindberghs. "I wish you had seen the little notebook she produced for hints on seaside gardens!"[2]

Harold Nicolson's prediction that the domestic arrangements on Illiec were bound to be rather "hugger mugger" proved all too accurate. Anne wasn't used to managing servants—the Morrows had housekeepers to do that—and she was repeatedly surprised when they failed to anticipate the family's needs. The plasterers and painters hired to redecorate the house had destroyed the best furniture and left the grounds awash in plaster dust. Before the mess was straightened out, summer guests began arriving—Evangeline Lindbergh, the newly married Constance and Aubrey Morgan, and Dwight junior with his bride Margot. Anne had hung curtains in Evangeline's room, but the windows in the other bedrooms were bare, so everyone woke up at sunrise. She forgot to order extra milk and food and then was irritated with the cook, who was struggling unsuccessfully to produce edible meals in the antiquated kitchen with inadequate provisions. Soon after this nightmare house party, the cook caught pneumonia and departed and the English nursemaid gave notice. Nevertheless the Lindberghs seemed outwardly content with their Swiss Family Robinson existence. Charles went diving for abalone, holding a knife in his teeth like a pirate, and he called Illiec the only home he had really loved since the Camp in Little Falls.

In America *The Culture of Organs* had just been published, and Lindbergh and Carrel were featured on the cover of the June 13 issue of *Time*. But even as Lindbergh's scientific accomplishments were being hailed by the public, their future was in grave doubt, and Carrel was becoming desperate over his inability to coax Charles and Anne to return home. As a Catholic he saw their situation as a spiritual crisis, and since he could not imagine a rationalist like Charles accepting the Church of Rome, he invited James Newton, a young American who was an organizer for Moral Re-Armament, to St. Gildas. Newton talked earnestly about his decision to surrender his life to God. Lindbergh, in turn, lectured Newton on geopolitics, suggesting that if England and France did nothing, Germany and the Soviet Union might eventually destroy each other. Madame Carrel, meanwhile, sent her husband out to the garden to bury the silver.

In August the American military attaché in Moscow asked Colonel Lindbergh to make a tour of aviation facilities in Russia. Anne dreaded the trip but could not imagine staying behind. "I must go," she wrote. "I must be part of C's life."[3] The Soviets entertained the Lindberghs lavishly, with heavy banquets and heavier doses of propaganda. Endless multicourse meals only made Anne and Charles more acutely aware of the shabby goods in the stores and the sullen, cowed expressions of the people in the streets. A silent man in plain clothes followed them everywhere, and American diplomats warned that even the embassy was bugged. The state of Soviet aviation was a dismal contrast to what Charles had seen in Germany. One new Soviet aircraft engine, trotted out with much fanfare, proved to be a copy of the Wright Whirlwind that had carried him from New York to Paris in 1927—and not a good copy either. Describing the visit in a letter to his cousin Jerry Land, Lindbergh complained that it was impossible to walk across the floor of a Russian factory without tripping over discarded tools and parts. And, he added, "Russian life is as close to hell on earth as it is possible for human beings to come."[4]

Charles and Anne returned home via Prague, where the American military attaché, a Major Riley, took them on an auto tour of the Sudetenland, which Hitler was threatening to reclaim for the Reich. The party of three stayed overnight at the palace of Prince Clary Aldringen. Over dinner, the prince delivered an impromptu lecture on Russian history, tracing the use of secret police, terror, and purges back to the despotism of the czars. The rest of the dinner guests assured the Lindberghs that they were far more afraid of the Czech Communists than of the Germans.

Returning to Europe, the Lindberghs found France and England prepared to go to war over Czechoslovakia. On a visit to London, they saw commuters lining up in Piccadilly Station to be fitted for gas masks. Charles was convinced that it was already too late to stop the Reich's expansion across Central Europe. The time to stop Germany had been in 1936, he reiterated in his letters to his cousin Jerry Land.

Ambassador Joseph Kennedy had worked closely with Jerry Land on the National Maritime Commission before his appointment to the Court of St. James's, and no doubt was well aware of Lindbergh's views even before they met at the Astors' country home. On September 22 Kennedy invited the Lindberghs to lunch at the embassy and explained that he was hoping to get the president to urge Prime Minister Neville Chamberlain and French Premier Édouard Daladier to fly to Munich and negotiate a settlement. At the ambassador's request, Lindbergh prepared a long letter summarizing the state of the German aircraft industry. Among other daunting assessments, the letter estimated that Germany was capable of producing up to 20,000 planes a year. This figure was too high—two years later, in 1940, the Germans managed to produce only 10,826 planes—however, it was not out of line with figures accepted by American and French military observers.

Lindbergh's problem was not lack of information but his pessimism, which led him to put everything he read and saw in the worst possible light. If he did not actually hate America, he was certainly disgusted with it. Group Captain John Slessor of the British Air Ministry, who met with Lindbergh that week at Kennedy's request, concluded that he was "an extremely likable person, transparently honest and sincere." But unfortunately, Lindbergh's sense of the situation was skewed by his disillusionment: "In general, his attitude struck me as being entirely sympathetic to the British.... He has an enormous admiration for the Germans and likes them personally though he says there is much in their policy and method he cannot forgive. He dwelt especially on the magnificent spirit in Germany of refusal to admit that anything was impossible, or that any obstacle was too much to be overcome; he said that this was the spirit which had formerly prevailed in the United States, but he was very much afraid that we were losing it in that country."[5]

Almost as soon as he returned to France, Colonel Lindbergh was asked by Ambassador William C. Bullitt to join a group that was working on a plan to establish factories in Canada to assemble planes for the French Air Force using American-made parts. Lindbergh was not enthusiastic. He thought the plan impractical, and in any case the French government was so inept and the French people so "decadent" that the lack of war matériel was the least of their problems.

Before its first meeting was over, Bullitt's committee also concluded that setting up factories in Canada would take too long. The French needed the war planes now.

"Why not buy some bombers from Germany?" Lindbergh suggested.

Everybody laughed.

That night Lindbergh slept in the American Embassy, in the same bed he had used on the night after his transatlantic flight. Unable to rest, he began brooding over his little joke and decided that it wasn't so silly after all. Of course the Germans would never sell planes to France unless there was also some political realignment, but since he believed that Germany's ambitions lay to the east, at least in the immediate future, that might not be impossible.

A few days later, on October 11, Anne and Charles flew to Berlin in their Mohawk, ostensibly to attend a meeting of the Lilienthal Aviation Society but actually at the request of Truman Smith and the newly appointed American ambassador, Hugh R. Wilson. There was no compelling justification for this third visit. According to Major Smith, the Colonel was invited mainly because Ambassador Wilson wanted a chance to meet informally with Göring about the Jewish refugee situation and hoped to use Lindbergh's presence to lure the *Reichsmarschall* to a stag dinner. Despite some claims to the contrary, Lindbergh was not told the nature of the subject Wilson wanted to discuss.

Sixteen guests were invited to the ambassador's dinner, including

Göring and his deputies Gen. Erhard Milch and General Udet. Göring arrived carrying a small red box, headed straight for Lindbergh, and informed him that the Reich was presenting him with the Order of the German Eagle, a civilian decoration, in recognition of his 1927 transatlantic flight. Lindbergh, observed Truman Smith, did not understand the speech until it was translated for him and then looked "nonplussed." Smith later insisted that neither he nor Ambassador Wilson had known in advance of Göring's plan. In any event, other Americans, including Henry Ford, had accepted similar decorations, so they saw no reason why Lindbergh should refuse it. Nor, it must be said, did Lindbergh. It was the 171st medal he had received in eleven years, and to the end of his days he would insist that as far as he was concerned he had no reason to believe that Göring's motives were less than sincere. Anne, who understood that the American press would never overlook Lindy's acceptance of a German medal, took one glance at it and called it "the albatross."

As before, when in Berlin the Lindberghs stayed at the Smiths' apartment. They were the easiest houseguests in the world, since they were always closeted in their room writing. Charles, Smith recalled, "spent time with [Anne] each day, seeking to perfect still further her literary style." (According to Lindbergh, he would never have presumed to criticize Anne's style. Anne, he said, had no confidence when it came to writing about the technical aspects of flying, and asked for his help, which he gave.)[6]

Far from weaning Anne from her diary, Charles had begun one of his own. Intended as a record of a critical period in European history, Charles's journal also provides an inadvertent portrait of a mind adrift. "Life throughout the civilized world has become so complex that it is difficult to think clearly, even when time exists for thinking," he reminded himself in a typical entry, yet clarity of thought continued to elude him. Seized by a vision of Armageddon, yet perversely attracted to the spirit and aviation prowess of the nation responsible for the threat, he was by turns confused, resentful, and almost pathetically grateful for acquaintances like the Chinese author-philosopher Lin Yutang, who had the power to lift him temporarily from his depression.[7]

The apparent purposefulness of the Germans was a rebuke to the lack of purpose in his own life. On some level Lindbergh grasped that this was a problem, yet he prated on about his need for more free time and was angry with those who urged him to return home and commit himself to a job in aviation or science. Although he could never admit it,

Nazi aggression also spoke to a reservoir of rage within himself. At one point he noted in passing that Hitler must relish being in position to wreak revenge on the nations responsible for Germany's suffering—though surely, he would not be "insane" enough to do so. Incapable of looking within himself to consider the real reasons why Germany had tapped such powerful and contradictory emotions, he concluded that the solution lay in further "study" of the German situation.

Truman Smith, on his part, was far from unaware of the evils of Nazism. Smith had interviewed Hitler back in 1922 and reported to Washington then that his "Racialist Party" (as Smith called the National Socialists) was no better than an "anti-Semitic gang." But the major had fallen prey to the occupational disease of the area specialist. He had devoted a good part of his life to studying Germany, and the possibility that nothing could be done to avert war was difficult for him to accept. No doubt Smith was also a bit carried away by having the great Charles Lindbergh "at his beck and call," as he put it. The experience was such a heady one that Smith was a bit slow to realize that Lindbergh was off on a mental tangent of his own. He was taken aback when Charles announced that he was thinking of spending the winter in Berlin with Anne and the boys so that he could further his "study" of the German scene. This was a decidedly bad idea, but Smith was about to learn that Lindbergh was a loose cannon, easy to set in motion but hard to control.

On October 13, at a private dinner party, Anne found herself sitting next to Prince Kinsky, the president of the Austrian Aero Club, who launched into a vicious tirade against the Jews. Previously, the Lindberghs' Nazi hosts had made sure they were insulated from this kind of talk, and the experience left Anne badly shaken. Still, she continued to inspect schools and houses, including one in a village which had posted a large sign on the road into town: Jews Not Wanted Here. Another house that she and Charles saw together was large and spacious, with lovely grounds, but, Lindbergh noted in his journal, there was "something strange" about the deal. The owners were abroad and wanted to be paid in foreign currency, and Colonel Wendland of the German Air Ministry said that rather than have the Lindberghs live there, Albert Speer would be pleased to build them a house on any site they chose. (The house the Lindberghs had seen belonged to a Jewish family that had emigrated, and the Nazis obviously did not want the Lindberghs living in a "Jewish" house.)

On October 29 Charles and Anne returned to Paris by train. Bad weather had forced them to leave the Mohawk in Berlin, and they planned to return for it when Colonel Wendland notified them that he had found more houses for them to inspect. A week later Germany exploded in the staged anti-Jewish riots of *Kristallnacht*, and on November 11 Lindbergh telephoned Major Smith from Paris to tell him that under the circumstances he was no longer considering bringing his family to Berlin.

Ironically, the criticism of Colonel Lindbergh in the press up to this time was not that he was pro-German but that he was anti-Soviet. The Stalinist journalist Claud Cockburn, writing in the British publication *The Week,* had made a virtual career of depicting Lord and Lady Astor's circle, the so-called Cliveden set, as a nest of traitors, and in one of these attacks Cockburn described a conversation at Cliveden in which Lindbergh had mocked the Soviet Air Force. The conversation had never taken place but was close enough to Lindbergh's true opinions, and he declined to issue a denial. This led to an attack on Lindbergh in *Pravda,* in the form of an open letter signed by eleven high-ranking military pilots. Following the *Pravda* attack, denouncing Lindbergh quickly became almost a cottage industry among American Communists and their sympathizers. Few journalists in the United States had any illusions about Hitler, but there were many who still romanticized Stalin as "Uncle Joe." Even in the mainstream press, the suggestion that the Soviet Air Force was vastly inferior to the Luftwaffe was viewed as outrageous, and, amazingly in retrospect, few publications questioned the credibility of the airmen's letter.

But the news of Lindbergh's acceptance of a medal from Göring, closely followed by reports that he and his family planned to live in Germany over the winter, provoked criticism of another order entirely. Even the couple's closest friends were shocked. Anne had returned to Illiec alone, leaving Charles behind in Paris, and had no idea how to reply to the wires and letters of protest that were pouring in. Dr. Carrel, who despite his flirtation with intellectual fascism, was a Frenchman after all and hated the Nazis, was now back at Rockefeller University and sent the Lindberghs a clipping from *The New Yorker* that summed up the reaction in the States: "With confused emotions we say goodbye to Colonel Charles A. Lindbergh, who wants to go and live in Berlin, presumably occupying a house that once belonged to Jews.... If he wants to experiment further with the artificial heart, his surroundings there should be ideal." Similar sentiments were expressed by political cartoonists who depicted Lindbergh wearing a medal in the form of a swastika-decorated heart.

In keeping with their policy of never explaining themselves to the press, the Lindberghs issued no statement saying that they had decided not to move to Berlin after all. Charles later told Carrel that he had changed his plans because he did not wish to give the impression that he approved of the events of November 9. However the public never heard this.

Charles, meanwhile, still had to return to Berlin to retrieve the Mohawk. Before he left he was summoned to a meeting with French Air Minister Guy la Chambre, who said that after some thought the French government had decided that it wanted to pursue the idea of buying airplane engines—as opposed to finished planes—from Germany. Lindbergh had already had second thoughts about this notion, and since he took it for granted that the deal would be a stalking horse for a political alliance, he was amazed that la Chambre was interested. Fifty years later one is still amazed. Perhaps la Chambre simply wanted to see how far the Nazis would go to impress Lindbergh. Possibly the mission was planned to keep them guessing as to France's true position.

Returning to Berlin by train, he called on Ernst Udet. The walls of Udet's apartment were literally covered with medals, mementos, pinup pictures, and hunting trophies, including an enormous stuffed rhinoceros head. Udet set up a small target box in the living room and challenged his guest to a shooting contest with a .22-caliber rifle. Lindbergh was a little nervous—an errant shot would have wreaked havoc on the garish display mounted on the wall behind the target box. Nevertheless he took up the challenge and fired away.

The following afternoon Göring's deputy, General Milch, assured Lindbergh that neither his boss nor Hitler was responsible for the anti-Jewish riots. (Lindbergh interpreted this to mean that Goebbels and Himmler had organized them without Hitler's approval.) Milch also suggested that the sale of airplane engines to France might be arranged after Christmas.

Lindbergh returned secretly to Berlin in January and was informed that the sale of Daimler Benz 1,250-horsepower engines to the French had been approved. He carried this message back to la Chambre, who told him he would be turning over the negotiations to the French air attaché in Berlin, Paul Stehlin. Udet was drunk, as usual, when Stehlin raised the subject with him, and he laughed uproariously. "I realized that the Germans had been bluffing all along," Stehlin later said. "They were amazed that Colonel Lindbergh had fallen for the idea." Stehlin added that when he returned to Paris and described Udet's reaction, Lindbergh was "quite angry and flared up at me."[8]

In his memoir, *Berlin Alert,* Truman Smith gives a different account of the collapse of the deal. According to Smith, la Chambre later told Lindbergh that he and Daladier had been quite serious about purchasing the Daimler engines but were overruled by the French Foreign Office. Smith also mentions a 1956 comment by Gen. Friedrich Hanesse, who recalled that Göring had indeed approved the negotiations with the French, but without consulting Hitler, who never would have allowed such an arrangement.

Whatever the truth may have been, Lindbergh was far over his head in the world of secret diplomacy. When, shortly before his final trip to Berlin, the Paris *Herald* ran a story headlined, LINDBERGH REPORTED PROVIDING U.S. WITH DATA ON REICH AIR FORCE, he was grievously offended by the implication that he was a spy, which he considered a slur on his honor. Lindbergh actually apologized for the story to Milch and Udet, giving them his personal assurance that he had never passed on military secrets. For all his "study" of the German situation, the essential point—that Hitler was a fanatic—had escaped Lindbergh's notice. The concept of honor was dead in Germany, as was, for that matter, rationality. (No wonder Udet laughed when discussing the engine negotiations with Stehlin!)

Complicating the situation was the experience of Dwight Morrow, Sr.'s, old friend George Rublee, who had been appointed by President Roosevelt to head the Inter-Governmental Refugee Committee. Rublee's mission was to negotiate a mass emigration of German Jews, who would be resettled in North America and in colonies in British Guiana, the Philippines, Tanganyika, and elsewhere.[9] Rublee and his wife Juliet were in Berlin when Lindbergh was there in January, and Charles warmly recommended his old family friend to General Milch and Udet. Shortly after Lindbergh departed, Rublee was told that the Reich was prepared to free 150,000 Jewish workers and their dependents in return for a cash indemnity. Further releases would follow until even the camps were emptied. No reason was given for this abrupt change in policy, but rumor had it that Göring was behind the plan. Elated, Rublee returned to London, only to run into a wall of hostility. British and U.S. officials were suspicious. Countries that had previously expressed a willingness to take part in the plan balked when they heard the numbers involved. Even Jewish philanthropists had second thoughts about the morality of paying the Reich to expel its own people. By late spring it was obvious that the plan would fail, and Nazi propaganda organs gleefully pointed out that the nations who criticized them didn't want the Jews either. It may be that the offer was a propaganda ploy from the beginning, but Rublee thought the Germans were serious and suspected that the Roosevelt administration and the British wanted war and therefore did not wish the plan to succeed. Lindbergh's journals do not comment on the collapse of the Refugee Committee's efforts, but Rublee's conclusions probably had much to do with his own suspicion that Roosevelt was maneuvering the world to the brink of war.

Since Illiec was uninhabitable during the coldest part of the winter, the Lindberghs were living temporarily in Paris. On a rare night out at the Tour d'Argent restaurant they were recognized by a party of Americans at an adjoining table who immediately fell into a loud argument over Hauptmann's guilt or innocence. Anne was upset ("Why can't we shrink down into ourselves and live our own little inconspicuous lives like these people?" she wondered unrealistically).[10] And Charles was frustrated and helpless over his inability to protect her from such experiences. To say anything to these people would have only created a scene in which he would come out in the wrong. The incident reinforced his anxiety about returning home, but with war on the horizon there appeared to be no alternative.

Less understandably the Lindberghs felt that the criticism of their visits to Berlin in the American press was irresponsible and unjustified. Anne in particular was stung by the *New Yorker* item, which she thought quite inaccurate—though, it would seem, the editors' speculation about the Lindberghs' house hunting had come awfully close to the mark. Charles wrote Henry Breckinridge complaining of the unfairness of the press and was stunned when Breckinridge replied that while some things that had been printed were unfair, there were other factors the newspapers weren't aware of. On balance, he thought the press had it about right.

While debating their next move, the Lindberghs were taking advantage of their sojourn in Paris to visit the galleries, and Anne had decided to have a portrait head modeled by the sculptor Charles Despiau. Modern art—like so many other things in their environment those days—disturbed them, especially some paintings by Dalí, which struck Charles as proof that the world was going mad. He was interested in the techniques of bronze casting, however, and struck up an acquaintance with the American sculptor Jo Davidson, who suggested that while Anne was sitting for Despiau he would like to do a portrait head of Charles.

Lindbergh liked Davidson very much, but when the sculptor persisted in denouncing the Munich agreement and ventured the opinion that totalitarianism might yet be defeated, he was irate and close to despair. The trouble with people like Davidson and Lin Yutang, he wrote in his journal, was that they insisted on living in a sort of "Platonic Utopia of their own." He, on the other hand, was a realist.

Davidson had a different analysis. "Your problem," he told Charles, "is that you always see and talk to the wrong people."

This was true enough, but the question was, Why?

It is impossible to read the Lindberghs' writings of this period without empathizing with their intense horror of war and violence and their frustration with acquaintances who insisted that the only rational response to the Nazis was all-out war. Still, Davidson, who had made up his mind that Hitler must be opposed at all costs, was the true realist. The Lindberghs' own attitude toward the Reich at this point was not so much conscious admiration (or even, on Anne's part, unconscious) but moral and psychological surrender. Their thinking was like that of hostages who come to identify with their captors while expressing suspicion and hostility toward the loved ones who have failed to rescue them. Charles had managed to convince himself that through talking nicely to the Nazi leaders and offering them a free hand in the East, they could be placated into leaving Western Europe alone. When he wrote of "studying" the German situation, what he really meant was internalizing the Nazi worldview to a point where he could mentally justify coexistence. If it hadn't been for the anti-Jewish riots of November 9, it seems likely that he would actually have gone through with his plan to move his family to Berlin, thus creating a situation in which he, Anne, and their children would, in fact, have been hostages. Once the Nazis had the Lindberghs under their physical control, it is difficult to imagine that they would have allowed such a propaganda bonanza to slip away from them.

Tempting as it is to ascribe the Lindberghs' state of mind to the traumatic aftereffects of the kidnapping and the Hauptmann trial, one can't help observing that in Charles's case, it was a continuation of a long-established pattern: Brought up under the influence of a father who believed that the Morgan bank was at the center of an antidemocratic conspiracy, Charles had wed the daughter of a Morgan partner— his first and only sweetheart—and proceeded to spend much of his married life residing, quite unhappily, in his in-laws' home. Convinced that his firstborn child had been kidnapped by gangsters, he promptly allowed the gangster Mickey Rosner to sleep under his roof and issue orders to his wife and his servants. He had never permitted himself a single expression of anger toward the man who was accused and convicted of killing his son. On the contrary, although Hauptmann had been a German, and the movement to exonerate him had been sponsored and financed by American Nazis, Lindbergh felt—almost from the moment he first set foot on German soil—a bewildering affinity for the Nazi regime.

Jo Davidson, who had known Charles Lindbergh for only a few days, diagnosed his problem as a surfeit of bad influences. Dr. Carrel, distraught over the effect of his own philosophical preoccupations on his friends the Lindberghs, saw them as suffering from a spiritual malaise that only God could cure. Harold Nicolson, a man not given to employing religious metaphors, complained that Charles had been converted to the Nazi "theology"—a word chosen advisedly in preference to *politics* or *ideology*. In the United States, meanwhile, apprehension over reports of the Lone Eagle's visits to Germany was mixed with the realization that he might still be a potent political force. Just as in 1927, the president of the United States had decided it was time to bring Charles Lindbergh home.

TWENTY-THREE

"America First"

*J*OE KENNEDY'S APPOINTMENT as ambassador to Great Britain meant that his former assistant commissioner Jerry Land had taken over his post as chairman of the National Maritime Council. Land's new job brought him into frequent contact with the president, who kept wanting to know what was going on with his cousin Lindbergh. Was there any danger that he would give up his American citizenship?

Land and Slim wrote each other fairly often—there was a long correspondence over an heirloom baby present that the admiral sent to his namesake Land Lindbergh—and Slim's views on the situation in Europe were invariably informative and reasonable in tone. It was on this basis that Land had helped arrange for Lindbergh to return to the United States to give a briefing to NACA in December 1937. By the summer of 1938, however, there appears to have been a question in Land's mind as to whether his cousin was quite well. Lindbergh's appointment to NACA was scheduled to expire in August, and Roosevelt asked Land on several occasions whether he should renew it. Was Lindbergh coming home? And if so, when? Land told Roosevelt to go ahead and sign the reappointment. "You may think I am assuming a lot," he wrote Charles, "but I felt it was essential for the interest of aviation."[1]

When Lindbergh still did not return, Roosevelt sent word through Juan Trippe that he was prepared to offer him the post of head of the Civil Aeronautics Administration (CAA). Lindbergh wasn't interested, but having accepted the NACA reappointment, he could hardly refuse when General H. H. ("Hap") Arnold, chief of the Army Air Corps, asked him to return to the States for a brief tour of active duty. Arnold's summons was undoubtedly arranged in consultation with Land, who wrote his family expressing satisfaction that he was finally getting Slim and the president to work together.

In April Charles booked passage on the liner *Aquitania;* among his fellow passengers were his new friends, Lin Yutang and his wife. The press had learned of Lindbergh's travel plans, and at least two hundred reporters and photographers were assigned to meet the ship when it docked in New York. Alexis Carrel, who knew Charles's state of mind better than anyone, was so apprehensive that he wrote to Secretary of the Treasury Henry Morgenthau, asking Morgenthau to arrange for himself and Madame Carrel to board the *Aquitania* before she cleared customs so that they could confer with Colonel Lindbergh "about important matters." Carrel didn't explain what was so important that it couldn't wait until the ship docked, but the obvious inference is that he was worried about what Lindbergh might say in the presence of so many reporters.[2]

With Morgenthau's help, Carrel, his wife, and Jim Newton were able to take a tug belonging to the chief of the Port of New York out to the ship. They were talking with Lindbergh in his cabin, waiting for the other passengers to disembark, when a *Daily Mirror* photographer broke down the door from an adjoining cabin and snapped their picture. (Ironically the editors of the *Mirror* subsequently failed to recognize the Carrels, who were identified only as "fellow passengers.") Minutes later the party stepped out into the corridor into a blaze of flashbulbs and fought their way down the gangplank behind a wedge of policemen. Carrel and Newton were lost in the crush. Madame Carrel was on the verge of fainting when Aubrey Morgan, who had been waiting on the dock, managed to shove her into a taxi.[3]

Lindbergh had come to view such occasions as a form of legalized assault and described the scene as both "ridiculous" and "barbaric." Although his attitude toward the press now approached paranoia, his anger on this occasion was hardly unjustified. In order to avoid an even-more-tumultuous scene he had been forced to leave Anne and the children in France, to follow on a later ship. Even so, when the family arrived in May, Arthur Springer was advised by the police to hire private security guards to help them get safely ashore.

Despite criticism of his acceptance of a medal from Göring, Charles

Lindbergh was still a hero. On the train to Washington, where he was to confer with General Arnold, high school students headed to the capital for spring field trips lined up outside his compartment door hoping to get his autograph. Republican leaders monitored such developments with interest, no doubt recalling his success in mobilizing opposition to Roosevelt during the airmail controversy of 1934.

At the first NACA meeting he attended, the Washington press corps sent a representative begging Colonel Lindbergh to pose for just one picture, promising, "on their word of honor," to leave him alone after that. He indignantly refused. "Imagine," he wrote in his diary. "The type of men who broke through the window in the Trenton morgue to open my baby's casket and photograph his body—they talk to me of honor."[4]

Lindbergh was still deeply depressed over what he saw as his inability to protect his family from harassment, and the talk of war was almost physically oppressive. However, his state of mind was only intermittently apparent to those around him. Jerry Land, with whom Lindbergh was staying in Washington, reported to his sister (whom he addressed in annoying Landish fashion as "Sister") that Slim looked and sounded awfully well. General Arnold apparently thought so, too, and promptly appointed Lindbergh to a committee that was studying the reorganization of NACA, as well as to the Kilner Board, which was to create a five-year plan for the development of new aircraft weapons and equipment. In addition Lindbergh began traveling to army and navy air bases around the country, briefing officers on the state of military aviation in Europe.

During his presentation to NACA the previous December, Lindbergh had urged the rapid expansion and modernization of American military aviation. This was what General Arnold and other senior officers of the Army Air Corps had been advocating for years, and now, for the first time since World War I, Congress and the president were prepared to listen. Lindbergh was in many respects ideally suited to play a leading role in this revitalization. He had a grasp of the technical issues and up-to-date information. His popularity would help convince the public to make the necessary sacrifices, and he had clout with the conservative wing of the Republican party, which was likely to oppose increased appropriations. Arnold told Lindbergh that the vice-chairmanship of NACA was his for the asking. A more prestigious title, he hinted, could be arranged. Lindbergh was in a position to dictate his terms.

His reaction was panic. The vice-chairmanship, Lindbergh noted in his journal, would commit him to a demanding schedule, frequent meetings, and constant travel. When would he think? When would he write in his diary? Although others seemed to cope with the stress that went along with such jobs, he couldn't imagine how they did it. His mind, he complained, was like a "spinning projectile" that did not change directions easily.

"Do you mind if I ask you a personal question?" asked the perplexed General Arnold. "What are you shooting at?" Lindbergh replied that he wasn't shooting at anything. He was just trying to take life as it came.

Rockefeller University, meanwhile, had notified Dr. Carrel that his laboratory would be closed down in July, and Lindbergh had decided that Highfields, his and Anne's former estate in Hopewell, would make an ideal site for Carrel's institute. This was contrary to the spirit of the deed of gift, which stipulated that the house would become a children's home, but apparently Lindbergh had begun discussing the change of plan with New Jersey authorities as early as 1935, at which time they were not unreceptive. Carrel was in correspondence with the New Jersey Board of Institutions and Agencies, which administered the property, and in March of that year its assistant chief E. P. Earle wrote Carrel asking, "When are you and Col. Lindbergh going to Vineland (a state mental institution) with Commissioner Ellis and me to look over some of our feeble-minded 'prospects'?" There followed a discussion of the relative merits of insulin-shock therapy and the drug xanthine. Since Carrel had neither seen patients nor worked with human research subjects for many years, and his field of specialization was completely unrelated to mental illness, the letter raises the question of what these patients were "prospects" for.[5] (For some time Lindbergh had expressed interest in moving on to experiments with hypothermia and whole-body perfusion—maintaining the blood circulation artificially in order to perform open-heart surgery, for example—but his discussions with various experts reflect his expectation that the research would be conducted with monkeys or apes.)

Whatever Carrel and Lindbergh had in mind, it was no doubt less bizarre by several orders of magnitude than the rumors that occasionally cropped up in the tabloids and popular press. There was talk that Carrel planned to experiment with whole-organ transplants. Carried away with the science-fiction implications of this idea, several magazine articles speculated about the development of a "Carrel-Lindbergh Robot"—a bionic man patched together from the organs of a number of human subjects. Carrel's files contain numerous letters from individuals, some pathetically sincere, volunteering themselves as human guinea pigs.

No doubt in reaction to such rumors, Lindbergh asked Carrel not to mention his name publicly in connection with the institute. However, a revised prospectus for the laboratory, now renamed the "Highfields Center for the Science of Man," promised potential donors that both Carrel and Colonel Lindbergh would devote a "substantial proportion" of their time to the center's work, which would specialize in virology and tissue-culture studies—work that "must be exclusively scientific, basing its proceeds and conclusions on observable data."[6] Jim Newton's attempts to raise funds on the basis of this proposal came to nothing, as did talks with other institutions such as the Kellogg's Battle Creek Sanitarium in Michigan. Lindbergh blamed the situation on the imminent possibility of war; donors, he noted, were reluctant to commit themselves to new projects. But unease over Carrel's—and, perhaps more to the point, Lindbergh's—political and philosophical views surely played a role in scaring off sponsors.

In May Anne and the boys arrived from France, taking up residence in a rented house in Lloyd Neck, a picturesque enclave on the North Shore of Long Island. Charles spent weekends with his family, swimming with Jon in Long Island Sound or at the local club pool and working on his oil paintings, a hobby that had replaced photography as his favorite means of relaxation.

Among the guests at Lloyd Neck that summer were Dwight junior and his wife Margot, who were about to depart on a six-month cruise, retracing the routes of Columbus with naval historian Professor Samuel Eliot Morison. Another visitor was the French aviator-poet Antoine de St.-Exupéry. "St. Ex," as Anne called him, was a fascinating conversationalist but spoke only French, which tended to exclude Charles from the conversation. Anne's attraction to the dashing Frenchman was so obvious that Charles told her he was jealous; he felt compelled to reassure himself in his diary that Anne and St.-Exupéry had spent not much more than half an hour alone together. His jealousy was not entirely irrational. Anne never saw "St. Ex" again, but she read her children *The Little Prince* and spoke of its author so often and so reverently that Jon wondered if "St. Ex." was a saint, like Saint John and Saint Peter.

A third visitor at the house quite frequently was the Carrels' friend Jim Newton. A former personal assistant to Harvey Firestone, founder of the Firestone Tire and Rubber Company, Newton was experienced in making himself useful to busy people and soon became part of the family circle. As he had in 1927, Lindbergh found release from his stressful situation in practical jokes. An avid amateur magician, Newton had mastered the trick of holding a lighted candle in his mouth for thirty seconds. While demonstrating this feat at Lloyd Neck, he dripped wax on his trousers, and Lindbergh talked him into removing them so the children's nursemaid could iron the wax off. Newton stepped into a closet under the staircase to wait for his pants to be returned. Minutes later the door opened a crack. Charles had located a teargas gun, given him years before by a British naval officer in China, and he fired a round onto the closet floor. Gasping for breath, Newton exploded out of the closet and sprinted, trouserless, through the house, much to the alarm of the nursemaid. Anne, it seems, took such carryings-on in stride and remained quite fond of Newton.[7]

Newton, however, was having little success interesting Charles in Moral Re-Armament. Although he thought MRA attracted "a fine type" of person (nondrinking and anti-Communist), Charles was put off by the MRA activists' blinding enthusiasm for the cause. For that matter, he couldn't quite figure out what the cause was. The MRAers appeared to believe that goodwill and positive thinking would solve all the world's problems. Newton arranged for Charles to meet a pair of leading MRA organizers, who explained the approach of their leader, Frank Buchman, to the troubled international situation. In a series of radio broadcasts here and abroad, Buchman was attempting to enlist a hundred million people who would promise to submit to God's will in international affairs.

Lindbergh was spending most of the week in Washington, and on August 23 he was invited to have dinner with William Castle, a former ambassador to Japan who had assisted him and Anne in planning their 1931 Great Circle flight. An assistant to the chairman of the Republican National Committee, Castle clung to the belief that Hitler's ambitions did not extend beyond territories occupied by ethnic Germans. When Lindbergh showed up at Castle's house he found another guest already present—Fulton Lewis, Jr., the Hearst columnist and broadcaster who had been his chief antagonist during the airmail crisis of 1934. Over dinner Lewis complained that "Jewish advertising firms" had threatened to boycott his radio show unless one of his commentaries was pulled from the air. Although polls consistently showed that 85 percent of Americans opposed involvement in any European war, Lewis complained, the national media were dominated by propaganda for the other side. Lewis suggested that Lindbergh was the one spokesman capable of representing the majority who favored nonintervention in the European situation.

In complaining about the media's pro-war bias, Lewis undoubtedly had in mind the very influential Walter Winchell, whose almost-daily attacks on Nazism and the German American Bunds had been, ironically enough, inspired by his outrage over the anti-Semitic character of the Hauptmann defense campaign. In hindsight Winchell's vocal anti-Nazism was the exception. Certainly the moving-picture industry, about which Lewis also complained, had been rather timid about dealing with the subject. (In 1934, following a visit to Germany, Irving Thalberg assured a group of Jewish film producers that the best policy was silence: "Hitler and Hitlerism will pass: the Jews will still be there."[8]) The mood of the media began to change dramatically only in 1939, when Warner Brothers' *Confessions of a Nazi Spy,* released with some trepidation lest it inspire an anti-Semitic backlash, was a tremendous popular success.

Uneasy about Lewis's penchant for blaming the Jews, Lindbergh nonetheless agreed that the American public was hearing only one side of the story. Commentators urging England and France to declare war on Germany failed to make clear that the military situation of the democracies was "hopeless." Even if the United States became involved, Lindbergh thought, a European war would probably end with a negotiated peace.

On September 1 the Wehrmacht swept into Poland, and England and France responded by declaring war. Two weeks later, on September 15, Lindbergh attended a meeting of the NACA special committee. Jerome Hunsaker pleaded with him to change his mind and accept the vice-chairmanship. Lindbergh testily turned him down. "They all seem to feel that because I have kept myself clear of the obligations... that they have tied themselves up with," he groused in his journal, "I am available to carry on whatever problems they feel need attention. ... How little people realize the necessity of keeping free time to think and to live!"

The importance of leisure time was not foremost in the minds of the NACA committee members at this juncture. Perplexed by Lindbergh's insistence that he was unable to devote himself full-time to NACA business, they suspected him of having other plans, possibly including a run for the presidency.[9]

Indeed, Lindbergh had already decided to take up Lewis's suggestion that he make a radio broadcast, which was scheduled for that very evening. Lewis's grumblings about bias to the contrary, all three major radio networks—Mutual, NBC, and Columbia—had decided to carry Lindbergh's talk.

Following the NACA meeting, Charles went back to his Washington *pied-à-terre*. While he was having lunch with Anne and Jim Newton, Truman Smith, now attached to the Military Intelligence Division (MID) of the Department of War, showed up with an urgent message, passed down through Secretary of War Woodring and General Arnold: If Lindbergh would desist from attacking the administration, the president was prepared to create a separate department of the air force and name him secretary. "So you see, they're worried," Smith crowed.[10]

Needless to say this was a strange way for the president to deliver such an important message. One can only assume that Roosevelt was just fishing. He did not expect Lindbergh to accept and wanted to be in a position to deny the offer was ever made.

That evening Americans gathered in front of their radios with excitement and anticipation. Lindy, whose 1927 speech at the Washington Monument had been the highlight of the first nationwide radio broadcast in America's history, had not addressed the public—except involuntarily through newsreel footage—since.

Breaking his silence after twelve years, he began:

> I speak tonight to those people in the United States of America who feel that the destiny of this country does not call for our involvement in European wars.... This country was colonized by men and women from Europe. The hatreds, the persecutions, the intrigues they left behind, gave them courage to cross the Atlantic Ocean to a new land. They preferred the wilderness to the problems of Europe. They weighted the cost of freedom from those problems and they paid the price. In this country, they eventually found a means of living peacefully together—the same nationalities that are fighting in Europe today.

Lindbergh went on to say that he was not a strict isolationist. He believed in the Monroe Doctrine, and if the Americas were attacked, he would fight. But, he warned, any departure from strict neutrality with respect to Europe would result in the United States being dragged into a conflict that would require the sacrifice of "a million men, possibly several million—the best of American youth."

Jerry Land had seen the text of this speech before the broadcast and managed to convince himself that Slim's and the president's positions were not so very far apart. His wife Betty—aware of Lindbergh's habit of letting his mail go unread—volunteered to go through the letters and telegrams that came pouring in over the next few days and reported that they were 95 percent favorable. On September 25, however, Admiral Land was present at a stag dinner at the Mayflower Hotel. Among the other guests were Postmaster General Jim Farley, the president's secretary Stephen Early, and several Democratic senators. Land was surprised to hear Early denounce Lindbergh's speech as a Republican plot. He was even more upset when several journalists told him that they considered the speech pro-Nazi and anti-Jewish.

Early was surely correct in thinking that William Castle, Fulton Lewis, and Truman Smith had urged Lindbergh to go on the radio in the hope that he would emerge as a potential opponent to Roosevelt, who would be running for an unprecedented third term in 1940. In the immediate aftermath of the speech, Lindbergh was aggressively courted by the Republican party's elder statesmen as well as anti-interventionist southern Democrats. Senator Harry Byrd (brother of Dick Byrd) invited Lindbergh to lunch in order to introduce him to Vice President John Nance Garner, and on another occasion Byrd arranged for Lindbergh to meet with seven Democratic congressmen who were considering breaking with the administration on the issue of aid for Britain. Senator William Borah, the rock-ribbed isolationist Republican from Idaho, asked Lindbergh to his congressional office to sound him out on the possibility of his running for president on the Republican ticket. Ex-president Herbert Hoover, Bill Castle, and several other conservative Republicans also raised the issue of a presidential race over lunch at the Harvard Club.

Hoover's luncheon group, however, wanted some assurances. Elements in Lindbergh's radio speech disturbed them. Surely they were referring to a passage that a number of editorials had singled out as objectionable:

There is no Genghis Khan or Xerxes marching against our Western nations. This is not a question of our banding together to defend the white race against foreign invasion. This is simply one more of those age old struggles within our family of nations—a quarrel arising from the errors of the last war.... We must not permit our sentiment, our pity, or our personal feelings of sympathy, to obscure the issue, to affect our children's lives. We must be as impersonal as the surgeon with his knife ... the gift of civilized life must still be carried on. It is more important than the sympathies, the friendships, the desires of a single generation.

Well, plenty of people thought there *was* a "Genghis Khan" loose in Europe. Neutrality toward Nazi Germany was simply not a viable position for a leader of either party. And what, exactly, did Lindbergh mean by his surgery simile? The luncheon ended with Lindbergh huffily declaring that he refused to compromise his views to accommodate politicians, Democratic or Republican.[11]

In subsequent radio speeches, Lindbergh made it clear that he was opposed not just to entering the war but to military aid for Britain. Moreover, he saw no great moral difference between the Axis powers and the Allies. Although the Germans were the aggressors, and guilty of many crimes, they were themselves the victims of the punitive Treaty of Versailles. Britain certainly wasn't in the war to champion the cause of humanity, but because it wanted to hold on to its own empire.

Jim Newton had a friend who was an editor at *Reader's Digest,* and he had arranged for both Carrel and Lindbergh to contribute articles. Carrel wrote on health topics—his first *Digest* piece advocated breast-feeding. Lindbergh's contribution was "Aviation, Race and Geography," which appeared in the November 1939 issue. Aviation, he wrote, was both the crowning achievement of Western civilization and a symbol of its overweening vanity—"man flung upward in the face of God; another Icarus to dominate the sky":

> It is a tool specially shaped for Western hands, a scientific art which others only copy in a mediocre fashion, another barrier between the teeming millions of Asia and the Grecian inheritance of Europe, one of those priceless possessions which permit the White race to live at all in a pressing sea of Yellow, Black and Brown.

But even for the white race, aviation and technology in general also had their dark sides—degradation of the environment, flabby children, "physical and spiritual mediocrity," and now, "terrible weapons of destruction." Just as Athens and Sparta had quarreled while the Persians marched: "while we stand poised for battle, Oriental guns are turning westward, Asia presses toward us on the Russian border, all foreign races stir restlessly. It is time to turn from our quarrels and build the White ramparts again."

* * *

This stew of Social Darwinist clichés was more shocking to Lindbergh's friends and admirers than anything he said in his radio speeches. What had become of the man who once predicted that aviation would ultimately break down the barriers of nationalism, class, and racial prejudice?

Lindbergh, as he always insisted, did not believe in the existence of an Aryan master race. When he spoke of the threat of "Asian" influences overwhelming Western civilization, he was not referring to Jews—as was very often the case with the Nazis—but to Japanese imperialism and, especially, Soviet Communism, which he had been told was just a modern variant of czarist or, rather, "Asian" despotism. As far as he was concerned, this meant that he was not a Nazi and entitled him to be highly offended by any suggestion that he was. But the line was pretty finely drawn. His racialist views certainly disposed him to accept Hitler's self-justifying claim that he was the defender of European civilization, the last hope of holding back the tide of Communism.

Such ideas do not spring full-blown into the mind of a thirty-seven-year-old man. Charles's father, and very probably his mother as well, believed in the intellectual superiority of whites, and Lindbergh undoubtedly had absorbed this notion at an early age. Just a year earlier, writing to Grace Nute, who had discovered the article C.A. wrote on race relations in 1904, Lindbergh commented that the piece "represents a portion of my father's outlook on life that I know always existed." He added that he was "extremely glad" Nute had come upon the article, since it would confound certain people who were trying to appropriate C.A. as their hero. But he also insisted that he did not remember ever having a single conversation with his father on the subject of race.[12]

A far-more-direct influence on Lindbergh's thinking was Carrel, who in turn was influenced by the protofascist theories of Houston Stewart Chamberlain, the English author of *The Foundations of the Nineteenth Century*, who married Richard Wagner's daughter Eva and spent the latter years of his life as the sage of Bayreuth. A number of Carrel's intellectual hobbyhorses, for example his observation that fascism at least attracted a better physical type than Communism, which was the refuge of the weak—a notion also expressed by Lindbergh in his journal—were direct borrowings from Chamberlain. Unlike Chamberlain, however, Carrel was less a white supremacist than a white inferiorist. Industrial society, he constantly implied, was so degenerate that Western civilization almost deserved to be destroyed.

An Olympian view of history as just a tic in the evolutionary process certainly made it easier to dismiss such mere contemporary realities as the concentration camps. In this respect, Lindbergh had much in common with American Marxists, whose "objective" understanding of the historical process enabled them to ignore the existence of Stalinist terrorism. For Lindbergh, however, ideology was never more than a thin veneer. Despite all his talk about "values," ideas for him were slippery rocks that he grabbed at in an effort to avoid being swept away by the rushing tide of events. Almost invariably his opinions were molded by personal experience, the abstract formulations tacked on later in order to justify his emotional responses. Lindbergh's vision of the white race as threatened by "a pressing sea of Yellow, Black and Brown," vividly recalls that moment on the Yangtze in 1931 when he stood aboard the Sirius and—overcoming his inhibitions, at the urging of his companion—fired warning shots to prevent the mob of starving peasants from swamping his plane. The Nazis' plaints about the fatherland being overwhelmed by "Asian" immigrants evoked his sympathy because he, too, had been victimized by an immigrant. Hauptmann, though a German, reportedly had been a Spartacist, and—according to some unconfirmed accounts—had been born in Romania of German parents. Moreover, in his native country Hauptmann had promptly been arrested and jailed for his crimes; in the freer climate of America, he had flourished.

In 1939 warnings about the menace of Japanese imperialism were frequently stated in terms even more explicitly racist than Lindbergh's, and the Reader's Digest article provoked less of a storm than one might imagine. But the obvious parallels between Lindbergh's thinking and the Nazi worldview made him a favorite target of liberal columnists. Dorothy Thompson, wife of Main Street author Sinclair Lewis, attacked Lindbergh relentlessly in a series of syndicated columns that mixed occasional shrewd insights with amateur psychologizing. On one occasion Thompson wrote that Lindbergh's 1927 flight to Paris had required "rigorous, even cruel, self-discipline." In the next breath, she opined that Clarence Chamberlin—who had not even organized the flight of the Columbia—had contributed more to aviation. Such nonsense, combined with the assumption that his anti-Communism was a major character flaw, would influence much future writing about Lindbergh.[13]

More justifiably Thompson guessed that Lindbergh was setting himself up to become president, or more accurately an American dictator, should the fortunes of war turn against the Allies. The truth, in some respects even sadder, was that Lindbergh did not want political power but saw himself as potential savior—the popular hero who, by holding himself above the fray (at times, against his own instincts), would be in a position to step in and rescue Western Europe from total destruction.

Lindbergh managed to preserve a sense of humor about Thompson's columns, as he seldom did when his critics hit closer to the mark. Checking into a hotel in Minneapolis and discovering that he had been assigned the "Nordic suite," he cracked, "Wait until Dorothy Thompson hears about this!"

There was not much, however, that he found amusing during this period. Never a drinker, he now discovered that he could scarcely tolerate being in a room with others who were drinking. At a party on Long Island, when a young woman became tipsy and threw herself at "Lindy," he recoiled in horror and disgust. Almost everything struck him as evidence of the degenerate state of American society, including the mediocre words and music of the new air corps hymn—which had emerged from a contest sponsored by Bernarr Macfadden, publisher of *Liberty* magazine, an enthusiastic propagator of conspiracy theories about the 1932 kidnapping.

The gossip in Washington was that the radio speeches and articles— so unlike the Lindbergh that Jerry Land and his air corps colleagues knew—were being written for him by Truman Smith, or perhaps by Bill Castle, an occasional contributor to a pro-German magazine called *Today's Challenge*. On the day after the second radio speech, Land asked Slim to lunch in order to sound him out about these rumors. "His ideas are his own and I doubt if anyone really has any control over those ideas," the admiral reported despairingly to "Sister" Land. The admiral and his wife, with whom Lindbergh had often stayed when he had business in Washington, were so upset that they no longer called or invited him to dinner. They would see Slim only twice during the coming year, and then briefly when their paths crossed by chance.[14]

Shortly after his argument with Land, Lindbergh stopped by the headquarters of the Morgan bank in New York to meet his financial adviser Harry Davison for lunch. While he was waiting in the reception room on the partners' floor, Jack Morgan and Tom Lamont came out of their offices and began to chide him for his opposition to aid for Britain. A furious Lindbergh complained in his journal that Morgan and Lamont's attitudes were all that could be expected from men who spent far too much time cooped up in the airless, unhealthy atmosphere of 23 Wall Street.

For all his murky obsessions, Lindbergh was quite correct in pointing out the major flaw in his opponents' arguments. Influential advocates of aid to Britain knew very well that they were starting the country down a slippery slope. As had happened in World War I, aiding the Allies meant that the United States would almost inevitably be drawn into the conflict sooner or later. The politicians, the columnists, and bankers like Lamont all refused to say as much openly—and, in fact, often denied it—on the grounds that the majority of Americans were not yet prepared to accept the necessity of war. To Lindbergh's way of thinking, this was a conspiracy against the public, pure and simple. And no one stood to benefit more than the House of Morgan, which was preparing to finance the Allies in this war as it had in the last.

In May 1940, as the German army swept through the Low Countries, Lindbergh went on the radio again, urging American neutrality and denouncing unnamed "powerful elements" that planned to profit from selling arms to the British. This was too much for Henry Breckinridge, who resigned as Charles and Anne's personal attorney. A year later, in a speech before the American Society of International Law, Breckinridge would denounce his former friend and client, saying, "Norway has its Quisling, France has its Laval, and the United States its equivalent."

Around this time the Lindberghs also became estranged from Harry Guggenheim. However, it is far from clear, as has often been assumed, that their differences were mainly political. Guggenheim had divorced his wife Carol, a great favorite of both Charles and Anne, and in 1940 he married Alicia Medill Patterson, whose family owned both the New York *Daily News* and the *Chicago Tribune*. Alicia Guggenheim's father, Col. Joseph Patterson, was a staunch isolationist, and the Patterson family newspapers, especially the *Tribune,* were vociferously pro-Lindbergh. Harry Guggenheim himself, for that matter, was briefly active in organizing Jews against intervention. But Guggenheim had never been slow to tell Charles when he thought he was making an ass of himself, and Lindbergh was in no mood to tolerate criticism of any sort. Although La Falaise and Lloyd Neck were only a few miles apart, Lindbergh and his onetime friend no longer saw each other.

For all his geopolitical speculations, Lindbergh's "powerful elements" speech made it obvious whom he really blamed for the war—his in-laws and their friends, the "anglophile" bankers. Not long after the speech, a distraught Betty Morrow invited her daughter to lunch at the Cosmopolitan Club and tried to reason with her. England might be invaded any day. Didn't she care about the fate of her British friends? What about her brother-in-law Aubrey's family? And Lord and Lady Astor, who had been so kind to her? Anne did care, but she also accepted Charles's argument that only a negotiated peace (in other words, surrender) could save Europe from devastation.

Mrs. Morrow had never had a good relationship with her son-in-law. They hadn't had a substantive conversation in years, and she was not about try to influence him now. In despair she turned to Tom Lamont saying that Anne was so "torn in spirit" her health was imperiled and begged him to intercede. Lamont wrote Lindbergh an avuncular letter, asking him to consider the toll his speeches were taking on the Morrow family.

Charles's reply was curt: "I intentionally did not specify individuals, groups, or organizations in my address because I still hope that it will not be necessary to do this," he wrote.[15]

The imperturbable Aubrey Morgan, recently appointed assistant head of the British Information Office in New York, was the only member of the Morrow clan who managed to remain philosophical. Asked why he didn't exert more influence over his brother-in-law, he quipped, "I am the living refutation of the invincibility of British propaganda."

Harold Nicolson, meanwhile, had already weighed in with his explanation of Lindbergh's behavior in an article that appeared in *The Spectator* in October of 1939. Lindbergh, he theorized, was suffering a delayed reaction to the twin traumas of his meteoric rise to fame and the murder of his firstborn child: "He identified the outrage to his private life first with the popular press and then by inevitable associations with freedom of speech and, almost, with freedom. He began to loathe democracy." Lindbergh's tragedy, Nicolson went on, was that he had come to believe his own publicity—"the legend of the kid from Minnesota whose head could not be turned." Now, reacting against pressures he found unbearable, he was transforming himself into a parody of his rigid, conspiracy-minded father.

Harsh as this was, Nicolson's article was a generally sympathetic attempt to make excuses for a man for whom he still felt great affection. "Let us not allow this incident to blind us to the great qualities of Charles Lindbergh," he concluded. "He is and always will be not only a schoolboy hero, but a schoolboy."

Lindbergh, it must be noted, did not agree that he was against free speech—in his view, he was exercising it. Opposition to involvement in European wars had been an axiom of American foreign policy since George Washington. And for better or worse, his opinions on other subjects were not out of line with what many, even a majority of, Americans believed. That such views were now considered traitorous only confirmed his opinion that the media had become a tool of the war propagandists.

Charles and Anne now dismissed Harold Nicolson as a "disillusioned idealist," a term that might have been better applied to themselves, but his article struck a nerve in both of them. For perhaps the only time in his life, Charles was able to admit to feelings of rejection. If Nicolson was such a "great friend," he wondered in his journal, why was it that he and Vita had had so little time for him and Anne when they were in England—"We never really knew them, or they us."[16]

When the Wehrmacht broke through the Maginot Line, Alexis Carrel found himself in the mid-Atlantic, returning from a visit to his homeland, where he had offered his services to assist in the organization of military hospitals. Refusing her husband's pleas to return with him to the States, Anne Carrel had insisted on remaining in France. A nurse, she was on a tour of hospitals near the front when the Germans broke through. For almost a month Carrel had no word of his wife and did not know whether she was alive or dead.

On hearing that Lindbergh was preparing his second radio speech of the month, Carrel telephoned Lloyd Neck and begged him to come out in favor of immediate and massive aid for the Allied nations. Lindbergh replied that American aid would only prolong the misery and contribute to the destruction of European civilization.

"It's the Nazis who are destroying western civilization!" screamed a furious Carrel. "It's the Nazis!"

Charles told his mentor that he was being irrational.

Shortly after this conversation Carrel showed up at the office of a certain well-regarded Manhattan psychiatrist named Schorr, asking for a consultation in his capacity as Colonel Lindbergh's private physician. Carrel told Dr. Schorr that he "did not like the trend Lindbergh's mind was taking." Lindbergh, he said, "hated the British, and next to them, he hates the United States." At this point Carrel realized that Schorr's nurse was listening in and insisted that the psychiatrist close his office door. The nurse, who happened to have a friend who was an FBI informant, reported the visit to the bureau's New York office.

Carrel's efforts to reason with Lindbergh were an utter failure. A few months later, he returned to France via Lisbon, ostensibly to deliver a shipment of vitamins for undernourished children, but really in the hope that he could persuade his wife to flee the country and come back to the United States with him. Madame Carrel's letters warning her husband not to return reached New York after his departure, and soon after Carrel entered occupied France, the Nazis issued a report that he had accepted the post of minister of health in the occupation government. Carrel's friends and his loyal American secretary, Katherine Crutcher, realized the report was untrue and began leaking smuggled correspondence from Carrel to the American media to counter the propaganda from Berlin. No one knew better than the Lindberghs that Carrel, for all his eccentricities, was no Nazi, yet they remained coolly aloof. In a conversation with Crutcher, Charles seemed satisfied that his mentor was in no great distress.

Charles Lindbergh would later insist that he did not remember this period of his life as especially stressful. And from his perspective, perhaps it wasn't. After years of keeping his emotions bottled up, he was expressing his anger toward his in-laws, the American public, and the press, and he was feeling rather pleased with himself. Although the Lindberghs' home in Lloyd Neck was the target of rowdies who drove by at night screaming taunts of "Nazi-lover," he no longer worried about the problem of security. Even letters threatening the lives of his sons were now dismissed as nasty annoyances.

By the end of 1939, the Lindberghs had moved up the road from their first rented house in Lloyd Neck, which did not have central heating, to a pre-Revolutionary-era farmhouse on the estate of Mrs. William Delano Wood, a distant relative of FDR. The Manor House, as it was called, had once been the headquarters of the Tory leader Count Rumford. It now became a gathering place for those who saw Lindbergh as the natural leader of the anti-interventionist cause.

Although Lindbergh's opposition to aid for the Allies and his refusal to condemn German aggression outright had alienated many potential supporters, opinion polls still showed that 80 to 85 percent of all Americans opposed entry into the war. In this sense Lindbergh was the spokesman for the majority, and there was no lack of activists eager to set up an organization around him. Perhaps the most enthusiastic was R. Douglas Stuart, Jr., the young heir to the Quaker Oats fortune. Stuart was a senior at Yale University's law school, and he and a group of fellow Yalies, including Sargent Shriver, Kingman Brewster, and Dwight

Morrow, Jr.'s, prep school friend Dick Bissell, joined forces with a former American Legion official from the Midwest named O. K. Arm-
strong to form the No Foreign Wars Campaign. The NFWC, as it was
called, was intended to be nonideological, a sort of umbrella organization that would coordinate the efforts of everyone from the Quakers
and the socialists to conservative midwestern businessmen and war veterans.

Charles Lindbergh took part in the discussions leading to the
NFWC's formation but never formally joined it and did not see himself
as the group's leader. This vacuum at the top had predictable consequences. Verne Marshall, an Iowa journalist recruited to serve as the
NFWC's secretary, turned out to be an ineffectual organizer with an
affinity for conspiracy theories. Stuart wished to exclude profascist
groups like the New World Movement, founded by Merwyn K. Hart,
head of the New York State Economic Council, but Lindbergh failed to
back him up. (Indeed, if the FBI's reports are accurate, Lindbergh actually met privately with Hart on several occasions.) Questionable characters like George Eggleston, whose magazine *Scribner's Commentator*
grew more anti-Semitic by the week, became steadily more influential,
driving the moderates out.

Even more than Eggleston, the most controversial presence in the
NFWC was Lawrence Dennis, a ruggedly handsome Philips Exeter
graduate and former *New Republic* columnist whose embittered expression and sarcastic turn of mind convinced Anne that he was nursing
some secret sorrow. Dennis was the author of *The Coming American
Fascism,* a work of political theory that predicted that the United States
would be forced to adopt what he called a "desirable fascism," a disci-
plined corporate state that would guarantee full employment and welfare benefits, albeit at the sacrifice of individual rights. A genuine intellectual, Dennis at times insisted that he was merely describing historical
trends, not advocating them, and complained that he had been unfairly
labeled "America's number one fascist." Nevertheless, he managed to
defend Hitler with considerable sophistry. In a 1938 article in the
American Mercury, for example, he suggested that Americans who condemned the Nazis' "virtually bloodless" occupation of Austria were
guilty of a double standard. "Have we forgotten our conquest of Mexico or our conquest of the continent from the Indians?"[17]

Charles's excuse for ignoring the extremists' takeover of the NFWC
was that he needed to keep his schedule free to work on his speeches—
he seldom gave more than two a month—and to preserve a "balance"

between private and public life. His insistence on spending time with Jon and Land, now eight and four, was no doubt admirable in its way, though his philosophy of child rearing occasionally took strange turns. A ram with a penchant for butting everything and everyone who came near was penned up in a neighbor's pasture, and Charles, in line with his belief in inculcating independence, took Jon into the field so that he could learn to handle himself in a confrontation with the feisty animal.

Another member of the household at this time was a fifty-eight-pound sea turtle Jim Newton had rescued from a man who planned to use it to make soup. The enormous turtle, whose jaws looked strong enough to snap off a child's finger, worried even Charles, and when it failed to thrive he decided that the only solution was to release it into Long Island Sound. As the poor beast slowly swam out of view, he and the boys watched from on shore, waving good-bye.

Meanwhile, Anne Lindbergh surveyed the collection of second-raters and lunatic-fringe types who gathered at her dinner table and wondered how she, who had once listened to her father discuss world affairs with the likes of Walter Lippmann and Jean Monnet, could have sunk so low. She did not like these people, though at times her objections appeared to be more aesthetic than political. ("All the intellectuals are against us!" she wailed in her diary.)

But Anne, however "torn" by the situation, actively supported her husband. Expecting her fourth child in October, she devoted the final months of her pregnancy to writing her own defense of anti-interventionism. Her small essay, entitled *The Wave of the Future: A Confession of Faith,* sold more than fifty thousand copies in two months, became a Book-of-the-Month Club selection, and rose to the top of the *Herald Tribune*'s bestseller list.

Charles later said that he never did manage to get through Lawrence Dennis's book. But Anne surely did. Her thesis, almost a gloss on Dennis's lengthier tome, was that the "democracies" (her quotes) had failed to solve the problems of unemployment, poverty, and social dislocation and must make way for a new order. Free elections and individual rights were luxuries that we in the "have nations" of the world would be forced to give up under pressure from "have not" nations, now demanding their fair share of the world's resources:

> What was pushing behind Communism? What behind Fascism in Italy? What behind Nazism? Is it nothing but a "return to barbarism," to be crushed at all costs by a "crusade"? Or is some new,

and perhaps even ultimately good, conception of humanity trying to come to birth, often through evil and horrible forms and abortive attempts?

Anne did not venture to guess what this "new conception" might be—she certainly didn't go so far as to label it "desirable fascism"—but whatever it was, she was sure it would be unstoppable: "The wave of the future is coming and there is no fighting it."[18]

Except for its assumption that fascism and Communism were two sides of the same coin—and, of course, the author's name—*The Wave of the Future* was potentially acceptable to both rightists and leftists. W. H. Auden was among those who sent Anne a note of congratulations. It was the anti-Communist liberals, the very people Anne hoped to persuade, who loathed the book. Charles Lindbergh at least talked about preserving the values of Western civilization, even if he didn't know what they were. Anne, on the other hand, was ready to sweep everything away—"the sacredness of property, the infallibility of the democratic way of life, the efficiency of the capitalistic system"—all in the name of some revolutionary "conception" that she could not define but ringingly pronounced irresistible.

Jerry Land, who had been out of touch with the Lindberghs for many months, wrote Anne congratulating her on the birth of a daughter, also called Anne, and expressing skepticism about her other recent "production": "To me it leaves much to be desired in the way of conviction and it causes many doubts to arise in the part of my cranium where my brain is supposed to be."[19]

According to aviation correspondent C. B. Allen, who interviewed Colonel Lindbergh for the *Saturday Evening Post* during this period, even he was privately dismayed by the book. And, surely, the last thing Charles wanted for the United States was a government that provided total security in exchange for restricting individual freedom.

It was a measure of Anne's political naïveté that she was genuinely surprised when reviewers charged her with justifying totalitarianism. Responding to her critics in the *Atlantic Monthly,* she reminded them that she had never called fascism the wave of the future but merely "the scum on the top of the wave." (However, she still did not say what the wave was.) No sooner had she put the *Atlantic Monthly* piece in the mail than she discovered that "my point of view has widened again." It occurred to her, apparently for the first time, that the interventionists upheld "the fundamental truth of our era—One must lose one's life to save it ... [but] Charles does not give in his talks an ideal to die for."[20]

Perhaps the most eloquent response to *The Wave of the Future* came from Anne's cousin Dick Scandrett, who frequently served as the Morrow family spokesman: "The speeches and articles by Charles have not been nearly as distressing to me as your articles, both because the expression of his thinking is direct and because he is the son of his own father rather than the son of your own father." Scandrett complained that Anne's was the sort of reasoning that convinced impressionable and idealistic people that they had a duty to support totalitarian regimes abroad out of guilt for their own affluence. "You are vague and fatalistic about what fascism has to contribute to a future social order for us all. In the meantime, your thesis seems to be that we should work hard, courageously and faithfully in and for America, to produce a very beautiful nut that you think would be extremely difficult for any foreign aggressor to crack."

Scandrett marshaled all the right arguments, but in the end he resorted to hectoring and scare tactics. First he reminded Anne that by loyally supporting her husband she was betraying the memory of her father. ("He [Morrow] may not have had a scientific mind but he ... liked people.") And he added that he favored an immediate declaration of war because then it would become possible for the government to "deal with" enemy sympathizers by prosecuting their "illegal and traitorous" acts.[21] Since a copy of this letter promptly made its way into FDR's personal files, one presumes that it was written less to convert Anne than to stake out the Morrow position.

By the end of 1940 the No Foreign Wars Campaign had become such a sink of fascist sympathizers that Douglas Stuart resigned to form an entirely new organization, called the America First Committee. Robert Wood, the chairman of Sears, Roebuck, agreed to serve as chairman. Sydney Hertzberg was publicity director. The board of directors included the socialist Norman Thomas, Dorothy Detzer of the Women's International League for Peace and Freedom, and Chester Bowles, chairman of the Benton & Bowles advertising agency. Lillian Gish, Philip La Follette of Wisconsin, and Adelaide Hunt Marquand, whose sister had been a classmate of Anne's at Miss Chapin's, were soon enlisted as platform speakers.

The committee's chief financial backer was Colonel Patterson, Harry Guggenheim's father-in-law. Lindbergh, who had expressed no ethical reservations about dealing with the likes of George Eggleston and Lawrence Dennis, was quite upset by this turn of events, but consoled himself with the thought that Patterson was perhaps not responsible for his newspaper's behavior during the kidnapping investigation.

Once again Charles and Anne declined to take any active leadership role. While America First was being organized, they were ill with chicken pox, which they had caught from Jon, and as soon as they recovered, they departed for a month's vacation in the Everglades with Jim Newton. When they returned in early April, Robert Wood pressed Charles to take over the chairmanship of the committee, but he refused. Lindbergh told Wood that he would address America First rallies but wanted complete autonomy as to the content of his speeches. Anne appeared on America First platforms with her husband, but like him, she never actually joined.

This arrangement did not bode well for the future of the organization. Although America First claimed three hundred thousand members, it had no leader of truly national stature except for Lindbergh who, on principle, refused to lead. The organization's board declared a policy of excluding known anti-Semites or fascist sympathizers and devoted much energy to debating individual cases—Avery Brundage of the American Olympic Committee and industrialist William R. Grace were ousted; Henry Ford was asked to resign, invited back on, then left again when he decided that the United States should sell arms to the Allies after all. These battles consumed a great deal of time and energy, but as long as Colonel Lindbergh refrained from denouncing the Nazis they were ultimately pointless. The committee could do nothing to prevent fringe groups like John T. McWilliams's American Destiny Party, William Pelley's Silver Shirts, and the Bunds from urging their members to infiltrate America First.

The book *Under Cover*, by John Roy Carlson, the result of several years' experience investigating pro-Nazi sects, gives a vivid glimpse of Lindbergh's appeal to such people. Carlson, who charged that William Castle was controlled by a Nazi agent, would have dearly loved to lay the same charge against Lindbergh. What he found was quite different. Lindbergh was viewed by the rank and file of these sects as the white knight who would step forward to lead them when the time came, but those in the know saw Lindbergh as disposable. Lawrence Dennis, when interviewed by Carlson, reluctantly allowed that he might be useful as a figurehead: "Lindbergh is excellent, but he is not well versed in politics. Surrounded by a circle of advisors of the nationalist type, Lindbergh would make an excellent nominal leader."[22]

This was devastating enough, and when Carlson's book appeared in 1943 an excited "Sister" Land wrote the admiral demanding to know if what it said about Slim was accurate. Jerry Land replied evasively that he hadn't read the book. His refusal to add a word of reassurance to ease the family's distress was more telling than any denunciation.

Despite rumors to the contrary, Lindbergh was writing his own talks, but during this period he did show advance drafts of his speeches to America First's New York chapter chairman, John T. Flynn, a former New Dealer whose books, including *Graft in Business, God's Gold,* and *Investment Trusts Gone Wrong!* would no doubt have found favor with C. A. Lindbergh. Under Flynn's influence no more was heard of manning the white ramparts, and Lindbergh's speeches began to stress traditional isolationist themes, including the fear that the United States would be forced to turn itself into a copy of the enemy—"a regimented nation, a militaristic nation that surpasses Germany itself in totalitarian efficiency." In one talk Lindbergh actually said, "I never wanted Germany to win this war."

Under the committee's auspices, Lindbergh addressed mass rallies in New York's Madison Square Garden, the Hollywood Bowl, and elsewhere. Once almost unnaturally youthful looking, he now seemed prematurely aged. (Anne, too, noted in her diary that she had gone from seeming much younger than all her contemporaries, and therefore perpetually promising, to feeling infinitely older and more tired.) Slightly stoop-shouldered, with a receding hairline, Colonel Lindbergh wore short-sleeved dress shirts with a collection of pens protruding from the lapel pocket and looked less like a dashing pilot than an engineer, ill at ease over being called away from his drafting board to deliver a political pep talk. His speeches, which he read word for word in a slightly high-pitched, nasal monotone, were dull rather than rabble-rousing and were addressed to all who felt overwhelmed by the changes of the past twenty years, which had made the world so much more stressful, violent, and confusing. The typical America First supporter was in no sense a radical, much less a Nazi, but a middle-aged resident of small-town or rural America. To such followers the war in Europe seemed far distant and they hoped that it would stay that way. Nevertheless, committee organizers noted uneasily that the rallies at which Lindbergh appeared were always jammed to overflowing, and that the most enthusiastic segment of the audience paid scant attention to the text of Lindbergh's talks, cheering loudest when he mopped his brow or cracked a rare smile.

The emergence of America First galvanized the Roosevelt administration. Interior Secretary Harold Ickes, who had made it almost a personal mission to discredit Lindbergh, harped relentlessly on his acceptance of a medal from the Germans, missing few opportunities to refer to Lindbergh as "that Knight of the German Eagle." Roosevelt himself, in a press conference on April 25, 1941, compared Lindbergh to Clement Vallandigham, the leader of a group of Union army renegades known as Copperheads during the Civil War, as well as to the "sunshine patriots" at Valley Forge who urged General Washington to surrender. FDR's comment was undoubtedly designed to goad his adversary into reacting, and if nothing else, it showed that he understood how thin-skinned Lindbergh could be. Complaining that he could not serve under a commander in chief who doubted his loyalty, Lindbergh resigned his commission in the reserves. It was left to the editorial writers to observe that the same man who saw nothing wrong with keeping a medal from Hitler now felt that service in an American uniform was incompatible with his sense of honor.

Harold Ickes had also fastened on the notion that Truman Smith was writing Lindbergh's speeches, perhaps on instructions from the chief German military attaché Friedrich von Boetticher. Smith, like so many others accused of controlling Lindbergh, only wished it were true. "In speech writing, as in flying, Charles Lindbergh is the 'lone wolf,' " he later wrote.

A fierce infighter, Ickes launched a campaign to discredit Smith through blind items leaked to Drew Pearson's "Washington Merry-Go-Round" column. Among other charges, Smith was said to have quipped at a cocktail party that Roosevelt was "paralyzed from the neck up." Smith, a diabetic who had been granted special permission to remain on active duty, was able to prove that he had been a patient in Walter Reed Hospital on the date in question.

Ickes' campaign was so relentless that in June 1940, Smith's superior, Gen. George C. Marshall, suggested to Smith that he and his wife leave town for a while. They retreated to the home of Gen. Albert Wedemeyer and his wife, Dade, near Fort Benning, Georgia. Shortly after their return to Washington, Kay Smith called the Lindberghs with a warning. A friend in the FBI had passed on the word that both the Smiths' and the Lindberghs' phones were being monitored by the FBI. Lindbergh advised America First staffers to speak clearly, so that the surveillance teams would have no trouble understanding them.

Roosevelt had, that same month, signed an executive order authorizing the attorney general to use wiretaps in connection with the investigation of persons suspected of "fifth column" activities. Nevertheless FBI files released through the Freedom of Information Act show no evidence that the Lindberghs' phone was ever tapped. Allowing for the possibility that the records have been suppressed, it would seem that Smith was misinformed. J. Edgar Hoover admired Lindbergh—a man who, like himself, was good to his mother—and perhaps wanted a more definite authorization before undertaking a surveillance that could have political repercussions unfavorable to the bureau.[23]

But Truman Smith's conversations with von Boetticher were being monitored by the counterintelligence section of MID, Smith's own agency, which was also looking into miscellaneous allegations against Lindbergh. These records remain classified, but German archives released after the war show that in June 1941 Smith asked von Boetticher to get the Nazi press to stop running articles praising Lindbergh. The chargé d'affaires, Hans Thomsen, promptly relayed this request to the chief of the German general staff, adding that "contacts with him [Lindbergh] are maintained through a group in the [American] General Staff." Most likely, this was pure braggadocio—if Thomsen really was in communication with a clique of pro-German generals in the U.S. Army, this would certainly have merited more than a brief aside. However, a few weeks after this conversation with von Boetticher, MID decided that Smith had to go; over the objections of General Marshall, Smith was forced to take medical retirement.

The Lindberghs, meanwhile, were being audited by the IRS, an inquiry they felt sure was politically inspired. It may well be that the IRS's curiosity was aroused by a tip that Walter Winchell had passed on to his friend J. Edgar Hoover. Winchell had sent Hoover a copy of a blind item from his column alleging that a certain "ho-humbug" (Lindbergh) had "sent his fortune to Germany to pay for South American propaganda." The Lindberghs did have a bank account with Morgan Cie in occupied France and were forwarding funds to pay the caretakers on Illiec, which may have inspired this improbable tale. In any event no charges were filed as a result of the IRS investigation, and its main result was to feed Charles's ever-mounting paranoia.

Another development that convinced Charles that the movement toward war was a Morgan plot was the Republicans' choice of the avidly pro-British Wendell Willkie as their candidate for president in 1940. Willkie was a relative unknown whose nomination had indeed been engineered almost singlehandedly by Tom Lamont. "We had no more chance to vote on the issue of peace than if we had been a totalitarian state ourselves," Lindbergh told an America First rally.

By June 1941 the Wehrmacht was pushing across the Soviet Union and was well entrenched in North Africa. Great Britain continued to hold out under relentless pounding. After every air raid, Harold Nicolson mailed his former friend a postcard with the message: "Do you still think we are soft?" (Lindbergh claimed later that he never saw them.) The battle against aid to the Allies had been lost. American shipping convoys were delivering arms to Britain and would soon be sending Lend-Lease supplies to the Soviet Union as well. Moreover, many of the predictions Lindbergh had made in 1938 and 1939 had already been disproved. In 1941 the United States would produce 19,445 combat airplanes, many of superior design to their German counterparts. The Germans turned out only 11,776 airplanes in all. Nazi totalitarianism only seemed efficient. The Germans were reluctant to put their economy on a total war footing for fear of spreading disaffection, and due to political interference and general incompetence, the best ideas of the Luftwaffe's aeronautical scientists were never utilized.

Lindbergh, however, was more convinced than ever that America was on the brink of anarchy. When he and Anne spent a weekend at the California ranch of novelist Kathleen Norris, an America First speaker, he was startled to learn that among the family group were four members of the Communist party. Far from being reassured by the fact that the America Firsters and the Communists were getting along just fine, he saw the divided Norrises as an omen of an ideological warfare that would soon tear America apart.

America First now claimed a membership of eight hundred thousand. But the figures were misleading. Novelist John P. Marquand, whose wife was a friend of Anne's, found himself hosting a benefit cocktail party for the Lindberghs and observed that Charles and the America First board appeared to be in a "mental fog," unable to grapple with the reality that entry into the war was now inevitable. The same, he thought, was true of their opposite number, the William Allen White Committee. Neither side could admit that America was being swept along by events beyond anyone's control. White's group insinuated that all anti-interventionists were motivated by anti-Semitism. On the other hand, Marquand noted, the America Firsters at the party were discussing a rumor that the White Committee was secretly funded by the British Secret Service.[24]

The atmosphere was so overheated that when Lindbergh asked in one speech, "Is it not time to turn to new policies and new leadership?"

the question was interpreted by some editorial writers as a call to violent revolution. In Oklahoma City, the city council refused to grant a permit for an America First rally in the municipal auditorium or anywhere else within the city limits; organizers shifted the location to a ballpark outside town, announcing the new site just hours in advance in order to thwart a violent counterdemonstration. Ten thousand people showed up anyway. The parallel between Lindbergh's speaking tours and the lonely 1918 campaign of C. A. Lindbergh, "the Gopher Bolshevist," was becoming more obvious by the day. Lindbergh professed not to see the connection, though he later wrote in another context, "I am certainly aware that there is much of my father in me. At times, I almost feel that I am my father."

On September 11 Roosevelt issued his "shoot on sight" order, authorizing the U.S. Navy to fire at any hostile vessel. That same night at a rally in Des Moines, Lindbergh departed from his usual call for "realism" to blast the three groups "responsible for changing our national policy of neutrality and independence to one of entanglement in foreign affairs." These were the Roosevelt administration; the British and those "capitalists, Anglophiles and intellectuals who believe in their future"; and, third, the Jews:

> It is not difficult to understand why the Jewish people desire the overthrow of Nazi Germany. The persecutions they suffered in Germany would be sufficient to make bitter enemies of any race. No person with a sense of the dignity of mankind can condone the persecution the Jewish race suffered in Germany. Certainly, I and my friends do not. But no person of honesty and vision can look on their pro-war policy here today without seeing the dangers in that policy, both for us and for them. Instead of agitating for war, the Jewish groups in this country should be opposing it in every possible way, for they will be among the first to feel its consequences. Tolerance is a virtue that depends upon peace and strength. History shows that it cannot survive war and devastation. A few very far-sighted Jewish people realize this and stand opposed to intervention. But the majority still do not. Their greatest danger to this country lies in their ownership and influence in our motion pictures, our press, our radio, and our government.

The speech touched off an uproar, largely because it appeared to confirm what many had long suspected. Lindbergh knew this would happen but did not really understand why. Anti-Semitism was certainly endemic among his social circle, but he had always been the exception to the rule. He recalled with bitterness that Henry Breckinridge, who now condemned him, had once remarked in his presence, "Whenever a Jew enters the room, he raises the tempo and lowers the tone." The constant plaints of Fulton Lewis and other anti-interventionists about Jewish control of the media had initially repelled him, though perhaps this had changed over time, especially considering that Wendell Willkie (that "tool" of Tom Lamont!) had been hired as counsel to the film industry.

It never seemed to occur to Lindbergh that there were people who supported France and Britain not out of some parochial interest but because they believed freedom for Western Europe was essential to a free America. Nor had he imagined that his remarks about the "consequences" for Jews of advocating intervention could be taken as a signal to the hatemongers. Informed of this he was shocked but not contrite. He was responsible only for his own comments—which both he and Anne insisted were "moderate." He noted in his journal that he had not meant the statement as a threat but only as a friendly warning, since the United States was obviously a more violent country than Germany.

Certainly, no one on the America First board considered Lindbergh anti-Semitic, and at first the board was inclined to blame John T. Flynn. The New York chapter chairman had been having a lot of trouble with Bundists in his organization, and they suspected him of using Lindbergh's speech to throw a bone to the extremists. But Lindbergh had purposely made sure that Flynn did not see an advance text of the Des Moines talk. He had shown the manuscript only to Anne, who protested "You can't say that!" but then did nothing to interfere.

After the speech an outraged Flynn wrote Lindbergh that it was one thing to complain of bias in the media, "But this is a far different matter from going out on the public platform and denouncing 'the Jews' as war makers. No man can do that without incurring the guilt of religious and racial intolerance which is poison in a community like ours." This distinction was lost on Lindbergh, who concluded that Flynn simply lacked the courage of his convictions. He ignored Flynn's furious demand that he issue a statement making it clear that he had been speaking for himself, not the committee.[25]

But perhaps Lindbergh understood more than he let on. As he recalled in an unpublished 1968 memo, "Months before, I had decided that before my country actually entered the war I would name the groups responsible for getting us into it. By September 1941, I realized that we were so involved in the war it was only a question of what incident would result in a formal declaration, the Des Moines address was scheduled, and I decided that if I waited any longer I might not have another opportunity."[26]

In other words, he was tired of the whole business but wanted to get a few things off his chest and didn't mind at all that he was pulling the plug on his own followers. For fourteen years the press had been badgering him to reveal his innermost thoughts—well, now he had. It was the perfect masochistic revenge.

Bizarrely enough, the harshest lecture Lindbergh received after the Des Moines speech was from Henry Ford, the former publisher of the notoriously racist and anti-Semitic *Dearborn Independent*. Lindbergh had donated some inventions from his grandfather Land's laboratory to the Dearborn Museum, and when he visited Detroit to discuss the gift, Ford shut his office door and berated Lindbergh for the better part of an hour. The rise of Nazism had motivated Ford to rethink his belief in the existence of an international Jewish conspiracy, at least so he claimed. Word of the tongue-lashing circulated around the Ford headquarters and inspired a call from the local FBI office. The lecture made little impression on Lindbergh, however, perhaps because Ford now thought that the DuPont family of Delaware was responsible for all the evil in the world.[27]

After the Des Moines speech, the America First board was so dispirited that they considered disbanding the organization altogether. A motion to dissolve was narrowly defeated, and the committee struggled on a while longer. Despite the resignation of key district leaders, Lindbergh's speeches continued to draw enthusiastic crowds. On October 3 Lindbergh told an audience in Fort Wayne, Indiana, that FDR was "moving toward" cancellation of the 1942 congressional elections. On October 30, in what would prove to be the committee's last hurrah, twenty thousand people showed up at a Madison Square Garden rally, and those who were unable to gain entrance held a peaceful demonstration outside while Lindbergh spoke. The final official action of America First was a letter sent by the Glendale, New York, chapter to President Roosevelt. "Dear Mr. President," it began, "What's all this saber rattling in connection with Japan?"[28]

The letter was dated December 6, 1941.

TWENTY-FOUR

War

*W*ELL, HE GOT US IN THROUGH THE BACK DOOR," was Robert Wood's comment when Charles Lindbergh called him to discuss the attack on Pearl Harbor.

Wood was referring to such recent activities as a patrol of Cam Ranh Bay by the U.S. Navy yacht *Isabel* at the beginning of December. Britain had been pressuring Washington for assurances that the United States would declare war on Japan in the event of a Japanese attack on British possessions in Asia. Congress and the public, having declined to go to war to defend Paris, were not entirely convinced they should do so over Malaya, and some America Firsters, along with, for that matter, some naval officers, suspected Roosevelt of trying to provoke the Japanese into an act of aggression against America's Asiatic fleet.

Lindbergh agreed that American actions in the Pacific had been provocative, but all that was now irrelevant. As it had promised at the time of its founding, the America First Committee responded to Congress's declaration of war by voting itself out of existence. Two days later Lindbergh wrote to General Arnold, asking for his help in getting his commission reinstated.

On December 16 Lindbergh was in Manhattan, where he attended a dinner party at the Beekman Place apartment of America First organizer Ed Webster, who was celebrating his forthcoming marriage to another committee volunteer. Webster had invited at least forty people who had been "street speakers" for the committee, and an argument promptly broke out between those who approved of the board's vote to disband and a rump faction in favor of antiwar agitation. Lindbergh tried to avoid getting caught up in the discussion but eventually took the floor and spoke for at least fifteen minutes.

Two of the guests, Amos and Cornelia Pinchot, later reported the gist of the speech to their friend Daisy Harriman. Lindbergh, they said, had told the group:

> There is really only one danger in the world—and that is the yellow danger. China and Japan are really bound together against the white race. There could only have been one efficient weapon against that alliance.... Germany itself could have been that weapon. The ideal set-up would have been to have had Germany take over Poland and Russia, in collaboration with the British [empire], as a bloc against the yellow people and the Bolsheviks. But instead, the British government and the fools in Washington had to interfere. The British envied the Germans and wanted to rule the world forever. Britain is the cause of all the trouble in the world today.

According to the Pinchots, Lindbergh went on to say, "Of course, America First cannot be active right now. But it should keep on the alert and when the large missing lists and losses are published the American people will realize how much they have been betrayed by the British and the Administration.... There may be a time soon when we can advocate a negotiated peace."

By unknown means Harriman's version of the speech made its way to FBI headquarters and was soon also reported in the national press. Another FBI informant who happened to be present at the Webster party vaguely confirmed the "yellow peril" remarks but said that Lindbergh had defended the committee's decision to vote itself out of existence. Lindbergh himself, in a third version, would hotly deny that he had ever mentioned the "yellow races" (it was Japanese expansionism, not race, he was worried about, he insisted), though he conceded that he had been pretty hard on the British.[1]

Now that war had been declared, such remarks were potentially seditious. The intelligence community, meanwhile, was already taking a closer look at Lindbergh in connection with an apparently unrelated event. Just four days before Pearl Harbor an unknown person had handed Senator Burton Wheeler a copy of a classified War Department contingency plan, code-named Project Victory, which projected that the

United States would enter the war in Europe no later than 1943. To the isolationist Wheeler this was the smoking gun, proof that FDR had never meant to keep the United States out of the European conflict, and he promptly leaked relevant portions of the report to the *Chicago Tribune*. In the aftermath of Pearl Harbor, the American public was in no mood to get excited about the Project Victory document, but many in the intelligence community believed that the leaked report played a critical role in Hitler's decision to declare war on the United States sooner rather than later, forcing America to fight on two fronts.

With hindsight, the America Firsters also thought the timing of the leak was suspicious. To those who were already convinced of the existence of a Roosevelt-Churchill plot, the leak proved that British and perhaps American intelligence as well had advance warning of the attack on Pearl Harbor. According to this theory an agent of the British Secret Service, knowing that the United States would be at war with Japan in a matter of days, had fed the report to Wheeler so that its publication would provoke the Germans and force the United States to devote a larger share of its resources to the European theater of operations.

The counterintelligence section of MID, for its part, had narrowed the source of the leak to eight officers in the Planning Division of the War Department and their staffs. Initially, at least, their prime suspect was Gen. Albert Wedemeyer, a 1938 graduate of the General Staff course at the German War College, a close friend of Truman Smith, and a Lindbergh supporter. Counterintelligence suspected that it was Lindbergh himself who had passed the report from Wedemeyer on to Wheeler. The FBI agreed, basing its judgment on a report from a source inside the Ford Motor Company. FBI agents now visited the company's headquarters, where they questioned Harry Bennett and Charlie Sorenson about Lindbergh's army contacts. What generals was he talking to? Who were his friends? Bennett and Sorenson insisted that they had no idea.

On December 12, just five days after Pearl Harbor, J. Edgar Hoover informed his assistant Clyde Tolson that he and the attorney general had already discussed calling Lindbergh to testify before a grand jury about the Project Victory leak. "I said that I believed he [Lindbergh] should either be made to put up or shut up," Hoover told Tolson. "The Attorney General stated that he believed if we could get a strong report on this it might give the President a chance to clean out some 'brass hats.'"[2]

MID eventually decided that the source of the leak was not Wedemeyer after all, and the investigation of Charles Lindbergh was dropped. In the meantime, however, the investigation squelched any chance of Lindbergh's getting back into uniform. On January 12, for example, Lindbergh went to see Secretary of War Henry L. Stimson to ask that his commission be restored. Stimson knew that Lindbergh's visits to Germany had been made in the service of Army Intelligence and felt that the criticism over his acceptance of the German medal had been basically unfair. Moreover, Stimson happened to know from personal experience the inside story of another action of Lindbergh's that had been dredged up as evidence of profascist leanings: In 1930, when antifascist demonstrators threatened to disrupt a state visit by the Italian foreign minister, Count Dino Grandi, Stimson had personally telegraphed Lindbergh, asking him to fly Grandi from New York to Washington in an amphibious plane, thus eluding the picketers at the airport. Lindbergh, who was scheduled to inaugurate Pan-Am's "Flying Boat" service to South America that very day, had agreed to postpone his plans and fly to New York purely to accommodate the government. (In the event, bad weather made the flight to Washington impossible, and Lindbergh did not meet Grandi on that occasion.)

Obviously pained, Stimson told Lindbergh that he regretted being unable to offer him a commission. The reason, he said, was that Lindbergh's America First speeches showed "that he took a very different view of our friends and enemies in the present war" and that he "evidently lacked faith in the righteousness of our cause." Further, in an obvious reference to the Harriman story, which was being circulated within the administration to justify keeping Lindbergh out of uniform, he accused Lindbergh of being "antagonistic" toward China.[3]

Obviously unhappy about being the one to deliver the bad news, Stimson was immensely relieved when Lindbergh suggested that he might best serve the war effort by becoming a technical consultant to the aviation industry. The secretary arranged for Lindbergh to discuss the matter with General Arnold the next day, but Arnold, who had previously advocated restoring Lindbergh's commission, was now evasive, and Lindbergh got the impression that his old friend had been ordered not to talk to him.

Lindbergh's next move was to call colleagues in private industry to offer his services. Harry Bixby, now a Pan-Am executive, Guy Vaughan of Curtiss-Wright, and Deac Lyman, the former aviation correspondent for the *Times* who had become vice president of United Aircraft, all told Lindbergh that they would be delighted to find a job for him. However, all three companies soon withdrew their offers under pressure from the government. As an embarrassed Juan Trippe put it in a phone call to Lindbergh, certain unforeseen "obstacles" had arisen, making it impossible to use his services. Only Henry Ford, who wasn't about to let the War Department tell him how to run his plant, dared to ignore the warnings against hiring Lindbergh. Ford offered him a sixty-six-dollar-a month position as a consultant on the manufacture of the B-24 bomber.

Lindbergh believed that the pressure against hiring him was strictly political, and he was deeply hurt that men who had been his colleagues in aviation since 1927 had failed to stand behind him. No doubt he would have been even more bitter if he knew the extent of the cooperation the government was receiving. Even Lindbergh's personal papers, which he had donated to Yale University's Sterling Library on the understanding that they would be shown only to researchers with his and Anne's specific authorization, were not immune. In November of 1942, Dr. Russell Pruden, the library's curator, told an agent from the FBI's New Haven office that he would be happy to allow the bureau access to the vault in order to examine the correspondence Lindbergh had received in connection with the America First campaign. Hoover declined the offer but passed the message on to the War Policies Unit of Army Intelligence.[4]

It wasn't easy to find housing in the Detroit area during wartime, and for some months after Charles began working for Ford, Anne and the children remained on the East Coast, occupying a rented cottage on Martha's Vineyard. The cottage was so dilapidated—and the rent so far above the normal rate—that a few neighbors, unfamiliar with the Lindberghs' domestic habits, were quite convinced that Anne was using the location to signal to German U-boats. Finally, in July, Charles managed to locate a large, handsome house in exclusive Bloomfield Hills, and Anne and the children were able to join him in Michigan.

The house, which the Lindberghs rented from the well-to-do Belknap family, boasted a kitchen full of gleaming modern appliances, reproductions of Impressionist paintings in the living room, a pink-and-white unupholstered chaise longue in the boudoir, and wall-to-wall carpeting throughout. For Anne, this encounter with Midwestern tastes was a shock. She complained that she felt as if she were living on a movie set and worried that the pristine carpets, satin drapes, and beige upholstery would not long survive the depredations of three active youngsters. Her apprehension was promptly justified when Jon and Land shot a skunk in the woods and dragged the stinking carcass into the house to show it off to their nursemaid.

Despite a run of such domestic disasters, the Lindberghs seemed well settled. Although Charles, too, thought the Belknaps' decor a bit overdone, he was delighted to have his family settled in a proper home—far from the New York press and his in-laws. He was also relieved to be near his mother, who had recently begun to suffer from a tremor of the hand, soon to be diagnosed as an early stage of Parkinson's disease. Evangeline insisted on doing all her own housework and had a phobia about doctors. Although "Brother" Land had so far been unsuccessful in convincing her to quit teaching and put herself under a doctor's care, Charles was more persuasive.

In August 1942, a month after the move, Anne gave birth to her fifth child, a boy whom she and Charles decided to call Scott. Anne used a picture postcard of a fifteenth-century Calusa Indian deer mask as a talisman to help her keep her mind off the labor pains, and Charles, present throughout his wife's labor and delivery as always, was deeply touched by her spirituality and courage. Christmas 1942, he wrote in his journal, was the happiest family holiday since his marriage.

Although as Charles himself often noted, he did not shift mental gears easily, once he was forced to change he was not one to mull over the past. For Anne, however, the repercussions of the America First period were far from over. The storm of criticism over *The Wave of the Future* had left her, by turns, angry and dejected. The fact that her message had been so cruelly misunderstood, she told friends, proved she was a failure as a writer. (On the contrary, the decline of the West and the obsolescence of democracy were intellectual clichés Anne's powerful prose style had brought vividly to life.) As usual, she also felt overwhelmed by the conflicting demands of running the house and trying to write. She tried to devote a certain number of hours each day to "awareness," but, she confessed, remaining aware could be awfully tiring.

Charles reminded his wife that the world was full of writers who turned out one book after another without receiving a fraction of the success, much less the attention, that came her way. The way to find time to write, he advised, was to stop devoting so much energy to unpacking and rearranging the house—a form of "mental prostitution," he called it—when no doubt they would be moving on in a few months anyway. It apparently did not occur to him that he might help out by taking on chores like making the baby's formula, and, practically speaking, he was not around often enough to make a difference.

His duties at Ford involved long hours and frequent business trips.

What upset Anne most about the response to *The Wave of the Future* was the social isolation. Many liberal intellectuals, the very people whose acceptance and respect she most wanted, were convinced that the Lindberghs were anti-Semites and refused to meet them socially. The writer Robert Nathan and his wife, informed that the Lindberghs would be present at a dinner party they were planning to attend, were appalled. The hostess responded by disinviting Charles and Anne. On another occasion, when Anne phoned Adelaide Marquand at the home of the playwright George S. Kaufman, Beatrice Kaufman was so furious that she ordered Adelaide out of her house. Almost as disturbing, the small circle of friends that she and Charles had enjoyed seeing as a couple, people like the Guggenheims and the Breckinridges, were now estranged. Anne foresaw that her husband's frequent absences were not merely a matter of wartime necessity. Their interests were rapidly diverging.[5]

Anne preferred to work in Spartan surroundings, and Charles soon obtained a battered old trailer from Henry Ford, which he installed on the grounds as a studio for Anne, no doubt to the horror of their Bloomfield Hills neighbors. Although it would seem at this point that Anne had nothing to lose by writing exactly what was on her mind, her reaction was the opposite. Drafts of stories too revealing of her bitterness toward her family and other unacceptable emotions were abandoned as unpublishable. Instead she set out to complete the final draft of her autobiographical story of Eve and Gerald's fogbound flight over the Alps. *The Steep Ascent* was the most self-revealing work Anne had produced so far, dealing with her negative feelings about flying, her guilt over being so often separated from her children, and her dedication to serving as a "bridge" between her misunderstood husband and the world.

But 1943 was not a good year for a book about the uses of fear as a spiritual tonic. Reviewers, as always, praised the delicacy and precision of Anne's style but were underwhelmed by the novel's contents. There was a pinched, inhibited quality about this 120-page book; in form, it was one long interior monologue, in which the heroine interacted with God and her conscience and hardly at all with her husband, not to mention the rest of the world. Having seen the results in real life, the critics condemned the heroine's concept of herself as a "bridge" as painfully naive, and one hostile newspaper reviewer called the story an illustration of "the dangerous position a romantic gets into." Anne characterized this comment as "so nasty that it is funny."[6]

Discouraged, Anne would not publish again for more than a decade. Instead, she began taking classes in sculpture at the Cranbrook Academy, a small art school presided over by the Swedish artist Carl Milles. Cranbrook was an insular community that provided Anne with a readymade circle of friends and restored her confidence, but she herself thought of the time she spent there as a form of escapism.

Charles, busy at Ford's Willow Run plant, was discovering that he had been all too right in thinking that he could never adapt to the demands of a full-time executive position. On his first day on the job he was appalled to learn that Ford's test pilots, and even some senior executives, were required to punch the time clock. He was able to get this policy changed, and he also persuaded Ford to lift his ban on smoking in the cafeteria. (As much as he hated cigarette smoke, Charles had noticed that visiting army brass smoked anyway and thought it unfair that employees were denied the same privilege.) But there was nothing he could do to alter Ford's basic management style. Charlie Sorenson and Harry Bennett were bitter rivals, and when not battling each other they swept through the factory at regular intervals, issuing contradictory orders and terrorizing middle management.

The company was tooling up to produce the B-24 based on a prototype developed by Republic Aircraft of California, but even though Ford had not manufactured planes for years, its executives were convinced that they had little to learn from outsiders. Lindbergh called the first B-24 produced at Willow Run, the worst example of metal airplane construction he had ever seen. His own assignment, to finalize plans for equipping the plane with armor and machine guns, was complicated by red tape and interfering generals, whose ignorance of aeronautical design did not prevent them from making demands that Lindbergh had no choice but to accept. The wartime emergency made speed the top priority. Still, he brooded that the decisions he was okaying would cost American airmen their lives.

Lindbergh was far from alone in finding it hard to adapt to the pressure. The daredevil pilots of the twenties were now entering cautious middle age and inclined to be pessimistic on the subject of American military aviation. After years of being condemned as zealots and radicals, the heirs of Billy Mitchell—a group that included Generals Hap Arnold, George C. Kenney, Carl Spaatz, and Jimmy Doolittle—were now in charge, but there were those among Lindbergh's contemporaries who feared the change had come too late. Phil Love, now an air corps colonel, considered the younger generation of pilots soft and refused a promotion to general because he did not want to be responsible for sending them into combat. (He was later killed in a stateside crash.)

Frustrated by the way things were going at Ford, Lindbergh refused his token salary, telling Bennett he wanted the freedom to take occasional days off. Anticipating that he might yet find a way to get into action, he put himself through a rigorous training course to update his license for multiengined planes. Next he arranged to join a party of Willow Run test pilots who were on loan to the Mayo Clinic's Aero-medical Laboratory as human guinea pigs, testing oxygen equipment for pilots. The subjects exercised on a treadmill while breathing pure oxygen, then entered a tank where the pressure was quickly lowered to simulate altitudes up to forty-five thousand feet. At forty-one Lindbergh was in excellent shape—during a routine physical in 1936 he had set a record by holding his breath for three full minutes—still, the tests were stressful and occasionally dangerous. During one experiment the tube on his oxygen bottle jammed, and before the controllers noticed that anything was amiss he had passed out.

By the beginning of 1944, the flap over Project Victory had been long forgotten. Al Wedemeyer was back in favor, and Lindbergh—who apparently never understood the nature of the suspicions against him—somewhat belatedly discovered that he would have no problem in getting clearance to work for other defense contractors. He promptly signed on with the Chance Vought Division of United Aircraft as a consultant on the single-engine F-4U Corsair fighter, which United was building for the navy and the marines. His real goal was to get into combat, and even this was now possible, thanks to friends at the Navy Bureau of Aeronautics who managed to get him approved as a civilian observer (also known as a "tech rep") representing United in the Pacific theater. Secretary of the Navy Frank Knox never saw the authorization papers and, presumably, no one in the cabinet knew that Lindbergh was headed to the front.

Lindbergh hitched his way across the Pacific on military planes as far as the Solomon Islands, where he was assigned a marine Corsair to fly as an observer. Soon, he was joining combat patrols over Rabaul and New Ireland. Since shooting down the Lone Eagle would have been a propaganda coup for the Japanese, he used the alias Jones in radio communications. Otherwise, he took full part in the missions, strafing targets on the ground and practicing skip-bombing techniques. All this was strictly against regulations, but to the men of military aviation, Lindbergh was still a hero—indeed, a rather high percentage of military officers had supported America First—and they were quite happy to abet the Lone Eagle's desire to see military action.

Moving on to the island of Emirau, Lindbergh flew in a three-plane mission to test a new bombing rack, dropping five-hundred-pound bombs on a reported Japanese antiaircraft position on Kavieng. Soon, he had twenty-five missions to his credit, and the senior officers in the sector, nearly all of whom had met Lindbergh personally and could hardly claim to be ignorant of what was going on, were becoming nervous.

It was time to move on, and Lindbergh caught a ride with an Australian pilot to New Guinea, where Army Air Corps Gen. Ennis Whitehead lent him a P-38 Lightning to fly to the forward air base in Hollandia. His borrowed plane happened to belong to the ace Dick Bong, and when the P-38 emblazoned with twenty-one enemy flags set down at Hollandia, everyone on the field sprinted over to meet their hero. The discovery that the pilot was not the great Dick Bong, who was on R & R in Australia, but an unknown fortyish civilian, provoked universal disappointment.

Lindbergh found this role reversal highly amusing. He presented himself at the tent of Col. Charles H. MacDonald, commander of the crack 475th Fighter Group, known as Satan's Angels, and mumbled his name along with the information that he had come from United Aircraft to learn how Lightnings performed in combat. MacDonald grumbled that he had enough problems without baby-sitting for visiting desk jockeys, and went on with his card game. Eventually it dawned on the colonel that his visitor was *the* Charles Lindbergh, but he didn't become really impressed until he learned that Lindbergh was getting a third more miles per gallon than any pilot in the group.

On one mission to the Waigeo Islands, MacDonald and the rest of the squadron ran low on fuel and returned home while Lindbergh and his wingman remained behind to strafe some camouflaged barges. Suddenly the wingman radioed that he, too, was low on fuel. "How much have you got?" Lindbergh asked. "About 175 gallons," came the panicky answer. He instructed the pilot to throttle down on his engine and switch his fuel mixture to auto lean. Flying together they made the nearest refueling base at Owi Island. The wingman's fuel gauge was on empty, but Lindbergh still had 260 gallons left in his tanks. After this sortie, Lindbergh began lecturing the squadrons on fuel economy. His methods were hardly novel, just the standard fuel-saving tricks used by the old-time gypsy fliers, but they were not recommended in the flight manuals everyone had been following so conscientiously.

As Walter S. Ross observed in his 1965 biography of Lindbergh, the snapshots taken of Charles in New Guinea tell a story of their own. The unself-conscious grin that had charmed the world in 1927 was back. Lindbergh was flying again, doing the job he had been trained for, and he was a happy man. But like many men drawn to military life, Lindbergh enjoyed everything about war except the fact that it involved killing. He was past forty when he had his first taste of combat, and he came equipped with a somewhat old-fashioned, or just naive, concept of the rules of war. When someone suggested to him that he use his fuel conservation skills to bomb Tokyo he replied, quite seriously, that he wouldn't have the heart for it—a battleship, yes; a city, never. For that matter he never strafed a jungle hut without wondering guiltily if the occupants were really Japanese soldiers, as the orders of the day claimed, or some terrified mother and her children.

He had been in New Guinea twenty-three days before word of his presence reached General Kenney, who ordered him to report immediately to command headquarters of the Fifth Air Force in Brisbane, Australia.

"Don't you know the Japs will chop your head off if you're shot down?" Kenney snapped.

The plainspoken general also had some choice comments to make about the navy officers in the Solomons who had shipped Lindbergh to an air corps unit without getting clearance from his office. Once Kenney was convinced that Lindbergh had made the move on his own, and that the navy wasn't setting him up to take the responsibility for its breach of regulations, he calmed down.

When the discussion turned to fuel saving, Kenney remarked that Lindbergh had performed quite a feat getting the *Spirit of St. Louis* to Paris with fuel to spare, and he wished that someone could tell his P-38 pilots how to perform the same miracle. Lindbergh told Kenney that with proper training, he believed squadrons could get a flying radius of 700 miles, and expert pilots 750. When he repeated these projections to General MacArthur and his chief of staff, Gen. Richard Sutherland, they were delighted.

Lindbergh soon increased even these estimates. A former member of the Satan's Angels recalled a lecture he gave shortly after his return from Brisbane: "He spoke informally on operational techniques and engine problems and fuel economy. However, when he claimed that the current P-38J-15-LO was good for an 800-mile operating radius and 10 hours flying time, it was generally felt that even if the engines could do that, it would be unwise to subject a fighter pilot to missions of such length." (The idea that ten hours of flying was too long, which might be taken as superficial proof of Phil Love's comment that the younger generation of pilots was soft, reflected the assumptions of training and specific conditions in that theater of war.)[7]

Lindbergh took every combat mission he could get, but the one he was scheduled for on July 28 was supposed to be an uneventful "milk run." All went smoothly until the final hours of the flight, when two Sonia-type Japanese fighters appeared out of nowhere. One of them flew head-on at Lindbergh, guns blazing. On a collision course at five-hundred miles per hour, Lindbergh fired back. At the last minute both pilots went into a climb, and the P-38 cleared the top of the Sonia by about ten feet, so close that Lindbergh could see the finning on the Japanese plane's engine cylinders. The Sonia, mortally wounded, spun out and crashed into the sea.

Three days later the tables turned. Banking to go to the rescue of his wingman, who was being harassed by a Zero, Lindbergh miscalculated and put too much distance between himself and the rest of the squadron. The Zero shifted his attention to this tempting target and opened fire at close range. Lindbergh was prepared to die. "I think of Anne—of the children.... There is an eternity of time. The world was never clearer." Inexplicably the Zero's fire missed, and MacDonald and two other squadron members came to Lindbergh's rescue. "The Jap must not have been too good a shot," MacDonald later reported.[8]

Lindy's narrow escape was the talk of New Guinea. A Passaic, New Jersey, newspaper, meanwhile, tipped off by a serviceman from the area, had published a story about Lindbergh shooting down a Japanese fighter. "It would raise one hell of a hullabaloo if you were shot down," Kenney told Lindbergh before issuing an order grounding him. He had flown a total of fifty combat missions.

To the men of military aviation, it seemed grossly unfair that the Lone Eagle had been denied a chance to serve in uniform. Some officers on MacArthur's staff were also in favor of pressuring the commander to remedy the situation, and MacArthur might well have been willing to raise the issue with the War Department. After all, the general's wife, Jean, had known Evangeline Lindbergh since 1929. Of course, there were officials in the Roosevelt administration who would sooner have climbed the stairs of the Washington Monument on their hands and knees than see Lindbergh's military rank restored to him. But with the ailing president campaigning for a fourth term, such a move would also have had certain advantages. Despite what he may or may not have said at the party in Webster's apartment, Lindbergh had steered clear of the rump America First organization led by the profascist Gerald L. K. Smith. The invasion of Europe was under way, and a battlefield commission in reward for service rendered would be far less controversial than it would have been earlier in the war.

Characteristically it was Lindbergh who vetoed the idea. He had no respect for FDR, and according to his rigid and bizarrely personalized sense of honor it would therefore be impossible for him to accept a commission.

Charles worked for United Aircraft in Connecticut until May of 1945, and shortly after V-E day, he joined a Naval Technical Mission in Europe as a civilian representative of the corporation. On his way to Germany, Lindbergh stopped in Paris, hoping to locate Anne Carrel. Dr. Carrel had died just days after the Liberation, his last hours tormented by an argument between factions of the resistance over his wartime cooperation with the Vichy regime. Madame, who had always maintained that she was too frail to join her husband in New York, had sailed for the States that very morning. She would outlive her husband by three decades.

Joining the Technical Mission in Munich, Lindbergh became part of a team of observers who drove their jeeps into territory where the Wehrmacht, defeated but not yet demobilized, was still in effective control. At the BMW aircraft factory a workman led them to a field where he had buried the plans for an experimental jet engine. Everywhere they went, the team sought out Germany's leading aeronautical scientists, debriefed them, and then tried to persuade them to defect to the Americans rather than the Russians. Lindbergh's group located Professor Willy Messerschmitt, who was living in a barn; Dr. Felix Kracht, the inventor of the rocket glider; Dr. Helmut Schelp, assistant head of development of the jet and rocket propulsion program; Dr. Franz Josef Neugebauer, who was working on a design for a nuclear-propelled aircraft; Dr. August Lichte, a developer of the Junker JU 004 turbojet engine; and Dr. Ulrich Henschke, who was working on artificial limbs capable of being controlled by neurological impulses.

A few days after Lindbergh spoke to him, Messerschmitt was

arrested when an SS officer's uniform was found hanging in the closet of his former home. Most of the scientists professed to be anti-Hitler and some told stories of relatives and colleagues who had either been arrested or mysteriously committed suicide during the final months of the war. An army sergeant who was traveling with the group carried snapshots from the recently liberated death camps that he showed to those who still thought the Nazis were "all right." Nearly all were desperate to escape the Russians. Even Schelp, whose wife and children were trapped in the Russian zone, came over.

In Nuremberg, Lindbergh and a Lieutenant Uellendahl were billeted in the home of a woman who wore a German air-raid warden's uniform. When he asked about it, she laughingly told him that she was half-Jewish but had evaded registration by keeping constantly on the move. Her husband and mother had been killed. She had heard nothing from her father since he had been shipped to Buchenwald ten years earlier and assumed he was long dead, too. The uniform had been given to her as "a joke."

Lindbergh recorded her story in his journal, along with abundant expressions of distaste at the Allied treatment of the Germans. He was shocked by soldiers who boasted of "liberating" (a euphemism for raping) German women and by the treatment of German prisoners of war. He protested against army regulations that forbade sharing food with the Germans—predicting correctly how no rule would prevent GIs from slipping candy bars to hungry children. He sympathized with a woman in Dessau who told him that she had been betrayed for twelve years by Hitler, and now the Americans were preparing to turn the town over to the Russians.

On June 11 the mission reached Camp Dora, which had provided forced labor for the V-2 rocket factory at Nordhausen. A seventeen-year-old prisoner from Poland showed them the crematorium, where, he said, twenty-five thousand bodies had been incinerated during the last year and a half. A pit eight feet long and six feet wide was filled to overflowing with human ashes and bone fragments.

"Of course, I knew these things were going on" Lindbergh wrote in his journal, "but it is one thing to have the intellectual knowledge, even to look at photographs someone else has taken, and quite another to stand on the scene yourself, seeing, hearing, feeling with your own senses. A strange sort of disturbance entered my mind. Where was it I had felt like that before?"

The entry continues with a catalog of the horrors of Biak—

Japanese soldiers incinerated in caves; others starving to death in the jungle because the Americans would not accept their surrender; the heads of dead Japanese buried in anthills to cleanse them of flesh so they could be used as souvenirs. "We, who claimed that the German was defiling humanity in his treatment of the Jew, were doing the same thing in our treatment of the Jap.... 'And why beholdest thou the mote that is in thy brother's eye, but considerest not the beam that is in thine own eye?'"

When Lindbergh's journals were published in 1970, the *New York Times* reviewer called this comparison between the occasional excesses of battle-weary combat troops and the systematic extermination campaign of the Nazis "grotesque." This is certainly true from the point of view of history, but Lindbergh was writing personally. To those who lived through it, "ordinary" combat, as practiced in the New Guinea campaign, was quite awful enough. Lindbergh's tolerance for moral ambiguities was nil at the best of times, and the enormity of the horror of Nazism was too much for him to grasp. He dealt with it by choosing to believe that the great majority of Germans, including those he had known and trusted, were not aware of what was going on. He passed up a chance to tour Dachau—in fact, he even avoided using the term *concentration camp* in his diaries, applying it only to American prisoner-of-war camps. (Those who imagine that blaming America first is a liberal reflex should consider the case of Lindbergh.) On the other hand, he applied the same rule to himself, and one can only admire his refusal to seize the occasion of the trip as an opportunity for issuing self-serving statements of the "if only I had known" variety.

It was harder for Lindbergh to turn his back on the mounting evidence that he had been deliberately deceived and lied to. Ernst Udet had died during the war, supposedly in a flying accident, but it soon came out that he had shot himself after a nervous breakdown partly induced by the disarray of the Luftwaffe's construction and development program, which was already in trouble at the time of Lindbergh's 1938 tour. Lindbergh also learned that the scientist who sat next to him at the stag dinner for Göring that year had been the head of the V-2 rocket project, a program whose existence was never revealed to him. Since Lindbergh had been an early proponent and supporter of Robert Goddard, this was no oversight, and on learning that much of the German work was based on patented processes stolen from the recently deceased Goddard, Lindbergh permitted himself a rare expression of outrage on his friend's behalf.

After the technical mission ended, Lindbergh purchased a Renault Quatre Chevaux and began driving through the ruined countryside of Western Europe. He covered about sixty thousand kilometers before his peregrinations were interrupted by an invitation from Gen. Carl Spaatz to join a top-secret weapons research project being organized at the University of Chicago. The report of the Navy Technical Mission, on which Lindbergh collaborated, had urged the U.S. government to commit itself to the development of rocketry, high-tech airplanes, and other advanced weapons. Convinced that the atomic bomb and supersonic bombers had made his noninterventionist beliefs obsolete, Lindbergh accepted Spaatz's invitation. He would devote much of the next ten years to serving as a dollar-a-year consultant on a variety of air force and army technical committees.

On the Chicago project, code-named CHORE, Lindbergh worked with nuclear physicists Enrico Fermi and Walter Bartky. The committee's discussions of advanced mathematics and physics were often over his head, and his chief function was to bring the scientists' flights of imagination back to earth by reminding them that high-tech jet fighters were still piloted by human beings and that combat conditions were likely to be distracting and unpredictable, no matter how perfect the equipment.

Lindbergh also served on a committee to reorganize the Strategic Air Command, chaired an inquiry into the relative performance of air force research facilities, and worked with John von Neumann on the Air Force Scientific Advisory Board's studies of ballistic missiles. He spent nearly two weeks on a nuclear-powered submarine and flew B-52 bombers, training with the 509th Atomic Bomb Group out of Walker Air Force Base. He made recommendations on the relative effectiveness of weapons systems, pilot training, personnel policies, and testing crew reactions under simulated combat conditions. In late 1948 and early 1949, he flew around the world, surveying possible sites for SAC bases. When the Berlin airlift began, he acted as a consultant, riding as a passenger on a number of flights over the Soviet corridor.[9]

In his rare public statements on defense issues, Lindbergh presented himself as the most resolute of Cold Warriors. In a 1954 *Saturday Evening Post* article, one of his rare published statements on defense issues, Lindbergh warned, "The hydrogen bomb and the supersonic missile have eliminated defensive security on the face of the earth." Since a nuclear first strike was "against the traditions and policies of the American people," our only security lay in the capacity to retaliate with overwhelming force—"Our weapons must be widely decentralized as well as extremely powerful and if we relax our vigilance even temporarily our civilization is likely to fall, with a loss of life that is staggering."

Privately Lindbergh readily admitted that the capability of the Soviets was often overestimated, while millions were wasted on redundant weapons systems. But the man the public still thought of as "Lucky Lindy" had always had a cautious streak. If risks were inevitable, he was prepared to take them. If not, he insisted on a margin of safety that others might consider excessive. As a military strategist, he was the most pessimistic American general since George Washington. His Cold War position was no more than a continuation of his prewar anti-interventionism. Once the United States had relied on the oceans for protection. Now it must rely on "character"—the nuclear arsenal, which he hoped we would never have to use, was merely the outward evidence of our determination.[10]

When Lindbergh met Willy Messerschmitt in 1945, the German aeronautical scientist told him that if it weren't for the war, he would already have created the first commercial transatlantic jet airplane. On his return from Europe Lindbergh relayed this information to Juan Trippe, and a few months later he rejoined Pan-Am as a technical consultant, working with a group of engineers on the problems of converting to jet propulsion. In 1952, while Lockheed and Boeing were developing prototype jets for the commercial market, most airline executives were still counting on turboprops to remain the industry standard for years to come. Juan Trippe, already converted to the advantages of jets by Lindbergh and the Pan-Am engineering department, was the exception. He saw the new technology not as a luxury for the few but as a way to move more passengers more cheaply and pressured Lockheed into modifying its plans for the 707, employing a more advanced engine and increased passenger capacity.

Trippe's announcement, in October 1955, that Pan-Am planned to spend $269 million on forty-five Lockheed and Douglas jets stunned the industry and made the transition to jets inevitable. He later told his biographer Robert Daley that no business decision in Pan-Am's history had been more carefully researched, and Lindbergh had been involved at every step of the way.[11]

To one degree or another Charles Lindbergh had been involved in almost every major development in commercial and military aviation since 1927. Since he was always a consultant, never the individual with the title, his contributions can be difficult to evaluate even in retrospect,

and they were certainly little known to the general public. It is the ultimate irony that Lindbergh, who longed to be accepted as an intellectual
and a writer, got his wish, often to the detriment of his reputation, and
is little remembered as the man who set up the infrastructure of the first
transcontinental airline, flew the first American airmail route to the
Caribbean, and (with Anne) mapped the major international routes.
Lindbergh's postwar work for the air force was even less well known and
in April 1954, when President Eisenhower restored his commission in
the reserves, promoting him to the rank of brigadier general, the honor
was presented as a belated acknowledgment of his wartime services.
Those inside the aviation industry knew better, as did members of
Congress who served on committees related to military aviation and the
defense budget. Lindbergh was frequently in the capital lobbying for
appropriations.

During these visits to Washington, he stayed at the Army-Navy
Club, and frequently dropped in at the Smithsonian, where he would
stand inconspicuously in the corner, staring up at the *Spirit of St. Louis*.
His receding hairline and a few extra pounds had changed his appearance dramatically, and Anne Lindbergh later commented to author Ron
Chernow that her husband was one of the rare men who found the
physical changes of middle age a blessing. For the first time in many
years he could venture out in public without being recognized, a situation he did his best to maintain. The advent of television was another
blessing. Lindbergh recognized early on that the press photographers
who had once been his bane no longer had the power to make or break
a celebrity. No one in the postwar world was truly famous unless he had
appeared on the small screen, and Lindbergh made it his business to
avoid the TV cameras.

Emory Land, who was not one to hand out undeserved compliments, even to a relative, rated his cousin Slim as one of the three most
influential figures in the growth period of American aviation. Land considered Jimmy Doolittle the best test pilot and all-around flyer and
Jerome Hunsaker of MIT the leader in aeronautical engineering. Lindbergh, in his estimation, bridged both worlds, at once an outstanding
pilot and major figure in commercial and military aviation.[12]

Yet, even as he took part in the planning of ballistic missile systems
and pushed commercial aviation into the jet age, Lindbergh was grappling with his own disenchantment with aviation. His old dream had
been fulfilled. The sky had indeed become the universal highway—but
instead of leading to brotherhood, peace, and prosperity, it often

seemed to be a conduit for social chaos and the ever-present threat of nuclear annihilation. In his 1948 essay *Of Flight and Life,* Lindbergh was perhaps the first to point out a phenomenon often noted by the pilots of high-performance jets—a feeling of almost godlike disassociation. It worried him that these same pilots were carrying nuclear weapons. *Of Flight and Life* also predicted that the ease of transportation in the modern world, in addition to creating a global economy and a unitary, mass culture, would stimulate massive population shifts. Overwhelmed by refugees, America would be forced to choose between its traditional commitment to welcoming the dispossessed of the earth and the preservation of its own political values and prosperity. Most reviewers had no idea what he was talking about and dismissed this passage in the essay as just another paranoid, white-supremacist fantasy.

Lindbergh, however, was the opposite of xenophobic. What he hated was that the nations of the world were losing their individual characters and coming more and more under the sway of homogenized, mass culture. During his 1948 visit to Japan, when his military hosts took him to dinner at the officer's club and proudly informed him that the ingredients of the meat-and-potatoes meal were all imported from the States, he was irate. The penchant of overseas Americans for creating little Ohios, New Yorks, and Californias wherever they went mystified him, especially since the effort condemned them to consuming canned and packaged food, and he complained that it was an insult to the Japanese staff to expect them to serve such meals.

The ultimate disillusionment came during an inspection visit to the SAC base in Fairbanks, Alaska, when Lindbergh was invited to come along on a reconnaissance flight over the North Pole. The adventure he had daydreamed about since childhood was now the stuff of a routine afternoon's patrol. Since a heated car drove him to and from the airfield, it wasn't even necessary to don a parka. He spent the flight seated on his parachute pack, working on the draft for a chapter of his autobiography.

TWENTY-FIVE

"The Mermaid and the Eagle"

*I*N 1946, AFTER SEVENTEEN YEARS OF MARRIAGE, Charles and Anne finally settled into a permanent home, purchasing a house on the shores of Long Island Sound in Scott's Cove near Darien, Connecticut. The eighty-thousand-dollar house, with nine bedrooms, six and a half baths, and three studies—one each for Charles and Anne and one for their secretary—was spacious enough for their family, which was enlarged in October that same year by the birth of a second daughter, Reeve. The America First debacle had freed Charles from the burden of being the all-American hero, and he and Anne at last enjoyed a modicum of privacy. Ironically but perhaps not surprisingly, at the very moment when they were free to live in relative peace, the Lindberghs' marriage began to show signs of strain.

During the months when Charles was in the Pacific, Anne had been on her own for the first time in her life, and she had managed rather well. When Charles returned from the war, he discovered a wife who had a newfound sense of independence. After giving birth for the sixth time, Anne, now forty, decided that her family was quite large enough, a disappointing decision for her husband, who had been much impressed by Ambassador Kennedy's large brood and often said that he considered twelve children the ideal family size. Nor did she feel driven any longer to prove herself by continuing as Charles's flying partner. In the future, when she flew, she would treat herself to the comfort and security of a scheduled Pan-Am flight, thank you.

With five children under fifteen to raise, Anne undoubtedly hoped that Charles would be content to stay closer to home once the war ended. After all, she had stood by him during the difficult days of the America First period, to the detriment of family peace and old friendships, and in 1945, when Charles came back to the States to work for United Aircraft, she had left Bloomfield Hills and returned east, leaving behind her new friends at the Cranbrook Academy.

But Charles, instead of settling down, had become more of a wanderer than ever. A real-life Peter Pan, he still defined freedom as the ability to fly off to some faraway destination on a moment's notice. He had managed rather successfully, if often messily, to avoid the sort of career commitments that tie most adults to a daily routine. Anne's decision to retire from aviation actually removed the last obstacle to total "freedom," since he now had a stable, well-ordered home to return to whenever he wished. "Lindbergh was not domesticated," observes one friend who sympathized completely with Anne. However, it is also true that he had made sacrifices for his family that most men are not called on to make, and a close reader of Anne's published diaries can't help coming to the conclusion that her loyalty may have been a gift that was not always easy to bear. The legendary character that Charles Lindbergh himself identified with was not Peter Pan but King Midas, whose golden touch destroyed everything and everyone he dared to love.

The decade after the war was a difficult period, made more so by Charles's deepening interest in military strategy and high-tech weaponry. Never strictly speaking a pacifist, Anne hated war and hated the atom bomb even more. Otherwise she tended to mirror her family and friends, who ranged from liberal Republicans to quite left wing. Dwight junior and his wife were members of the NAACP during the forties, long before civil rights was a fashionable cause. Corliss Lamont, with whom Anne remained on friendly terms, was being investigated by the FBI, and ban-the-bomb and anti-McCarthyite sentiment was running high among Smith alumnae and intellectuals in general. In these circles marriage to a man who was a consultant to the Strategic Air Command was not something to be proud of; indeed, Charles's resolute anti-Communism was less socially acceptable than his near isolationism had been in the years before the war.

Knowing that it was useless to try to change her husband's mind on any subject by arguing with him, Anne mounted a more subtle campaign, on occasion clipping articles she found especially persuasive and leaving them on his pillow. To an extent this strategy worked. Charles came to share his wife's distaste for the demagoguery of Joe McCarthy and in 1952, for the first time in his life, he voted for a Democratic presidential candidate, supporting Adlai Stevenson over Gen. Dwight D. Eisenhower. (Lindbergh's preference may not have been known to Eisenhower when he restored his army rank and promoted him to general.)

If politics often divided them, the Lindberghs were held together during this period by their devotion to their children. Although from reading Anne Lindbergh's diaries one might easily get the impression that she was a frazzled, nervous parent, her children thought of her as supportive and patient, if perhaps a bit overindulgent. Unlike some women who make a show of loving babies indiscriminately, Anne had the ability to accept and enjoy her children's individual personalities from a very early age. Charles, who had an almost phobic abhorrence of public displays of affection and was too self-conscious even to take part in social dancing, seemed to lose his inhibitions among young children and become almost a child himself. When Jim Newton sent the children a variety of animal tails that they wore pinned to the seat of their jeans or playsuits, Charles tried the raccoon tail on himself and concluded that it made a definite improvement in his appearance. Indeed, he wrote Jerry Land, wearing the tail had made him aware of an aspect of his character previously unknown to him—"hidden vanity." For the first time in his life he understood how a woman feels when she tries on a new and very becoming hat.[1]

Charles expected his children to be highly independent and had myriad strategies for inculcating the values of promptness, honesty, and frugality. He paid Jon five cents a pound for his catches of fish until the basement freezer was so stuffed with seafood there was no room for other groceries. A little later, when Jon's aluminum canoe had been replaced by a small motorboat, he got a dollar for every load of dirt and sand he brought home; he and his father used the landfill to build a small beach at the north end of their property. Lindbergh taught his children to swim, shoot, climb trees, and use tools, and he put each of them in turn through a program of driving lessons that included learning to put the car into a controlled skid.

At times his methods of teaching his children to take calculated risks struck other adults as extreme. Harold Nicolson had looked on in horror as Charles, attempting to teach three-year-old Jon to swim, flung him repeatedly into the deep end of the Morrows' swimming pool. Kay Smith told of a visit to the Eiffel Tower during the late thirties when, as they were descending the stairs, she automatically reminded Jon to hold on to the railing and watch his step. She was aghast to be overruled by Charles who ordered, "Jon, let go of the railing and run down." Lindbergh's reply to such comments was that most parents overprotected their children when they were young and then provided no discipline at all as soon as they got a little older. Of the Eiffel Tower incident, he explained that they were already near the bottom of the tower when he said this and Jon was justifiably restless, having been denied a trip to the top because Smith's daughter threw a tantrum on the first-stage landing.

In general Lindbergh was a man of many rules—from ideas about the unhealthfulness of refined sugar and the importance of getting enough fiber to the all-purpose maxim: "Do the difficult things first." All these rules were made to be broken on occasion, though it took the children a while to figure this out, and at times even other adults were taken aback by Lindbergh's peremptory manner. One air force officer who was invited to dine with Lindbergh at the Army-Navy Club in Washington was startled when the general countermanded his instructions to the waiter. "You haven't ordered any fruit," Lindbergh intoned. The officer meekly asked the waiter to bring him some stewed prunes—and ate them. In more relaxed moments, Lindbergh himself had a sweet tooth and much preferred rich desserts, especially chocolate or angel food cake as made by the family's longtime cook, Martha Knecht. Even his lifelong shunning of alcohol was not entirely a matter of principle. "I would like to enjoy wine," he once confessed. "I just don't. Wine glasses on a table look so nice, and the wine smells so nice, and even tastes nice, but when I start drinking it seems awful! It must be great fun to like wine and to travel through France sampling the wine of various areas."[2]

Lindbergh had a temper and he himself admitted that he spanked all his children on occasion, but on the whole, he was less a martinet than an enthusiastic, often very competitive, playmate. He was good at inventing games. One of the children's favorites was "Wild Cats," played inside a "cave" constructed by draping a sheet or blanket over some chairs. Charles would crawl inside the cave with the "cats" and distribute treats. But even when the children were very young, it would not have occurred to Lindbergh to deliberately let them win a game or contest—to do so would be dishonest—and even after Jon and Land were grown up and parents themselves, he still took pride in being able to best them in a foot race.

He encouraged his children to believe there was nothing they could not accomplish if they set their minds to it, and set an example of fearlessness and toughness. Several times every winter, he would plunge naked into the frigid waters of Scott's Cove then enjoy an invigorating run along the beach. As a small-plane pilot, he continued to enjoy a remarkable record of injury-free miles; once, while flying with ten-year-old Reeve as a passenger, he lost engine power over the Connecticut woods and side-slipped into a clearing so narrow that the mechanics had to remove the plane's wings to extricate it.

Jon, far from being discouraged by his early swimming lessons, loved the water and by the time he entered his teens was spending long hours tooling around the sound in a small outboard. He enjoyed extraordinary freedom for his age. On one occasion when still in his midteens, he was given permission to make a three-day boat trip on his own.

Charles took credit for steering his older sons away from aviation, warning them that flying was no longer as exciting as it had been in his day and they would always have the burden of being compared with their famous father. Jon switched from air force to navy ROTC early in his career at Stanford and completed training as a navy frogman. He and his wife Barbara, whom he married when he was twenty-two, settled in Seattle, where he and inventor Edwin Link formed a company called Ocean Systems, Inc., to develop equipment for undersea exploration. In 1964 Jon broke the record for an extended dive—spending forty-nine consecutive hours at a depth of 432 feet. Lanky, quiet Land, the son who most resembled his famous father, also married young; he settled in Greenough, Montana, where he became the owner and manager of the Lindbergh Cattle Co.

For the younger children, "Father," as he was always called—never "Dad"—was a somewhat more remote figure. Daughter Anne, a toddler during the months Charles spent at the Pacific front, was the child who took his frequent absences most to heart. Charles was amazed and a little hurt to discover that when he came home after a brief absence, Anne regarded him with wide-eyed suspicion. Two years later, when he returned from a weeklong business trip, Anne greeted him with the instruction, "Take off your coat—are you going to stay?"[3]

Anne grew up to become the author of a series of whimsical fantasies for children, and she has acknowledged in one interview that she drew on her memories of her famous parent in creating the mildly eccentric father figure of the book *Nobody's Orphan,* who is given to quoting aphorisms that he attributes to his favorite politician, Calvin Coolidge. "Father was very high on Calvin Coolidge," says Anne. Even more obviously drawn from life is the character of Mr. Sweeny in Anne's 1982 novel, *The People in Pineapple Place.* A middle-aged Peter Pan who combs his hair across the top of his head to hide a bald spot, exactly as Charles Lindbergh began doing in his late fifties, Mr. Sweeny suffers from a disease known as "chronic cyclical anticipatory motion discomfort" which, we are told, began forty-three years earlier when he was "worried about the war in Europe [and] afraid the United States would get involved." As a result of this condition, Mr. Sweeny never gets any older but travels back and forth in space and time, taking the children of Pineapple Place with him. The children find these repeated dislocations educational, if a trifle disconcerting.[4]

As had been the case since 1927, most of the work that occupied Charles's time was either unpaid or performed for a salary that was a fraction of what he should have been earning. After the war, Juan Trippe proposed that Lindbergh rejoin Pan-Am for a consultancy fee of ten thousand dollars a year, on the understanding that he would devote one-tenth of his time to the airline. Charles insisted on taking less since he hated the idea of committing such a large percentage of his time. In the end, by his own account, far more than a tenth of his working hours were devoted to Pan-Am business, but the contract was not renegotiated. Charles's almost-pathological aversion to getting paid—he could not accept that he deserved the money and saw contracts as an abridgment of his freedom—must have been frustrating for Anne. They were hardly poor, but there was far less family wealth than most people supposed, and the fact that Charles's frequent absences had little to do with earning money can only have made them more irritating.

Ironically Charles would soon be earning more as a writer than from aviation. He had been working since the late thirties on the manuscript of *The Spirit of St. Louis,* an account of his 1927 flight with autobiographical flashbacks. Over thirteen years, the manuscript had taken shape from bits and pieces written on airplanes, in his room in the Army-Navy Club in Washington, and even in the New Guinea jungles while waiting to go into combat. Disdainful of the articles and newspaper stories written about him, Lindbergh had never made any secret of his opinion that he could do a better job of writing about his adventures than most professional writers. Irritatingly enough, from the writers' point of view, *The Spirit of St. Louis* would prove he was right.

By any standards, and certainly in comparison with *We*, his previous book, *The Spirit of St. Louis* is an amazing accomplishment. It has the pacing of an adventure novel and a complex narrative structure, describing the flight hour by hour with flashbacks so skillfully employed that the reader never questions that they represent the scenes from the pilot's past that actually flashed before his eyes during the critical moments of his adventure. Moreover, as Brendan Gill has observed, the book is written in the historical present indicative, a tense most writing teachers consider inadvisable for a beginner and certainly impossible to sustain over the course of a five-hundred-page work of nonfiction.

Charles dedicated the work to his wife, "who will never realize how much of this book she has written." More than a few reviewers have suspected that this was a coy way of acknowledging that Anne had, in fact, written all or most of it. Anne denied this, insisting that she did not read drafts of the various chapters until they had assumed more or less their final shape, and that she had actually tried to talk Charles out of using the present tense, which gives the book its energy and intensely personal flavor. And, in fact, an examination of the manuscript, now part of the collection of the Library of Congress, leaves no doubt that the book was Charles's own work. He had literally taught himself to write, and only after the manuscript had been through numerous drafts did he begin sending it out for criticism—not only to old friends like Bud Gurney and Don Hall, who were asked to check for accuracy, but to publishing professionals who could give him pointers on style.[5]

By the time *The Spirit of St. Louis* appeared in 1953, Charles Lindbergh had been in the public eye for a quarter of a century, yet the book offered the first uncensored portrait of Lindbergh the man—one that, as the *New York Times* reviewer observed, "brings him into the company of his fellow mortals." Among the book's revelations was Lindbergh's description of the "phantoms" that visited the cabin during the latter stages of the transatlantic flight.

Nevertheless, like most autobiographies, *The Spirit of St. Louis* had its self-mythologizing aspects. The most serious distortion, as Gill also notes, was that Evangeline Lindbergh was reduced to a cartoon of the conventional homemaker, far different from the brilliant, erratic woman she actually was. During the period when the final draft of *The Spirit of St. Louis* was being prepared for submission to a publisher—Lindbergh did not use an agent but solicited free advice from several—Evangeline was lying paralyzed in her modest home in Grosse Pointe Park, suffering from the final stages of Parkinson's disease. Lindbergh visited his mother as often as he could, but the burden of caring for her had fallen on the ever-loyal "Brother." One can well understand that for Lindbergh to publish anything critical about his parents at this point would have made her final months more painful.

This does not quite explain why the book avoids discussing Evangeline's scientific interests or her role as his primary teacher. For that matter, as in all his later writings, Lindbergh devotes so much space to nostalgic reminiscences about Little Falls, to the exclusion of his life in Washington, that one almost forgets that Minnesota was only where he spent his summer vacations. It was Lindbergh himself who longed to remember his childhood as idyllic and who objected to any suggestion by other writers that it was otherwise. The modern biographer is inclined to assume that Lindbergh, who practiced the art of closing his mind to subjects too hurtful to think about throughout his life, was suppressing some childhood trauma. On the other hand, early drafts of the manuscript reveal that he made some attempts to treat his childhood more honestly, but the anecdotes he came up with never seemed quite proportionate to the feelings of deprivation they were meant to illustrate. At the same time, a note of unintended bitterness crops up in anecdotes intended to be about something else entirely—his youthful shyness or his dislike of city life. Although it would seem that CA was the one more responsible in refusing to give Evangeline her freedom, it was his mother toward whom Charles felt a deep, if always carefully suppressed, resentment.

Lindbergh must have realized that he had given short shrift to the Land side of the family in *The Spirit of St. Louis*. When the book was awarded the Pulitzer Prize for biography, he donated the monetary award to Dr. Laszlo Schwartz, a member of the Columbia University faculty who had announced his intention of writing a biography of Charles H. Land. Unfortunately the book was never completed.

Evangeline Lindbergh died in September 1954. In November, Betty Morrow, still an indefatigable fund-raiser at the age of eighty-one, was honored at a banquet at the Waldorf-Astoria for her fifty years of volunteer work on behalf of the Community Service Society. A few days later Mrs. Morrow suffered a paralytic stroke, lingering in a coma for eight weeks before she finally passed away on January 23, 1955. Charles, who had been in Europe on army business, managed to return in time for the funeral.

Mrs. Morrow had lived well, traveled extensively, and given generously to her favorite charities. When Dwight Morrow died in 1931, he left an estate on which the New Jersey inheritance tax alone was more than a million dollars, an amount in that depression year sufficient to rescue the state treasury from a threatened bankruptcy. Twenty-three years later, Mrs. Morrow's entire estate came to less than $10,000,000. In her will she bequeathed Next Day Hill to the Little School, which was renamed the Elisabeth Morrow School. The bulk of her portfolio went to Dwight junior, who, after recurrent hospitalizations for mental illness and a stint as a dairy farmer in Carmel, California, during the war, finally earned his Ph.D. in history in 1951. Amicably divorced from Margot, by whom he had three children, Dwight taught at Lincoln University in Pennsylvania and then at Temple before returning to Carmel, where he established himself as an expert on the history and technology of the winemaking industry. Never quite resigned to his role as "the forgotten Morrow," Dwight often remarked sarcastically that he had finally managed to fulfill his father's lifelong ambition of becoming a history teacher.

Betty Morrow died just a few months too soon to witness the astounding success of Anne's next book, *Gift from the Sea,* an essay on the role of women inspired by Virginia Woolf's *A Room of One's Own,* which Mrs. Morrow once called "the most important book in English since *Uncle Tom's Cabin." Gift from the Sea* appeared that March and shot to the top of the bestseller lists, where it remained for fifty-one weeks. Astoundingly it is still being offered thirty-eight years later as a selection of the Book-of-the-Month Club. In the interim it has sold in excess of seven million copies. According to the publisher's spokesperson, Mrs. Lindbergh continues to receive, on average, about fifteen letters a week from readers who have been inspired by the book's message, and in a 1991 survey for which a sample of Americans were asked to name the book that had influenced their lives most strongly, it tied for ninth place with Betty Friedan's *Feminine Mystique* and several other titles.

Anne Lindbergh thought of *Gift from the Sea* as her "feminist essay," yet—amazingly, considering its enormous popularity—this deceptively graceful book has been ignored by feminist critics and teachers of women's studies. In his 1976 biography of Charles Lindbergh, Leonard Mosley dismissed the book as "an anodyne for masses of fretful women" and "the Bible of the Middle American Housewife," a fair summary of prevailing opinion, and prior to publication an editor at Pantheon—not seriously, one hopes—suggested changing the title to *Quiet Desperation,* a reference to the well-known quotation from Thoreau. Far from being a social critic, much less an advocate of rebellion in the name of self-expression, Lindbergh advocated that women seek change within themselves, through contemplation and self-renewal.

But the self-effacing prose of *Gift from the Sea* conveyed a revolutionary message. In a decade when the women's magazines were filled with articles advocating "togetherness," and the ideal woman was a housewife who kept an immaculate home, served as a Cub Scout den mother, ran the car pool, and still found time to make centerpieces out of pine cones and last year's Christmas ribbons, Lindbergh ventured to suggest that many traditional women's tasks are simply not worth doing and, moreover, that women cannot and should not depend on their husbands to fulfill all their emotional and intellectual needs. Nearly four decades later, the ideal of the executive in an apron having been replaced by that of the corporate lawyer with a Filofax, who manages to spend "quality time" with her family and still work out an hour a day, Mrs. Lindbergh's warning against frittering away one's life in pursuit of someone else's definition of perfection is as relevant as ever.

Whether Mrs. Lindbergh profited from her own advice is another question. Certainly she believed she had. In a 1978 speech at Smith College, significantly titled "The Journey Not the Arrival Matters," Lindbergh would recall with wry humor how far she had come since the early years of her marriage, when her idea of liberation consisted of playing "the devoted page, serving my knight." But as a practical matter, as Charles's travels became ever more frequent and unpredictable, she was left at home to deal with the day-to-day responsibilities of running the house and bringing up their five children.

Anne's feeling of being weighed down by the unending and often inconsequential chores of daily living was not necessarily the result of overwork. While it is true that no mother of five can ever be said to have it easy, the Lindberghs had a live-in cook and part-time cleaning woman, and on occasion, a nursemaid and a secretary as well. As Anne herself was the first to admit, she had never been efficient when it came to dealing with schedules and errands. A writer of slow and methodical habits, she needed uninterrupted blocks of time, and when sunk in what she called her "well of concentration," details like picking up one of the children from school were often forgotten.

Charles, despite his own troubles shifting mental gears, was exasperated by his wife's inability to cope. "He was baffled by my difficulty in changing from one role to another," Anne later said.[6]

One of Anne's reasons for giving up aviation after the war was that she was struggling to find her own voice—"and it was not the voice of a radio operator." Charles had long believed that his wife had the makings of a great novelist and hoped that she would use her "retirement" from flying to write a big "social" novel. As he had in Detroit, he tried to encourage her by constructing a studio, in this instance made from an old toolshed that he found abandoned by the side of Route 1. But months, sometimes years, went by, during which Anne found no time at all to write, and—curiously, considering the promise of her early short stories—she seemed overwhelmed by the prospect of launching into a full-length novel.

An orderly man, Charles had been an enthusiastic housekeeper in his bachelor days and still knew his way around a kitchen. He continually advised his wife to simplify her routine in order to avoid becoming bogged down in minutiae—advice she was not always good at applying but which, ironically, was incorporated into *Gift from the Sea*. There was, for example, the unending problem of the mail. As Charles once explained to Jerry Land, his "conscience" would not permit him to sign letters composed by a secretary. Since he continued to receive thousands of pieces of mail every year, more than any one person could respond to personally, he dealt with the overflow by depositing the majority of his letters, unopened, in cardboard boxes, which he eventually piled in the back of the family station wagon and delivered to Yale, for inclusion among his personal papers. Unfortunately Anne's conscience dictated that mail ought to be answered, and much of the burden of handling the correspondence fell to her by default. It was she who wrote the personal notes that went out to friends along with complimentary copies of *The Spirit of St. Louis*, as it was she who handled certain business and personal requests that could not be ignored. When Jerry Land passed away at the age of ninety-three Anne wrote the sympathy letter to the family, mentioning (with no apparent irony) that, next to Evangeline, the admiral had been the relative Charles felt closest to.

Charles's supportiveness did not extend to rearranging his schedule so that he could be at home to take over certain responsibilities. One must admit, however, that Anne's view of domestic life as a spiderweb that grew more intricate (and stickier) with each passing year, was not very inviting. Just as he had once escaped from an unhealthily close relationship with his mother, Charles now found activities that drew him away from Connecticut. Military aviation was especially convenient since it often involved classified subjects, and it was not only possible but necessary to be a little vague about the nature of the business that called him away.[7]

After the remarkable success of *Gift from the Sea,* Anne's literary career did not flourish. In 1956 Pantheon released a slender collection of her lyric poems entitled *The Unicorn.* While not overtly autobiographical, a number of selections, written over a twenty-year period, were obviously inspired by the death of Charles Lindbergh, Jr., and the isolation of the America First period. The title poem depicted the unicorn—"His bright invulnerability/Captive at last." Reviewers for some reason seemed not to see the resemblance between this wounded mythical creature and Charles Lindbergh, yet few could doubt that another of the lyrics, describing Hans Christian Andersen's "Little Mermaid," who left her happy undersea playground and the companionship of her laughing sisters only to learn "the price one pays for mortal love," was meant to reflect the poet's own experience.

The Unicorn received generally favorable notices, including coverage on the front page of the *New York Times* Sunday book section, and quickly made an appearance on the bestseller lists, only to be blindsided by a January 12, 1957, review by John Ciardi, poetry editor of the *Saturday Review,* damning the poems as "low-grade poetry and low-grade humanity," as well as "inept, jingling, slovenly, illiterate even and puffed up with the foolish afflatus of a stereotyped high-mindedness." (Even at that, Ciardi's review had been toned down. He had wanted it to appear under the title "The Slovenly Unicorn," but was overruled by the magazine's editor, Norman Cousins, and in subsequent published remarks he called Mrs. Lindbergh's imprecise diction "akin to Original Sin.") Not surprisingly, many readers of the normally polite *Saturday Review* concluded that Ciardi was motivated by personal or political animosity. Hundreds wrote to protest, and the furor became so intense that Cousins took the extraordinary step of publishing a statement defending his decision not to fire his poetry editor.

From today's perspective, perhaps the most amazing aspect of this contretemps was that a review of a book of poems could inspire such passionate public debate. Sadly, Ciardi was basically correct. The author of *The Unicorn,* while by no means lacking in natural gifts, was a constricted talent. Lindbergh relied overmuch on romantic clichés. She had never learned to edit her own work and could certainly have benefited from the unsparing appraisals that most apprentice poets receive from their peers, not to mention from teachers and magazine editors. As Ciardi's rebuttal to his accusers made clear, what really riled him was that a book by a celebrity had been released by a major trade house and was receiving major bookstore presentation as well as gentle reviews, all at a time when many accomplished poets were lucky to see their work in print at all. Ironically, considering her earlier fears that her writing would be received as just another "Lindbergh stunt," Anne Lindbergh had walked into that very trap. She wrote as an amateur—"for therapy," as she told one interviewer—yet published as a professional.

Just as Charles Lindbergh's personality served as a lightning rod, Anne's charm and sensitivity inspired a chivalrous overprotectiveness. Ciardi at least paid Mrs. Lindbergh the compliment of taking her seriously as an artist, even though he thought her a very bad one. Many writers would have found the experience of being at the center of a literary cause célèbre not entirely unpleasant, especially considering that her book was outselling by a wide margin all other works of poetry published that year. Moreover, a careful reading of *The Unicorn* makes it clear that Anne Lindbergh's devoted fans were not simply hypnotized by her celebrity. What made Anne Lindbergh's writing interesting was not its gentleness at all but its undertone of anger, which occasionally flared up into violent imagery. "Plunge deep/Into the sky/O wing/Of the soul" begins one poem, which then quickly degenerates into mush about "The pale cloud-pastures/Of the mind." Perhaps if it had come a few years earlier, Ciardi's attack would have had a liberating effect. Instead it only made Anne warier of self-revelation. She published no more books of poetry but began work on a novel whose theme was a defense of the institution of marriage—a reply to a criticism no one had made.

In some respects the Lindberghs remained a close-knit clan. There were frequent family vacations—ski trips, holidays in the Florida Keys, and a two-week stay in the Bahamas—and after Jon and Land married the group was extended to include their wives and children. But closeness did not necessarily mean communication. Lindbergh could be quite garrulous when he was enjoying himself, but he had a tendency to compartmentalize his interests. Exactly what Father did for the military was always mysterious to his wife and children; nor was he much given to reminiscing about past exploits. In the 1960s, when Land arranged for his father to speak to the Montana state constitutional convention, he was amazed by the fuss; though he knew his father was famous it was the first time he had ever seen him in the presence of an adoring crowd.

Of course, "that business in New Jersey," as Lindbergh preferred to call it, was a taboo subject. Indeed, Lindbergh wrote in an unpublished memo that he had never discussed the kidnapping even with his wife. He appeared surprised that anyone should think this necessary—"after all, she lived through it"—a comment that leads one to wonder how two people could go through life side by side without talking about the subject that surely haunted them both. The younger Anne first learned about the kidnapping when she answered the door one day and found herself face to face with a deranged man who insisted that he was her brother, Charles Augustus Lindbergh, Jr. (Individuals claiming to be the Lindbergh baby arrived in Darien every few months or so, but most were spotted by drivers from the local car service, who had been warned to notify the police.) Scott, the next child in line, learned of the crime for the first time at the age of ten when he came across a library book on the subject.

Less understandably the America First period was another area that was not discussed. In 1956, when producer Leland Hayward began filming the movie version of *The Spirit of St. Louis* he quickly discovered that many people in the business had neither forgotten nor forgiven Lindbergh's Des Moines speech of 1941. Lindbergh had arranged for Bud Gurney to serve as technical adviser on the film, and he himself paid only a few visits to the set. (Surprisingly enough the screenwriters' insertion of purely fictional incidents into his life story—including the famous scene in which Jimmy Stewart is kept awake by a fly buzzing around inside the cabin of the plane—did not bother him at all.) A few weeks before the film was scheduled to open, however, Lindbergh received a call from his attorney, Walter Fletcher of Davis, Polk, Wardwell, Sunderland and Kiendl. According to Lindbergh, Fletcher told him that he had been contacted by the legal department of Warner Brothers, which had received protests from Jewish theater owners who were reluctant to exhibit a film glorifying Charles Lindbergh. As an exercise in damage control, the company attorneys suggested that Lindbergh put on his general's uniform, fly to Israel, and "make an official inspection of the Israeli army."

If this was indeed the producers' suggestion, Lindbergh was right to dismiss it as ridiculous. What he could not see, however, was that the public might deserve some reassurance that he was not a Nazi. After two years as a highly visible and controversial spokesman for the anti-interventionists, Lindbergh had dropped from sight shortly after the war began. Aside from an article in *Collier's* by Charles MacDonald and a piece by *Times* correspondent Deac Lyman, almost nothing had been published about his wartime service. Many Americans had no idea what had become of Charles Lindbergh after December 1941, and the minority who had read his often inscrutable musings in *Of Flight and Life* can hardly have been reassured. Even if he did not see fit to recant his prewar views or issue an apology, a well-placed interview or two expressing some awareness of the horrors of Nazism, for example, would have gone a long way to mollify the public.

Lindbergh, however, had never—even at the height of his fame—been good at ingratiating himself. The whole idea of public relations repulsed him. He refused to cooperate with biographers, but years after their books appeared he prepared lengthy memos annotating their alleged errors. (On more than a few points, the verdict must go to the biographers.) He could never quite decide which he wanted most—to be understood or to be let alone. So he did, and said, nothing.

The fears of the executives at Warner Brothers were realized when *The Spirit of St. Louis* did disappointing business at the box office—only partly, one suspects, because of the theater owners' lack of enthusiasm. Jimmy Stewart was in many respects the ideal actor to play Lindbergh. A fan of long standing, Stewart was a skilled pilot who had risen to the rank of general in the air corps reserves through merit rather than the favoritism often accorded Hollywood stars. In personality, posture, and speech patterns, if not in actual looks, his resemblance to Lindbergh was almost uncanny. (A journalist who was introduced to General Lindbergh at a diplomatic reception some years after seeing the movie said recently that his first impression was of being in the presence of a man who was doing a Jimmy Stewart imitation.) But Stewart was simply too old to play the youthful Lindbergh convincingly. The Lindy of 1927, for all his often-reported wholesomeness, had more in common with James Dean, and the casting of an older actor only served to remind the moviegoing public of certain disillusioning events that the film, like the book it was based on, chose to ignore.

The film's release was a missed opportunity for Charles Lindbergh to make some sort of peace with the media and the American public. "I guess I'm just a stubborn Swede," he told *New York Times* reporter Alden Whitman some years later. This explanation is not as frivolous as it may seem. Self-revelation does not come easily to the Swedish character, and there is a definite tradition, exemplified by Lindbergh's own grandfather, of reacting to attacks on one's reputation by retreating into the role of the aloof, misunderstood exile.

For that matter Lindbergh was extraordinarily touchy even when it came to private criticism, as editors who worked with him on magazine articles, book forewords, and other projects soon learned. No one was more conscientious about revising manuscripts and soliciting the opinions of friendly readers, but once a piece of work was officially submitted it was a hard pull to get him to accept even minor copy-editing changes. In the offices of the *Reader's Digest,* this attitude earned the general the nickname the Lone Ego—a good pun but an inaccurate diagnosis. A true egotist has no fear of self-contradiction. Lindbergh did not know who he was and thus had felt threatened by the attempts of others, friendly or otherwise, to define him.

To the extent that he had to play any public role, Lindbergh was more comfortable cast as the antihero than the hero. Both his father and grandfather had made careers of battling the Establishment. Ever since his childhood, when someone put into his head the notion that his grandfather Land's laboratory was the devil's workshop, Lindbergh had been fascinated with the devil, especially the fallen angel of *Paradise Lost.* His problem with Christianity was it did not accept that the devil was necessary, and in his later years he became a student of the Tao Te Ching, which teaches: "The whole world recognizes the beautiful as the beautiful, yet this is only the ugly; the whole world recognizes the good as the good, yet this is only the bad." Lindbergh needed the consolation of such philosophy since aviation, the religion of his youth, had proved so disillusioning. Again and again over the years, he had found himself supporting policies—passenger airlines as opposed to individual ownership of airplanes, the routinization of the pilot's job, the purchase of jumbo jets, the creation of a Strategic Air Corps equipped with death-dealing weapons—that seemed practical and even necessary but which negated the vision that had drawn him to flying in the first place.

Anne Lindbergh's ability to empathize with this existential dilemma undoubtedly played a role in her decision to remain in a marriage that was often difficult. Unlike Charles, however, she did not enjoy the role of the contrarian. Years after the war she still dreaded meeting strangers for fear she might run into one who would take it upon himself to chastise her for the views she had expressed in *The Wave of the Future.* Such attacks left her by turns mortified and furious with what she called the American penchant for "devil baiting." Running into Corliss Lamont at a tea given by her mother's friend Amey Aldrich, Anne commented that their situations were in some ways similar. "You know," commiserated Corliss, "one gets tired of being smeared." (An interesting remark, this, since Lamont usually gave the impression that he thrived on it.)

Some months later Anne reopened the subject in a letter:

> I *do* know! It is the most difficult thing on earth. Having one's words, one's deeds perhaps misunderstood. Calumny. Distrust. Hate. Isolation. I have tasted them all. The hardest part of it is not simply *standing* it. I think we are both still Puritan-Presbyterian enough to *stand* things pretty well.... The difficult thing is to bear it without armor, so to speak, to carry it and still remain open-hearted, generous, believing, hopeful and of course, still vulnerable.[8]

Isolation was the operative term. The Lindberghs seldom appeared in public. With fewer friends in common every year, they did not go to parties or out to dinner. They did not see many films and never watched television. Their joint social life consisted mainly of attending seminars and conferences at Aspen and similar places where intellectuals like Robert K. Hutchins of the University of Chicago lectured on various problems of the day. Through Jim Newton and his wife, the former Ellie Forde, an MRA activist whom he had married in 1942, they were also drawn into the orbit of the Moral Re-Armament Movement. MRA, whose motto was "Change Begins Within Me," taught that social conflicts, including labor-management disputes and the Third World's drive to shake off the fetters of colonialism, could be resolved nonviolently if both sides pledged themselves to sincere self-examination and honest communication. This platform suited the optimistic mood of the postwar years, when even serious political scientists were (somewhat prematurely, as it turned out) announcing "the end of ideology." An outgrowth of Oxford Movement Christianity—a religious movement that began at Oxford University in England earlier in the century—MRA received favorable coverage in the *Reader's Digest* and other American publications, but its chief strength was in Europe, where it attracted mainly well-heeled, well-educated conservatives.

Dr. Carrel's hope that the Lindberghs would find peace of mind through the solace of religion had begun to bear fruit during the war years. Charles had begun carrying a copy of the New Testament in his suitcase. Anne continued to read the works of Teilhard de Chardin and other Catholic philosophers, prayed regularly, and was attracted to images of the Madonna in art and sculpture. Nevertheless both of them were far from orthodox believers in any sense, and they neither joined nor attended any church. MRA's emphasis on public testimony was alien to Anne's instinctive feeling that religion was an intensely private experience, and Charles had expressed reservations about the intellectual vacuity of the MRA philosophy as early as 1939. He had second thoughts in 1950, however, after MRA negotiators successfully intervened to settle a bitter strike against National Airlines. For several summers he and Anne rented a chalet in Vevey, Switzerland, near MRA's international conference center in Caux.

Recruiting the Lindberghs would have been a major coup for MRA, whose publicity somewhat forlornly cited the actor Joel McCrea and a grandson of Mahatma Gandhi as the organization's most famous adherents. Charles and Anne resisted all appeals, but the influence of MRA teachings is evident in Anne's writing, especially *Gift from the Sea*. Charles, for his part, was drawn to MRA's message of conciliation—at one point, at least according to James Newton, he actually considered the possibility of apologizing to the press. But the most obvious attraction of Caux was the opportunity to mix with congenial people in a setting where they had no fear of embarrassing encounters with hostile strangers. Frank Buchman, the Oxford Movement's American founder, had also attended the Berlin Olympics in 1936, and longtime members were themselves sensitive to the charge that the movement had been soft on Nazism.

By the late 1950s, however, some MRA-watchers had begun to report that the movement was taking on some of the more alarming characteristics of a cult. Promising young trade union leaders and Third World politicians who had attended MRA conferences on scholarships complained that the group's recruiting tactics—overwhelming the newcomer with fixed smiles and displays of aggressive goodwill—amounted to a polite form of brainwashing. Moreover, during group meditation sessions, some members were receiving "Guidances from God." A strikingly large number of these "Guidances" centered on the difficulty of achieving the MRA standard of "Absolute Purity." God, it seems, had sent word that the absolutely pure must not indulge in sexual intercourse except for purposes of procreation, even within marriage. A British journalist sitting in on one MRA discussion group heard a participant tearfully announce: "There is something I want to share with you. This morning, my wife tried to seduce me."

"Absolute Purity" held zero appeal for Charles. For that matter, he even had doubts about the corollary MRA principle of "Absolute

Love." Even God was not "absolutely loving," he told Ellie Newton; if he were, he would never allow the devil to "work his way" with humankind. This assertion led to such a furious argument that Mrs. Newton later wrote to apologize. "I'm sorry if I was too much on the Devil's side," Charles answered, "but I suspect that God smiles on him, at times, at least, with more benevolence than you do.... If I didn't think there was a touch of sin and humor in heaven, I'd much prefer to live in hell—I feel sure I'd find plenty of old friends there." And he could not resist adding, "You'll wave to me anyway, won't you?"[9]

In the spring of 1961, when Jim Newton sent an invitation to the summer conference at Caux, Charles wrote again, reminding his friend that he had severe doubts about both the "ideology" and the "effectiveness" of MRA. Nevertheless the Lindberghs were in Switzerland that summer, and Charles attended a number of official MRA functions. Among the speakers at the conference that year was an Oxford-educated Kenyan, John Ole Koncellah. Lindbergh was intrigued by Koncellah's account of his youth on the Masai Mara Reserve, and especially of the lion hunt, a test of courage that traditionally marked the coming of age of the Masai warrior. During a dinner meeting organized by Newton, Lindbergh plied Koncellah with questions, and the Masai leader politely invited Lindbergh to visit the reserve.

Some months later Koncellah's young son Ben was startled to see a dusty Volkswagen approaching the family *enkang* (encampment) in a remote corner of the vast reserve. The driver was Charles Lindbergh. Locating the *enkang* without benefit of a guide was no mean feat in itself, and Lindbergh's request to be allowed to live for a time in the camp in order to study Masai ways was perhaps even more disconcerting. The traditionalist Masai, all too familiar with the tendency of some visitors to view them as picturesque curiosities, are generally suspicious of such requests, but Koncellah was not exactly a typical Masai and Lindbergh no ordinary visitor. Aside from being a tireless walker, he was good listener, capable of keeping his mouth shut for hours at a time. Lindbergh was assigned his own hut, complete with an elderly woman to keep house for him, and blended into the daily routine, happily subsisting on the traditional diet of fresh milk mixed with blood drawn from the vein of living cow and served in a gourd rinsed in animal urine. Lindbergh, who had never encountered a cuisine he didn't relish, pronounced this diet quite "enjoyable." Indeed, he fit in so effortlessly that Koncellah later told an American interviewer, Dr. Richard Logan, that he had found Lindbergh to be "very much like the Masai."[10]

It may seem a large leap from a "fascination" with the Third Reich to enchantment with the Masai. In fact, the differences are not so great. Both are (or in the case of the Reich, were) warrior societies and, as Lindbergh saw it, victims of British colonialism. Contrary to the view of Lindbergh's first biographer, Kenneth S. Davis, who once called him a "totalitarian personality," Lindbergh was a romantic reactionary, constantly searching for some idyllic society in which courage and individualism still mattered and adventure was not mere self-indulgence but an integral part of the daily struggle for existence. With hindsight, he was horrified to think that he had ever perceived elements of this society in Nazi Germany, which had turned out to be obsessed with regimentation, coercion, and technologically efficient extermination. But this monumental error did not convince him that the search was futile.

In a 1973 letter to Wayne S. Cole, a historian who was writing a book on the history of the America First movement, Lindbergh summarized the evolution of his thinking on the influence of race and biology in history. He still believed in "the average intellectual superiority of the white race" and "the sensate superiority of the black race." But he now thought too much emphasis on intellect had a negative survival value— "it is quite possible that the black race will achieve a better balance of life eventually."[11]

During his stay with the Masai, Lindbergh discovered that the reserve was far from a utopia. There were many problems, beginning with poverty, malnutrition, intertribal violence, and the appalling prevalence of disease, including endemic syphilis. But the Masai, he noted, were not true primitives any more than twentieth-century Americans were. Aside from the Masai's recent history of contacts with the British and others, their own culture was the product of a long evolution, giving rise to customs and taboos that interfered with the natural wisdom of biology. Still—and despite the fact that the Masai's numbers continued to dwindle and even many Kenyans considered them a sad anachronism—Lindbergh found in them a "vitality" that had been missing in his own life.

"You speak of freedom in your country," one tribal elder told him. "But we have known a freedom far greater than yours."

For Charles Lindbergh, this was the siren call. "Soon I wanted to renounce civilization. Why had I waited so long?"[12]

TWENTY-SIX

"After D'Fall"

*T*O THE WORLD AT LARGE, Charles and Anne Lindbergh were inexplicable and often infuriating personalities. To immerse oneself in the writings of these compulsive diarists is to think often of the "telescopic philanthropy" of Dickens's Mrs. Jellyby, whose family went to rack and ruin while she immersed herself in correspondence on behalf of the natives of faraway Borrioboola-Gha. But, unlike Mrs. Jellyby, the Lindberghs were neither nonentities nor fools. They were the last great amateurs in a world in which amateurism had become obsolete. Born introverts, they found themselves caught in the spotlight of history—and their reaction was to stare back at it like a pair of wild deer mesmerized by the headlights of an oncoming car.

Others who have come under the spell of the romance of aviation seem to understand the Lindberghs best. Michael Parfit, a pilot who retraced the route of Charles's 1927 Guggenheim tour, a quest he described in a book entitled *Chasing the Glory,* has written: "Flying is like standing up in a room full of children and finding out that you're a giant. You think you see everything, and the squabbles down around the floor look small."[1]

Indeed, as the utopian dream of air-mindedness soured, a significant number of pilots were converted to what has come to be known as New Age consciousness. To cite just one example, Donald Keyhoe, the marine pilot who was Lindbergh's official escort in 1927, became convinced that the mysterious lights known as "foo-fighters," which Allied airmen reported seeing during World War II, were actually flying saucers and that the U.S. Air Force was engaged in a massive coverup to prevent the public from learning that extraterrestrials representing a vastly superior civilization had already landed in the Arizona desert. Keyhoe wrote eight books on the subject of flying saucers, and as director of a group called the National Investigations Committee on Aerial Phenomena did more than any other single individual to popularize the concept. Charles Lindbergh was interested enough in Keyhoe's flying saucer theory to review the air force's Project Blue Book report on UFOs and discuss the matter with Gen. Carl Spaatz and even, at one point, to enlist Pan-Am pilots in assisting with Keyhoe's "research," but he concluded in short order that the idea was nonsense. (In fact, Keyhoe's claim that Sen. Barry Goldwater was a believer may have influenced Lindbergh's decision to vote for Johnson in 1964.)[2]

The Lindberghs represented the more rational, moderate side of New Age thinking. They studied Jung, but were dismayed, on meeting the great man in person, to discover that he, too, believed that UFOs were controlled by visitors from outer space. Anne continued her study of the literature of mysticism and Charles of Taoism. Their interest in Native American cultures, pre-Columbian myths, and yoga dated back to the 1930s. Along with many small-plane pilots of their generation, they were among the first to become alarmed by the deterioration of the environment; what looked liked progress at ground level could be seen, from the air, as depredation—the disappearance of forests, the draining of wetlands, the rapid decline of bird life, and the degeneration of air quality so that the pall of pollution, once limited to the air over big cities, now covered whole regions.

Certainly nothing could have been more in tune with New Age thinking than the Lindberghs' relentless self-scrutiny. They spent their whole lives finding themselves. No development was too momentous in its own right to be swept into the maw of their self-referential quest. Others were destroyed by the Nazis; the Lindberghs were psychologically devastated by their confusion about Nazism. Other white Americans of their background responded to the civil rights movement of the 1960s by reexamining their prejudices and accepting integration; Charles Lindbergh was in Africa drinking cow's blood and anticipating the triumph of the black race in the evolutionary struggle. Still, unlike others who only brooded, the Lindberghs also did. At their best they could be grand. And however muddled their politics, there was something gallant in their insistence that democracy must mean more than the supine glorification of materialism.

The results of Charles's sojourn with the Masai illustrate the bewildering turns his search for "values" could take. Though he had not actually seen a lion hunt during his stay at Masai Mara, he had become intrigued by the notion that a one-to-one confrontation with a charging wild animal was one of the few tests of valor that still had any authenticity. Searching for the "primitive" within himself, he went on safari, hunting big game with guides like Denis Zaphiro, who some years earlier had taken Ernest Hemingway on a similar expedition.

Lindbergh had shot grouse or ducks as an adult, usually on occasions arranged by others, but he was hardly an avid sportsman. This sudden passion for hunting now that he was in his sixties was a striking development, and one can't help but recall the trip in quest of "big game" that he and his father had talked about so many years earlier—one of many promises to his son that CA made in good faith but never got around to keeping. Whatever inspired it, Lindbergh's career as a big-game hunter did not last long. The animals were so beautiful—perfect in a way that mere human beings like himself were not—that he found it hard to justify killing them. For one trip with Zaphiro, he managed to obtain a permit to shoot a rhino, already an endangered species, but when the moment came he put his rifle aside.

On subsequent visits to East Africa (at least a half dozen of them during the course of the decade), he carried neither gun nor camera. Once an avid photographer, Charles had concluded that his heavy bag of photographic gear was just one more example of the impedimenta of civilization that he could profitably do without. Instead he explored the countryside by road and from the air, on one occasion landing a borrowed plane in the Olduvai Gorge in order to pay a surprise visit to the camp of anthropologist Mary Leakey.

The next step—from admirer of animals to environmental activist—was far from an obvious one. Lindbergh, at this stage of his life, was a sometime consultant on space medicine to NASA, part of a technical committee at Pan-Am that was working with the developers of the SST, and still devoting a substantial amount of time to the air force. His experiences during the anti-interventionist campaign, moreover, had left him deeply suspicious of anything that smacked of radicalism and reluctant to lend his name to any cause. As Lindbergh himself told it, the decision to take a public stand on environmental issues was made rather casually. In late 1964 or early 1965 he happened to read about the formation of an American chapter of the Geneva-based World Wildlife Fund in the *New York Times* and phoned the chairman, Ira Gabrielson, to offer his services. According to some WWF activists, however, the general's involvement owed a great deal to Anne Lindbergh. Anne had purchased L'Argonaute, a chalet overlooking Lake Geneva, and had numerous acquaintances in Switzerland. Reportedly also, she had been quietly giving to environmental causes for some years—as had Corliss Lamont—and she encouraged her husband to get involved in the hope that working to save wild animals would be an effective therapy for his aimlessness and disillusionment. Charles Lindbergh himself acknowledged elsewhere he was influenced by his children, who made sure that he was aware of the arguments that the SST would be too noisy and a polluter of the upper atmosphere as well as serving no useful purpose. However it came about, in environmentalism both the Lindberghs found a cause whose facts at least arguably justified their free-floating pessimism.

The first public statement of Charles Lindbergh's conversion appeared in the form of a 1964 *Reader's Digest* article entitled "Is Civilization Progress?" The miracle of aviation, he wrote, made it possible for him to be in New York one day, discussing the development of the new supersonic jet airplane at a Pan-Am board meeting, and camping in the African bush the next. But the price of this great freedom was technology's assault on natural beauty: "Where civilization is most advanced, few birds exist. I realized that if I would have to choose, I would rather have birds than airplanes."

As usual, Lindbergh in print sounded more extreme than he actually was. Far from making such a choice, he thought that good science was necessary to the development of enlightened environmental policies. The argument that environmentalism is the last refuge of upper-class misanthropy has often been made, and there was certainly more than a touch of this in the Lindberghs' attitudes. Anne's occasional essays and speeches on the subject reveal a patrician disdain for shopping malls. Charles was given to snorting, "Man is the dirtiest creature on Earth," and his unsuccessful campaign against granting landing rights in the United States for the French and British-operated Concordes showed that the prickly isolationist in him had not quite been extinguished. "To what extent do we control our own destiny?" he asked in a letter to the *New York Times*. "Having decided not to put SST's into operation, must we still do so because of the pressure of foreign governments?"[3] On the whole, however, the positions that he and

Anne took on specific issues were moderate and well reasoned. Never mere sentimentalists, they understood that the survival of wild species was a marker of the overall health of the environment.

Charles, especially, made it clear that he was not opposed to technology or growth per se, but only to the inappropriate use of technology. The average family sedan in the early sixties, he liked to point out, had a more powerful engine than the *Spirit of St. Louis*. In fact, his conversion to environmentalism coincided with his return to the scientific laboratory after a gap of many years. A group of scientists at the Naval Research Institute in Bethesda, Maryland, had become interested in taking up the work on the perfusion pump abandoned by Carrel and Lindbergh in 1939. Charles visited Bethesda for a briefing on the research and volunteered to collaborate with Dr. Theodore Malinin on a larger pump that would make use of modern synthetic materials.

Malinin seems to have been skeptical at first but soon became enthusiastic about Lindbergh's contribution. When Lindbergh was available to work, he and Malinin would stay in the lab for fourteen hours at a stretch, surviving on Kentucky Fried Chicken that Charles ordered by the bucketful. The two men coauthored an article on the redesigned apparatus for the journal *Cryobiology,* and it was later manufactured for sale to researchers by Corning Glass.

Environmentalism was very much a Lindbergh family project. In the mid-1960s, eager to share his African experiences, Charles organized a safari for his wife and several of the children—Reeve, Jon and his wife, Barbara, and Land and his wife, Susan. The party traveled in Land Rovers, without a guide, revisiting the highlights of Father's previous trips.

It was in the Serengeti that Anne, arising early for a solitary stroll through the field next to the campsite, unexpectedly found herself sharing the shade of a grove of acacia trees with a pair of lions. To her surprise she was not at all afraid. "I feel honored that they have not considered me worth running away from—or towards," she wrote. The spell was broken only when Jon, emerging from his tent, shouted, "Father, there are two lions in the field and Mother is there with them!" At the sound of Jon's voice, the lioness and her mate rose from their resting place and made a dignified exit.[4]

A few winters later, Jon organized a whale-watching expedition off the coast of Baja California. He and his parents, joined by Land and Susan, rented a forty-foot fishing boat to explore the gray whale nursery at Laguna San Ignacio. When Jon, the professional diver, donned a wet suit to go for a swim among the whales, his sixty-seven-year-old father insisted on coming along. Much to his alarm, Jon soon found himself being butted by a very playful gray whale calf. The baby was having a grand time, but as Jon well knew, a mother gray whale, normally a placid creature, can become hostile if she suspects her offspring are threatened. As Jon swam for the boat, his overfriendly companion close behind, he saw the mother gray whale rise out of the water.

"Meanwhile," Jon wrote, "my father had jumped in and was swimming over to join the fun. I watched with horror as the mother whale broke the surface and blotted him from sight. This must be the attack! I vaulted up into the skiff and we sped over to help. When we reached the scene the whales were gone. Father couldn't understand what the fuss was about. He'd been swimming on his back and hadn't even seen a whale."

The Baja trip, which resulted in other, more satisfying close encounters with gray whales, was described by Jon in a major article in *Life* magazine, a piece that also happened to be one of the first to describe the eerie "songs" of the humpback whale for a popular audience. The African safari had been written up by Anne for an earlier issue of *Life*, which also featured an essay by Charles entitled "The Wisdom of Wildness." In the meantime Charles had been appointed by the National Union for the Conservation of Nature to attend the 1966 conference of the International Whaling Commission. After the meeting ended Lindbergh went to see Peru's president Fernando Belaúnde Terry to request protection for the humpback and blue whales being caught off the shores of his country. Somewhat to his chagrin he learned that one of the companies involved was based in Minnesota and was headed by a Swedish American whose family had been close to the Melrose and Little Falls Lindberghs. His personal appeal to the chairman resulted in the company's decision to give up the harpooning of endangered whales.

Unfortunately the portrait of a harmonious family pioneering together in the realm of ecotourism projected in the *Life* magazine articles was incomplete. The younger children did not remember the America First period, and since it was never discussed at home, each of them had to learn about it for the first time under rather unpleasant circumstances. Reeve was a freshman at Radcliffe when she heard that the roommate of one of her boyfriends had said, "Well, I don't mind meeting her, but you'll never get me to shake hands with her father." She had no idea what this remark referred to, but she guessed that it had something to do with the standoffish attitude she had sensed in certain adults she met. A little independent research turned up the information that these people believed her father to be anti-Semitic. The discovery was a shock, leaving her angry and confused about just whom to be angry with. Not that she believed the charge—she didn't for a minute. "Nothing [such people thought] corresponded to *my* view of my father," she later told Julie Nixon Eisenhower (an interviewer who had cause to empathize), "so that each experience of this kind was a crazy kind of nightmare."[5]

The children dealt with the situation by assiduously avoiding the spotlight.

Anne Spencer Lindbergh, a shy, pretty blond who bore a distinct resemblance to her father's half-sister Eva, was married in 1963 to Julien Feydy, whom she met while studying in Paris. The couple settled in the Feydy family château in Douzillac, in the Dordogne region. Anne did not return to the United States until 1976. By that time her first marriage had ended, and she and her second husband, the Polish American composer Jerzy Sapieyevski, purchased a town house in the Georgetown section of Washington, D.C. Anne had long written poetry for her own enjoyment, and Sapieyevski set some of her verse to music, creating a song cycle called "Love Poems," which premiered at the Phillips Gallery, and another called "Nocturnes," performed at the National Gallery. They were an extraordinarily handsome couple, "so much in love that it was an experience to be in the same room with them," recalled one friend who did not wish to be identified, "but I'm afraid she's a bolter." At any rate there was another divorce, and in 1988 Anne married her third husband, the author and Dartmouth English professor Noel Perrin.

Reeve, meanwhile, married Richard Waldron Brown, a photographer, and settled in northern Vermont, where she taught school. She wrote short stories and produced a picture book, illustrated by her husband's photos, but her career did not begin to take off until the late eighties, by which time she, too, was remarried, to Nathaniel Tripp.

Scott, born in 1942, was the only child to become openly estranged from his father. Always a nonconformist, he showed no interest whatsoever in emulating his father's example of strenuous competitiveness. After attending Amherst, he moved to England to study philosophy at Cambridge University and spent his vacations exploring Europe in his somewhat battered Volkswagen. A fast driver, he eventually acquired an MG sports car (over his father's objections) and a pet

Great Dane, who became his inseparable companion. In 1967 Scott met Alika Watteau, a Belgian film actress, painter, and passionate animal rights activist, opposed to animal experimentation, the pet trade, and zoos. Alika owned two monkeys, rescued from owners who had found them unmanageable, and after she and Scott were married in 1968, their collection of simian charges grew.

In 1971 Scott and his wife moved to a seventeenth-century manor house in the Dordogne, near the town of Bergerac, which they converted into a primate center. The Lindberghs studied the scientific literature on maintaining primates in captivity but were convinced that it was not enough to maintain the animals, mainly red and black howlers and other South American species, at a survival level. To thrive they needed to be happy, a state they encouraged by allowing the animals a free choice of mates, an overabundance of fresh food so that they could graze at will (a practice known as saturation feeding), and free access to the out-of-doors, achieved by dividing their estate's grounds into a maze of fenced-in enclosures—which separated the territories of dominant males but did not prohibit the animals from having free run of the one-hundred-acre grounds.

Maintaining the monkeys was an expensive business, and the Lindberghs' unorthodox methods, as well as their lack of conventional credentials and professional associations, placed them outside the network of funding sources. A journalist who visited the manor house during the 1970s found the monkeys living in comfortable, temperature-controlled quarters while Scott and his wife shivered in two underheated rooms. Over the mantel of the sitting room hung a painting by Alika depicting Scott as St. Hubert the huntsman, who according to legend entered a cloister after his encounter with a stag bearing a crucifix.

Mrs. Lindbergh's second novel, published in 1962, reveals that she had given serious consideration to the question of whether or not her marriage was worth preserving. *Dearly Beloved* was fiction, but as the critic Elise Mayer has noted, in Anne's hands the machinery of the novel was never more than a "thin veil" thrown over material that was obviously intensely personal. The character in the novel who most resembles the author is Deborah McNeil, a petite, still-girlish matron who has striven mightily to be "the perfect wife, the perfect mother." Her husband John, considered a prime catch by all Deborah's girlfriends, is a cold, hypercritical man who cannot tolerate failure in himself or in her and who demands too much of his sons and spoils his daughters. On the day of their eldest child's wedding, Deborah realizes that John is as much a stranger to her as he was on their wedding day. Another female character, Beatrice, is divorced from a newspaper correspondent who used home as "a place to hole up between assignments." ("She sometimes suspected him of inventing the crises abroad, or ferreting them out, so that he had to leave.") A third woman, Frances, less easy to identify with the author since she is married to an alcoholic, recalls that she first thought of divorce soon after the wedding but did not want to disappoint her mother. Years later ("Mother was dead then") Frances launches into an affair, but when she suggests to her lover that they divorce their spouses and marry each other he recoils in horror: "Oh my dear, you're not trying to make it your whole existence, are you?"[6]

Dearly Beloved was a richer, more accomplished novel than *The Steep Ascent,* but it was a story in which, as one critic complained, "nothing happens," and its view of married life was too pessimistic for most readers. True love, even true communication, are elusive, the author suggests, but the institution is worth preserving because it symbolizes the possibility that they might be achieved. Anne had found great solace in the words of Rilke: "It does not occur to anyone to expect a single person to be 'happy'—but if he marries, people are much surprised if he *isn't*! … a good marriage is that in which each appoints the other guardian of his solitude."

Possibly this philosophy represented the best form of marriage two intensely introspective people could hope for. On the other hand, it could also be a rationale for remaining the all-accommodating, "perfect" spouse, and there are hints that Anne paid a physical price for her acceptance. She was among the first group of patients to be diagnosed with temporomandibular joint dysfunction syndrome, a painful condition caused by the habitual clenching of the jaw muscles; although it is now known to be rather common, some specialists have suggested that the condition is unusually prevalent among highly affluent and educated married women. Anne had become active in the affairs of Smith College, where she is remembered by former students as a warm and gracious person whose faculty for precise observation made her a stimulating conversationalist. Nevertheless a few acquaintances came to wonder whether her cultivation of solitude, which soon extended to periodic retreats at a Benedictine monastery, was producing an unhealthy detachment. A friend of General Lindbergh's, inquiring about the welfare of a woman who had been employed by Anne for a number of years, was startled when she replied off-handedly, "Oh, she died." End of conversation. Whether this reflected actual indifference to the fate of a mere servant, as he suspected, or simply a habit of emotional distance, the effect was chilling.

In 1963, after their youngest daughter entered Radcliffe, the Lindberghs scaled back their domestic arrangements and evolved a routine that appeared to accommodate their divergent interests. They sold the big Scott's Cove house and moved to a much more modest one a few hundred yards away. Much of the valuable antique furniture they had inherited from Anne's mother was sold off or put in storage. The living room of the new house was dominated by a pair of Vlaminck still lifes they had purchased in Paris before the war but was otherwise sparsely appointed. There was no carpet on the steps and no curtains—though the house did have window shades. "Ever since the kidnapping, I've always been very careful to draw the shades at night," Anne explained to one acquaintance.

In some respects the Lindberghs' existence was almost Spartan. They were not collectors; in fact their goal was to own as few possessions as possible. Charles, who had driven the Franklin touring car he received in 1927 for twelve years, believed that automobiles should be maintained to last. He was loyal to Fords and did not even buy the most expensive models of those—one family car was a brown Pinto station wagon. On the other hand, the Lindberghs' peripatetic life-style was not everyone's idea of simplicity.

In addition to Anne's chalet overlooking Lake Geneva, the Lindberghs had acquired a home on Maui. The Maui house was really more of a cottage, lacking all but the most basic conveniences, but it was situated on a lot with a breathtaking view of the Pacific and was adjacent to the property of Sam Pryor, a Pan-Am vice president with whom Charles had worked closely over the years. Their usual schedule was to spend the spring and fall in Connecticut, the summer in Switzerland—Anne's favorite residence—and two winter months on Maui, which Charles much preferred.

Moreover, in addition to trips to Africa, the whale-watching expedition off Baja, and family visits, the Lindberghs now occasionally appeared together at official functions. Charles was a great admirer of John F. Kennedy's personality, if not his politics, and he and Anne, normally great refusers of social invitations, happily appeared at the state dinner hosted by the president and the first lady in honor of André Malraux in May 1962. They went to Cape Kennedy to observe Apollo launchings and attended another state dinner in 1968, in honor of the Apollo astronauts.

But if Anne ever hoped that working for the environment would cure her husband's restlessness she was to be disappointed. During the latter part of the sixties, even as Charles cut down on his activities on behalf of Pan-Am and the army, his commitments to the movement rapidly multiplied. Of numerous organizations he was associated with, none proved more congenial than the Geneva-based World Wildlife Fund. Though not a grass-roots organization, the WWF is a highly effective one. "We don't bother with politics," says board member Francis Kellogg. "We go directly to the people at the top." Lindbergh joined the WWF's "Committee of 100," a panel of internationally known figures, including Prince Bernhard of the Netherlands and Prince Charles of Britain, who lobbied heads of state for emergency measures to save endangered wildlife and habitats. Ironically Lindbergh's reputation as a semirecluse and a prickly character made him especially effective in this role. VIPs who were jaded when it came to meeting the usual run of famous faces were curious about Lindbergh and quite impressed to find themselves on the receiving end of the charming personality and skillful salesmanship that Lindbergh was capable of when he really wished to win someone over to his way of thinking.[7]

By the latter part of the decade, Lindbergh had begun to concentrate his activities in Asia and the South Pacific, partly as a result of his growing friendship with British anthropologist Tom Harrisson, best known to the public as the man who parachuted cats into Borneo. At Harrisson's suggestion he went to Indonesia to persuade President Sukarno to offer some protection to the Javanese rhinoceros and successfully lobbied Ferdinand Marcos for preserves for the tamarau, a wild buffalo native to the island of Mindoro, and the endangered monkey-eating eagle. Lindbergh was highly effective in persuading Ferdinand Marcos to set aside a preserve for the tamarau—as usual, the pitch leaned heavily on the twin motivations of national pride and international prestige for the Marcos regime. What amazed Harrisson was that Lindbergh was also willing to take part in the physically challenging and time-consuming task of touring Mindoro by helicopter in order to sell the concept of conservation to the people: "It meant hopping out of the craft at every village, waving to the crowd, making speeches, and going through all sorts of boring ceremonials....Not only did Lindbergh do it all, but he looked positively happy doing it."[8]

For the first time since 1941, he was even willing to speak in public, as Lowell Thomas, Jr., learned in 1968. Thomas, then a member of the Alaska legislature, was sponsoring a bill to revoke the bounty on wolves and asked his father-in-law, Sam Pryor, if Lindbergh would agree to speak on behalf of the bill. To Pryor's amazement Charles not only said yes, he was ready to clear his schedule and go to Anchorage right away. A few days later he addressed a hastily organized joint session of the legislature, reminding the lawmakers that Alaska was one of the last unspoiled places on earth and its survival was dependent on their stewardship. "I have always felt that Lindbergh's speech was the turning point in attitudes of most Alaskans," says Thomas.[9]

Lindbergh did not see much of the Alaskan wilderness on this occasion, but a little more than a year later he returned to explore the Kenai Peninsula with Thomas in the latter's single-engine seaplane. Alaska had long held a special place in Charles's imagination. He could still recite all sixty-nine lines of "The Cremation of Sam McGee," a poem he had memorized as a child, and was ready to prove it if challenged. But the willingness to take off on a moment's notice on errands he could hardly have found enjoyable made him an organizer's dream. When John Paul Getty decided to endow a conservation prize, Frank Kellogg called to ask if Lindbergh would be available to fly to London for the announcement, an event expected to generate important publicity for the WWF.

"I was just about to leave for Maui, which is my favorite place in all the world," Lindbergh said. "My car is already in the driveway. But if you need me I'll come."

"There will be photographers present," Kellogg warned. "This might not be the sort of thing you want to do."

"I'll be there on one condition. No television. I don't care at all how many photographers there are."

In the event, the occasion produced enough photos and clippings to fill two souvenir scrapbooks. These were presented to Getty, for whom Lindbergh was still the Columbus of the Air, a world-historical figure. "When I'm feeling low, I get down those books and browse through them," he confessed later.

Lindbergh, one can be sure, also enjoyed meeting Getty. Part of him was greatly impressed by rank, titles, and enormous wealth, and he valued his association with other WWF sponsors such as Prince Bernhard. At the same time, however, the fact that the rest of the world was also impressed by appearances never failed to annoy him. When traveling, Lindbergh dressed like a slightly down-at-the-heels college professor in wash-and-wear suits—typically often washed and well worn—with nylon shirts. His canvas carry-on (the man responsible for designing the first commercial coast-to-coast luggage service never risked checking a bag) was equipped with a shoeshine kit he used to clean his sturdy, army-issue shoes. Another of his space-saving strategies was to have oversize pockets sewn into the lining of his overcoat. These, he boasted, were large enough to hold an extra pair of trousers and a safari shirt or even a dress suit! Although as a Pan-Am director he was entitled to free first-class air travel, he avoided Clipper Club lounges and usually sat in coach, listed on the flight manifests under a pseudonym—often, simply August Lindbergh.

Oddly, considering that he was not at all flexible when it came to ideas and emotions, Lindbergh was an endlessly adaptable traveler. One of the great omnivores, he enjoyed meat-and-potatoes meals, topped off by angel food or chocolate cake. In the cities he sought out Chinese restaurants but could make do nicely with diner food. When abroad, he ate the local cuisines with gusto, and if raw seafood or other exotic ingredients were involved, so much the better. Anne, always an abstemious eater, lived on yogurt, fruit, and other health foods, and one suspects that Charles, when at home, was equally restrained.

Nevertheless the ability of this six-foot two-inch man who had never worked out in his life to eat his way around the world while remaining fit and energetic left other men his age, and even some quite a few years younger, in awe. (This factor is mentioned so often by men who knew Lindbergh that one almost feels that for them, digestive prowess had replaced sexual or athletic feats as the measure of middle-aged machismo in our society.) In the jungles he could live off the land. "He ate wild boar, and picked fruit off the trees and didn't ever seem to get worried about brackish water," Tom Harrisson recalled some years after their tour of Mindoro, adding that Lindbergh could "doss down anywhere in the jungle, on the floor of a plane, in a bug-ridden hut, and just go to sleep."[10]

Lindbergh had come to prefer sleeping on the floor even when other accommodations were available. In 1971, during a visit to the Lindbergh Historical Site in Little Falls, he expressed a desire to spend the night in his childhood home. The site supervisor explained that the beds in the restored house were not made up but offered to see about getting some sheets and blankets brought in. "Don't bother," Lindbergh replied. "I'll just stretch out here on the kitchen floor." And he did.

While strangers occasionally interpreted such behavior as either macho one-upmanship or a form of religious asceticism, Charles was apparently having fun. A friend who dropped in at the Scott's Cove house the day after an ice storm had knocked out the electric power and the furnace, found the general camping out in a sleeping bag in the living room. As delighted as a small boy by the unforeseen adventure, Charles proudly pointed out pie tins filled with water that he had arranged in circle around the sleeping bag, explaining that they were a kind of homemade thermostat—if the water began to freeze during the night he would know it was necessary to get up and drain the pipes.

Such spontaneity kept Charles feeling young, though it did not necessarily have the same effect on the rest of the family. Since he disliked making phone calls and writing letters, "Mother" (as he called Anne) and the children often didn't know where he was. On one occasion, very possibly the time he decided to fly to London to meet Getty, Anne was waiting in Maui for his arrival and didn't hear from him for almost a month. This was not especially convenient for her, since the cottage was Charles's idea of paradise but not hers. The roughly finished lava walls gave shelter to a variety of creeping and skittering forms of life, including lizards and wild rats, and the nearest store was eleven miles away on a road passable only by Jeep. However, Anne was beyond being alarmed or even upset over these derelictions. "You know Charles, he'll be here when he's here," she told an acquaintance.

Lindbergh's work for environmental organizations had never entirely distracted him from his personal quest for a society that realized the ideal of freedom, as he saw it. By the end of the decade, these activities were brought together in his work as the most active outside director of the Filipino foundation known as PANAMIN, the Private Association for National Minorities. Lindbergh liked the Philippines and he very much liked PANAMIN's founder Manuel Elizalde, Jr. Harvard-educated, the scion of one of the islands' wealthiest families, Elizalde—or Manda, as he was called—was a hard-drinking playboy whose interest in tribal peoples had begun when he sponsored a hospital boat to deliver medical services. What began as a rich man's hobby had gradually taken over Elizalde's life, and by the time Lindbergh met him, Elizalde had sworn off liquor, adopted more than fifty orphans and was working to establish a reserve for the Tboli, a large tribe on Mindanao.

Saving primitive peoples from extermination was a popular cause abroad but hotly controversial in the Philippines, where the population explosion was generating tremendous competition for land and resources. As expanding farm settlements encroached on the jungle, bloody confrontations between the farmers and tribesmen, accused of rustling cattle or other crimes, were not uncommon. PANAMIN's greatest challenges were, first, to convince farmers and villagers to accept the existence of the reserve and, second, to set up councils as a mechanism for resolving disputes. In 1969 and again in 1970, Lindbergh visited the reserve, not only meeting the Tboli themselves but shaking hands with the mayors, attending village ceremonies, even posing for photographs wearing a peasant-style conical hat.

The political situation in the Philippines being what it was, many Filipinos were deeply suspicious of Elizalde's motives for putting himself forward as a champion of the minorities. Some speculated that the reserve was really a front for an attempt to secure valuable logging and mineral rights. Others—no doubt with some justification—saw a plan to build up a political base among the tribes, either on his own behalf or as an agent for Marcos. After it became known that Elizalde had given guns to some tribesmen—he said for self-defense—the rumors intensified, and there was talk that one village mayor had put out a contract on Elizalde's life. Needless to say Elizalde's close relationship with Charles Lindbergh, a brigadier general in the reserves known to have undertaken special projects for various branches of the U.S. military, provided more grist for the rumor mills. During his travels on Mindanao in the spring of 1970, Lindbergh was accompanied by Alden Whitman, who was working on a magazine feature about Lindbergh's environmental activism. Meanwhile, another member of the party, photographer Edgar Needham, was secretly taking notes for an unauthorized profile that would eventually appear in *Esquire*.

Although Needham hinted that Lindbergh was on a secret mission to develop counterinsurgency bases for the CIA, even he did not take such speculation seriously. His profile presents Lindbergh not so much as an "ugly American" as a bumbling one, a "midwestern bumpkin" acting out some cowboys-and-Indians fantasy, crashing through the bush with a submachine gun and trying to impress the locals by demonstrating a trick method of cracking coconuts. Alden Whitman, according to Needham, was armed with a revolver that kept slipping out of his back pocket at the most inopportune moments.

Having sized up Lindbergh as a right-wing nut, Needham cited lengthy snatches of his conversation to prove it. Meeting the general as he was returning from a swim in the ocean, Needham commented, "You certainly dried off fast." To which Lindbergh replied, "I never get very wet when I go into the water." Later, asked what he thought of student protests in the States, Lindbergh said:

I get pushed farther to the right than I like to go by this type of movement. The left always pushes me to the right and the right always pushes me to the left. Now I'm right of center and farther to the right, because of the student movement, than I like to go. And when I get out on Long Island and see some of those restaurants that you speak of [Whitman and I had been discussing the tabs in Manhattan's eateries] this pushes me left again. On Long Island I could easily become a Communist, if I hadn't had too much contact with Communism.

Some days later, following a stay with the Agta, a Negrito minority, Lindbergh remarked, "Y'know, if I could choose my skin color, I'd choose brown, it's really the most beautiful color for skin." This prompted Needham to ask, "How far away is your nearest Negro neighbor? ... Do you really think you'd be able to keep your house if you were brown?"

Busy catering to the then fashionable standards of radical chic, Needham was hardly an objective observer. For example, he found Elizalde's wife ridiculous because she wore heavy eye makeup and snacked on Cheez Doodles. (One suspects that if she had appeared in a camouflage suit spouting Marxist dogma she would have been more in line with his image of a politically correct Third World woman.) It was fairly well known among American journalists in Asia that General Lindbergh had visited Vietnam under army auspices in 1967 and had not liked what he saw. This can hardly have been surprising—for all his postwar role as a defender of American power, he did not like war when he came face to face with it and had always believed that the United States had no business getting involved in imperialist adventures. By the same token, few who knew Lindbergh's history could blame him for declining to go public as an opponent of the conflict. Nevertheless, Needham had great fun provoking Lindbergh, who called Vietnam "a bad battlefield, badly chosen" and then backtracked by saying, "I don't think we can just step out. ... But not having had the responsibility, not having specialized in that field, I'm very hesitant, as I say, to reach an opinion.... Saigon to me is the most depressing occupied city I've ever seen."[11]

Two decades later many of the statements that Needham quoted as examples of Lindbergh's fatuity seem less foolish than his own liberal posturing. Even the remark "I never get very wet when I go into the water" is actually a good comeback to an inane question. Nor, it turns out, was Lindbergh's comment about brown skin exactly spontaneous.

"That fellow kept asking me what color skin I liked best," he later complained. "I knew whatever answer I gave would be wrong. I just didn't know what to say."[12]

Although Needham portrayed Elizalde's insistence on arming the male members of the party as childish provocation, he perhaps had a more realistic notion of the risks of traveling in a region where gunbattles were not uncommon and, reportedly, a ten-thousand-dollar reward had been offered for his death. The dangers were illustrated by an incident that occurred as the PANAMIN group was returning to the reserve from a wedding near Cotabuto City. The delegation was divided between two chartered buses, the first carrying Elizalde, his wife, Lindbergh, and several journalists. Most of the men were armed, Lindbergh with a 9-mm Swiss HK submachine gun.

"As we passed through Surallah," Lindbergh later wrote, "we noticed that the streets were unusually quiet. A few miles further on, we came to a village and saw in front of us a truck drawn across the road to form a block. The night was dark. When we stopped close to the truck, we saw vaguely on each side of the road men armed with rifles, and we heard the rattle of gun bolts behind the figures we could see.... Obviously, the situation was tense, with fingers on triggers on both sides."[13]

The standoff was ended when a uniformed soldier of the Philippine Constabulary descended from the bus, his M-14 rifle aimed and ready to fire. The truck blocking the road slowly backed up, and the PANAMIN bus was allowed to proceed.

Elizalde promptly radioed a story to UPI saying that Lindbergh and the rest of the party had escaped an "ambush" on a deserted road. Lindbergh, more accurately, called the encounter a "show of force" staged by the mayor of Surallah, who had been feuding with PANAMIN. Although there was obviously a potential for the confrontation to get out of hand, the idea was to send a message to Elizalde, not to harm him. Nevertheless Lindbergh did not see fit to issue a correction. At the end of the expedition, moreover, he approved a document written by the PANAMIN staff that was released to the press under the title, "Lindbergh's Statement."

Needham's *Esquire* article, mockingly entitled "Travels with Charlie," was skewed, but it must be said that Lindbergh had asked for it. His habit of thinking out loud, not to mention his tendency to let others do his thinking for him, made him an inviting target for journalistic ambushes, if not actual ones. However worthy PANAMIN's aims, most figures of international repute would have hesitated to identify themselves so closely with a highly controversial operation, run at the whim of one man.

John Nance, then AP bureau chief in the Philippines, met Lindbergh for the first time in Manila shortly after the Cotabuto incident. Like Needham, he found that Lindbergh's stream-of-consciousness monologues could be mystifying at times. (The sight of a helicopter rotor, for instance, prompted a discourse on molecular structure—"Do you ever wonder why all those spinning molecules don't just fly apart? I think about it all the time.") However, like Tom Harrisson and other activists who worked with Lindbergh on various projects, he had an opportunity to see the positive side of Lindbergh's association with PANAMIN. Not merely a celebrity passing through, Lindbergh put in many hours studying the issues and advising Elizalde on his dealings with international organizations. "He was not just for show. He went in there and did the work," says Nance. According to Nance, Lindbergh was well aware of the questions being asked in Manila and elsewhere about Elizalde's motives, but he liked Manda because he had "missionary zeal" without the accompanying disease of "missionary dogma." Dogma was a trait of which he had become very suspicious indeed. "And, I'll tell you," he warned Nance, "I think you've got to be very careful, *very careful,* about looking into motives. Why does anyone do anything?"

In defense of Lindbergh's approach, he was willing to work with indigenous organizations, subordinating his own interests to their goals, rather than using his contacts to burnish his own celebrity—a criticism often made of some other well-known conservation spokesmen. At the same time he passed up opportunities to accomplish much more. For example, he rejected numerous offers to host television documentaries and to do major interviews with Barbara Walters and others.

At seventy Charles Lindbergh bore little resemblance to the grinning Lindy the public knew, and many acquaintances thought his precautions against being recognized in airports and on the street approached paranoia. Nevertheless he was spotted amazingly often. Nance recalls arriving with Lindbergh at a hotel in Davos City, so grimy and disheveled from a trip to the interior that he would have thought they would be unrecognizable even to their best friends. No sooner had they approached the desk to check in than a middle-aged American tourist made a beeline in Lindbergh's direction.

"Say, aren't you Charles Lindbergh?"

"Yes I am. And who are *you?*"

For the next ten minutes, Lindbergh amiably interrogated the stranger about his family, his home, and his experiences in the Philippines. Finally, however, it proved impossible to prevent the man from launching into a lengthy anecdote: "I remember exactly what I was doing when I heard you had made it to Le Bourget. I was in the kitchen, and my mother was cooking pancakes. And she said ..."

"People always insist on telling me what they were doing that day, right down to the dialogue," a grinning Lindbergh told Nance later. "And you'd never *guess* what some of them were doing!"

Lindbergh appeared to enjoy this conversation, and he said elsewhere that what he really disliked about such encounters was that so many people, especially the ones he was likely to meet in first class, had favors to ask—causes to be endorsed, speeches to be made, and so on. He had no desire to do these things but didn't feel comfortable saying no.

"Lindbergh travels to get away from being Lindbergh," said Elizalde.

In the spring of 1971, there was dramatic news from the Philippines that would open the final chapter in Charles Lindbergh's quest for a lost Eden. Villagers of the Blit tribe, pushed deeper into the forests by encroaching settlements, had come into contact with a small forest-dwelling tribe who had never heard of rice, taro, or tobacco. The tiny band, numbering no more than twenty-five individuals, lived in caves and survived by gathering fruit, roots, and tadpoles; had no weapons; were unfamiliar with metal; and had no words in their language for "war" or "enemy." The Tasaday, as they called themselves, were possibly the last Stone Age culture on earth.

A few months later Lindbergh flew in from New York to join the first expedition to the isolated forest caves the Tasaday called home. The party would consist of eight people, including Elizalde, a *National Geographic* editor and photographer, John Nance of the Associated Press, and two anthropologists—one American and one Filipino. Before the adventure got under way, there was a meeting with the mayor of Surallah, and Lindbergh, to cement a truce between the mayor and PANAMIN, accepted an appointment as honorary police chief of the village. The mayor cheerfully admitted that he had been present the night PANAMIN's bus was stopped and pointed out the spot where he had been standing. Lindbergh decided it would not be tactful to mention that the spot was directly opposite the window of his seat on the bus, and exactly where he would have aimed his fire if shooting had broken out.

PANAMIN's release of a report on the Tasaday by Dr. Robert Fox, a well-known American anthropologist and the association's chief research adviser, already had the academic community in turmoil. There were conflicts over who should be chosen to study the Tasaday, and how. Lindbergh, too, worried about the ethical implications of intrusion on a vulnerable culture, but the group was already beginning to come into contact with other tribes as they moved out of their traditional hunting territories.

Just getting the PANAMIN group to the Tasadays' home grounds proved a problem. A trek through the jungle would be long and arduous. Clearing a landing space large enough for a helicopter was judged too disruptive of the Tasaday's environment. After a long debate, an advance party of Tboli was sent ahead to construct a treetop landing platform. Lindbergh argued that this idea was too risky, and in the event, the platform, nearly one hundred feet off the ground and roughly the size of a Ping-Pong table, wobbled alarmingly when swept by the downdraft of the incoming chopper. As the copter hovered five feet above the platform, each member of the party leapt onto the swaying, none-too-sturdy-looking platform, descended through a trapdoor, and climbed down a rope ladder to the jungle floor. As one might expect the Tasaday were nervous about the sudden intrusion into their lives of so many strangers, but they were also inclined to see Elizalde as an almost godlike figure, especially since their little group was short on marriageable women and they hoped that Elizalde would arrange for one of their number to find a bride from a neighboring tribe. For the next two weeks the PANAMIN party camped some distance from the Tasaday caves, spending at most three hours a day with the tribe.

The Tasaday called Lindbergh Kakay Shalo (friend Charles) and honored him with a sample of one of their favorite delicacies—a kind of brown grub that they gathered from the undersides of rotting logs. He popped the treat into his mouth and managed a smile. "Not too bad," he pronounced, "like an oyster ... a very tough oyster."

During the course of his travels, Lindbergh had gotten into the habit of carrying small items that could serve as conversation pieces. He produced a magnet from his pack for the children to play with and cheerfully gave them piggyback rides. Though Lindbergh could be temperamental on occasion, John Nance observed, "He knew how to be very gentle with gentle people."[14]

In long discussions with Nance and another member of the expedition, anthropologist Carlos Fernandez, Lindbergh discoursed on his belief that modern technology, with its "insatiable commercial demands" and "fantastic destructive powers," was endangering the very survival of the human race. "The rise of intellect has coincided with the decline of natural life," he told them. "The rate of change was at first very slow, but in recent times it has accelerated to the point where, if you were to plot it on a graph, the curve would make a long, low slightly rising line covering eons of time, but then would turn rapidly upward. Modern man is at the point where the curve is almost perpendicular to the base line—and before it becomes perpendicular, it must bend or break."[15]

Lindbergh added somewhat sorrowfully that the group's early contacts with an Ubud-Blit hunter named Dafal had ended their Edenic existence forever. "He brought the apple and they bit it, no question about that. Now there's no turning back, but great care can be taken to see that the Tasaday are not destroyed or allowed to destroy themselves."

Robert Fox had already suggested that the Tasaday's history could be divided into two periods—B.D. for "before Dafal" and A.D. for "after Dafal." After listening to Lindbergh, Fernandez observed, "I guess you could say that A.D. also stands for 'after d'fall.'"[16]

When it came time for the group to leave the jungle after their two-week visit, they received word that PANAMIN's chartered helicopter was out of commission. Since it would take two weeks for replacement parts to arrive from Manila, and the expedition was not carrying provisions for an extended stay, a PANAMIN staffer arranged for Clark Air Force Base to send one of its Chinook helicopters to ferry the group out. The story was picked up by the international media, which reported melodramatically Charles Lindbergh had been "rescued" from the jungle by the U.S. Air Force. Five days later, after Lindbergh had departed for the United States, President Marcos signed a decree creating a reserve of 46,299 acres for the Tasaday and Manubo-Blit tribes. The size of the reserve was at least partly the result of Lindbergh's coaching Elizalde in the fund-raising principle that it never pays to ask for too little. On the theory that Marcos would reap international prestige by positioning himself as a defender of indigenous peoples, and that politicians are automatically inclined to cut all requests by 50 percent, Lindbergh had urged Elizalde to go for broke—"Ask for twice as much land as you want. Ask for 100,000 acres!"

Marcos's quick action generated mainly favorable publicity abroad and resentment at home, where many suspected him of trying to curry favor with the Philippines' minority peoples during an election year even while asserting his regime's claim to a potentially valuable tract of virgin timberland. Suspicion over the timing of the discovery of the Tasaday heightened some months later after an incident that occurred during a tour of the provinces by Imelda Marcos. Mrs. Marcos had expressed a desire to meet with representatives of the Tasaday. Anthropologists connected with the foundation were horrified—one simply did not pluck cave dwellers out of their environment to parade them before visiting VIPs, but as PANAMIN's patroness Imelda could not be denied. In a panic, some staffers resorted to substituting two members of the Tboli tribe, a ruse that quickly backfired when opponents of the reserve began claiming that the Tasaday were a hoax—a group of Tboli tribesmen dressed up (or down) in G-strings made of vines and coached to pretend ignorance of such basic items as rice and sugar.

Although PANAMIN's close relationship to the Marcos regime was sufficient, Charles Lindbergh's connection to the Tasaday discovery helped generate controversy in the American media, and the hoax charges were widely disseminated through an ABC documentary and numerous articles. The ABC team, according to one observer, arrived in the Philippines prepared to expose Lindbergh's collusion with Marcos and found their prejudices supported when they innocently hired guides who were agents of the Communist insurgents.

The hoax charge is still being vigorously argued in international journals, but its supporters appear to be driven more by politics than by the scientific evidence. The sixteen anthropologists who actually studied the Tasaday agree that they were and are indeed "real," and speak a language quite distinct from that of the Tboli. The experts differ, however, in their views of the Tasaday's history. Some consider them true survivors of the Stone Age; others theorize that they were isolated from a more developed tribal group in relatively recent times, perhaps as little as 150 years ago.

These disagreements were unknown to Lindbergh, who believed at the time of his visit that he was meeting representatives of a Stone Age people unsullied by civilization. In some ways what he saw confirmed his own romantic notions of the primitive. The Tasaday were well nourished and generally healthy, free from diseases like schistosomiasis that are endemic in the Philippines. Generous and affectionate, they had little experience of conflict and few words in their vocabulary to describe unpleasant personal relationships.

Although Lindbergh told Nance that his stay with the Tasaday was "one of the great experiences" of his life, comparable to his 1927 flight, his comments suggest that he was also profoundly disappointed. Free from the constraints of laws, religious taboos, and the drive to acquire material goods, the Tasaday used their freedom to do nothing at all. "They've not made one single mark in improving their places, for sleeping, for entering," Lindbergh commented wonderingly. "Why not make it easier? And don't they wonder what is beyond the next mountain?"

When Lindbergh remarked, "I'm puzzled by the lack of a spirit of adventure," Nance innocently suggested, "Necessity is the mother of invention." This adage, cliché though it might be, was also the perfect refutation of Lindbergh's notion that civilization had "uprooted" the human race from some ideal state of nature. His quest for the primitive had reached a dead end.

TWENTY-SEVEN

"Witnesses"

*N*OTHING IRRITATED CHARLES LINDBERGH so much as the charge that he had no real friends. From his point of view he had, if anything, far too many. One of the consequences of great fame is never being allowed to outgrow a friendship, and for a naturally introverted man, he had lived a highly public life.

Lindbergh often complained that friends and acquaintances tended to turn their slightest contacts with him into anecdotes, which mutated in the course of retellings, making him sound more eccentric than he actually was. Still, there is no denying that he was a difficult man to get to know and those who worked and traveled with Lindbergh during the final decades of his life often seem to be describing completely different individuals. Some found his conversation rambling and disorganized; others insist that he was "an intellectual chess player" who could be hard to follow only because his mind was always two or three jumps ahead of what was actually being said. Some found him humorless ("I never heard him crack a joke or laugh at one," says Frank Kellogg); others praise his wry wit—a disparity possibly explained by his deadpan delivery, which he himself called the "Swedish sense of humor."

All agree that Lindbergh, in his personal relationships, could be extraordinarily courteous, even diffident. To discuss him is to hear of hundreds of small kindnesses, too inconsequential to relate in detail but highly memorable to those who witnessed them. Frank Kellogg recalls a

WWF committee meeting in Manhattan to which one representative, recently recovered from an illness, had come directly from the airport, bringing his suitcase with him. After the session ended, several members of the committee were walking up Fifth Avenue together when they were abashed to see that Lindbergh, the oldest man present by some years, had taken over the heavy suitcase. What impressed Kellogg was not just Lindbergh's thoughtfulness in carrying another man's bag but that he had managed to appropriate it so unobtrusively as to avoid calling attention to its owner's weakness in front of the others.

Lindbergh, in fact, could be a bit of a mother hen. He fetched people's coats for them, ran all sorts of errands that others of his age and stature would have thought beneath them, and made it his business to steer the conversation away from topics that might hurt the feelings of anyone present. A guest invited to Scott's Cove for dinner failed to follow Lindbergh's characteristically precise directions and arrived very late, more than a little nervous about the reception he would receive, only to find the general busy in the kitchen, cheerfully warming up a home-cooked meal of chicken and dumplings.

Even the rare journalist who managed to establish a personal connection with Lindbergh found him unusually helpful when it came to writing letters of recommendation and otherwise furthering his career. "He was kind to me in ways I didn't know about until after his death," says John Nance.

One suspects that Lindbergh's charm was a by-product of his habit of intense concentration. It is always flattering to have another human being's complete attention, and when that person happens to be famous the effect can be positively dizzying. Unfortunately quite a few acquaintances came to assume that Lindbergh held them in especially high regard and were later hurt by the discovery that with Lindbergh, friendship was very much a matter of "out of sight, out of mind." As Lindbergh's interests turned away from aviation, many "old friends" who had known him in that context discovered that his interest in them had waned as well. Declining invitations to official functions, including a dinner organized by colleagues to celebrate the fortieth anniversary of his New York–to–Paris flight, Lindbergh invariably explained that life was too short to waste it eating catered food and listening to dull speeches. He would suggest meeting for a private lunch instead, but in fact his schedule was so unpredictable that such meetings were rarely possible to arrange, and when they did take place Lindbergh's boredom was so evident that they were rarely repeated.

Ironically Lindbergh himself often mistook superficial charm for friendship, and his poor judgment on this score made it easy for the likes of Mickey Rosner and Ernst Udet to deceive him. The people whose opinion he really cared about, moreover, were the very sort who, in the long run, found his awkwardness and stubborn naïveté difficult to tolerate—fortune's favorite children, like the brilliant, subtle Dwight Morrow, who had become a multimillionaire without trying (at least, so he claimed); Harry Guggenheim ("always a gentleman," as Lindbergh put it); and Harold Nicolson, whose social acceptability was so secure that his barbed wit and unconventional behavior only enhanced his reputation.

It is no exaggeration to say that Lindbergh never really got over being rejected by Nicolson. The depth of his feelings was almost that of a spurned lover—not literally, there being no evidence that Lindbergh was even aware of Nicolson's bisexuality, much less of any such tendencies in himself—but at least metaphorically. Although he had long made a practice of ignoring works written about him by others, Lindbergh wasted no time in perusing the first volume of Nicolson's *Diaries and Letters* when it appeared in 1966, and he was stunned by the passage with which Nicolson, after their argument over German air power at Sissinghurst Castle, described Lindbergh as having internalized "the Nazi theology."

Since the Lindberghs had read Nicolson's 1939 *New Statesman* article at the time of its publication, it is difficult to imagine that this characterization came as a complete surprise. What really rankled, one suspects, was Charles's discovery that Nicolson had considered him (and for that matter, Anne) unsophisticated. Among the dozen-odd other passages Lindbergh found offensive was one in which Nicolson described him as entering the library at Next Day Hill through a "window"—the ingress in question was what the British sometimes call French windows and Americans know as French doors.

Furious, Lindbergh demanded a retraction. Nicolson, who was in his eighties and in feeble health, was in no condition to reply, and his son Nigel, who had edited the volume on his father's behalf, politely declined. Letters flew back and forth across the Atlantic. Lindbergh, who began by threatening a libel suit, was soon plaintively soliciting Nigel Nicolson's advice on how he could repair the damage the book had done his reputation. Nigel helpfully suggested he try writing a letter to some sympathetic American newspaper.

The strangest aspect of this contretemps, which Leonard Mosley was not free to mention in his 1976 biography of Lindbergh, was that Nigel, anticipating that the Lindberghs might object to the passages in question, had requested their permission to publish them. His letter had been answered by Mrs. Lindbergh, who raised no objections. Thus Anne was placed in the acutely embarrassing position of having her judgment repudiated by her husband.

Unfortunately Charles did not simply follow Nigel Nicolson's advice. Instead he drove to Yale to reread his journals of the period and concluded, to his own satisfaction, that they did not support the charge that he had been a Nazi sympathizer. Harcourt Brace Jovanovich's publisher, William Jovanovich, agreed to bring the journals into print, not quite in their entirety but in vast, largely unedited swaths. The result was a massive tome—1,038 pages covering just seven years, and those far from comprehensively.

The decision to publish this personal material was a difficult one for Charles. Despite his flair for self-deception, Lindbergh realized that the journals did not present a flattering portrait. "I could have gone back and cleaned them up but I didn't," he later told John Nance.

By the time the book appeared in the stores, however, it had acquired eight pages of prefatory material that seemed calculated to offend and enrage the very people who might be interested enough to wade through it. Although the journals can best be read as the record of a proud man having a nervous breakdown in public, William Jovanovich, in a brief introduction, professed to find them "rigorous and bracing." The remainder of the preface consisted of a letter from Lindbergh in which he called World War II a net defeat for the cause of civilization: The war had cost millions of lives. Yet Poland, over which the Allies had gone to war, was still not free; the British empire had disintegrated, and Communism held sway from the Baltics to the Pacific. He did not spell out just how the status of civilization might have been improved if England had made a negotiated peace with Hitler. In theory all wars are avoidable, and many historians would agree with Lindbergh that the policies of the Allies from 1918 on pushed Germany into chaos and made war inevitable. What was ludicrous about Lindbergh's statement was his setting himself up as the voice of reason, an advocate of "clarification" of the issues, when after thirty years he still seemed unable to grasp that there was no reasoning with Nazism.

The journals themselves were such a muddle that the critics could find support for almost any interpretation. Those who believed Lindbergh was a Nazi all along were now convinced. *The New Republic*'s

Reed Whittemore saw idealism and a horror of violence. Louis Berg, writing in *Commentary*, observed the traditional military mind trying to grapple with the reality of totalitarianism and noted perceptively that Lindbergh's attitudes had much in common with the self-deception of the Junker generals. Jean Stafford, detecting a stew of "warmly nursed grievances," bluntly labeled him a "goony bird."

Anne, who had seen to it that dozens of acquaintances received free copies of her husband's earlier books, declined to send out this one. A number of the couple's friends were told that the volume was "too expensive."

The final verdict on the *Wartime Journals* cannot be rendered until the world learns the exact nature of the material that was omitted. However, given the amount of unflattering material included, there is no reason to doubt Lindbergh and Jovanovich's assurances that the elisions were made largely for reasons of length. The great revelation of the *Journals* was not that Charles Lindbergh loved Nazism—but that he was so terrified of it that he could see no alternative but submission and appeasement, spiritual as well as political. Sadly, for all his physical bravery he was a moral coward. One can most kindly attribute this to a reaction to the events of 1932.

Yet the publication of the *Wartime Journals* was not quite the act of masochism it seemed at the time. A good critic of other people's writing, Charles recognized that Harold Nicolson's gifts as a raconteur gave his version of events authority. While from his own point of view an anecdote embellished for dramatic effect was a lie, it was the well-turned anecdote the public remembered. Fortunately he also had a gifted diarist in his own family. Anne's personal writings, which he had long viewed as a waste of time and a distraction, suddenly promised to become her masterpiece. The project of gathering her letters and excerpting them and her diaries for publication was one Anne undertook with great reluctance. There were too many painful memories—of the premature deaths of her father and Elisabeth, Dwight's illnesses, and her own difficulties adjusting to life as a public figure, not to mention the grim weeks following the kidnapping. Charles urged her to put everything into print, including her reactions to what he still called "that business in New Jersey."

Even with this encouragement, Anne, with her gift for procrastination, might have drawn out the task had not the publication of her husband's journals and the round of harsh reviews that followed given her an impetus. Now there were grandchildren in school, old enough to hear the taunts that once pursued Jon and Land. *Bring Me a Unicorn,* the first volume of her writings, appeared just a year after the *Wartime Journals.* The second, *Hour of Gold, Hour of Lead,* followed in 1973 and the third, *Locked Rooms and Open Doors* in 1974.

"I never get tired," Charles Lindbergh liked to boast, "though every once in a while I do get sleepy." But in his seventieth year, he was often tired. When he said good-bye to the Tasaday, he had promised to visit them again soon, but in late 1972 he postponed plans to return to Mindanao, canceled another trip to Asia, where he was to meet with Tom Harrisson, and began missing WWF board meetings. Charles excused himself on the grounds that he was suffering from a bad case of shingles, then pneumonia. In fact his doctors had diagnosed lymphoma during a routine checkup. At first they held out hope of recovery, but within a year, the cancer had metastasized.

For years now he had been impatient with reminders of his early career in aviation, but in 1973 he seemed eager to reclaim the past. When he learned that George Dade, the former Roosevelt Field mechanic whom he had not seen in decades, had discovered his old Jenny moldering in a barn in Iowa and had it shipped back to New York, Lindbergh promptly drove to Dade's house on Long Island to confirm the identification. He arrived with the trunk of his station wagon filled with books, free copies he had received from various publishers, which he planned to deliver to La Falaise, now opened to the public under the terms of Harry Guggenheim's will. To the surprise of Dade, who was aware of Lindbergh's dislike for reminiscing, he invited himself to lunch and seemed eager to talk over the old days at Roosevelt Field. Before he left he examined the Jenny and found his initials, which he had carved into the fabric of the fuselage during a forced layover in a farmer's field.

With characteristic thoroughness, he was researching death. He paid a visit to Arlington National Cemetery then peppered an acquaintance knowledgeable about military protocol with questions: Who was eligible to buried there? (As a Congressional Medal of Honor winner, he was.) Why were some headstones different from others? How were the gravesites assigned? It was not uncommon for Lindbergh to interrogate people he knew on arcane subjects, and he never mentioned having a personal motive for wanting to know. Even after he had lost more than twenty pounds and was obviously failing, Lindbergh did not allude to his illness, and many assumed, wrongly, that he was being kept in the dark by his doctors. This would have been impossible even if they had wished it; few laymen knew more about medical diagnosis than Lindbergh.

In the spring of 1974, Lindbergh resigned from the boards of the World Wildlife Fund and Pan-Am. While resting at his cottage on Maui he managed to complete the foreword to John Nance's book *The Gentle Tasaday,* and a few weeks later he returned to New York, where he was admitted to Columbia Presbyterian Hospital. His plan was to fight the cancer and live, if possible, and when Nance visited him early that summer he talked enthusiastically of returning to the Philippines.

When the doctors acknowledged that their best hope was to prolong his life for a few more months, Lindbergh insisted on checking out of the hospital and returning to Hawaii. A panel of physicians gathered in his room to argue against the idea. One of the younger physicians even threatened that the hospital would deny him permission to leave. He brushed their objections aside. "It isn't a medical problem now, it's a philosophical problem."

Sam Pryor arranged for Lindbergh to return to the islands on a commercial flight, his stretcher placed across a row of seats in the first-class compartment. By happenstance, the plane's captain was the stunt pilot who had flown the replica of Lindbergh's plane in the movie version of *The Spirit of St. Louis.*

Few individuals, at least among those who have enjoyed perfect health over a long life, can have spent as much time thinking about death as Charles Lindbergh. The subject had interested him since childhood, when he saw his grandfather Land replacing bones and flesh with porcelain, and wondered about the limits of medical technology. Working at the Naval Research Institute in the sixties he had discussed the future of cryobiology with specialists there and fantasized that someday it might be possible to close the gap between the galaxies by sending human beings into space in a state of suspended animation. Although it has been suggested by an earlier biographer that he would have preferred a "hero's death," one can be sure that, on the contrary, Lindbergh thought of death as an interesting natural phenomenon and felt fortunate to have a chance to observe all its stages, in control of the great experiment to the end.

Rapidly weakening, Lindbergh spent his last days planning his departure from life with meticulous care. He reviewed Anne's suggestions for the funeral service, choosing hymns sung in Hawaiian and a Native American poem. He had decided that he wanted to be buried in the graveyard of the century-old Palapala Hoomau Congregational Church in Kipahulu. After consulting with neighbors in Hana, he worked on the design for a Hawaiian-style burial vault, fifteen feet square and lined with lava rock. The bottom of the vault was covered with a layer of ili'ili stones, gathered from the foot of Maui's scenic cliffs. Although the design was traditional, the scale was not—it was, in the words of the construction supervisor, not for a "small man—more like a president." Nor did custom sanction digging a man's grave while he was still alive. Mr. Kahaleuahi, a neighbor and the same contractor who had built the Lindberghs' cottage, had difficulty convincing his work crew that the job would not bring them bad luck, and with Father growing impatient, his sons lent a hand with the work.[1]

At the borrowed cottage near Hana where the Lindberghs were staying—their own home was too inaccessible for the nurses—Charles spent his last days tinkering with the oxygen system that had been installed in his bedroom. Anne, who was with her husband in his last moments, later said that even as his consciousness began to ebb, he was trying to readjust his oxygen mask.

Several times that week he had been near death, and Anne had asked him to describe the experience so that she would know what to expect when her turn came. He found it impossible to put into words. But he did leave a note. Found on his nightstand after he breathed his last, it said: "I know there is infinity beyond ourselves. I wonder if there is infinity within."[2]

Ironically the grave of Charles Lindbergh, which would no doubt be a site of only passing interest if it were located in Arlington, ranks as a major tourist attraction in remote, picturesque Kipahulu, where it is regularly visited by tour buses. It is impossible to know whether Lindbergh intended this, but he did take care to arrange who his neighbors in the churchyard would be—buried next to the Lindbergh bier are four apes, Sam Pryor's beloved pet gibbons whom he had hand-raised in captivity. Pryor loved his pets so much that he wanted them to be buried in consecrated ground, a plan Lindbergh knew of when he and Pryor jointly signed an application for adjacent family plots. This, one feels, is the ultimate Lindbergh statement. Unable to decide whether he wished to be buried as a hero or just another primate, he managed to have it both ways.

"I was *glad* when he died," confesses a friend of Anne Lindbergh who for obvious reasons wishes not to be identified. "I thought, well, at least she has a few good years left. She can be herself now."

Anne, with more wisdom, not to mention more love, understood that a marriage of forty-five years is not necessarily over because one partner has passed away. For one thing, before her husband's will could be settled it was necessary to dispose of challenges from two men who claimed to be the long deceased Charles Lindbergh, Jr. (Other claimants continue to come forward, most recently a black woman who says that her color and sex were changed by the FBI in an effort to conceal her identity!) Moreover, the fiftieth anniversary of "the flight" was approaching, and with it, invitations to a plethora of commemorative events. Anne attended a few, including the dedication of a Pan-Am Clipper in her husband's honor, but daughter Reeve represented the family at the largest celebration, at Roosevelt Field on Long Island. The most important of the official commemorations, a symposium held in the main hall of the Air and Space Museum in Washington, D.C., came to a tragic and unexpected end when aviator John Grierson suffered a fatal stroke even as he was delivering the final words of the keynote address.

The estate, meanwhile, had authorized a book celebrating the flight by Brendan Gill, and a group of friends, spearheaded by James Newton, had announced plans to organize a scholarship foundation in Lindbergh's memory. The Lindbergh Fund, headquartered in Minneapolis, gives grants to scientists whose work promotes sound ecological values. Another project close to the heart of some of Lindbergh's admirers has been the donating of Lindbergh statues to localities connected with him in life. Minnesota, where Lindbergh is remembered as a favorite son, accepted the offer to place a sculpture on the State House grounds in St. Paul, but other venues, including St. Louis, where feelings about Lindbergh remain decidedly mixed, have been less enthusiastic.[3]

Shortly after Richard Nixon resigned the presidency, Anne Lindbergh wrote to his daughter Julie Nixon Eisenhower, whom she knew from Smith College functions, urging her to think of herself as a "living witness" for her father. Mrs. Lindbergh's letter made plain that she had taken on this function on behalf of her late husband and, moreover, intended to pass the charge onto her offspring—"I feel that our children are and will be living witnesses for my husband, long after his death and mine," she explained.[4]

Given that Charles Lindbergh missed few opportunities to express his contempt for hero-worshippers and repeatedly advised his children to refrain from defending his reputation in print, one might surmise that he would have disliked this business of statues and anniversary symposia, not to mention a family burdened with the dubious burden of "witnessing." Lindbergh, however, was a complex, often inscrutable man, and it may well be that he would have welcomed having others do for him what he could not or would not do for himself. It is not surprising, however, that the Charles Lindbergh legacy has proved to be somewhat confusing. Although the *New York Times* announced on May 19, 1977, that Lindbergh's papers at Yale would henceforth be open to researchers, this turned out not to be the case. A promised book on Lindbergh's environmental activities by Alden Whitman never appeared, nor did an edition of Lindbergh's letters. A posthumous autobiography, edited with evident care and dedication by William Jovanovich and Judith Schiff of Yale University, was filled with cotton-wool musings on the "life stream," evolution, and the indestructibility of molecules ("I am the stars") but not a single tender word from Lindbergh for his wife of forty-five years. (Rather, embarrassingly, he discusses his choice of a wife in terms of breeding.) In a muddle that recalls the genesis of Nicolson's life of Dwight Morrow, there is even some confusion over whether Lindbergh has one authorized biographer or two—a retired army colonel and military historian named Raymond Fredette says he was chosen by Lindbergh himself and has a contract from Harcourt Brace Jovanovich that appears to uphold his claim, while, more recently, Mrs. Lindbergh has named Scott Berg as the authorized biographer.

In the late seventies, Anne Lindbergh occasionally expressed an interest in writing a book on widowhood, a sort of sequel to the meditations of *Gift from the Sea*. Often alone during the final decades of her marriage, she had perhaps begun to do some hard thinking about this status even before she had personal experience of it, and she once jokingly told a group of Smith College students about a conversation on the subject with an elderly Welshwoman who told her, "For true happiness, there is nothing like being a childless widow!" However, the project was often postponed, and when Julie Eisenhower was shown Mrs. Lindbergh's studio during a visit to Scott's Cove, she found the desk covered with a layer of dust, obviously untouched for months.

When Mrs. Lindbergh did find time to turn to writing, it was not to her book on widowhood but to a project she admitted that she approached with something akin to dread—editing the fourth and fifth volumes of her diaries and letters, covering the years 1936 through 1944. Oddly enough, the penultimate entry in volume 5 consists of a long meditation on the death of Antoine de St.-Exupéry, who had been declared missing in action after his plane disappeared during a reconnaissance flight over southern France. In 1942, writing to Jim Newton on the occasion of his forthcoming marriage, Anne had called Charles "the sun" in her life; now, just two years later, he had been demoted. "Charles is earth to me," Anne writes in October 1944, while St.-Exupéry, whom she had met only once, is "a sun or a moon or stars which light earth." (No wonder Charles was jealous and perplexed!)[5] The next and final entry, written later that same month, has Charles striding in the door, home from his war service in the Pacific, and—his only recorded words—consoling Anne, who is still grieving for "St.-Ex." Somehow, her closing statement that separation had helped create a common ground for carrying the marriage forward is not convincing.

This was the end of the saga. Although Mrs. Lindbergh reportedly continued to keep a diary at least sporadically into her eighties, there have been no more volumes. The complete diaries, covering six decades in the life of an exceptional and influential American woman, must surely be a unique literary and historical document. One can only regret that their creator saw fit to cut their publication short at the moment when she began to see her husband as a fallible human being rather than an icon.

During the 1970s and 1980s, Mrs. Lindbergh was often described as a recluse; however, this is a relative term. She served a number of years on the board of Harcourt Brace Jovanovich, remained active in Smith College affairs, and gave occasional interviews to scholars. Until the end of the decade, when her health began to fail, she spent every summer at her chalet in Switzerland and paid frequent visits to her five children and more than a dozen grandchildren, spending much time in northern Vermont, where her two daughters are now settled. (The Maui house, never her favorite, remained in the family until 1990, when it was sold to Mike Love, formerly of the Beach Boys.)

Nevertheless two former employees came up with exactly the same phrase to describe Anne Lindbergh—"the loneliest woman in the world."

In an almost eerie parallel, Bruno Richard Hauptmann also had his living witness. Anna Hauptmann and her son Mannfried had retired into obscurity after the trial, living first in the Bronx, where she ran a small mail-order business, and later in New Jersey and the Philadelphia area. Years after the execution she continued to receive letters—"thousands of them," she later said—from people who believed her husband was innocent. She was also approached by numerous "famous detectives," journalists, and amateur sleuths who assured her that they had proof that her husband had been framed. By the late 1930s she had begun to work with a private investigator named Julius A. Braun, who claimed to have traveled more than 140,000 miles tracking down clues in the case.

Mrs. Hauptmann became disillusioned with one would-be champion after another and found solace in religion. But her faith in her husband's innocence never failed her. Indeed, her image of Richard became more idealized over the years. She remembered him as a paragon of virtues, a hardworking carpenter, and a devoted husband and father. When journalist Anthony Scaduto visited Mrs. Hauptmann during the early 1970s, she told him that she had suspected her husband was up to something in the garage but had suppressed her curiosity because she thought he was building a wardrobe for the baby and did not want to spoil the surprise. After his arrest, Richard had told her that he was drying ransom bills, which he claimed to have obtained from Isidore Fisch.

Scaduto's own view of Bruno Richard Hauptmann is summarized by the title of this 1977 book, *Scapegoat,* which, as *Kirkus Reviews* observed, "turns the 'beast' and 'baby killer' into a figure of almost tragic integrity, whose character in these pages outshines even Lindbergh's."

Willing to point the finger of blame everywhere but at Hauptmann, Scaduto revived a number of old theories. Eager to show that the NYPD had not been idle during the kidnapping investigation, Lieutenant Finn later reminisced about the case in an article in *Liberty* magazine, revealing that there had been an intensive investigation of the Giessler and Leipold families. (The saga of Duane Bacon, who had escaped from under the noses of the New York Police, presumbly did not make such a good story.) The theory of the Giesslers' involvement was later taken up by Alan Hynd, a writer for *True* magazine. A more colorful theory about the Plymouth Apartments connection had been put forth even during the trial in a series of broadsides by the so-called "Committee of Witnesses," whose organizer was a former army intelligence officer named Hal Walton. Walton, who apparently had connections with the Robert Thayer and Bill Donovan law firms, concluded that the kidnapping had been organized by agents of the German airline holding company Luft Hansa, in retaliation for the Lindberghs' 1931 visit to China, which enabled Juan Trippe to compete with the Germans for landing rights in major Chinese cities. According to one Committee of Witnesses brochure, the Giesslers' neighborhood was a nest of "old German imperial types and high school teachers"—the latter group suspect because Frederick Muentzer, who had attempted to assassinate Jack Morgan in 1915, was a professor of German. Scaduto revived the notion of the Giesslers' involvement, though he never managed to link them up with his other favorite suspects, Isidore Fisch and Paul Wendel.[6]

The present author is in total disagreement with Scaduto's contention that Bruno Richard Hauptmann was the victim of a frameup. Hauptmann undoubtedly wrote the ransom notes and ended up with a goodly share of the payoff. The Giesslers and Henry Leipold had nothing to do with the crime. Nor, for that matter, did Hohenzollern spies, Luft Hansa, or high school teachers. Allegations by Scaduto and others that Charles Lindbergh deliberately lied about recognizing Bruno Hauptmann's voice or in some other way conspired to frame a man he knew to be innocent are equally without foundation. But Scaduto was right about one thing: Lindbergh did know that the evidence pointed to more than one perpetrator and to a probable link to the Next Day Hill servants. Living in England, cut off from the scientific career he had worked so hard to establish, Lindbergh had ample time to brood over his inability to establish a safe home for his family in America or even to uncover the full truth about the murder of his son. His mother-in-law's efforts to defend her employees' privacy had frustrated the police and left many questions about the possible complicity of Charles Ellerson and the other servants unanswered. Even more disturbing, perhaps, was the possibility that the child had been targeted first of all because Hauptmann had a grudge against the Morgan bank. Lindbergh insisted to the end of his life that he never believed in the existence of the evil Money Trust, yet the almost physical disgust he felt upon visiting 23 Wall Street after his return to the United States surely was not entirely caused by his disagreement with the bankers' position on aid to Britain or even his belief that the architects of the Treaty of Versailles had caused the travails of Europe, for which the Germans were taking the blame. A feeling, perhaps never consciously articulated, that he, too, was a victim, underlay his rage against the "anglophile" bankers

Although *Scapegoat* portrayed her husband as an injured innocent, Mrs. Hauptmann felt used by Anthony Scaduto, and by 1981 she had acquired a new champion, attorney Robert Bryan, who had formerly represented "Lindbergh baby" Kenneth Kerwin. Bryan was successful in getting the state of New Jersey to release its files on the Lindbergh case, including a cache of papers discovered in the garage of the late Governor Harold Hoffman. Bryan also filed a one-hundred-million-dollar suit in Anna Hauptmann's name against David Wilentz and the state of New Jersey.

In a 1981 interview Mrs. Hauptmann told William Geist of the *New York Times*, "I would like to meet Mrs. Lindbergh." She described Richard as a man who cried when their pet dog Lottie died and, wrote Geist, "tells of a time when she ran up the stairs to berate him for playing the mandolin after the baby was asleep and found him playing the Brahms lullaby as the baby looked on approvingly. 'It was beautiful, but then they [the police] came, and it was a different world.'"

And ten years later, lawsuits and calls for a pardon having proved unavailing, Mrs. Hauptmann, aged ninety-four, returned to the Flemington, New Jersey, area for the first time to give a press conference in which she stated, "It is my duty to fight for my husband as long as I live."[7] Rebuffed by the governor, Mrs. Hauptmann reiterated her desire to meet with Anne Lindbergh, to explain to her why Bruno was innocent, a call she repeated in early 1992 during an appearance on the TV show "A Current Affair."

As typically happened in such cases, Mrs. Hauptmann's statement inspired assorted case mavens to beat a path to Scott's Cove where Anne Lindbergh lay seriously ill and often disoriented. At the age of eighty-five, Mrs. Lindbergh could no longer remember much about her triumphs as an aviatrix and author. The one event of the past that remained indelibly fixed in her memory was "the New Jersey business," and these visits from strangers were so threatening to her peace of mind that the family was forced to remove her to a secret location.

A widow's faith cannot wipe away the evidence or change Bruno Richard Hauptmann retroactively from a cold-blooded kidnapper into an innocent man. Nonetheless Mrs. Hauptmann's impassioned pleas (of which she undoubtedly believes every word) have had an impact. Many Americans today have only a vague idea of what Charles Lindbergh was famous for, and few know much about his and Anne's joint contributions to the world of aviation. Fewer still can conceive of a time when aviation was associated with idealistic values like peace, brotherhood, and international cooperation. But it is difficult to find anyone who does not know about the Lindbergh kidnapping and has not "heard" that Bruno Hauptmann was innocent; an amazing number are prepared to argue vigorously the guilt of their favorite candidates, from Violet Sharpe and poor Elisabeth Morrow to Charles Lindbergh himself.

One is tempted to conclude that this denouement proves the truth of Alexis Carrel's complaints that the modern world is more fascinated by villains than heroes and nurtures the abnormal at the expense of the normal. But it was Lindy's very normality, his all-American image, that the public responded to in 1927. It is not so much that people no longer desire heroes but that anyone who becomes a hero through the mass-media celebrity system must be willing at least to go through the rituals of pretending to be a regular guy. Neither Charles Lindbergh, who had more in common with eccentric, curmudgeonly geniuses like Henry Ford and Thomas Edison, nor his esthete wife was willing or able to accept the rules of the game. As John Gregory once wrote, what the country wanted from Lindy was "those bits of homely color, those human interest stories which prove we are all akin to the hero.... We long to see the loveable boy."[8] Well, he wasn't there.

A NOTE ON SOURCES

Charles and Anne Morrow Lindbergh present a special set of problems for any would-be biographer. On the one hand, both have written at great and revealing length about their public and private lives. Anne Morrow Lindbergh's diaries and letters have appeared in a five-volume series. General Lindbergh wrote three biographies: *We, The Spirit of St. Louis,* and the posthumously published *Autobiography of Values.* He discussed his changing feelings about the field of aviation in the long essay *Of Flight and Life* (New York: Scribner's, 1948). *The Wartime Journals of Charles A. Lindbergh* devotes a thousand pages to the period between March 1938 and June 1945.

On the other hand, despite their long public careers as aviators, authors, memoirists, and, on occasion, advocates of controversial causes, the Lindberghs have often resented the efforts of others to write about them. Access to the Lindbergh Papers at Yale University's Sterling Library has been limited to a very few researchers, and almost twenty years after Charles Lindbergh's death there is still no authorized biography, although one has been promised before the end of the decade.

Under the circumstances, what is the justification for a new biography now? From the biographer's point of view, the answer is obvious: One chooses a subject about which one has something new to say.

The era when aviation was glamorous and adventurous is now but a dim memory. It is even more difficult to realize that there were people, including the young Charles Lindbergh, who seriously believed that it would bring about peace, prosperity, and social equality. Lindbergh's attraction to this vision goes far to explain his later search for substitute utopias. Early issues of aviation magazines such as *Western Flying, Popular Aviation, Flying,* and *Aero Digest* provided me with many interesting examples of air-minded thinking, and Joseph J. Corn's *The Winged Gospel: America's Romance with Aviation, 1900–1950* gives an intriguing and scholarly overview.

Both Charles and Anne Lindbergh were children of charismatic fathers, a circumstance that makes it easy to underestimate their unusually close relationships to their mothers. The papers of Emory Scott Land in the Library of Congress provided important insights into the family of Charles A. Lindbergh's mother and the relationship between Admiral Land and his famous cousin. Dr. William S. Chase, DDS, and the American Dental Association were especially helpful in tracking down biographical information about Dr. Charles Henry Land.

The most obvious difference between this and previous biographies of Charles Lindbergh is in the amount of space devoted to the 1932 kidnapping of Charles Augustus Lindbergh, Jr. The desire of the Lindbergh family to put their memories of this tragic crime behind them is more than understandable; nevertheless, an objective biographer must acknowledge that this unfortunate affair altered the course of the Lindberghs' lives forever. Unlike some previous researchers who have approached the official archives looking for evidence that would exculpate Bruno Richard Hauptmann, I was mainly interested in what the files would tell me about Charles Lindbergh's role in administering the investigation. In a situation unusual if not unique in the annals of American crime, the Lindberghs' home became a temporary police headquarters, and Colonel Lindbergh served as the unofficial but acknowledged coordinator of the efforts of state, federal, and local officials. The FBI's CALNAP files proved most helpful in this regard, yielding in addition a vivid portrait of life at the Morrows' Englewood mansion. These files run to more than three hundred thousand pages, although much of these consist of field-office reports on obviously unproductive tips from the public. The Lindbergh case archives at the New Jersey State Police Headquarters near Trenton were also extremely useful, especially for information about Bruno Richard Hauptmann, the forensic evidence, and the often-surreal second investigation conducted by Gov. Harold Hoffman.

Although in most cases it has not been possible to quote from these sources, the Charles A. Lindbergh (Senior) and Family Papers in the collection of the Minnesota Historical Society and the Dwight Whitney Morrow Papers at Amherst provided much important information. The Minnesota archive also houses papers of historian Grace Nute, and Lynn and Dora Haines, covering their research into C. A. Lindbergh's career. The Sophia Smith Collection, Smith College; the Sackville-West Papers at the Lilly Library, University of Indiana at Bloomington; and the Thomas W. Lamont Papers at the Harvard Business School's Baker Library also yielded useful material.

The Lindbergh collection in the Manuscript Division of the Library of Congress is limited mainly to the manuscripts of *The Spirit of St. Louis* and related correspondence but also contains two lengthy memorandums (seventy-nine and seventy-six pages respectively) of Lindbergh's annotations on biographies of him by Kenneth S. Davis and Walter S. Ross. Lindbergh's comments on the Ross book were written on various dates in August 1968, those on the Davis book in August 1969. These memorandums clarify a number of confusing incidents, debunk many untrue or exaggerated anecdotes, and give insights into Lindbergh's perspective on major events. In a number of instances Lindbergh's memory proved less reliable than the documented assertions of Davis and Ross.

The Lindbergh files at the research library of the Air & Space Museum, a division of the Smithsonian Institution, consist mainly of clippings; however, the files associated with the careers of others are more informative. Longtime Pan-Am pilot Basil Rowe's account of flying the Caribbean with Lindbergh was especially interesting.

The Alexis Carrel Papers at Georgetown University answered some questions about the enigmatic Dr. Carrel and raised others. Also useful in understanding Carrel were Father Joseph Durkin's *Hope for Our Time: Alexis Carrel on Man and Society* (New York: Harper & Row, 1965) and Theodore Malinin's *Surgery and Life: The Extraordinary Career of Alexis Carrel*, cited hereafter in the notes.

The Franklin D. Roosevelt Library in Hyde Park, New York, was consulted for background on the America First movement and Lindbergh's battles with the Roosevelt administration. Examination of the Records of the German-American Bunds, part of the Records of the Alien Property Office in the National Archives, Suitland, Maryland, turned up examples of anti-British and anti-Morgan bank propaganda pamphlets and cartoons.

A bibliography of articles by and about the Lindberghs would be a publishing undertaking in itself. Readers are invited to consult Perry D. Luckett's *Charles A. Lindbergh: A Bio-bibliography* (New York: Greenwood Press, 1986). Kenneth S. Davis's bibliography for his 1958 life of Lindbergh, *The Hero*, remains unsurpassed for the years covered. Among the most interesting articles not cited in the footnotes to individual chapters were those of Lauren D. Lyman, especially "The Lindbergh I Know," *Saturday Evening Post*, Apr. 4, 1953; C. B. Allen's "The Facts About Lindbergh," *Saturday Evening Post*, Dec. 28, 1940; and Alden Whitman's "The Price of Fame," *New York Times Magazine*, May 8, 1977.

Both Lyman and Whitman wrote for the *Times*, Charles Lindbergh's favorite newspaper and the source of much of the best-informed coverage of his and Anne Lindbergh's career over the years. The *Times* also had the most expansive and generally reliable reporting on the transatlantic air race of 1927, the Violet Sharpe suicide, and the arrest and trial of Hauptmann.

Of the many books written about the 1932 kidnapping, Jim Fisher's *The Lindbergh Case* is the most objective and best documented; however, Fisher relied primarily on the New Jersey State Police archives and his conclusions differ from my own. Although a number of investigators associated with the case later published articles in *Liberty* magazine and elsewhere, these pieces were frequently ghostwritten and are largely disappointing.

At the beginning of my research, Anne Morrow Lindbergh had agreed to grant an interview. That meeting never came about because of Mrs. Lindbergh's declining health, and her subsequent decision to appoint an authorized biographer made it impossible for me to interview certain close friends and family members. Others who knew the Lindberghs asked for anonymity. On the whole I sympathize with General Lindbergh's complaints about the unreliability of anecdotal evidence, especially concerning events that took place decades ago.

Of those who spoke without conditions, special thanks to John Nance, the Honorable L. Francis Kellogg, George Dade, and George T. Rutledge, who recalled working with Slim Lindbergh during his airmail-pilot days at Lambert Field. Also, thanks to Dr. Brashier for his tour of Highfields; Donald Westfall of the Lindbergh Historical Site in Little Falls, Minnesota; Sheriff Jim Marino of Hunterdon County, New Jersey; Sgt. Thomas DeFeo and Dolores Raisch of the New Jersey State Police Museum; Lowell Thomas, Jr.; Gore Vidal; Nigel Nicolson; Dr. Richard Logan; Denis Zaphiro; Robert Ball; Jim Fisher; Patterson Smith; Mr. and Mrs. Godfrey Rockefeller; Donn Coddington; Caroline Crockett; Michael Parfit; Dr. H. Berton McCauley; the American Heritage Center of the University of Wyoming; the reference staffs of the Forbes Library in Northampton, Massachusetts, and the New Jersey State Library in Trenton; Reeve Lindbergh Tripp; and Anne Spencer Lindbergh.

NOTES

Key to abbreviations used in the notes:

A&S   Research Library of the Air & Space Museum, Smithsonian Institution, Washington, D.C.

COH   Oral History Research Office, Columbia University, New York, N.Y.

DWM   Dwight Whitney Morrow Papers, College Archives, Amherst College, Amherst, Mass.

FBI   Federal Bureau of Investigation, Washington, D.C.

FDR   Franklin Delano Roosevelt Presidential Library, Hyde Park, N.Y.

GU   Alexis Carrel Papers, Georgetown University, Washington, D.C.

HB   Thomas W. Lamont Papers, Baker Library, Harvard Business School, Boston, Mass.

HC   Hunterdon County Historical Society, Flemington, N.J.

LC   Manuscript Division of the Library of Congress, Washington, D.C.

LL   Vita Sackville-West Papers, Lilly Library, University of Indiana, Bloomington, Ind.

MHS   Charles A. Lindbergh (Senior) and Family Papers, Grace Nute Papers, Lynn and Dora B. Haines Papers, Minnesota Historical Society, St. Paul, Minn.

NJSP   New Jersey State Police Archives, Trenton, N.J.

SS   Sophia Smith Collection, Smith College, Northampton, Mass.

Chapter 1   Prophets

1. Willard Glazier, *Down the Great River* (Philadelphia: Hubbard Brothers, 1988), esp. pp. 153–54.
2. Charles A. Lindbergh, *Boyhood on the Upper Mississippi: A Reminiscent Letter* (St. Paul: Minnesota Historical Society, 1972), pp. 1–2.
3. For excerpts from these letters, see Brendan Gill, *Lindbergh Alone* (New York: Harcourt Brace Jovanovich, 1977), pp. 55–56.

4. Interestingly, in his last book, C.A. inserted a footnote—quite irrelevant to the text—condemning *Main Street*. Lewis's novel, he complained, was based on the "ridicule of certain country people." See *The Economic Pinch* (1923; reprint, Hawthorne, Calif.: Omni, 1988), p. 177.

5. C..A to Eva, July 9, 1914, Lindbergh Papers, MHS; see also Bruce L. Larson, *Lindbergh of Minnesota: A Political Biography* (New York: Harcourt Brace Jovanovich, 1973), p. 31.

6. Ibid., p. 44.

7. Ibid., p. 55.

8. Russel Blaine Nye, *Midwestern Progressive Politics* (East Lansing: Michigan State University Press, 1959), p. 247.

9. Lindbergh, *The Economic Pinch*. The answer to the first question, according to chapter 9, is that only bankers do business with other people's money.

10. Ibid., p. 22.

11. Folder 137, Box 23, Lindbergh Papers, LC.

12. Larson, *Lindbergh of Minnesota*, p. 31; memo of Aug. 4, 1969, p. 5, Lindbergh Papers, LC; Lynn Haines and Dora B. Haines, *The Lindberghs* (New York: Vanguard Press, 1931), p. 45.

13. Dr. Jerry Herschfield, DDS, "Charles H. Land and the Science of Porcelain in Dentistry," *Bulletin of the History of Dentistry*, 34, 1, (Apr. 1986); also L. Laszlo Schwartz, DDS, "The Life of Charles Henry Land: Address before the American Academy of the History of Dentistry." Schwartz's address was subsequently reprinted in the *Journal of the American College of Dentists*, 24, 1 (1957), pp. 33–51.

14. Schwartz, ibid.

15. This revealing comparison was made by Lindbergh in several early drafts of *The Spirit of St. Louis*. See Box 23, Lindbergh Papers, LC.

Chapter 2   "I Worshipped Science"

1. Charles A. Lindbergh, *The Spirit of St. Louis* (Charles Scribner's Sons, New York, 1953; reprint, New York: Avon, 1985), p. 292.

2. Haines and Haines, *The Lindberghs,* p. 209. The story of pulling rank on a Capitol guard is from Charles A. Lindbergh, *Autobiography of Values,* ed. William Jovanovich and Judith A. Schiff (San Diego, Calif.: Harcourt Brace Jovanovich, 1978), pp. 54–55.

3. *New York Times,* June 15, 1927, p. 2.

4. Box 4, File 23, Lindbergh Papers, LC.

5. Kenneth S. Davis, *The Hero* (Garden City, N.Y.: Doubleday, 1958), p. 60. The quote from Juno Butler is from an interview that originally appeared in the *Minneapolis Tribune,* May 21, 1927. Additional reminiscences of Charles's Little Falls childhood come from a *Tribune* article of May 20, 1936.

6. Davis, *The Hero,* p. 59.

7. For C.A. on religion, see Larson, p. 34; the experience of being caught in a downpour is from CA to Eva, Aug. 11, 1921, Lindbergh Papers, MHS.

8. Lindbergh, *Boyhood on the Upper Mississippi*, p. 14.
9. *Congressional Record*, 64th Congress, 1st sess., appendix, pp. 497–98.
10. Ibid., p. 666.
11. Charles A. Lindbergh, *Of Flight and Life* (New York: Charles Scribner's Sons, 1948), p. 50.
12. Haines and Haines, *The Lindberghs*, p. 252.
13. Larson, *Lindbergh of Minnesota*, p. 237.

Chapter 3   "This Strange Unmortal Space"

1. Davis, *The Hero*, p. 75. Davis takes the quote on grades from Louis La Coss, author of one of the better-researched instant newspaper bios, which appeared as a supplement to the *St. Louis Globe-Democrat* on June 19, 1927. The story of shooting at coins was told by Lindbergh to Alden Whitman. See "The Return of Charles Lindbergh," *New York Times Magazine*, May 23, 1971, pp. 28–29 and ff.
2. Several of Lindbergh's college papers were later reprinted in George Buchanan Fife, *Lindbergh, the Lone Eagle* (New York: Burt, 1927), pp. 130–40.
3. Lindbergh, *Autobiography of Values*, p. 121.
4. Lindbergh, *The Spirit of St. Louis*, p. 235.
5. Don Dwiggins, *The Barnstormers* (Blue Ridge Summit, Pa.: Tab, 1981), p. 51.
6. Davis, *The Hero*, p. 81. Davis's source was an Associated Press interview with Page, datelined May 21, 1927.
7. Lindbergh, *The Spirit of St. Louis*, pp. 240–41. Lindbergh says (p. 246) that the parachute jump marked the end of his nightmares about falling, but he stresses that "love of adventure" was his chief motivation.
8. See Joseph J. Corn, *The Winged Gospel: America's Romance with Aviation, 1900–1950* (New York: Oxford University Press, 1983), chap. 2, passim.
9. *Autobiography of Values*, p. 121. In 1940 an anonymous tipster told the FBI that Lindbergh had had several girlfriends in Montana and had proposed marriage to two of them, both "laundresses." Since the source got most of his facts wrong, including Lynch's first name, the information can hardly be taken seriously; however, his additional claim that Lynch flew bootleg whiskey across the border as a sideline confirms plausible speculation from other sources. Lindbergh "had principles" against hard liquor, as the saying went in those days, but was not censorious in his choice of friends.
10. Larson, *Lindbergh of Minnesota*, p. 271.
11. Charles A. Lindbergh, *We* (New York: Putnam's, 1927), p. 55.
12. *St. Cloud Daily Times*, Aug. 19, 1989. A clipping of this story, along with a related article from the *Morrison County Record*, was obtained during my visit to the Lindbergh Historical Site, Little Falls, Minn.
13. Lindbergh, *We*, p. 75.
14. Quoted in Bruce L. Larson, "Barnstorming With Lindbergh," *Minnesota History*, Summer 1991. This article was reprinted in the Winter 1991–92 issue of the Charles A. Lindbergh Fund, Inc., newsletter. Slim's belief that

the control wires were cut is reflected in letters he received from Bud Gurney and H. J. Lynch, commenting on his account. See esp. H. J. Lynch to C. A. Lindbergh [the younger], Aug. [?], 1923, Lindbergh Papers, MHS.

15. "M" [Mother] to "C," Apr. 17, 1923, Lindbergh Papers, MHS.

Chapter 4   Cadet and Airmail Pilot

1. A vivid if fitful portrait of the mechanical, financial, and romantic pitfalls of barnstorming emerges in letters to Lindbergh from his flying buddies. See especially HB [Heston Benson] to "Slender," Nov. 28, 1923, and "Buddie" [Gurney] to Slim, n.d. but apparently Sept. 1923. Evangeline's letter worrying about Charles getting enough to eat, while praising his "grit," is Nov. 29, 1923. Lindbergh Papers, MHS.
2. Marvin Northrop, "Lindbergh, the Jenny Pilot," *Western Flying*, May 1937, pp. 18–19. Leonard Mosley, in his biography, *Lindbergh* (Garden City, N.Y.: Doubleday, 1976), quotes additional comments made by Northrop in a personal interview, pp. 55–56.
3. Folder 25, Box 5, Lindbergh Papers, LC.
4. *St. Louis Post-Dispatch,* Oct. 8, 1923, p. 3.
5. Randy Enslow, "Barnstorming with Lindy," *Popular Science Monthly,* Oct. 1929, pp. 19–21.
6. Memo of Aug. 12, 1969, pp. 35–36, Lindbergh Papers, LC. Additional information about Lindbergh's cadet-school experiences—practical jokes, like a "snipe hunt" in which the victim was advised to don a flying suit and goggles to keep the snipe from scratching him, and such boring courses as "Army Paperwork" come from Slim's letters to CA: Mar. 21, Apr. 4, and Apr. 24, 1924, Lindbergh Papers, MHS.
7. Lindbergh, *We,* p. 128.
8. A copy of Cadet C. A. Lindbergh's original handwritten report on the crash can be found in the Lindbergh file, A&S.
9. Charles A. Lindbergh, "He Does It Again," *National Aeronautic Association Review,* 4 (Nov. 1926), pp. 174–75.

Chapter 5   The "Walled Garden"

1. Harold Nicolson, *Dwight Morrow* (New York: Harcourt Brace and Company, 1935), p. 17.
2. Ibid., p. 40.
3. Ibid., p. 71; see also Constance Morrow Morgan, *A Distant Moment: The Youth, Education & Courtship of Elizabeth Cutter Morrow* (Northampton, Mass.: Smith College, 1977).
4. Nicolson, *Dwight Morrow,* p. 110.
5. Reminiscences of Corliss Lamont, COH.
6. Nicolson, *Dwight Morrow,* pp. 158–63.

7. Thomas Lamont to Harold Nicolson, Box 114, Folder 4, p. 6, Thomas Lamont Papers, HB.

8. For an overview of Lamont's rise to power at J. P. Morgan and his role in international affairs see Ron Chernow's *The House of Morgan: An American Banking Dynasty and the Rise of Modern Finance* (New York: Atlantic Monthly Press, 1990), esp. pp. 225–29.

9. Thomas Lamont to Nicolson, p. 8, Lamont Papers, HB.

Chapter 6   "Don't Take Yourself Too Seriously"

1. Masefield's tribute, "Some Memories of Thomas William Lamont and Florence Corliss Lamont," appears in Corliss Lamont, ed., *The Thomas Lamonts in America* (South Brunswick, N.J.: A. S. Barnes, 1971), pp. 137–44. This volume incorporates reminiscent essays by members of the Lamont family. Constance Morrow Morgan, *A Distant Mirror,* gives an account of the Morrow family's early years. Far better known, of course, is Anne Morrow Lindbergh's *Bring Me a Unicorn: Diaries and Letters, 1922–1928.* Although first published by Harcourt Brace Jovanovich (New York: 1971), the British edition (London: Chatto & Windus, 1972) is now easier to obtain and references are to that edition. For Anne Lindbergh's comments on the "walled garden," see her introduction, pp. xv–xxv.

2. Reminiscences of Corliss Lamont, COH.

3. See, for example, Dwight Morrow to Elisabeth Morrow, Dec. 15, 1926, Series XIII, Personal and Family Papers, Box 3, Folder 12: Elisabeth Morrow, DWM.

4. Anne Morrow Lindbergh, *North to the Orient* (San Diego, Calif.: Harvest/ HBJ, 1963), p. 13.

5. Julie Nixon Eisenhower, *Special People* (New York: Simon & Schuster, 1977), p. 127.

6. Constance joked about her unsuccessful rebellion in a speech before prospective Smith students, as reported in the *New York World-Telegram* and *New York Herald Tribune* on April 29, 1933, clippings, Constance Morrow Morgan alumnae file, SS. Anne's rebellion against Smith is described in *Bring Me a Unicorn,* pp. 5–7.

7. Lamont to Nicolson, p. 7, HB.

8. Masefield, "Some Memories," p. 145.

9. Chernow, *The House of Morgan,* pp. 193–95 and chap. 11 passim.

10. Morrow to Elisabeth, Mar. 16, 1920, Series XIII, Personal and Family Papers, Box 3, Folder 12: Elisabeth Morrow, DWM.

11. See Morrow to Elisabeth, May 21, 1925, Series XIII, Personal and Family Papers, Box 3, Folder 12: Elisabeth Morrow, DWM. Constance's remarks are from the *New York World-Telegram,* Apr. 29, 1933.

12. Dwight senior to junior, Sept. 20, 1924, Series XIII, Personal and Family Papers, Box 3, Folder 10: Dwight W. Morrow, Jr., DWM. The statement that Dwight was persecuted by bullies and "heard voices" was made by Mrs. Morrow to Harold Nicolson.

13. Anne Morrow Lindbergh recalled her reaction to the dean's suggestion in a speech entitled "Earth Values," given at Smith College, Feb. 20, 1970, SS.

14. Morrow to Anne, Jan. 28, 1926, Series XIII, Box 3, DWM. Morrow's summary of the plot of *Kim* was a bit muddled, but he may have understood the moral better than he knew. Interestingly, Prof. Raymond Carney points out in his preface to the Signet Classic edition (New York: New American Library, 1984) that *Kim* is not merely an amusing children's story but "a profound response to a deep-seated sense of modern alienation, emotional estrangement and perpetual homelessness. The novel is a kind of desperate whistling in the dark."

15. Reminiscences of Marjorie Hope Nicolson, COH. Mary Cooke's comment is from a newspaper story, datelined Feb. 14, 1929, by Evelyn Seeley, a staff writer for the *New York Telegram,* quoted from a clipping in the Anne Morrow Lindbergh alumnae file, SS.

16. "Caprice," *Smith College Monthly,* 34, 1 (Oct. 1926), p. 16.

17. Nicolson, *Dwight Morrow,* p. 233.

18. *Hearings Before the President's Aircraft Board, September 21 to October 16, 1925,* 4 vols. Mitchell's articles appeared in the *Saturday Evening Post* between Dec. 10, 1924, and Mar. 14, 1925, and were later published as *Winged Defense* (New York: Putnam's, 1925). For a lively, highly pro-Mitchell view of the controversy, see Isaac Don Levine's *Mitchell: Pioneer of Air Power,* rev. ed. (New York: Duell, Sloan & Pearce, 1958).

Chapter 7   "Like Brave Lochinvar Out of the West"

1. For Sikorsky's own account of the Fonck attempt, see *The Story of the Winged-S* (New York: Dodd, Mead & Co., 1938). For additional information, including flight specifications, see Dorothy Cochrane, Von Hardesty and Russell Lee, *The Aviation Careers of Igor Sikorsky* (Seattle: University of Washington Press, 1989).

2. This was Lindbergh's belief and arguably true; according to Cochrane, Hardesty, and Lee, test flights of the S-35 had shown it was able to "maintain flight" on two engines.

3. Lindbergh, *The Spirit of St. Louis,* p. 181.

4. Ev Cassagneres, *The Spirit of Ryan* (Blue Ridge Summit, Pa. Tab, 1982), p. 45.

5. Ibid., p. 48.

6. The *New York Times*'s Lindbergh story of May 24, pp. 1–4, reported that the woman had collected on her bet. For a good overview of the air race preparations at Curtiss Field, see Richard Montagu, *Oceans, Poles and Airmen: First Flights over Wide Waters and Desolate Ice* (New York: Random House, 1971), esp. p. 65 on the reaction of the public to Lindbergh.

7. Harry Bruno, *Wings over America: The Story of American Aviation* (Garden City, N.Y.: Halcyon House, 1944), p. 173.

8. John Frogge's recollections are from the *New York Times,* May 20, 1977, sec. 2, p. 3, and May 22, sec. 21, p. 3.

9. Harry Bruno, "Lindbergh, the Famous Unknown," *Saturday Evening Post,* Oct. 21, 1933, p. 23 and ff.

10. Lindbergh, *The Spirit of St. Louis,* p. 284.

11. Davis, *The Hero,* p. 209, gives the hapless American's name as Henry Wheeler, based on a May 23, 1927, account in the Paris *Herald.* The *New York Times's* coverage of the *Spirit's* landing, May 22, 1927, also describes this misunderstanding, as does Lindbergh in *We* and *The Spirit of St. Louis.*

Chapter 8   "The Glory"

1. Janet Flanner, *Paris was Yesterday: 1925–1939,* ed. Irving Drutman (San Diego: Harvest/HBJ, 1988), pp. 22–23.

2. *New York Times,* May 26, 1927, p. 3.

3. Lindbergh, unaware of the unwritten law that one does not reveal the nature of private conversations with the royal family, related the conversation to someone in his entourage, and the story was promptly reported in the press. For the benefit of the similarly curious, Lindbergh had a container that he ditched over the Atlantic; other (male) aviators of the time used a rubber tubing and bottle arrangement.

4. Lindbergh, Memo of August 12, 1969, p. 39, Lindbergh Papers, LC.

5. Reminiscences of Vice Adm. Emory Scott Land, U.S.N. Ret., COH.

6. Bruno, with Dutton, "Lindbergh, the Famous Unknown." Commenting on this account in *Autobiography of Values,* Lindbergh insists that the decision not to wear the uniform was his, not Blythe's.

7. Emory Scott Land, *Winning the War with Ships: Land, Sea and Air—Mostly Land* (New York: Robert M. McBride Co., 1958), p. 125.

8. Lindbergh, *We,* pp. 292–93.

9. An inveterate list maker, Lindbergh reviews his honors in an appendix to *The Spirit of St. Louis.* A more selective and thus inevitably less intriguing catalog is *The Lindbergh Collection* (St. Louis: Missouri Historical Society, 1977).

10. Memo of Aug. 1, 1968, p. 30, Lindbergh Papers, LC.

Chapter 9   "Save Him from the Wolves"

1. Milton Lomask, *Seed Money: The Guggenheim Story* (New York: Farrar, Straus & Giroux, 1964), p. 92. For a slightly different account, see also Harry F. Guggenheim, *The Seven Skies* (New York, Putnam's, 1930), pp. 74–75. In a 1970 letter to his father's biographer, Bruce L. Larson, Lindbergh commented, "I wasn't much worried about the 'wolves' and felt well able to take care of myself in this respect." See Larson, "Lindbergh's Return to Minnesota, 1927," *Minnesota History,* 42, 4 (Winter 1970), pp. 141–52.

2. Robert Daley, *An American Saga: Juan Trippe and His Pan Am Empire* (New York: Random House, 1980), p. 62.

3. Anne Morrow Lindbergh, *Bring Me a Unicorn,* p. 208, quotes Charles as saying, "I don't think anything is going to stop people that want to fly from

flying. To have someone else crack up isn't going to stop them.'"

4. In his *Autobiography of Values,* Lindbergh states that this meeting took place in the fall of 1927; the Dwight Morrow Papers (DWM) indicate that it must have occurred before the Guggenheim Tour, probably in June.

5. Knight to Morrow, June 29, 1927, Series I Business Affairs and Public Activities Files, 1900–1931, Folder: Charles A. Lindbergh, DWM.

6. Morrow to Knight, June 29 and 30, 1927, ibid.

7. Bruno, with Dutton, *Lindbergh, the Famous Unknown.*

8. William Randolph Hearst, *Selections from the Writings and Speeches of William Randolph Hearst* (San Francisco: privately published, 1948), pp. 61–62.

9. Memo of August 1, 1968, pp. 6–8, Lindbergh Papers, LC.

10. Mitchell's letter and Warner's statement were reprinted in the *New York Times,* along with Lindbergh's absolution of the navy, June 16, 1927, p. 4.

11. Lindbergh, *The Spirit of St. Louis,* p. 453.

12. Donald Keyhoe's account of the tour, along with many photos, appeared as "Seeing America with Lindbergh," *National Geographic,* Jan. 1928, pp. 1–46. Other incidents from the tour discussed in this section are from Keyhoe's book *Flying with Lindy* (New York: Putnam's, 1928), and the official papers of the Daniel F. Guggenheim Fund for the Promotion of Aeronautics, LC, especially the unpublished history of the fund by R. F. Mayo, Box 20. The *New York Times* accorded the tour extensive coverage, reporting Lindbergh's smoking (Aug. 9, p. 11), his denials of smoking (Aug. 10, p. 13, Aug. 11, p. 10), his rebuff of the teenager who wanted to kiss him (Aug. 24, p. 5), and his Memphis press conference, chiding reviewers for misunderstanding the title of *We* (Oct. 5, p. 4). The recollection of Eva Lindbergh Christie Spaeth is from the transcript of a 1976 conversation with a group of Minnesota historians, Oral History Collection, OH 35, Box 3, MHS.

13. Morris Markey, "Young Man of Affairs," *The New Yorker,* Sept. 20, 1930. This was the first of a two-part profile, continued in the Sept. 27 issue.

14. Corn, *The Winged Gospel,* pp. 21–24; 52–53. The Goldstein study appeared in *Prospects: An Annual of American Cultural Studies,* 5 (1980), p. 294. Bibliographer Perry D. Luckett lists more than seventy-five published musical compositions inspired by Lindbergh. Among the more curious of these was "Der Lindberghflug," a cantata on the theme of Charles's transatlantic flight, with a libretto by Bertolt Brecht and music by Paul Hindemith and Kurt Weill.

15. Keyhoe, *Flying with Lindy,* pp. 208–9; also Donald Keyhoe, "Has Fame Made Lindy High Hat?" *Popular Science Monthly,* July 1929, pp. 32–40.

16. Lindbergh, *Autobiography of Values,* p. 122.

17. Ibid., p. 320; also memo of Aug. 13, 1969, p. 46, Lindbergh Papers, LC.

18. Land, *Winning the War with Ships,* p. 131.

19. Ochs to Morrow, Dec. 20, 1927, Series X, Ambassador to Mexico, 1927–1930, Box 3, Folder 17: Charles A. Lindbergh, DWM. In addition to

Juan Trippe, whose contacts with Lindbergh were closer than was known at the time, Harry Guggenheim, soon to be named ambassador to Cuba, played a role in encouraging his interest in a Pan-American tour. Like Morrow, Guggenheim appears to have had second thoughts after various Coolidge administration officials urged a moratorium on long-distance flights.

Chapter 10   "The Last of the Gods"

1. Reminiscences of George Rublee, COH.
2. Lindbergh, *Autobiography of Values,* p. 87.
3. Constance Morrow to "Rhea and Anne," undated, Series XIII, Personal and Family Papers, 1882–1954, Box 3, Folder 9: Constance Morrow, DWM.
4. Land to Morrow, Dec. 19, 1927, Series X, Ambassador to Mexico, 1927–1930, Box 3, Folder 17: Charles A. Lindbergh, DWM.
5. Anne Morrow Lindbergh, *Hour of Gold, Hour of Lead: Diaries and Letters, 1929–1932* (New York: Harcourt Brace Jovanovich, 1973), p. 256.
6. *Northampton Gazette,* Jan. 20, 1928. The *Gazette* ran lengthy front-page stories on the Smith case almost daily for two months, beginning on Jan. 16. The *New York Mirror* and *Boston Herald* were among the papers publishing the most sensationalized accounts of the crime. The case was also reviewed by Dr. Lydiard H. Horton in the *New England Journal of Medicine,* Dec. 5, 1929. Horton concluded that Smith had accidentally fallen off a railroad bridge near the campus while in a semidazed condition induced by a hormonal disturbance associated with female adolescence. Horton's article, like the reactions of many police officials and the college administration, reflected a reluctance to accept that an eighteen-year-old woman with no known financial or romantic problems would take her own life. One must also consider the possibility that Smith was murdered, perhaps by a motorist who picked her up while she was hitchhiking and who later tossed the body off a bridge. This solution, too, got short shrift from the authorities. (The remains of Alice Corbett were never found.)
7. Endicott Peabody to Betty Morrow, Mar. 2, 1927. Series 13, Personal and Family Papers, 1882–1954, Box 3, Folder 10: Dwight Morrow, Jr., DWM.
8. Dwight W. Morrow, Jr., to Morrow, April 5, 1928, ibid.
9. Anne Morrow Lindbergh, *Bring Me a Unicorn,* pp. 113, 124, 130.
10. "'Lida Was Beautiful," *Smith College Monthly,* 37, 9 (June 1928), pp. 5–8.
11. "Madame d'Houdetot," *Smith College Monthly,* 26, 1 (Oct. 1928), pp. 21–34.

Chapter 11   "Anne and Lindy Wed"

1. Morrow to Charles Lindbergh, 2/14/28, Series X, Ambassador to Mexico, 1927–1930, Box 3, Folder 17: Charles A. Lindbergh, DWM.

2. Phone interview with John Nance, Apr. 17, 1991.

3. Corn, *The Winged Gospel*, pp. 91–111. Corn cites an influential article on this subject by Lindbergh's friend Dick Blythe that appeared in the September 1922 issue of *Aerial Age*.

4. Lauren D. Lyman, "Lindbergh Will Aid Aviation," May 27, 1928, *New York Times*, sec. 9, p. 17. My account of TAT's formation and the work of the technical committee draws on Lyman's reporting in the *Times*, including Apr. 25, 1929, p. 31, and June 18, 1929, p. 45; as well as Robert J. Serling's *Howard Hughes' Airline* (New York, St. Martin's Press, 1983).

5. Bruno, *Wings over America*, p. 251. Lindbergh discusses his desire to sue in his memorandum of Aug. 1, 1969, p. 45, Lindbergh Papers, LC.

6. Phone interview with George Dade, May 11, 1991.

7. Lindbergh, *Autobiography of Values*, p. 123.

8. *New York World*, Feb. 13, 1929, p. 1 and *ff.*

9. Chernow, *The House of Morgan*, p. 295. From Chernow's interview with AML.

10. Anne Morrow Lindbergh, *Bring Me a Unicorn*, p. 216.

11. Transcript of David McCullough interview with AML for the American Experience documentary series, A&S.

12. Anne Morrow Lindbergh, *Bring Me a Unicorn*, p. xxv.

13. D. W. Morrow, senior to junior, Oct. 17, 1928, Box XIII, Series 3, Dwight Morrow, Jr., DWM.

14. *Amherst*, 24, 2 (Fall 1976), p. 62, DWM.

15. Mitch Mayborn, "Lindbergh Flies the Mail to Panama," *American Aviation Historical Society Journal* (Spring 1961). In *Autobiography of Values*, p. 107, Lindbergh says he made the contract with Trippe in the summer of 1928; however, the announcement did not come until some months later.

16. Anne Morrow Lindbergh, *Bring Me a Unicorn*, p. 223.

17. A photostat of the extortion note is in the files of the New Jersey State Police, NJSP.

18. Markey, "Young Man of Affairs." Lindbergh disputed several aspects of Markey's description, saying that he did not need the reporters' help and was stuck for much less than an hour; nevertheless, it was more unusual sixty years ago than today for journalists to describe such incidents in print, and Markey's decision to air his grievances—in the pages of *The New Yorker*, no less—is evidence of the depth of the press's antagonism.

19. See Edward Dean Sullivan, *The Snatch Racket* (New York: Vanguard Press, 1932).

Chapter 12　"Our First Romancers of the Air"

1. Edward Moffat Weyer, Jr., "Exploring Cliff Dwellings with the Lindberghs," *World's Work*, 56 (Dec. 1929), pp. 52–57.

2. Anne Morrow Lindbergh, *Hour of Gold, Hour of Lead*, p. 101.

3. Charles Lindbergh also made numerous flights without Anne. It was typical of the times that both TAT and Pan-Am acquired Anne's services for nothing.

4. Anne Morrow Lindbergh, *Hour of Gold, Hour of Lead,* p. 51.

5. Lomask, *Seed Money,* p. 142.

6. Anne uses these terms in *North to the Orient,* p. 74. She consistently disclaimed any feminist role, but despite her self-effacing words, Anne was quite proud of her accomplishments. See also Amelia Earhart, *The Fun of It* (New York: Harcourt, Brace, 1932), pp. 174–75; and Doris L. Rich, *Amelia Earhart* (Washington, D.C: Smithsonian, 1989), pp. 100–101.

7. George Palmer Putnam, *Soaring Wings* (New York: Harcourt, Brace, 1939), pp. 183–84. Lindbergh said later that the glass contained water, not buttermilk, but he admitted that his memory of the incident was vague.

8. Memorandum for Charles Fay, Sept. 14, 1929, Series III, Personal and Family Papers, 1882–1954, Box 5, Folder 32: Trusts—Anne S. Morrow Lindbergh, 1926–1936, DWM.

9. Anne Morrow Lindbergh, *Hour of Gold, Hour of Lead,* p. 9.

10. See "The High Cost of Fame," *New Republic,* June 12, 1929; and "Feet of Clay—Or Eyes of Envy," *North American Review,* July 1929. Also "Crippling His Wings," *New Republic,* February 29, 1928. The contention that Lindbergh's calls for privacy were part of a psychological drive to manipulate the press is a major theme of Kenneth Davis's 1959 biography *The Hero.* Although Davis's interpretations are consistently hostile to Lindbergh, he was quite correct in observing that Lindbergh's complaints about the press had little to do with the straightforward desire to be let alone.

11. Charles Lindbergh continued to deny years later that Anne had been sick at all. She told the whole story in her filmed interview with David McCullough, A&S.

12. When a photo of the Lindbergh baby did become available, the *Daily Mirror,* in a snide reference to the rumors, commented that the child was "like any other baby after all."

13. The five newspapers were the New York *American,* the *Evening Journal,* and the *Mirror*—all Hearst-owned—and the *Daily News* and the *Post.* Bernarr Macfadden's *Daily Graphic,* sometimes called the "porno-graphic," was bankrupt and published its last issue on July 7, so it was no longer a factor.

14. Marlen Pew, *Editor & Publisher,* July 26, 1930, p. 60.

15. International News Photos to Dwight W. Morrow, July 9, 1930. Series X, Ambassador to Mexico, 1927–1930, Box 3, Folder 17: Charles A. Lindbergh, DWM.

16. Anne Morrow Lindbergh, *Hour of Gold, Hour of Lead,* p. 146.

17. Alexis Carrel, *Man, the Unknown* (New York: Harper & Brothers, 1935), pp. 141, 143; additional background on Carrel is from his papers, GU.

18. Lindbergh, *Autobiography of Values,* p. 134.

19. Charles A. Lindbergh, "A Method for Washing Corpuscles in Suspensions," *Science,* 75 (1932), p. 415; also, Lindbergh, "An Apparatus for the Culture of Whole Organs," *Journal of Experimental Medicine,* 62 (1935), p. 409; and Carrel and Lindbergh, "The Culture of Whole Organs," *Science,* 81 (1935), p. 2112.

20. Theodore I. Malinin, *Surgery and Life: The Extraordinary Career of Alexis Carrel* (New York: Harcourt Brace Jovanovich, 1979), p. 232.
21. Michael Parfit, *Chasing the Glory* (New York: Collier Books/Macmillan, 1989), pp. 208–29. Parfit interviewed Keyhoe shortly before his death but actually heard this story from his wife.
22. McCullough interview, A&S. A slightly different version of the conversation appears in *North to the Orient,* p. 31.
23. Ibid., chap. 12.
24. In addition to the account of this incident in *North to the Orient,* Lindbergh described the experience in a letter to historian Grace Nute, Nute Papers, MHS.
25. Mrs. Elizabeth Morrow to Nelson Johnson, Oct. 5, 1931, Series XIII, Personal and Family Papers, 1882–1954, Box 3, Folder 2: Anne Morrow Lindbergh, DWM.
26. Reminiscences of Marjorie Nicolson, pp. 316–20, COH.

Chapter 13   "The Eaglet Is Taken"

1. John Mosedale, *The Men Who Invented Broadway* (New York: Marek, 1981), p. 192.
2. The events of the evening of March 1 are reconstructed primarily from the files of the FBI and of the New Jersey State Police.
3. Statement of Anne M. Lindbergh to Lt. John J. Sweeney, March 11, 1932, NJSP.
4. Statement of Col. Charles A. Lindbergh to John J. Sweeney, March 11, 1932, NJSP.
5. Statement of Mrs. Anne Lindbergh to John J. Sweeney and Hugh Strong, Newark PD, March 13, 1932, NJSP.
6. Cpl. Joseph A. Wolf, "Major Initial Report," March 1, 1932, NJSP.
7. The original note is in the possession of the New Jersey State Police. For a photostat see J. Vreeland Haring, *The Hand of Hauptmann* (Plainfield, N.J.: Hamer, 1937), p. 16.
8. Daniel J. Boorstin, *Hidden History* (New York: Harper & Row, 1987), p. 293.
9. "Summary Report re Unknown Subjects" (62-3057), pp. 51, 52, 106, FBI.
10. Ibid., pp. 112–22.
11. Close readers of CAL's writings will note the number of times he says he "chose not to think" about painful or ambiguous situations. A number of these instances are discussed elsewhere in this biography, but by no means all of them.

Chapter 14   The "Inner Circle"

1. "Summary Report," pp. 142–43, FBI. The account of Pratt's call to Donovan comes from a report made by H. Norman Schwarzkopf to an FBI con-

ference on May 13, 1932; Donovan and Thayer gave signed statements providing additional information on Jan. 17, 1934. Quotations in this section, unless otherwise footnoted, are from the FBI files. In a few instances, reported conversations have been reframed as direct quotes, but no dialogue or incidents have been invented.

2. Laura Vitray, *The Great Lindbergh Hullabaloo* (New York: William Faro, 1932).
3. Anne Morrow Lindbergh, *Hour of Gold, Hour of Lead*, p. 231.
4. Haring, *The Hand of Hauptmann*, pp. 27–28. Haring reprints photostats of all the ransom notes. In the notes, it is often difficult to distinguish between sloppy handwriting and actual misspellings. In all but a few instances, I follow Haring's interpretation.
5. Ibid., pp. 35–36.
6. Evalyn Walsh McLean with Boyden Sparkes, *Father Struck It Rich* (Boston: Little Brown, 1936), p. 251. See also McLean's article in *Liberty,* July 2, 1938.
7. Land, *Winning the War with Ships,* p. 141.
8. Earlier that same day Betty Morrow made a quick trip to Washington to attend a meeting of the YMCA's board of trustees. It was later reported in the press that she met privately with Ogden Mills and asked him to consider arranging bail for Capone. The Lindberghs angrily denied these reports.
9. Elmer Irey with William J. Slocum, *The Tax Dodgers* (New York: Greenberg Publishing Co., 1948), p. 69.

Chapter 15 "Jafsie"

1. Leo Braudy, *The Frenzy of Renown* (New York: Oxford University Press, 1986), p. 23.
2. Another friend later told Condon that the same symbol had been printed on the targets used by German machine gunners during the war. This remains the best explanation for its origin.
3. John F. Condon, *Jafsie Tells All* (New York: Jonathan Lee, 1936), p. 29.
4. Ibid., p. 72 and *ff.* According to Condon's subsequent statements from the FBI files, Graveyard John also claimed that he was acting on behalf of some unnamed government official: "There is a very high man in this case—one of the smartest men."
5. In 1932 there were two mail deliveries a day, and all postmarks gave the time as well as the date. Condon later confided his suspicions about the sleeping suit to a reporter.
6. Born in Italy, Berritella was a former shoemaker who characterized himself as a "divine power healer." Agent Frank Wilson (later chief of the Secret Service under FDR) suspected Berritella of being the "swarthy" man Al Reich saw outside Woodlawn Cemetery, and Mary Cirrito answered the general description of the "violin prospect." Berritella had deposited thirty-

five dollars in his bank account the day after he and Cirrito went down to Princeton and twenty-five dollars on several occasions over the next few weeks. However, at the time he wrote his final report on the case, on November 11, 1933, Wilson had been unable to establish that either of them had received any of the ransom money.

In retrospect it seems almost unbelievable that Berritella and Cirrito—the only links the authorities had to the crime—were not pursued more industriously. The New Jersey authorities had no jurisdiction. The New York Police Department did not get a chance to question Berritella until after Owney Madden had seen him, and they seem to have been influenced by the New Jersey investigators' idea that the couple was working for Rosner. Meanwhile Frank J. Wilson, who was responsible for checking them out, was officially removed from the case in the summer of 1932, after the president transferred the investigation to the FBI. Some months passed before the bureau became interested in the pair, calling their visit to Princeton "an important clue" the New York Police Department had failed to follow up. In general, competition among the various agencies was intense, and investigators often seemed more intent on defending their own turf than sharing information.

7. Irey, with Slocum, *The Tax Dodgers*, p. 75.

8. Mrs. Lindbergh alludes to this incident in *Hour of Gold, Hour of Lead* but describes Garsson as "a city official." Irey gives a more complete account. Garsson was later convicted on an unrelated charge of bribing a congressman.

9. Curtis's story that the baby was being held on a boat first appeared in the press a few days after the kidnapping and no doubt inspired Graveyard John to make a similar claim.

10. The extraordinary circumstance that Condon chose to call the kidnapper by his own name, John, struck some investigators as a tip-off that the two men were confederates. Condon's reasoning on this point remains mysterious— "Dr. Condon is not an easy man to interview," complained the author of one FBI report. However, John was also Curtis's first name, and it may be that the alias was originally the kidnapper's idea—a clumsy attempt to throw suspicion onto Curtis.

11. Anne Morrow Lindbergh, *Hour of Gold, Hour of Lead*, p. 240.

12. For the autopsy report, as well as police reports from the discovery scene and a taped 1977 interview with Walter Swayze, see NJSP.

13. Report of an interview with Pat Candido, George Foster to Harold Hoffman, Feb. 24, 1936, NJSP.

14. Lindbergh, *Autobiography of Values*, p. 140. Lindbergh devotes less than two pages to the kidnapping—he never mentions the name of his child's killer—but recalls this incident with bitterness.

15. *New York Times*, May 18, 1932, p. 1. Also Lloyd Fisher, "The Case New Jersey Would Like to Forget," *Liberty*, Aug. 1, 8, 15, 22, 29 and Sept. 5 and 12.

Chapter 16   "Life Is Getting So Sad"

1. Sadly, as it turned out, many friends who wrote letters of sympathy at the time of Dwight Morrow's death made the point that Mrs. Morrow could draw comfort from the recent birth of her first grandchild.
2. Charles Lindbergh later wrote in his own journal that he had no idea how deeply unhappy his wife was during this period until several years later, when she gave him some of her old diaries to read. Had he known, he added, he would have taken her abroad to live much sooner than he did.
3. J. E. Seykora, "Unknown Subjects," May 10, 1934, serial 7-1-3760; see also Seykora, April 13, 1934, FBI.
4. Ibid.
5. "Summary Report," FBI.
6. Anne Morrow Lindbergh, *Hour of Gold, Hour of Lead,* p. 273.
7. The police were hard put to figure out what charges to bring against Curtis since he had never actually asked Lindbergh for money, and under the New Jersey penal code at the time, giving false information to the police was not a felony. Prosecutor Anthony Hauck went to the bizarre lengths of arguing that Curtis had been in touch with the actual Lindbergh kidnappers and had misled the police as to their whereabouts. The jury convicted, but Hauck's bizarre case did not reflect well on the New Jersey justice system. For the best account of the Curtis hoax and its handling by the prosecutors see Jim Fisher's *The Lindbergh Case* (New Brunswick, N.J.: Rutgers University Press, 1987).
8. Reminiscences of Marjorie Nicolson, pp. 316–20, COH.
9. Lamont, *The Thomas Lamonts in America,* p. 128.
10. Malinin, *Surgery and Life,* p. 111.
11. Quoted comments by Carrel are from his papers; see Box 37, Folders 5 and 6 and Box 38, Folder 1, GU. Perhaps the best popular article on Carrel and Lindbergh's partnership—though both had some reservations about its accuracy—is Arthur Train's "More Will Live," *Saturday Evening Post,* July 23, 1938, pp. 5–7, 67–70.

Chapter 17   "Around the North Atlantic"

1. Harold Nicolson, *Diaries and Letters: 1930–1939,* ed. Nigel Nicolson (New York: Atheneum, 1966), pp. 131–32.
2. Anne Morrow Lindbergh, *Locked Rooms and Open Doors: Diaries and Letters, 1932–1935* (New York: Harcourt Brace Jovanovich, 1974), p. 13.
3. Dudley D. Shoenfeld, *The Crime and the Criminal: A Psychiatric Study of the Lindbergh Case* (New York: Covici-Friede, 1936), p. 46.
4. Leigh Matteson had an account of the meeting directly from Shoenfeld; see Matteson's unpublished manuscript, p. 114, NJSP.
5. "Summary Report," p. 233, FBI.

6. At this point the NYPD had twenty-three detectives and five sergeants assigned to the case full-time under the supervision of Lieutenant Finn and Insp. John J. Lyons; the New Jersey State Police had four troopers and thirteen detectives working under Lieutenant Keaten and Capt. John J. Lamb. The IRS Enforcement Division had been relieved of official responsibility, much to Elmer Irey's disgust, but Frank Wilson and others continued to consult with the NYPD. The FBI had thirteen special agents working on the case in the New York–New Jersey area. In addition, agents in other field offices spent countless hours checking out tips from citizens who believed that radicals, foreign agents, or even their own neighbors were implicated in the crime. This thankless task left many field officers eager to accept the theory that Hauptmann had acted alone, a view they urged on headquarters in numerous memos.

7. Daley, *An American Saga*, p. 129. See also John Grierson, *Challenge to the Poles: Highlights of Arctic and Antarctic Aviation* (London: Foulis, 1964), which reprints CAL's official report in an appendix.

8. McCullough interview, A&S. The Lindberghs' stay in Greenland is also described at length in Anne Morrow Lindbergh's article "Flying Around the North Atlantic," *National Geographic*, Sept. 1934, pp. 2537–259.

9. Anne Morrow Lindbergh, *Locked Rooms and Open Doors*, pp. 89–90.

10. Grierson, *Challenge to the Poles*, p. 325.

11. Anne Morrow Lindbergh, *Listen! the Wind* (New York: Harcourt Brace, 1938), p. 230.

12. McCullough interview, A&S.

13. *New York Times*, Feb. 12, 1934, p. 1.

14. Ibid., Mar. 4, 1934, p. 3. For background on the controversy and Lindbergh's Senate testimony, see Henry Ladd Smith's *Airways: The History of Commercial Aviation in the United States* (New York: Russell & Russell, 1965), chaps. 13 through 21, and Arthur M. Schlesinger, Jr.'s *The Coming of the New Deal* (Boston: Houghton Mifflin, 1958), pp. 446–55.

15. Lindbergh's own account of the controversy in *Autobiography of Values* reveals that after thirty years his views were as simplistic as ever: "I knew many of the men who had taken part in the conference. They were not lawbreakers. They had been asked by a cabinet officer of the United States government to attend a meeting....There had been too much duplication of routing. The airlines were losing money."

Chapter 18   "Unknown Subject #5"

1. The suicide of Henry Carl Leipold occurred in Arthursburg, Dutchess County, New York, on August 20, 1933.

2. Fisher, *The Lindbergh Case*, p. 188.

3. Matteson manuscript, p. 132.

4. See Leon Turrou, *Where My Shadow Falls* (Garden City, N.Y.: Doubleday, 1949), p. 127.

5. *New York Times,* Sept. 24, 1934, p. 1 and ff.
6. Mrs. Hauptmann's decision to turn to Whitney for help did not please her cousin Wally Freirmuth, who was his second wife, and described her husband to the police as "a rat." "Report of Sgt. John Wallace," Dec. 4, 1934, NJSP. Whitney's offers to sell his solution to the case were reported to the FBI by editors of both the *Herald Tribune* and the *Daily News.* Interestingly, the source of the story was the same contractor who later provided an alibi witness for Hauptmann at the trial.
7. "Statement of Anna Hauptmann to Ellis Parker, Jr.," Apr. 20, 1935, NJSP.

Chapter 19   "It Was Enough to Make Me Want to Cable Hitler"

1. Author's interview with Maurice Sendak. For a novel based on the fantasy of identification with the Lindbergh baby, see John Vernon's *Lindbergh's Son* (New York: Viking, 1987).
2. Background on Flemington in this section, as well as miscellaneous quotations from newspaper coverage, is derived primarily from a clippings scrapbook kept by the Hunterdon County Historical Society. Some clippings are undated or missing page numbers, HC.
3. *New York Times,* Jan. 3, 1935, p. 4.
4. *New York Journal,* Jan. 26, 1935.
5. Undated clipping, HC.
6. *Sunday Mirror,* Jan. 6, 1935.
7. One prosecution expert, John F. Tyrrell, unwittingly provided inspiration for latter-day conspiracy theorists when he described the shakier, more slanted handwriting in the so-called nursery note as "extravagantly disguised." In fact, the kidnapper had no motive to disguise his handwriting in this note but not the others since success in collecting a ransom depended on convincing the parents that letters two through eighteen came from the same individual who wrote the nursery note. Examination of the notes does not support the conclusion that the handwriting in the first note was deliberately disguised. More likely this note was simply written in haste and under stressful and/or difficult physical circumstances (using a toolbox as a makeshift desk, for example). In any event, the syntax, identifying symbol, and even the paper and ink match those used in subsequent notes.
8. Hugo Adam Bedau and Michael L. Radelet, "Miscarriages of Justice in Potentially Capital Cases," *Stanford Law Review,* 40 (1987), p. 21.
9. Lupica also insisted that the car he saw was a 1929 Dodge. A car buff, he based his identification on the style of the radiator grille and hood ornament. The prosecution, relying on New York State registration records, believed Hauptmann's Dodge to be a 1930 model. Interestingly, FBI records variously identify the car as being a 1929, 1930, and even a 1931 Dodge. There is similar confusion in both primary and secondary sources

about the color: Ludovic Kennedy's *The Airman and the Carpenter* (New York: Viking, 1985) calls the Dodge dark blue (p. 75) and green (p. 76). Hauptmann bought the Dodge "new" from a dealer in 1931 but registered it as a 1930 car. While the confusion over color appears to be a matter of semantics, it is possible that the vehicle had some features not typical of the standard 1930 sedan.

10. Biographical information on Hauptmann is from his statement to Lloyd Fisher, Dec. 6, 1934, and police interrogations of Sept. 19 and 20, NJSP, and the trial transcript, FBI.

11. Stenographers rendered Deibisch's name variously as Deibig, Diebeg, and Irish. For Lena Aldinger's background, see Jos. Meade memos of Nov. 20 and following, NJSP.

12. Statement of Clayton Moul, Sept. 24, 1934. Serial 7-1-4636, FBI.

13. The sources were two Fisch acquaintances, Oscar Bruchman and Henry Uhlig. Uhlig said he had heard the story from an unnamed private detective. Many years later, Lindbergh case researcher Anthony Scaduto made contact with a man named Arthur S. Trost, who confirmed this story. Curiously, Scaduto dismissed the possibility that Fisch was laundering the money for his friend Bruno Hauptmann.

14. "Statement of James B. Russell," Oct. 5, 1934, Serial 7-1-5096, 12 pp., FBI.

15. "Deposition of Anna Hauptmann to Ellis Parker, Jr.," Apr. 20, 1935, NJSP. Another account of this incident is found in Anthony Scaduto's *Scapegoat: The Lonesome Death of Bruno Richard Hauptmann* (New York: Putnam's, 1976), p. 429.

16. *New York Times,* Dec. 27, 1946.

17. The anecdote is apocryphal, but for background on the Lonergan murder case see Meyer Berger's essay, "Mom, Murder Ain't Polite," in *Treasury of Brooklyn,* ed. Mary Ellen Murphy, Mark Murphy, and Ralph Foster Weld (New York: William Sloane, 1949). Berger observes that Irish juries in Brooklyn were notoriously disinclined to convict their own, enabling Reilly to become "famous in Irishtown as a deliverer of oppressed gunmen and beautiful ladies with homicidal tendencies."

18. Matteson manuscript, p. 160, NJSP. Fisher, *The Lindbergh Case,* p. 327.

19. *New York Times,* Oct. 7, 1932.

20. The only trip Hauptmann would have taken in the weeks after the kidnapping would have been to New Jersey to retrieve the sleeping suit. There is no evidence to suggest that the jury drew this implication, but one juror, Philip Hockenberry, later said that the panel had argued over Anna's response to Achenbach's testimony. Some thought she was acting, in a misguided attempt to display injured innocence; others assumed she was furious that a longtime acquaintance testified for the prosecution.

21. Paul Hutchinson, "Trial by Newspaper," *Scribner's Magazine,* Jan. 1936, unpaged clipping, NJSP.

Chapter 20   "House of Atreus"

1. The conversation with Mina Curtiss is from Nicolson to Sackville-West, Sept. 27, 1934. For Nicolson's descriptions of the Morrows and Next Day Hill, see letters of Sept. 22 and Oct. 1, 1934, Sackville-West Papers, LL.

2. Nicolson to Sackville-West, Sept. 30, 1934, ibid.; this passage also appears in *Diaries and Letters,* pp. 180–81.

3. Quotations in the previous paragraph are from Oct. 5, Nov. 9, Nov. 30, Sept. 30, Oct. 14, ibid.

4. Jul. 10, 1935, ibid.

5. Oct. 31 and Oct. 13, ibid.

6. Oct. 1, ibid.

7. Nov. 6, ibid.

8. Nov. 25, ibid.

9. Nicolson, *Diaries and Letters,* pp. 196–97.

10. *New York Times,* Feb. 23, 1935, p. 18.

11. Memorandum of Aug. 6, 1968, p. 38, LC.

12. Transcripts and a clipping of the 1936 *Cosmopolitan* interview with Anne New are from Box 37, Folder 6, of Dr. Carrel's papers, GU; see also, *New York Times,* Sept. 18, 1935, p. 25.

13. Anne Morrow Lindbergh, *Locked Rooms and Open Doors,* p. 323.

14. Roger Butterfield "Lindbergh: A Stubborn Young Man of Strange Ideas Becomes the Leader of the Wartime Opposition," *Life,* Aug. 11, 1941, p. 65. Butterfield does not cite the source of this quote; a reasonable guess would be that it came from Deac Lyman, the *New York Times* correspondent who interviewed Lindbergh days before he left the United States. Lindbergh, in an unpublished memorandum, calls the quote "inaccurate," a word that in his vocabulary meant a good deal less than untrue. See Lauren D. Lyman, "Lindbergh Family Sails for Europe," *New York Times,* Dec. 23, 1935, pp. 1 and 3.

15. Fisher, *The Lindbergh Case,* p. 409.

16. For Liebowitz's interview with Hauptmann, see Quentin Reynolds's *Courtroom: The Samuel S. Liebowitz Story* (New York: Farrar Straus, 1950), pp. 330–34.

17. A distant relative of Paul Wendel believed that the family had been cheated out of an inheritance by a conspiracy involving the Astor family, the Morgan bank, and Drew University. This other Wendel was a sometime member of the Friends of New Germany and a notorious writer of crank letters to FDR, among others. There is no evidence that Paul Wendel shared in these delusions, but Ellis Parker, who had known his victim for many years, may have seen an opportunity to build a motive. See Paul H. Wendel, *The Lindbergh-Hauptmann Aftermath* (Brooklyn, N.Y.: Loft, 1940).

18. Carrel's statements to friends and foreign newspaper correspondents were cited in a story by Hearst commentator Lew Wedeman, dated Oct. 10, 1936.

When Wedeman asked Carrel to confirm his comments for the record, Carrel said, "If Col. Lindbergh decides to run for the high office of President, he will surely be elected." Carrel Papers, Box 42, Folder 19, GU.

Chapter 21   Exile

1. Anne Morrow Lindbergh, *The Flower and the Nettle: Diaries and Letters, 1936–1939* (New York: Harcourt Brace Jovanovich, 1976), pp. 124–26.
2. Malinin, *Surgery and Life,* p. 149.
3. Nicolson to Sackville-West, May 6, 1936, Sackville-West Papers, LL.
4. Sackville-West to Nicolson, Sept. 2, 1936; Dec. 7, 1937; June 14, 1938, ibid.
5. Anne Morrow Lindbergh, *The Steep Ascent* (New York: Harcourt Brace, 1944,) pp. 59, 96–97 and passim.
6. Truman Smith, *Berlin Alert,* ed. Robert Hessen (Stanford, Calif.: Hoover Institution, 1984), pp. 89–90.
7. Ibid., p. 92.
8. William L. Shirer, *Berlin Diary: The Journal of a Foreign Correspondent, 1939–1941* (Boston: Little Brown, 1940), p. 65. Shirer also writes (p. 64) that during their visit the Lindberghs had avoided meeting the American press corps, which could usually be relied on to brief visitors on the facts about the regime, and, he adds, "We have not pressed for an interview."
9. Wayne S. Cole, *Charles A. Lindbergh and the Battle Against American Intervention in World War II* (New York: Harcourt Brace Jovanovich, 1974), p. 38.
10. Ibid., pp. 34–38.
11. Nicolson to Sackville-West, Dec. 10, 1936, Sackville-West Papers, LL; see also Nicolson, *Diaries and Letters: 1930–1939,* p. 283.
12. Charles A. Lindbergh, *The Wartime Journals of Charles A. Lindbergh* (New York: Harcourt Brace Jovanovich, 1970), p. 12.

Chapter 22   Mission to Berlin

1. General James H. ("Jimmy") Doolittle, *I Could Never Be So Lucky Again* (New York: Bantam, 1991), pp. 26–29.
2. Sackville-West to Nicolson, May 24, 1938, Sackville-West Papers, LL.
3. Anne Morrow Lindbergh, *The Flower and the Nettle,* p. 336.
4. Slim to Land, Dec. 9, 1938, Box 6: Lindbergh Material, Emory Scott Land papers, LC.
5. Davis, *The Hero,* pp. 378–89.
6. Smith, *Berlin Alert,* p. 30.
7. Lindbergh, *The Wartime Journals,* p. 137.
8. Leonard Mosley, *Lindbergh: A Biography* (Garden City, N.Y.: Doubleday, 1976), p. 240.
9. Ironically, this project became known in some circles as the "Kennedy plan." Kennedy originally opposed Rublee's efforts and became involved

only belatedly, Rublee interview, COH; see also Richard J. Whalen, *The Founding Father: The Story of Joseph P. Kennedy* (New York: NAL, 1964), pp. 253–56.

10. Anne Morrow Lindbergh, *The Flower and the Nettle,* p. 457.

Chapter 23 "America First"

1. Land to Slim, Aug. 17, 1938, Box 6: Lindbergh Material, Emory Scott Land Papers, LC.
2. Carrel to Morgenthau, May 1939, Box 42, Folder 19, Carrel Papers, GU.
3. Lindbergh, *The Wartime Journals,* p. 183.
4. Ibid., p. 187.
5. E. P. Earle to Carrel, Mar. 14, 1935, Box 75, Sec. 311, Carrel Papers, GU.
6. Prospectus of July 7, 1939, ibid.
7. James Newton, *Uncommon Friends* (San Diego: Harcourt Brace Jovanovich, 1987), p. 215.
8. Neal Gabler, *An Empire of Their Own* (Garden City, N.Y.: Anchor, 1989), p. 338.
9. Ibid., p. 256.
10. This offer is mentioned in Newton, p. 212, as well as by Lindbergh in his journals.
11. Lindbergh, *Wartime Journals,* p. 271.
12. Charles Lindbergh to Nute, Mar. 24, 1938, Nute Papers, MHS. In *Autobiography of Values,* Lindbergh hints that his first awareness of racial differences came from his mother.
13. A good example is John Lardner's much-praised essay, "The Lindbergh Legends." Lardner actually suggests that Lindbergh was a coward because, as an airmail pilot, he waited until the last minute to bail out of a disabled DH. What really riled him, however, is that Lindbergh, following his 1937 visit, found nothing good to say about the Soviet Union.
14. Emory Land to "Sister" (Dolly DeKay), Oct. 16, 1939, Box 27: Family Correspondence, 1927–71, Emory Scott Land Papers, LC.
15. Chernow, *The House of Morgan,* p. 446.
16. Lindbergh, *Wartime Journals,* p. 279.
17. Lawrence Dennis, "Propaganda for War," *American Mercury,* May 1938, p. 7.
18. Anne Morrow Lindbergh, *The Wave of the Future: A Confession of Faith* (New York: Harcourt, Brace, 1940), pp. 15–16, 37.
19. Land to Anne Morrow Lindbergh, Oct. 14, 1940, Box 27, Emory Scott Land Papers, LC.
20. Anne Morrow Lindbergh, *War Within and Without, Diaries and Letters, 1939–1944* (New York: Harcourt Brace Jovanovich, 1980), p. 183.
21. Scandrett to Mrs. Lindbergh, 1/22/41, Franklin D. Roosevelt, Papers as President, President's Personal File, 1933–1945, 1080, Folder: Lindbergh. FDR.
22. John Roy Carlson, *Under Cover* (New York: E. P. Dutton, 1943), p. 465.
23. Hoover wrote General Lindbergh a letter of condolence at the time of

Evangeline's death in 1954; a note appended to this letter reiterates that no active background investigation of Lindbergh was undertaken until he applied for a security clearance in 1953. One can only wonder what Hoover's motives might have been for going on record about this.

24. Millicent Bell, *Marquand: An American Life* (Boston: Atlantic Monthly Press, 1979), pp. 295–97.
25. Flynn to Lindbergh, Sept. 21, 1941, quoted in Ronald Radosh, *Prophets on the Right* (New York: Simon & Schuster, 1975), p. 224.
26. Memo of August 5, 1968, Lindbergh Papers, LC.
27. Edward A. Tamm, "Memorandum for the Director," Dec. 13, 1941, FBI. Following up on earlier reports from the Ford plant, Tamm had asked Agent Bugas in Detroit to interview Ford. He reported: Henry Ford told Bugas that he had heard a speech Lindberg [*sic*] had made several nights before, and Ford did not like some of the things which Lindberg had said about the Jews. Accordingly, he asked Lindberg to come out and see him so that he could give some views on that score. Lindberg was out there about four weeks ago." Lindbergh, in *Wartime Journals,* p. 553, mentions visiting Ford on Nov. 11, 1941, but says only that he and Ford discussed "the war and trends in this country." In later entries in the journals Lindbergh discusses Ford's strange theories, including (p. 712) Ford's obsession with the Du Ponts.
28. Roosevelt, Papers as President, Official File, 1933–1945, 4330, FDR.

Chapter 24   War

1. Copies of both versions of the speech are in Charles A. Lindbergh's FBI file.
2. Memorandum for Mr. Tolson, Ladd & Tamm, December 12, 1941, 65-11449-115, Charles A. Lindbergh file, FBI.
3. Lindbergh, *Wartime Journals,* pp. 580–81. Although Lindbergh was convinced that Stimson was acting under orders, Stimson says in a letter to the president of January 13 that, despite Lindbergh's past service, he "heartily" agrees with FDR's position.
4. R. H. Simons, SAC, New Haven, to Hoover, Nov. 13, 1942, 65-11449-155; also Hoover to L. M. C. Smith, Dec. 16, 1942, Lindbergh file, FBI.
5. Anne Morrow Lindbergh, *War Within and Without,* pp. 170–71; Leonard Mosley, *Lindbergh,* pp. 319–20.
6. Anne Morrow Lindbergh, *War Within and Without,* p. 419.
7. Martin Caidin, *The Forked Tailed Devil: The P-38* (New York: Bantam, 1990), p. 283.
8. Lindbergh, *Wartime Journals,* p. 892; Charles H. MacDonald, *Colliers,* Feb. 23, 1946, pp. 26 and *ff.* Part one of this article appeared in the Feb. 16 issue. An excellent overview of Lindbergh's New Guinea service, based on reminiscences of fighter group veterans, is provided in chapter 6 of Ronald W. Yoshino's *Lightning Strikes: The 475th Fighter Group in the Pacific War, 1943–1945* (Manhattan, Kans.: Sunflower University Press, 1988).

9. For more on Lindbergh's contributions to military and commercial aviation, see, *Charles A. Lindbergh: An American Life,* ed. Tom D. Crouch (Washington, D.C.: National Air and Space Museum, 1977), especially the chapters contributed by Paul Ignatius, Richard Hallion, and Judith L. Schiff. Lindbergh also discussed these activities in his *Autobiography of Values.*

10. Charles A. Lindbergh, "Our Best Chance to Survive," *Saturday Evening Post,* July 17, 1954, p. 25; see also Charles A. Lindbergh, "The Fourth Dimension of Survival," *Saturday Review,* Feb. 27, 1954, pp. 11–12.

11. Daley, *An American Saga,* p. 513.

12. Reminiscences of Emory Scott Land, COH.

Chapter 25   "The Mermaid and the Eagle"

1. Lindbergh to Jerry Land, Dec. 21, 1949, Box 27: Personal and Family Correspondence, 1927–1971, Emory Scott Land Papers, LC.

2. Memo of Aug. 8, 1968, Lindbergh Papers, LC.

3. Anne Morrow Lindbergh, *War Within and Without,* p. 407.

4. Barbara Gamerikan, "Her Words, His Music," *New York Times,* Feb. 24, 1985, sec.1, p. 49; Anne Spencer Lindbergh, *The People in Pineapple Place* (San Diego: Harcourt Brace Jovanovich, 1982).

5. Gill, *Lindbergh Alone,* p. 129.

6. Anne Morrow Lindbergh, "The Journey Not the Arrival Matters," reprint from *Smith Almunae Quarterly* (Aug. 1978), SS.

7. For the spiderweb analogy as well as the remark, "It was not the voice of a radio operator," see ibid.

8. Corliss Lamont, *Yes to Life* (New York: Horizon Press, 1981), p. 26.

9. Newton, *Uncommon Friends,* p. 312.

10. Dr. Logan, who had become interested in Lindbergh's Kenya experience while himself a resident there in the 1960s, is on the faculty of Wisconsin State University in Green Bay, where Ben Koncellah was a student.

11. Cole, *Charles A. Lindbergh and the Battle Against American Intervention,* p. 81.

12. Lindbergh, *Autobiography of Values,* pp. 272, 274.

Chapter 26   "After D'Fall"

1. Parfit, *Chasing the Glory,* p. 12.

2. Keyhoe's *Flying Saucers: Top Secret* (New York: Putnam's, 1960) lists Senator Goldwater and Carl Jung as NICAP members, along with actress Gloria Swanson.

3. *New York Times,* July 27, 1972, p. 31.

4. Anne Morrow Lindbergh, "Immersion in Life: Journey to East Africa," *Life,* Oct. 1966, pp. 88–90 and *ff.*

5. Eisenhower, *Special People,* p. 134.

6. Elsie F. Mayer, *My Window on the World: The Works of Anne Morrow Lindbergh* (Hamden, Conn.: Archon, 1988), p. 109; Anne Morrow Lindbergh, *Dearly Beloved* (New York: Harcourt, Brace & World, 1962), pp. 108–9, 148 and passim.

7. Interview with Francis Kellogg, New York, March 19, 1990.

8. Mosley, *Lindbergh,* p. 376.

9. Lowell Thomas, Jr., to author, Mar. 6, 1990.

10. Mosley, *Lindbergh,* p. 375.

11. Edgar Needham, "Travels with Charlie," *Esquire,* Mar. 1971.

12. Nance interview.

13. John Nance, *The Gentle Tasaday* (New York: Harcourt Brace Jovanovich, 1975), p. 43. The description is from a written account supplied to Nance by Lindbergh.

14. Nance interview.

15. Nance, *The Gentle Tasaday,* pp. 235–36.

16. Ibid.

Chapter 27   "Witnesses"

1. *Honolulu Star-Bulletin,* Aug. 27, 1974, p. 6.

2. Newton, *Uncommon Friends,* p. 350.

3. Lindbergh's emergence as the spokesman for anti-interventionism caused consternation in St. Louis, a city that was home to a large German American population as well as a substantial number of recent refugees from Nazi persecution. At that time the director of the Historical Society had doubts about his institution's treatment of the Lindbergh Collection, which had been maintained for many years by Miss Beauregard as a virtual shrine. Miss Beauregard's successor, a woman who had devoted many volunteer hours to accessioning the enormous agglomeration of flight memorabilia was let go. The then director's strong feelings on the subject of America First undoubtedly influenced Lindbergh's decision to donate his papers to Yale.

4. Eisenhower, *Special People,* p. 139.

5. Anne Morrow Lindbergh, *War Within and Without,* p. 447.

6. See "Committee of Witnesses, New York," mounted circulars in the collection of the New York Public Library. Lieutenant Finn's series, "How I Captured Hauptmann," as told to Thomas D. Curtin, ran in *Liberty* between Oct. 12 and Nov. 23, 1935. Alan Hynd's best-known article on the kidnapping appeared in the March 1949 issue of *True.* See also, Anthony Scaduto, *Scapegoat,* pp. 304–10 and the final chapter.

7. *New York Times,* Oct. 11, sect. 2, p. 26; Oct. 15, sect. 2, p. 18; Oct. 20, sect. 2, p. 2; and Nov. 23, sect. 2, p. 2—all 1981; also Oct. 5, 1991, sect. 2, p. 24.

8. In the same article Gregory claimed that some newspapers already had their Charles Lindbergh obituaries on file, "teeming with human interest items which can never be disputed." See John Gregory, "What's Wrong with Lindbergh?" *Outlook,* Dec. 3, 1931, pp. 532–34.

INDEX

CL = *Charles Lindbergh;* AML = *Anne Morrow Lindbergh*